# THE FIFTH Garfield Fat Cat 3-Pack

BY: JIM DAVIS

**Ballantine Books • New York**

A Ballantine Book
Published by The Random House Publishing Group

GARFIELD FOOD FOR THOUGHT copyright © 1987 by Paws, Incorporated
GARFIELD SWALLOWS HIS PRIDE copyright © 1987 by Paws, Incorporated
GARFIELD WORLDWIDE copyright © 1988 by Paws, Incorporated
GARFIELD Comic Strips copyright 1985, 1986, 1987 by Paws, Incorporated

All rights reserved under International and Pan-American Copyright
Conventions. Published in the United States by The Random House Publishing Group,
a division of Random House, Inc., New York, and simultaneously
in Canada by Random House of Canada Limited, Toronto.

Ballantine and colophon are registered trademarks of Random House, Inc.

www.ballantinebooks.com

Library of Congress Catalog Card Number: 95-95061

ISBN 0-345-40404-1

Manufactured in the United States of America

First Edition: January 1996

20  19  18  17  16  15  14  13  12  11

# Garfield food for thought

BY: JIM DAVIS

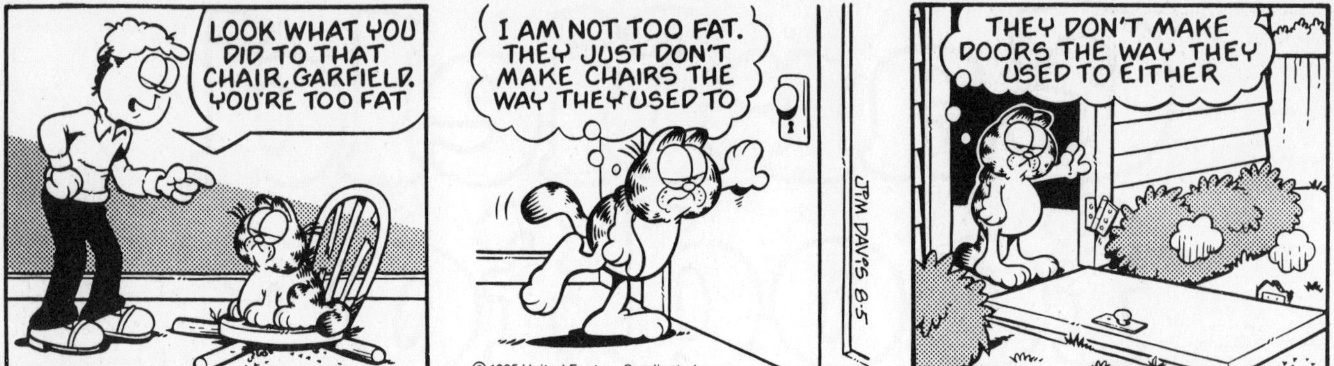
LOOK WHAT YOU DID TO THAT CHAIR, GARFIELD. YOU'RE TOO FAT
I AM NOT TOO FAT. THEY JUST DON'T MAKE CHAIRS THE WAY THEY USED TO
JIM DAVIS 8-5
THEY DON'T MAKE DOORS THE WAY THEY USED TO EITHER



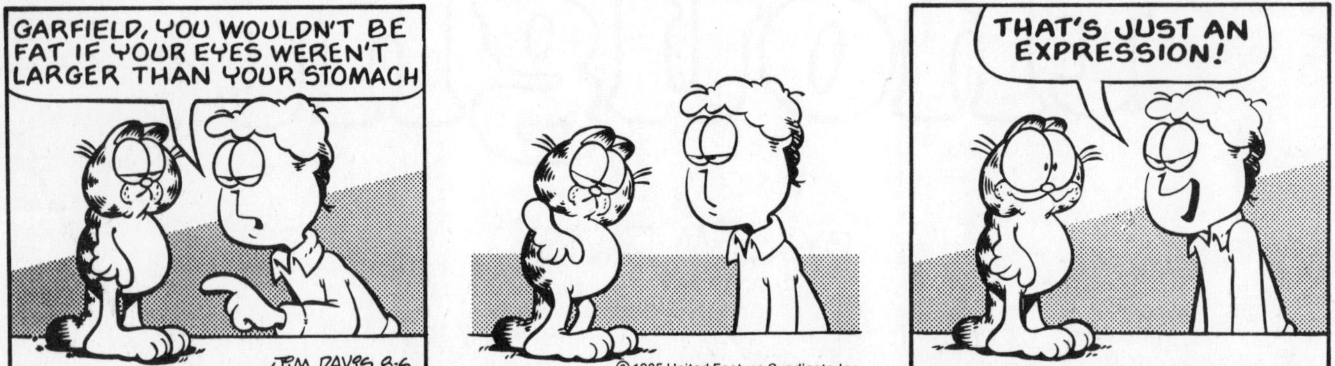
GARFIELD, YOU WOULDN'T BE FAT IF YOUR EYES WEREN'T LARGER THAN YOUR STOMACH
JIM DAVIS 8-6
THAT'S JUST AN EXPRESSION!

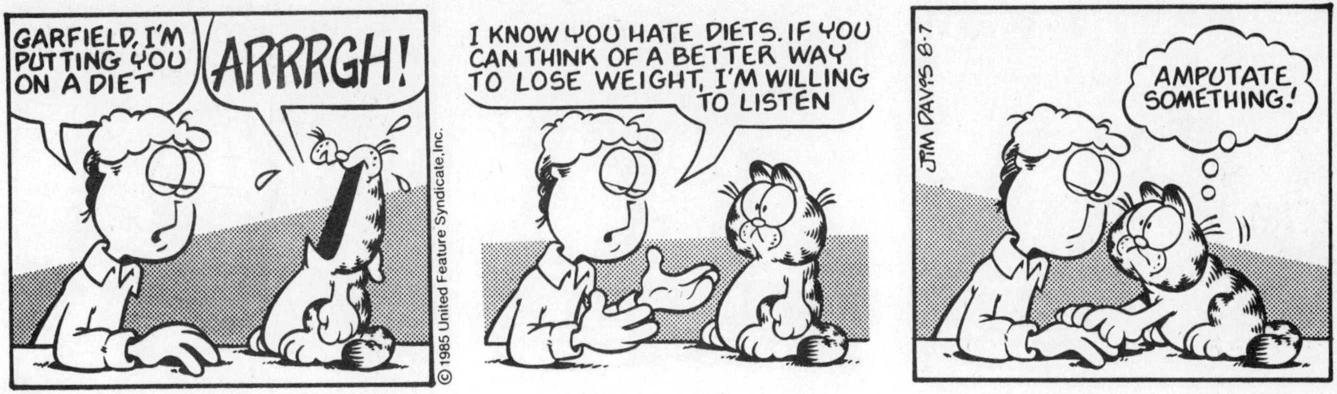
GARFIELD, I'M PUTTING YOU ON A DIET
ARRRGH!
© 1985 United Feature Syndicate, Inc.
I KNOW YOU HATE DIETS. IF YOU CAN THINK OF A BETTER WAY TO LOSE WEIGHT, I'M WILLING TO LISTEN
JIM DAVIS 8-7
AMPUTATE SOMETHING!

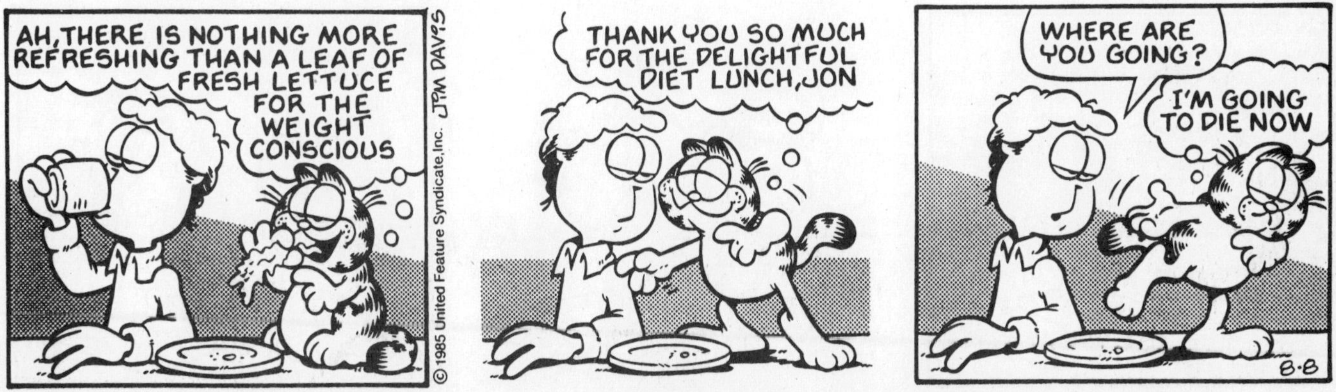
AH, THERE IS NOTHING MORE REFRESHING THAN A LEAF OF FRESH LETTUCE FOR THE WEIGHT CONSCIOUS
JIM DAVIS
© 1985 United Feature Syndicate, Inc.
THANK YOU SO MUCH FOR THE DELIGHTFUL DIET LUNCH, JON
WHERE ARE YOU GOING?
I'M GOING TO DIE NOW
8-8

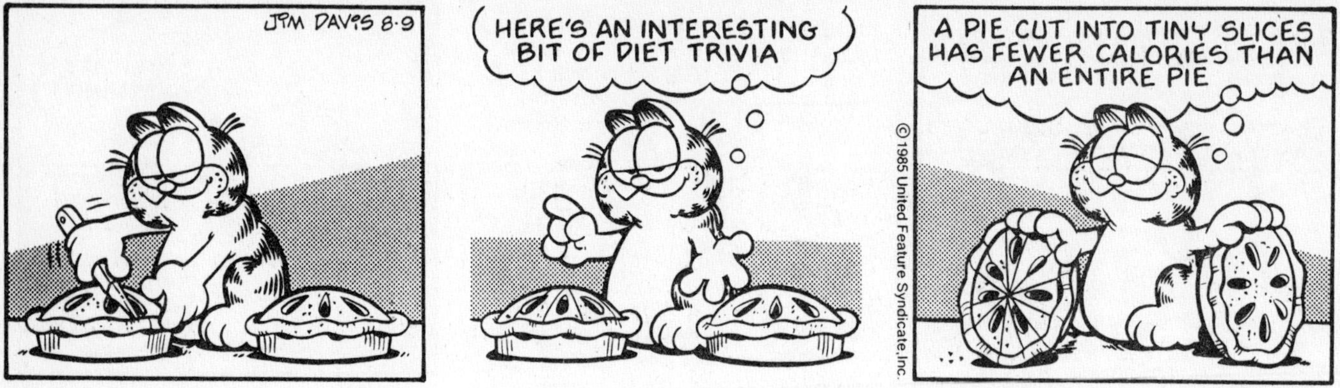
JIM DAVIS 8-9
HERE'S AN INTERESTING BIT OF DIET TRIVIA
A PIE CUT INTO TINY SLICES HAS FEWER CALORIES THAN AN ENTIRE PIE


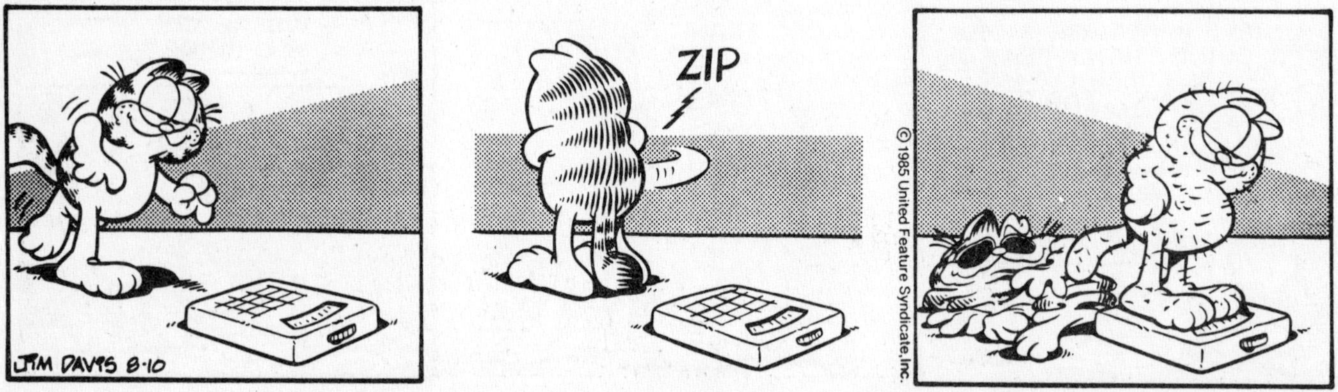
JIM DAVIS 8-10
ZIP

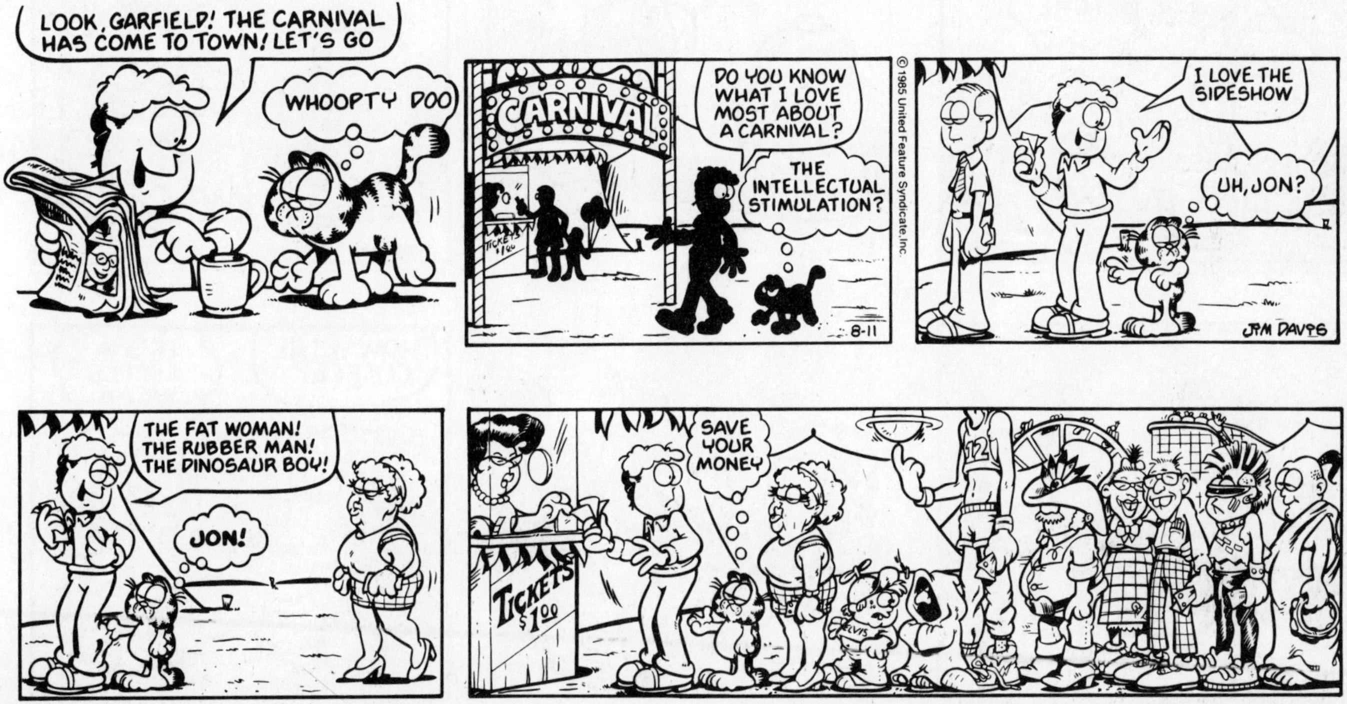
LOOK, GARFIELD! THE CARNIVAL HAS COME TO TOWN! LET'S GO
WHOOPTY DOO
CARNIVAL
TICKETS $1.00
DO YOU KNOW WHAT I LOVE MOST ABOUT A CARNIVAL?
THE INTELLECTUAL STIMULATION?
8-11
© 1985 United Feature Syndicate, Inc.
I LOVE THE SIDESHOW
UH, JON?
JIM DAVIS
THE FAT WOMAN! THE RUBBER MAN! THE DINOSAUR BOY!
JON!
TICKETS $1.00
SAVE YOUR MONEY
12
ELVIS

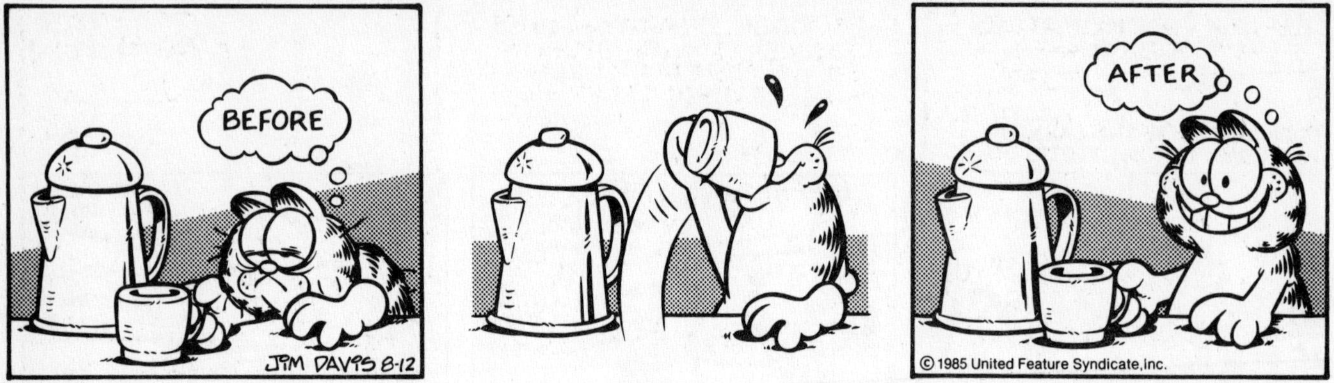
BEFORE
AFTER
JIM DAVIS 8-12
© 1985 United Feature Syndicate,Inc.

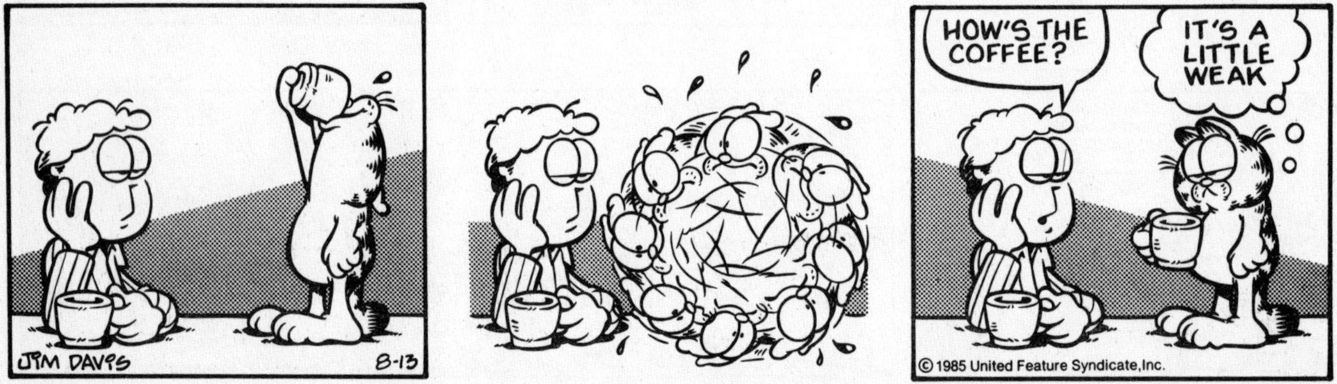
HOW'S THE COFFEE?
IT'S A LITTLE WEAK
JIM DAVIS 8-13
© 1985 United Feature Syndicate,Inc.

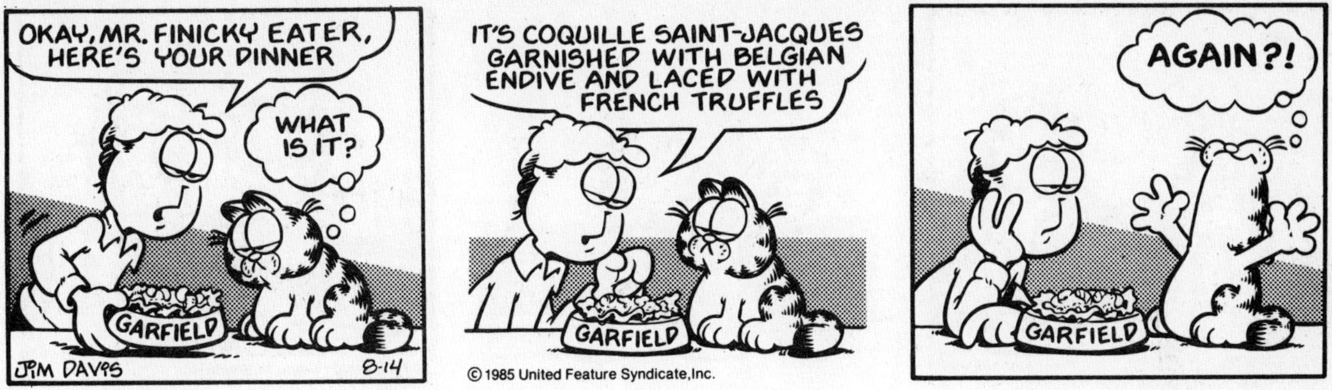
OKAY, MR. FINICKY EATER, HERE'S YOUR DINNER
WHAT IS IT?
GARFIELD
JIM DAVIS
8-14
IT'S COQUILLE SAINT-JACQUES GARNISHED WITH BELGIAN ENDIVE AND LACED WITH FRENCH TRUFFLES
GARFIELD
AGAIN?!
GARFIELD



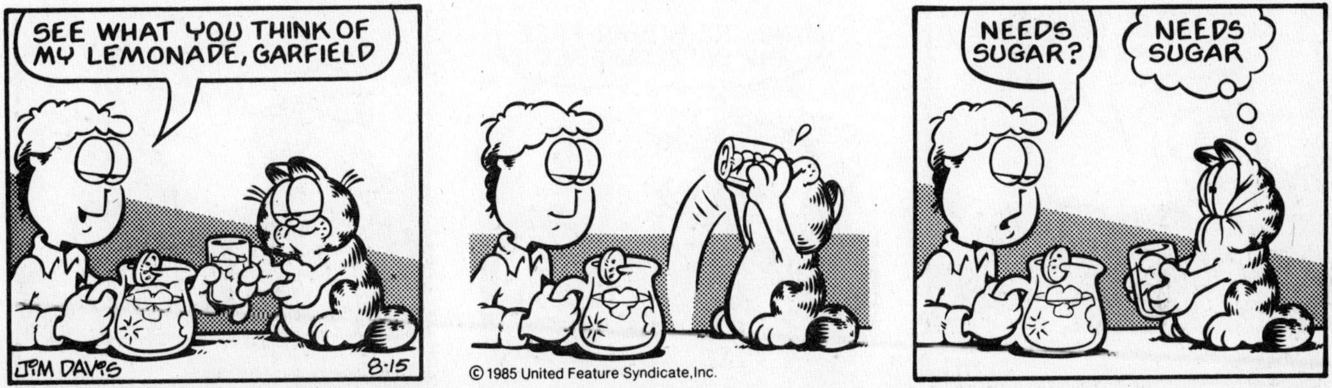
SEE WHAT YOU THINK OF MY LEMONADE, GARFIELD
JIM DAVIS
8-15
NEEDS SUGAR?
NEEDS SUGAR

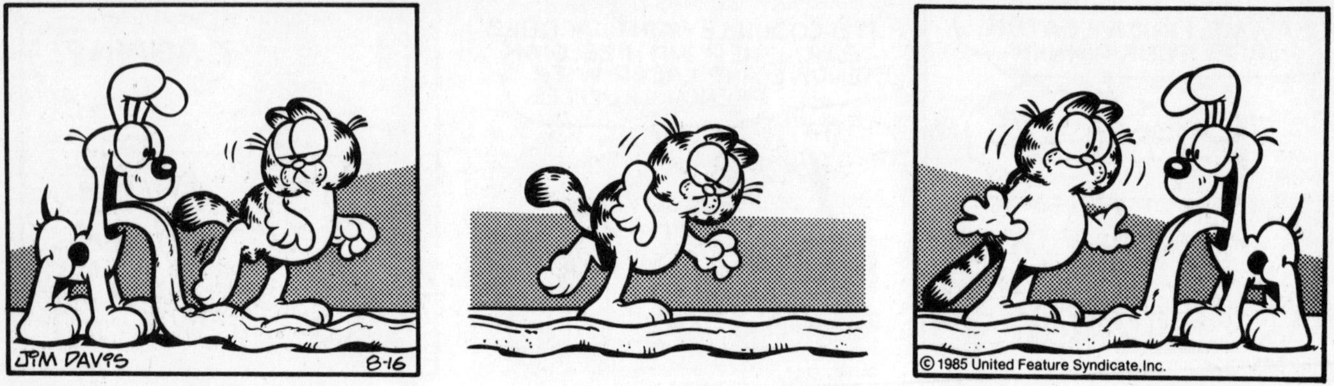
JIM DAVIS
8-16
© 1985 United Feature Syndicate, Inc.

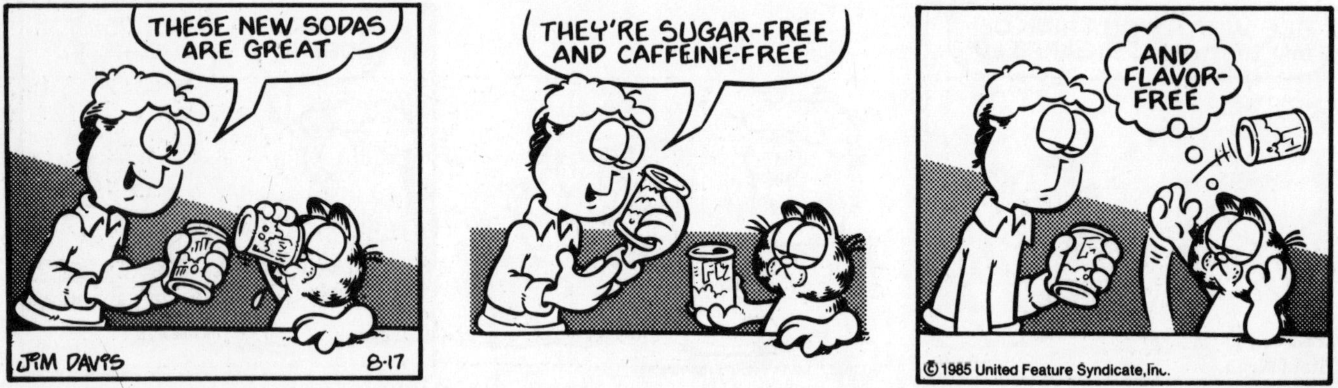
THESE NEW SODAS ARE GREAT
JIM DAVIS
8-17
THEY'RE SUGAR-FREE AND CAFFEINE-FREE
AND FLAVOR-FREE
© 1985 United Feature Syndicate, Inc.

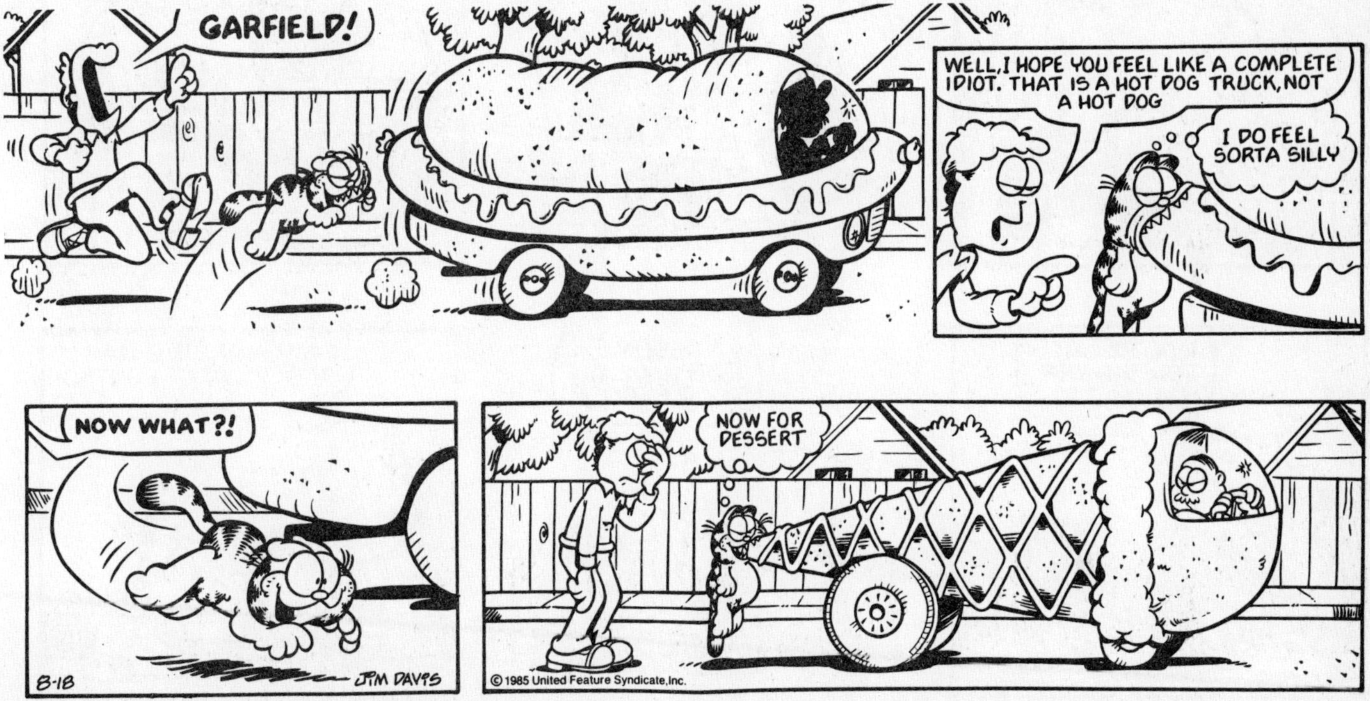
GARFIELD!
WELL, I HOPE YOU FEEL LIKE A COMPLETE IDIOT. THAT IS A HOT DOG TRUCK, NOT A HOT DOG
I DO FEEL SORTA SILLY
NOW WHAT?!
NOW FOR DESSERT
8-18
JIM DAVIS
© 1985 United Feature Syndicate, Inc.

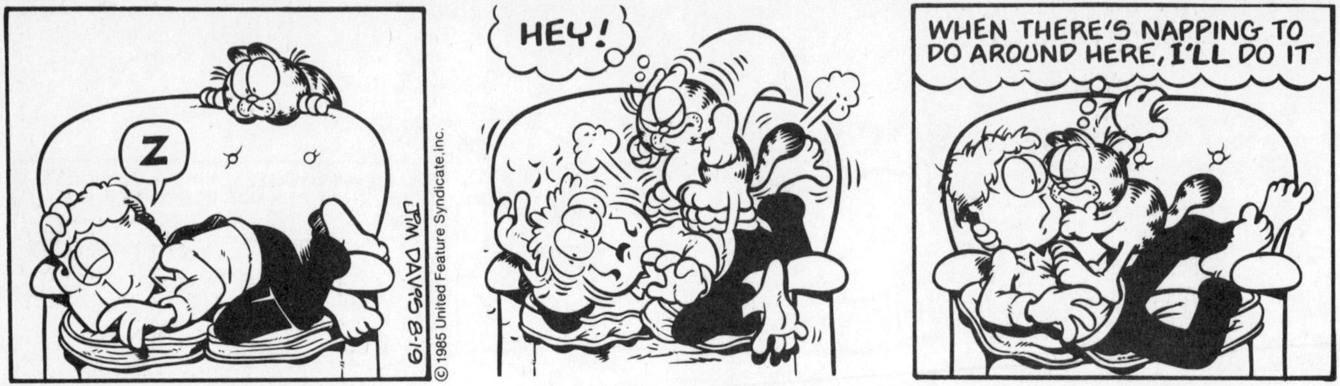
Z
JIM DAVIS 8-19
© 1985 United Feature Syndicate, Inc.
HEY!
WHEN THERE'S NAPPING TO DO AROUND HERE, I'LL DO IT

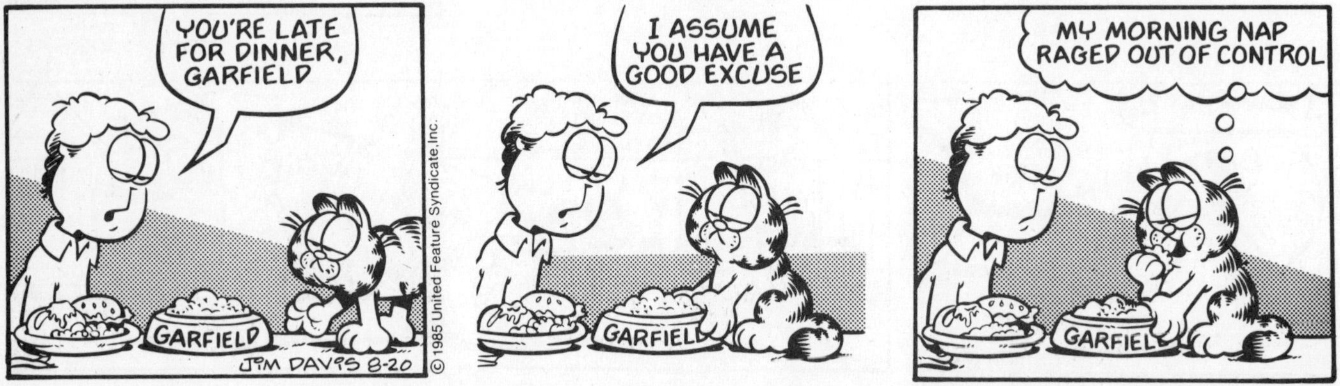
YOU'RE LATE FOR DINNER, GARFIELD
GARFIELD
JIM DAVIS 8-20
© 1985 United Feature Syndicate, Inc.
I ASSUME YOU HAVE A GOOD EXCUSE
GARFIELD
MY MORNING NAP RAGED OUT OF CONTROL
GARFIEL

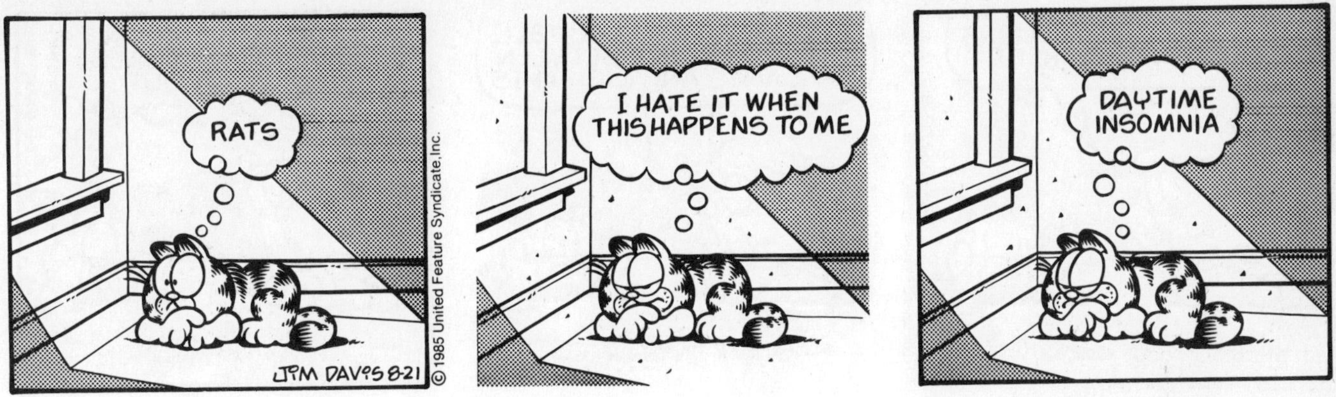
RATS
JIM DAVIS 8-21
I HATE IT WHEN THIS HAPPENS TO ME
DAYTIME INSOMNIA



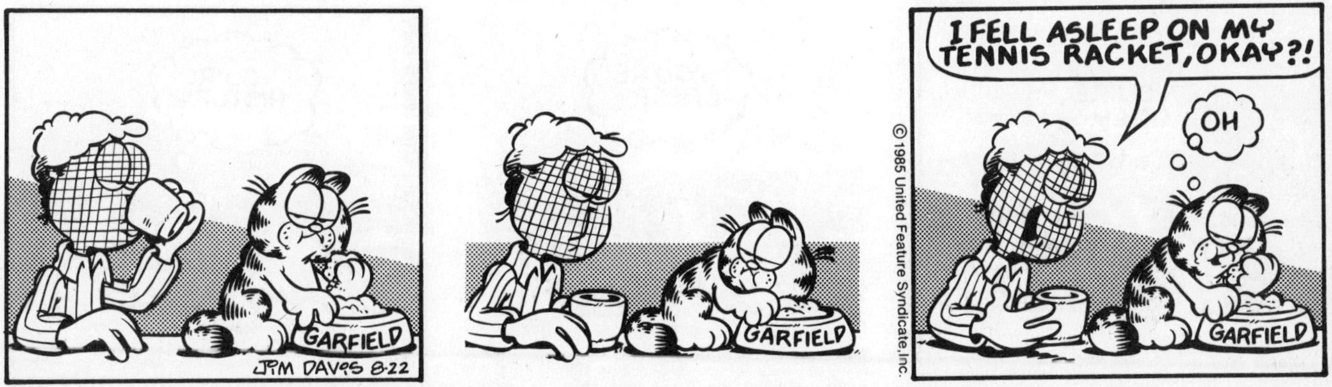
GARFIELD
JIM DAVIS 8-22
GARFIELD
I FELL ASLEEP ON MY TENNIS RACKET, OKAY?!
OH
GARFIELD

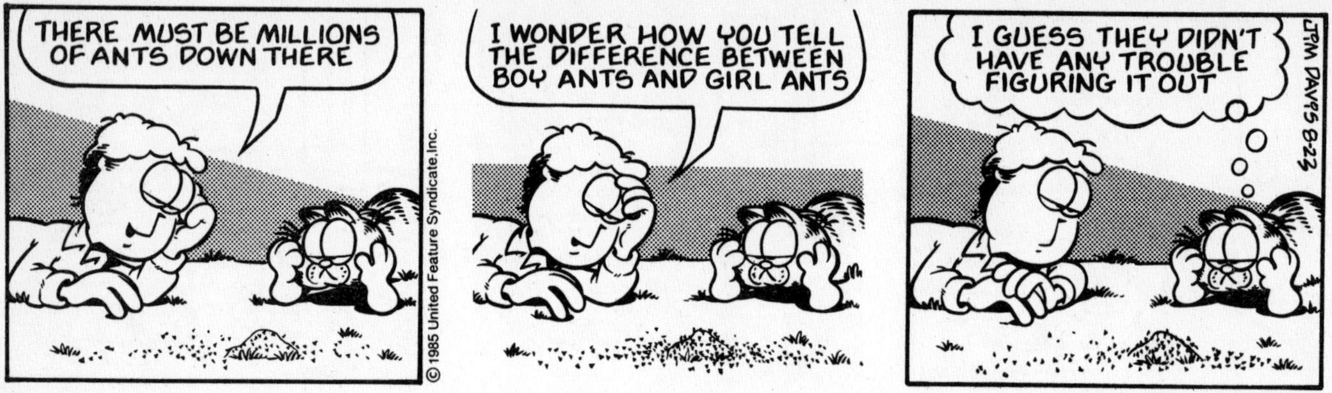
THERE MUST BE MILLIONS OF ANTS DOWN THERE
© 1985 United Feature Syndicate, Inc.
I WONDER HOW YOU TELL THE DIFFERENCE BETWEEN BOY ANTS AND GIRL ANTS
I GUESS THEY DIDN'T HAVE ANY TROUBLE FIGURING IT OUT
JIM DAVIS 8-23

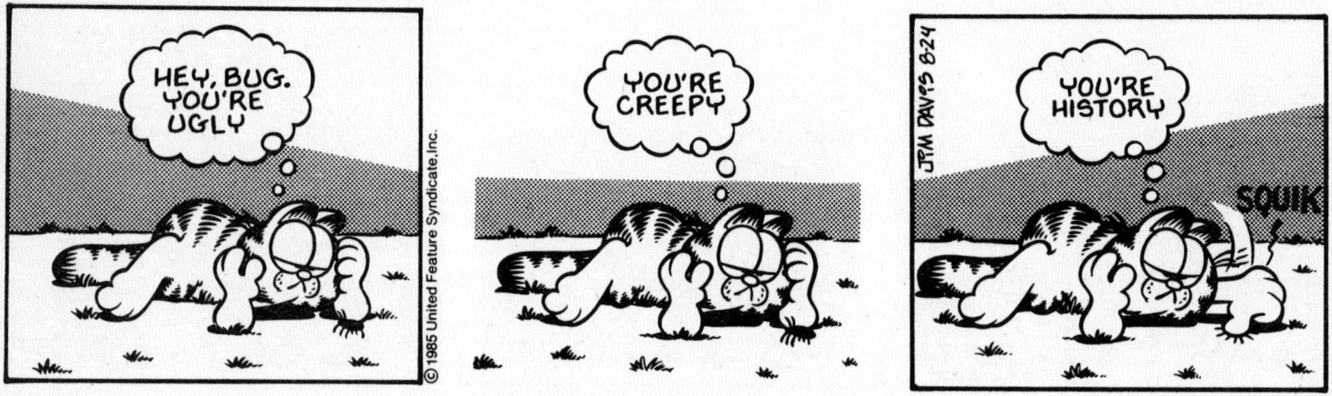
HEY, BUG. YOU'RE UGLY
© 1985 United Feature Syndicate, Inc.
YOU'RE CREEPY
JIM DAVIS 8-24
YOU'RE HISTORY
SQUIK

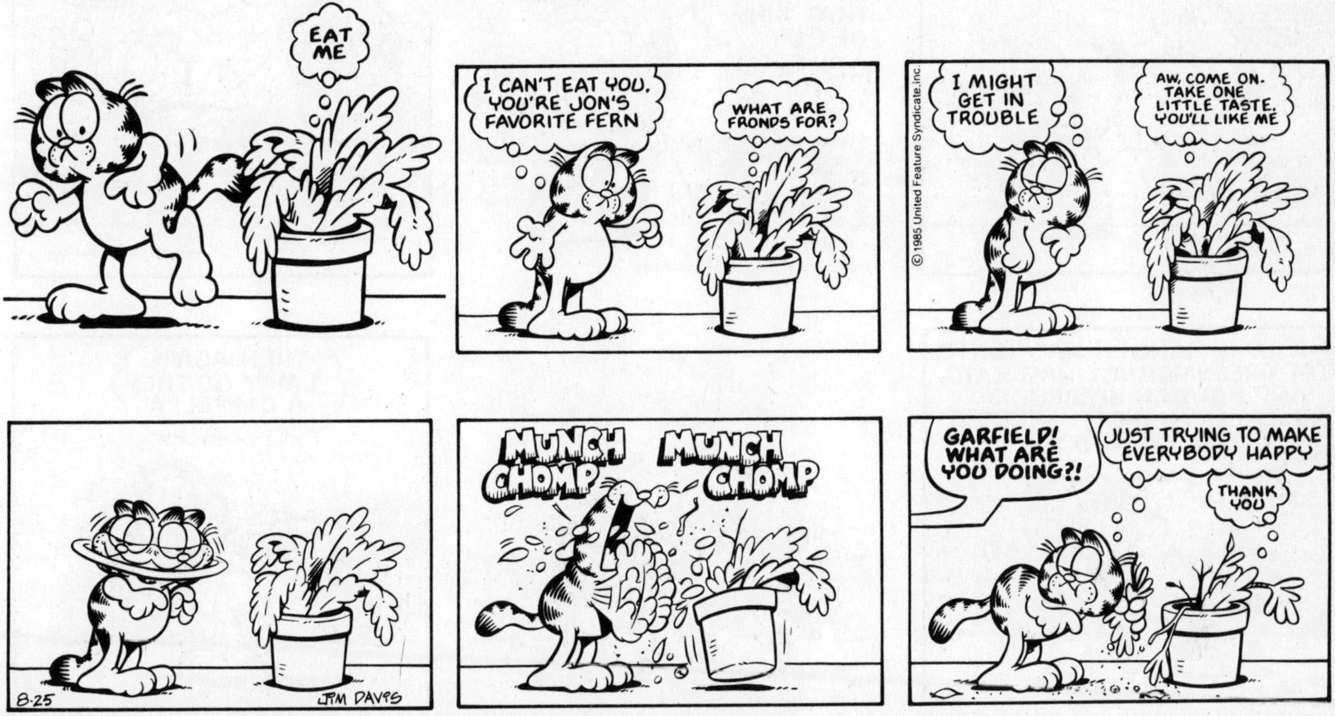
EAT ME
I CAN'T EAT YOU. YOU'RE JON'S FAVORITE FERN
WHAT ARE FRONDS FOR?
I MIGHT GET IN TROUBLE
AW, COME ON. TAKE ONE LITTLE TASTE. YOU'LL LIKE ME
© 1985 United Feature Syndicate, inc.
8-25
JIM DAVIS
MUNCH CHOMP MUNCH CHOMP
GARFIELD! WHAT ARE YOU DOING?!
JUST TRYING TO MAKE EVERYBODY HAPPY
THANK YOU

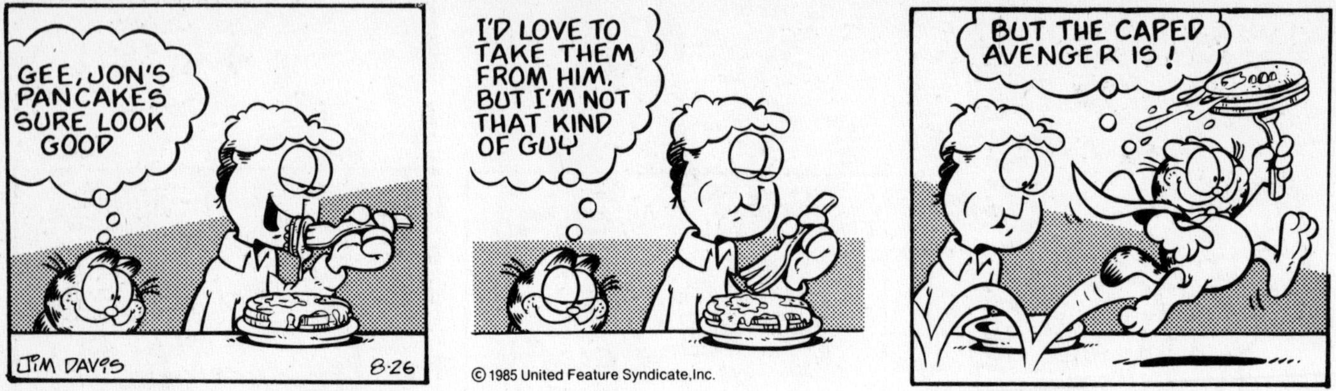
GEE, JON'S PANCAKES SURE LOOK GOOD
JIM DAVIS
8·26
I'D LOVE TO TAKE THEM FROM HIM, BUT I'M NOT THAT KIND OF GUY
BUT THE CAPED AVENGER IS!



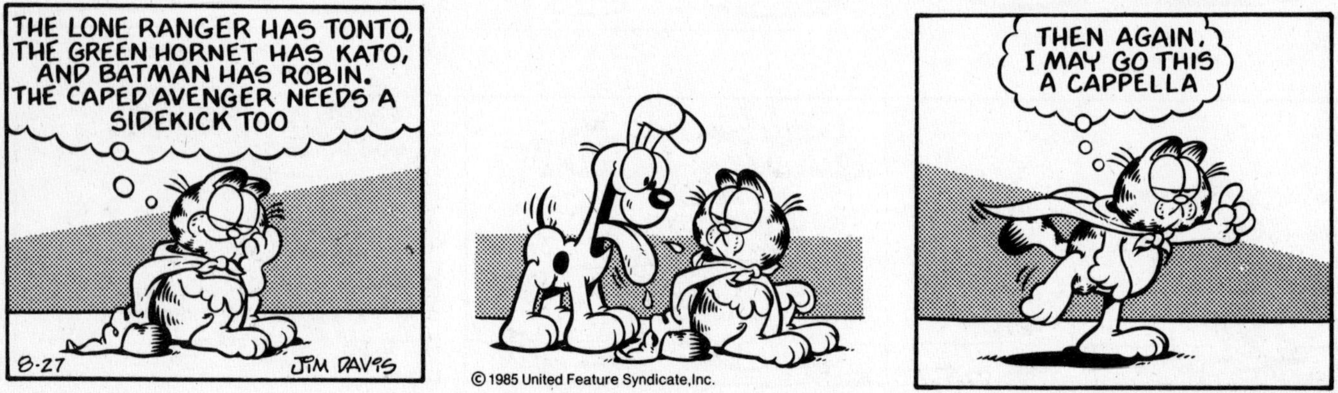
THE LONE RANGER HAS TONTO, THE GREEN HORNET HAS KATO, AND BATMAN HAS ROBIN. THE CAPED AVENGER NEEDS A SIDEKICK TOO
8·27
JIM DAVIS
THEN AGAIN, I MAY GO THIS A CAPPELLA

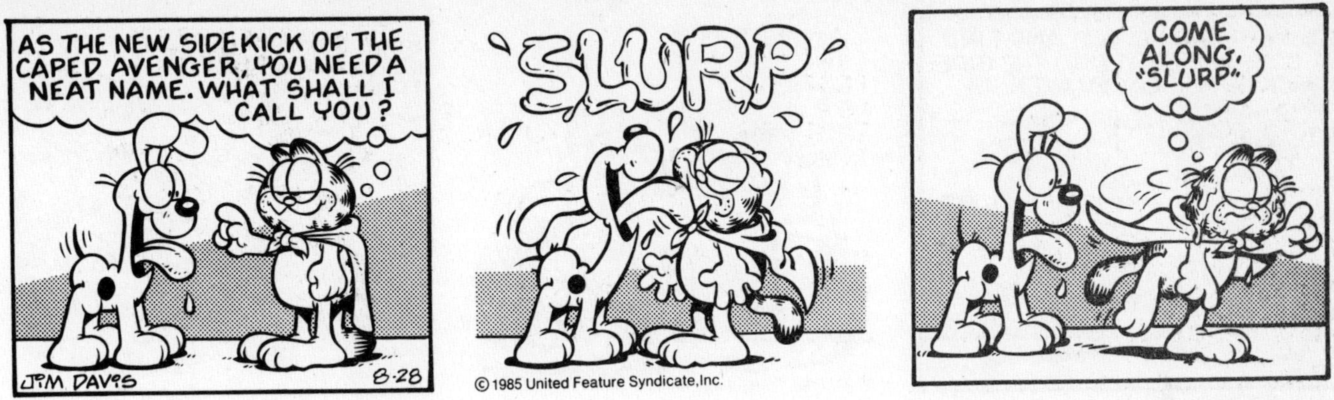
AS THE NEW SIDEKICK OF THE CAPED AVENGER, YOU NEED A NEAT NAME. WHAT SHALL I CALL YOU?
SLURP
COME ALONG, "SLURP"
JIM DAVIS
8-28


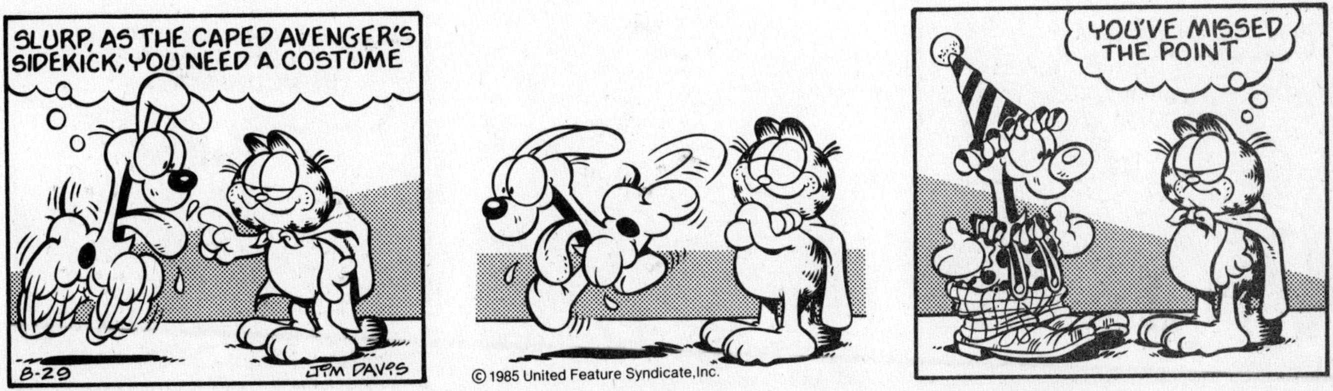
SLURP, AS THE CAPED AVENGER'S SIDEKICK, YOU NEED A COSTUME
YOU'VE MISSED THE POINT
8-29
JIM DAVIS

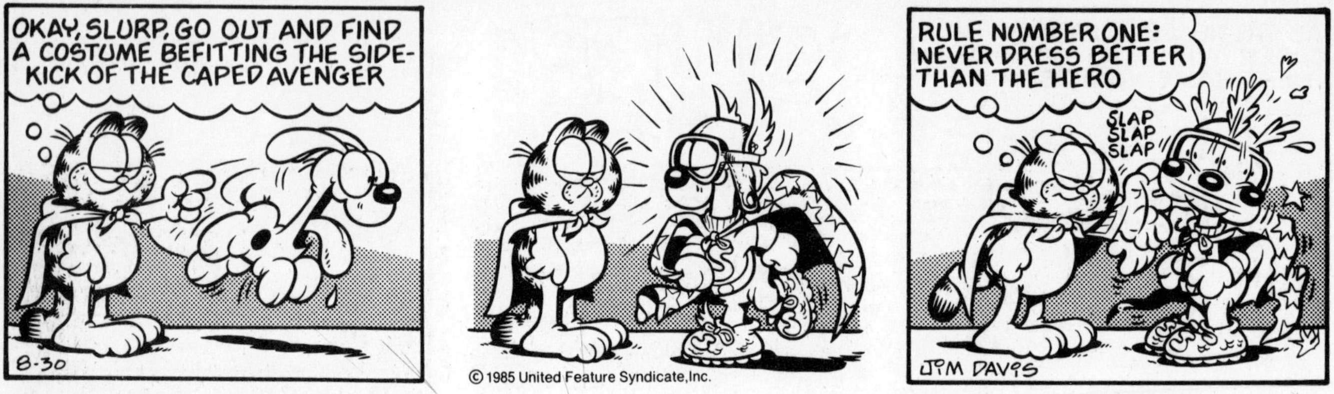
OKAY, SLURP, GO OUT AND FIND A COSTUME BEFITTING THE SIDE-KICK OF THE CAPED AVENGER
8-30
© 1985 United Feature Syndicate, Inc.
RULE NUMBER ONE: NEVER DRESS BETTER THAN THE HERO
SLAP SLAP SLAP
JIM DAVIS

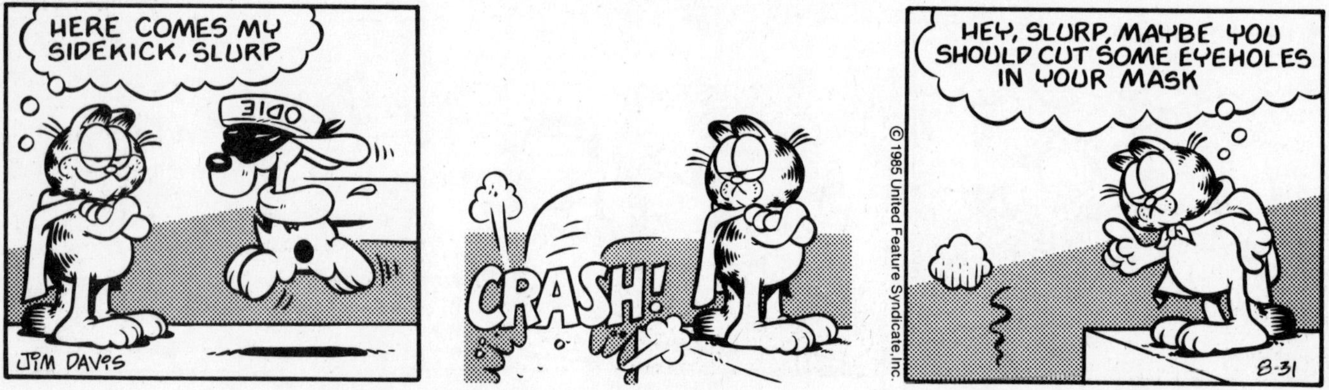
HERE COMES MY SIDEKICK, SLURP
ODIE
JIM DAVIS
CRASH!
© 1985 United Feature Syndicate, Inc.
HEY, SLURP, MAYBE YOU SHOULD CUT SOME EYEHOLES IN YOUR MASK
8-31

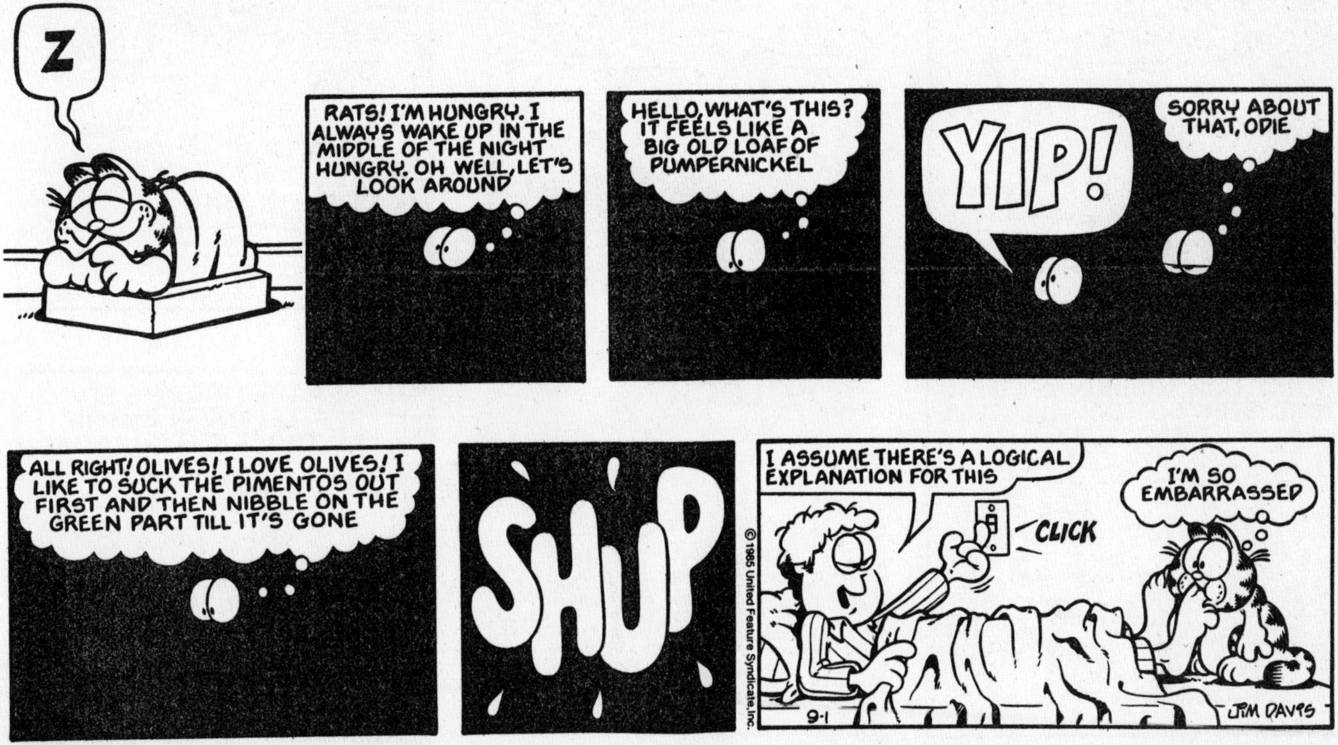
Z
RATS! I'M HUNGRY. I ALWAYS WAKE UP IN THE MIDDLE OF THE NIGHT HUNGRY. OH WELL, LET'S LOOK AROUND
HELLO, WHAT'S THIS? IT FEELS LIKE A BIG OLD LOAF OF PUMPERNICKEL
YIP!
SORRY ABOUT THAT, ODIE
ALL RIGHT! OLIVES! I LOVE OLIVES! I LIKE TO SUCK THE PIMENTOS OUT FIRST AND THEN NIBBLE ON THE GREEN PART TILL IT'S GONE
SHUP
I ASSUME THERE'S A LOGICAL EXPLANATION FOR THIS
CLICK
I'M SO EMBARRASSED
© 1985 United Feature Syndicate, Inc.
9-1
JIM DAVIS

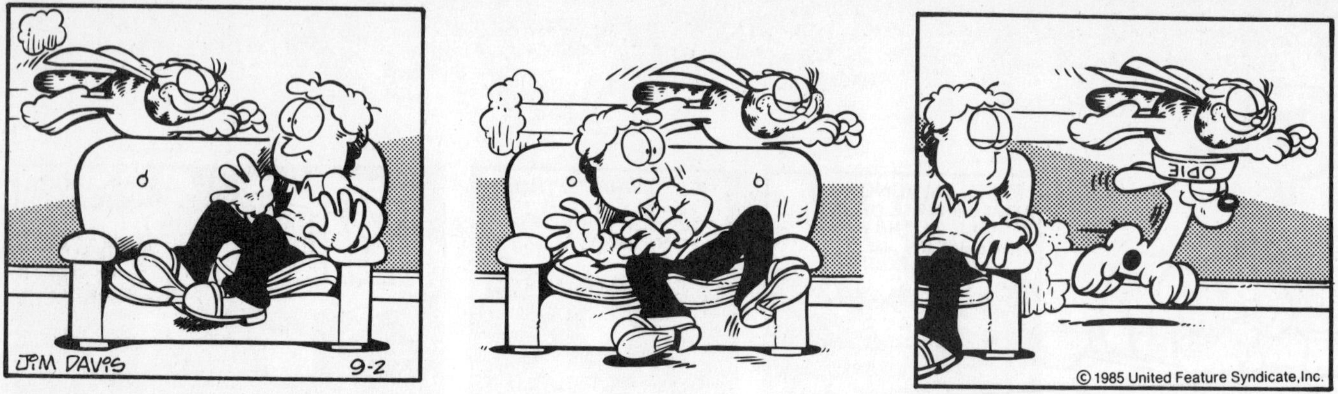
JIM DAVIS
9-2
ODIE


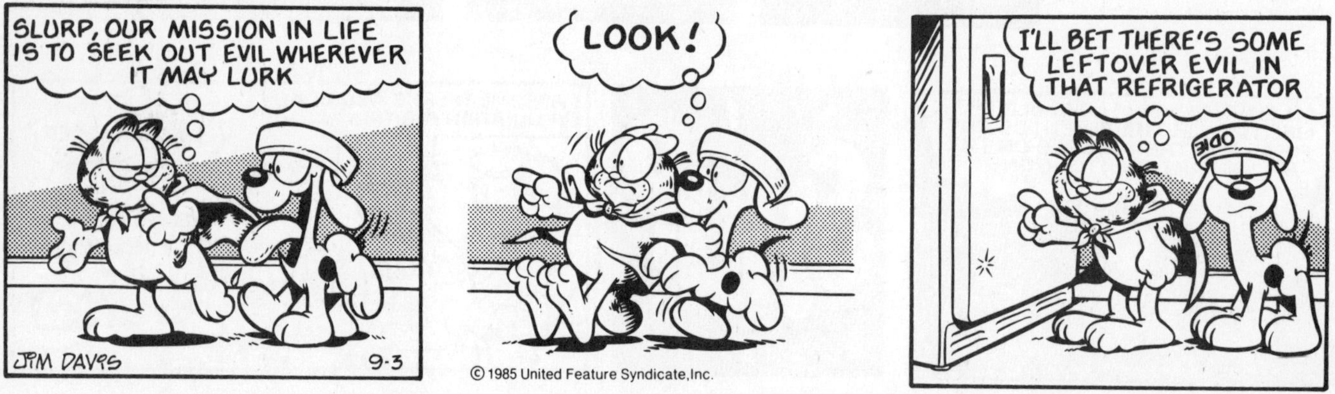
SLURP, OUR MISSION IN LIFE IS TO SEEK OUT EVIL WHEREVER IT MAY LURK
JIM DAVIS
9-3
LOOK!
I'LL BET THERE'S SOME LEFTOVER EVIL IN THAT REFRIGERATOR
ODIE

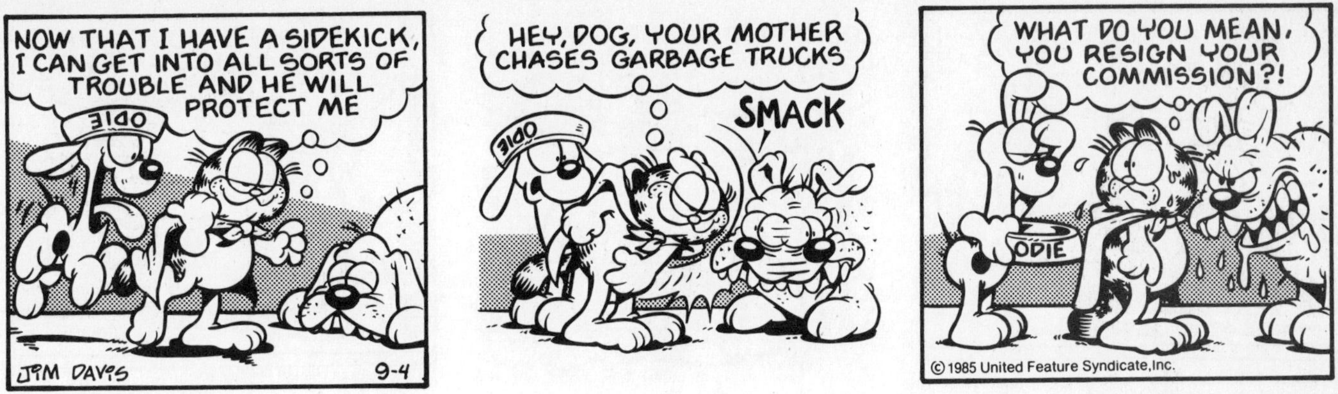
NOW THAT I HAVE A SIDEKICK, I CAN GET INTO ALL SORTS OF TROUBLE AND HE WILL PROTECT ME
JIM DAVIS
9-4
HEY, DOG, YOUR MOTHER CHASES GARBAGE TRUCKS
SMACK
WHAT DO YOU MEAN, YOU RESIGN YOUR COMMISSION?!
ODIE
© 1985 United Feature Syndicate, Inc.

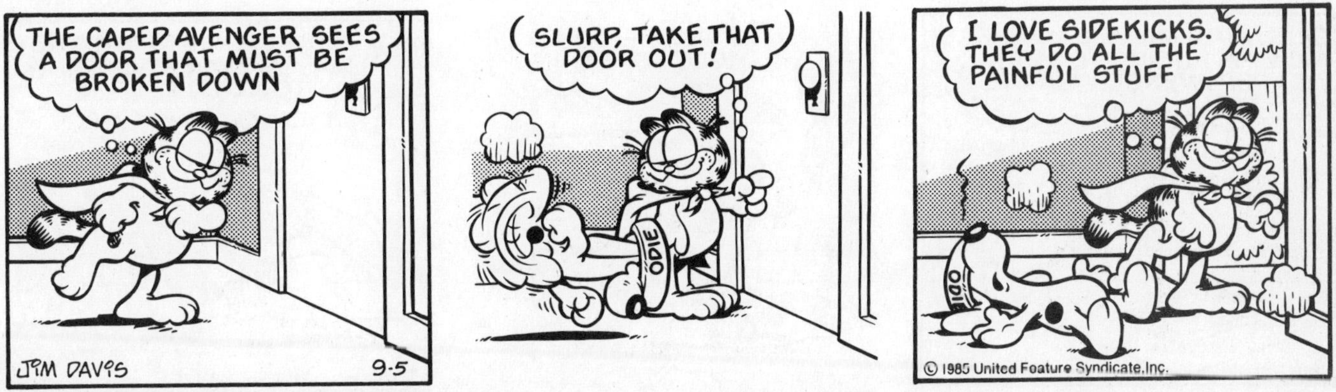
THE CAPED AVENGER SEES A DOOR THAT MUST BE BROKEN DOWN
JIM DAVIS
9-5
SLURP, TAKE THAT DOOR OUT!
ODIE
I LOVE SIDEKICKS. THEY DO ALL THE PAINFUL STUFF
© 1985 United Feature Syndicate, Inc.

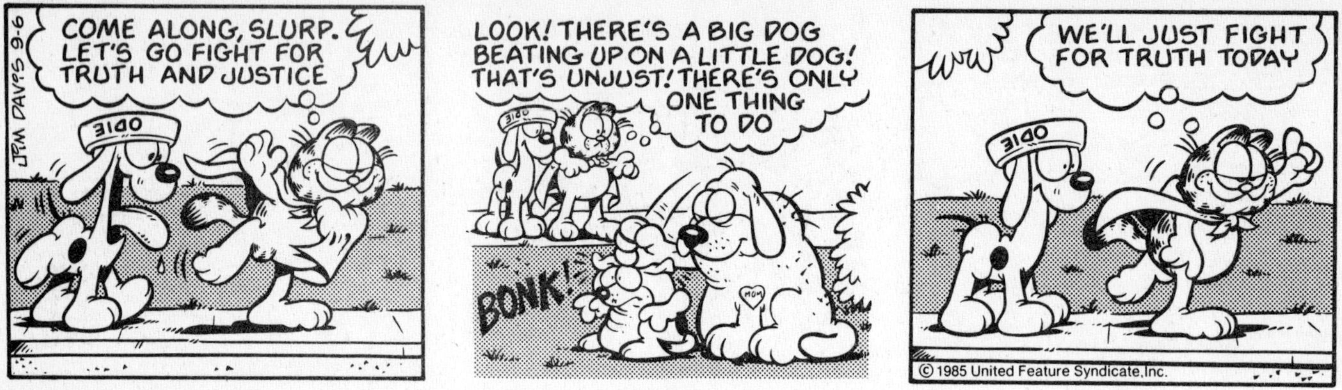
JIM DAVIS 9-6
COME ALONG, SLURP. LET'S GO FIGHT FOR TRUTH AND JUSTICE
LOOK! THERE'S A BIG DOG BEATING UP ON A LITTLE DOG! THAT'S UNJUST! THERE'S ONLY ONE THING TO DO
BONK!
MOM
WE'LL JUST FIGHT FOR TRUTH TODAY
© 1985 United Feature Syndicate, Inc.

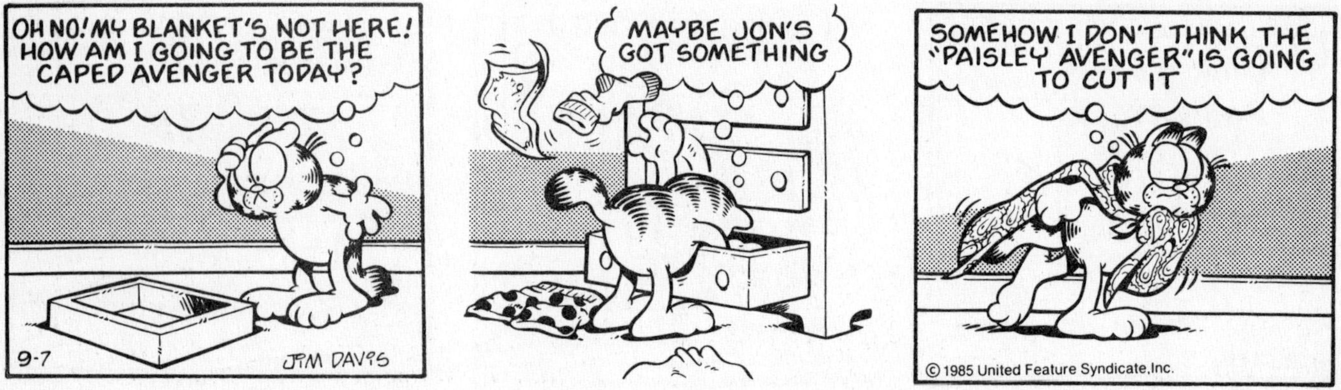
OH NO! MY BLANKET'S NOT HERE! HOW AM I GOING TO BE THE CAPED AVENGER TODAY?
9-7
JIM DAVIS
MAYBE JON'S GOT SOMETHING
SOMEHOW I DON'T THINK THE "PAISLEY AVENGER" IS GOING TO CUT IT
© 1985 United Feature Syndicate, Inc.

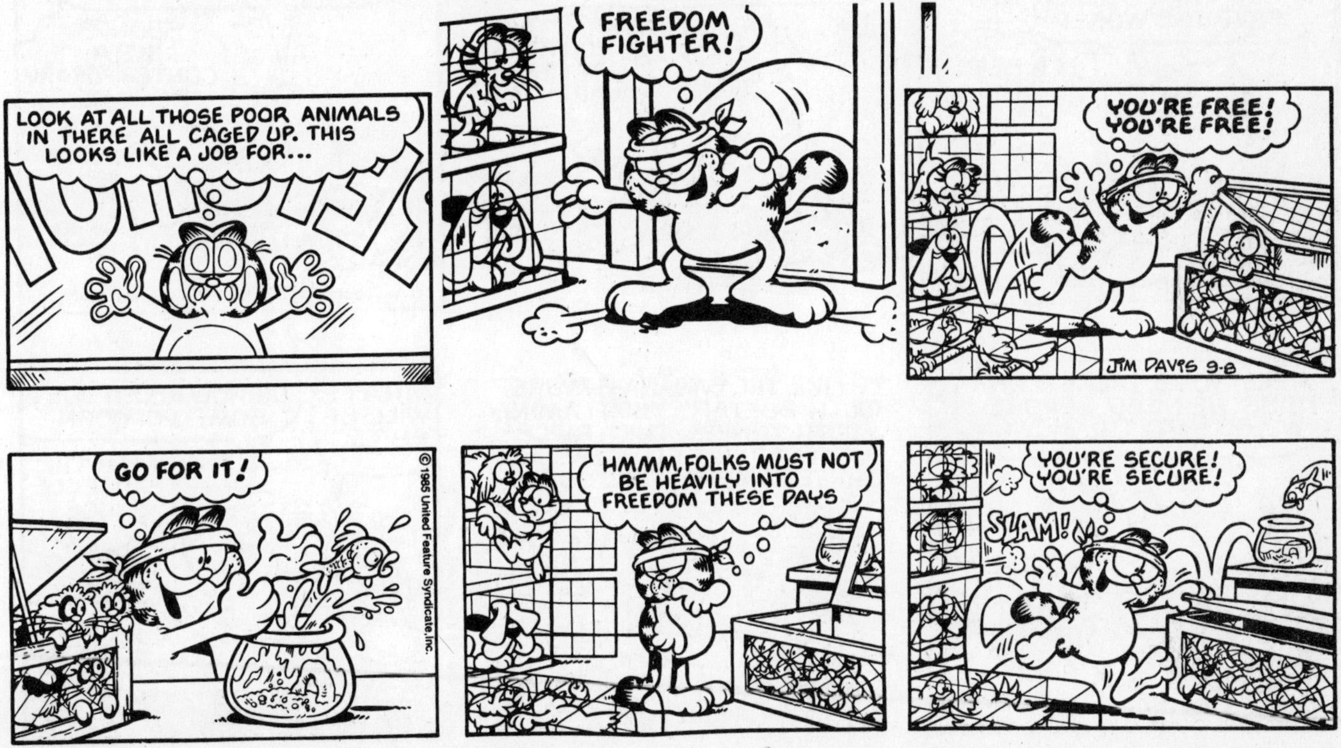
LOOK AT ALL THOSE POOR ANIMALS IN THERE ALL CAGED UP. THIS LOOKS LIKE A JOB FOR...
FREEDOM FIGHTER!
YOU'RE FREE! YOU'RE FREE!
JIM DAVIS 9-8
GO FOR IT!
© 1985 United Feature Syndicate, Inc.
HMMM, FOLKS MUST NOT BE HEAVILY INTO FREEDOM THESE DAYS
YOU'RE SECURE! YOU'RE SECURE!
SLAM!

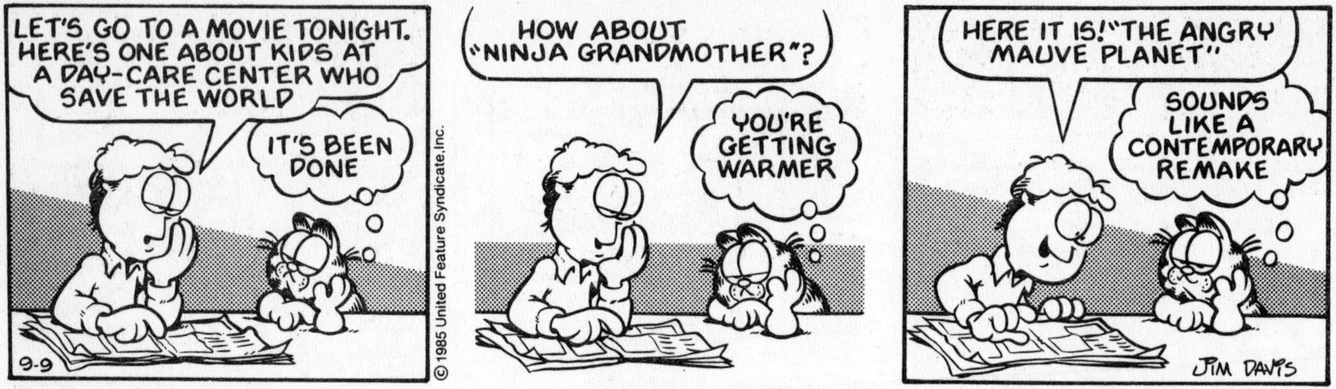
LET'S GO TO A MOVIE TONIGHT. HERE'S ONE ABOUT KIDS AT A DAY-CARE CENTER WHO SAVE THE WORLD
IT'S BEEN DONE
9-9
HOW ABOUT "NINJA GRANDMOTHER"?
YOU'RE GETTING WARMER
HERE IT IS! "THE ANGRY MAUVE PLANET"
SOUNDS LIKE A CONTEMPORARY REMAKE
JIM DAVIS


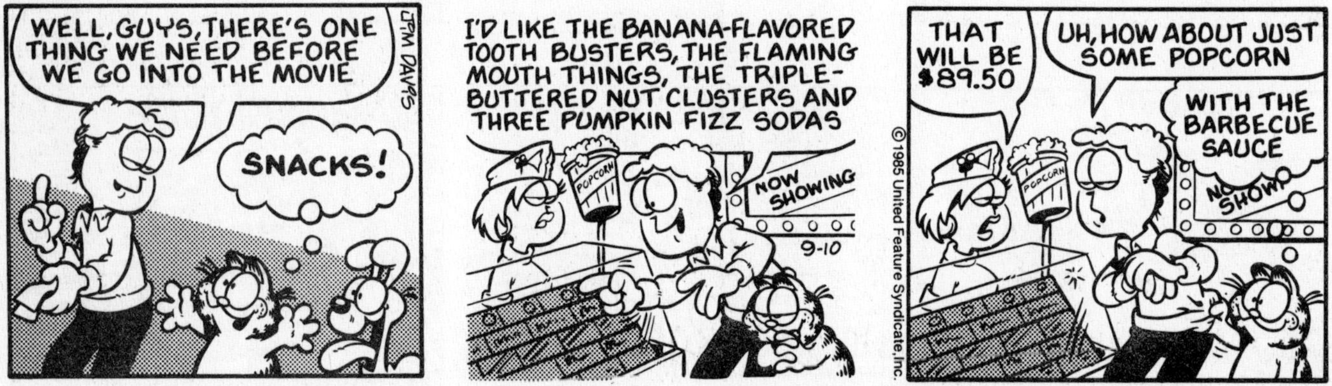
WELL, GUYS, THERE'S ONE THING WE NEED BEFORE WE GO INTO THE MOVIE
SNACKS!
JIM DAVIS
I'D LIKE THE BANANA-FLAVORED TOOTH BUSTERS, THE FLAMING MOUTH THINGS, THE TRIPLE-BUTTERED NUT CLUSTERS AND THREE PUMPKIN FIZZ SODAS
POPCORN
NOW SHOWING
9-10
THAT WILL BE $89.50
UH, HOW ABOUT JUST SOME POPCORN
WITH THE BARBECUE SAUCE
POPCORN

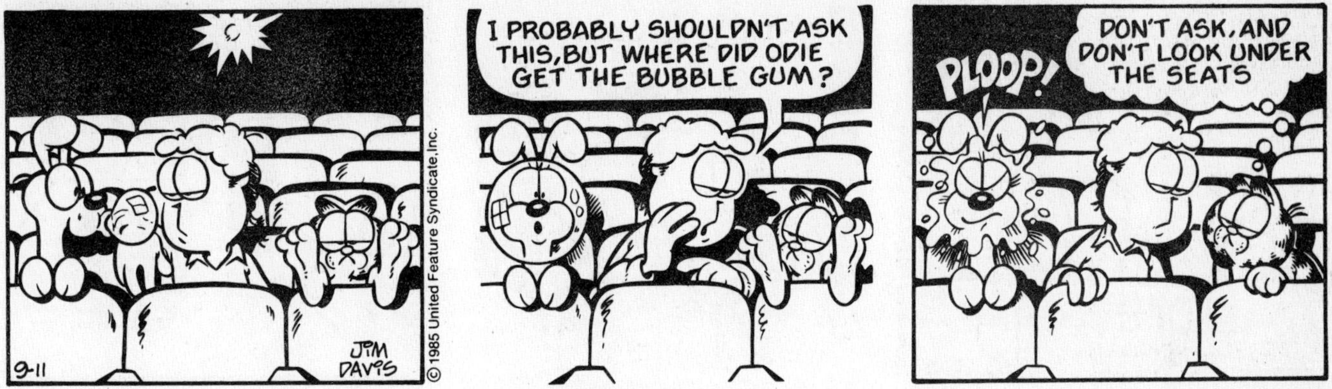
9-11
JIM DAVIS
© 1985 United Feature Syndicate, Inc.
I PROBABLY SHOULDN'T ASK THIS, BUT WHERE DID ODIE GET THE BUBBLE GUM?
PLOOP!
DON'T ASK, AND DON'T LOOK UNDER THE SEATS

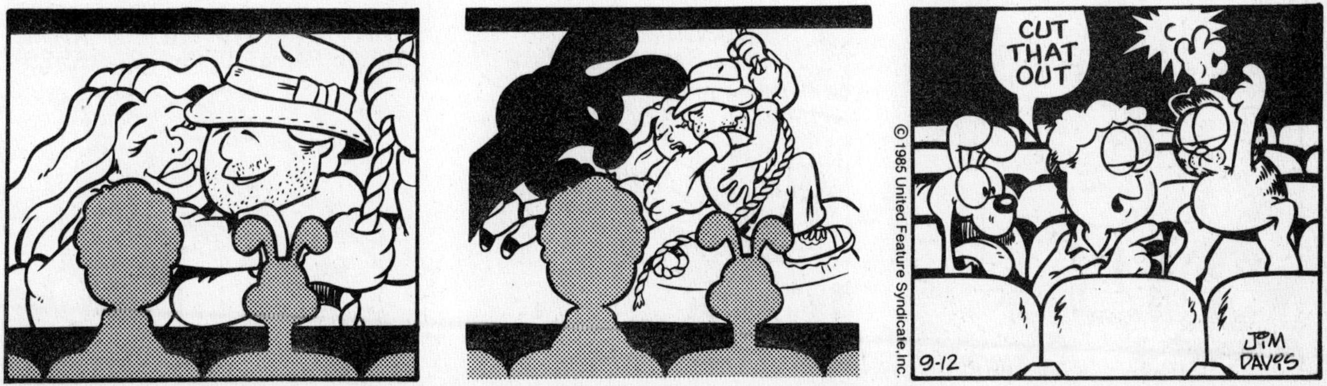
© 1985 United Feature Syndicate, Inc.
CUT THAT OUT
9-12
JIM DAVIS

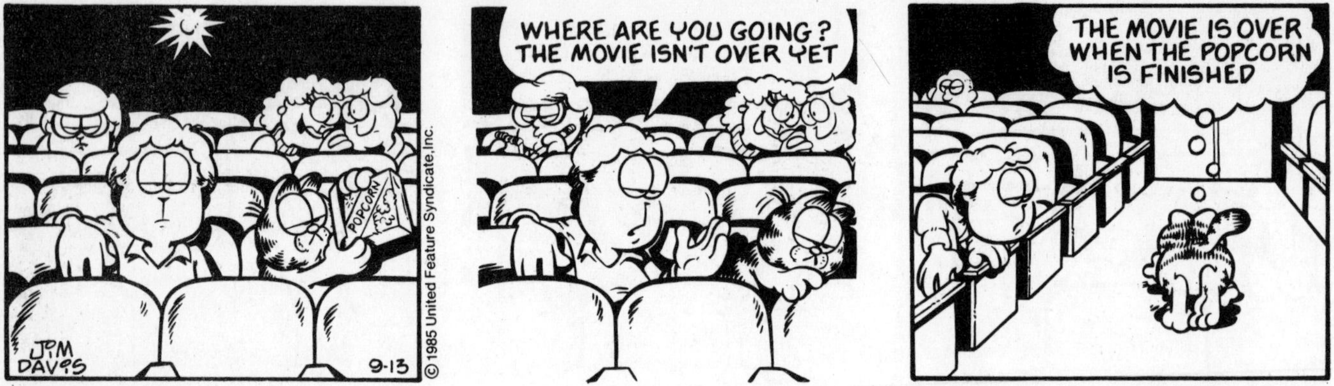

POPCORN
JIM DAVIS
9-13
© 1985 United Feature Syndicate, Inc.
WHERE ARE YOU GOING? THE MOVIE ISN'T OVER YET
THE MOVIE IS OVER WHEN THE POPCORN IS FINISHED


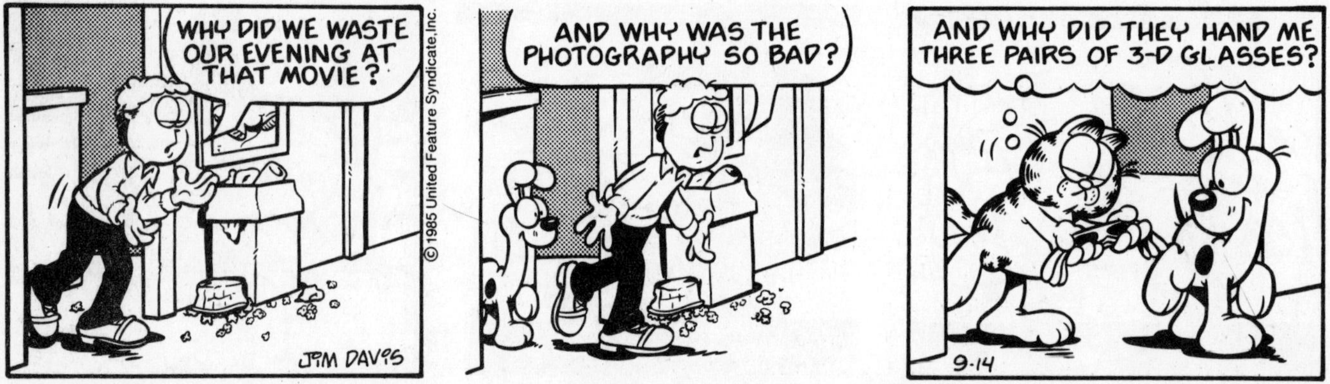

WHY DID WE WASTE OUR EVENING AT THAT MOVIE?
JIM DAVIS
© 1985 United Feature Syndicate, Inc.
AND WHY WAS THE PHOTOGRAPHY SO BAD?
AND WHY DID THEY HAND ME THREE PAIRS OF 3-D GLASSES?
9-14

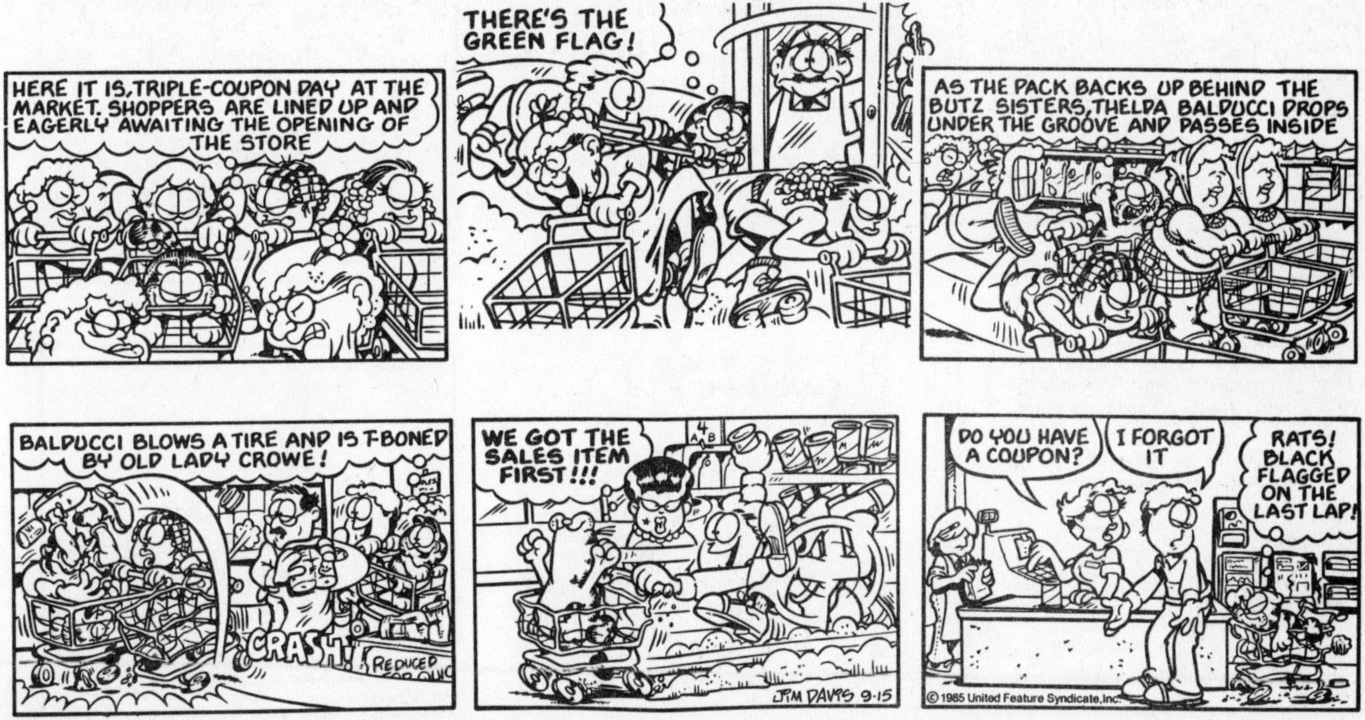
HERE IT IS, TRIPLE-COUPON DAY AT THE MARKET. SHOPPERS ARE LINED UP AND EAGERLY AWAITING THE OPENING OF THE STORE
THERE'S THE GREEN FLAG!
AS THE PACK BACKS UP BEHIND THE BUTZ SISTERS, THELDA BALDUCCI DROPS UNDER THE GROOVE AND PASSES INSIDE
BALDUCCI BLOWS A TIRE AND IS T-BONED BY OLD LADY CROWE!
CRASH!
REDUCED
WE GOT THE SALES ITEM FIRST!!!
JIM DAVIS 9-15
DO YOU HAVE A COUPON?
I FORGOT IT
RATS! BLACK FLAGGED ON THE LAST LAP!
© 1985 United Feature Syndicate, Inc.

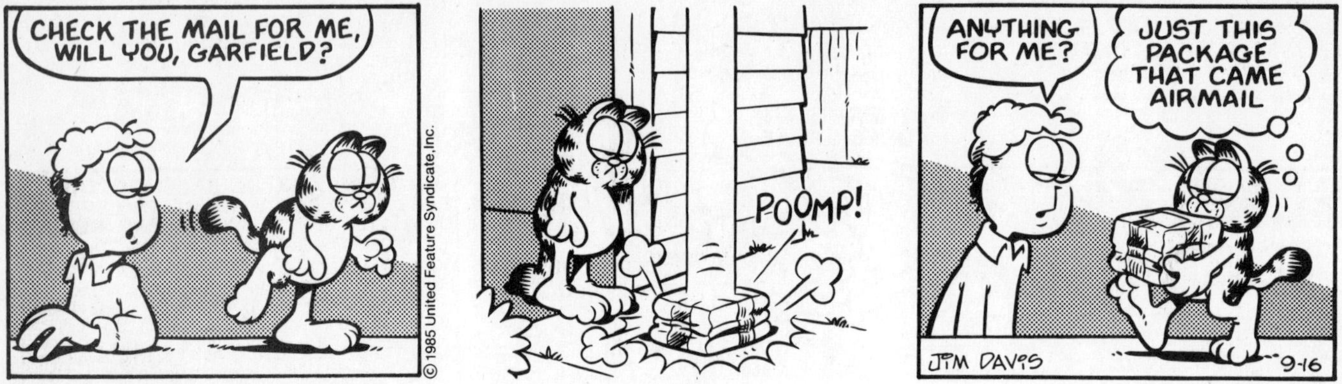
CHECK THE MAIL FOR ME, WILL YOU, GARFIELD?
POOMP!
ANYTHING FOR ME?
JUST THIS PACKAGE THAT CAME AIRMAIL
JIM DAVIS 9-16



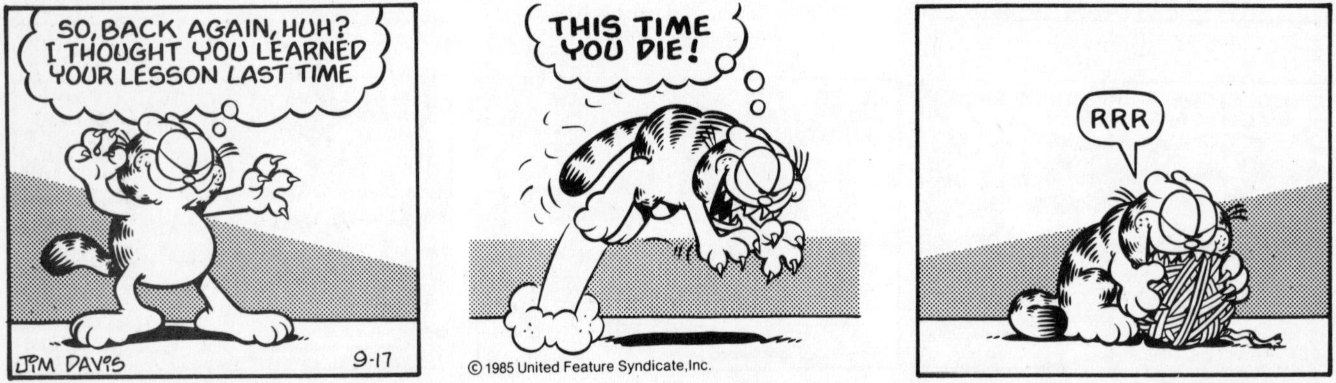
SO, BACK AGAIN, HUH? I THOUGHT YOU LEARNED YOUR LESSON LAST TIME
THIS TIME YOU DIE!
RRR
JIM DAVIS 9-17

I HAVE SOME BAD NEWS, GARFIELD. I RAN OUT OF YOUR FAVORITE CAT FOOD
I'LL SURVIVE
ODIE CHEWED UP YOUR SCRATCHING POST
BIG DEAL
AND FRANK LEFT MARCIA FOR STEPHANIE
HOW COULD HE?!
9-18
JIM DAVIS

THERE'S A MOUSE IN THE HOUSE. WHAT ARE YOU GOING TO DO ABOUT IT?
JIM DAVIS
9-19
LIGHTEN UP, JON. HOW MUCH CAN ONE LITTLE MOUSE EAT?
CAN WE TALK?
NNGH!

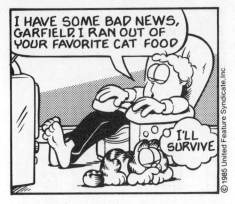

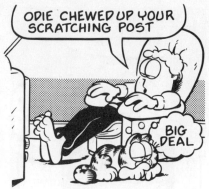

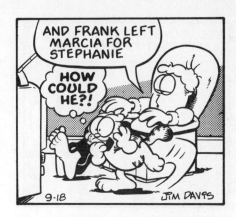

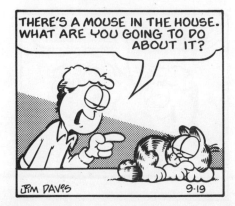

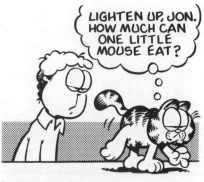

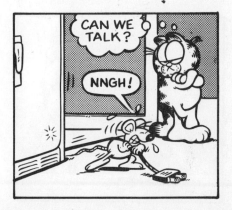

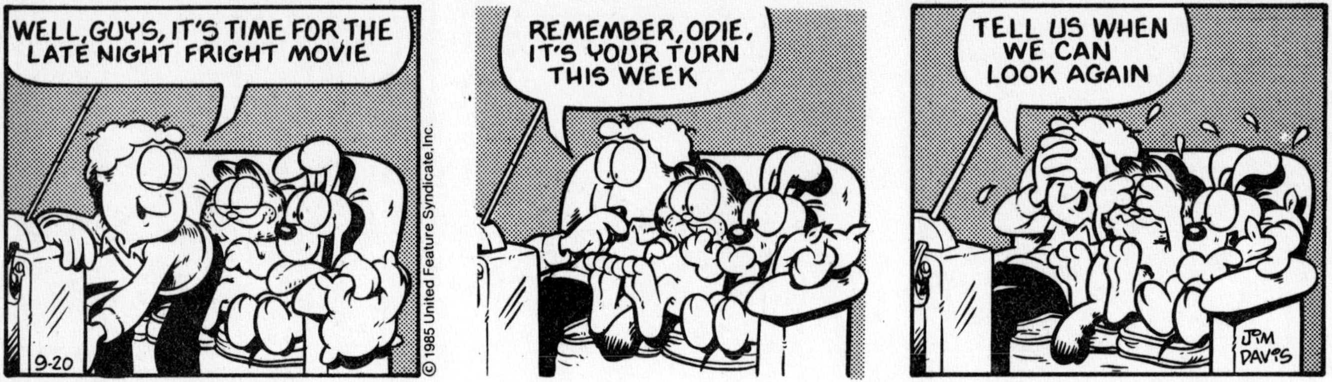
WELL, GUYS, IT'S TIME FOR THE LATE NIGHT FRIGHT MOVIE
9-20
© 1985 United Feature Syndicate, Inc.
REMEMBER, ODIE, IT'S YOUR TURN THIS WEEK
TELL US WHEN WE CAN LOOK AGAIN
JIM DAVIS

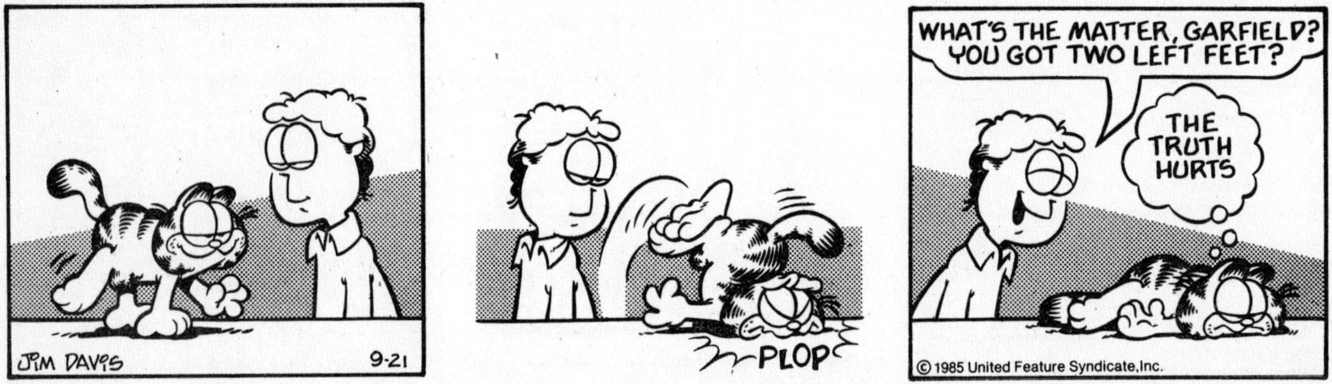
JIM DAVIS
9-21
PLOP
WHAT'S THE MATTER, GARFIELD? YOU GOT TWO LEFT FEET?
THE TRUTH HURTS
© 1985 United Feature Syndicate, Inc.

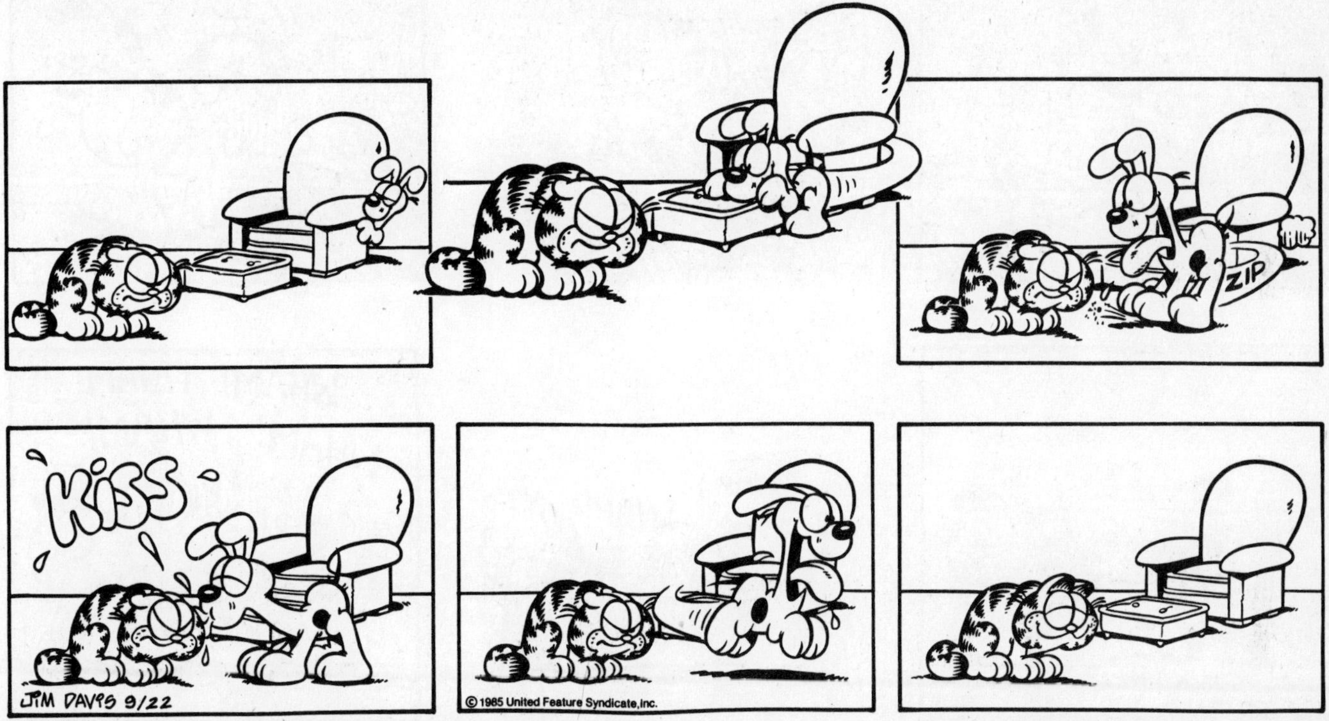
ZIP
KISS
JIM DAVIS 9/22
© 1985 United Feature Syndicate, Inc.

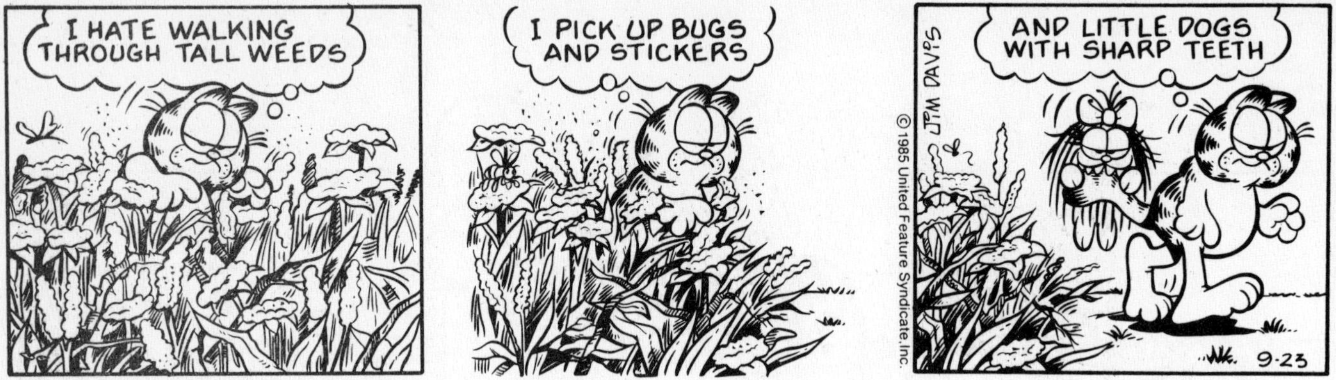
I HATE WALKING THROUGH TALL WEEDS
I PICK UP BUGS AND STICKERS
AND LITTLE DOGS WITH SHARP TEETH
JIM DAVIS
© 1985 United Feature Syndicate, Inc.
9-23

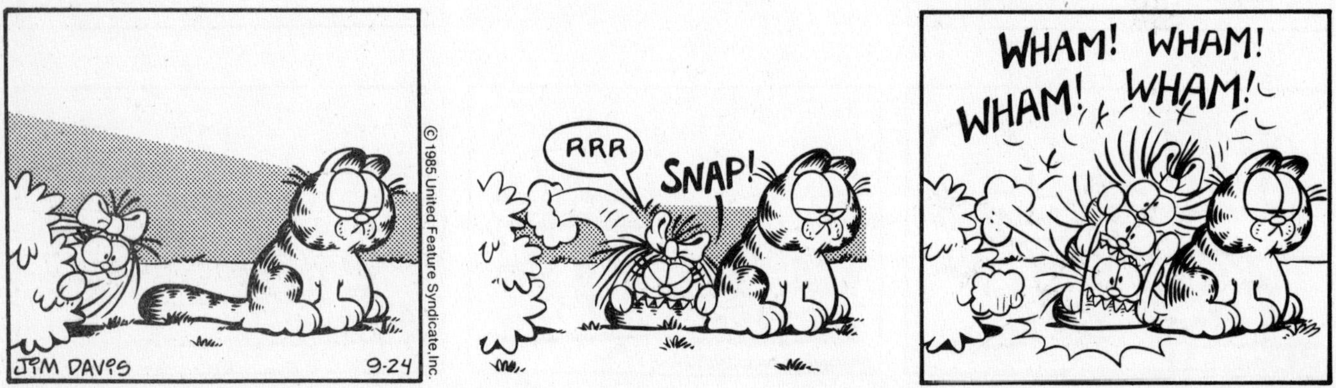
JIM DAVIS
9-24
© 1985 United Feature Syndicate, Inc.
RRR
SNAP!
WHAM! WHAM!
WHAM! WHAM!

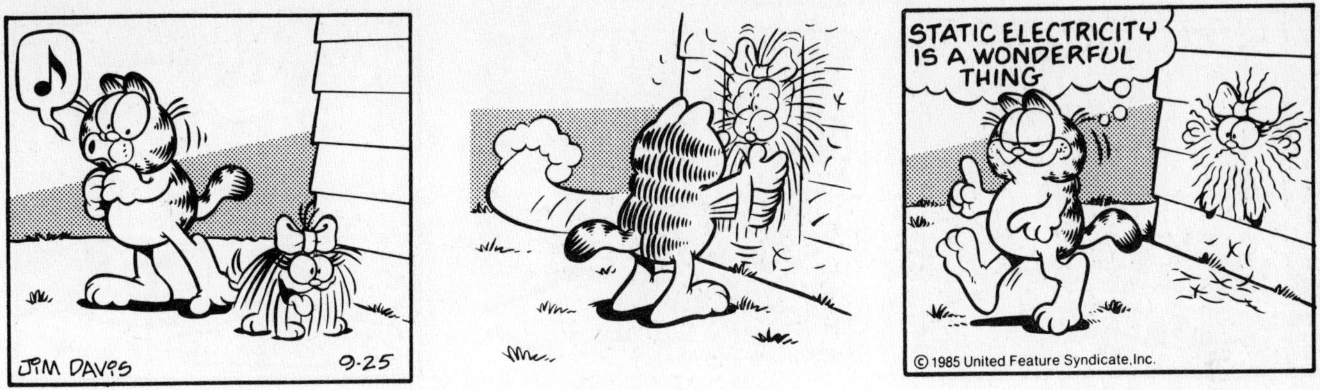
JIM DAVIS
9-25
STATIC ELECTRICITY IS A WONDERFUL THING
© 1985 United Feature Syndicate, Inc.

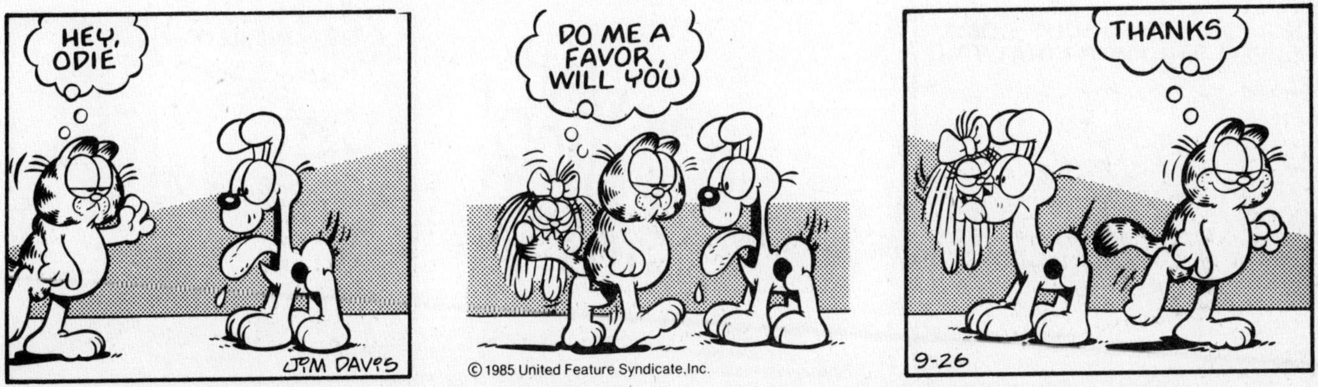
HEY, ODIE
JIM DAVIS
DO ME A FAVOR, WILL YOU
© 1985 United Feature Syndicate, Inc.
THANKS
9-26

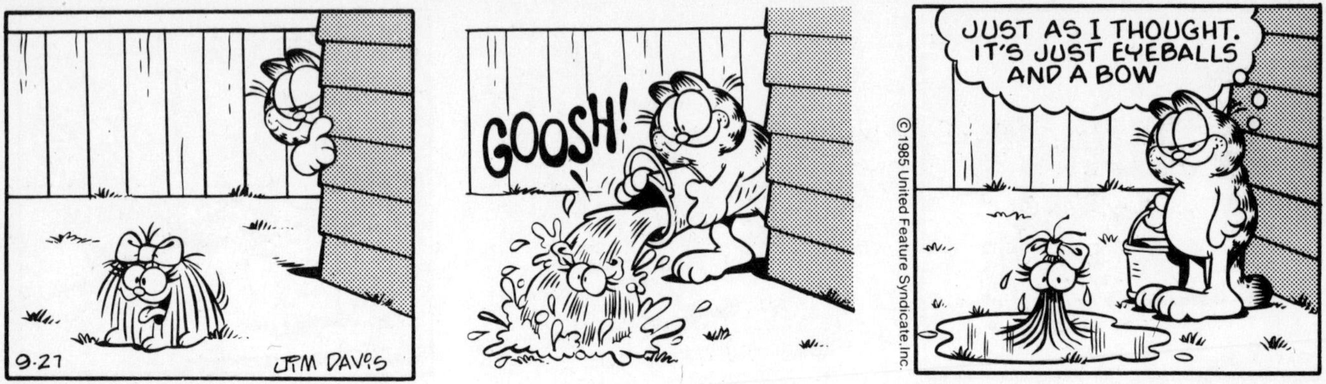
9-27
JIM DAVIS
GOOSH!
JUST AS I THOUGHT. IT'S JUST EYEBALLS AND A BOW



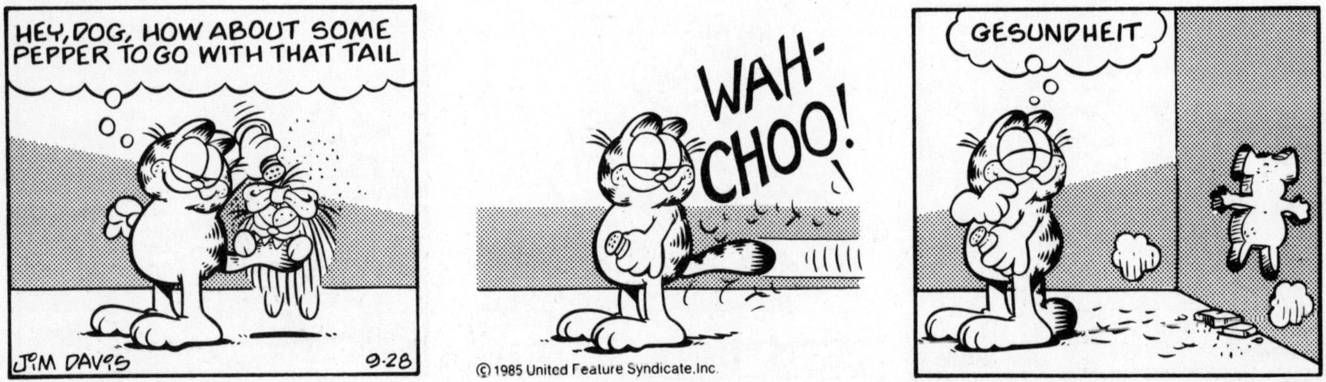
HEY, DOG, HOW ABOUT SOME PEPPER TO GO WITH THAT TAIL
JIM DAVIS
9-28
WAH-CHOO!
GESUNDHEIT

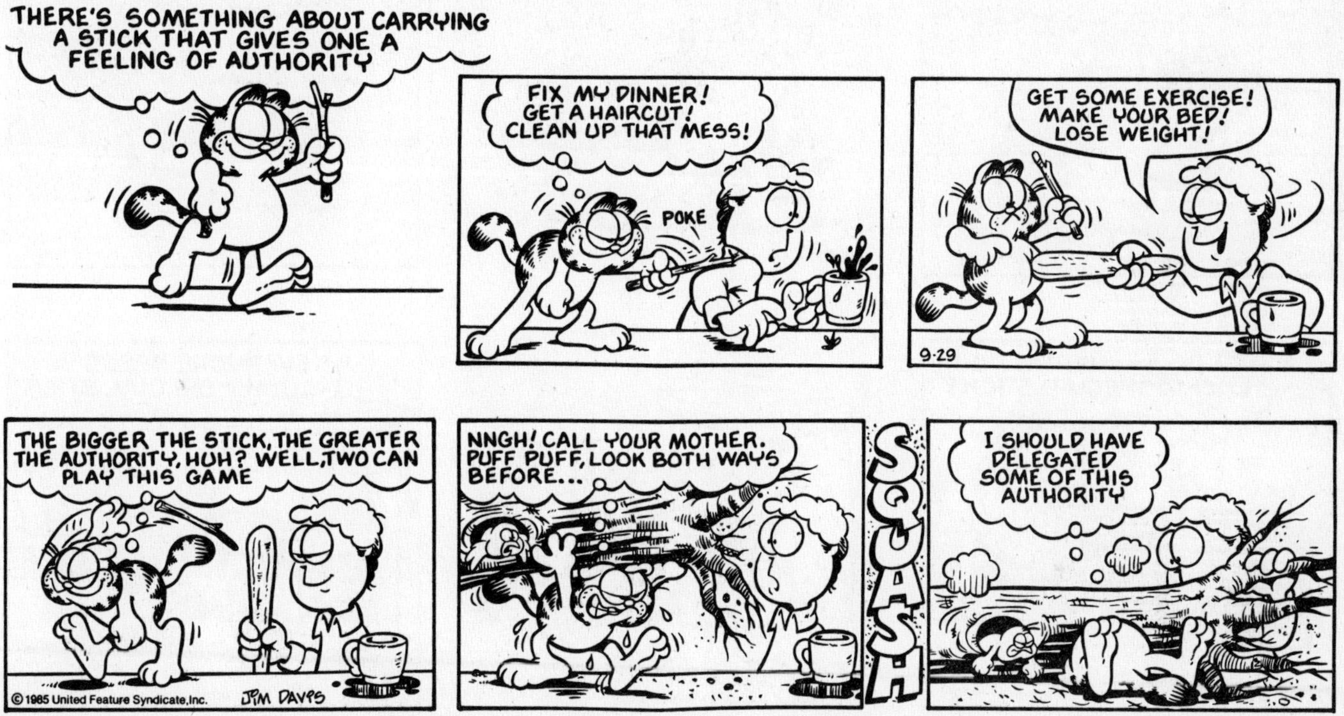
THERE'S SOMETHING ABOUT CARRYING A STICK THAT GIVES ONE A FEELING OF AUTHORITY
FIX MY DINNER! GET A HAIRCUT! CLEAN UP THAT MESS!
POKE
GET SOME EXERCISE! MAKE YOUR BED! LOSE WEIGHT!
9-29
THE BIGGER THE STICK, THE GREATER THE AUTHORITY, HUH? WELL, TWO CAN PLAY THIS GAME
© 1985 United Feature Syndicate, Inc.
JIM DAVIS
NNGH! CALL YOUR MOTHER. PUFF PUFF, LOOK BOTH WAYS BEFORE...
SQUASH
I SHOULD HAVE DELEGATED SOME OF THIS AUTHORITY

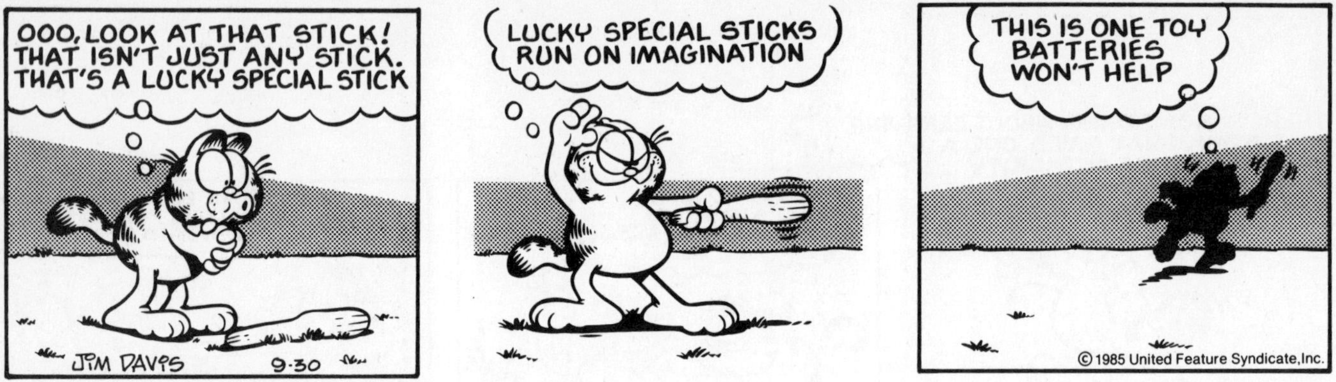
OOO, LOOK AT THAT STICK! THAT ISN'T JUST ANY STICK. THAT'S A LUCKY SPECIAL STICK
JIM DAVIS
9-30
LUCKY SPECIAL STICKS RUN ON IMAGINATION
THIS IS ONE TOY BATTERIES WON'T HELP
© 1985 United Feature Syndicate, Inc.

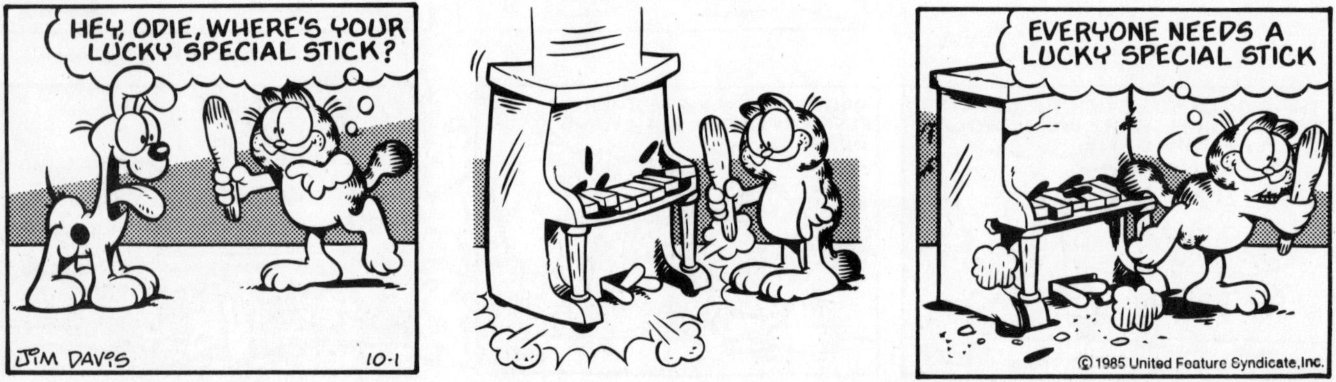
HEY, ODIE, WHERE'S YOUR LUCKY SPECIAL STICK?
JIM DAVIS
10-1
EVERYONE NEEDS A LUCKY SPECIAL STICK
© 1985 United Feature Syndicate, Inc.

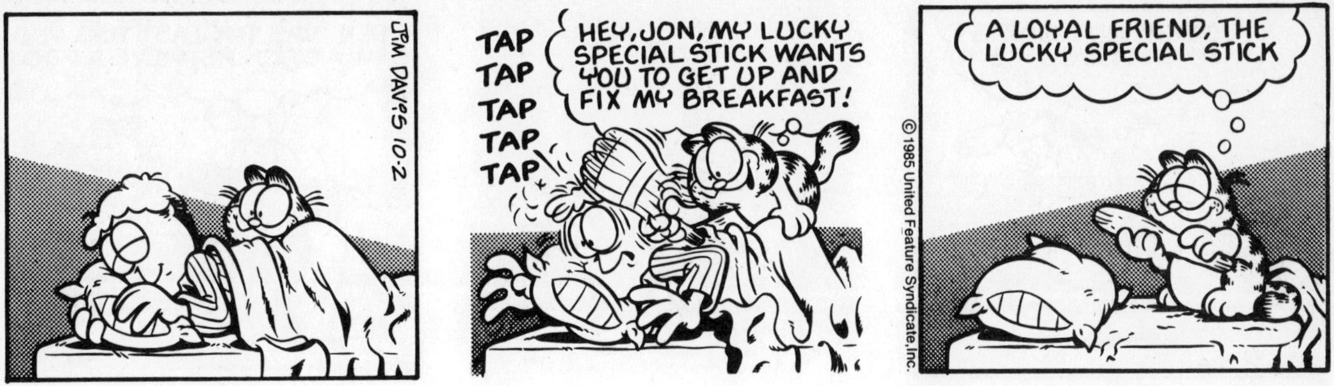
JIM DAVIS 10-2
TAP TAP TAP TAP TAP
HEY, JON, MY LUCKY SPECIAL STICK WANTS YOU TO GET UP AND FIX MY BREAKFAST!
A LOYAL FRIEND, THE LUCKY SPECIAL STICK
© 1985 United Feature Syndicate, Inc.

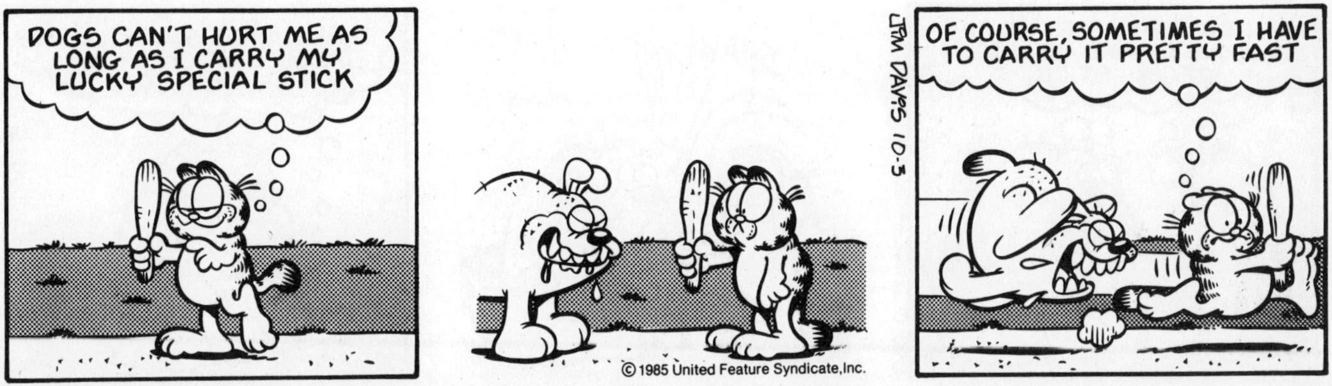
DOGS CAN'T HURT ME AS LONG AS I CARRY MY LUCKY SPECIAL STICK
JIM DAVIS 10-3
OF COURSE, SOMETIMES I HAVE TO CARRY IT PRETTY FAST
© 1985 United Feature Syndicate, Inc.

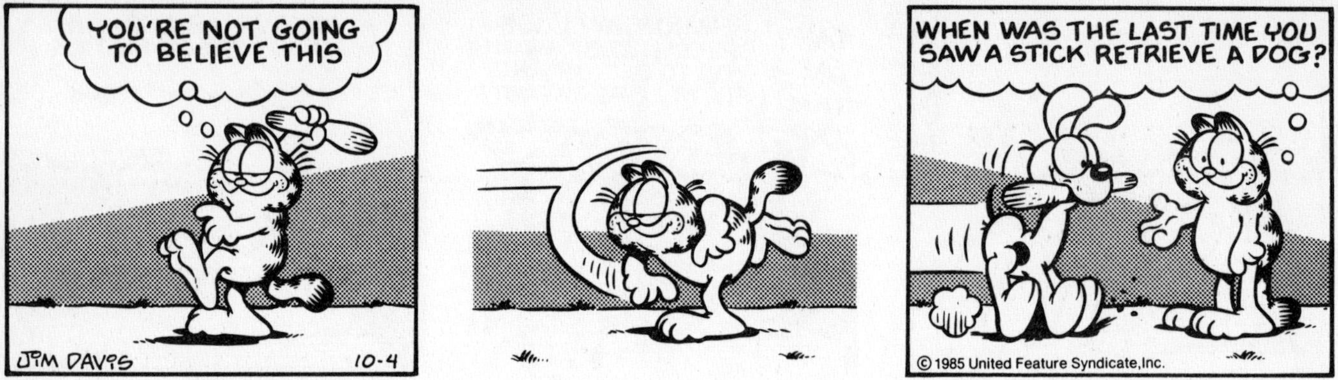
YOU'RE NOT GOING TO BELIEVE THIS
JIM DAVIS
10-4
WHEN WAS THE LAST TIME YOU SAW A STICK RETRIEVE A DOG?
© 1985 United Feature Syndicate, Inc.

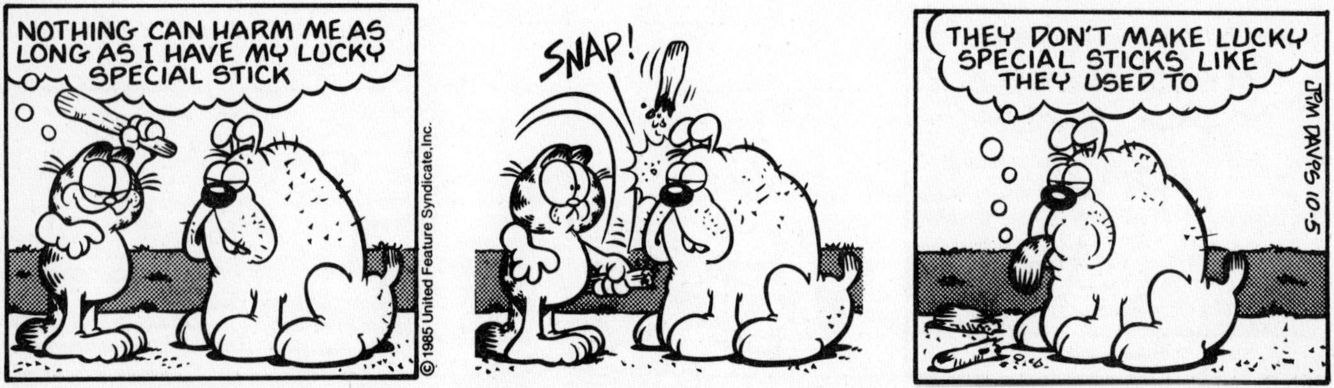
NOTHING CAN HARM ME AS LONG AS I HAVE MY LUCKY SPECIAL STICK
© 1985 United Feature Syndicate, Inc.
SNAP!
THEY DON'T MAKE LUCKY SPECIAL STICKS LIKE THEY USED TO
JIM DAVIS 10-5

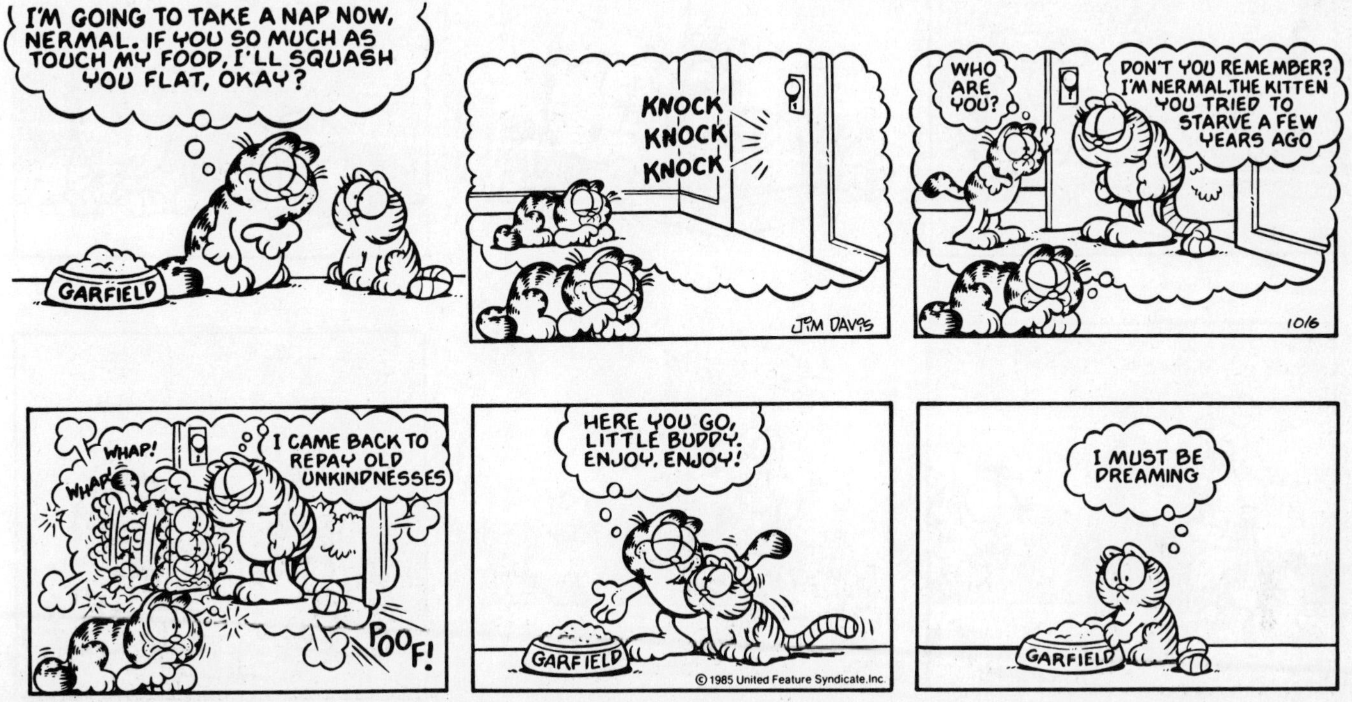
I'M GOING TO TAKE A NAP NOW, NERMAL. IF YOU SO MUCH AS TOUCH MY FOOD, I'LL SQUASH YOU FLAT, OKAY?
GARFIELD
KNOCK KNOCK KNOCK
JIM DAVIS
WHO ARE YOU?
DON'T YOU REMEMBER? I'M NERMAL, THE KITTEN YOU TRIED TO STARVE A FEW YEARS AGO
10/6
WHAP!
WHAP!
I CAME BACK TO REPAY OLD UNKINDNESSES
POOF!
HERE YOU GO, LITTLE BUDDY. ENJOY, ENJOY!
GARFIELD
© 1985 United Feature Syndicate, Inc.
I MUST BE DREAMING
GARFIELD

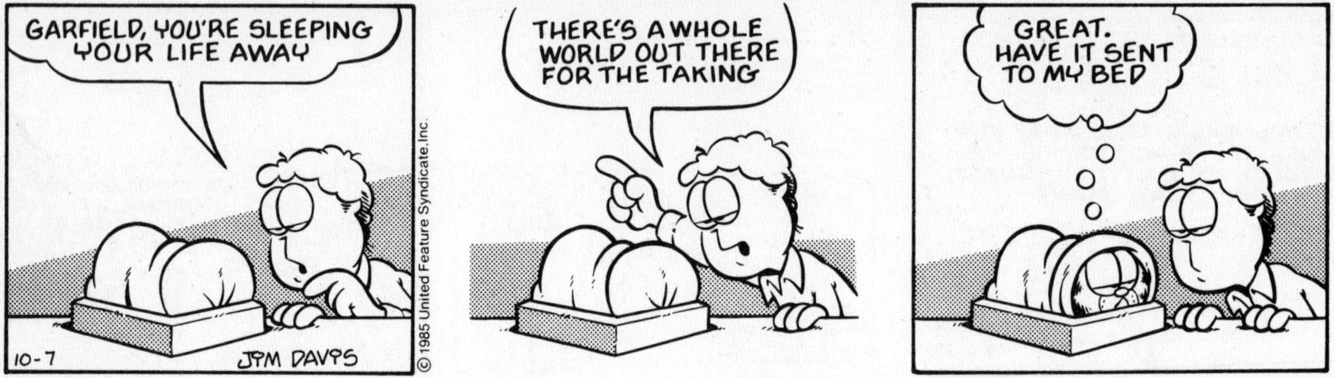
GARFIELD, YOU'RE SLEEPING YOUR LIFE AWAY
THERE'S A WHOLE WORLD OUT THERE FOR THE TAKING
GREAT. HAVE IT SENT TO MY BED
10-7
JIM DAVIS
© 1985 United Feature Syndicate, Inc.

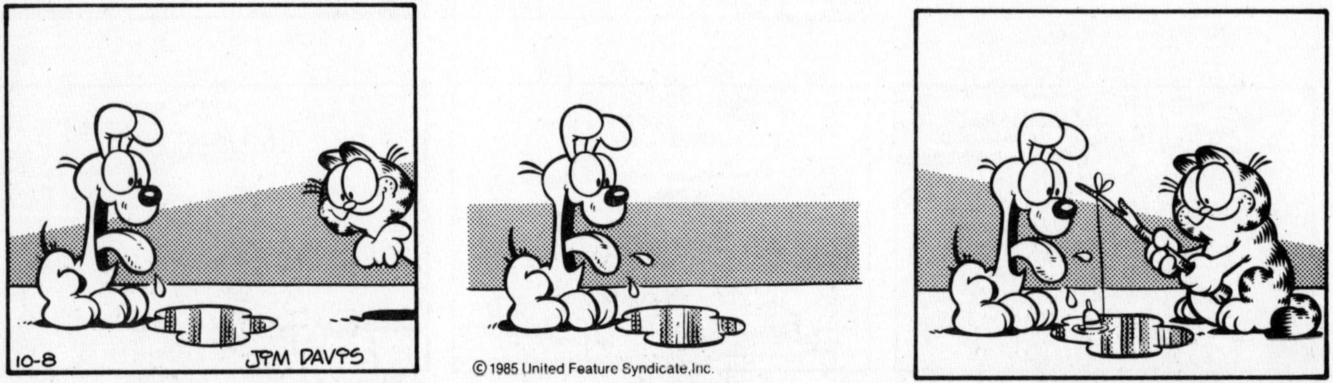
10-8
JIM DAVIS
© 1985 United Feature Syndicate, Inc.

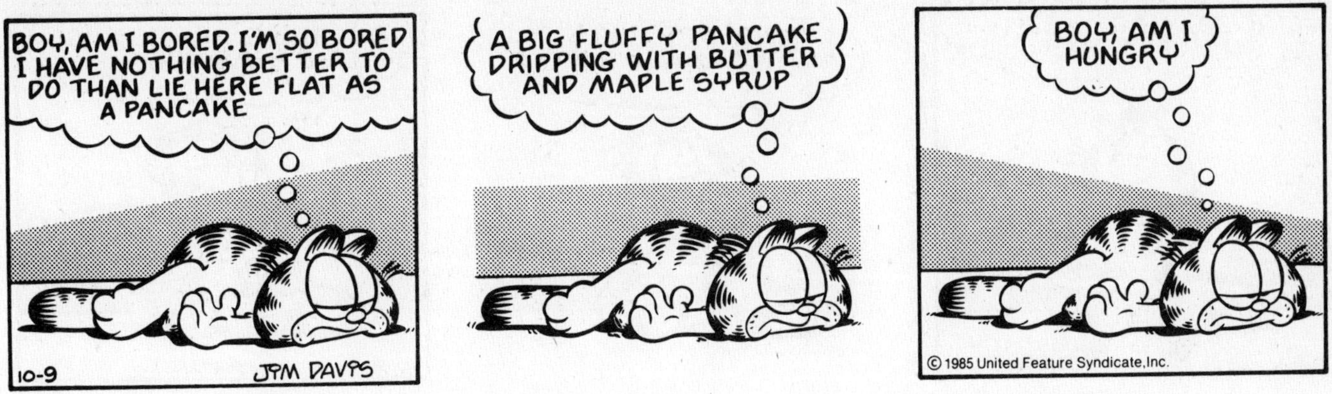
BOY, AM I BORED. I'M SO BORED I HAVE NOTHING BETTER TO DO THAN LIE HERE FLAT AS A PANCAKE
10-9
JIM DAVIS
A BIG FLUFFY PANCAKE DRIPPING WITH BUTTER AND MAPLE SYRUP
BOY, AM I HUNGRY
© 1985 United Feature Syndicate, Inc.

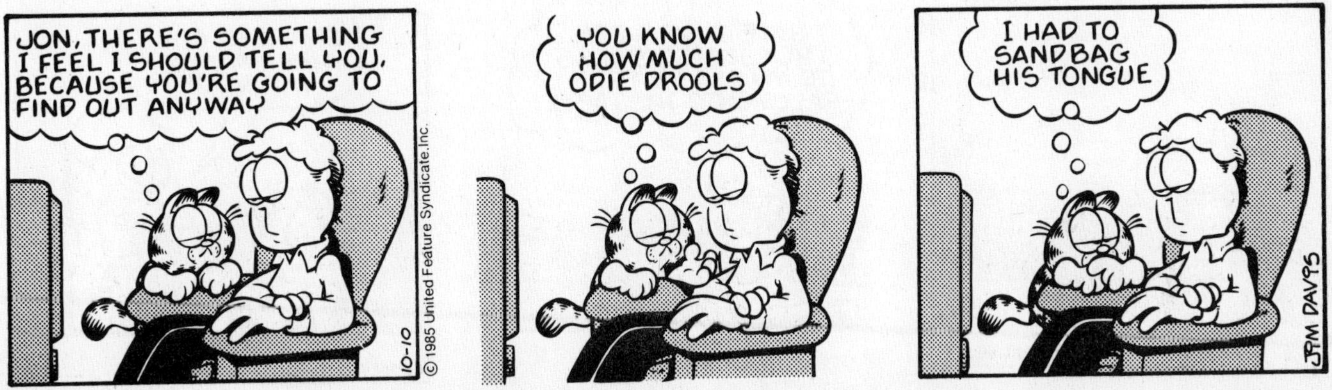
JON, THERE'S SOMETHING I FEEL I SHOULD TELL YOU, BECAUSE YOU'RE GOING TO FIND OUT ANYWAY
10-10
© 1985 United Feature Syndicate, Inc.
YOU KNOW HOW MUCH ODIE DROOLS
I HAD TO SANDBAG HIS TONGUE
JIM DAVIS

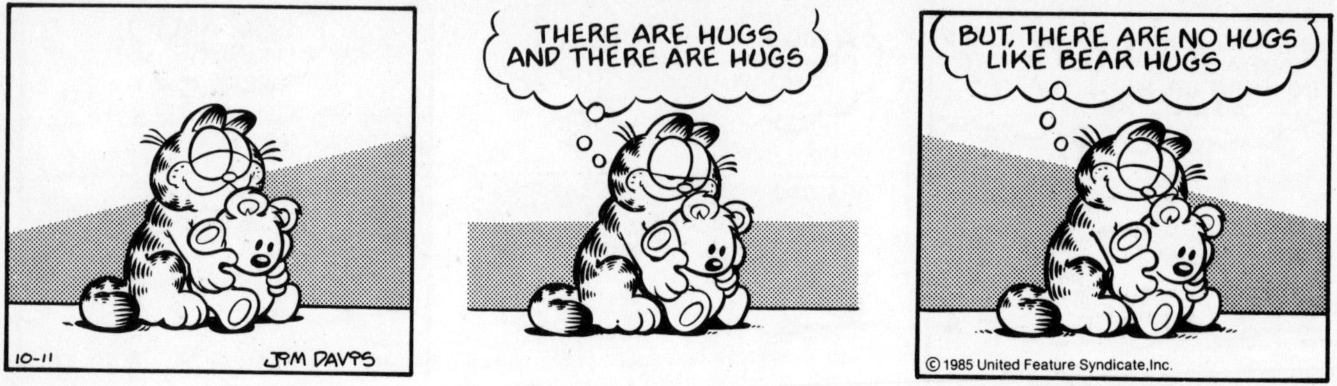
10-11
JIM DAVIS
THERE ARE HUGS AND THERE ARE HUGS
BUT, THERE ARE NO HUGS LIKE BEAR HUGS
© 1985 United Feature Syndicate, Inc.

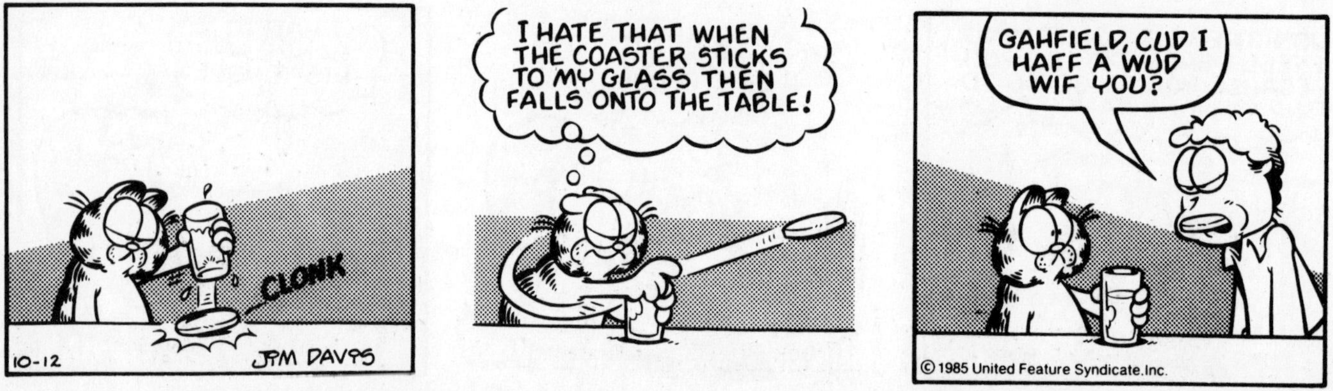
CLONK
10-12
JIM DAVIS
I HATE THAT WHEN THE COASTER STICKS TO MY GLASS THEN FALLS ONTO THE TABLE!
GAHFIELD, CUD I HAFF A WUD WIF YOU?
© 1985 United Feature Syndicate, Inc.

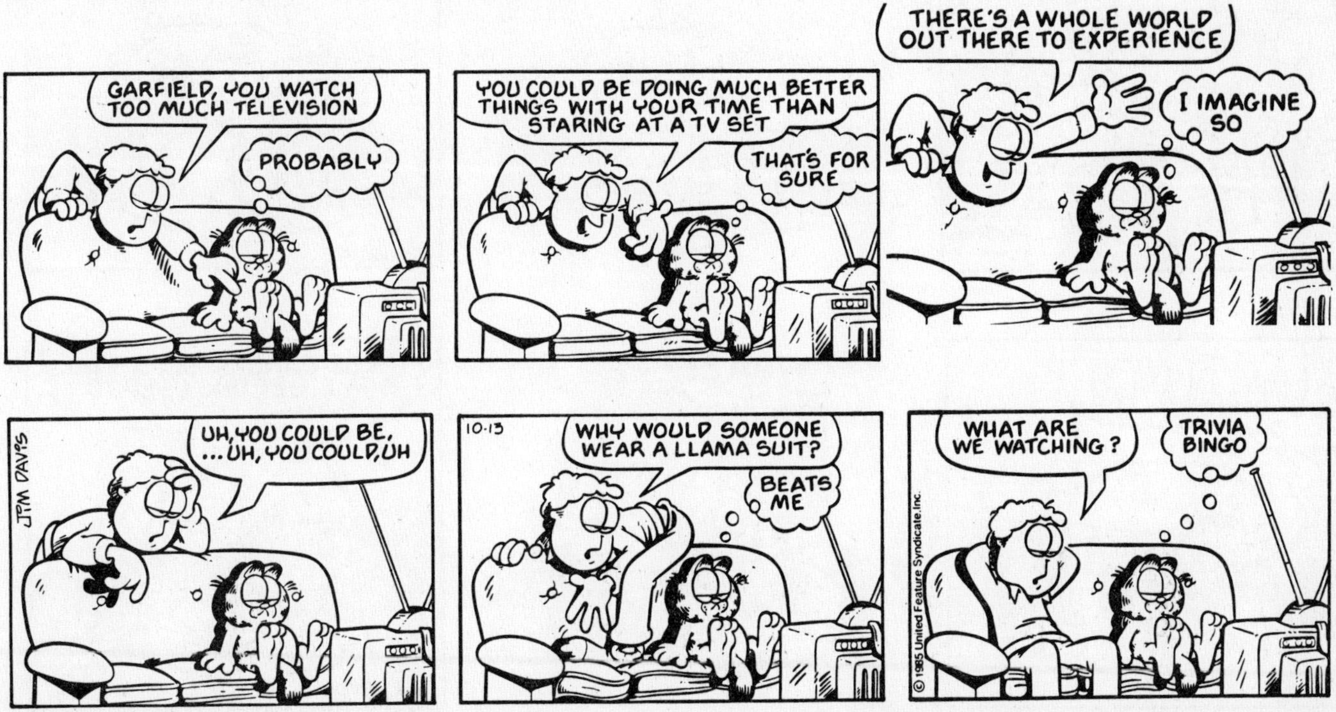
GARFIELD, YOU WATCH TOO MUCH TELEVISION
PROBABLY
YOU COULD BE DOING MUCH BETTER THINGS WITH YOUR TIME THAN STARING AT A TV SET
THAT'S FOR SURE
THERE'S A WHOLE WORLD OUT THERE TO EXPERIENCE
I IMAGINE SO
JIM DAVIS
UH, YOU COULD BE, ...UH, YOU COULD, UH
10-13
WHY WOULD SOMEONE WEAR A LLAMA SUIT?
BEATS ME
WHAT ARE WE WATCHING?
TRIVIA BINGO
© 1985 United Feature Syndicate, Inc.

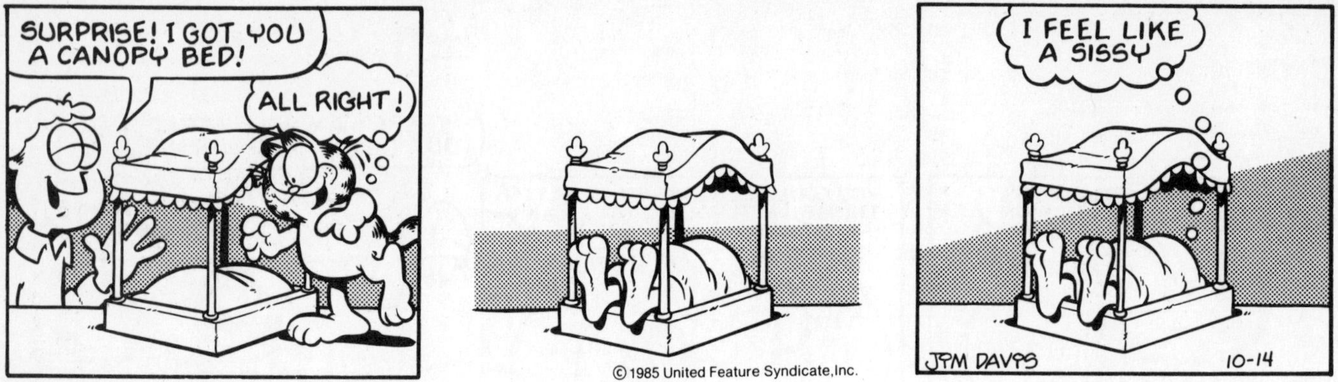
SURPRISE! I GOT YOU A CANOPY BED!
ALL RIGHT!
I FEEL LIKE A SISSY
JIM DAVIS
10-14



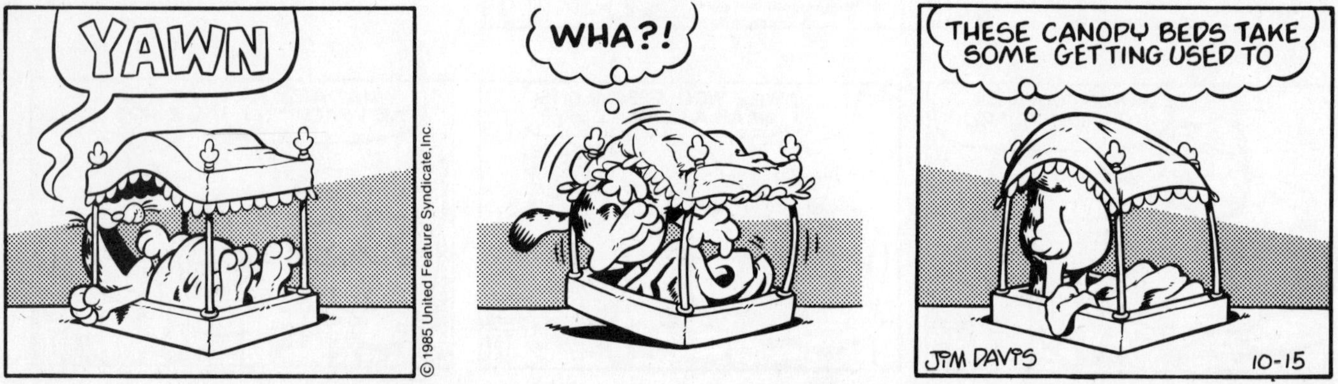
YAWN
WHA?!
THESE CANOPY BEDS TAKE SOME GETTING USED TO
JIM DAVIS
10-15

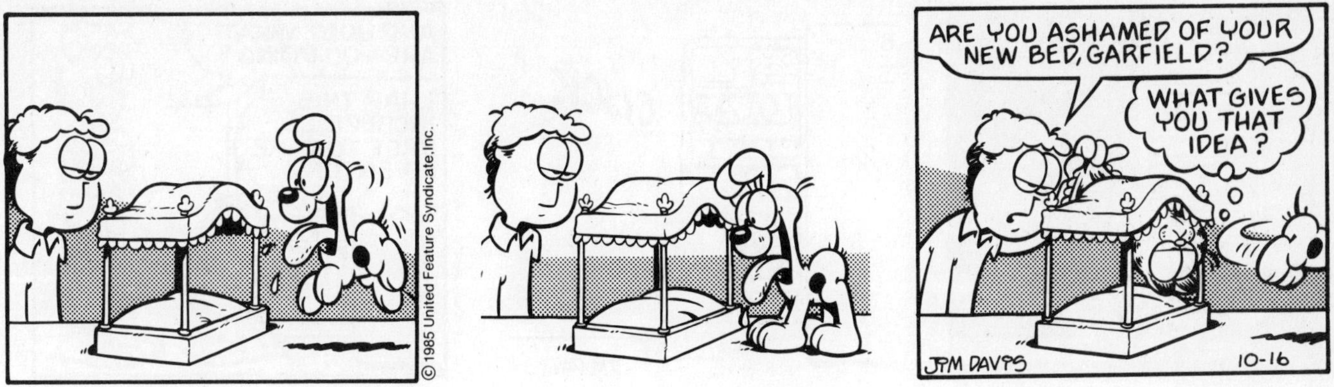
ARE YOU ASHAMED OF YOUR NEW BED, GARFIELD?
WHAT GIVES YOU THAT IDEA?
JPM DAVPS
10-16



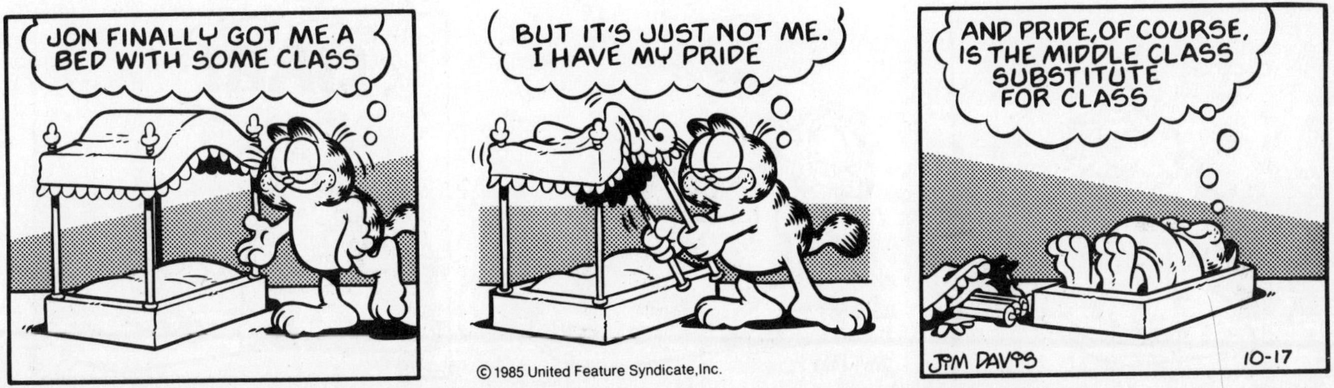
JON FINALLY GOT ME A BED WITH SOME CLASS
BUT IT'S JUST NOT ME. I HAVE MY PRIDE
AND PRIDE, OF COURSE, IS THE MIDDLE CLASS SUBSTITUTE FOR CLASS
JPM DAVPS
10-17

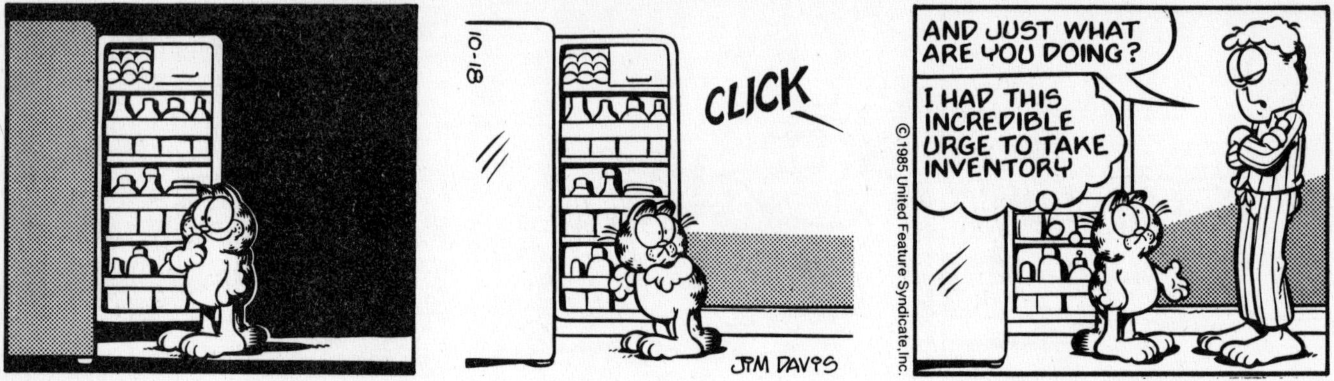
10-18
CLICK
JIM DAVIS
AND JUST WHAT ARE YOU DOING?
I HAD THIS INCREDIBLE URGE TO TAKE INVENTORY
© 1985 United Feature Syndicate, Inc.

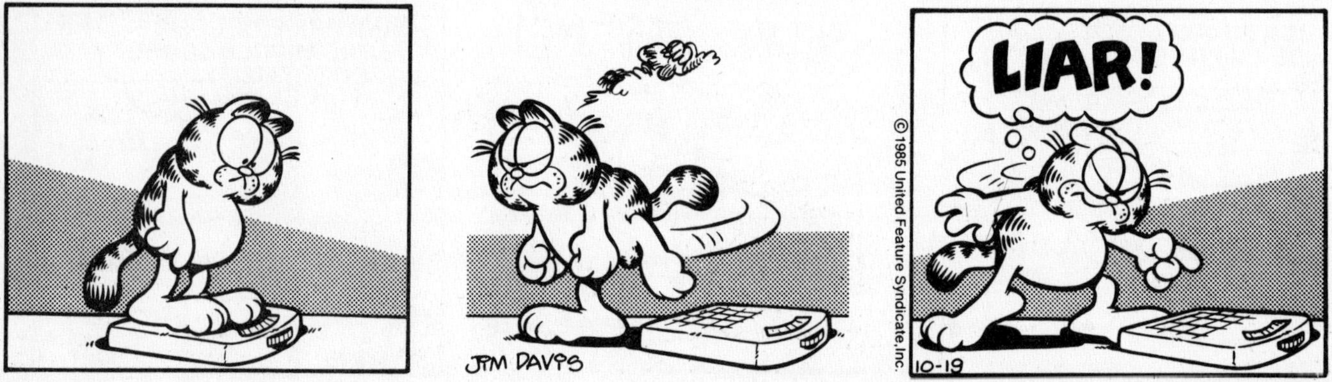
JIM DAVIS
LIAR!
© 1985 United Feature Syndicate, Inc.
10-19

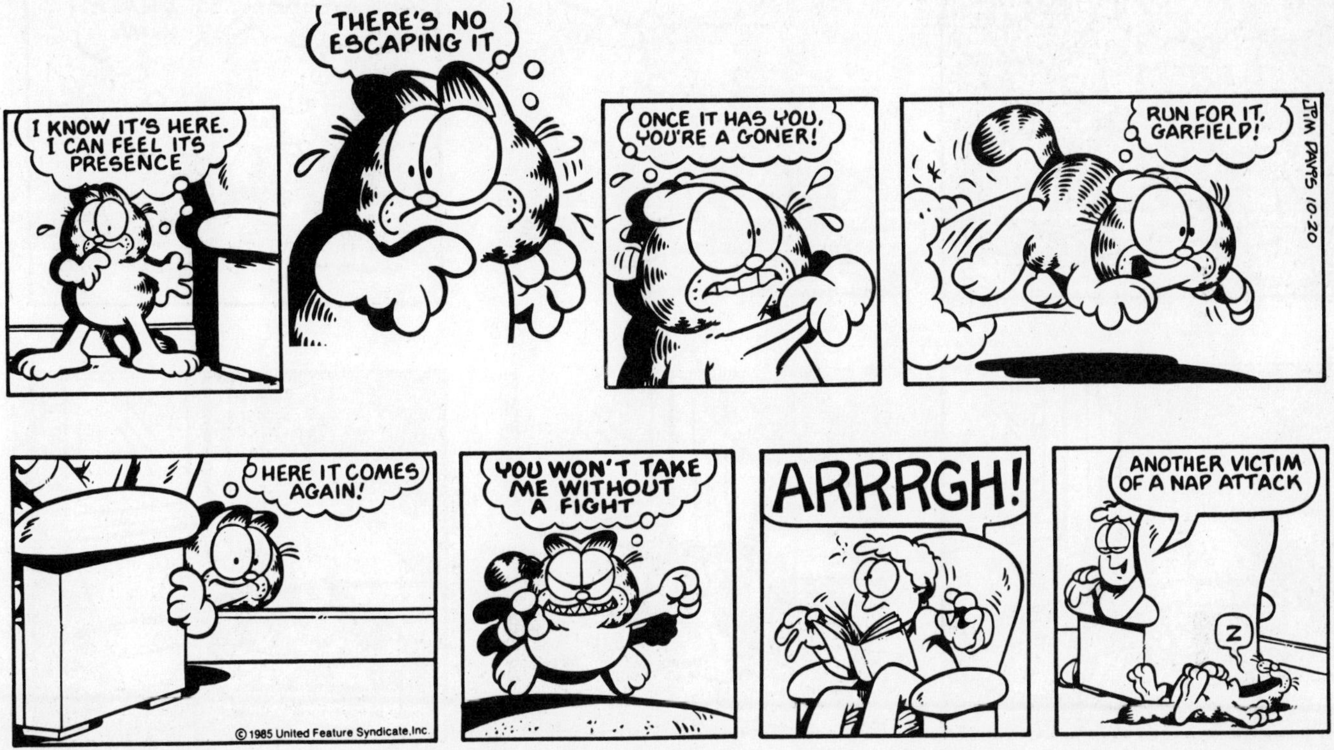
I KNOW IT'S HERE. I CAN FEEL ITS PRESENCE
THERE'S NO ESCAPING IT
ONCE IT HAS YOU, YOU'RE A GONER!
RUN FOR IT, GARFIELD!
JIM DAVIS 10-20
HERE IT COMES AGAIN!
© 1985 United Feature Syndicate, Inc.
YOU WON'T TAKE ME WITHOUT A FIGHT
ARRRGH!
ANOTHER VICTIM OF A NAP ATTACK
Z

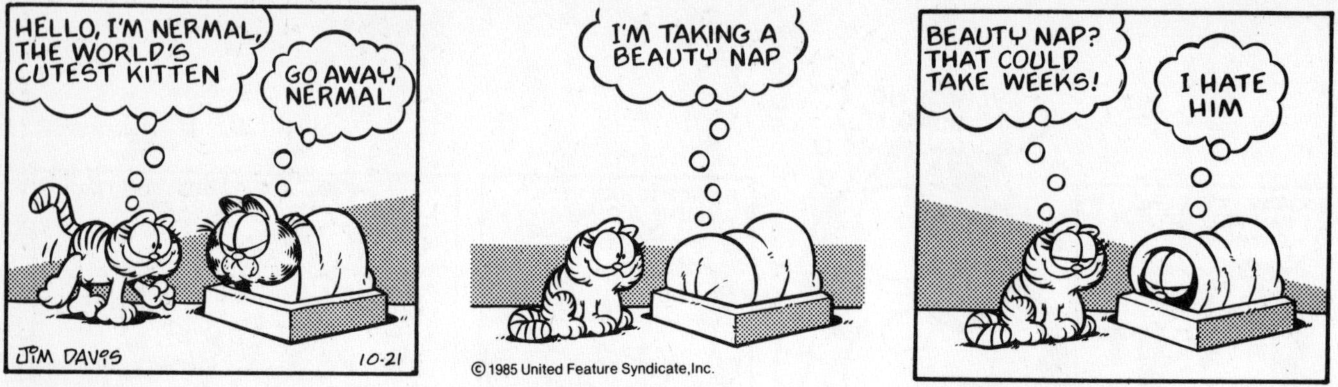
HELLO, I'M NERMAL, THE WORLD'S CUTEST KITTEN
GO AWAY, NERMAL
JIM DAVIS
10-21
I'M TAKING A BEAUTY NAP
© 1985 United Feature Syndicate,Inc.
BEAUTY NAP? THAT COULD TAKE WEEKS!
I HATE HIM

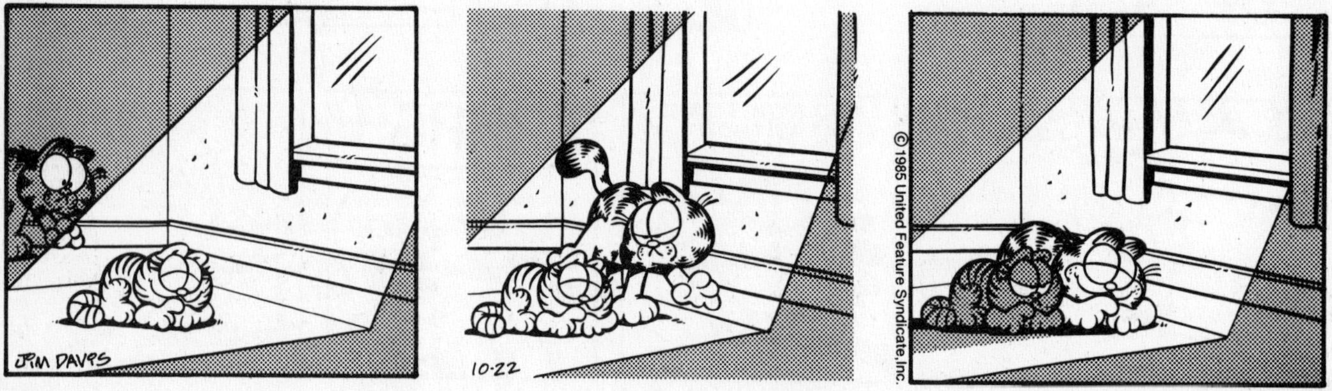
JIM DAVIS
10-22
© 1985 United Feature Syndicate,Inc.

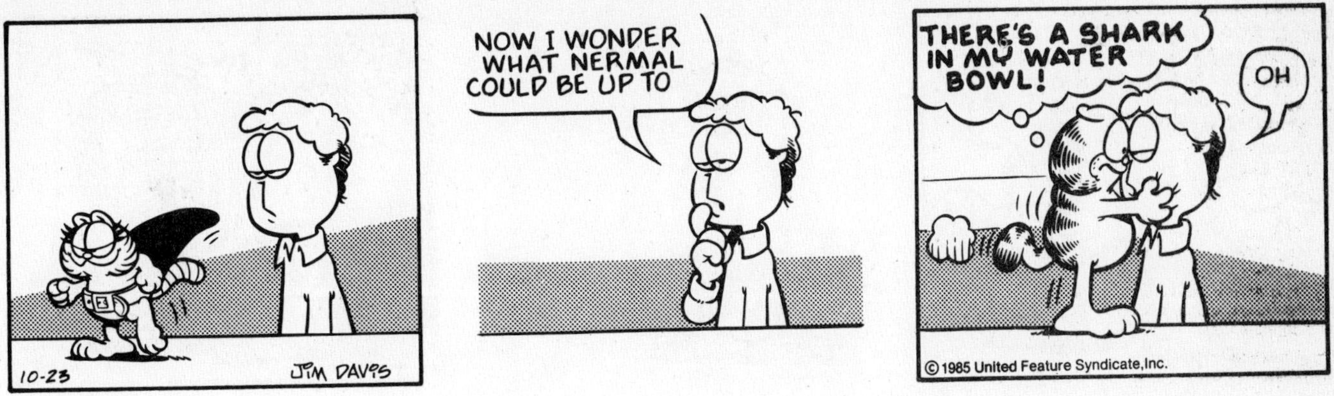
10-23
JIM DAVIS
NOW I WONDER WHAT NERMAL COULD BE UP TO
THERE'S A SHARK IN MY WATER BOWL!
OH
© 1985 United Feature Syndicate, Inc.

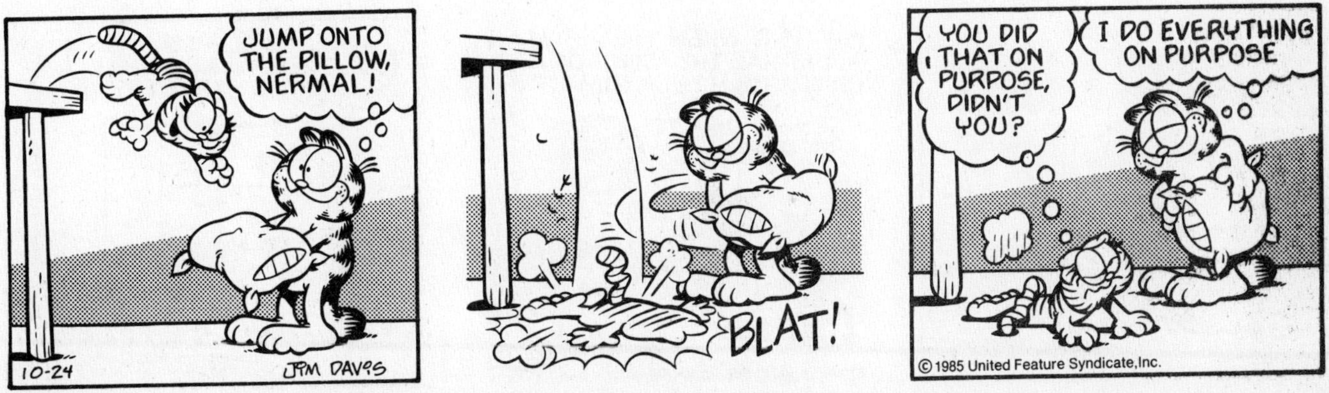
JUMP ONTO THE PILLOW, NERMAL!
10-24
JIM DAVIS
BLAT!
YOU DID THAT ON PURPOSE, DIDN'T YOU?
I DO EVERYTHING ON PURPOSE
© 1985 United Feature Syndicate, Inc.

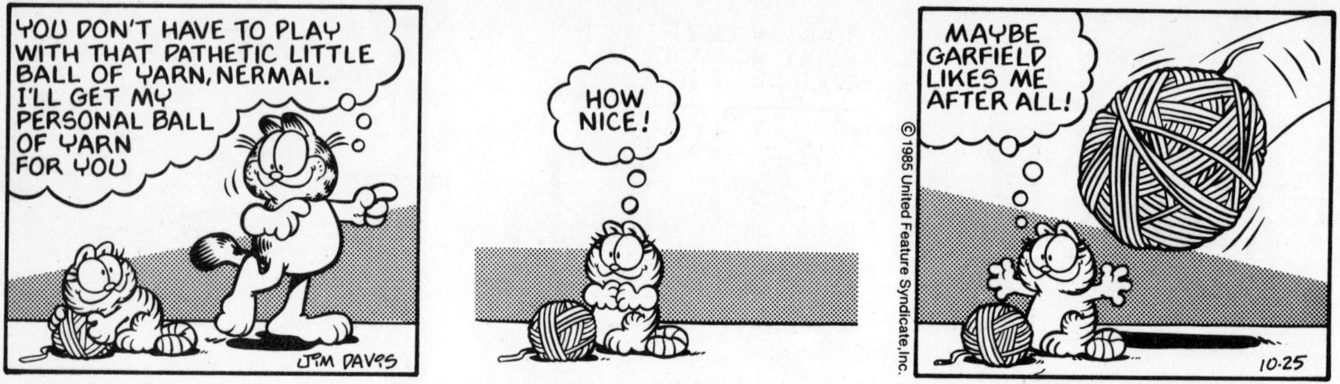
YOU DON'T HAVE TO PLAY WITH THAT PATHETIC LITTLE BALL OF YARN, NERMAL. I'LL GET MY PERSONAL BALL OF YARN FOR YOU
JIM DAVIS
HOW NICE!
© 1985 United Feature Syndicate,Inc.
MAYBE GARFIELD LIKES ME AFTER ALL!
10-25

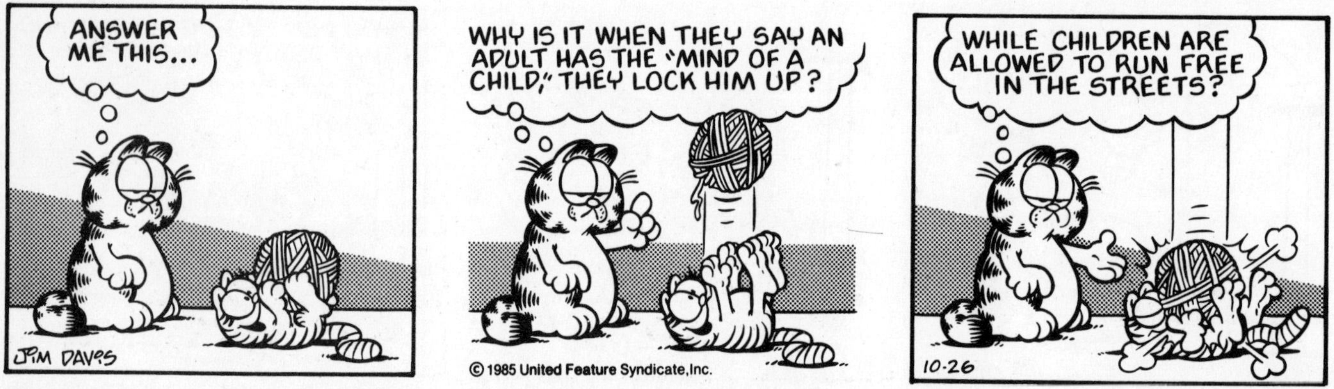
ANSWER ME THIS...
JIM DAVIS
WHY IS IT WHEN THEY SAY AN ADULT HAS THE "MIND OF A CHILD," THEY LOCK HIM UP?
© 1985 United Feature Syndicate,Inc.
WHILE CHILDREN ARE ALLOWED TO RUN FREE IN THE STREETS?
10-26

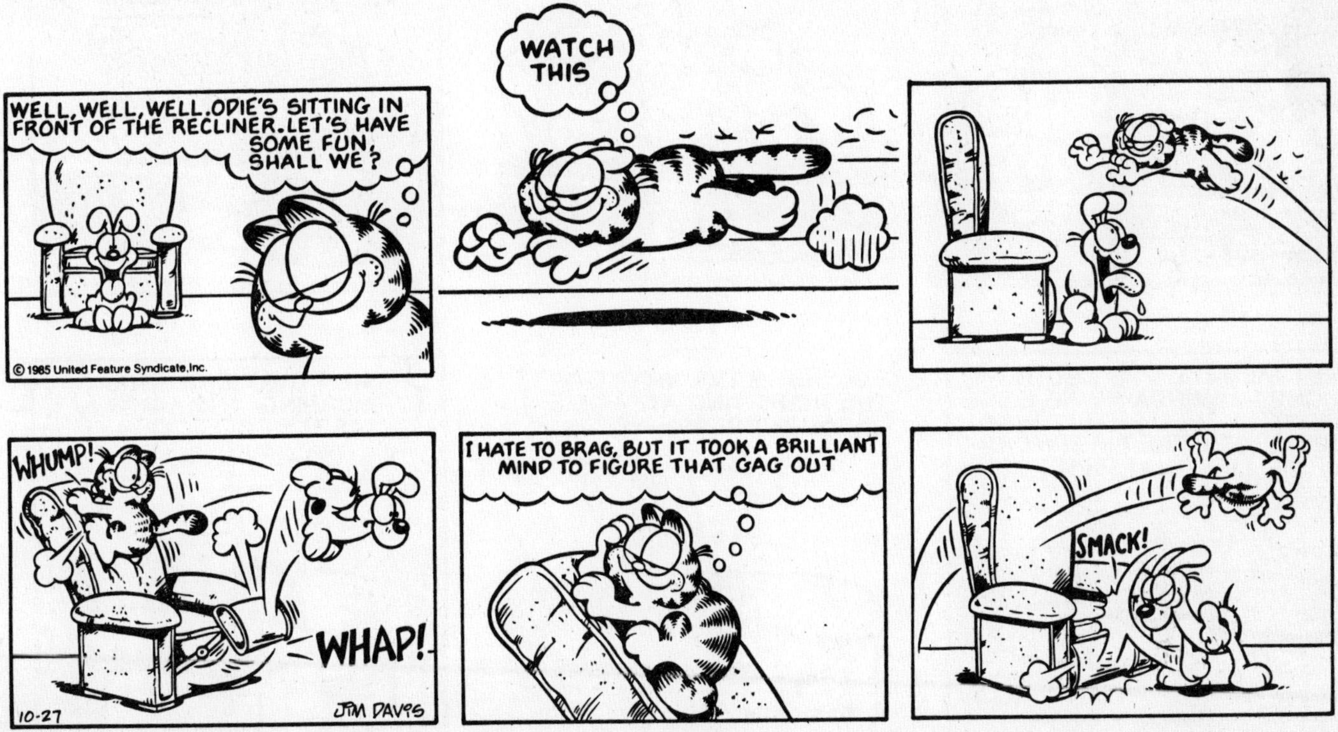

WELL, WELL, WELL. ODIE'S SITTING IN FRONT OF THE RECLINER. LET'S HAVE SOME FUN, SHALL WE?
© 1985 United Feature Syndicate, Inc.
WATCH THIS
WHUMP!
WHAP!
10-27
JIM DAVIS
I HATE TO BRAG, BUT IT TOOK A BRILLIANT MIND TO FIGURE THAT GAG OUT
SMACK!

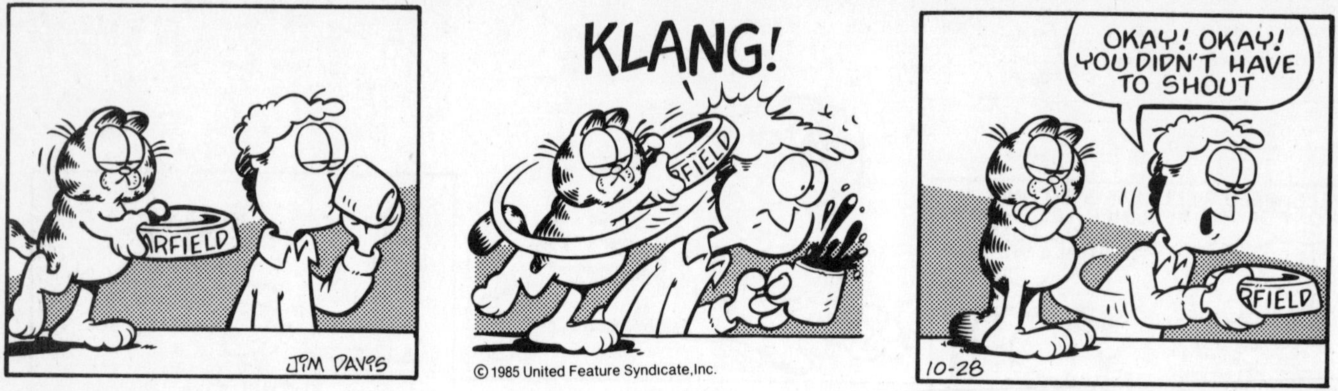

RFIELD
JIM DAVIS
KLANG!
FIELD
© 1985 United Feature Syndicate, Inc.
OKAY! OKAY! YOU DIDN'T HAVE TO SHOUT
RFIELD
10-28


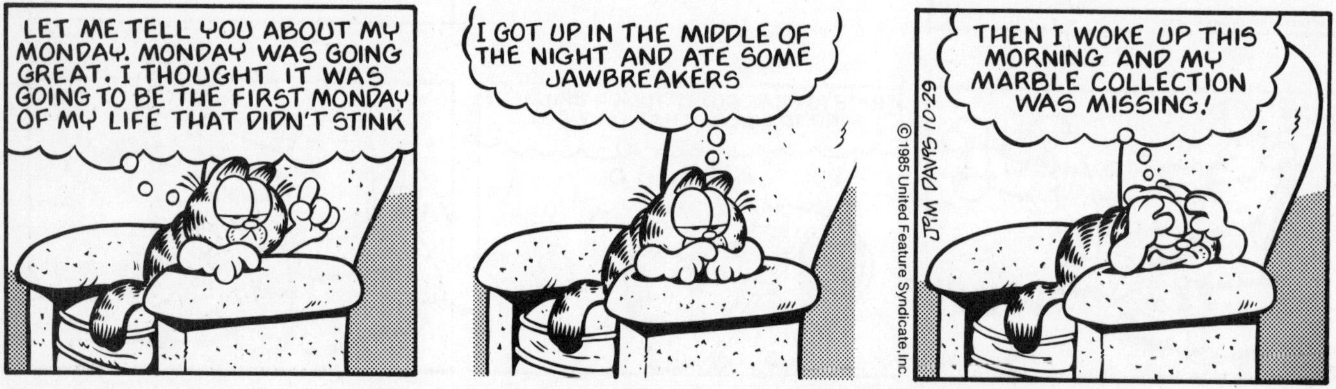

LET ME TELL YOU ABOUT MY MONDAY. MONDAY WAS GOING GREAT. I THOUGHT IT WAS GOING TO BE THE FIRST MONDAY OF MY LIFE THAT DIDN'T STINK
I GOT UP IN THE MIDDLE OF THE NIGHT AND ATE SOME JAWBREAKERS
JIM DAVIS 10-29
© 1985 United Feature Syndicate, Inc.
THEN I WOKE UP THIS MORNING AND MY MARBLE COLLECTION WAS MISSING!

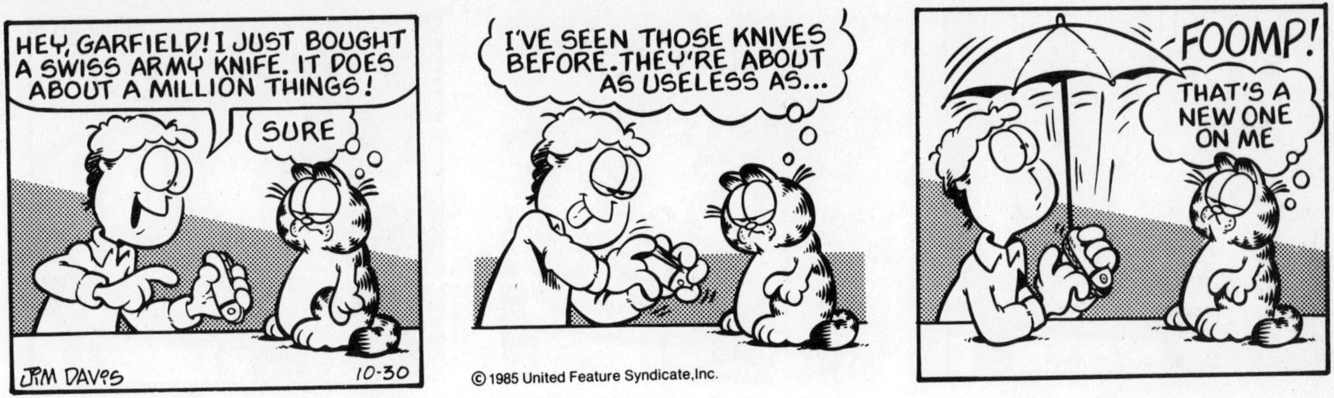
HEY, GARFIELD! I JUST BOUGHT A SWISS ARMY KNIFE. IT DOES ABOUT A MILLION THINGS!
SURE
I'VE SEEN THOSE KNIVES BEFORE. THEY'RE ABOUT AS USELESS AS...
FOOMP!
THAT'S A NEW ONE ON ME
JIM DAVIS
10-30


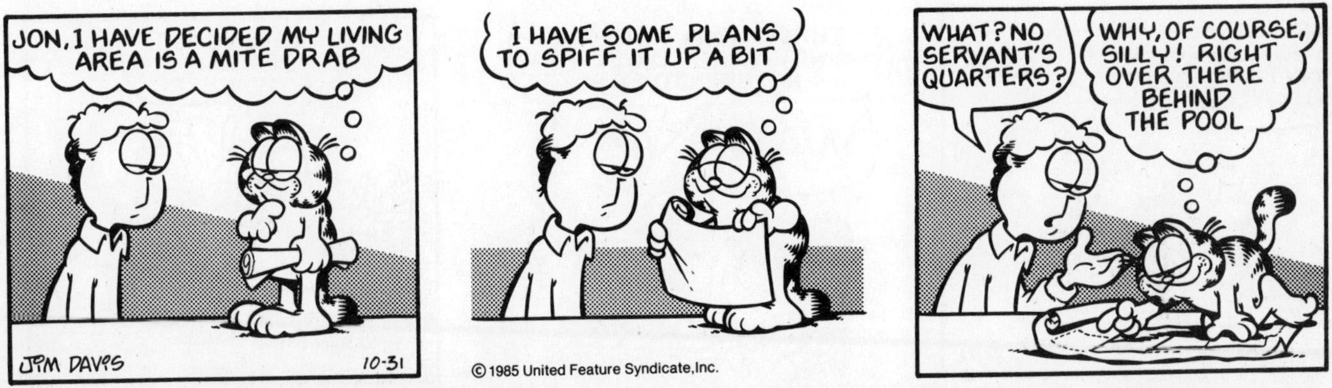
JON, I HAVE DECIDED MY LIVING AREA IS A MITE DRAB
I HAVE SOME PLANS TO SPIFF IT UP A BIT
WHAT? NO SERVANT'S QUARTERS?
WHY, OF COURSE, SILLY! RIGHT OVER THERE BEHIND THE POOL
JIM DAVIS
10-31

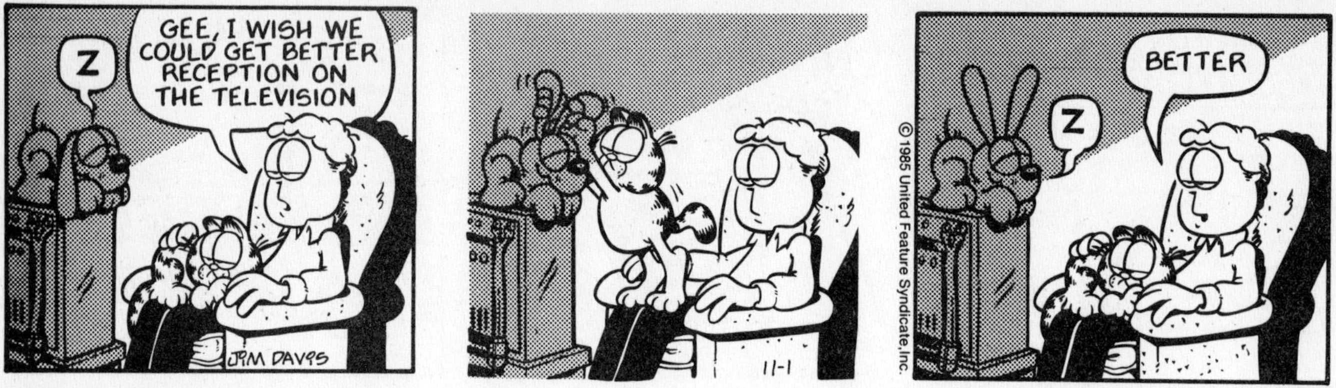
Z
GEE, I WISH WE COULD GET BETTER RECEPTION ON THE TELEVISION
JIM DAVIS
11-1
© 1985 United Feature Syndicate,Inc.
Z
BETTER

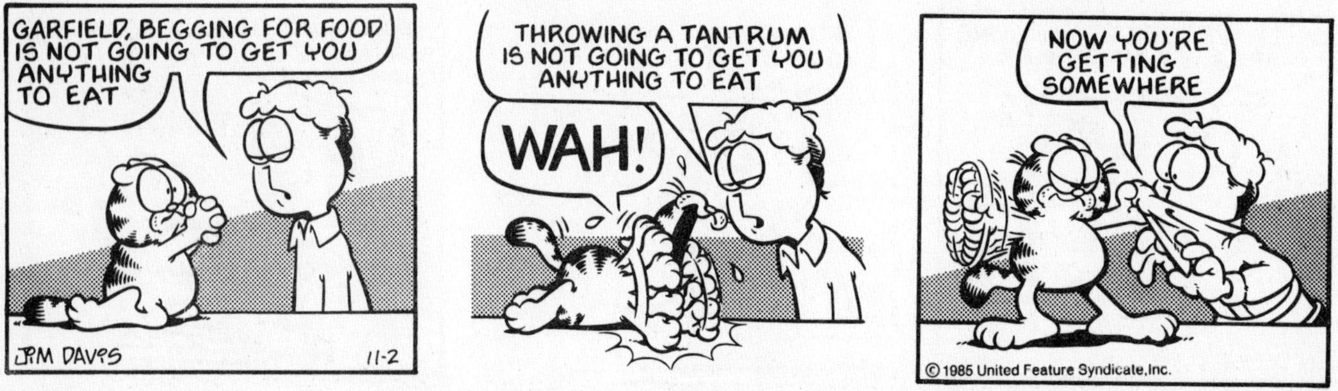
GARFIELD, BEGGING FOR FOOD IS NOT GOING TO GET YOU ANYTHING TO EAT
JIM DAVIS
11-2
THROWING A TANTRUM IS NOT GOING TO GET YOU ANYTHING TO EAT
WAH!
NOW YOU'RE GETTING SOMEWHERE
© 1985 United Feature Syndicate,Inc.

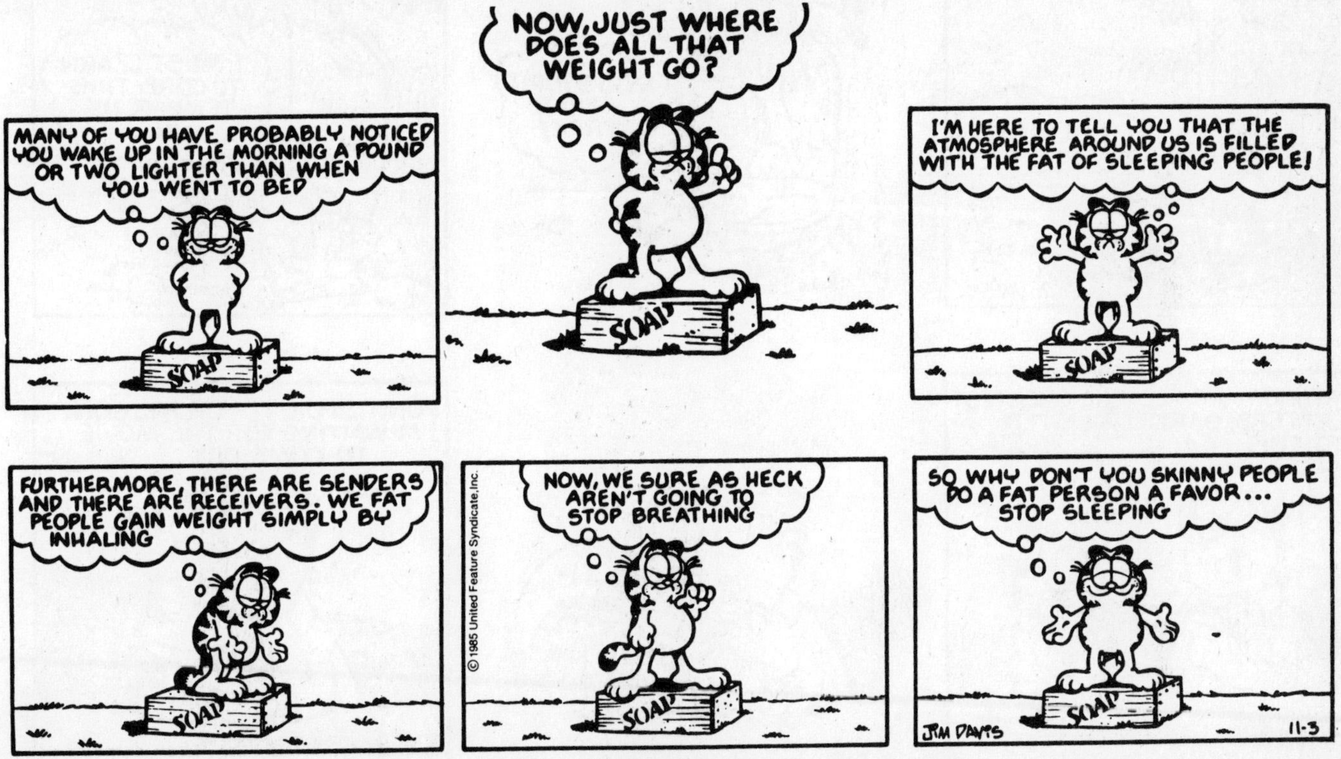
NOW, JUST WHERE DOES ALL THAT WEIGHT GO?
MANY OF YOU HAVE PROBABLY NOTICED YOU WAKE UP IN THE MORNING A POUND OR TWO LIGHTER THAN WHEN YOU WENT TO BED
I'M HERE TO TELL YOU THAT THE ATMOSPHERE AROUND US IS FILLED WITH THE FAT OF SLEEPING PEOPLE!
FURTHERMORE, THERE ARE SENDERS AND THERE ARE RECEIVERS. WE FAT PEOPLE GAIN WEIGHT SIMPLY BY INHALING
NOW, WE SURE AS HECK AREN'T GOING TO STOP BREATHING
SO WHY DON'T YOU SKINNY PEOPLE DO A FAT PERSON A FAVOR... STOP SLEEPING
SOAP
© 1985 United Feature Syndicate, Inc.
JIM DAVIS
11-3

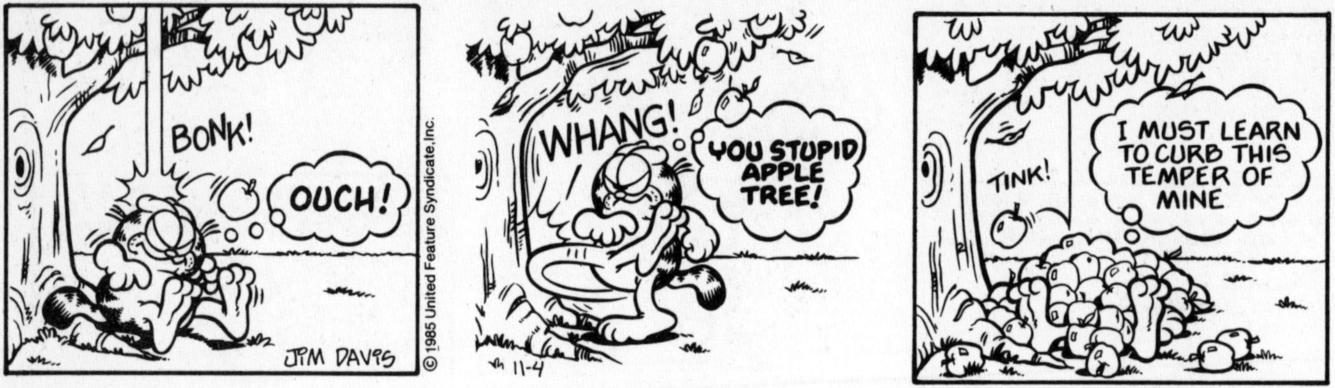
BONK!
OUCH!
JIM DAVIS
© 1985 United Feature Syndicate,Inc.
WHANG!
YOU STUPID APPLE TREE!
11-4
TINK!
I MUST LEARN TO CURB THIS TEMPER OF MINE

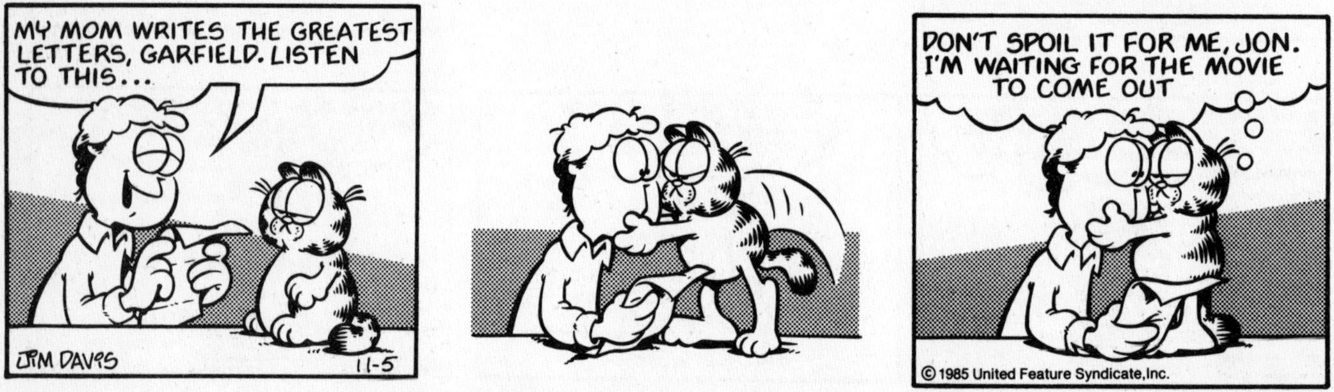
MY MOM WRITES THE GREATEST LETTERS, GARFIELD. LISTEN TO THIS...
JIM DAVIS
11-5
DON'T SPOIL IT FOR ME, JON. I'M WAITING FOR THE MOVIE TO COME OUT
© 1985 United Feature Syndicate,Inc.

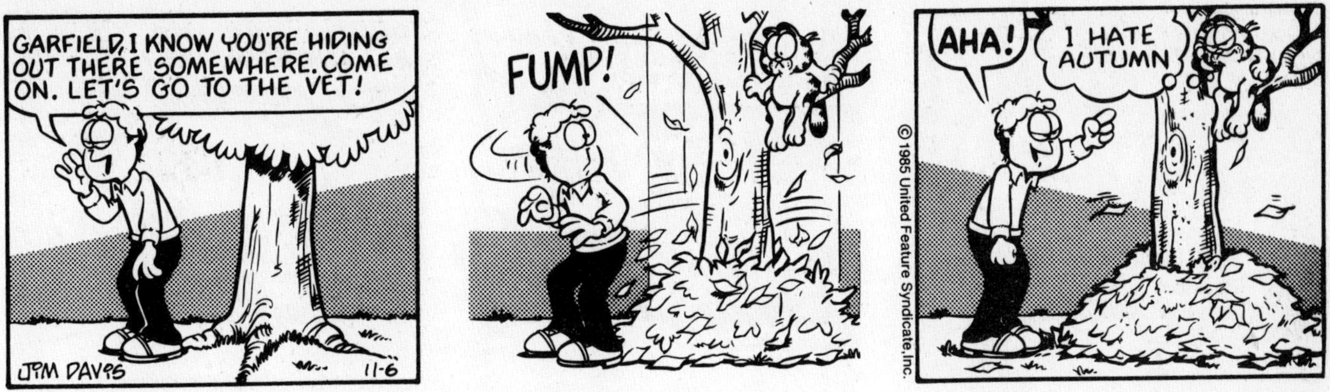
GARFIELD, I KNOW YOU'RE HIDING OUT THERE SOMEWHERE. COME ON. LET'S GO TO THE VET!
JIM DAVIS
11-6
FUMP!
AHA!
I HATE AUTUMN
© 1985 United Feature Syndicate, Inc.

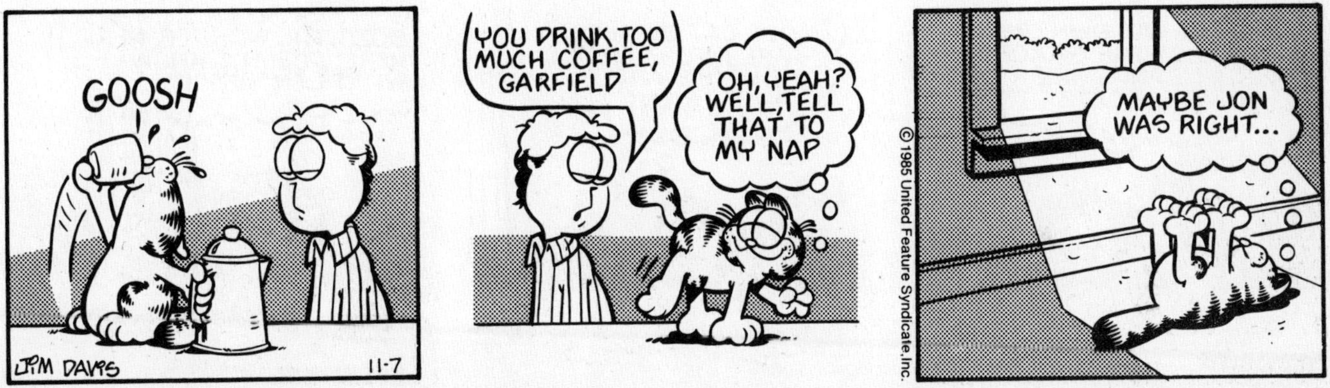
GOOSH
JIM DAVIS
11-7
YOU DRINK TOO MUCH COFFEE, GARFIELD
OH, YEAH? WELL, TELL THAT TO MY NAP
MAYBE JON WAS RIGHT...
© 1985 United Feature Syndicate, Inc.

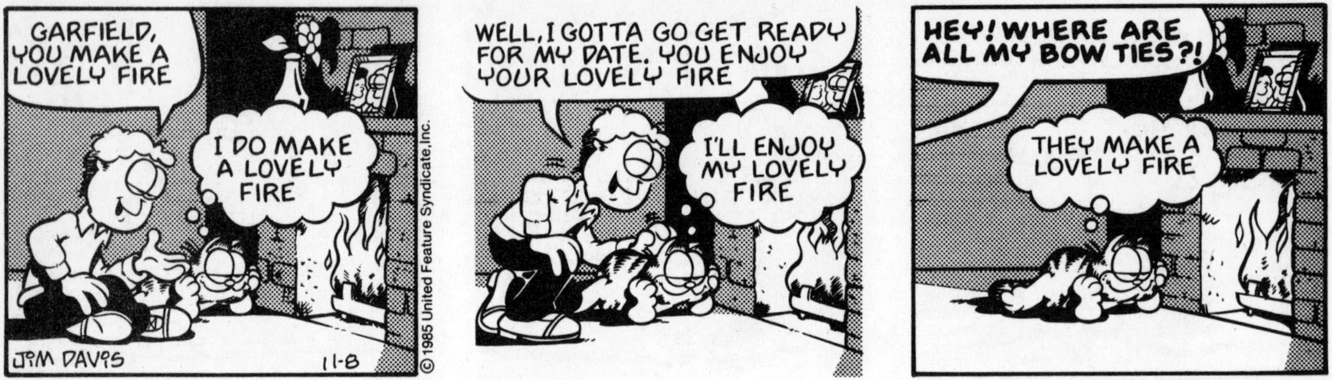
GARFIELD, YOU MAKE A LOVELY FIRE
I DO MAKE A LOVELY FIRE
JIM DAVIS
11-8
© 1985 United Feature Syndicate, Inc.
WELL, I GOTTA GO GET READY FOR MY DATE. YOU ENJOY YOUR LOVELY FIRE
I'LL ENJOY MY LOVELY FIRE
HEY! WHERE ARE ALL MY BOW TIES?!
THEY MAKE A LOVELY FIRE

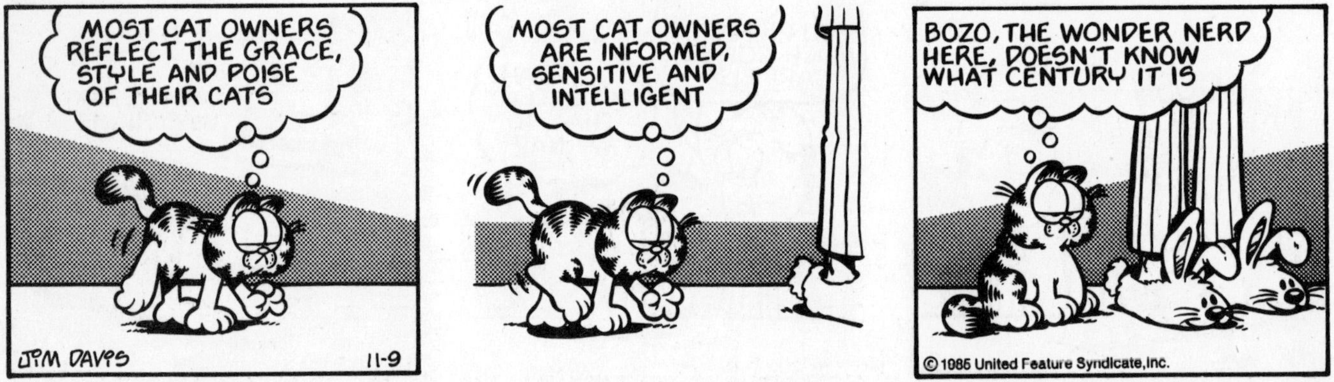
MOST CAT OWNERS REFLECT THE GRACE, STYLE AND POISE OF THEIR CATS
JIM DAVIS
11-9
MOST CAT OWNERS ARE INFORMED, SENSITIVE AND INTELLIGENT
BOZO, THE WONDER NERD HERE, DOESN'T KNOW WHAT CENTURY IT IS
© 1985 United Feature Syndicate, Inc.

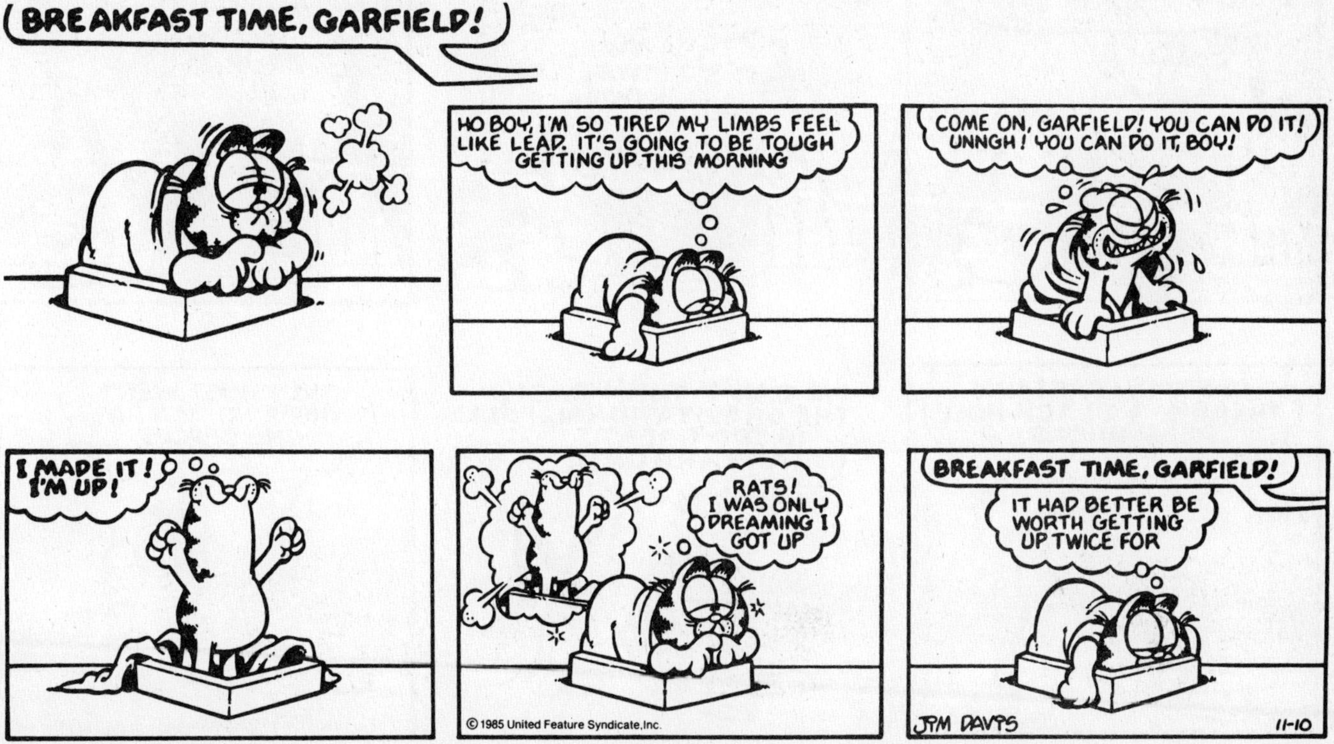
BREAKFAST TIME, GARFIELD!
HO BOY, I'M SO TIRED MY LIMBS FEEL LIKE LEAD. IT'S GOING TO BE TOUGH GETTING UP THIS MORNING
COME ON, GARFIELD! YOU CAN DO IT! UNNGH! YOU CAN DO IT, BOY!
I MADE IT! I'M UP!
RATS! I WAS ONLY DREAMING I GOT UP
BREAKFAST TIME, GARFIELD!
IT HAD BETTER BE WORTH GETTING UP TWICE FOR
© 1985 United Feature Syndicate, Inc.
JIM DAVIS
11-10

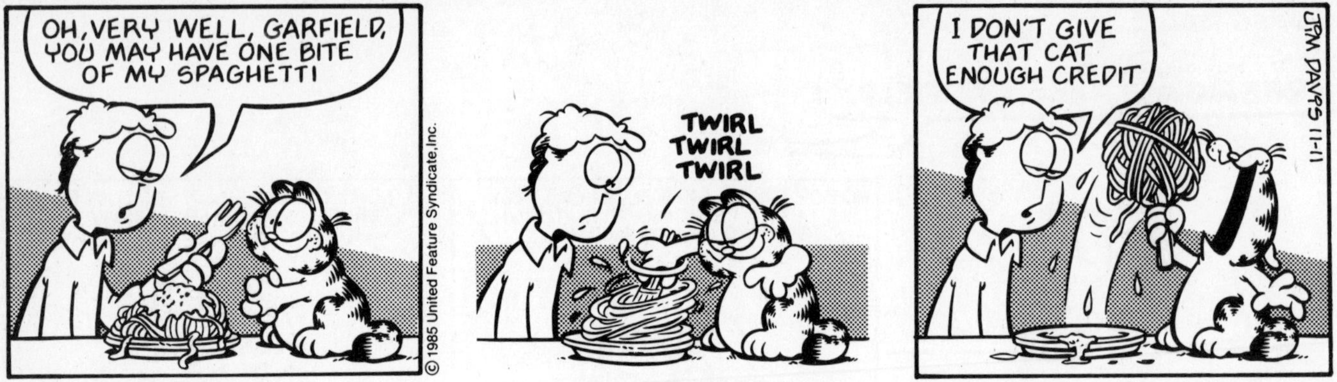
OH, VERY WELL, GARFIELD, YOU MAY HAVE ONE BITE OF MY SPAGHETTI
© 1985 United Feature Syndicate, Inc.
TWIRL TWIRL TWIRL
I DON'T GIVE THAT CAT ENOUGH CREDIT
JIM DAVIS 11-11

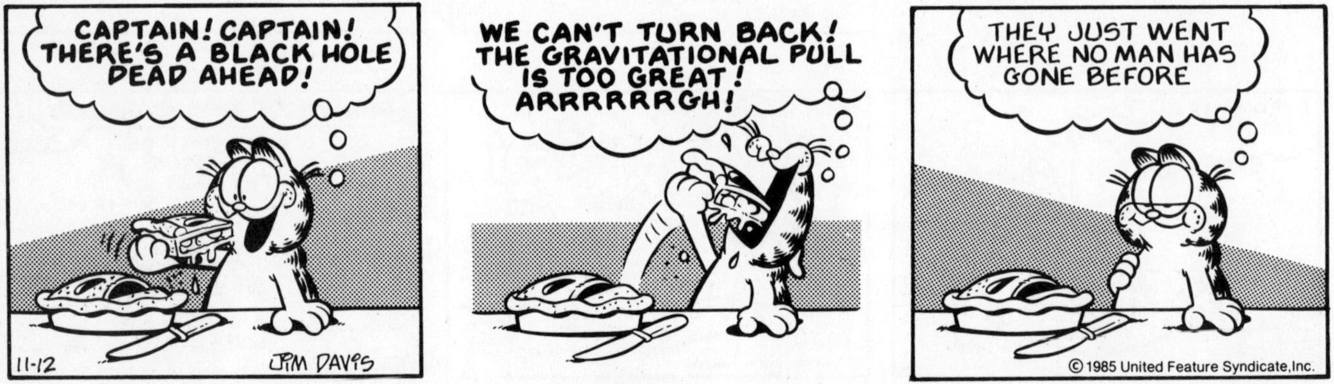
CAPTAIN! CAPTAIN! THERE'S A BLACK HOLE DEAD AHEAD!
11-12
JIM DAVIS
WE CAN'T TURN BACK! THE GRAVITATIONAL PULL IS TOO GREAT! ARRRRRRGH!
THEY JUST WENT WHERE NO MAN HAS GONE BEFORE
© 1985 United Feature Syndicate, Inc.

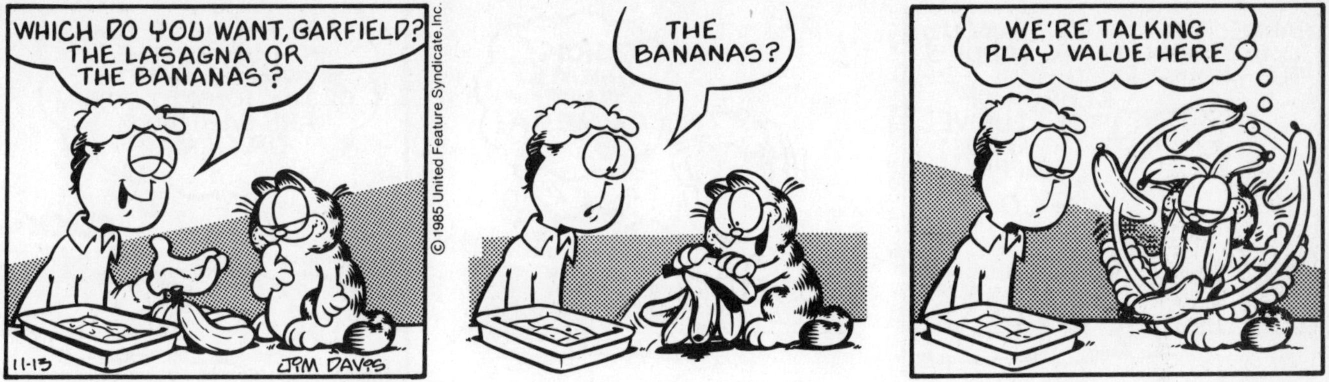
WHICH DO YOU WANT, GARFIELD? THE LASAGNA OR THE BANANAS?
11-13
JIM DAVIS
© 1985 United Feature Syndicate, Inc.
THE BANANAS?
WE'RE TALKING PLAY VALUE HERE

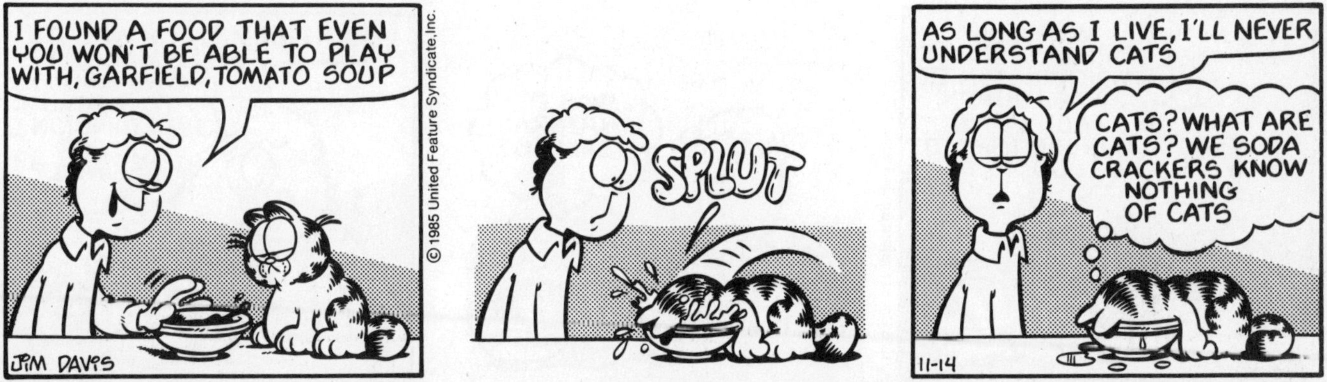
I FOUND A FOOD THAT EVEN YOU WON'T BE ABLE TO PLAY WITH, GARFIELD, TOMATO SOUP
JIM DAVIS
© 1985 United Feature Syndicate, Inc.
SPLUT
AS LONG AS I LIVE, I'LL NEVER UNDERSTAND CATS
CATS? WHAT ARE CATS? WE SODA CRACKERS KNOW NOTHING OF CATS
11-14

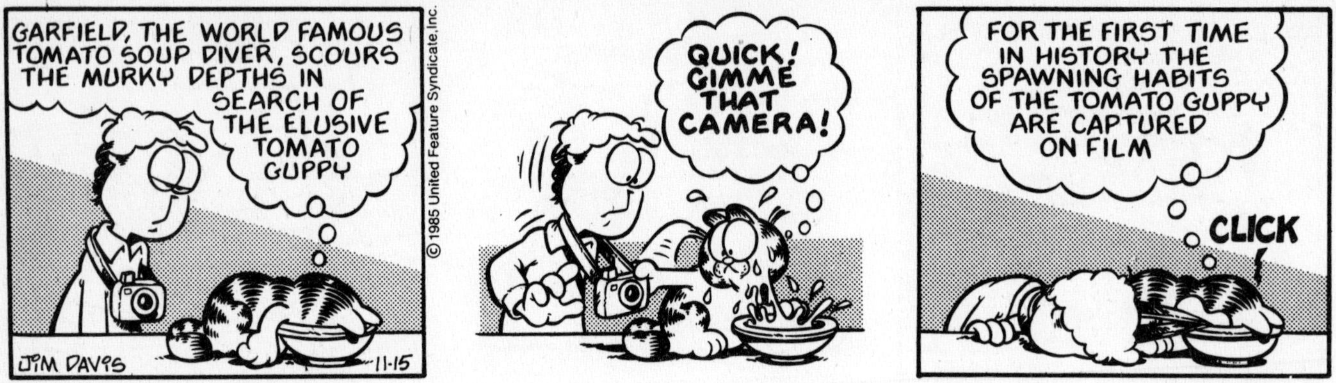
GARFIELD, THE WORLD FAMOUS TOMATO SOUP DIVER, SCOURS THE MURKY DEPTHS IN SEARCH OF THE ELUSIVE TOMATO GUPPY
JIM DAVIS
11-15
© 1985 United Feature Syndicate, Inc.
QUICK! GIMME THAT CAMERA!
FOR THE FIRST TIME IN HISTORY THE SPAWNING HABITS OF THE TOMATO GUPPY ARE CAPTURED ON FILM
CLICK

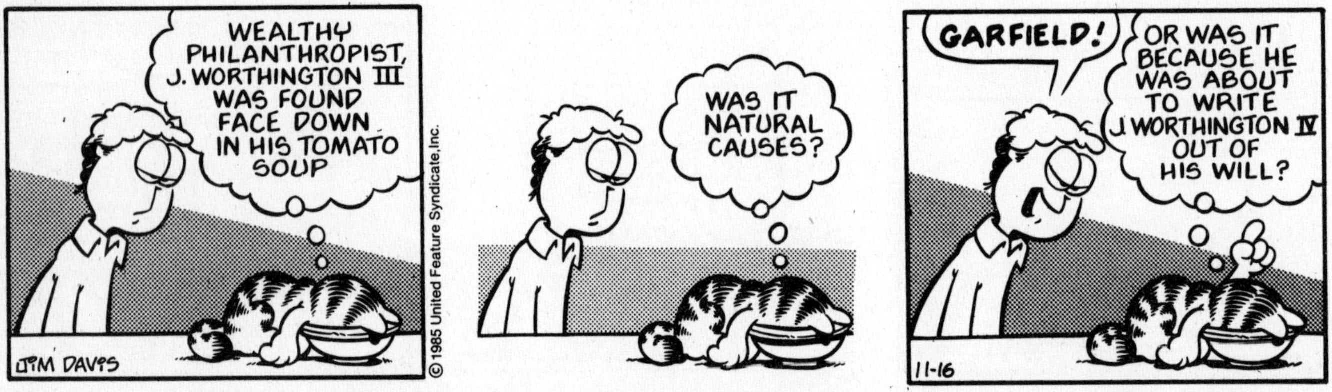
WEALTHY PHILANTHROPIST, J. WORTHINGTON III WAS FOUND FACE DOWN IN HIS TOMATO SOUP
JIM DAVIS
© 1985 United Feature Syndicate, Inc.
WAS IT NATURAL CAUSES?
GARFIELD!
OR WAS IT BECAUSE HE WAS ABOUT TO WRITE J. WORTHINGTON IV OUT OF HIS WILL?
11-16

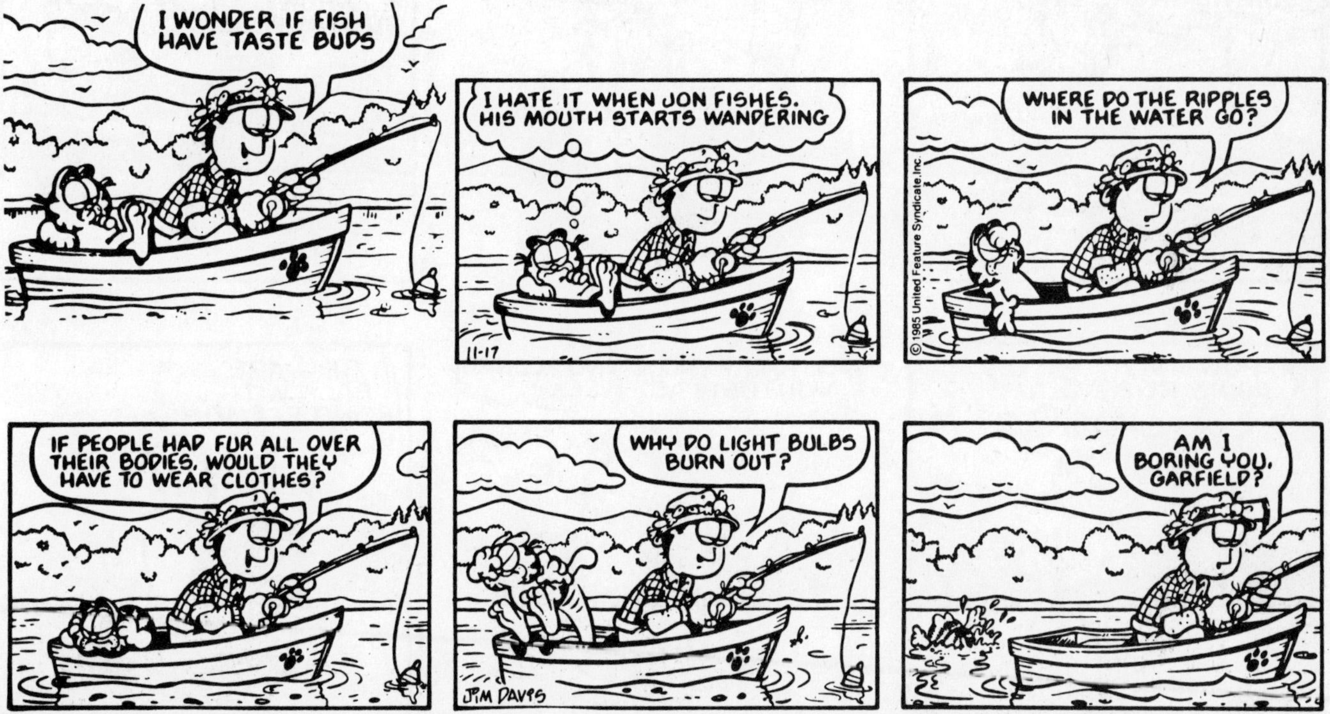
I WONDER IF FISH HAVE TASTE BUDS
I HATE IT WHEN JON FISHES. HIS MOUTH STARTS WANDERING
11-17
WHERE DO THE RIPPLES IN THE WATER GO?
© 1985 United Feature Syndicate, Inc.
IF PEOPLE HAD FUR ALL OVER THEIR BODIES, WOULD THEY HAVE TO WEAR CLOTHES?
WHY DO LIGHT BULBS BURN OUT?
JIM DAVIS
AM I BORING YOU, GARFIELD?

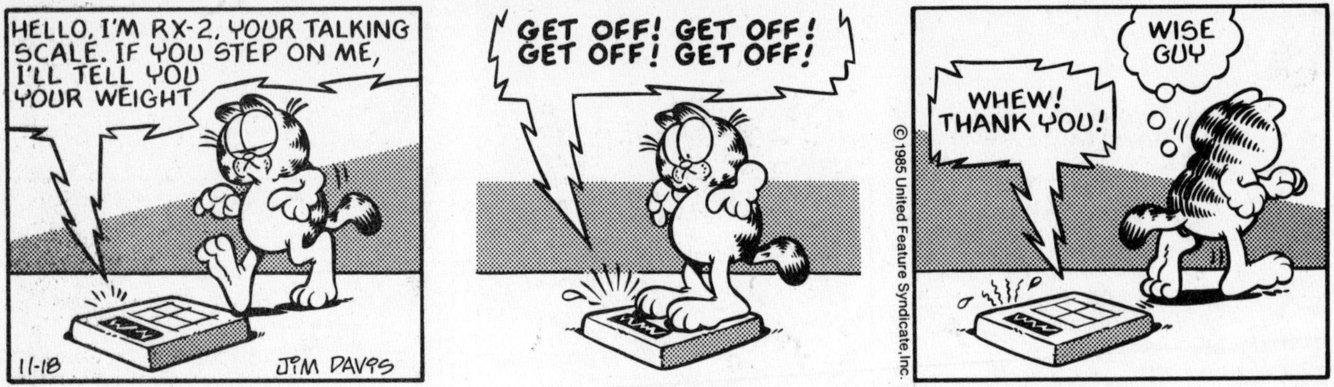
HELLO, I'M RX-2, YOUR TALKING SCALE. IF YOU STEP ON ME, I'LL TELL YOU YOUR WEIGHT
11-18
JIM DAVIS
GET OFF! GET OFF! GET OFF! GET OFF!
WHEW! THANK YOU!
WISE GUY
© 1985 United Feature Syndicate, Inc.

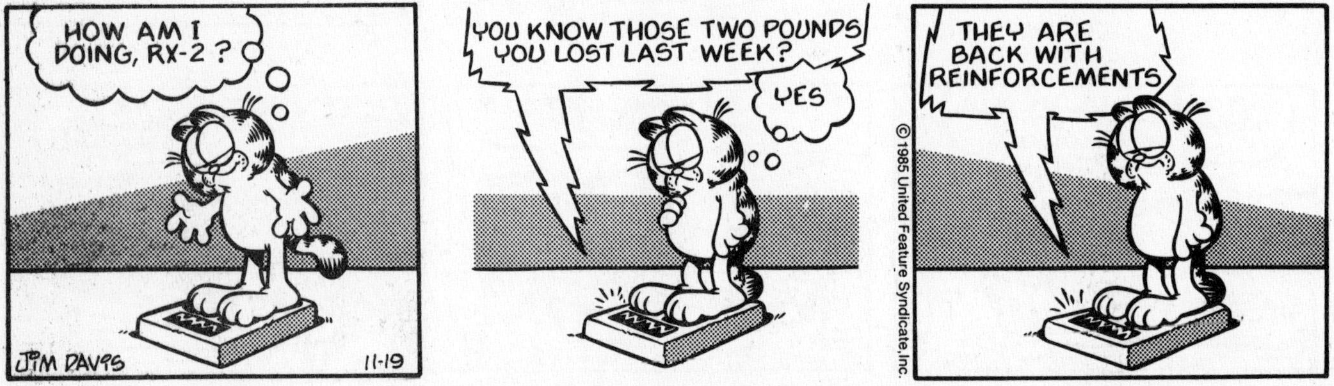
HOW AM I DOING, RX-2 ?
JIM DAVIS
11-19
YOU KNOW THOSE TWO POUNDS YOU LOST LAST WEEK?
YES
THEY ARE BACK WITH REINFORCEMENTS
© 1985 United Feature Syndicate, Inc.

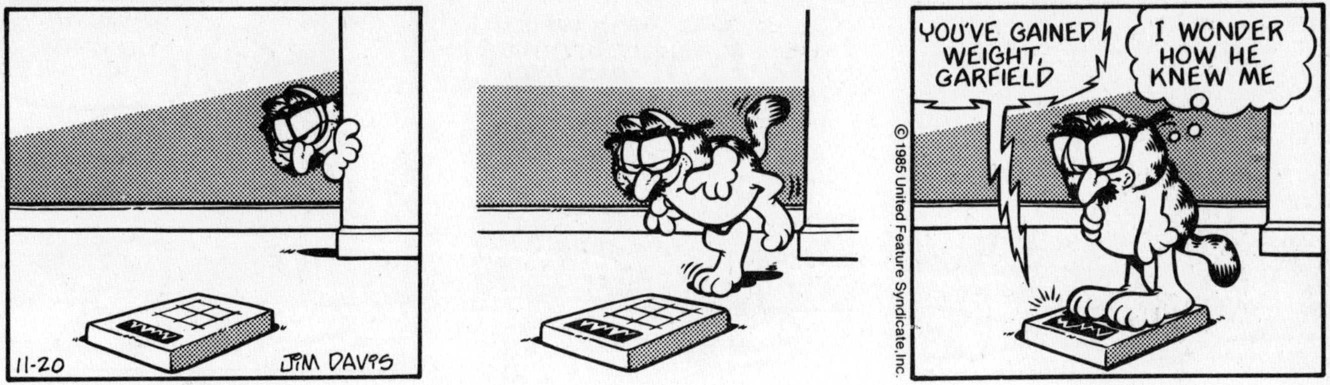
11-20
JIM DAVIS
YOU'VE GAINED WEIGHT, GARFIELD
I WONDER HOW HE KNEW ME


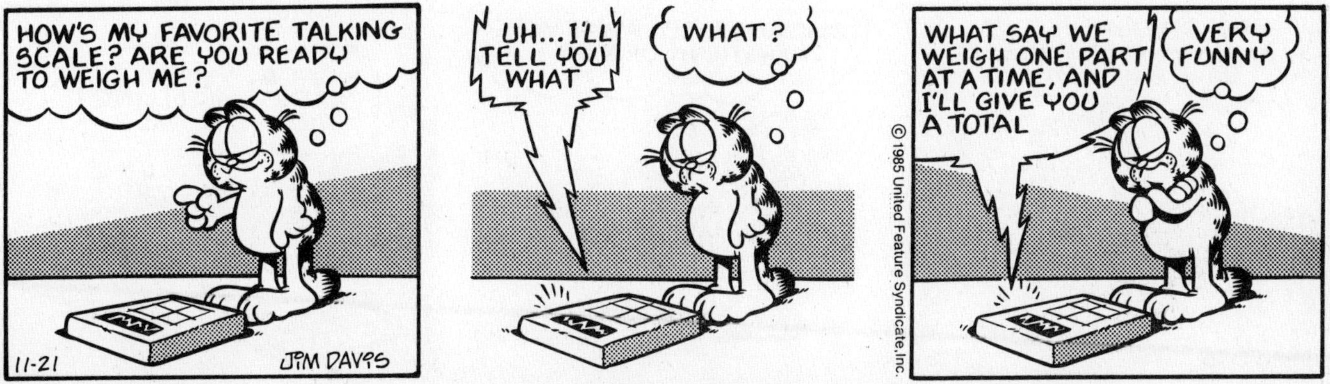
HOW'S MY FAVORITE TALKING SCALE? ARE YOU READY TO WEIGH ME?
11-21
JIM DAVIS
UH... I'LL TELL YOU WHAT
WHAT?
WHAT SAY WE WEIGH ONE PART AT A TIME, AND I'LL GIVE YOU A TOTAL
VERY FUNNY

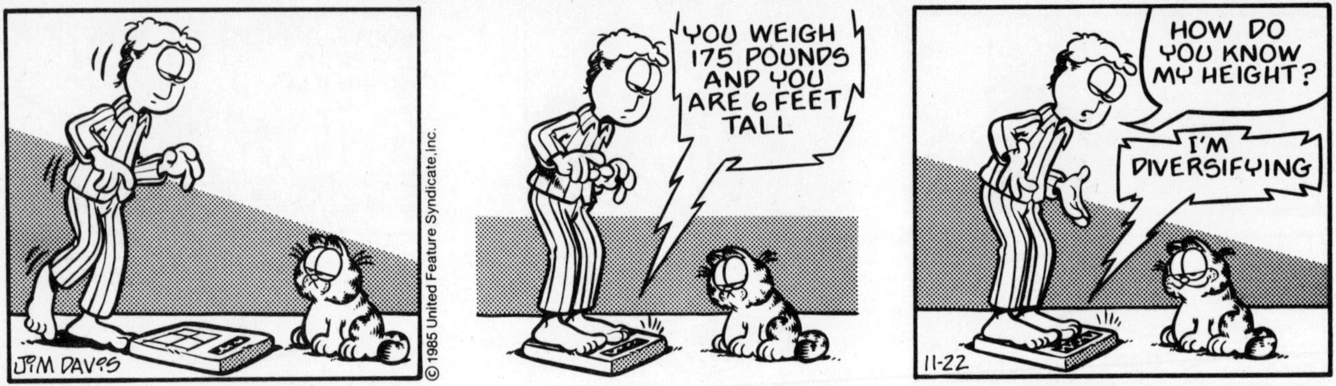
JIM DAVIS
© 1985 United Feature Syndicate, Inc.
YOU WEIGH 175 POUNDS AND YOU ARE 6 FEET TALL
HOW DO YOU KNOW MY HEIGHT?
I'M DIVERSIFYING
11-22

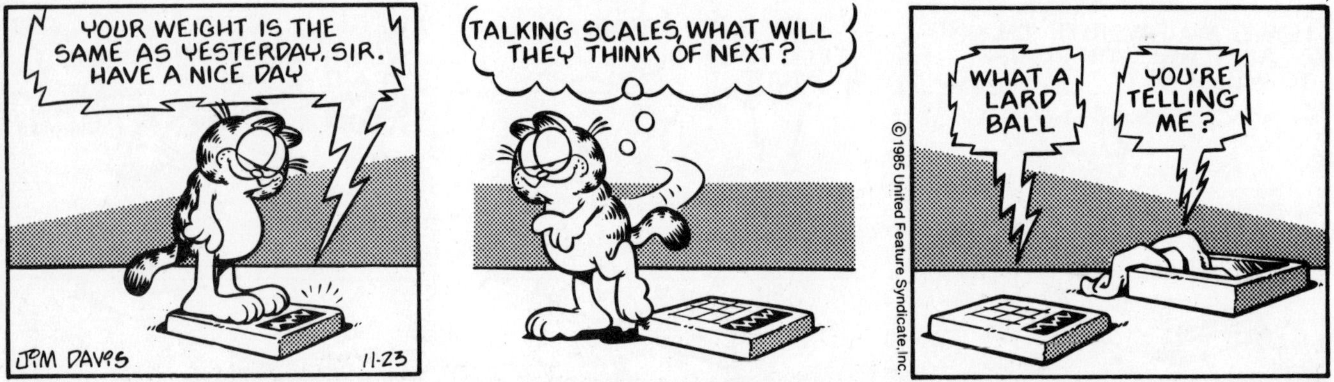
YOUR WEIGHT IS THE SAME AS YESTERDAY, SIR. HAVE A NICE DAY
JIM DAVIS
11-23
TALKING SCALES, WHAT WILL THEY THINK OF NEXT?
© 1985 United Feature Syndicate, Inc.
WHAT A LARD BALL
YOU'RE TELLING ME?

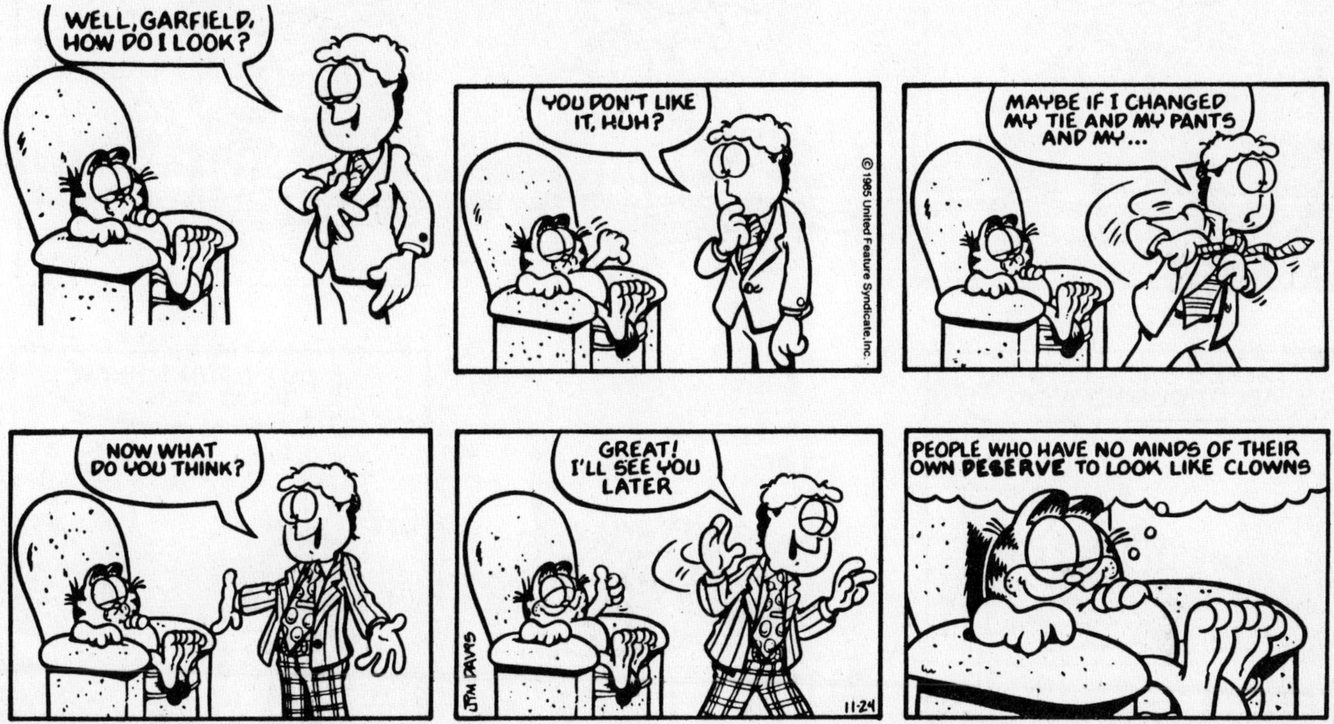
WELL, GARFIELD, HOW DO I LOOK?
YOU DON'T LIKE IT, HUH?
© 1985 United Feature Syndicate, Inc.
MAYBE IF I CHANGED MY TIE AND MY PANTS AND MY...
NOW WHAT DO YOU THINK?
GREAT! I'LL SEE YOU LATER
JIM DAVIS
11-24
PEOPLE WHO HAVE NO MINDS OF THEIR OWN DESERVE TO LOOK LIKE CLOWNS

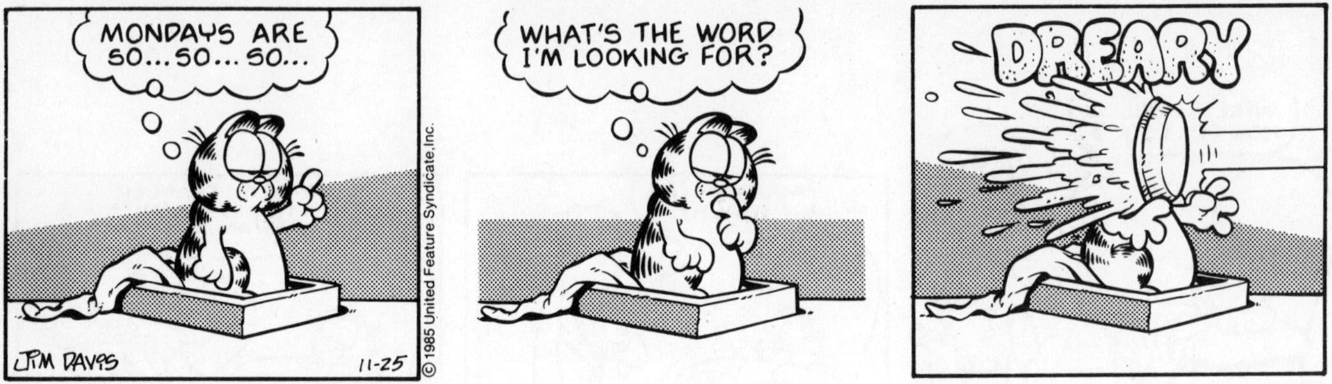
MONDAYS ARE SO... SO... SO...
JIM DAVIS
11-25
© 1985 United Feature Syndicate, Inc.
WHAT'S THE WORD I'M LOOKING FOR?
DREARY

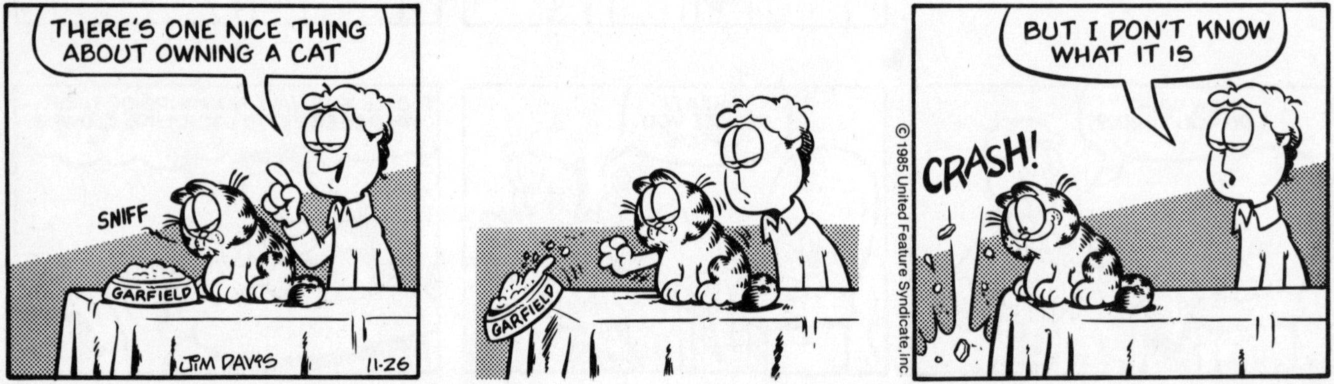
THERE'S ONE NICE THING ABOUT OWNING A CAT
SNIFF
GARFIELD
JIM DAVIS
11-26
GARFIELD
© 1985 United Feature Syndicate, Inc.
BUT I DON'T KNOW WHAT IT IS
CRASH!

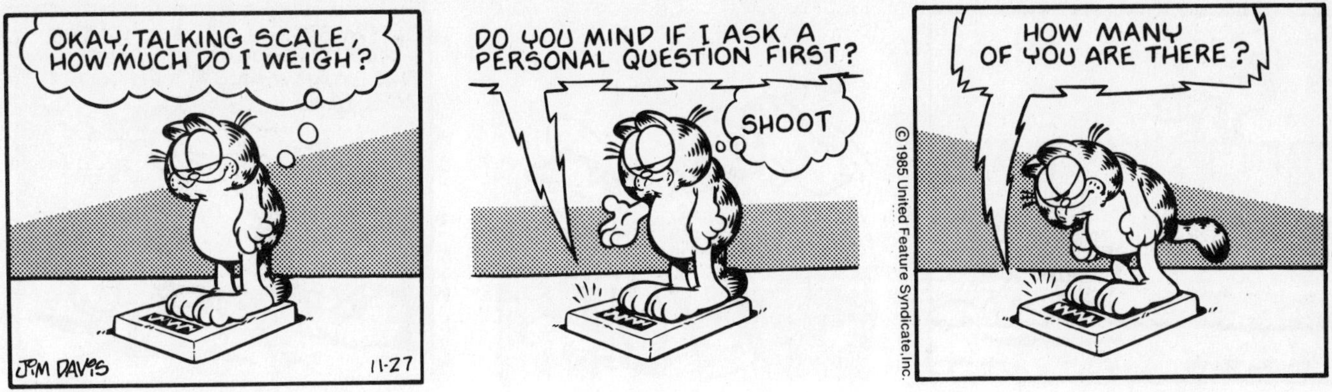
OKAY, TALKING SCALE, HOW MUCH DO I WEIGH?
JIM DAVIS
11-27
DO YOU MIND IF I ASK A PERSONAL QUESTION FIRST?
SHOOT
© 1985 United Feature Syndicate,Inc.
HOW MANY OF YOU ARE THERE?

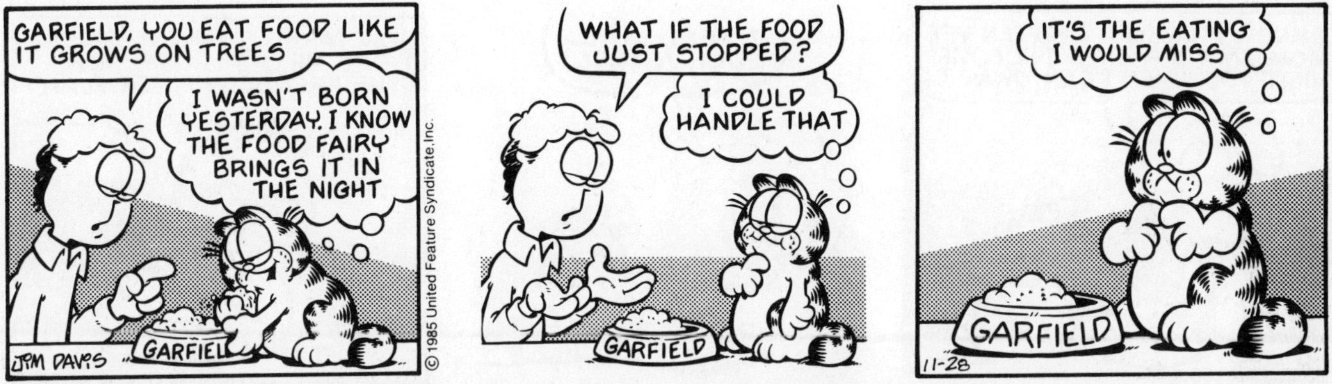
GARFIELD, YOU EAT FOOD LIKE IT GROWS ON TREES
I WASN'T BORN YESTERDAY. I KNOW THE FOOD FAIRY BRINGS IT IN THE NIGHT
JIM DAVIS
GARFIELD
© 1985 United Feature Syndicate,Inc.
WHAT IF THE FOOD JUST STOPPED?
I COULD HANDLE THAT
GARFIELD
IT'S THE EATING I WOULD MISS
GARFIELD
11-28

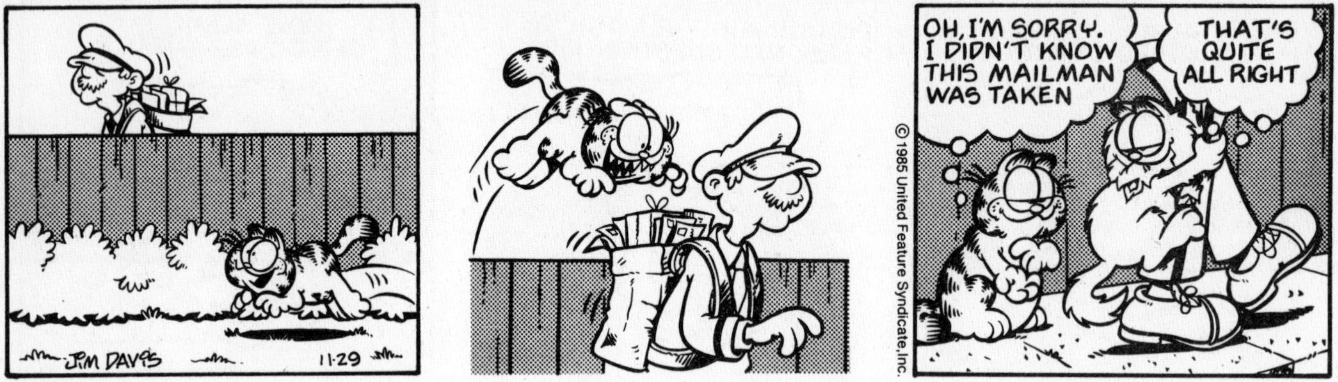
JIM DAVIS
11-29
OH, I'M SORRY. I DIDN'T KNOW THIS MAILMAN WAS TAKEN
THAT'S QUITE ALL RIGHT
© 1985 United Feature Syndicate, Inc.

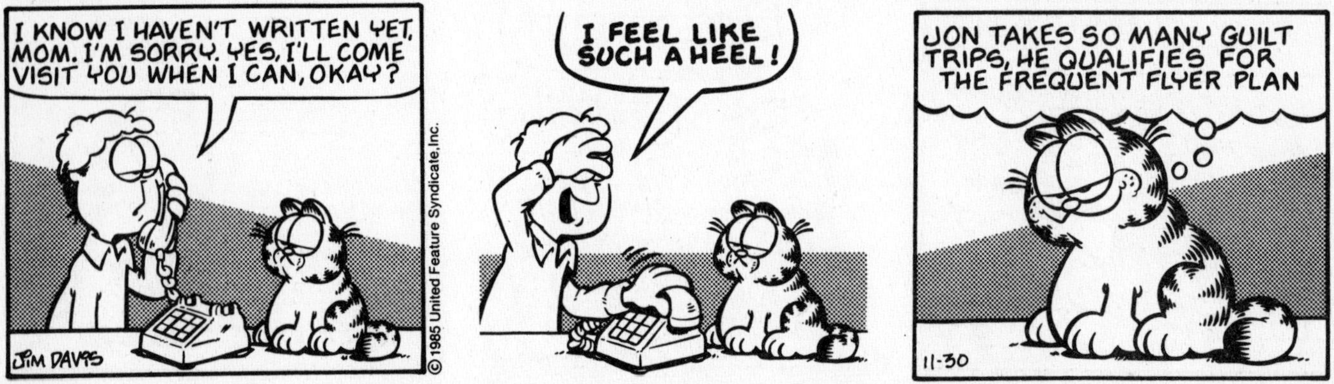
I KNOW I HAVEN'T WRITTEN YET, MOM. I'M SORRY. YES, I'LL COME VISIT YOU WHEN I CAN, OKAY?
JIM DAVIS
© 1985 United Feature Syndicate, Inc.
I FEEL LIKE SUCH A HEEL!
JON TAKES SO MANY GUILT TRIPS, HE QUALIFIES FOR THE FREQUENT FLYER PLAN
11-30

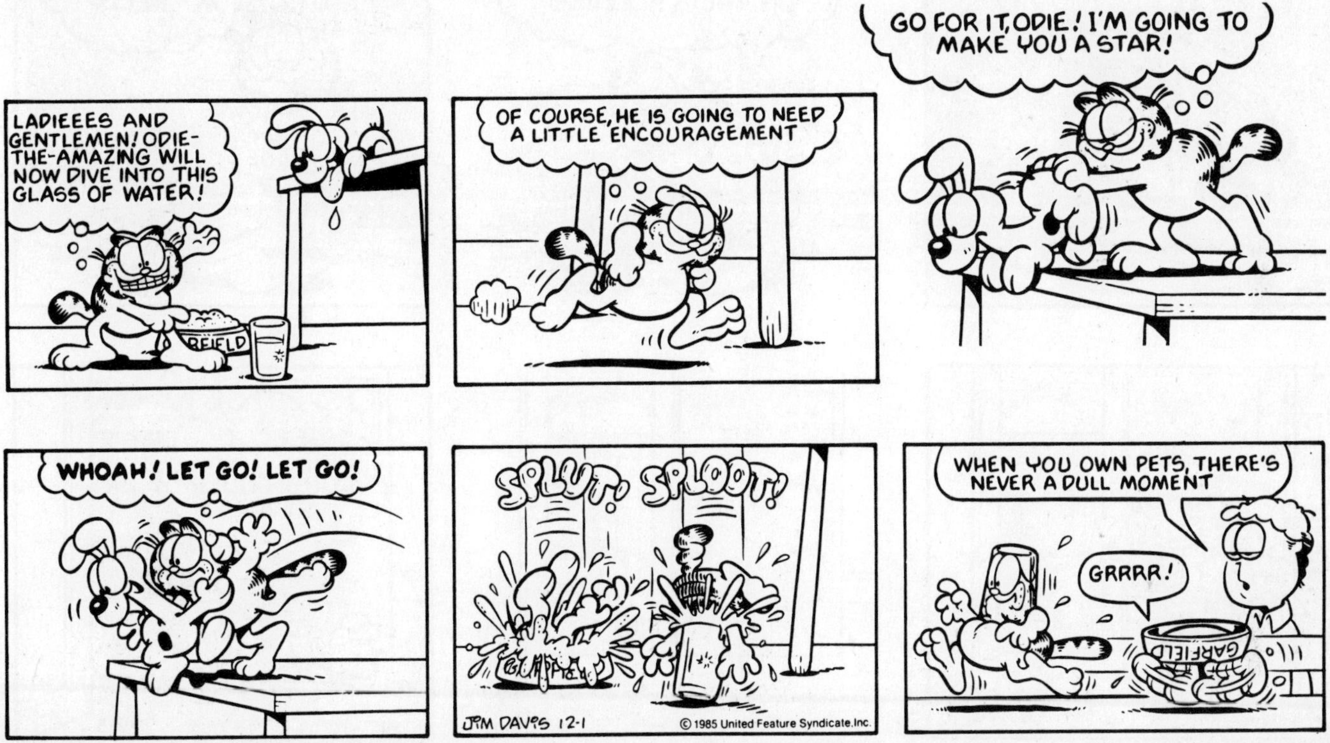

LADIEEES AND GENTLEMEN! ODIE-THE-AMAZING WILL NOW DIVE INTO THIS GLASS OF WATER!
OF COURSE, HE IS GOING TO NEED A LITTLE ENCOURAGEMENT
GO FOR IT, ODIE! I'M GOING TO MAKE YOU A STAR!
WHOAH! LET GO! LET GO!
SPLUT! SPLOOT!
JIM DAVIS 12-1
© 1985 United Feature Syndicate, Inc.
WHEN YOU OWN PETS, THERE'S NEVER A DULL MOMENT
GRRRR!
GARFIELD

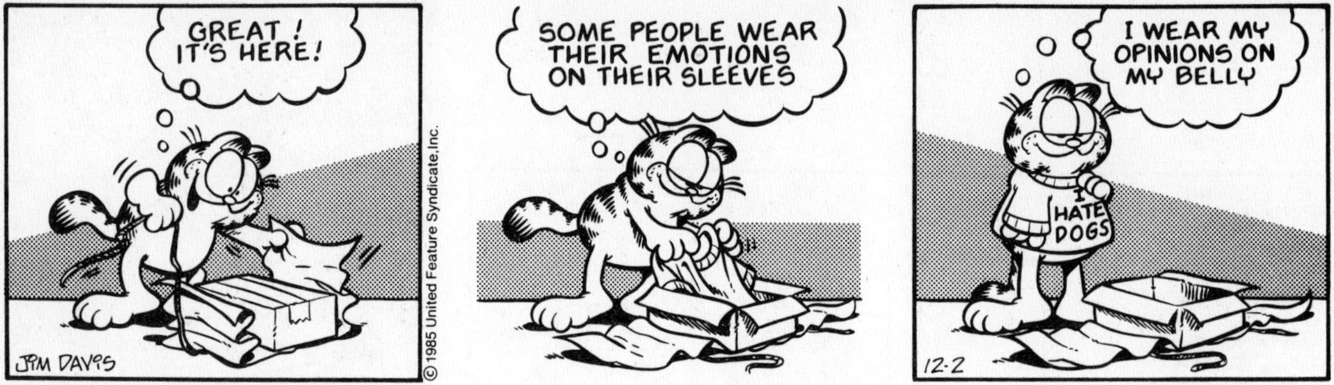
GREAT! IT'S HERE!
JIM DAVIS
© 1985 United Feature Syndicate, Inc.
SOME PEOPLE WEAR THEIR EMOTIONS ON THEIR SLEEVES
I WEAR MY OPINIONS ON MY BELLY
I HATE DOGS
12-2

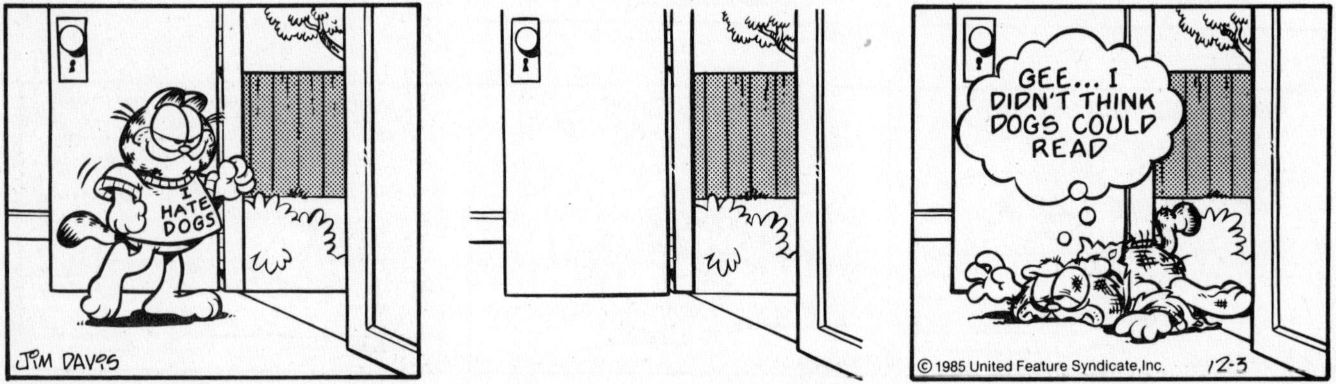
I HATE DOGS
JIM DAVIS
GEE... I DIDN'T THINK DOGS COULD READ
© 1985 United Feature Syndicate, Inc.
12-3

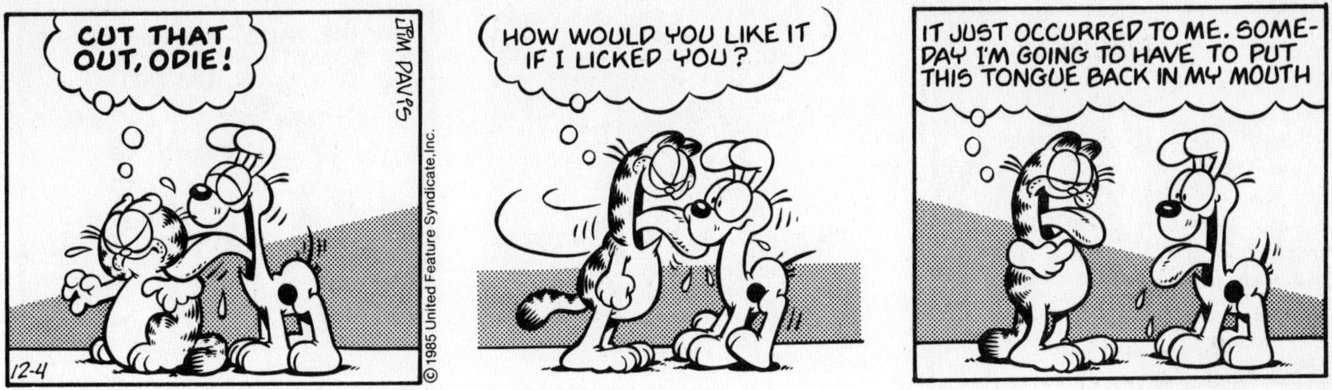
CUT THAT OUT, ODIE!
JIM DAVIS
12-4
© 1985 United Feature Syndicate, Inc.
HOW WOULD YOU LIKE IT IF I LICKED YOU?
IT JUST OCCURRED TO ME. SOMEDAY I'M GOING TO HAVE TO PUT THIS TONGUE BACK IN MY MOUTH

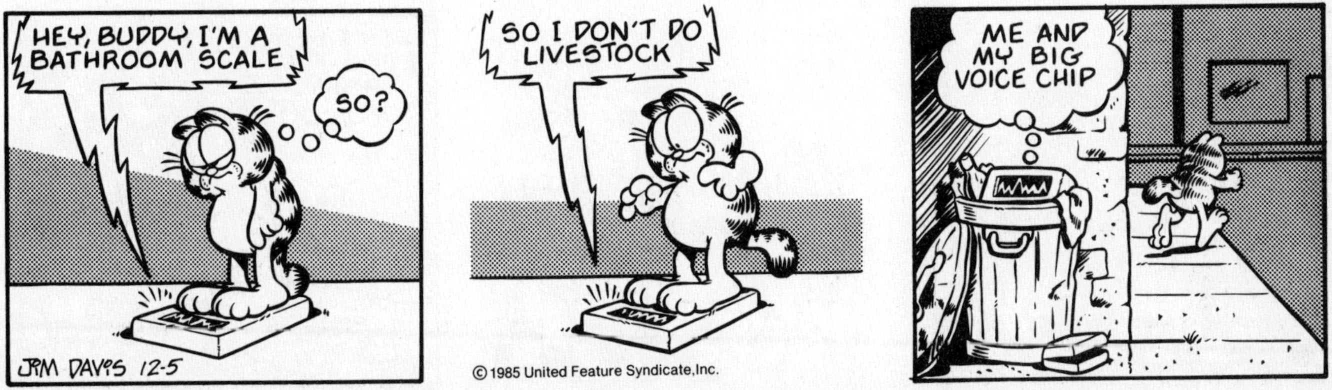
HEY, BUDDY, I'M A BATHROOM SCALE
SO?
JIM DAVIS 12-5
SO I DON'T DO LIVESTOCK
© 1985 United Feature Syndicate, Inc.
ME AND MY BIG VOICE CHIP

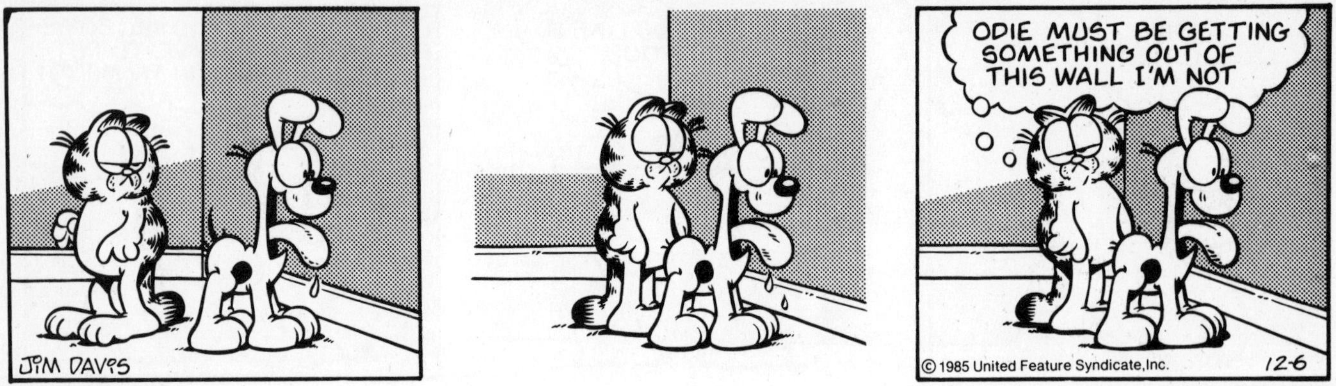
JIM DAVIS
ODIE MUST BE GETTING SOMETHING OUT OF THIS WALL I'M NOT
© 1985 United Feature Syndicate,Inc.
12-6

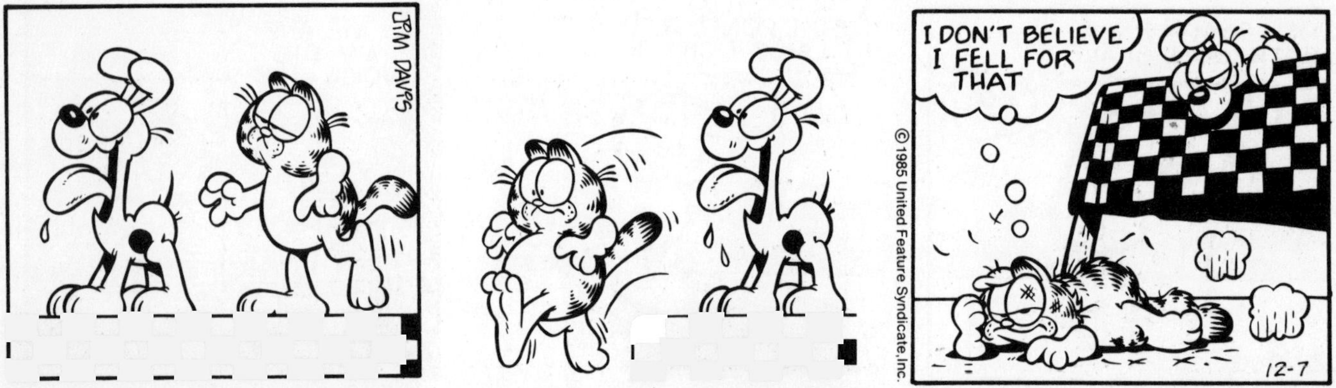
JIM DAVIS
© 1985 United Feature Syndicate,Inc.
I DON'T BELIEVE I FELL FOR THAT
12-7

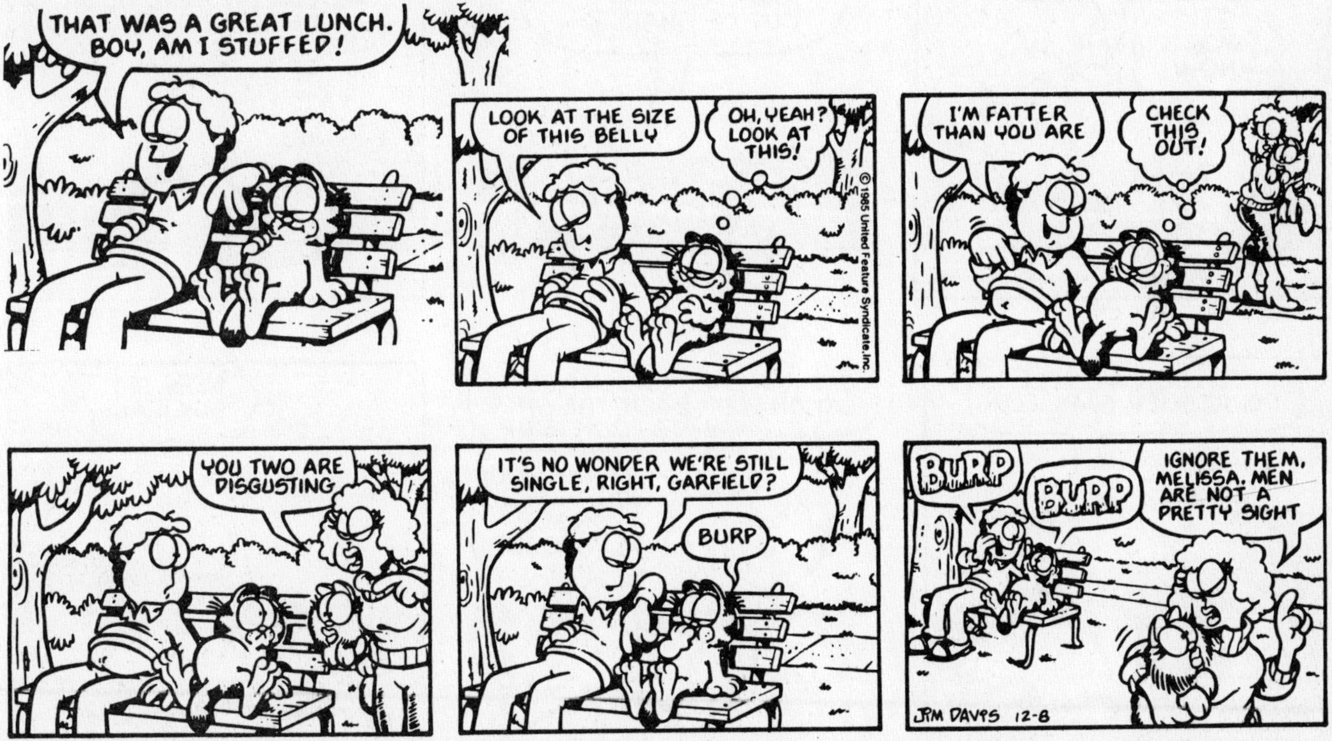
THAT WAS A GREAT LUNCH. BOY, AM I STUFFED!
LOOK AT THE SIZE OF THIS BELLY
OH, YEAH? LOOK AT THIS!
© 1985 United Feature Syndicate, Inc.
I'M FATTER THAN YOU ARE
CHECK THIS OUT!
YOU TWO ARE DISGUSTING
IT'S NO WONDER WE'RE STILL SINGLE, RIGHT, GARFIELD?
BURP
BURP
BURP
IGNORE THEM, MELISSA. MEN ARE NOT A PRETTY SIGHT
JIM DAVIS 12-8

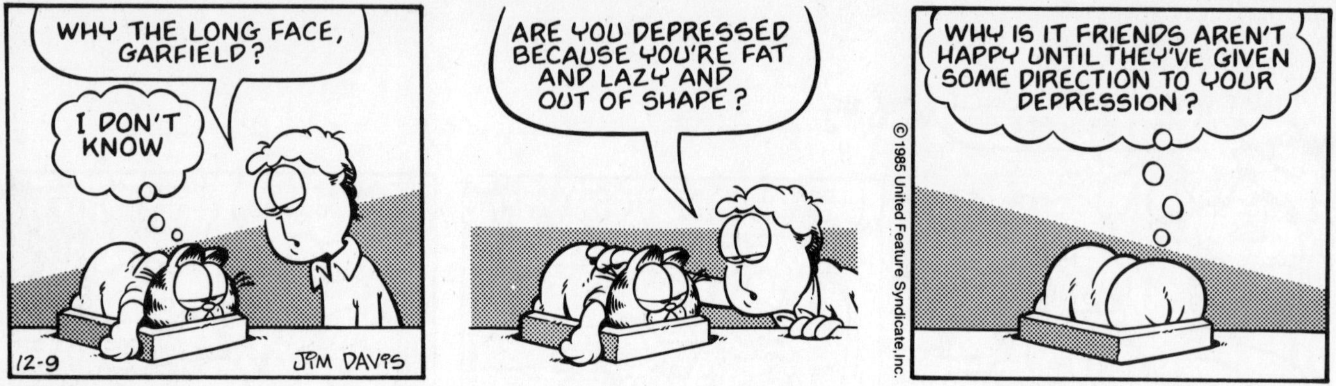
WHY THE LONG FACE, GARFIELD?
I DON'T KNOW
12-9
JIM DAVIS
ARE YOU DEPRESSED BECAUSE YOU'RE FAT AND LAZY AND OUT OF SHAPE?
© 1985 United Feature Syndicate,Inc.
WHY IS IT FRIENDS AREN'T HAPPY UNTIL THEY'VE GIVEN SOME DIRECTION TO YOUR DEPRESSION?

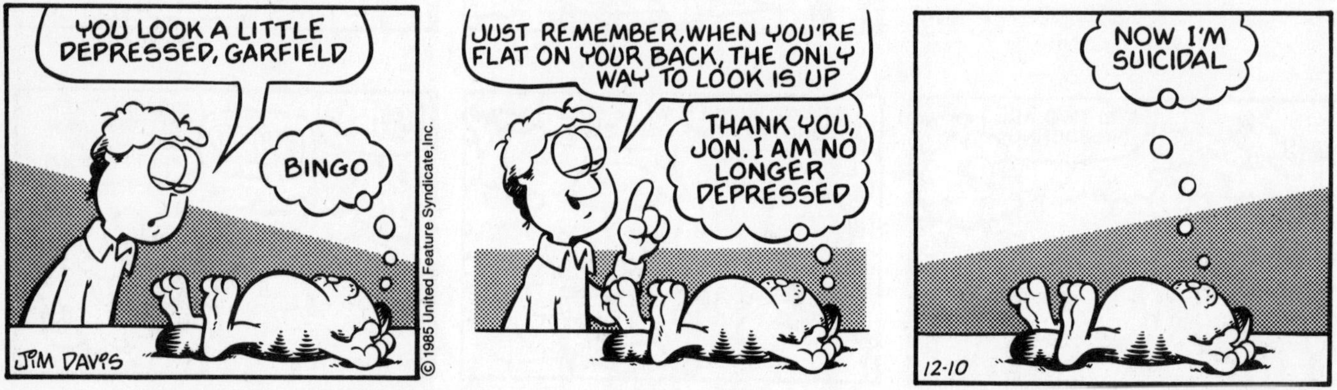
YOU LOOK A LITTLE DEPRESSED, GARFIELD
BINGO
JIM DAVIS
© 1985 United Feature Syndicate,Inc.
JUST REMEMBER, WHEN YOU'RE FLAT ON YOUR BACK, THE ONLY WAY TO LOOK IS UP
THANK YOU, JON. I AM NO LONGER DEPRESSED
NOW I'M SUICIDAL
12-10

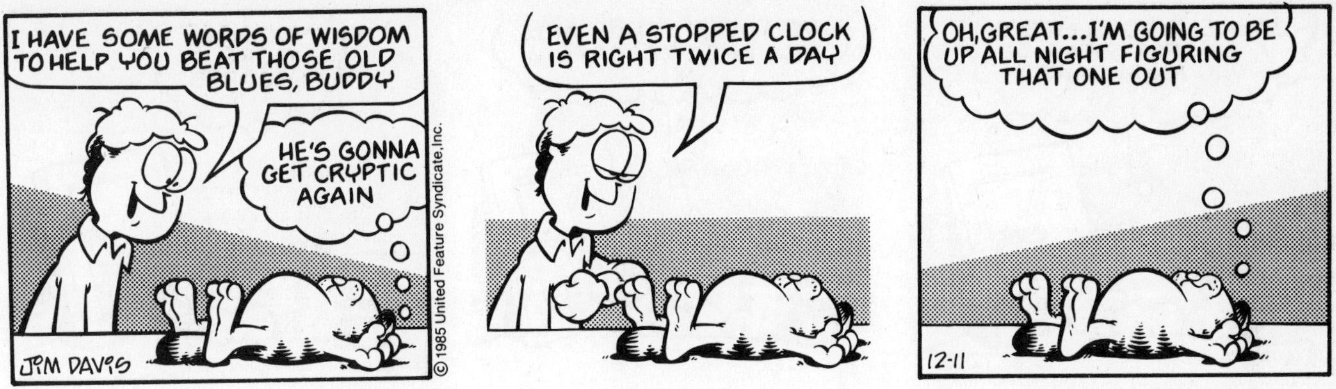

I HAVE SOME WORDS OF WISDOM TO HELP YOU BEAT THOSE OLD BLUES, BUDDY
HE'S GONNA GET CRYPTIC AGAIN
JIM DAVIS
© 1985 United Feature Syndicate, Inc.
EVEN A STOPPED CLOCK IS RIGHT TWICE A DAY
OH, GREAT... I'M GOING TO BE UP ALL NIGHT FIGURING THAT ONE OUT
12-11


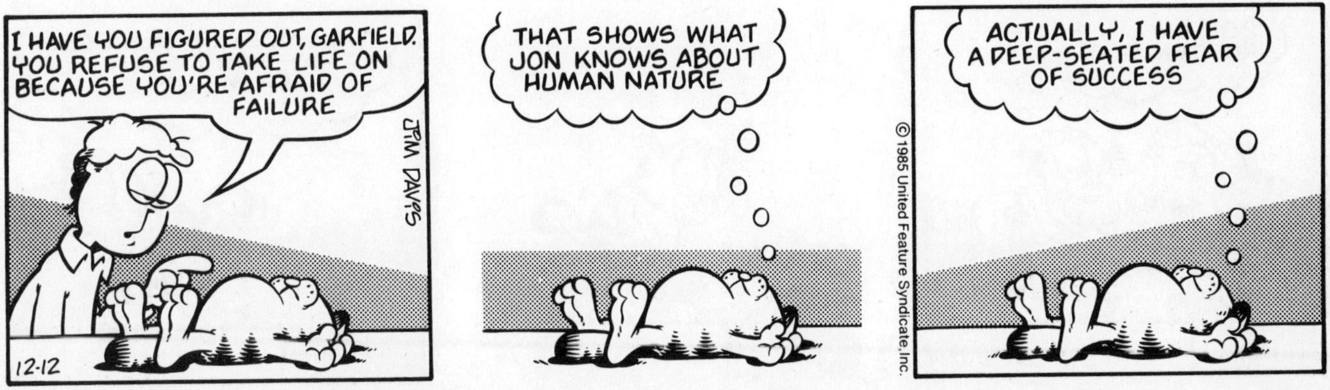

I HAVE YOU FIGURED OUT, GARFIELD. YOU REFUSE TO TAKE LIFE ON BECAUSE YOU'RE AFRAID OF FAILURE
JIM DAVIS
12-12
THAT SHOWS WHAT JON KNOWS ABOUT HUMAN NATURE
© 1985 United Feature Syndicate, Inc.
ACTUALLY, I HAVE A DEEP-SEATED FEAR OF SUCCESS

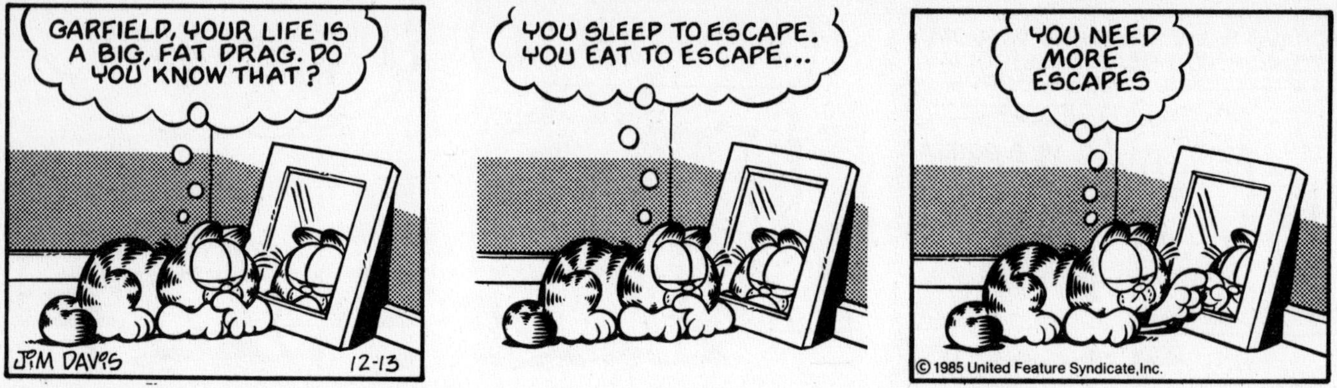
GARFIELD, YOUR LIFE IS A BIG, FAT DRAG. DO YOU KNOW THAT?
JIM DAVIS 12-13
YOU SLEEP TO ESCAPE. YOU EAT TO ESCAPE...
YOU NEED MORE ESCAPES
© 1985 United Feature Syndicate, Inc.

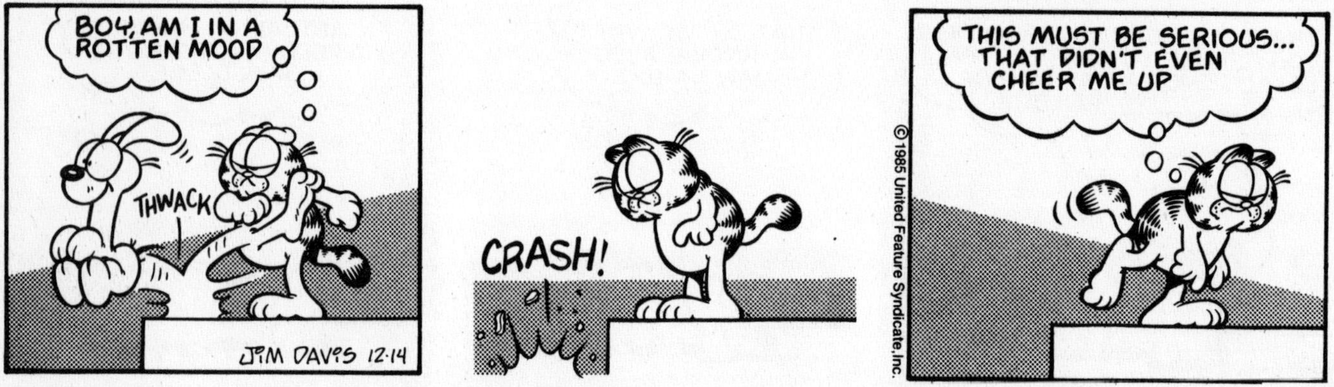
BOY, AM I IN A ROTTEN MOOD
THWACK
JIM DAVIS 12-14
CRASH!
© 1985 United Feature Syndicate, Inc.
THIS MUST BE SERIOUS... THAT DIDN'T EVEN CHEER ME UP

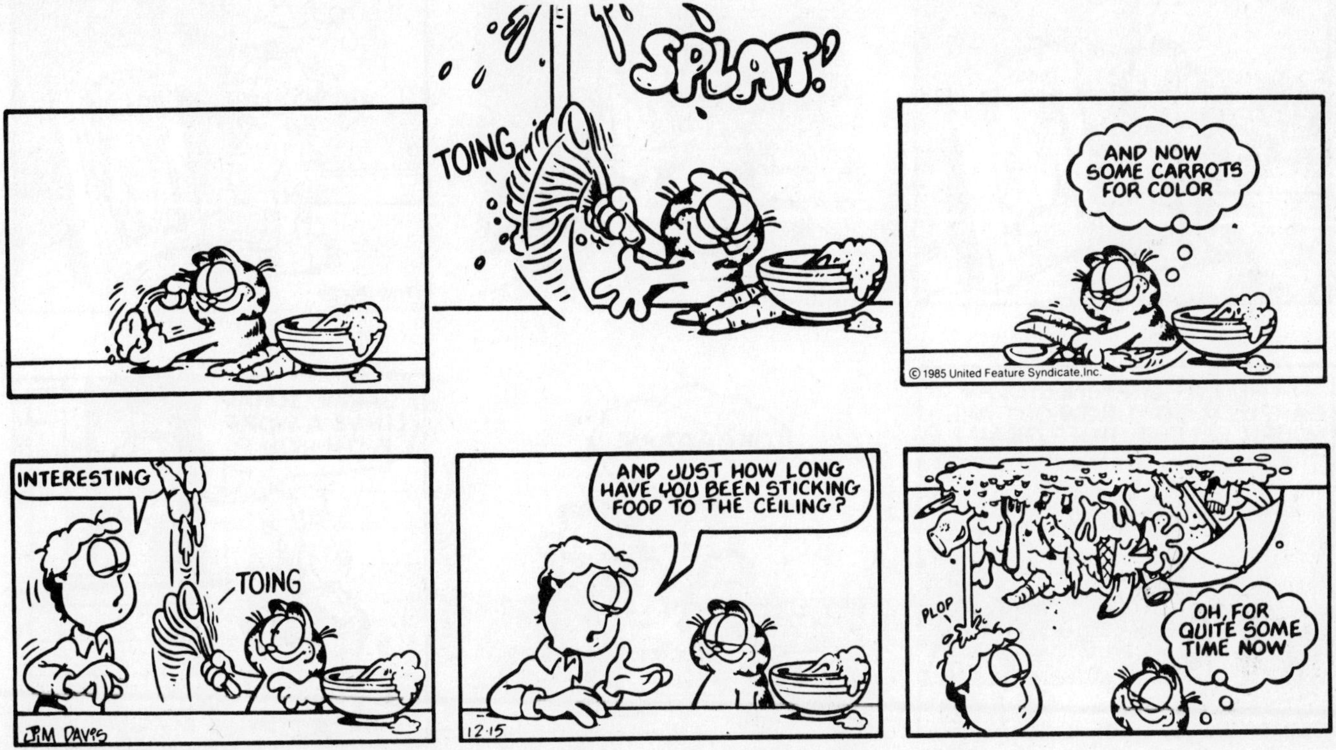
TOING
SPLAT!
AND NOW SOME CARROTS FOR COLOR
© 1985 United Feature Syndicate, Inc.
JIM DAVIS
INTERESTING
TOING
AND JUST HOW LONG HAVE YOU BEEN STICKING FOOD TO THE CEILING?
12·15
PLOP
OH, FOR QUITE SOME TIME NOW

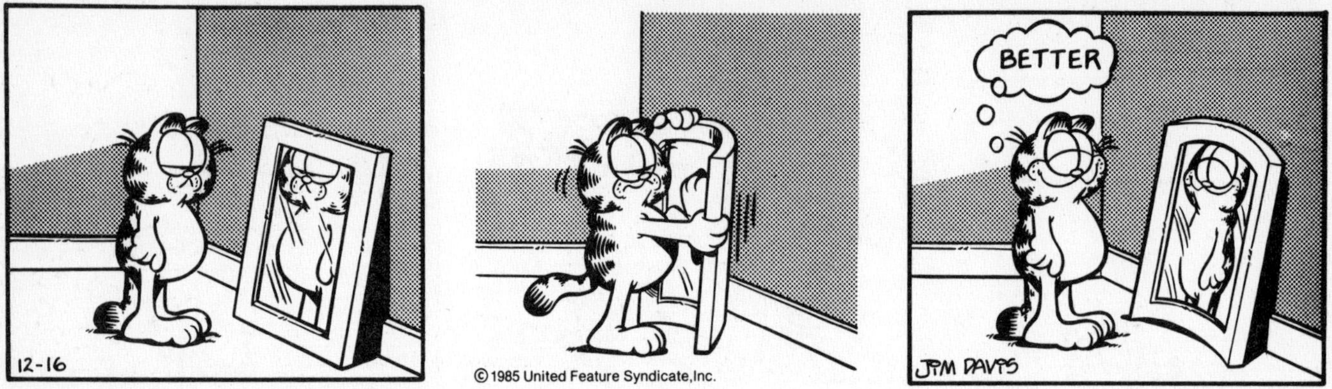
12-16
BETTER
JIM DAVIS


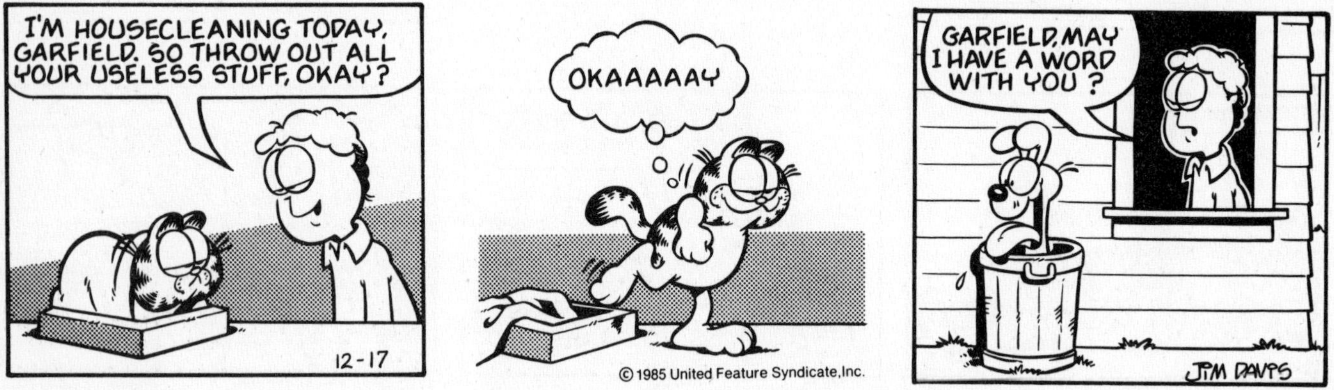
I'M HOUSECLEANING TODAY, GARFIELD. SO THROW OUT ALL YOUR USELESS STUFF, OKAY?
12-17
OKAAAAAY
GARFIELD, MAY I HAVE A WORD WITH YOU?
JIM DAVIS

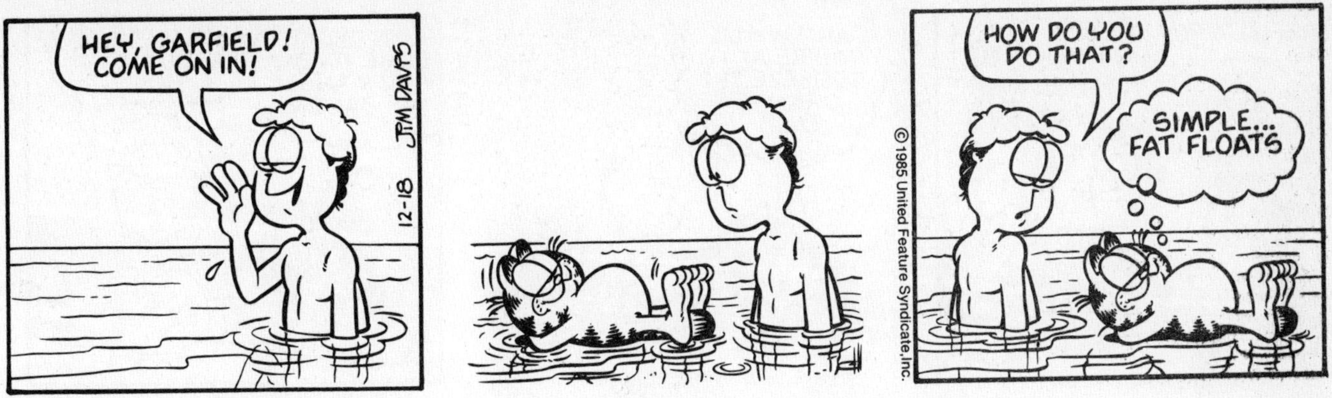
HEY, GARFIELD! COME ON IN!
JIM DAVIS
12-18
HOW DO YOU DO THAT?
SIMPLE... FAT FLOATS
© 1985 United Feature Syndicate,Inc.

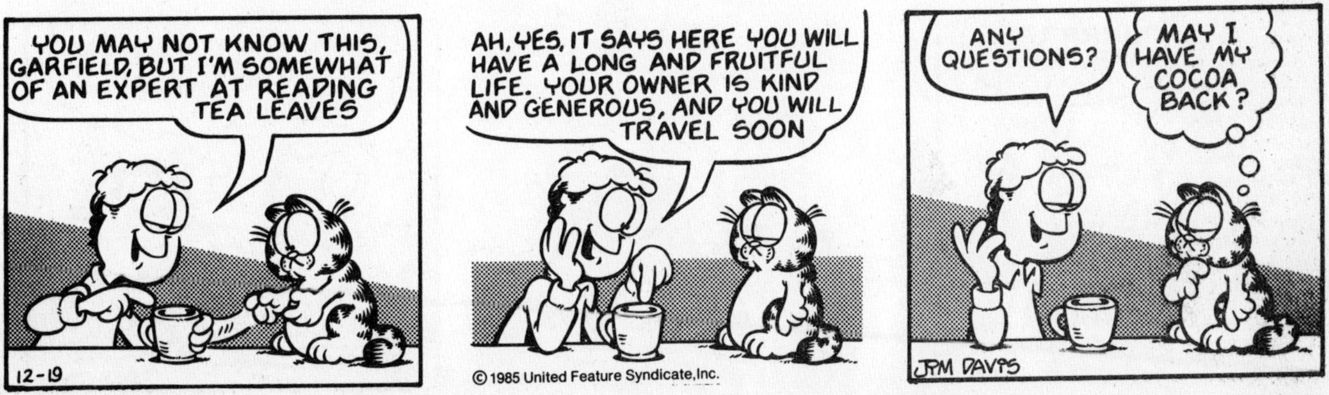
YOU MAY NOT KNOW THIS, GARFIELD, BUT I'M SOMEWHAT OF AN EXPERT AT READING TEA LEAVES
12-19
AH, YES, IT SAYS HERE YOU WILL HAVE A LONG AND FRUITFUL LIFE. YOUR OWNER IS KIND AND GENEROUS, AND YOU WILL TRAVEL SOON
© 1985 United Feature Syndicate,Inc.
ANY QUESTIONS?
MAY I HAVE MY COCOA BACK?
JIM DAVIS

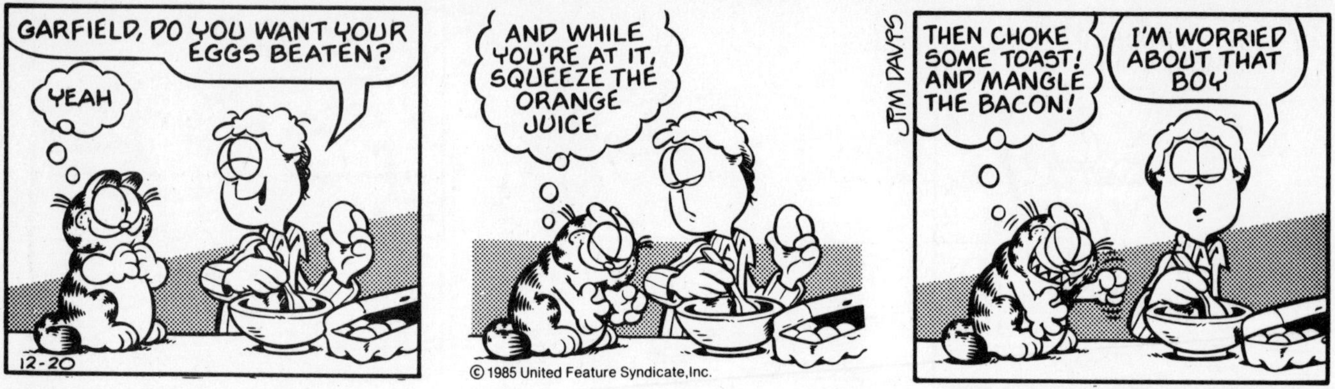
GARFIELD, DO YOU WANT YOUR EGGS BEATEN?
YEAH
AND WHILE YOU'RE AT IT, SQUEEZE THE ORANGE JUICE
THEN CHOKE SOME TOAST! AND MANGLE THE BACON!
I'M WORRIED ABOUT THAT BOY
JIM DAVIS
12-20


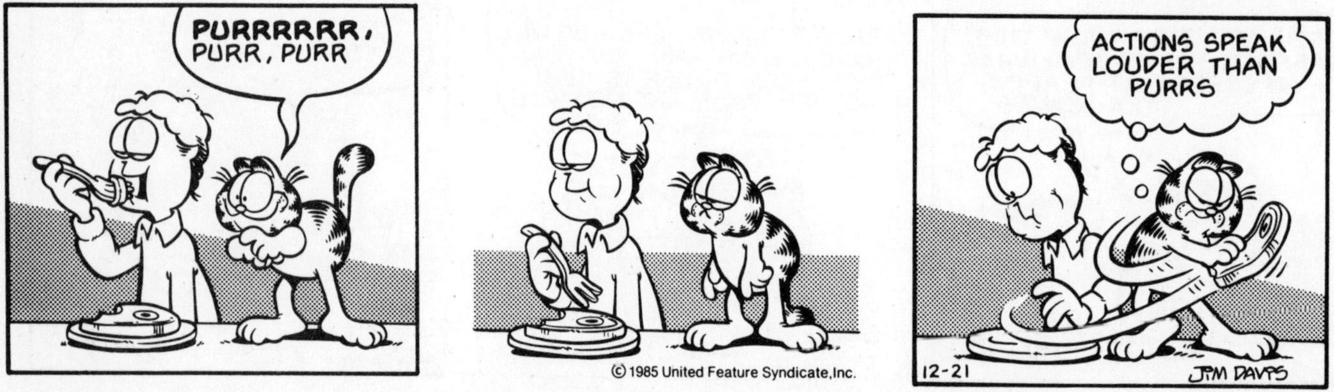
PURRRRRR, PURR, PURR
ACTIONS SPEAK LOUDER THAN PURRS
12-21
JIM DAVIS

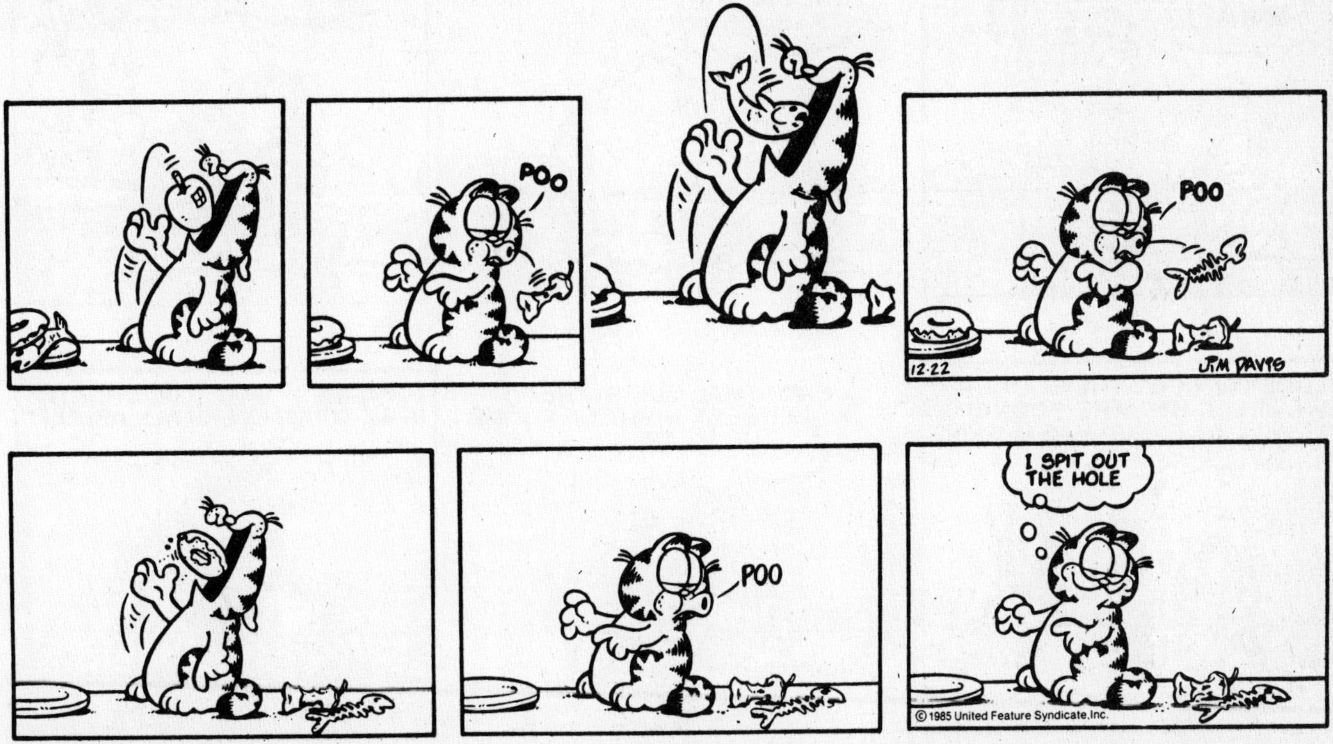
POO
POO
12·22
JIM DAVIS
POO
I SPIT OUT THE HOLE
© 1985 United Feature Syndicate, Inc.

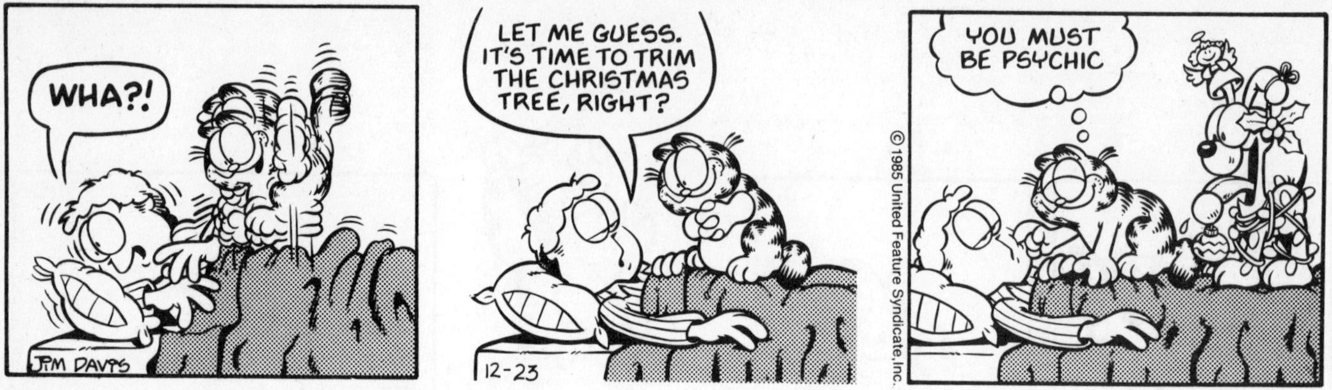
WHA?!
JIM DAVIS
LET ME GUESS. IT'S TIME TO TRIM THE CHRISTMAS TREE, RIGHT?
12-23
© 1985 United Feature Syndicate, Inc.
YOU MUST BE PSYCHIC

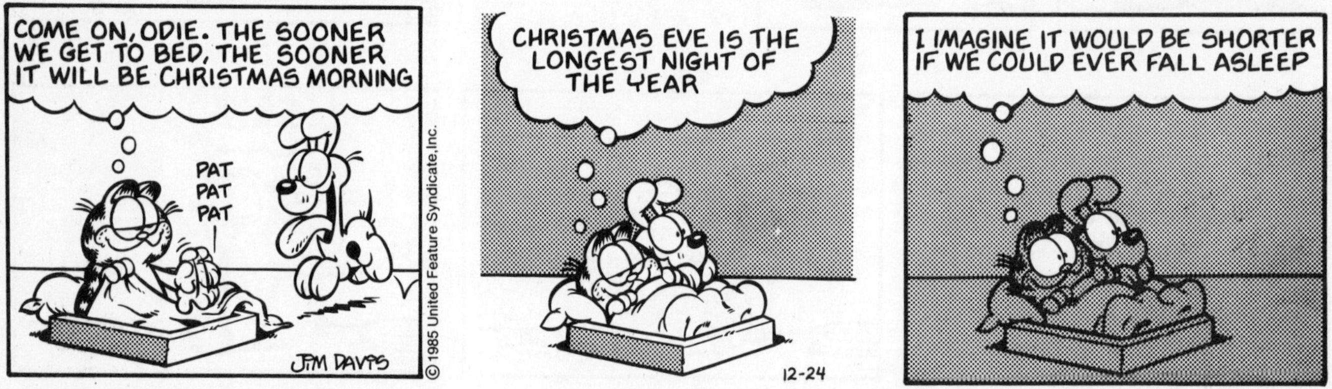
COME ON, ODIE. THE SOONER WE GET TO BED, THE SOONER IT WILL BE CHRISTMAS MORNING
PAT PAT PAT
JIM DAVIS
© 1985 United Feature Syndicate, Inc.
CHRISTMAS EVE IS THE LONGEST NIGHT OF THE YEAR
12-24
I IMAGINE IT WOULD BE SHORTER IF WE COULD EVER FALL ASLEEP

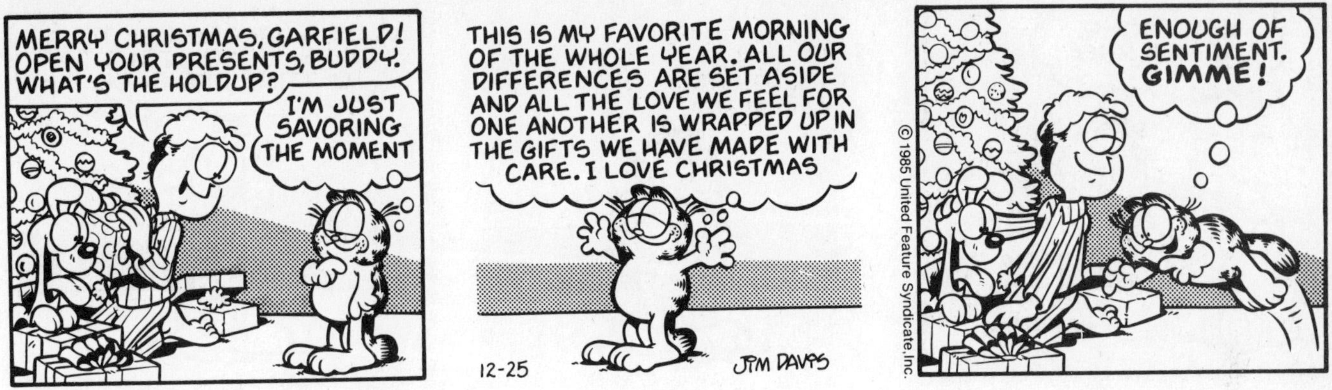
MERRY CHRISTMAS, GARFIELD! OPEN YOUR PRESENTS, BUDDY. WHAT'S THE HOLDUP?
I'M JUST SAVORING THE MOMENT
THIS IS MY FAVORITE MORNING OF THE WHOLE YEAR. ALL OUR DIFFERENCES ARE SET ASIDE AND ALL THE LOVE WE FEEL FOR ONE ANOTHER IS WRAPPED UP IN THE GIFTS WE HAVE MADE WITH CARE. I LOVE CHRISTMAS
12-25
JIM DAVIS
© 1985 United Feature Syndicate, Inc.
ENOUGH OF SENTIMENT. **GIMME!**

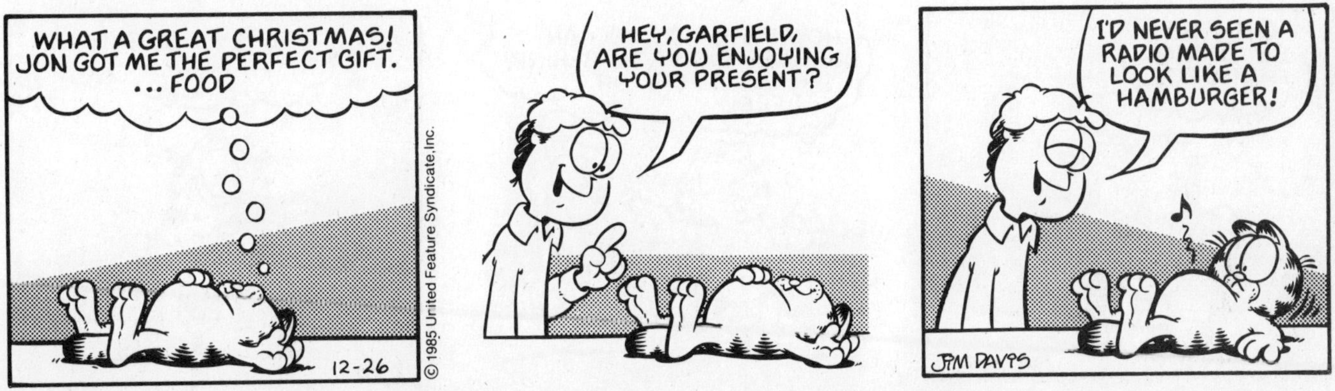
WHAT A GREAT CHRISTMAS! JON GOT ME THE PERFECT GIFT. ... FOOD
12-26
© 1985 United Feature Syndicate, Inc.
HEY, GARFIELD, ARE YOU ENJOYING YOUR PRESENT?
I'D NEVER SEEN A RADIO MADE TO LOOK LIKE A HAMBURGER!
JIM DAVIS

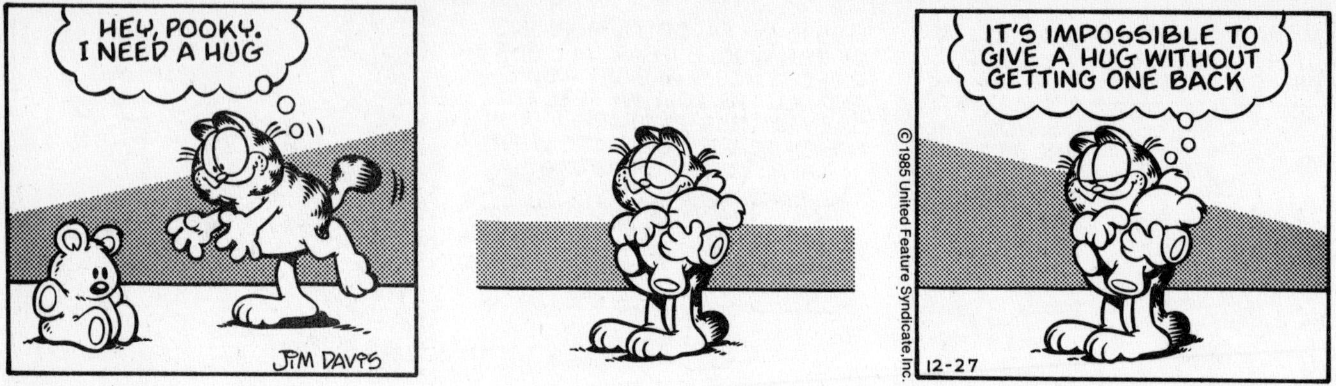
HEY, POOKY. I NEED A HUG
JIM DAVIS
IT'S IMPOSSIBLE TO GIVE A HUG WITHOUT GETTING ONE BACK
© 1985 United Feature Syndicate, Inc.
12-27

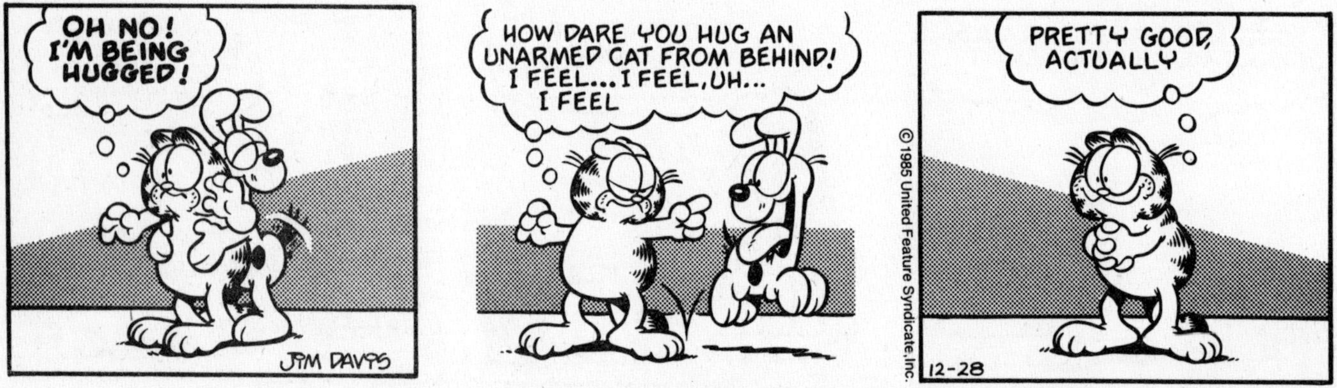
OH NO! I'M BEING HUGGED!
JIM DAVIS
HOW DARE YOU HUG AN UNARMED CAT FROM BEHIND! I FEEL... I FEEL, UH... I FEEL
PRETTY GOOD, ACTUALLY
© 1985 United Feature Syndicate, Inc.
12-28

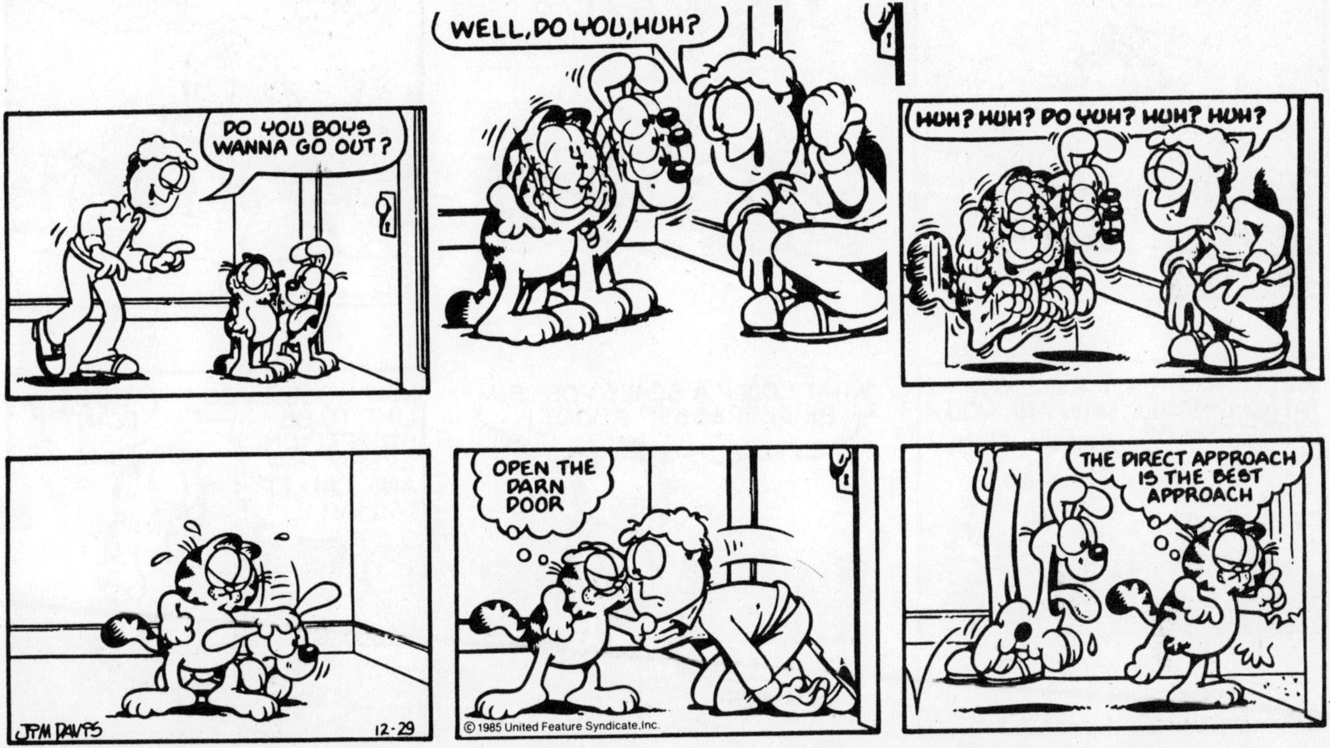

DO YOU BOYS WANNA GO OUT?
WELL, DO YOU, HUH?
HUH? HUH? DO YUH? HUH? HUH?
JIM DAVIS
12-29
OPEN THE DARN DOOR
© 1985 United Feature Syndicate, Inc.
THE DIRECT APPROACH IS THE BEST APPROACH

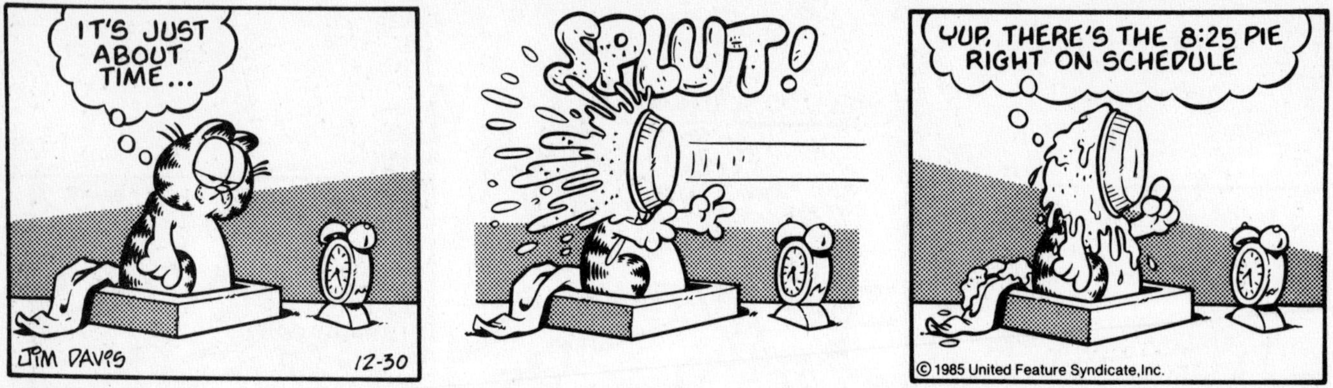
IT'S JUST ABOUT TIME...
JIM DAVIS
12-30
SPLUT!
YUP, THERE'S THE 8:25 PIE RIGHT ON SCHEDULE
© 1985 United Feature Syndicate, Inc.

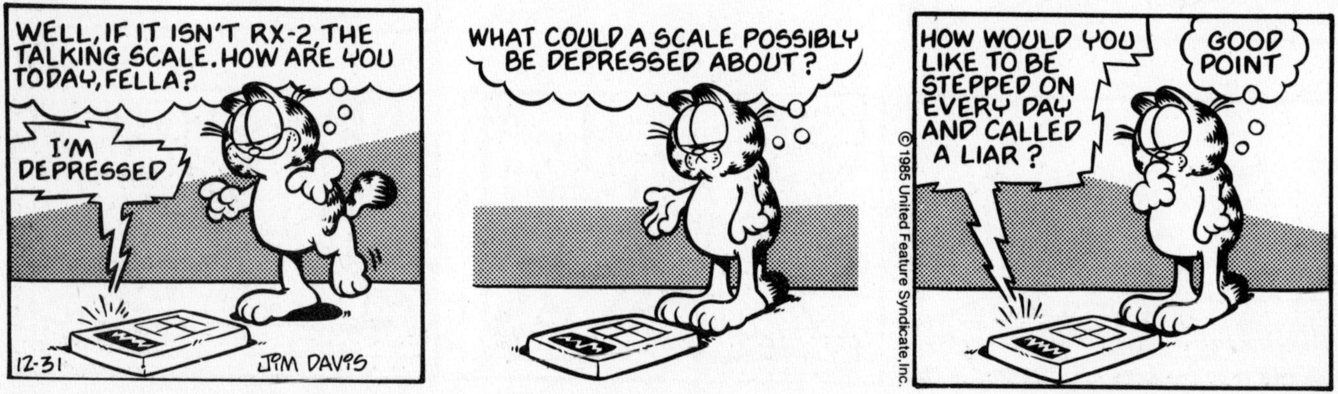
WELL, IF IT ISN'T RX-2, THE TALKING SCALE. HOW ARE YOU TODAY, FELLA?
I'M DEPRESSED
12-31
JIM DAVIS
WHAT COULD A SCALE POSSIBLY BE DEPRESSED ABOUT?
© 1985 United Feature Syndicate, Inc.
HOW WOULD YOU LIKE TO BE STEPPED ON EVERY DAY AND CALLED A LIAR?
GOOD POINT

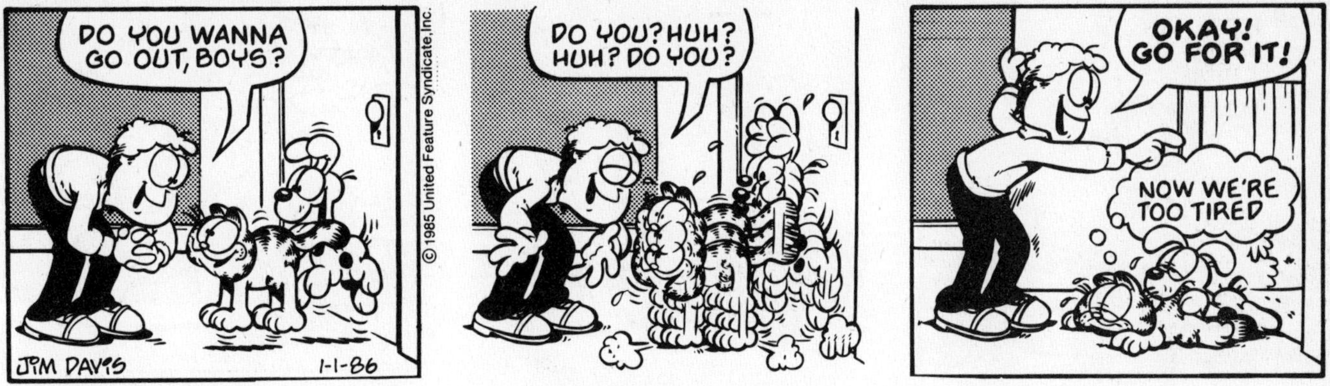
DO YOU WANNA GO OUT, BOYS?
DO YOU? HUH? HUH? DO YOU?
OKAY! GO FOR IT!
NOW WE'RE TOO TIRED
JIM DAVIS
1-1-86
© 1985 United Feature Syndicate, Inc.

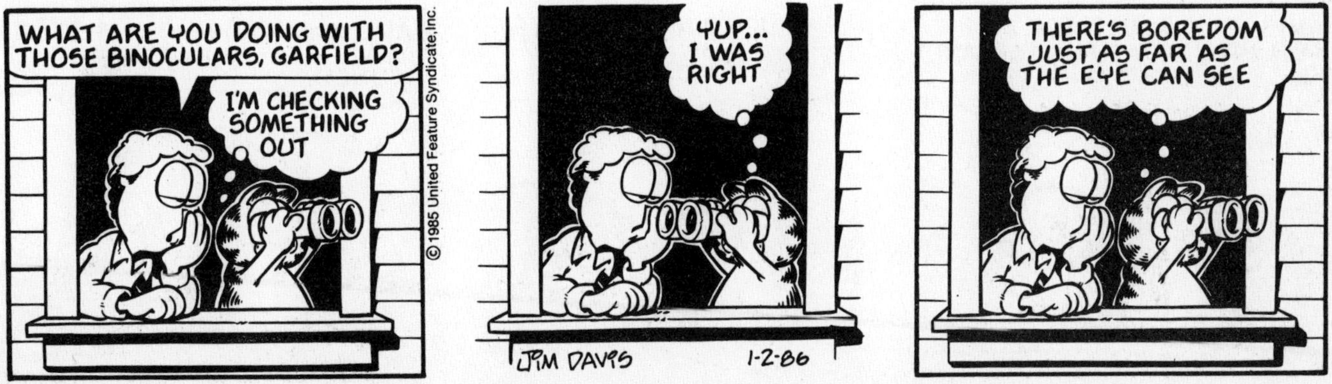
WHAT ARE YOU DOING WITH THOSE BINOCULARS, GARFIELD?
I'M CHECKING SOMETHING OUT
YUP... I WAS RIGHT
THERE'S BOREDOM JUST AS FAR AS THE EYE CAN SEE
JIM DAVIS
1-2-86
© 1985 United Feature Syndicate, Inc.

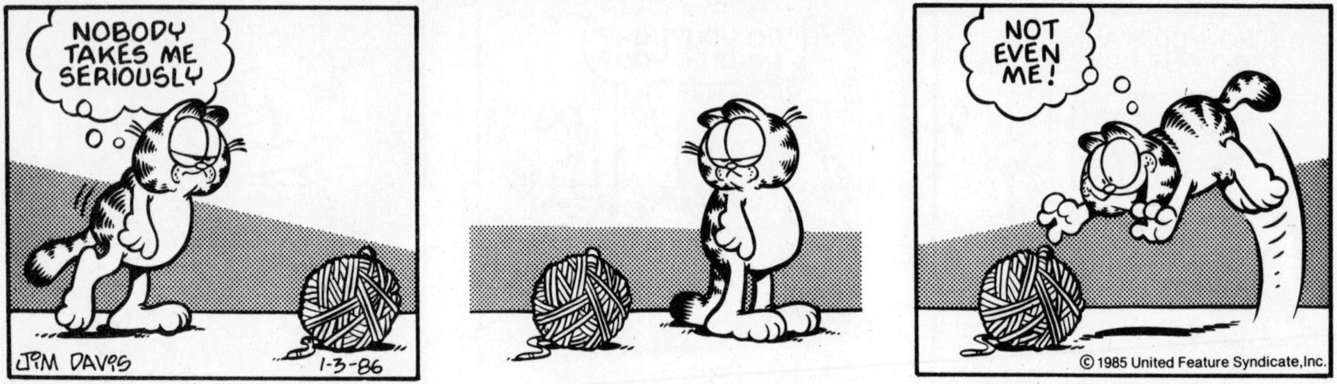
NOBODY TAKES ME SERIOUSLY
JIM DAVIS
1-3-86
NOT EVEN ME!
© 1985 United Feature Syndicate, Inc.

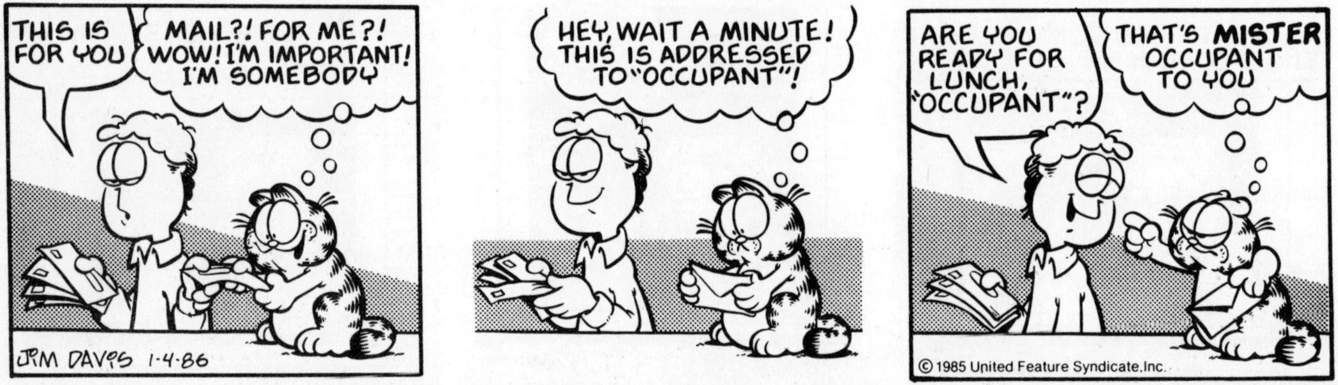
THIS IS FOR YOU
MAIL?! FOR ME?! WOW! I'M IMPORTANT! I'M SOMEBODY
JIM DAVIS 1-4-86
HEY, WAIT A MINUTE! THIS IS ADDRESSED TO "OCCUPANT"!
ARE YOU READY FOR LUNCH, "OCCUPANT"?
THAT'S **MISTER** OCCUPANT TO YOU
© 1985 United Feature Syndicate, Inc.

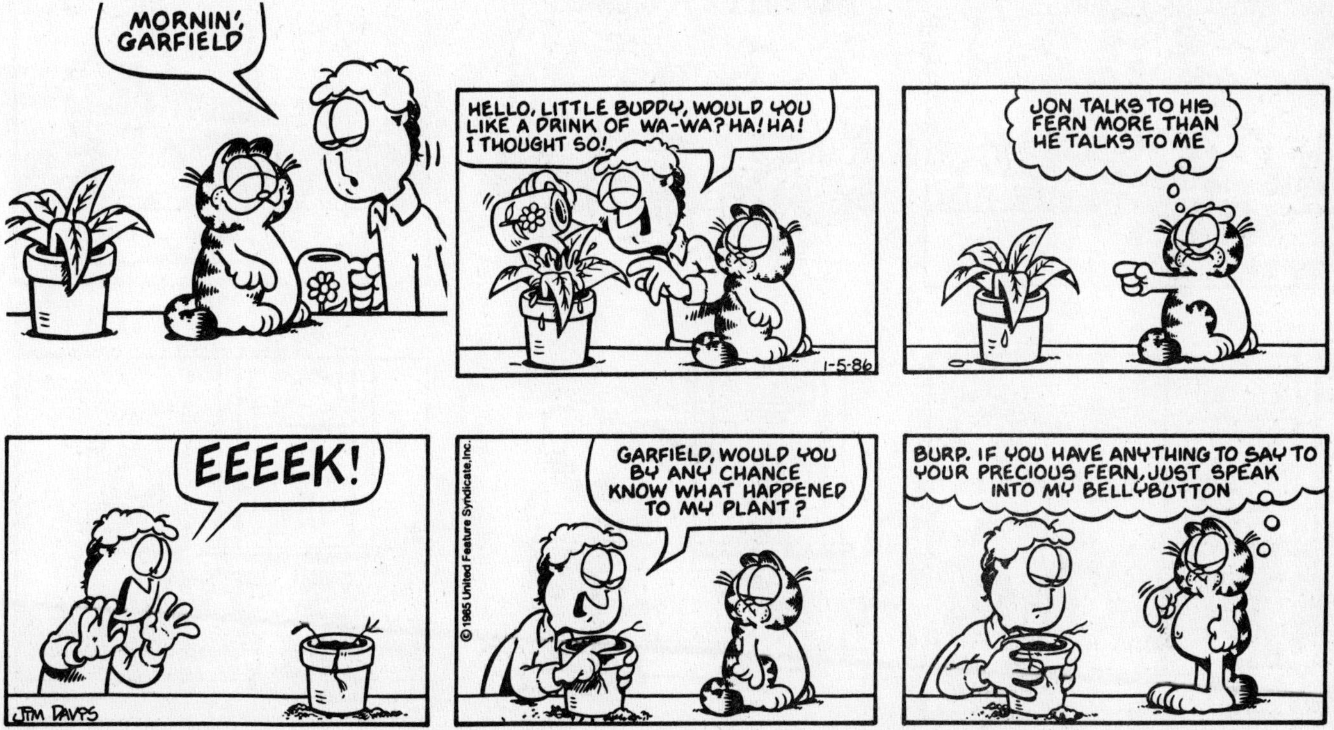
MORNIN', GARFIELD
HELLO, LITTLE BUDDY, WOULD YOU LIKE A DRINK OF WA-WA? HA! HA! I THOUGHT SO!
1-5-86
JON TALKS TO HIS FERN MORE THAN HE TALKS TO ME
EEEEK!
JIM DAVIS
© 1985 United Feature Syndicate, Inc.
GARFIELD, WOULD YOU BY ANY CHANCE KNOW WHAT HAPPENED TO MY PLANT?
BURP. IF YOU HAVE ANYTHING TO SAY TO YOUR PRECIOUS FERN, JUST SPEAK INTO MY BELLYBUTTON

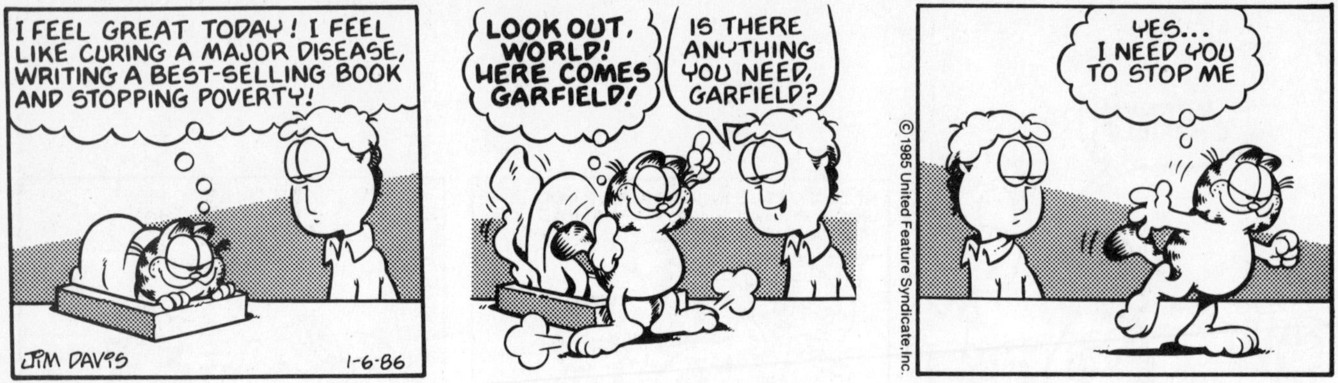
I FEEL GREAT TODAY! I FEEL LIKE CURING A MAJOR DISEASE, WRITING A BEST-SELLING BOOK AND STOPPING POVERTY!
JIM DAVIS
1-6-86
LOOK OUT, WORLD! HERE COMES GARFIELD!
IS THERE ANYTHING YOU NEED, GARFIELD?
© 1985 United Feature Syndicate, Inc.
YES... I NEED YOU TO STOP ME

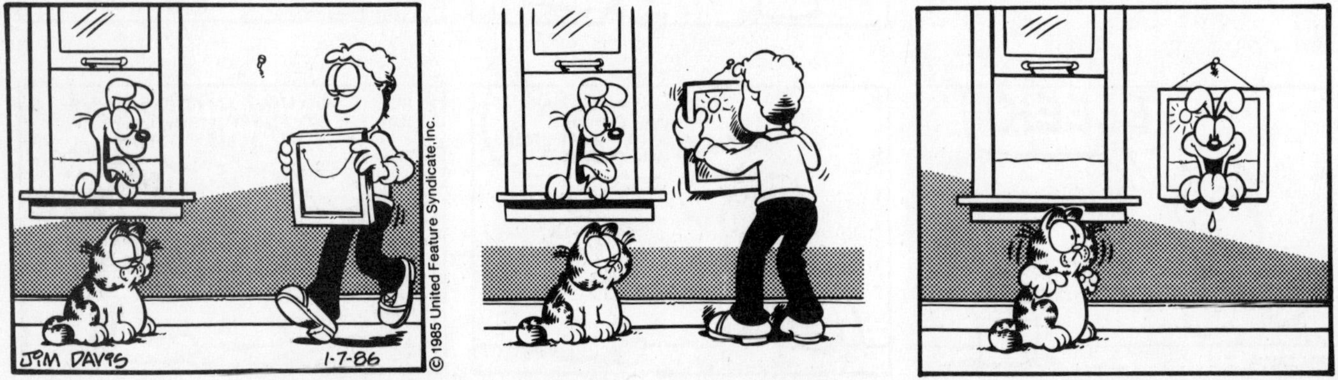
?
JIM DAVIS
1-7-86
© 1985 United Feature Syndicate, Inc.

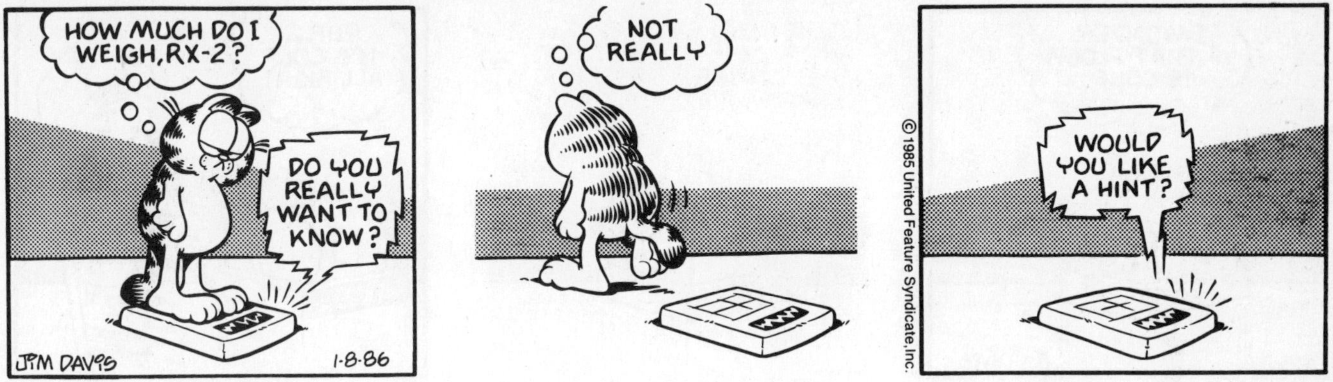
HOW MUCH DO I WEIGH, RX-2?
DO YOU REALLY WANT TO KNOW?
JIM DAVIS
1-8-86
NOT REALLY
WOULD YOU LIKE A HINT?
© 1985 United Feature Syndicate, Inc.

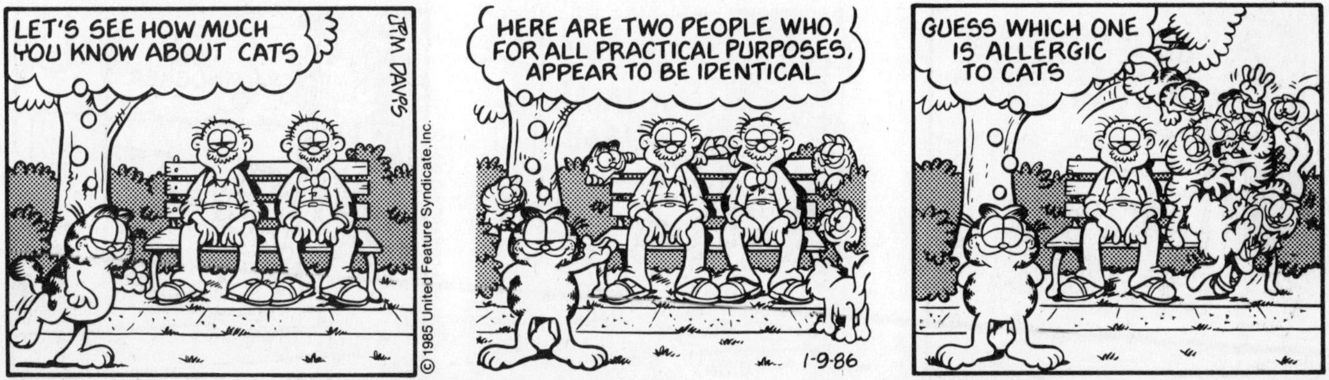
LET'S SEE HOW MUCH YOU KNOW ABOUT CATS
JIM DAVIS
© 1985 United Feature Syndicate, Inc.
HERE ARE TWO PEOPLE WHO, FOR ALL PRACTICAL PURPOSES, APPEAR TO BE IDENTICAL
1-9-86
GUESS WHICH ONE IS ALLERGIC TO CATS

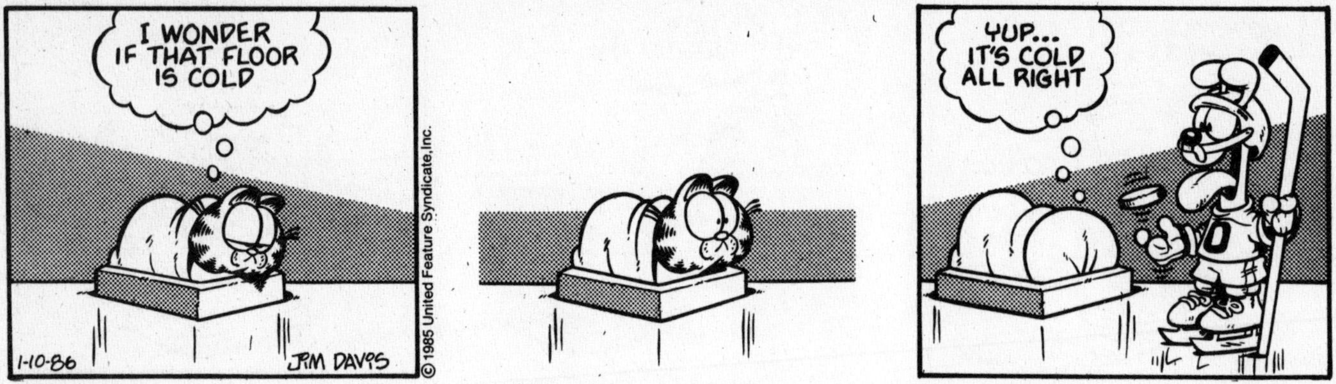
I WONDER IF THAT FLOOR IS COLD
1-10-86
JIM DAVIS
© 1985 United Feature Syndicate, Inc.
YUP... IT'S COLD ALL RIGHT
D

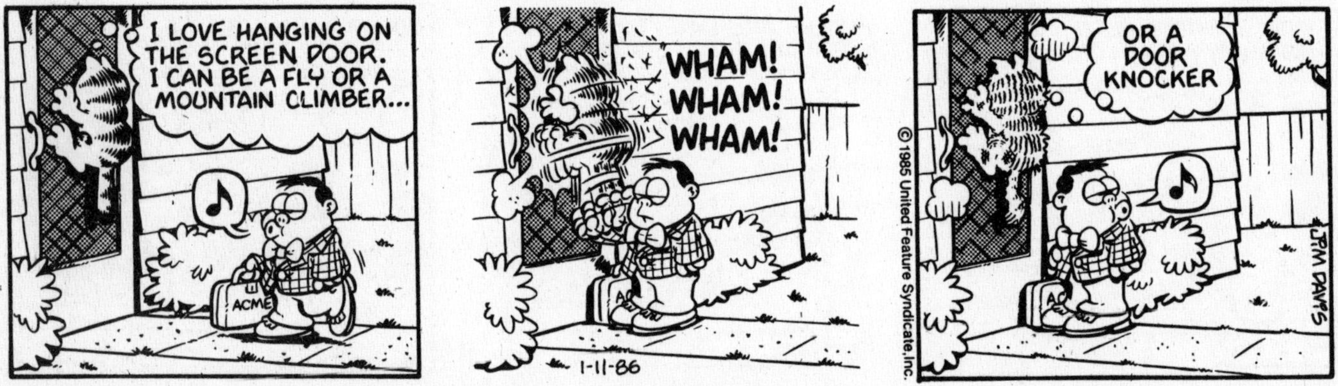
I LOVE HANGING ON THE SCREEN DOOR. I CAN BE A FLY OR A MOUNTAIN CLIMBER...
ACME
WHAM! WHAM! WHAM!
1-11-86
© 1985 United Feature Syndicate, Inc.
OR A DOOR KNOCKER
JIM DAVIS

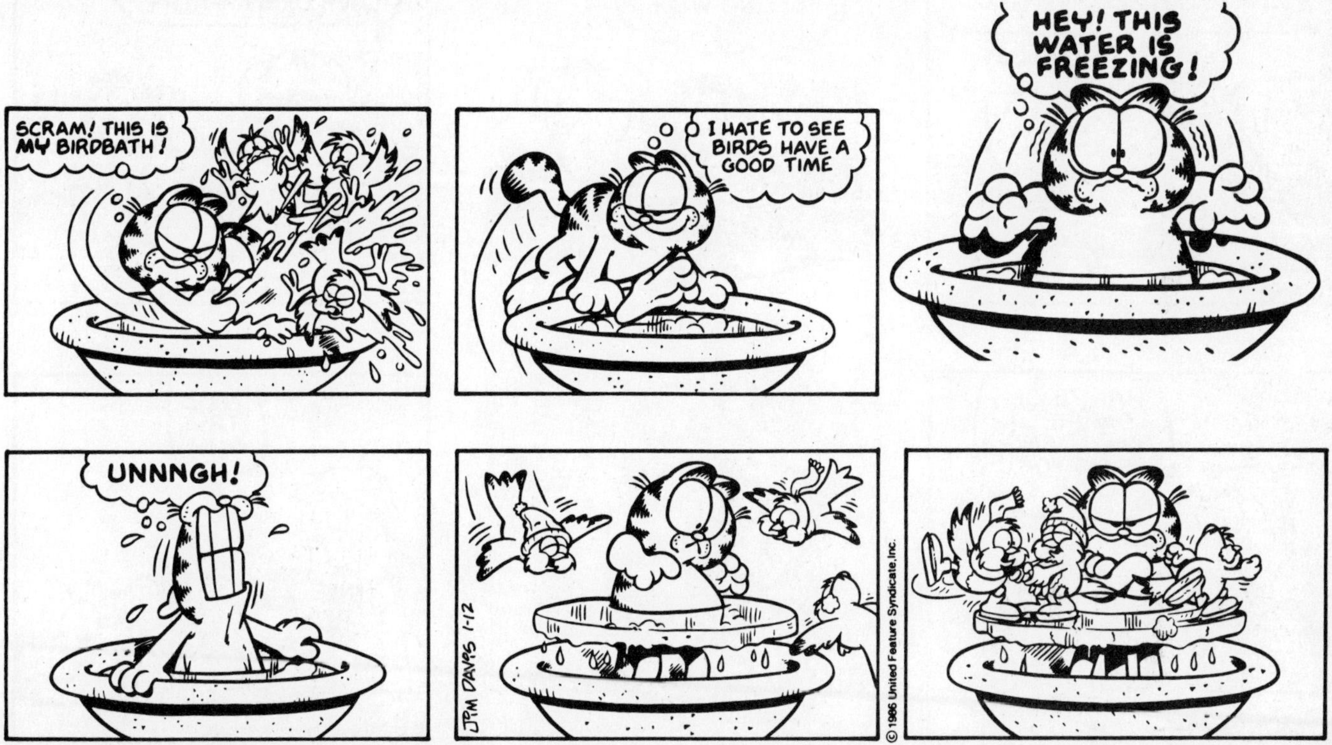
SCRAM! THIS IS MY BIRDBATH!
I HATE TO SEE BIRDS HAVE A GOOD TIME
HEY! THIS WATER IS FREEZING!
UNNNGH!
JPM DAVIS 1-12
© 1986 United Feature Syndicate, Inc.

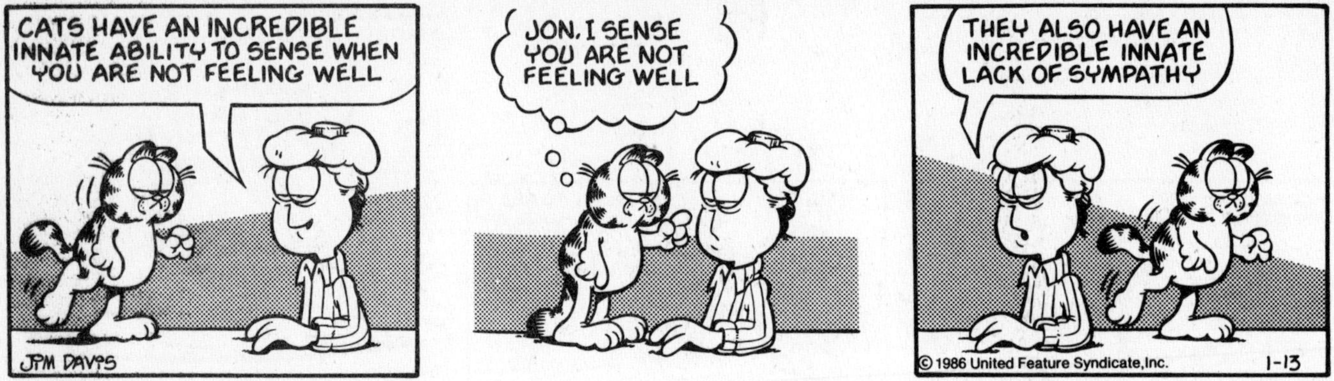
CATS HAVE AN INCREDIBLE INNATE ABILITY TO SENSE WHEN YOU ARE NOT FEELING WELL
JON, I SENSE YOU ARE NOT FEELING WELL
THEY ALSO HAVE AN INCREDIBLE INNATE LACK OF SYMPATHY
JIM DAVIS
© 1986 United Feature Syndicate, Inc.
1-13

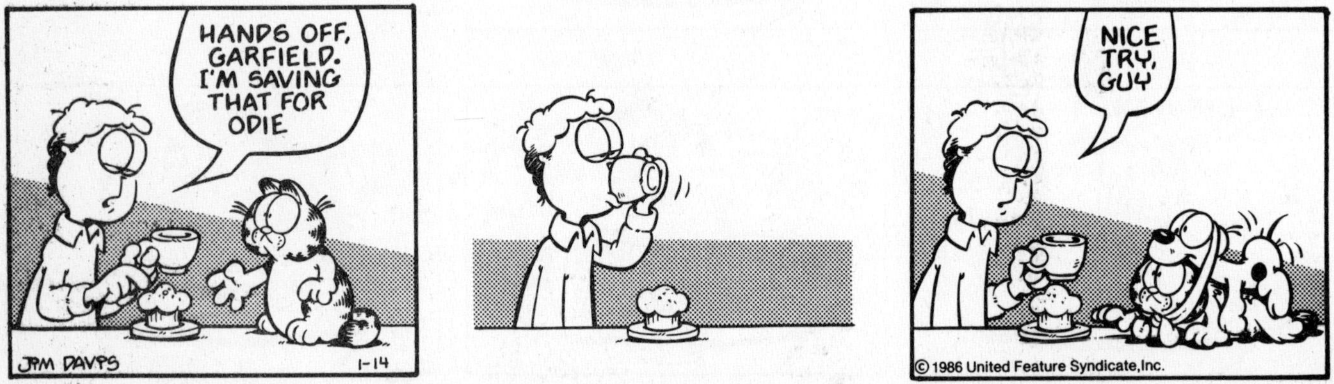
HANDS OFF, GARFIELD. I'M SAVING THAT FOR ODIE
NICE TRY, GUY
JIM DAVIS
1-14
© 1986 United Feature Syndicate, Inc.

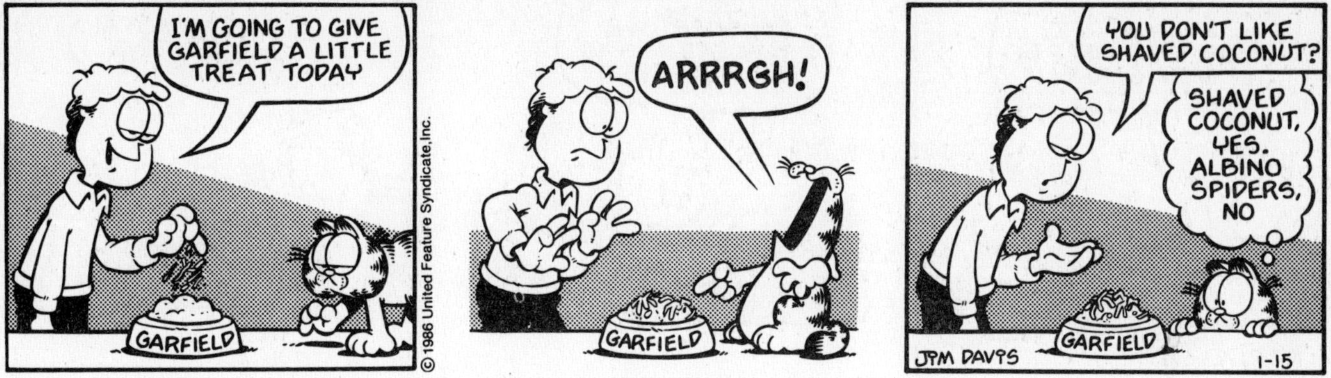
I'M GOING TO GIVE GARFIELD A LITTLE TREAT TODAY
GARFIELD
© 1986 United Feature Syndicate, Inc.
ARRRGH!
GARFIELD
YOU DON'T LIKE SHAVED COCONUT?
SHAVED COCONUT, YES. ALBINO SPIDERS, NO
GARFIELD
JIM DAVIS
1-15

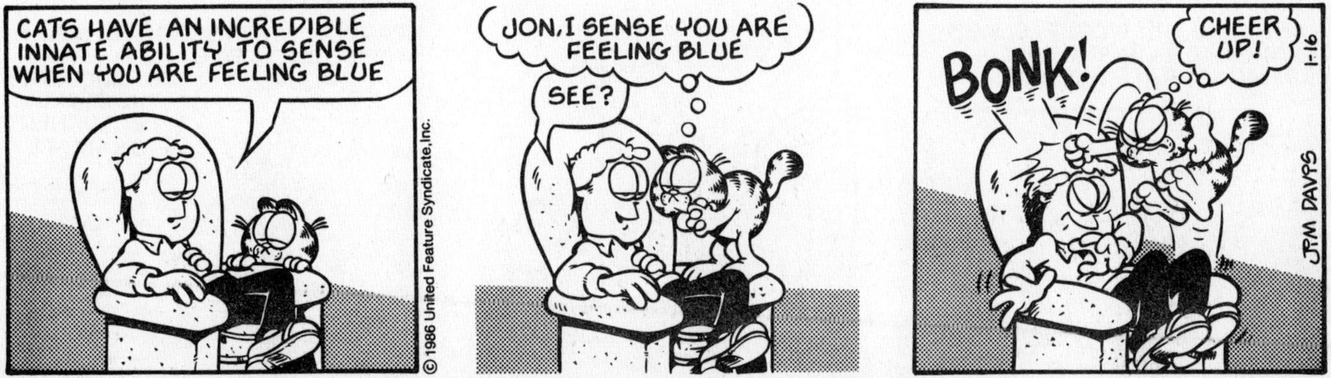
CATS HAVE AN INCREDIBLE INNATE ABILITY TO SENSE WHEN YOU ARE FEELING BLUE
© 1986 United Feature Syndicate, Inc.
JON, I SENSE YOU ARE FEELING BLUE
SEE?
BONK!
CHEER UP!
1-16
JIM DAVIS

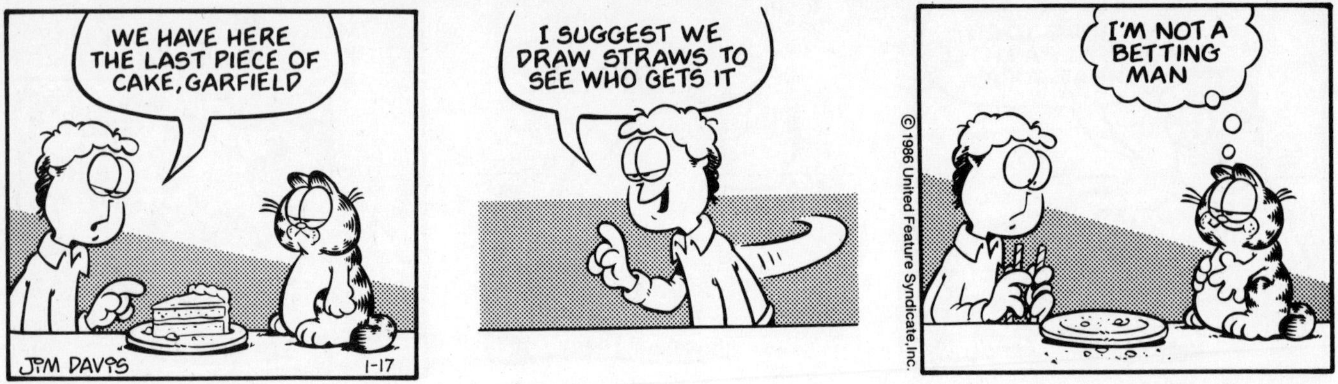
WE HAVE HERE THE LAST PIECE OF CAKE, GARFIELD
I SUGGEST WE DRAW STRAWS TO SEE WHO GETS IT
I'M NOT A BETTING MAN
JIM DAVIS
1-17
© 1986 United Feature Syndicate, Inc.

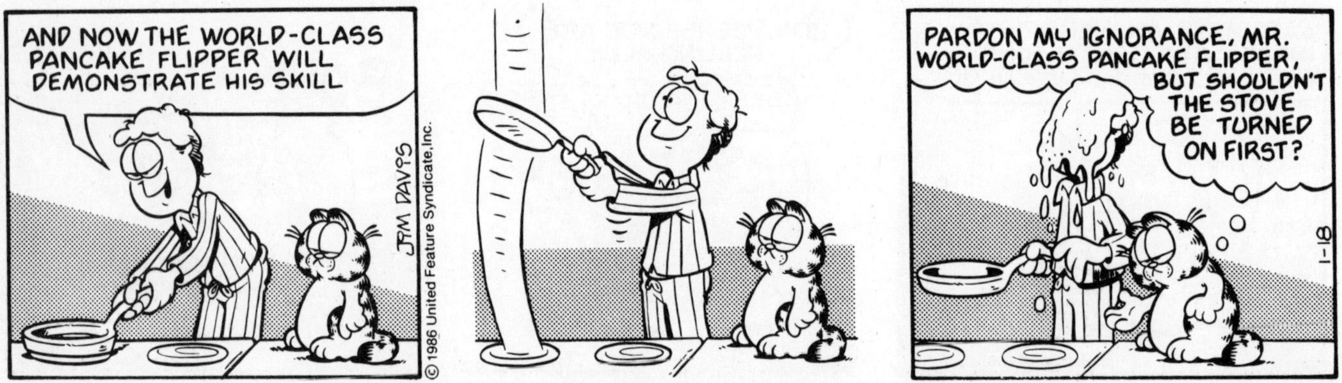
AND NOW THE WORLD-CLASS PANCAKE FLIPPER WILL DEMONSTRATE HIS SKILL
JIM DAVIS
© 1986 United Feature Syndicate, Inc.
PARDON MY IGNORANCE, MR. WORLD-CLASS PANCAKE FLIPPER, BUT SHOULDN'T THE STOVE BE TURNED ON FIRST?
1-18

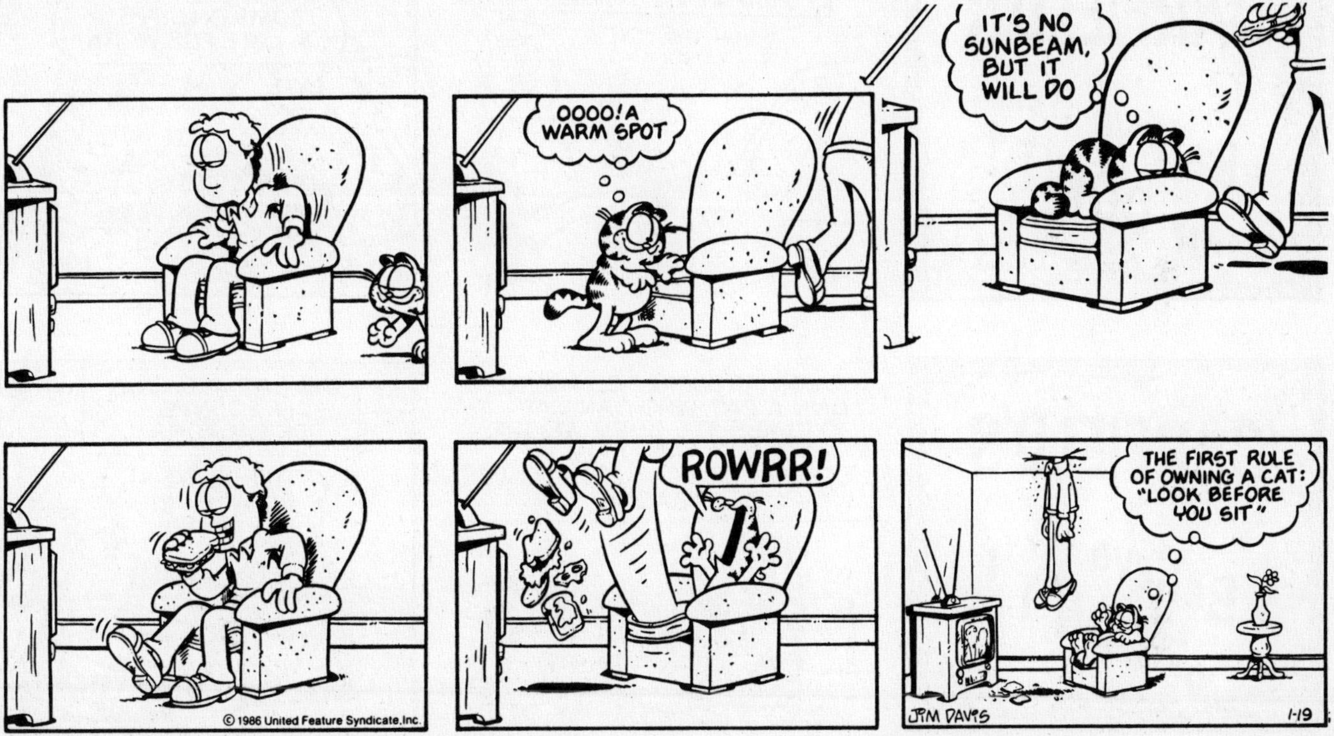
OOOO! A WARM SPOT
IT'S NO SUNBEAM, BUT IT WILL DO
ROWRR!
THE FIRST RULE OF OWNING A CAT: "LOOK BEFORE YOU SIT"
JIM DAVIS
1-19

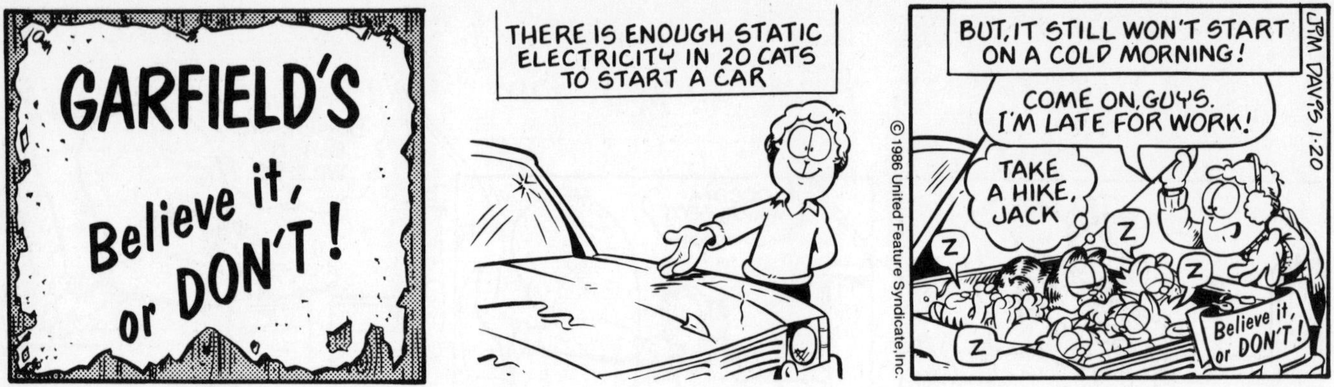
GARFIELD'S
Believe it, or DON'T!
THERE IS ENOUGH STATIC ELECTRICITY IN 20 CATS TO START A CAR
© 1986 United Feature Syndicate, Inc.
BUT, IT STILL WON'T START ON A COLD MORNING!
COME ON, GUYS. I'M LATE FOR WORK!
TAKE A HIKE, JACK
Z
Z
Z
Z
Believe it, or DON'T!
JIM DAVIS 1-20

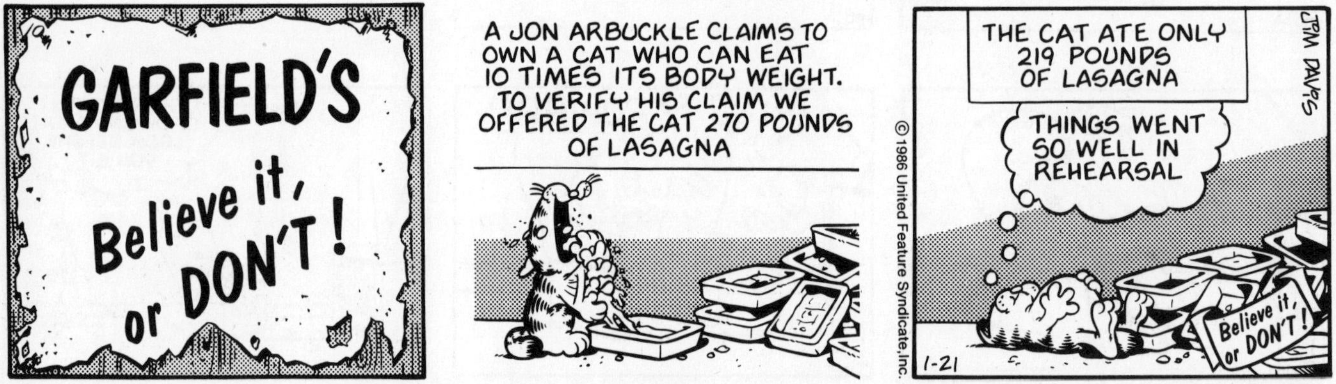
GARFIELD'S
Believe it, or DON'T!
A JON ARBUCKLE CLAIMS TO OWN A CAT WHO CAN EAT 10 TIMES ITS BODY WEIGHT. TO VERIFY HIS CLAIM WE OFFERED THE CAT 270 POUNDS OF LASAGNA
© 1986 United Feature Syndicate, Inc.
THE CAT ATE ONLY 219 POUNDS OF LASAGNA
THINGS WENT SO WELL IN REHEARSAL
Believe it, or DON'T!
JIM DAVIS
1-21

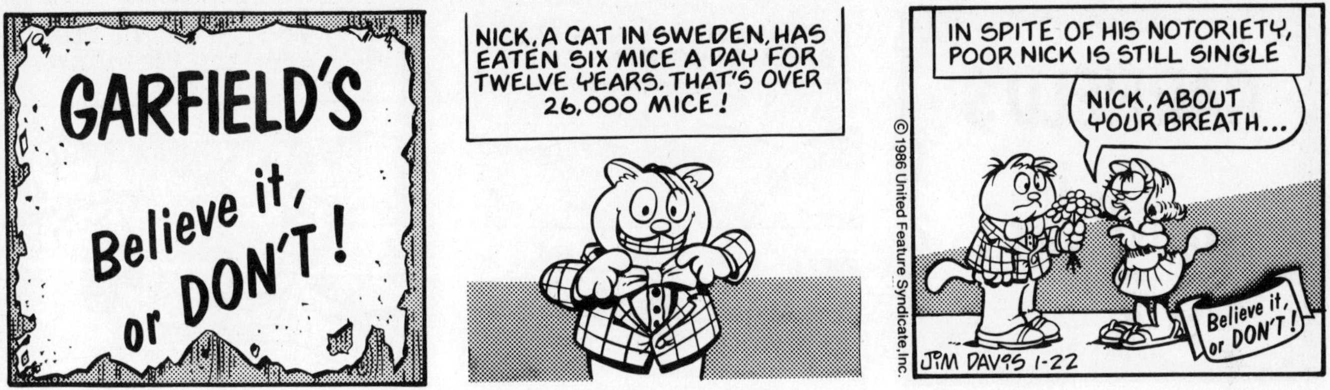
GARFIELD'S
Believe it, or DON'T!
NICK, A CAT IN SWEDEN, HAS EATEN SIX MICE A DAY FOR TWELVE YEARS. THAT'S OVER 26,000 MICE!
IN SPITE OF HIS NOTORIETY, POOR NICK IS STILL SINGLE
NICK, ABOUT YOUR BREATH...
Believe it, or DON'T!
JIM DAVIS 1-22
© 1986 United Feature Syndicate, Inc.

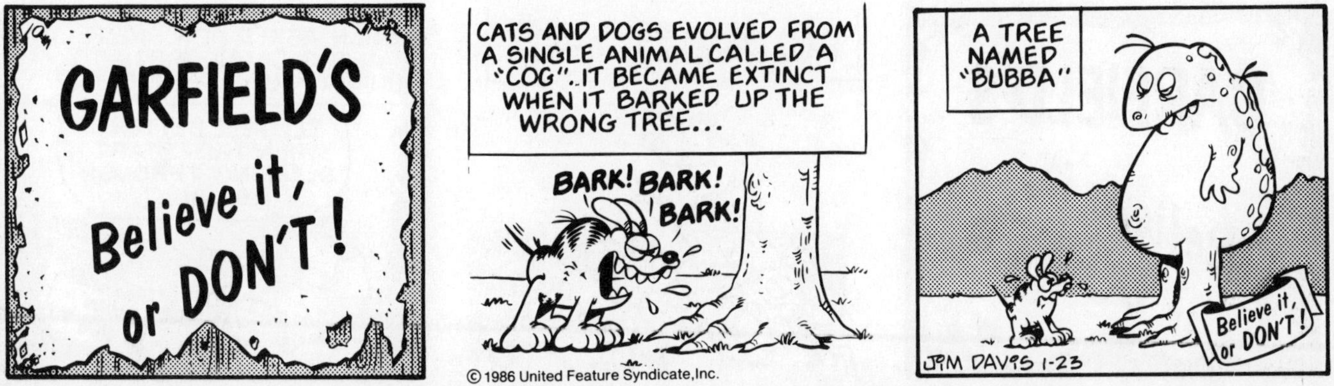
GARFIELD'S
Believe it, or DON'T!
CATS AND DOGS EVOLVED FROM A SINGLE ANIMAL CALLED A "COG". IT BECAME EXTINCT WHEN IT BARKED UP THE WRONG TREE...
BARK! BARK! BARK!
A TREE NAMED "BUBBA"
Believe it, or DON'T!
JIM DAVIS 1-23

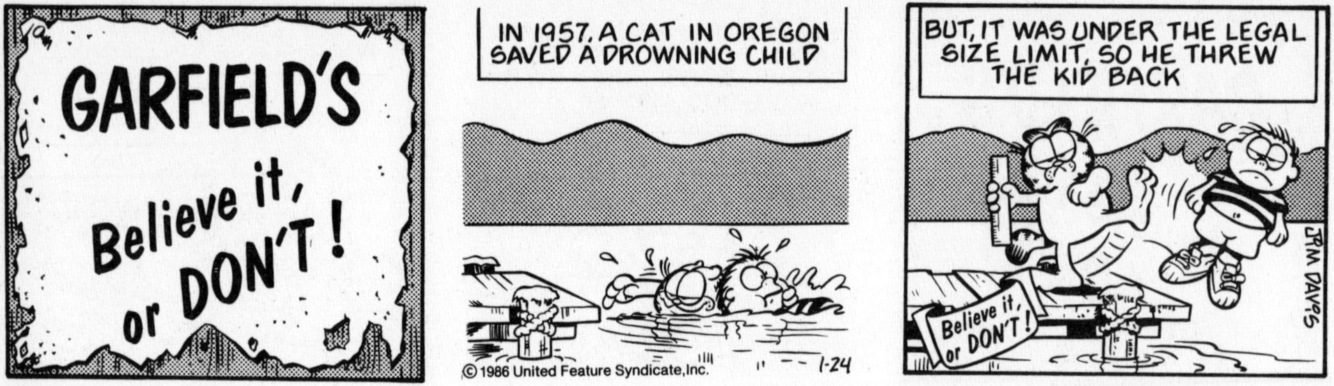
GARFIELD'S
Believe it, or DON'T!
IN 1957, A CAT IN OREGON SAVED A DROWNING CHILD
© 1986 United Feature Syndicate, Inc.
1-24
BUT, IT WAS UNDER THE LEGAL SIZE LIMIT, SO HE THREW THE KID BACK
Believe it, or DON'T!
JIM DAVIS

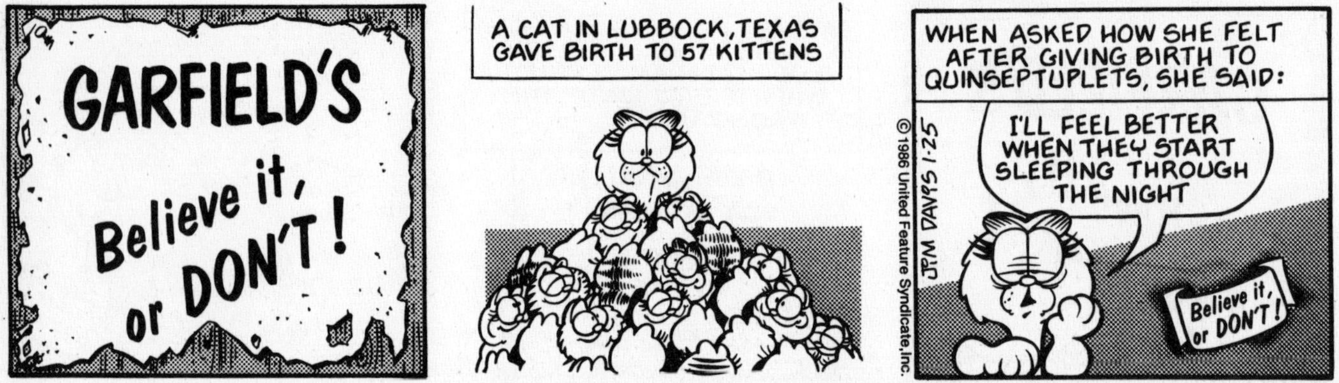
GARFIELD'S
Believe it, or DON'T!
A CAT IN LUBBOCK, TEXAS GAVE BIRTH TO 57 KITTENS
© 1986 United Feature Syndicate, Inc.
JIM DAVIS 1-25
WHEN ASKED HOW SHE FELT AFTER GIVING BIRTH TO QUINSEPTUPLETS, SHE SAID:
I'LL FEEL BETTER WHEN THEY START SLEEPING THROUGH THE NIGHT
Believe it, or DON'T!

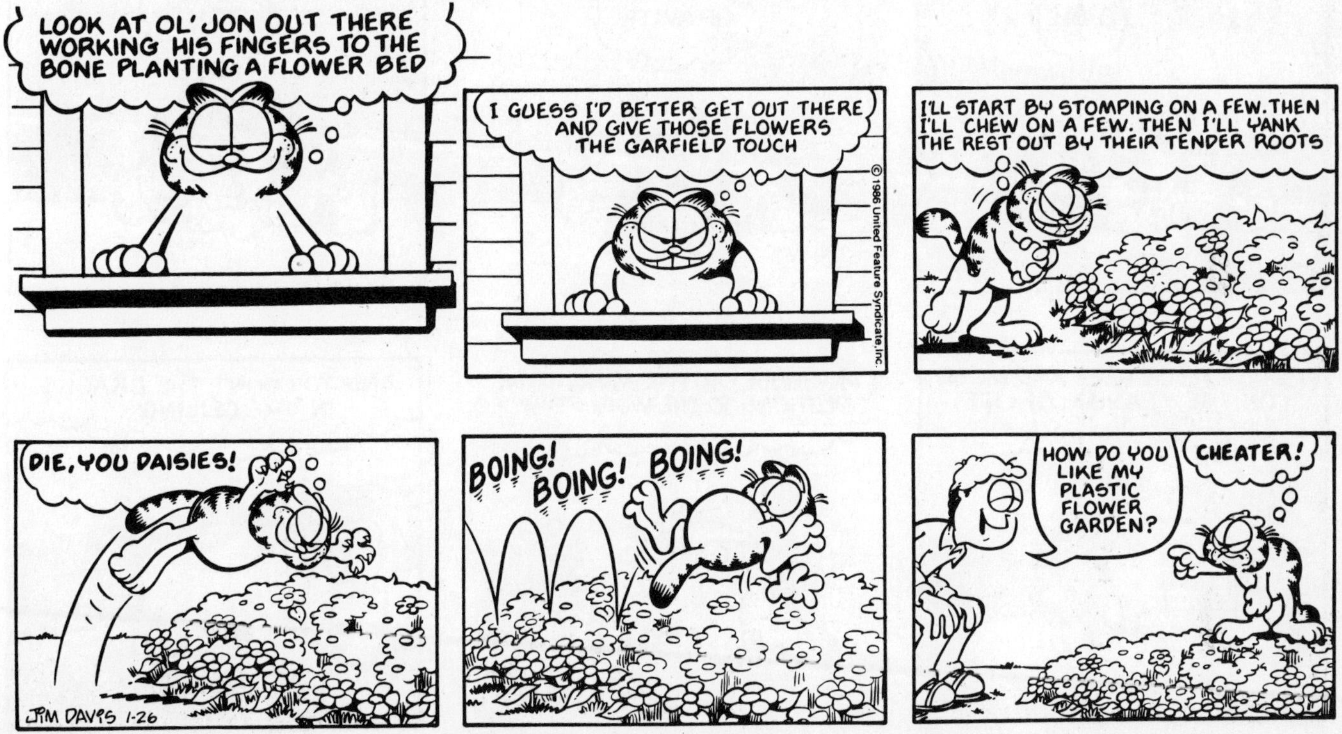

LOOK AT OL' JON OUT THERE WORKING HIS FINGERS TO THE BONE PLANTING A FLOWER BED
I GUESS I'D BETTER GET OUT THERE AND GIVE THOSE FLOWERS THE GARFIELD TOUCH
© 1986 United Feature Syndicate, Inc.
I'LL START BY STOMPING ON A FEW. THEN I'LL CHEW ON A FEW. THEN I'LL YANK THE REST OUT BY THEIR TENDER ROOTS
DIE, YOU DAISIES!
JIM DAVIS 1-26
BOING! BOING! BOING!
HOW DO YOU LIKE MY PLASTIC FLOWER GARDEN?
CHEATER!

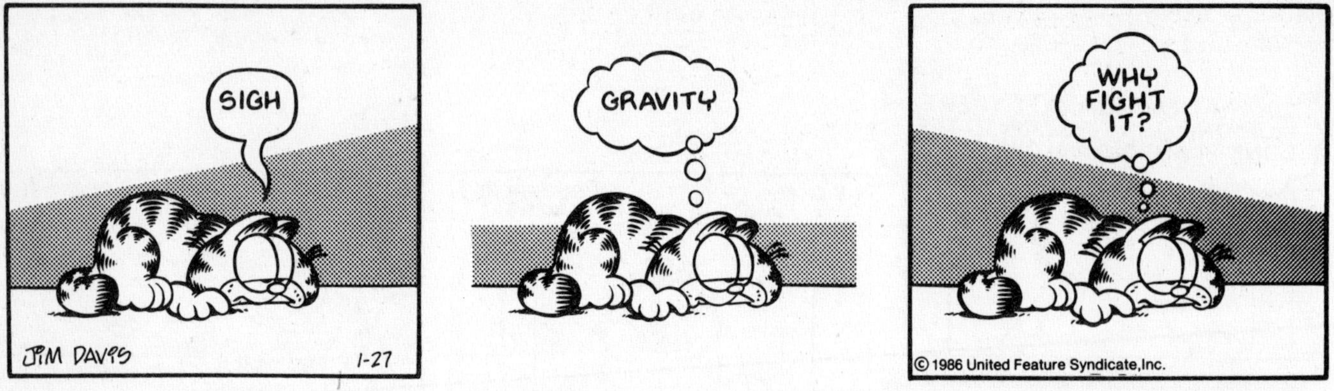
SIGH
GRAVITY
WHY FIGHT IT?
JIM DAVIS
1-27
© 1986 United Feature Syndicate,Inc.

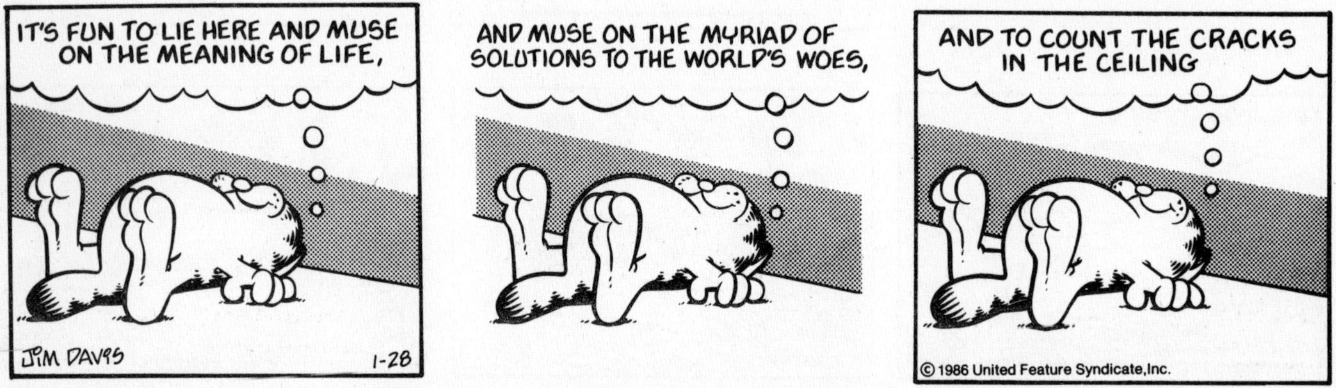
IT'S FUN TO LIE HERE AND MUSE ON THE MEANING OF LIFE,
AND MUSE ON THE MYRIAD OF SOLUTIONS TO THE WORLD'S WOES,
AND TO COUNT THE CRACKS IN THE CEILING
JIM DAVIS
1-28
© 1986 United Feature Syndicate,Inc.

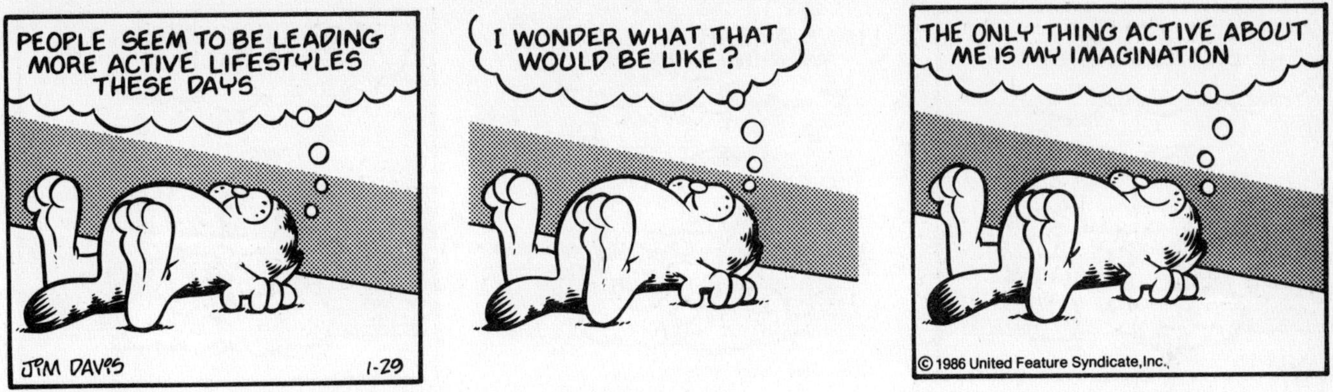
PEOPLE SEEM TO BE LEADING MORE ACTIVE LIFESTYLES THESE DAYS
JIM DAVIS
1-29
I WONDER WHAT THAT WOULD BE LIKE?
THE ONLY THING ACTIVE ABOUT ME IS MY IMAGINATION
© 1986 United Feature Syndicate,Inc.

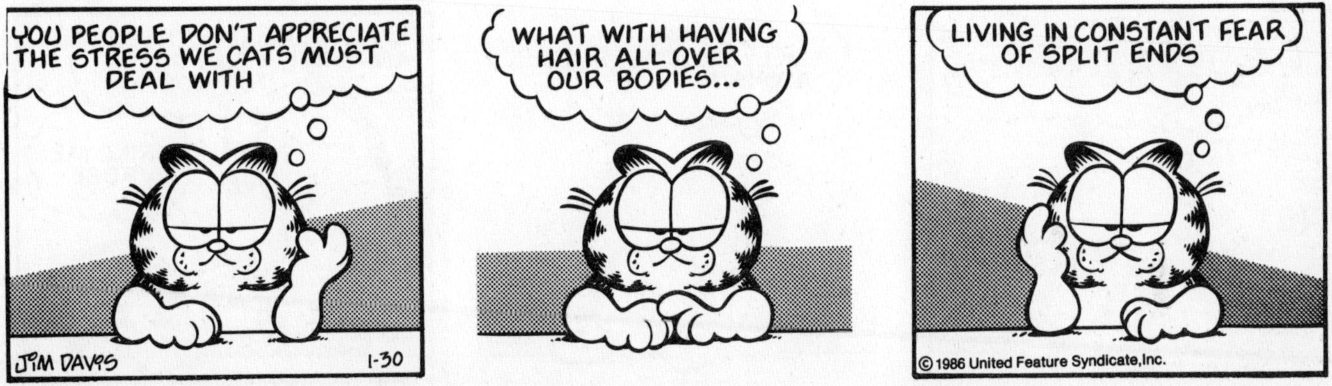
YOU PEOPLE DON'T APPRECIATE THE STRESS WE CATS MUST DEAL WITH
JIM DAVIS
1-30
WHAT WITH HAVING HAIR ALL OVER OUR BODIES...
LIVING IN CONSTANT FEAR OF SPLIT ENDS
© 1986 United Feature Syndicate,Inc.

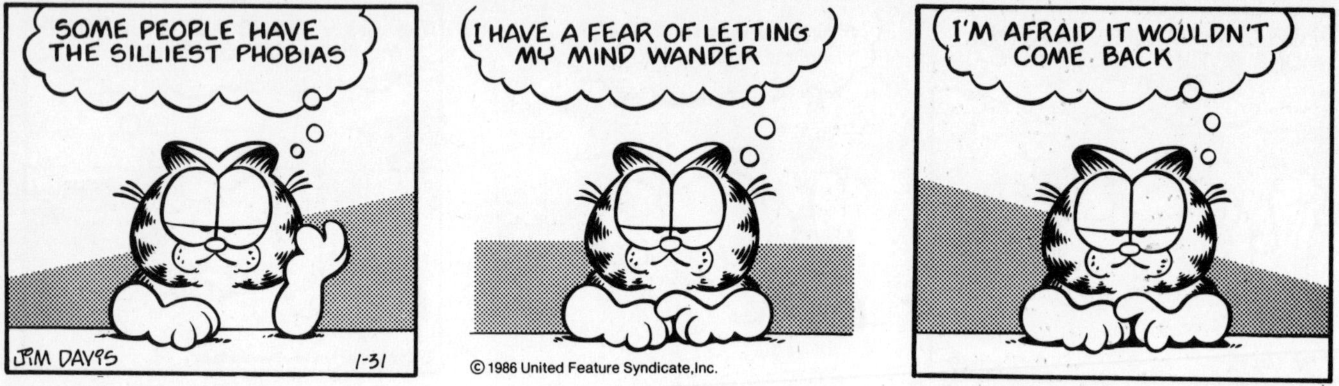
SOME PEOPLE HAVE THE SILLIEST PHOBIAS
JIM DAVIS
1-31
I HAVE A FEAR OF LETTING MY MIND WANDER
© 1986 United Feature Syndicate,Inc.
I'M AFRAID IT WOULDN'T COME BACK

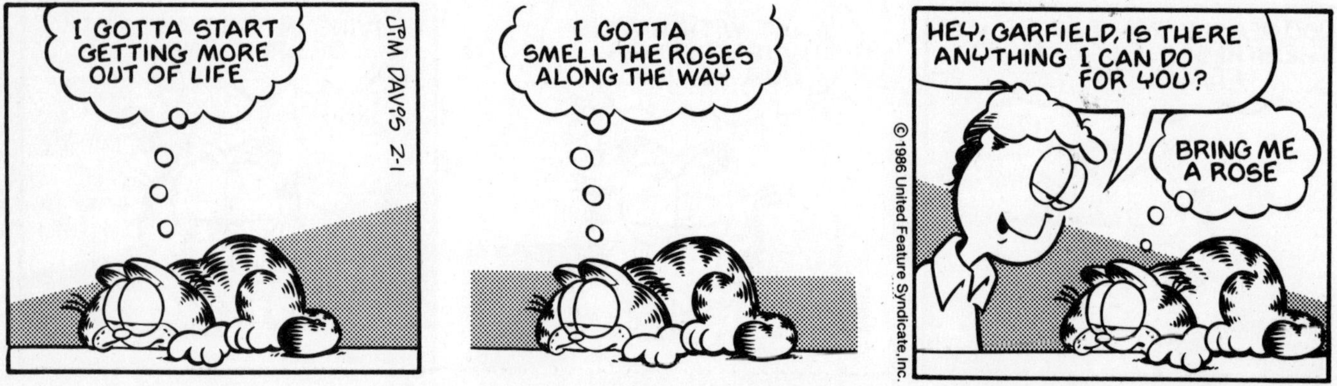
I GOTTA START GETTING MORE OUT OF LIFE
JIM DAVIS 2-1
I GOTTA SMELL THE ROSES ALONG THE WAY
© 1986 United Feature Syndicate,Inc.
HEY, GARFIELD, IS THERE ANYTHING I CAN DO FOR YOU?
BRING ME A ROSE

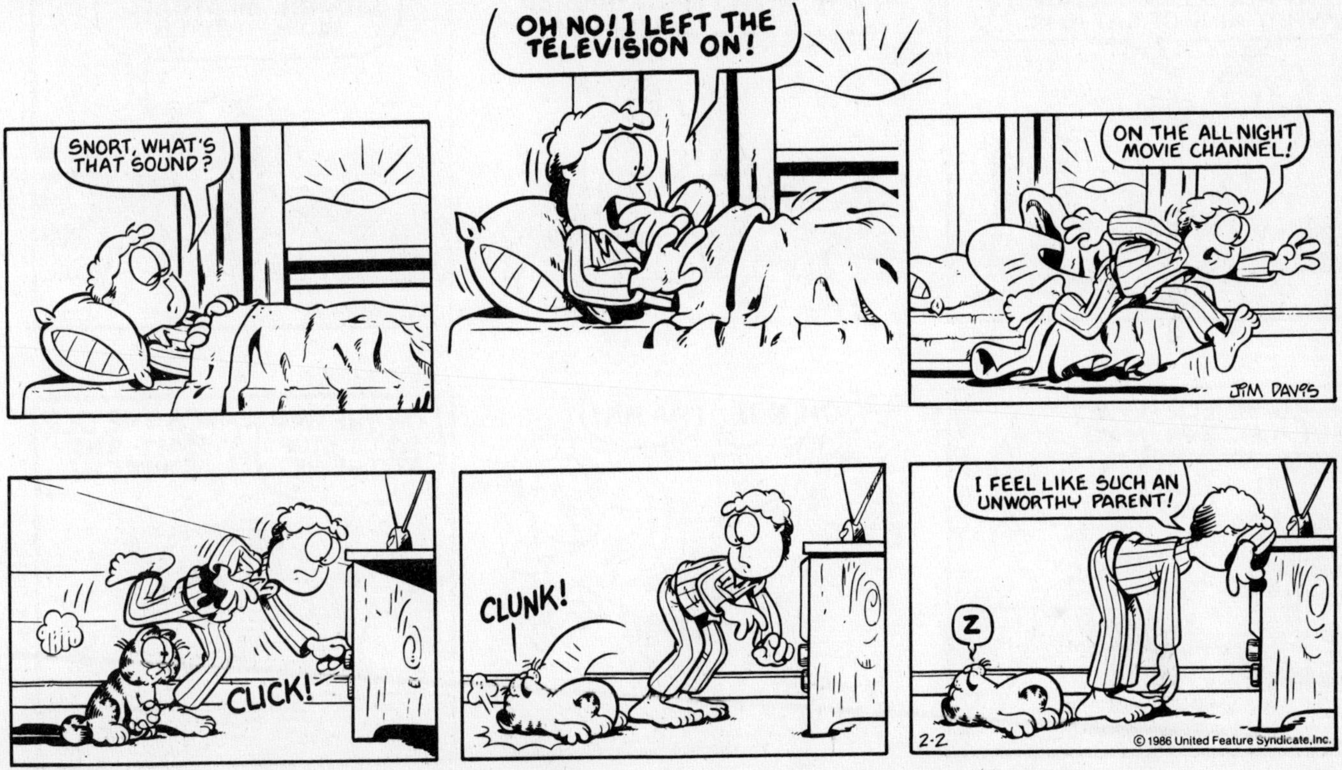
SNORT, WHAT'S THAT SOUND?
OH NO! I LEFT THE TELEVISION ON!
ON THE ALL NIGHT MOVIE CHANNEL!
JIM DAVIS
CLICK!
CLUNK!
I FEEL LIKE SUCH AN UNWORTHY PARENT!
Z
2-2
© 1986 United Feature Syndicate, Inc.

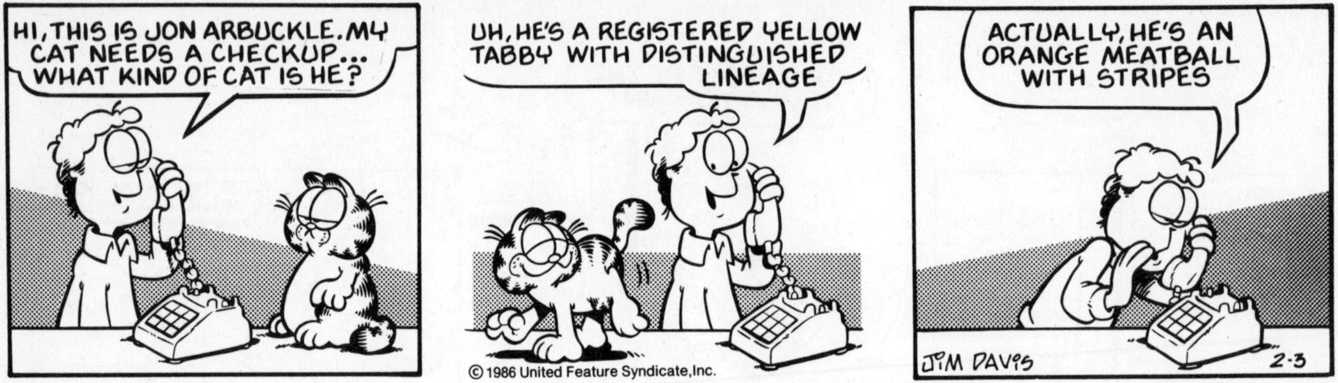
HI, THIS IS JON ARBUCKLE. MY CAT NEEDS A CHECKUP... WHAT KIND OF CAT IS HE?
UH, HE'S A REGISTERED YELLOW TABBY WITH DISTINGUISHED LINEAGE
ACTUALLY, HE'S AN ORANGE MEATBALL WITH STRIPES
JIM DAVIS
2-3



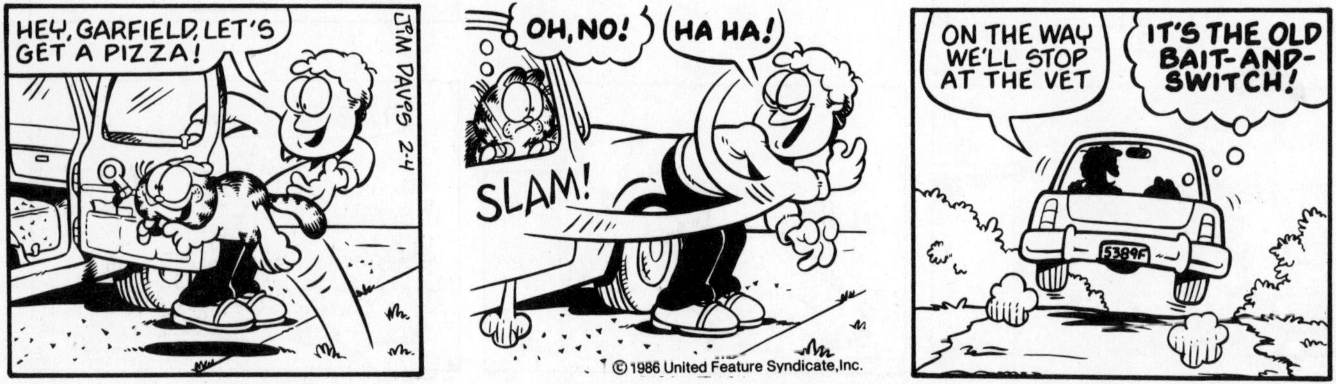
HEY, GARFIELD, LET'S GET A PIZZA!
JIM DAVIS 2-4
OH, NO!
HA HA!
SLAM!
ON THE WAY WE'LL STOP AT THE VET
IT'S THE OLD BAIT-AND-SWITCH!
5389F

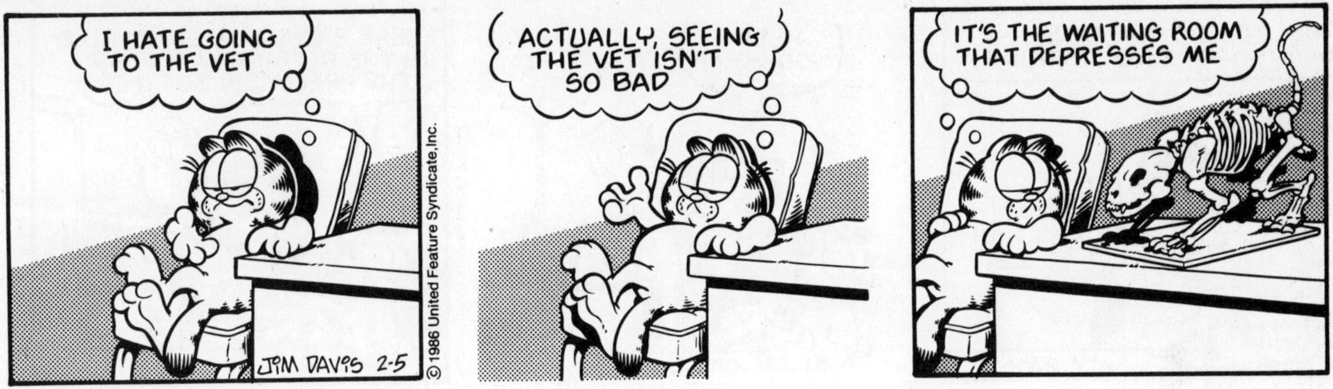
I HATE GOING TO THE VET
JIM DAVIS 2-5
ACTUALLY, SEEING THE VET ISN'T SO BAD
IT'S THE WAITING ROOM THAT DEPRESSES ME


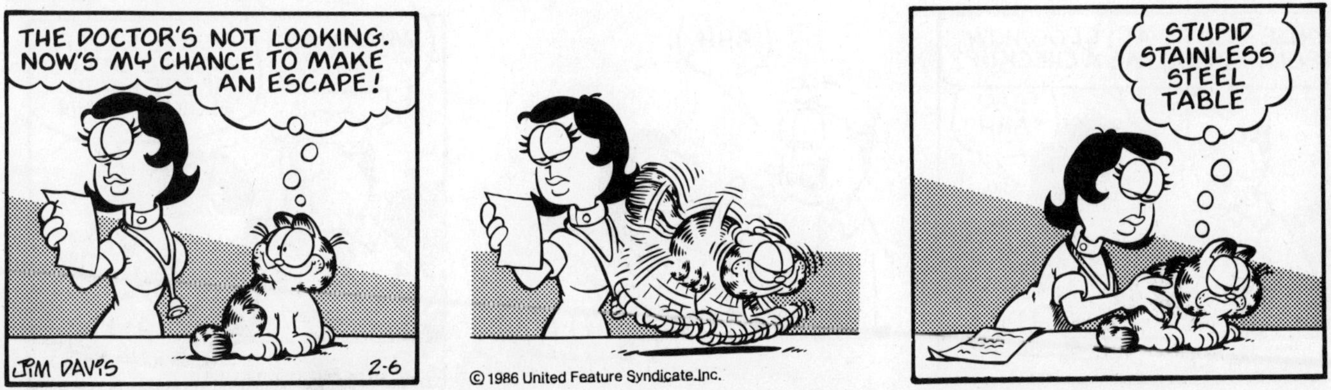
THE DOCTOR'S NOT LOOKING. NOW'S MY CHANCE TO MAKE AN ESCAPE!
JIM DAVIS
2-6
STUPID STAINLESS STEEL TABLE

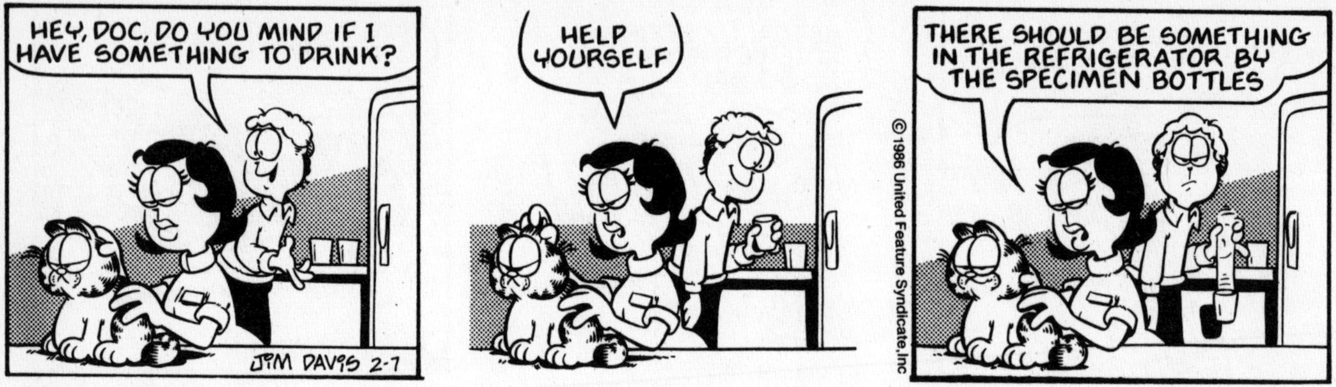
HEY, DOC, DO YOU MIND IF I HAVE SOMETHING TO DRINK?
JIM DAVIS 2-7
HELP YOURSELF
THERE SHOULD BE SOMETHING IN THE REFRIGERATOR BY THE SPECIMEN BOTTLES
© 1986 United Feature Syndicate, Inc

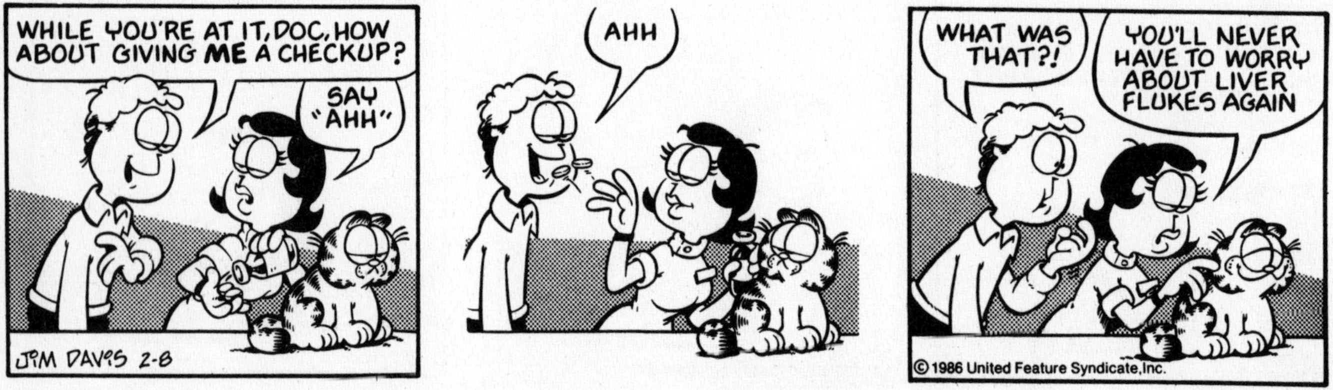
WHILE YOU'RE AT IT, DOC, HOW ABOUT GIVING **ME** A CHECKUP?
SAY "AHH"
JIM DAVIS 2-8
AHH
WHAT WAS THAT?!
YOU'LL NEVER HAVE TO WORRY ABOUT LIVER FLUKES AGAIN
© 1986 United Feature Syndicate, Inc.

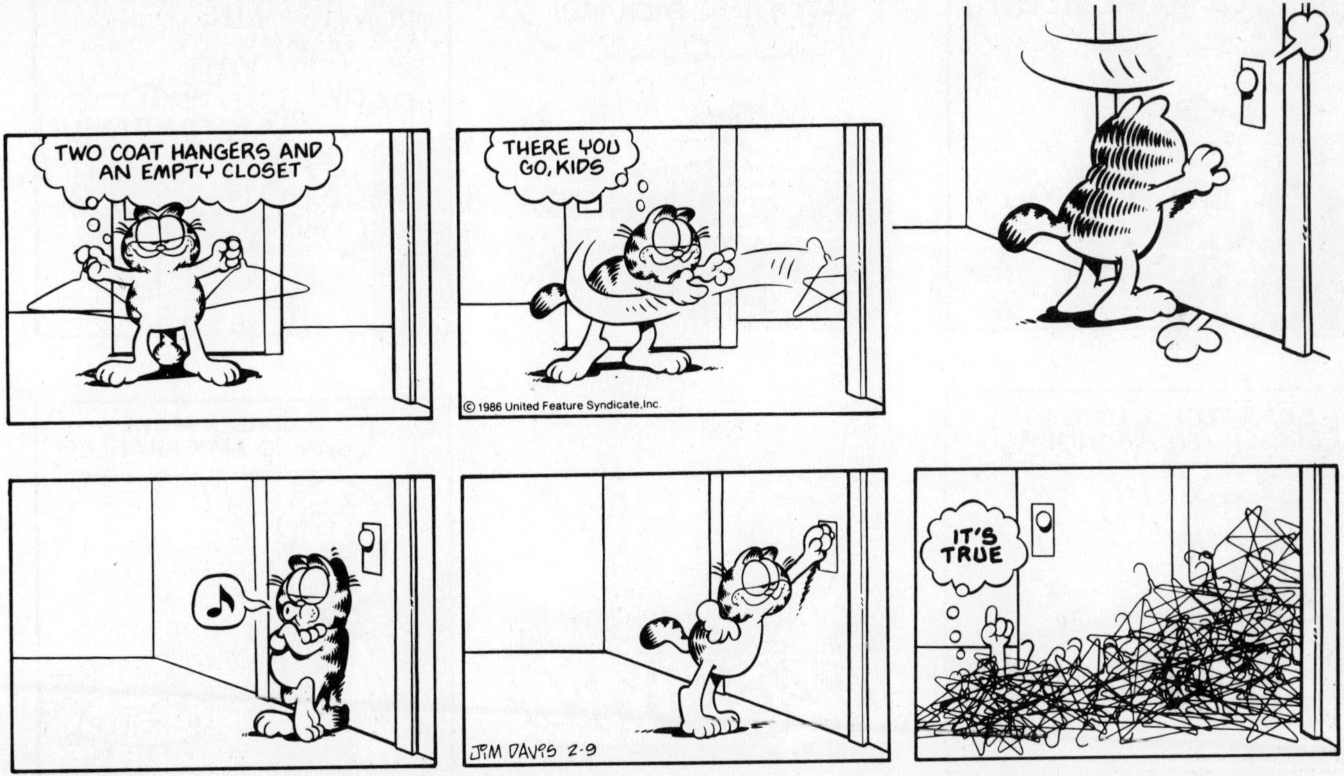
TWO COAT HANGERS AND AN EMPTY CLOSET
THERE YOU GO, KIDS
© 1986 United Feature Syndicate, Inc.
♪
JIM DAVIS 2-9
IT'S TRUE

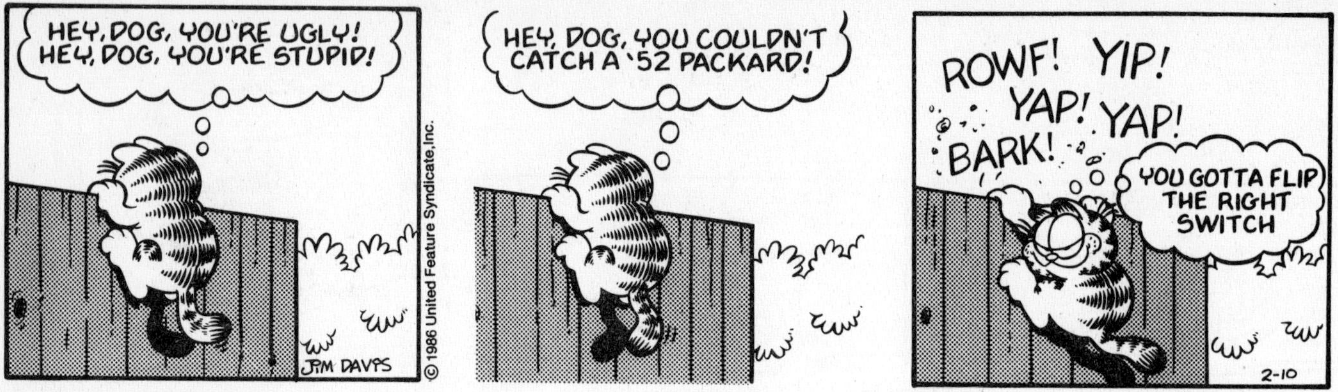
HEY, DOG, YOU'RE UGLY! HEY, DOG, YOU'RE STUPID!
JIM DAVIS
© 1986 United Feature Syndicate, Inc.
HEY, DOG, YOU COULDN'T CATCH A '52 PACKARD!
ROWF! YIP! YAP! YAP! BARK!
YOU GOTTA FLIP THE RIGHT SWITCH
2-10

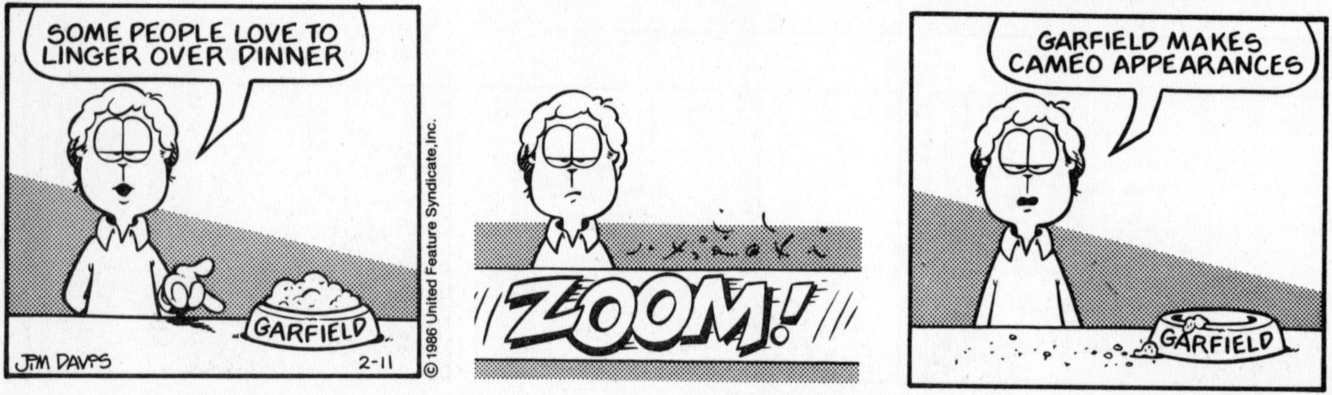
SOME PEOPLE LOVE TO LINGER OVER DINNER
GARFIELD
JIM DAVIS
2-11
© 1986 United Feature Syndicate, Inc.
ZOOM!
GARFIELD MAKES CAMEO APPEARANCES
GARFIELD

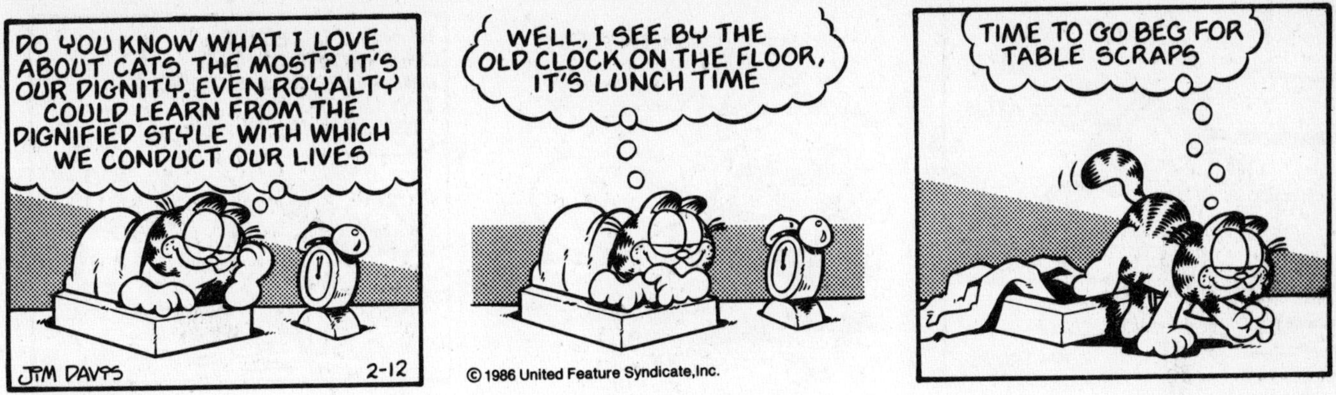
DO YOU KNOW WHAT I LOVE ABOUT CATS THE MOST? IT'S OUR DIGNITY. EVEN ROYALTY COULD LEARN FROM THE DIGNIFIED STYLE WITH WHICH WE CONDUCT OUR LIVES
JIM DAVIS
2-12
WELL, I SEE BY THE OLD CLOCK ON THE FLOOR, IT'S LUNCH TIME
© 1986 United Feature Syndicate, Inc.
TIME TO GO BEG FOR TABLE SCRAPS

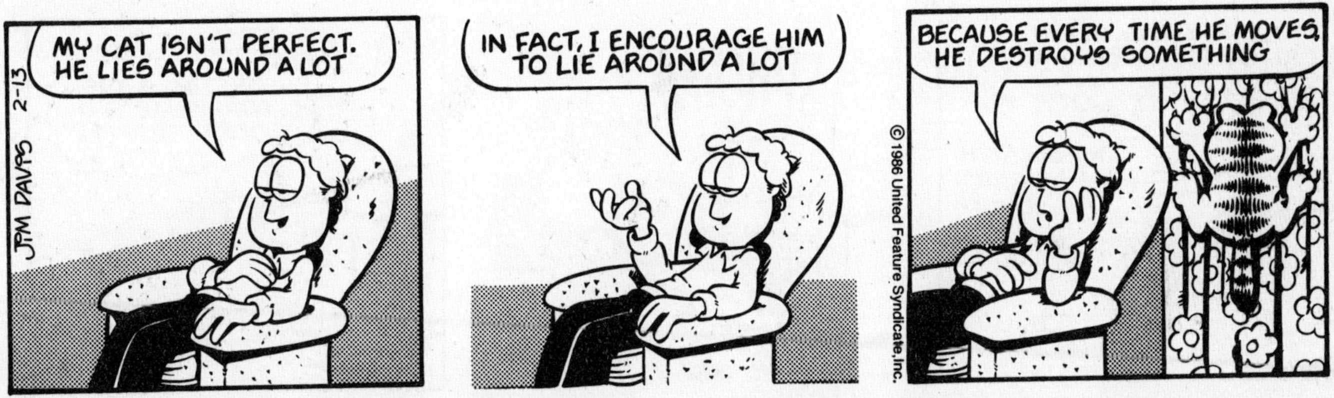
MY CAT ISN'T PERFECT. HE LIES AROUND A LOT
JIM DAVIS 2-13
IN FACT, I ENCOURAGE HIM TO LIE AROUND A LOT
BECAUSE EVERY TIME HE MOVES, HE DESTROYS SOMETHING
© 1986 United Feature Syndicate, Inc.

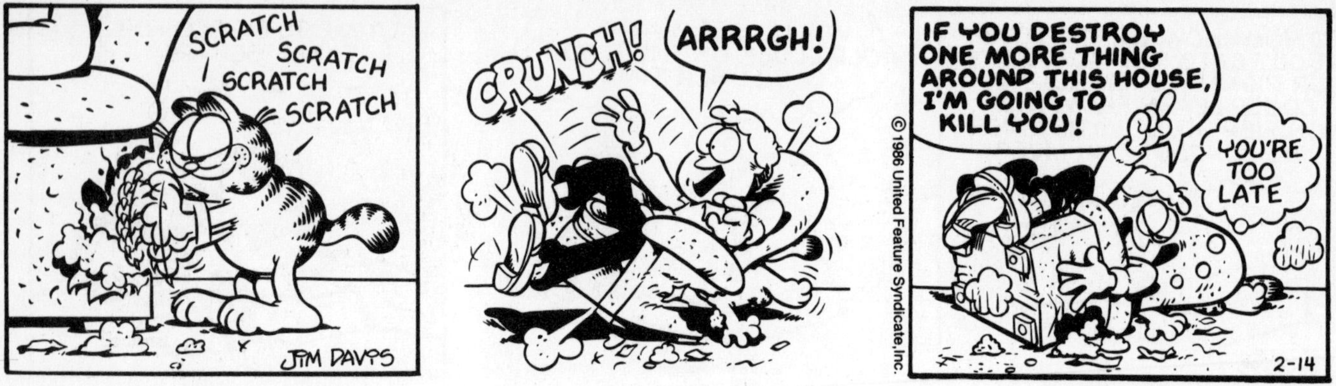
SCRATCH
SCRATCH
SCRATCH
SCRATCH
JIM DAVIS
CRUNCH!
ARRRGH!
IF YOU DESTROY ONE MORE THING AROUND THIS HOUSE, I'M GOING TO KILL YOU!
YOU'RE TOO LATE
2-14



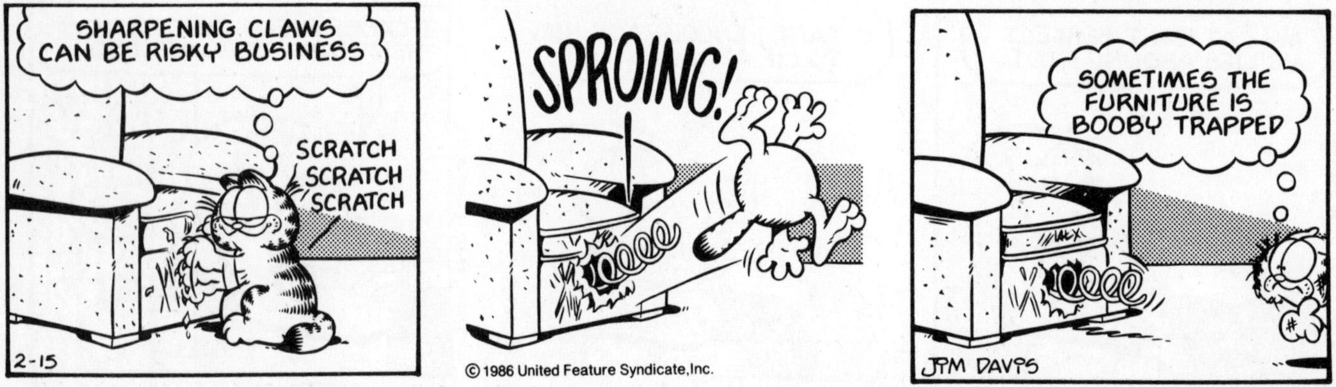
SHARPENING CLAWS CAN BE RISKY BUSINESS
SCRATCH
SCRATCH
SCRATCH
2-15
SPROING!
SOMETIMES THE FURNITURE IS BOOBY TRAPPED
JIM DAVIS

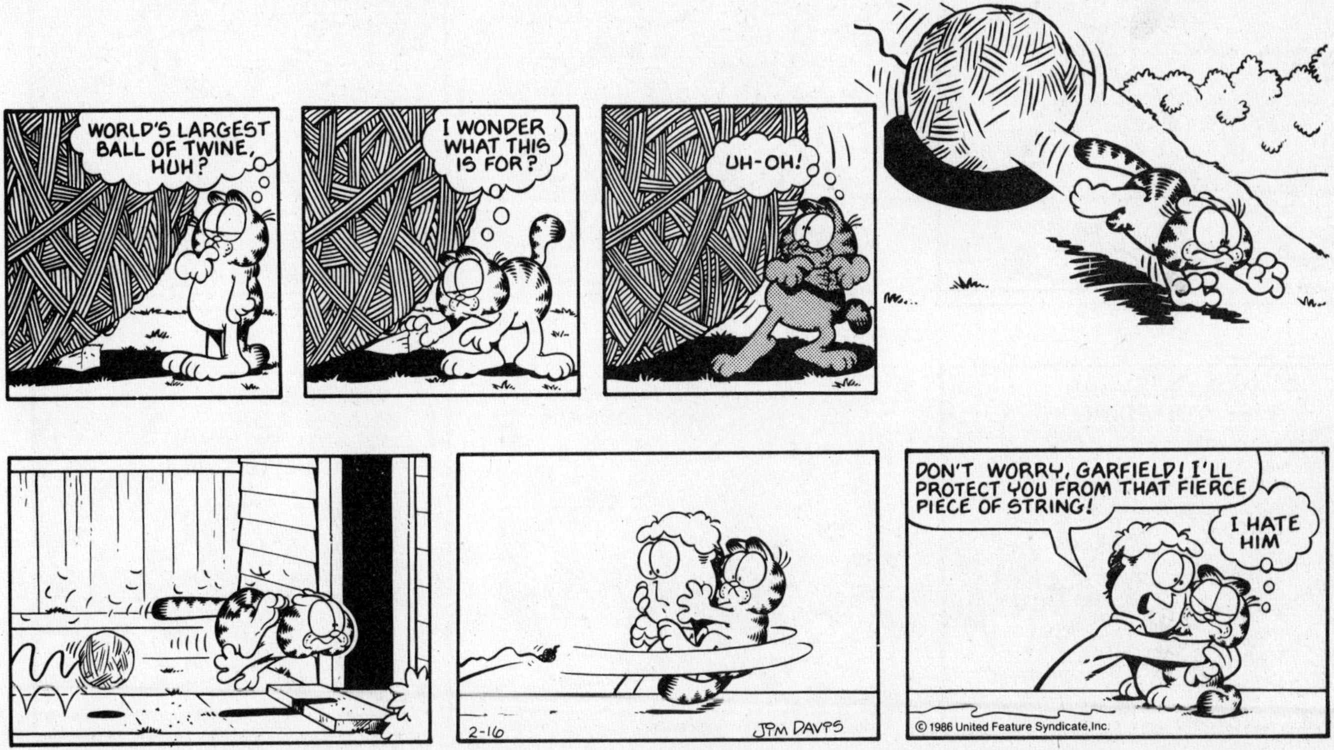
WORLD'S LARGEST BALL OF TWINE, HUH?
I WONDER WHAT THIS IS FOR?
UH-OH!
DON'T WORRY, GARFIELD! I'LL PROTECT YOU FROM THAT FIERCE PIECE OF STRING!
I HATE HIM
2-16
JIM DAVIS
© 1986 United Feature Syndicate,Inc.

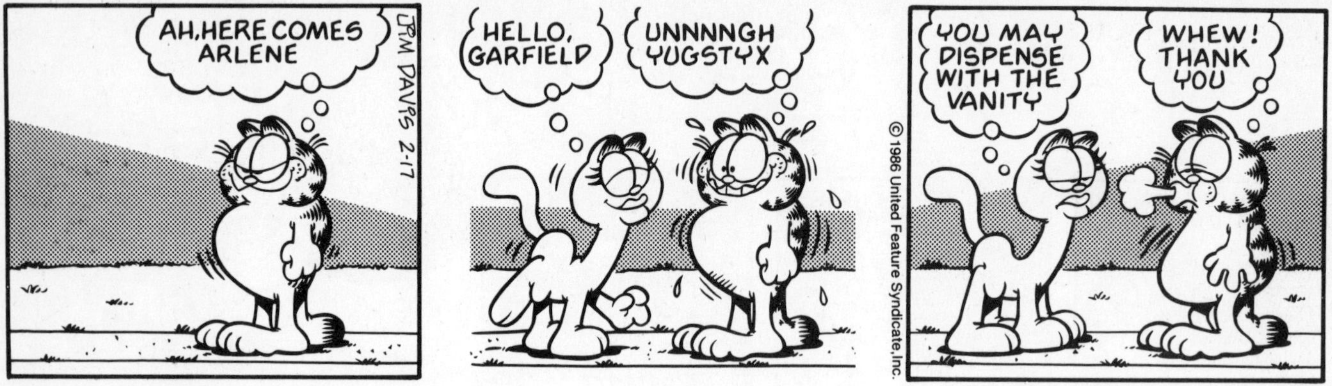
AH, HERE COMES ARLENE
JIM DAVIS 2-17
HELLO, GARFIELD
UNNNNGH YUGSTYX
YOU MAY DISPENSE WITH THE VANITY
WHEW! THANK YOU


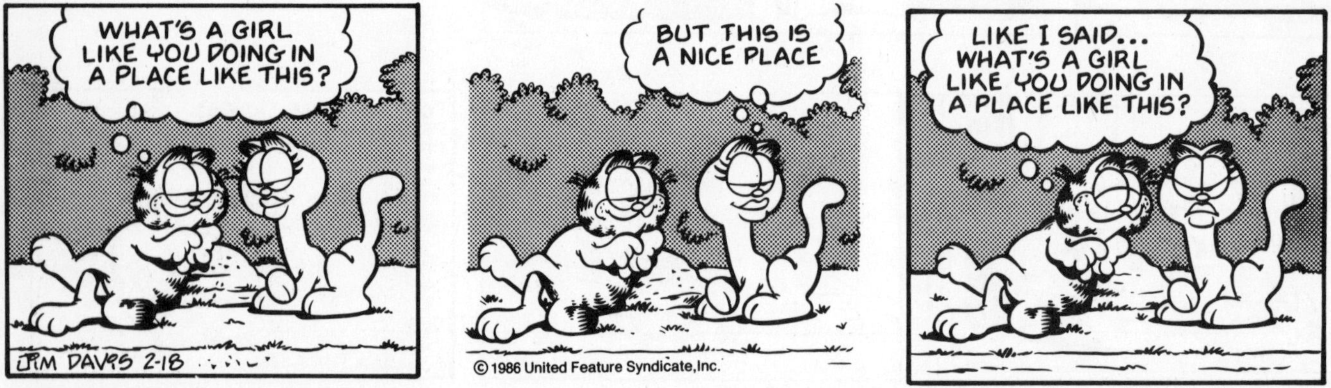
WHAT'S A GIRL LIKE YOU DOING IN A PLACE LIKE THIS?
JIM DAVIS 2-18
BUT THIS IS A NICE PLACE
LIKE I SAID... WHAT'S A GIRL LIKE YOU DOING IN A PLACE LIKE THIS?

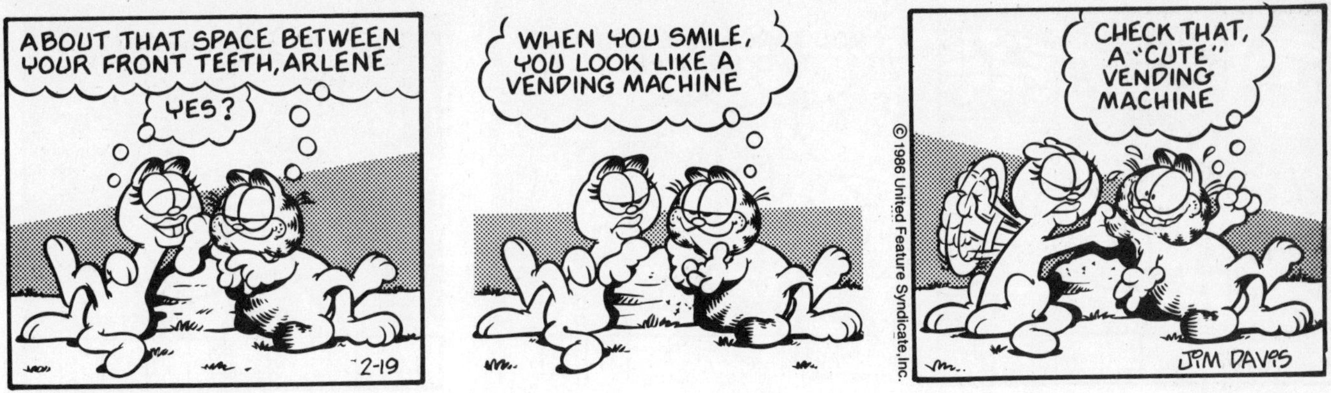

ABOUT THAT SPACE BETWEEN YOUR FRONT TEETH, ARLENE
YES?
2-19
WHEN YOU SMILE, YOU LOOK LIKE A VENDING MACHINE
© 1986 United Feature Syndicate, Inc.
CHECK THAT, A "CUTE" VENDING MACHINE
JIM DAVIS


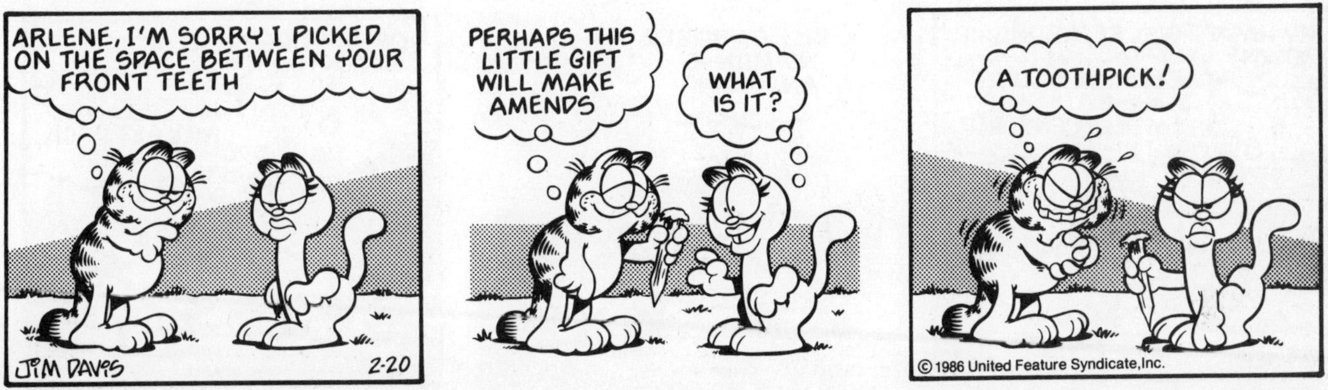

ARLENE, I'M SORRY I PICKED ON THE SPACE BETWEEN YOUR FRONT TEETH
JIM DAVIS
2-20
PERHAPS THIS LITTLE GIFT WILL MAKE AMENDS
WHAT IS IT?
A TOOTHPICK!
© 1986 United Feature Syndicate, Inc.

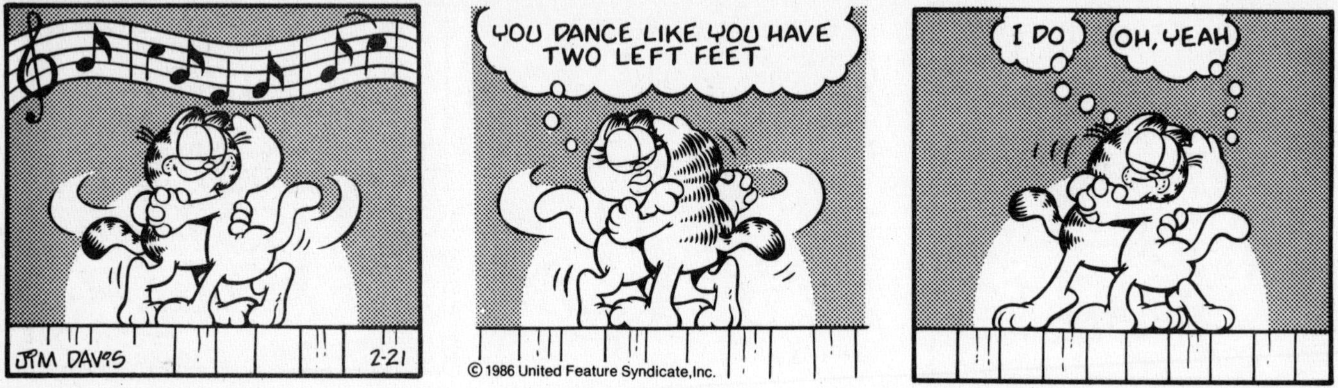
JIM DAVIS
2-21
YOU DANCE LIKE YOU HAVE TWO LEFT FEET
I DO
OH, YEAH
© 1986 United Feature Syndicate, Inc.

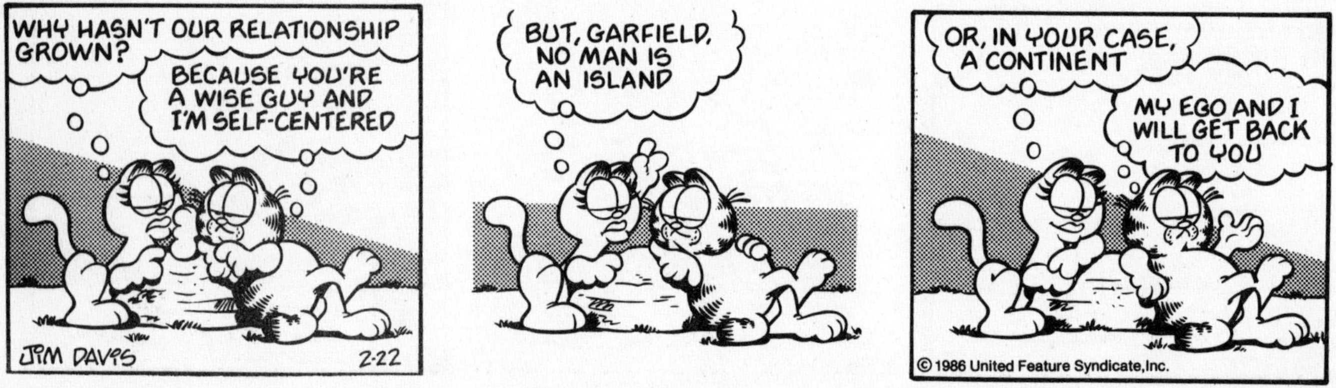
WHY HASN'T OUR RELATIONSHIP GROWN?
BECAUSE YOU'RE A WISE GUY AND I'M SELF-CENTERED
JIM DAVIS
2-22
BUT, GARFIELD, NO MAN IS AN ISLAND
OR, IN YOUR CASE, A CONTINENT
MY EGO AND I WILL GET BACK TO YOU
© 1986 United Feature Syndicate, Inc.

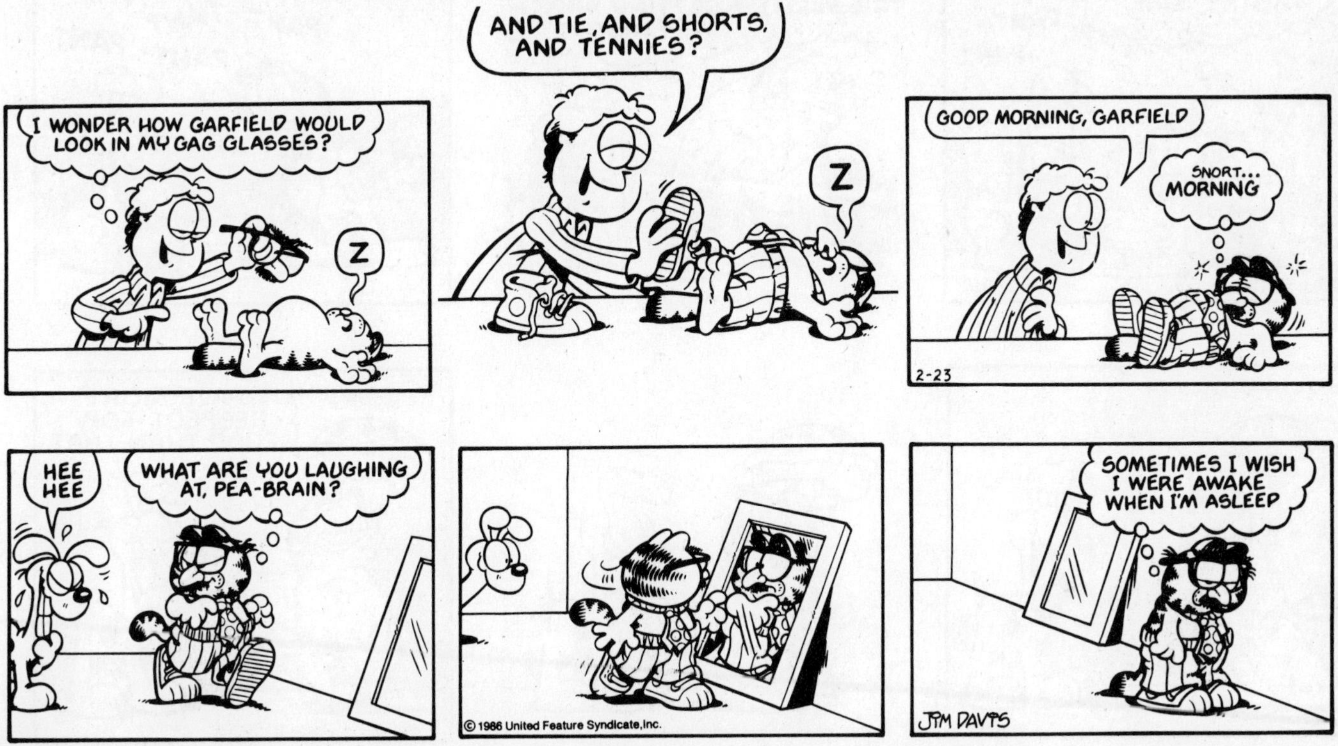
I WONDER HOW GARFIELD WOULD LOOK IN MY GAG GLASSES?
Z
AND TIE, AND SHORTS, AND TENNIES?
Z
GOOD MORNING, GARFIELD
SNORT... MORNING
2-23
HEE HEE
WHAT ARE YOU LAUGHING AT, PEA-BRAIN?
© 1986 United Feature Syndicate, Inc.
SOMETIMES I WISH I WERE AWAKE WHEN I'M ASLEEP
JIM DAVIS

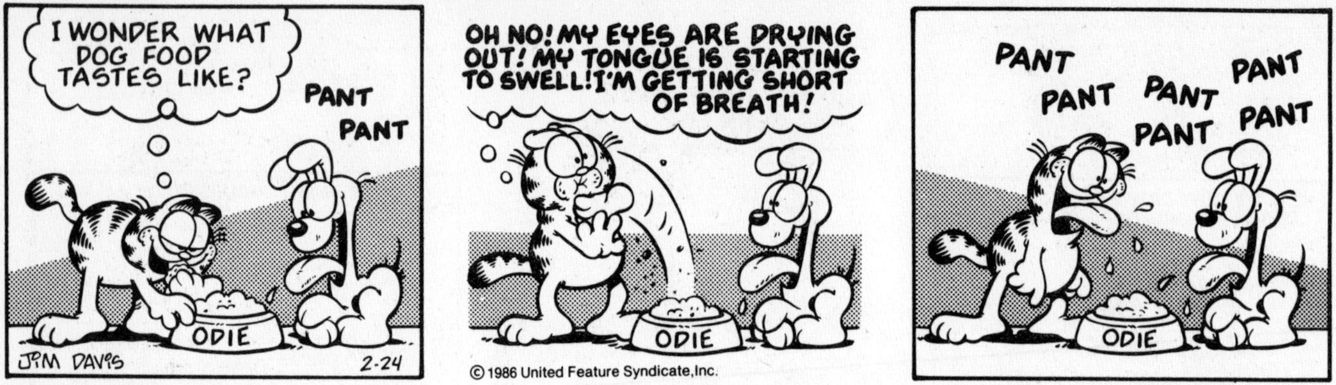
I WONDER WHAT DOG FOOD TASTES LIKE?
PANT PANT
ODIE
JIM DAVIS
2-24
OH NO! MY EYES ARE DRYING OUT! MY TONGUE IS STARTING TO SWELL! I'M GETTING SHORT OF BREATH!
ODIE
PANT PANT PANT PANT PANT PANT
ODIE



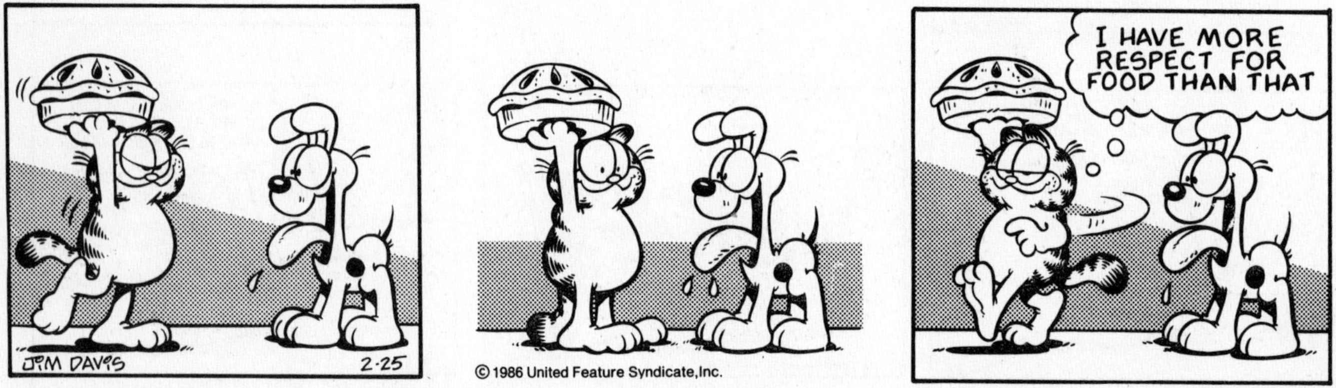
JIM DAVIS
2-25
I HAVE MORE RESPECT FOR FOOD THAN THAT

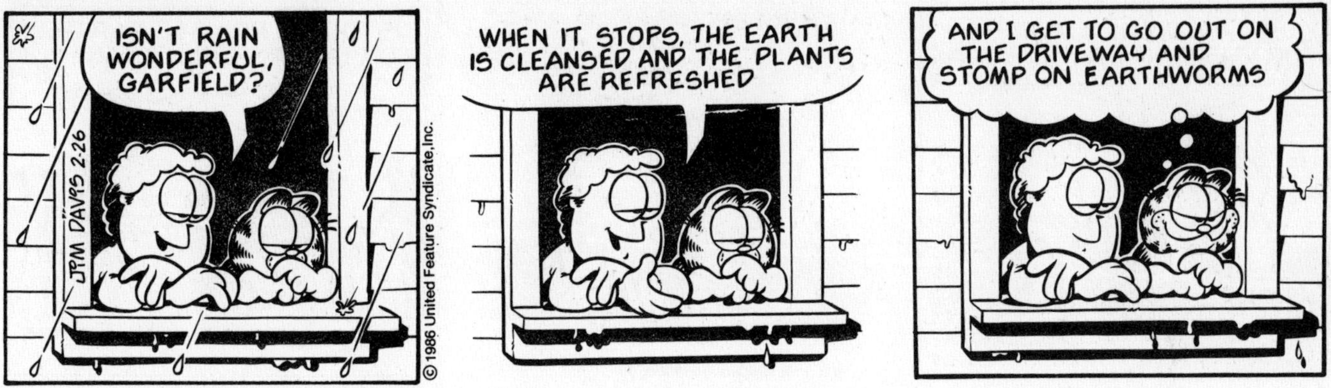
ISN'T RAIN WONDERFUL, GARFIELD?
JIM DAVIS 2-26
© 1986 United Feature Syndicate,Inc.
WHEN IT STOPS, THE EARTH IS CLEANSED AND THE PLANTS ARE REFRESHED
AND I GET TO GO OUT ON THE DRIVEWAY AND STOMP ON EARTHWORMS

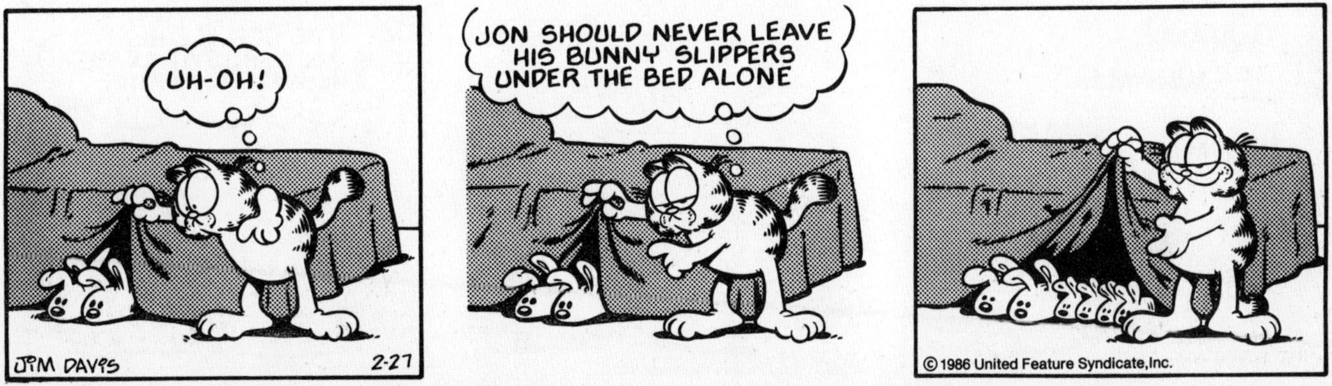
UH-OH!
JIM DAVIS
2-27
JON SHOULD NEVER LEAVE HIS BUNNY SLIPPERS UNDER THE BED ALONE
© 1986 United Feature Syndicate,Inc.

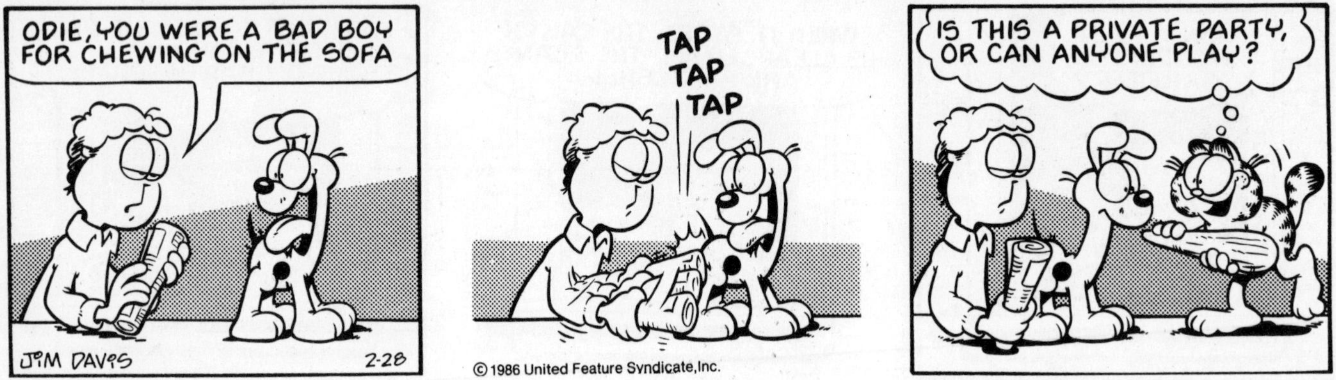
ODIE, YOU WERE A BAD BOY FOR CHEWING ON THE SOFA
JIM DAVIS
2-28
TAP
TAP
TAP
IS THIS A PRIVATE PARTY, OR CAN ANYONE PLAY?



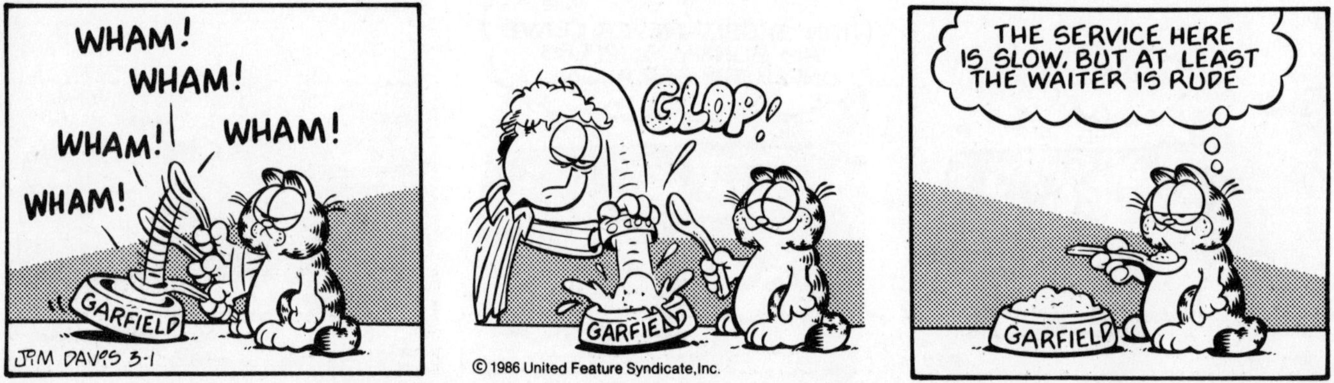
WHAM!
WHAM!
WHAM!
WHAM!
WHAM!
GARFIELD
JIM DAVIS 3-1
GLOP!
GARFIELD
THE SERVICE HERE IS SLOW, BUT AT LEAST THE WAITER IS RUDE
GARFIELD

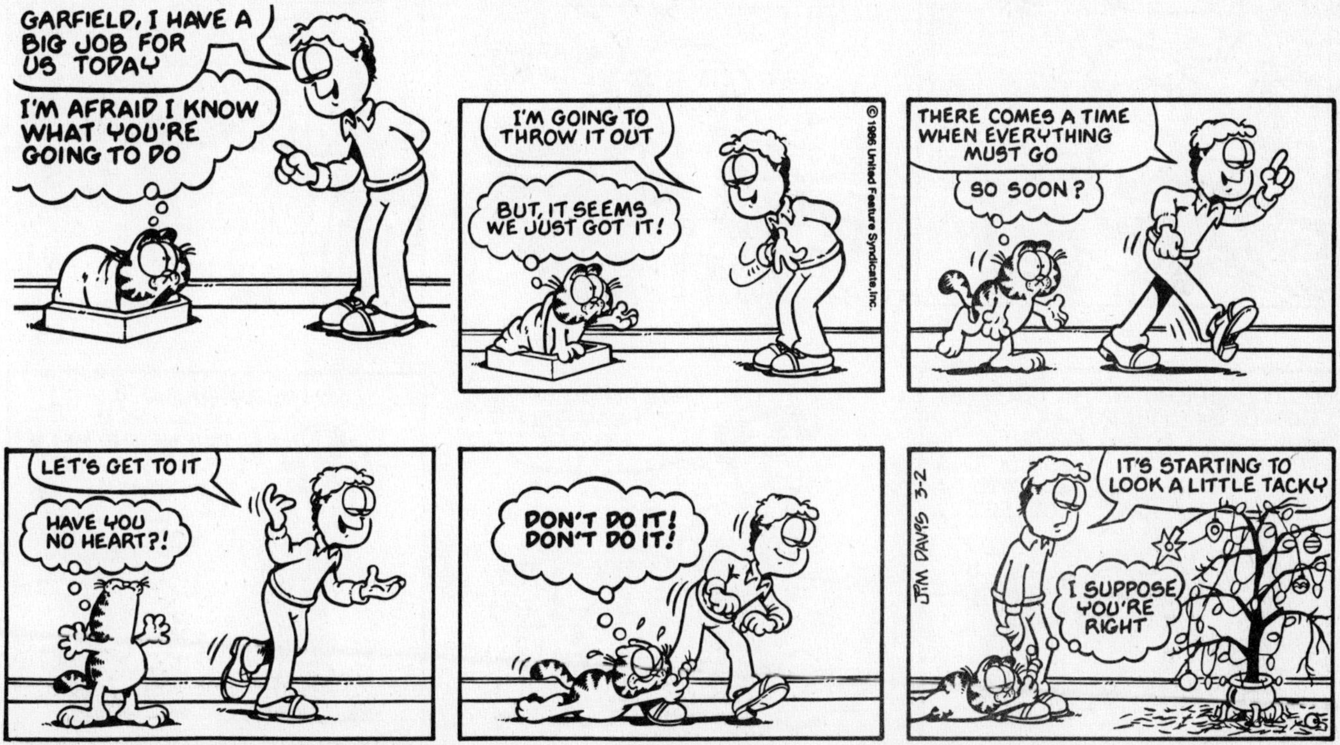

GARFIELD, I HAVE A BIG JOB FOR US TODAY
I'M AFRAID I KNOW WHAT YOU'RE GOING TO DO
I'M GOING TO THROW IT OUT
BUT, IT SEEMS WE JUST GOT IT!
© 1986 United Feature Syndicate, Inc.
THERE COMES A TIME WHEN EVERYTHING MUST GO
SO SOON?
LET'S GET TO IT
HAVE YOU NO HEART?!
JIM DAVIS 3-2
DON'T DO IT! DON'T DO IT!
IT'S STARTING TO LOOK A LITTLE TACKY
I SUPPOSE YOU'RE RIGHT

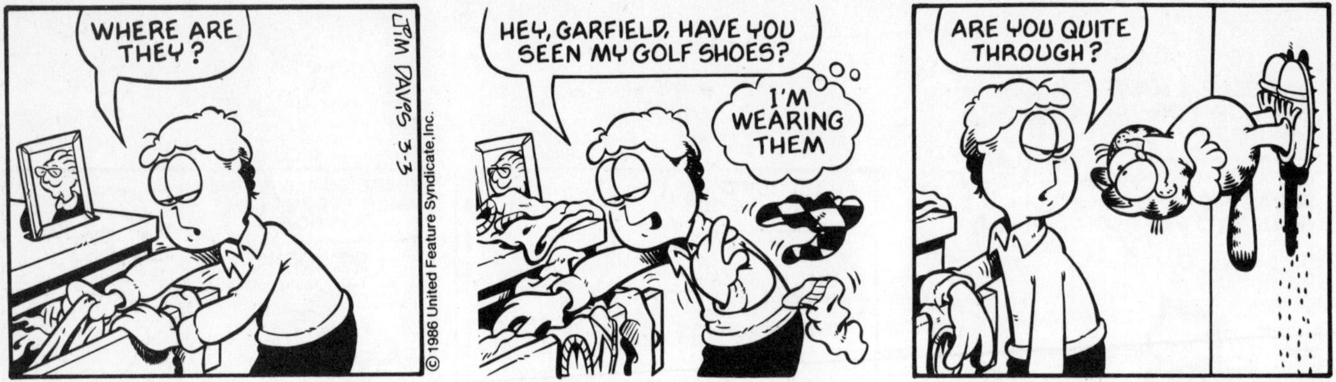
WHERE ARE THEY?
JIM DAVIS 3-3
© 1986 United Feature Syndicate, Inc.
HEY, GARFIELD, HAVE YOU SEEN MY GOLF SHOES?
I'M WEARING THEM
ARE YOU QUITE THROUGH?

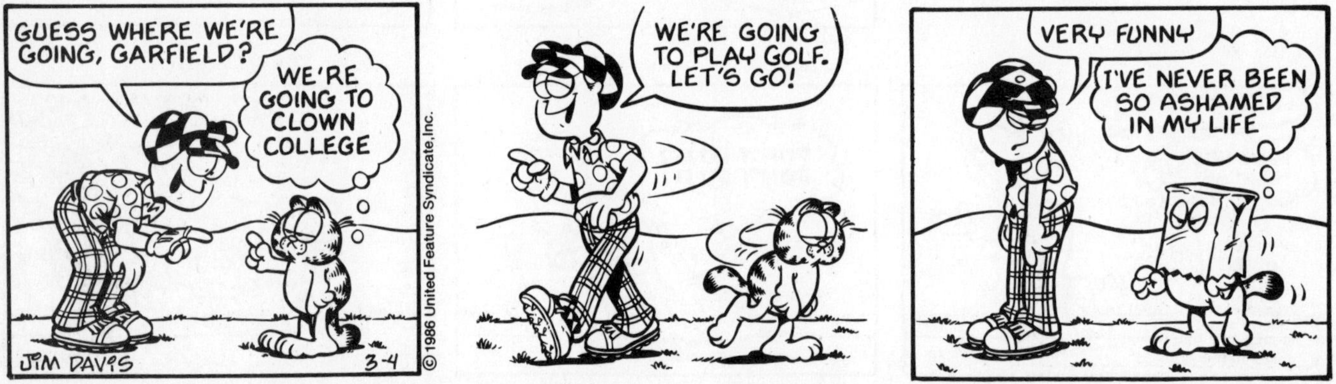
GUESS WHERE WE'RE GOING, GARFIELD?
WE'RE GOING TO CLOWN COLLEGE
JIM DAVIS
3-4
© 1986 United Feature Syndicate, Inc.
WE'RE GOING TO PLAY GOLF. LET'S GO!
VERY FUNNY
I'VE NEVER BEEN SO ASHAMED IN MY LIFE

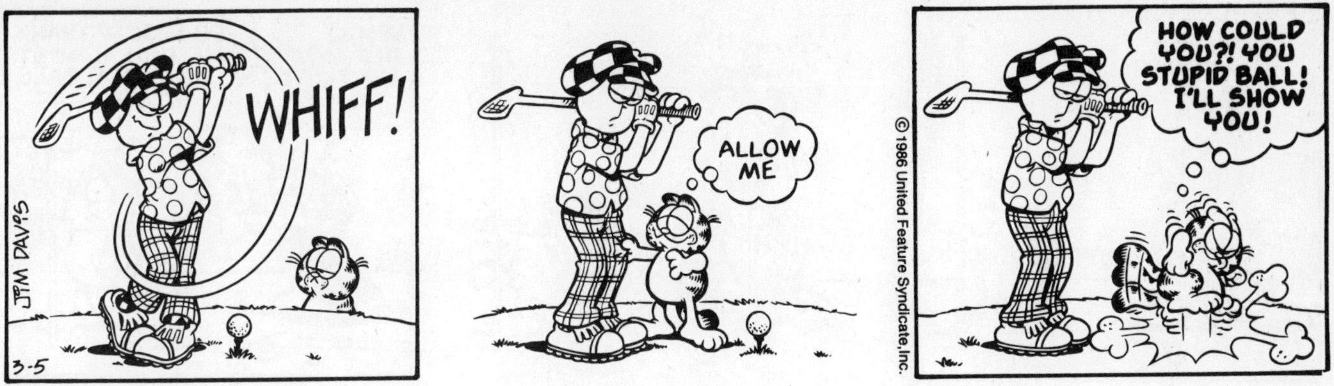
JIM DAVIS
3-5
WHIFF!
ALLOW ME
© 1986 United Feature Syndicate,Inc.
HOW COULD YOU?! YOU STUPID BALL! I'LL SHOW YOU!

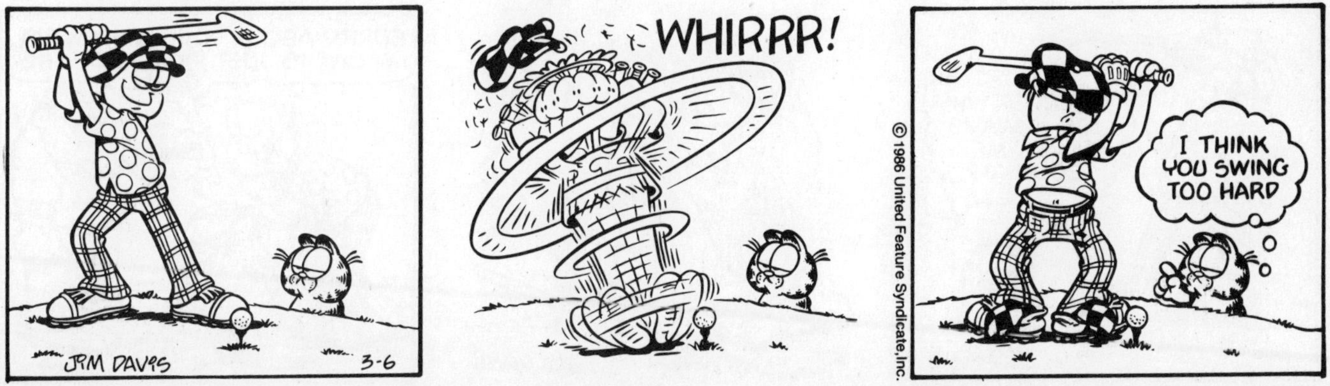
JIM DAVIS
3-6
WHIRRR!
© 1986 United Feature Syndicate,Inc.
I THINK YOU SWING TOO HARD

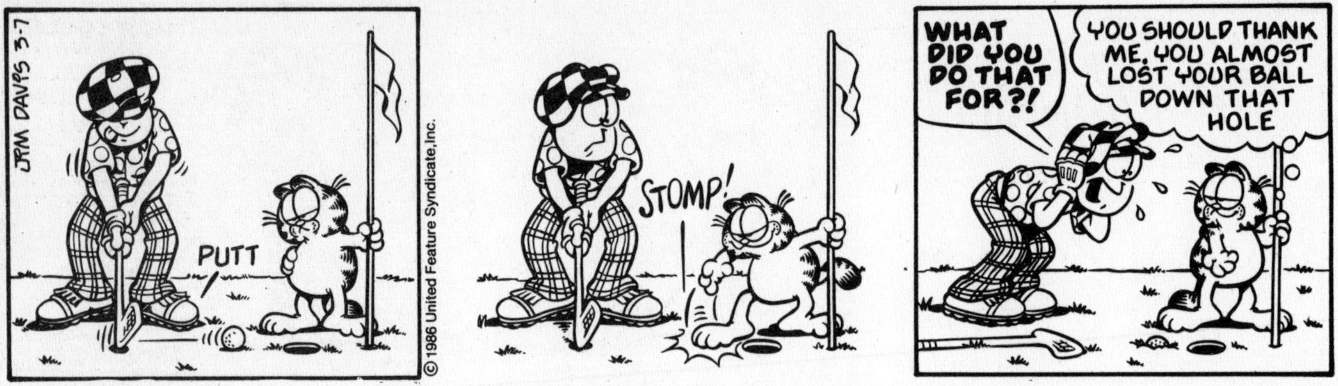
JIM DAVIS 3-7
PUTT
© 1986 United Feature Syndicate, Inc.
STOMP!
WHAT DID YOU DO THAT FOR?!
YOU SHOULD THANK ME. YOU ALMOST LOST YOUR BALL DOWN THAT HOLE

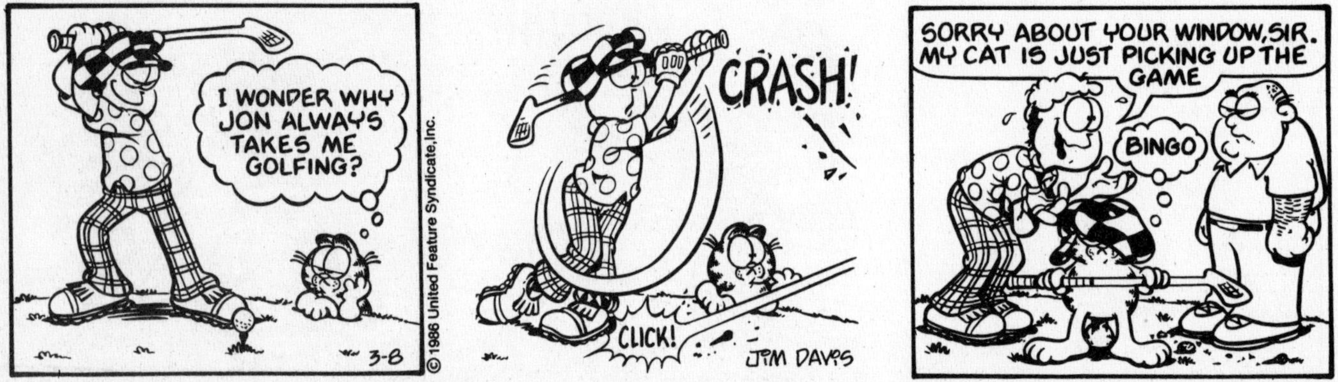
I WONDER WHY JON ALWAYS TAKES ME GOLFING?
3-8
© 1986 United Feature Syndicate, Inc.
CRASH!
CLICK!
JIM DAVIS
SORRY ABOUT YOUR WINDOW, SIR. MY CAT IS JUST PICKING UP THE GAME
BINGO

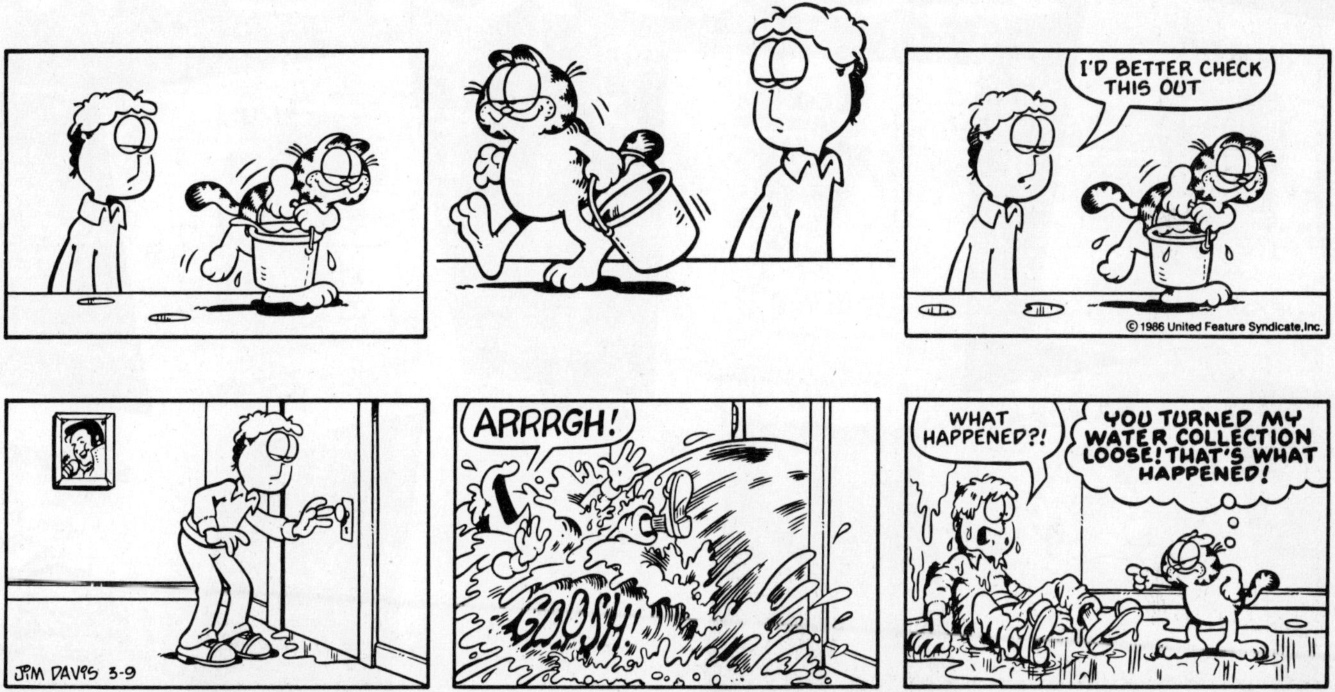
I'D BETTER CHECK THIS OUT
© 1986 United Feature Syndicate, Inc.
JIM DAVIS 3-9
ARRRGH!
GLOOSH!
WHAT HAPPENED?!
YOU TURNED MY WATER COLLECTION LOOSE! THAT'S WHAT HAPPENED!

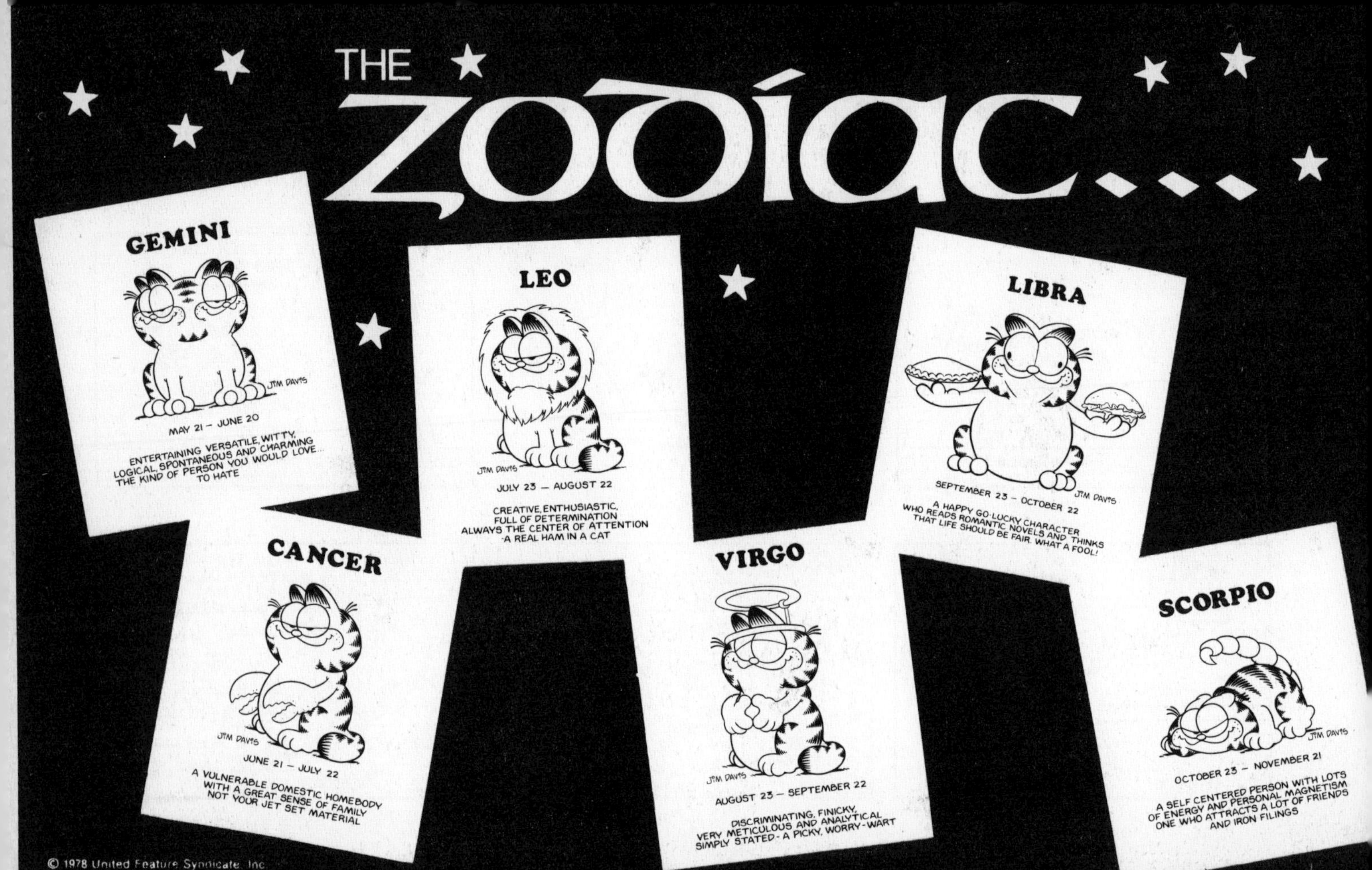
THE ZODIAC...
GEMINI
JIM DAVIS
MAY 21 — JUNE 20
ENTERTAINING VERSATILE, WITTY, LOGICAL, SPONTANEOUS AND CHARMING THE KIND OF PERSON YOU WOULD LOVE... TO HATE
LEO
JIM DAVIS
JULY 23 — AUGUST 22
CREATIVE, ENTHUSIASTIC, FULL OF DETERMINATION ALWAYS THE CENTER OF ATTENTION A REAL HAM IN A CAT
LIBRA
JIM DAVIS
SEPTEMBER 23 — OCTOBER 22
A HAPPY GO-LUCKY CHARACTER WHO READS ROMANTIC NOVELS AND THINKS THAT LIFE SHOULD BE FAIR. WHAT A FOOL!
CANCER
JIM DAVIS
JUNE 21 — JULY 22
A VULNERABLE DOMESTIC HOMEBODY WITH A GREAT SENSE OF FAMILY NOT YOUR JET SET MATERIAL
VIRGO
JIM DAVIS
AUGUST 23 — SEPTEMBER 22
DISCRIMINATING, FINICKY, VERY METICULOUS AND ANALYTICAL SIMPLY STATED - A PICKY, WORRY-WART
SCORPIO
JIM DAVIS
OCTOBER 23 — NOVEMBER 21
A SELF CENTERED PERSON WITH LOTS OF ENERGY AND PERSONAL MAGNETISM ONE WHO ATTRACTS A LOT OF FRIENDS AND IRON FILINGS

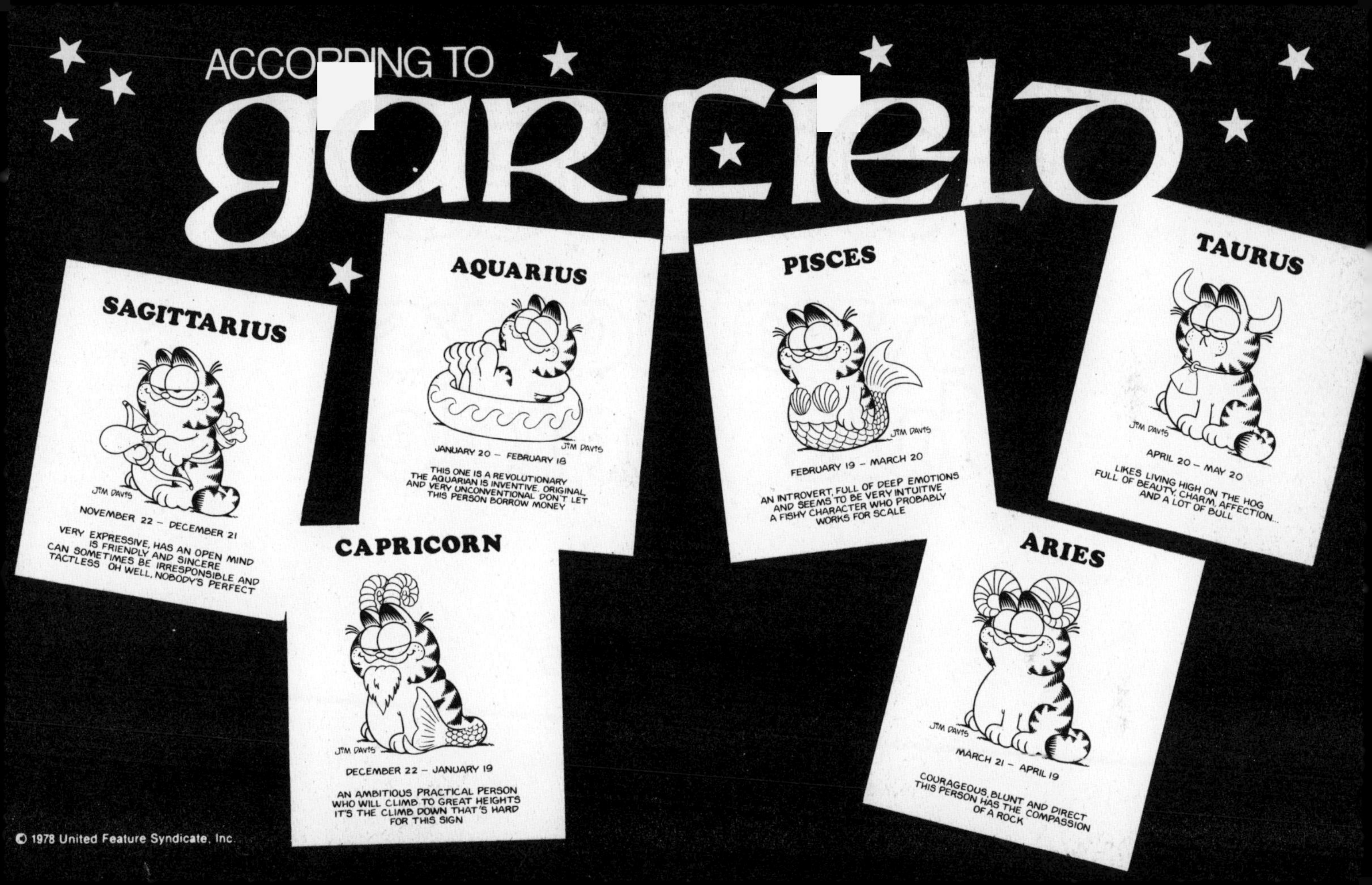
ACCORDING TO
garfield
SAGITTARIUS
JIM DAVIS
NOVEMBER 22 – DECEMBER 21
VERY EXPRESSIVE, HAS AN OPEN MIND IS FRIENDLY AND SINCERE CAN SOMETIMES BE IRRESPONSIBLE AND TACTLESS OH WELL, NOBODY'S PERFECT
AQUARIUS
JIM DAVIS
JANUARY 20 – FEBRUARY 18
THIS ONE IS A REVOLUTIONARY THE AQUARIAN IS INVENTIVE, ORIGINAL AND VERY UNCONVENTIONAL DON'T LET THIS PERSON BORROW MONEY
PISCES
JIM DAVIS
FEBRUARY 19 – MARCH 20
AN INTROVERT, FULL OF DEEP EMOTIONS AND SEEMS TO BE VERY INTUITIVE A FISHY CHARACTER WHO PROBABLY WORKS FOR SCALE
TAURUS
JIM DAVIS
APRIL 20 – MAY 20
LIKES LIVING HIGH ON THE HOG FULL OF BEAUTY, CHARM, AFFECTION... AND A LOT OF BULL
CAPRICORN
JIM DAVIS
DECEMBER 22 – JANUARY 19
AN AMBITIOUS PRACTICAL PERSON WHO WILL CLIMB TO GREAT HEIGHTS IT'S THE CLIMB DOWN THAT'S HARD FOR THIS SIGN
ARIES
JIM DAVIS
MARCH 21 – APRIL 19
COURAGEOUS, BLUNT AND DIRECT THIS PERSON HAS THE COMPASSION OF A ROCK

# Garfield swallows his pride

BY: JIM DAVIS

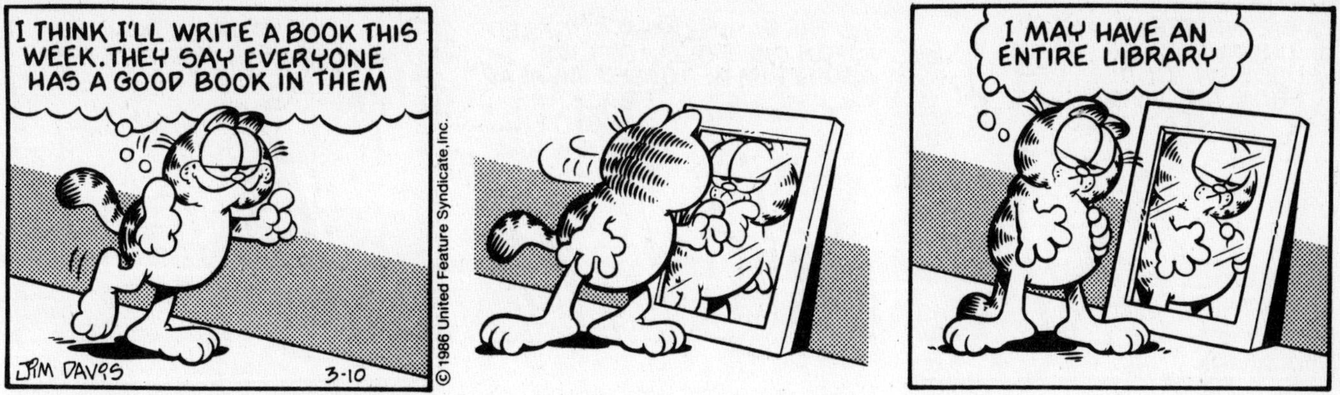
I THINK I'LL WRITE A BOOK THIS WEEK. THEY SAY EVERYONE HAS A GOOD BOOK IN THEM
JIM DAVIS
3-10
I MAY HAVE AN ENTIRE LIBRARY

© 1986 United Feature Syndicate, Inc.

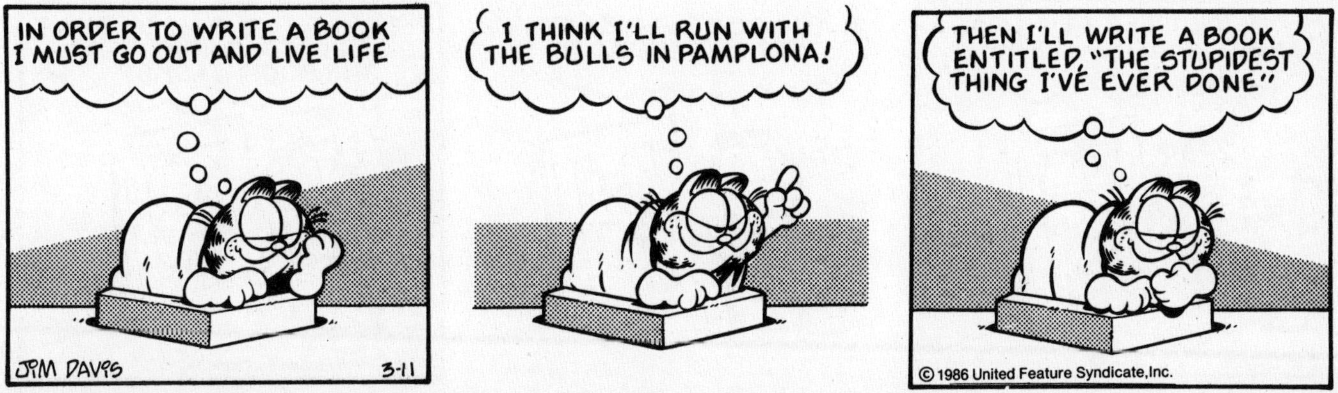
IN ORDER TO WRITE A BOOK I MUST GO OUT AND LIVE LIFE
JIM DAVIS
3-11
I THINK I'LL RUN WITH THE BULLS IN PAMPLONA!
THEN I'LL WRITE A BOOK ENTITLED, "THE STUPIDEST THING I'VE EVER DONE"

© 1986 United Feature Syndicate, Inc.

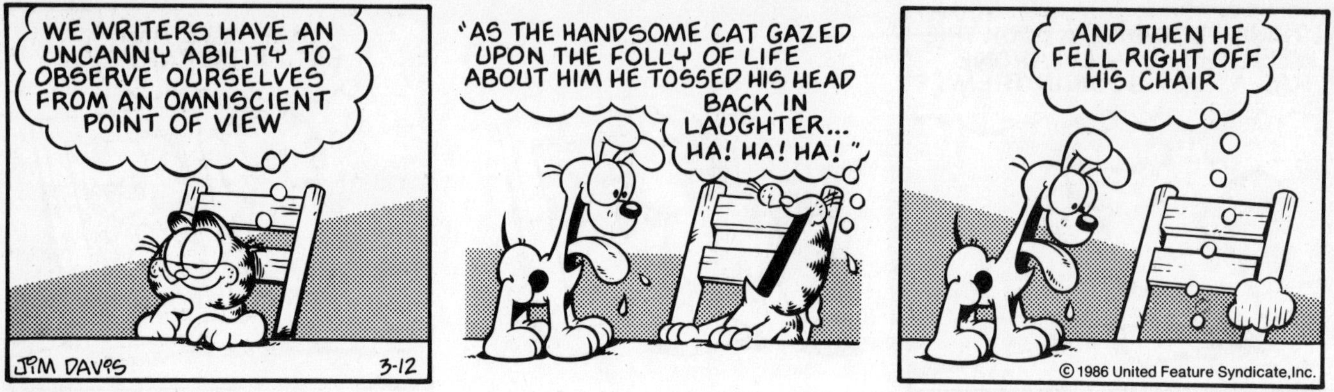
WE WRITERS HAVE AN UNCANNY ABILITY TO OBSERVE OURSELVES FROM AN OMNISCIENT POINT OF VIEW
"AS THE HANDSOME CAT GAZED UPON THE FOLLY OF LIFE ABOUT HIM HE TOSSED HIS HEAD BACK IN LAUGHTER... HA! HA! HA!"
AND THEN HE FELL RIGHT OFF HIS CHAIR
JIM DAVIS 3-12
© 1986 United Feature Syndicate, Inc.

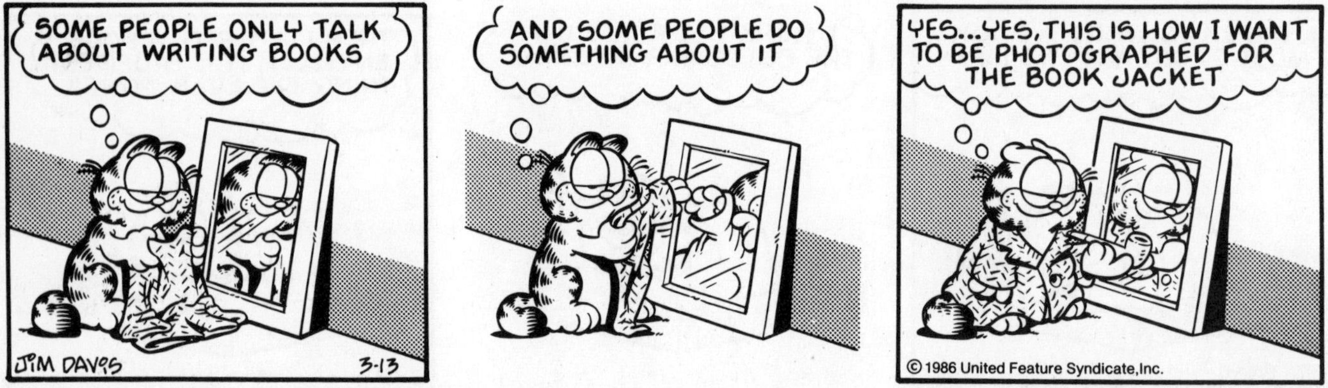
SOME PEOPLE ONLY TALK ABOUT WRITING BOOKS
AND SOME PEOPLE DO SOMETHING ABOUT IT
YES...YES, THIS IS HOW I WANT TO BE PHOTOGRAPHED FOR THE BOOK JACKET
JIM DAVIS 3-13
© 1986 United Feature Syndicate, Inc.

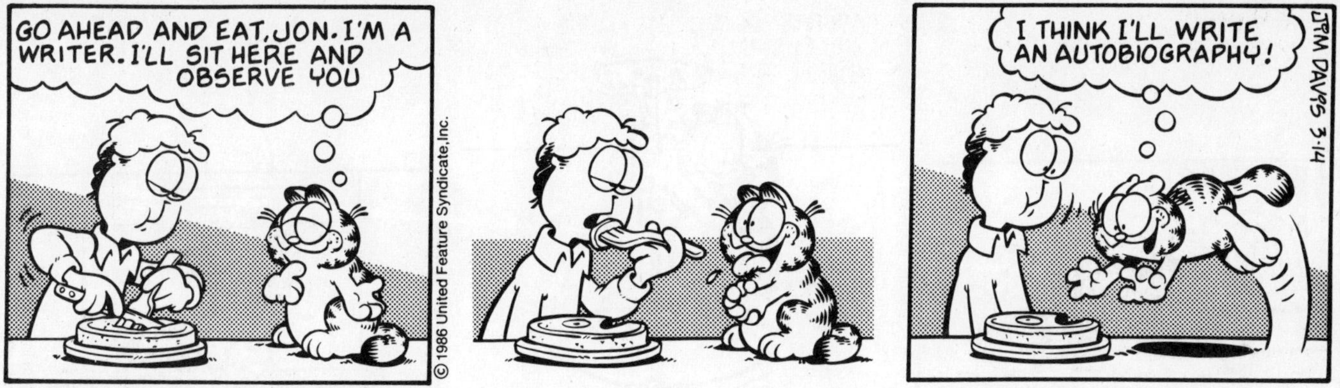
GO AHEAD AND EAT, JON. I'M A WRITER. I'LL SIT HERE AND OBSERVE YOU
© 1986 United Feature Syndicate, Inc.
I THINK I'LL WRITE AN AUTOBIOGRAPHY!
JIM DAVIS 3-14

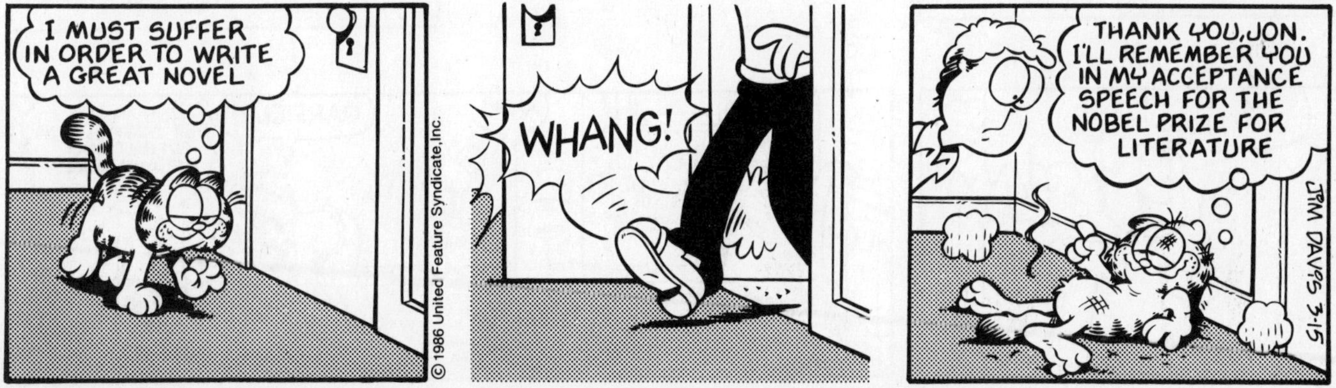
I MUST SUFFER IN ORDER TO WRITE A GREAT NOVEL
© 1986 United Feature Syndicate, Inc.
WHANG!
THANK YOU, JON. I'LL REMEMBER YOU IN MY ACCEPTANCE SPEECH FOR THE NOBEL PRIZE FOR LITERATURE
JIM DAVIS 3-15

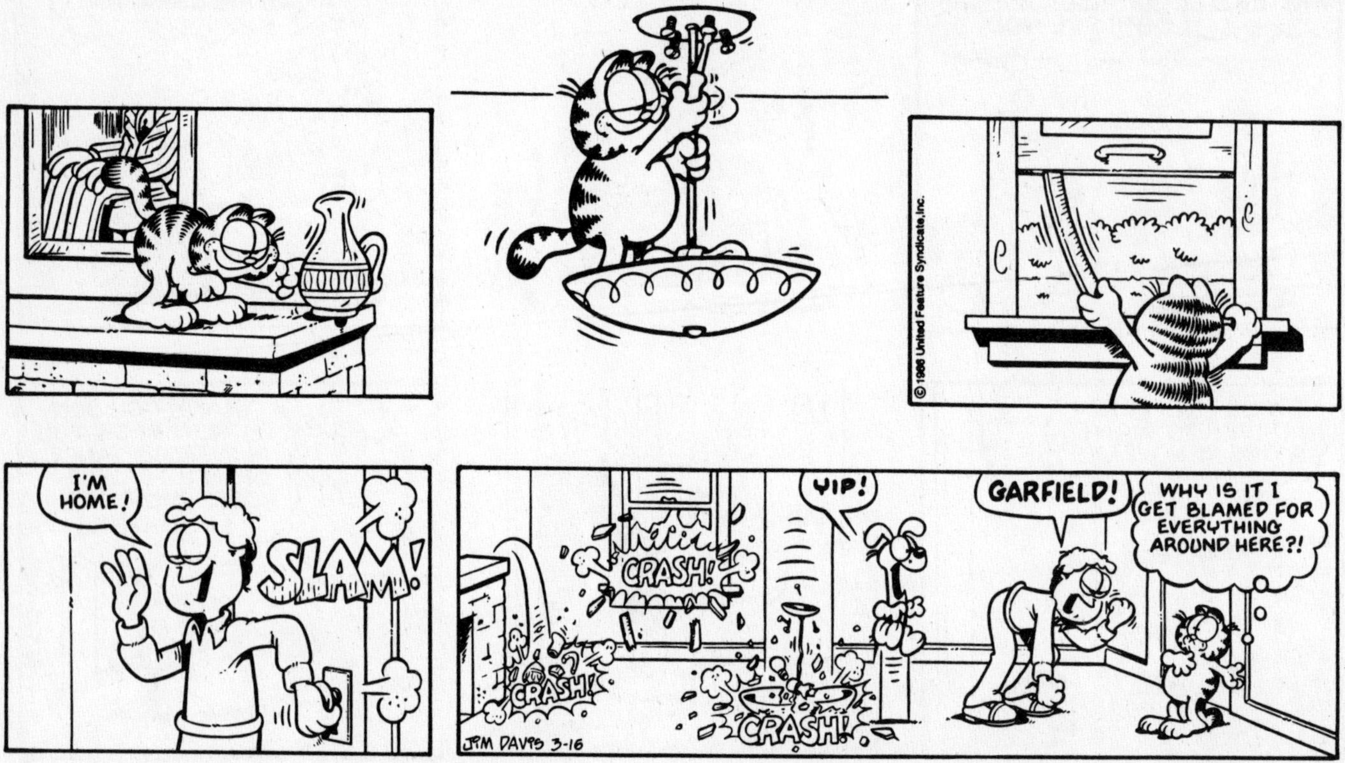

© 1986 United Feature Syndicate, Inc.
I'M HOME!
SLAM!
CRASH!
CRASH!
CRASH!
YIP!
GARFIELD!
WHY IS IT I GET BLAMED FOR EVERYTHING AROUND HERE?!
JIM DAVIS 3-16

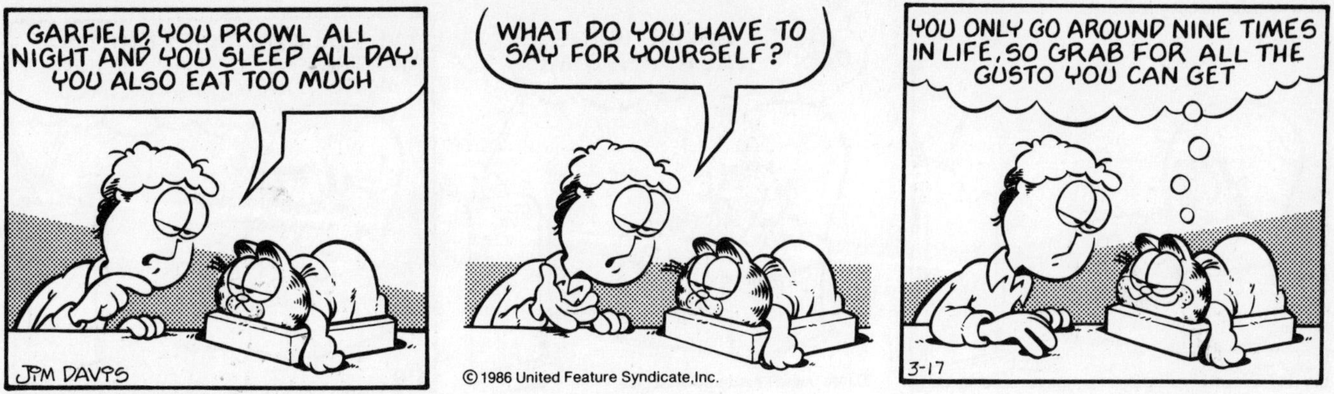
GARFIELD, YOU PROWL ALL NIGHT AND YOU SLEEP ALL DAY. YOU ALSO EAT TOO MUCH
WHAT DO YOU HAVE TO SAY FOR YOURSELF?
YOU ONLY GO AROUND NINE TIMES IN LIFE, SO GRAB FOR ALL THE GUSTO YOU CAN GET
JIM DAVIS
© 1986 United Feature Syndicate, Inc.
3-17

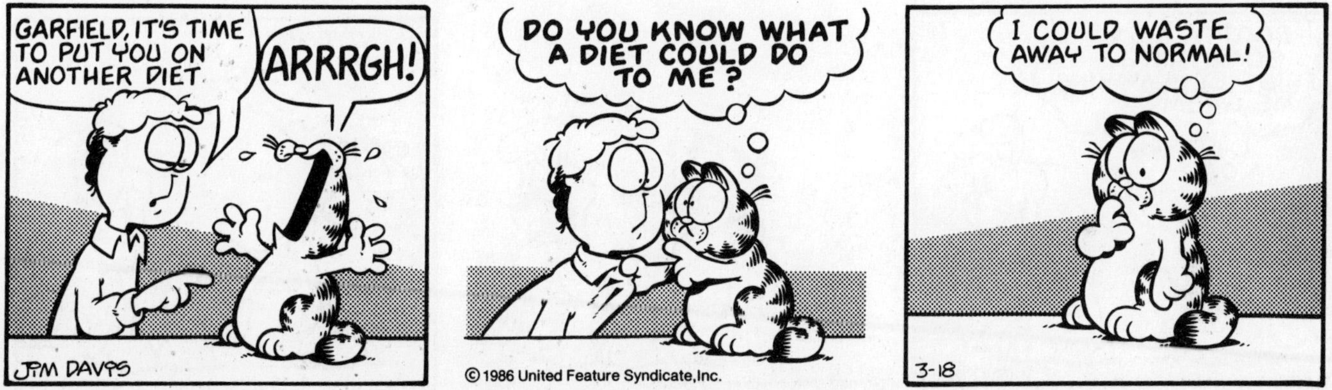
GARFIELD, IT'S TIME TO PUT YOU ON ANOTHER DIET
ARRRGH!
DO YOU KNOW WHAT A DIET COULD DO TO ME?
I COULD WASTE AWAY TO NORMAL!
JIM DAVIS
© 1986 United Feature Syndicate, Inc.
3-18

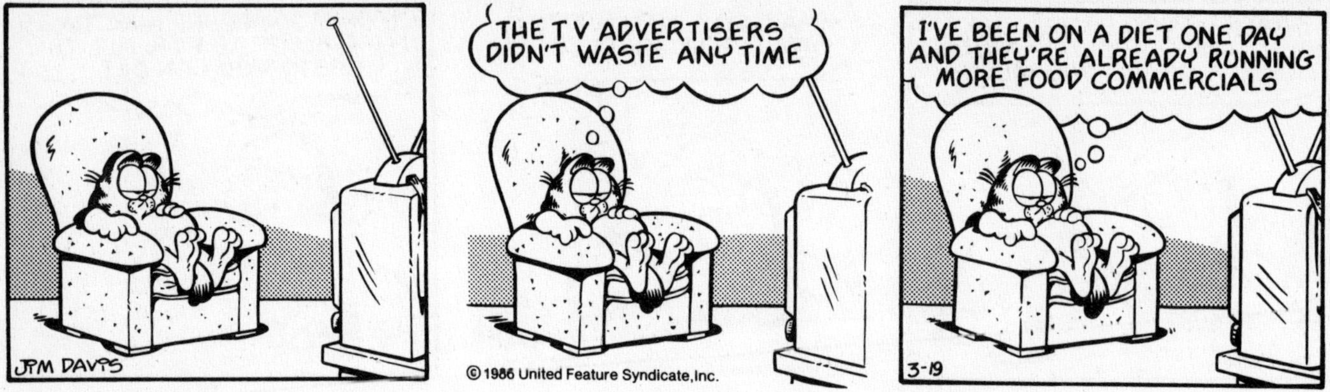
JIM DAVIS
THE T V ADVERTISERS DIDN'T WASTE ANY TIME
© 1986 United Feature Syndicate, Inc.
I'VE BEEN ON A DIET ONE DAY AND THEY'RE ALREADY RUNNING MORE FOOD COMMERCIALS
3-19

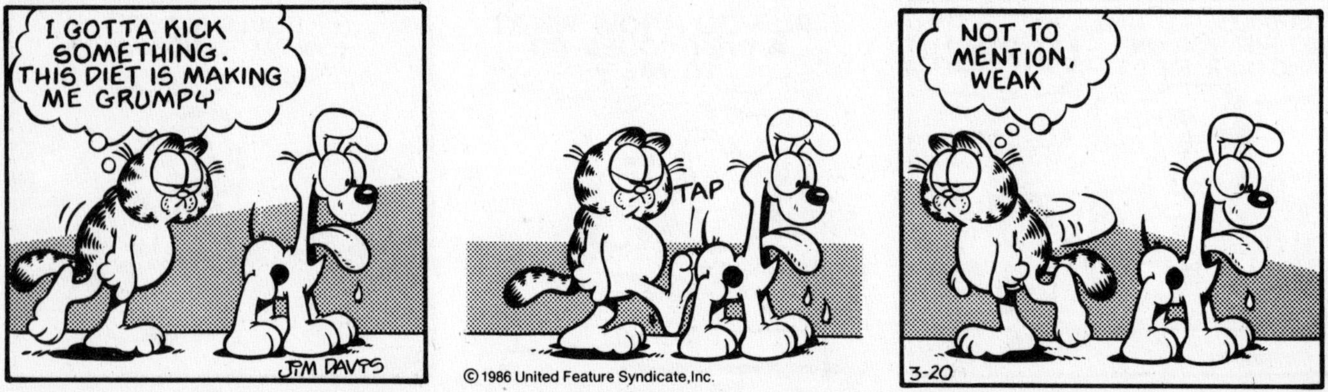
I GOTTA KICK SOMETHING. THIS DIET IS MAKING ME GRUMPY
JIM DAVIS
TAP
© 1986 United Feature Syndicate, Inc.
NOT TO MENTION, WEAK
3-20

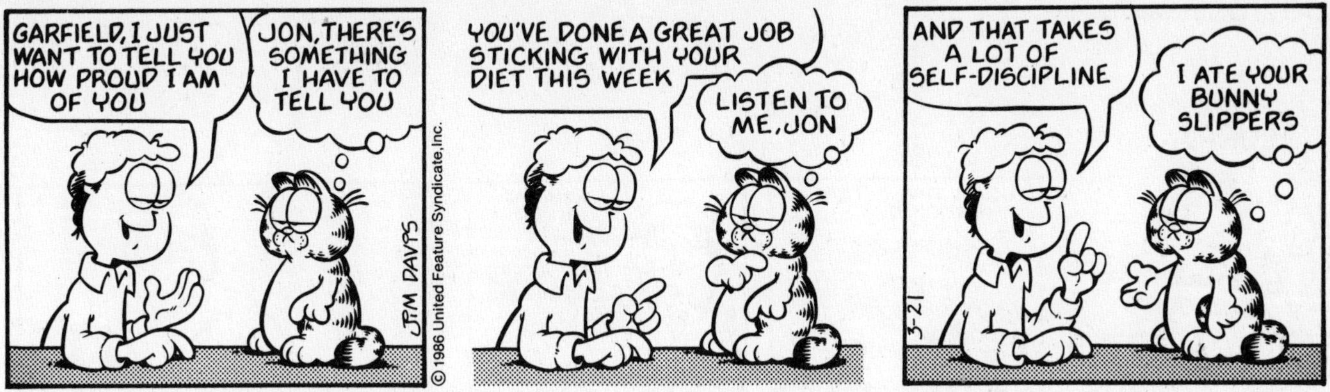
GARFIELD, I JUST WANT TO TELL YOU HOW PROUD I AM OF YOU
JON, THERE'S SOMETHING I HAVE TO TELL YOU
JIM DAVIS
© 1986 United Feature Syndicate, Inc.
YOU'VE DONE A GREAT JOB STICKING WITH YOUR DIET THIS WEEK
LISTEN TO ME, JON
3-21
AND THAT TAKES A LOT OF SELF-DISCIPLINE
I ATE YOUR BUNNY SLIPPERS

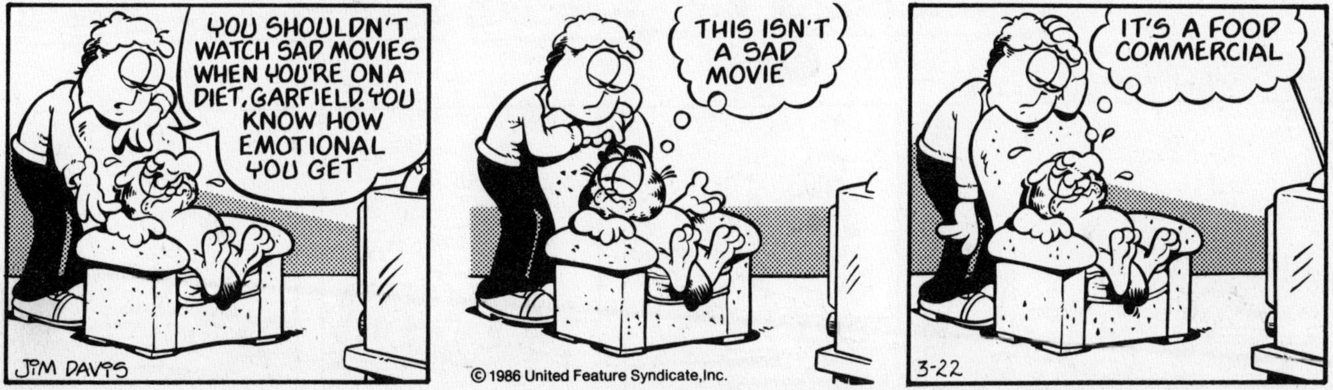
YOU SHOULDN'T WATCH SAD MOVIES WHEN YOU'RE ON A DIET, GARFIELD. YOU KNOW HOW EMOTIONAL YOU GET
JIM DAVIS
THIS ISN'T A SAD MOVIE
© 1986 United Feature Syndicate, Inc.
IT'S A FOOD COMMERCIAL
3-22

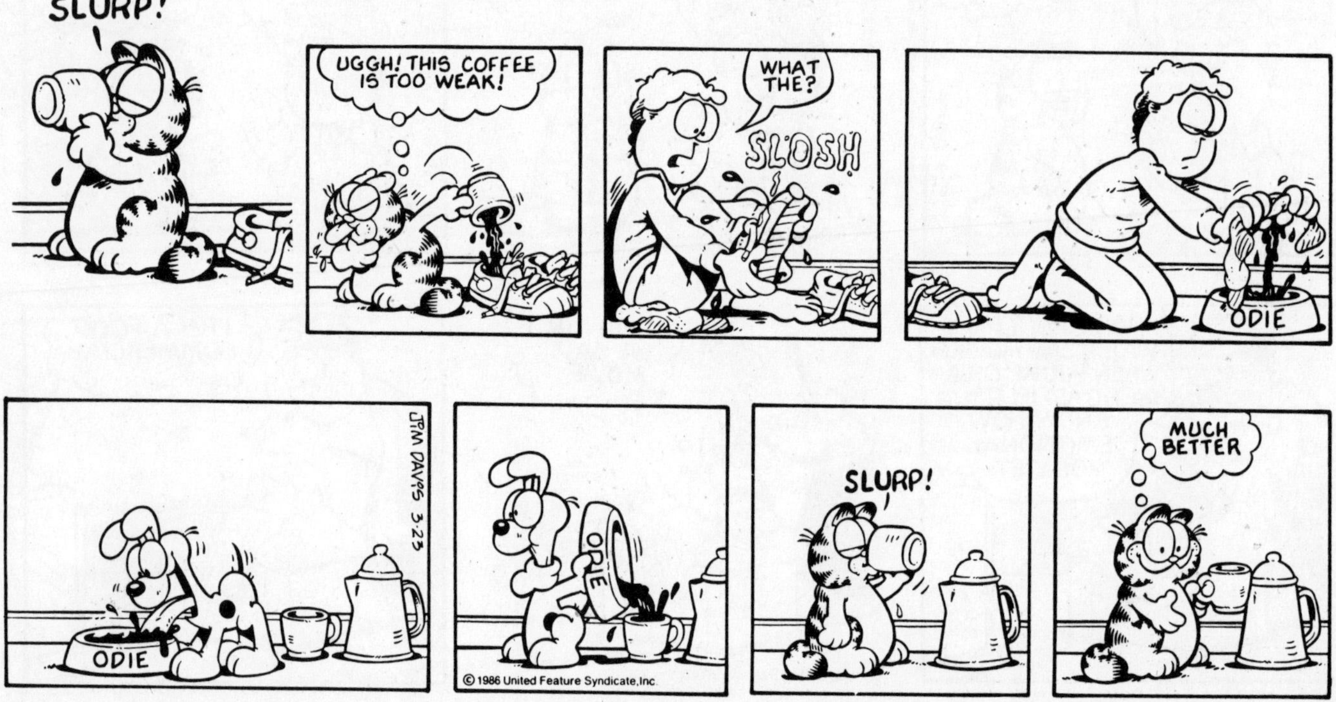

SLURP!
UGGH! THIS COFFEE IS TOO WEAK!
WHAT THE?
SLOSH
ODIE
JIM DAVIS 3-23
ODIE
ODIE
© 1986 United Feature Syndicate, Inc.
SLURP!
MUCH BETTER

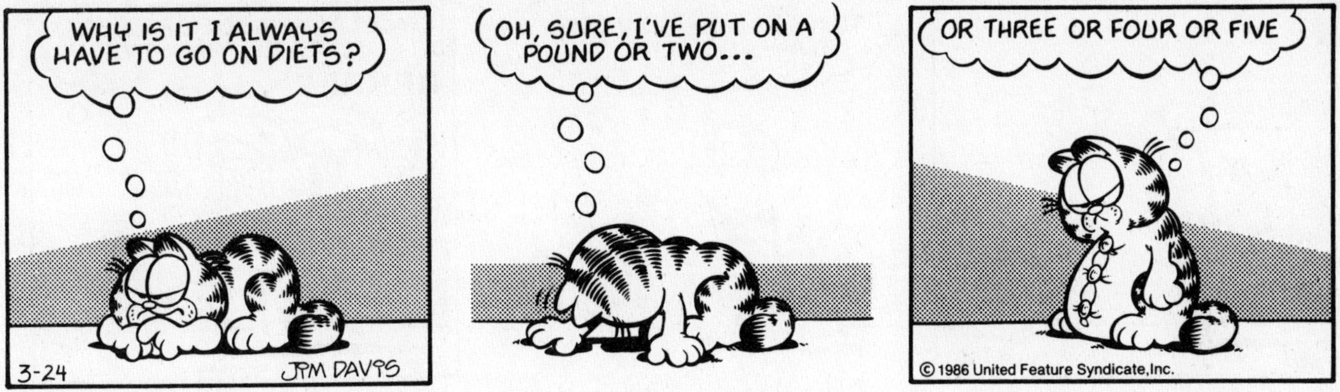
WHY IS IT I ALWAYS HAVE TO GO ON DIETS?
OH, SURE, I'VE PUT ON A POUND OR TWO...
OR THREE OR FOUR OR FIVE
3-24
JIM DAVIS
© 1986 United Feature Syndicate, Inc.

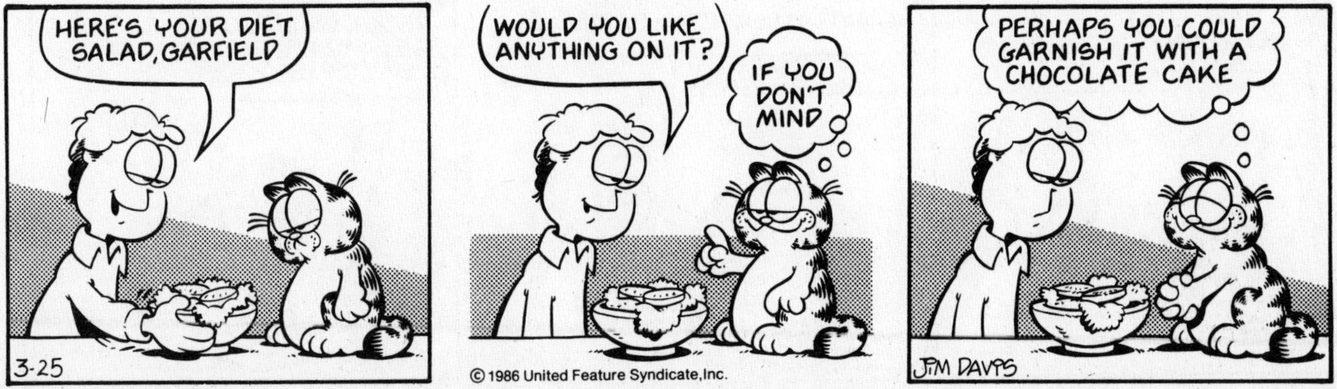
HERE'S YOUR DIET SALAD, GARFIELD
WOULD YOU LIKE ANYTHING ON IT?
IF YOU DON'T MIND
PERHAPS YOU COULD GARNISH IT WITH A CHOCOLATE CAKE
3-25
© 1986 United Feature Syndicate, Inc.
JIM DAVIS

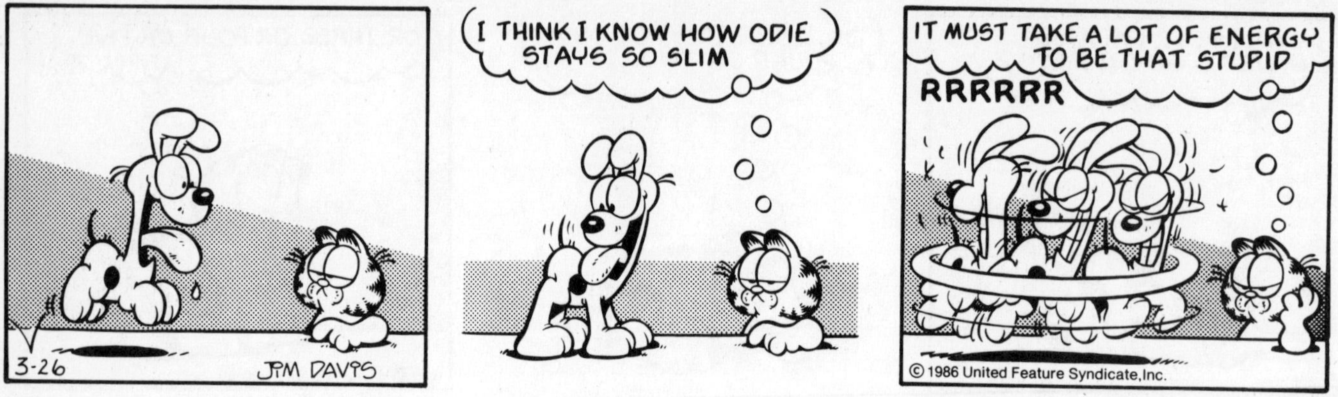
3-26
JIM DAVIS
I THINK I KNOW HOW ODIE STAYS SO SLIM
IT MUST TAKE A LOT OF ENERGY TO BE THAT STUPID
RRRRRR
© 1986 United Feature Syndicate, Inc.

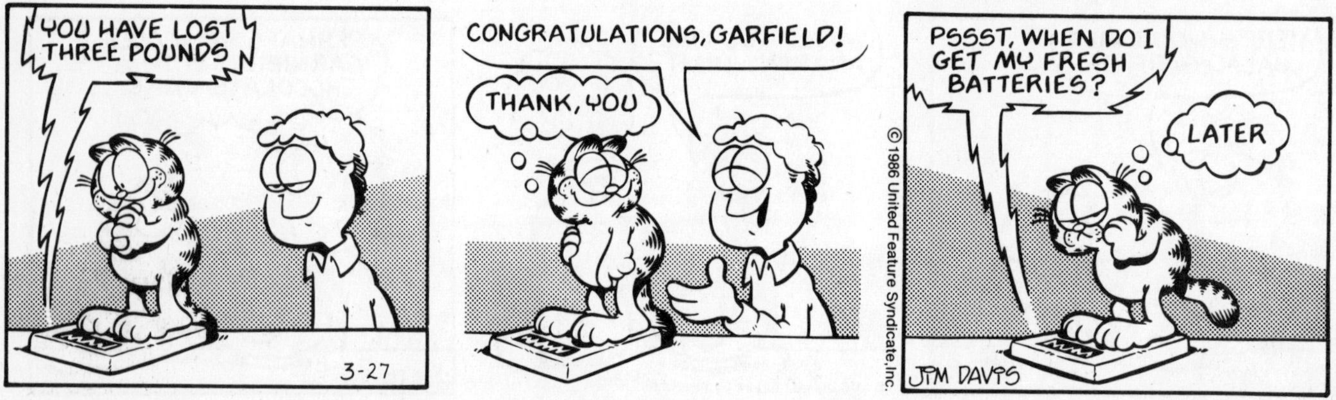
YOU HAVE LOST THREE POUNDS
3-27
CONGRATULATIONS, GARFIELD!
THANK, YOU
© 1986 United Feature Syndicate, Inc.
PSSST, WHEN DO I GET MY FRESH BATTERIES?
LATER
JIM DAVIS

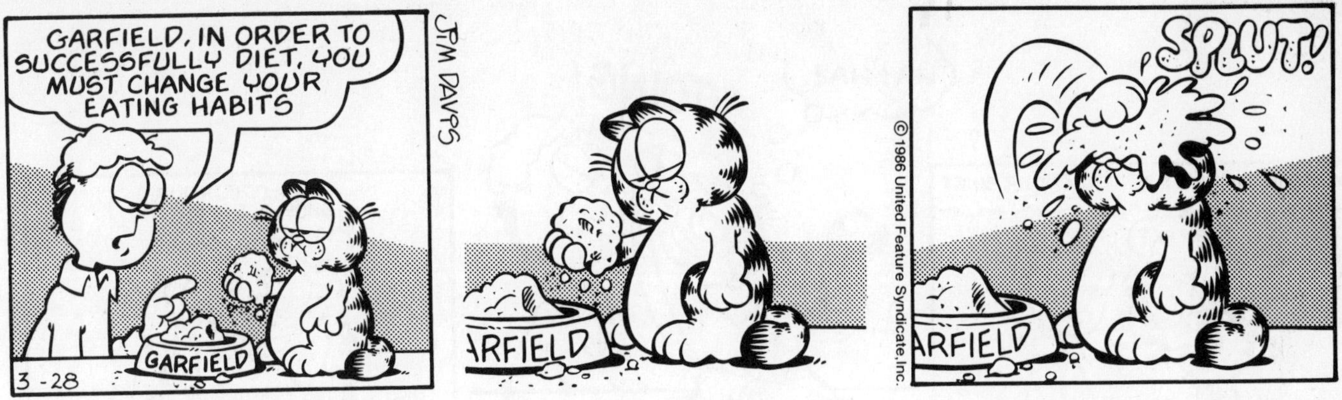
GARFIELD, IN ORDER TO SUCCESSFULLY DIET, YOU MUST CHANGE YOUR EATING HABITS
JIM DAVIS
GARFIELD
3-28
ARFIELD
SPLUT!
ARFIELD


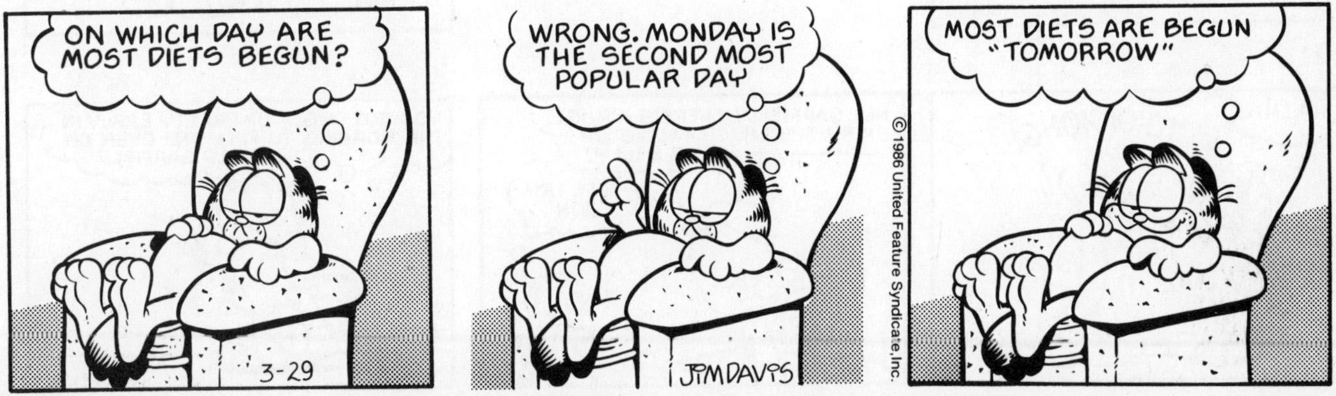
ON WHICH DAY ARE MOST DIETS BEGUN?
3-29
WRONG. MONDAY IS THE SECOND MOST POPULAR DAY
JIM DAVIS
MOST DIETS ARE BEGUN "TOMORROW"

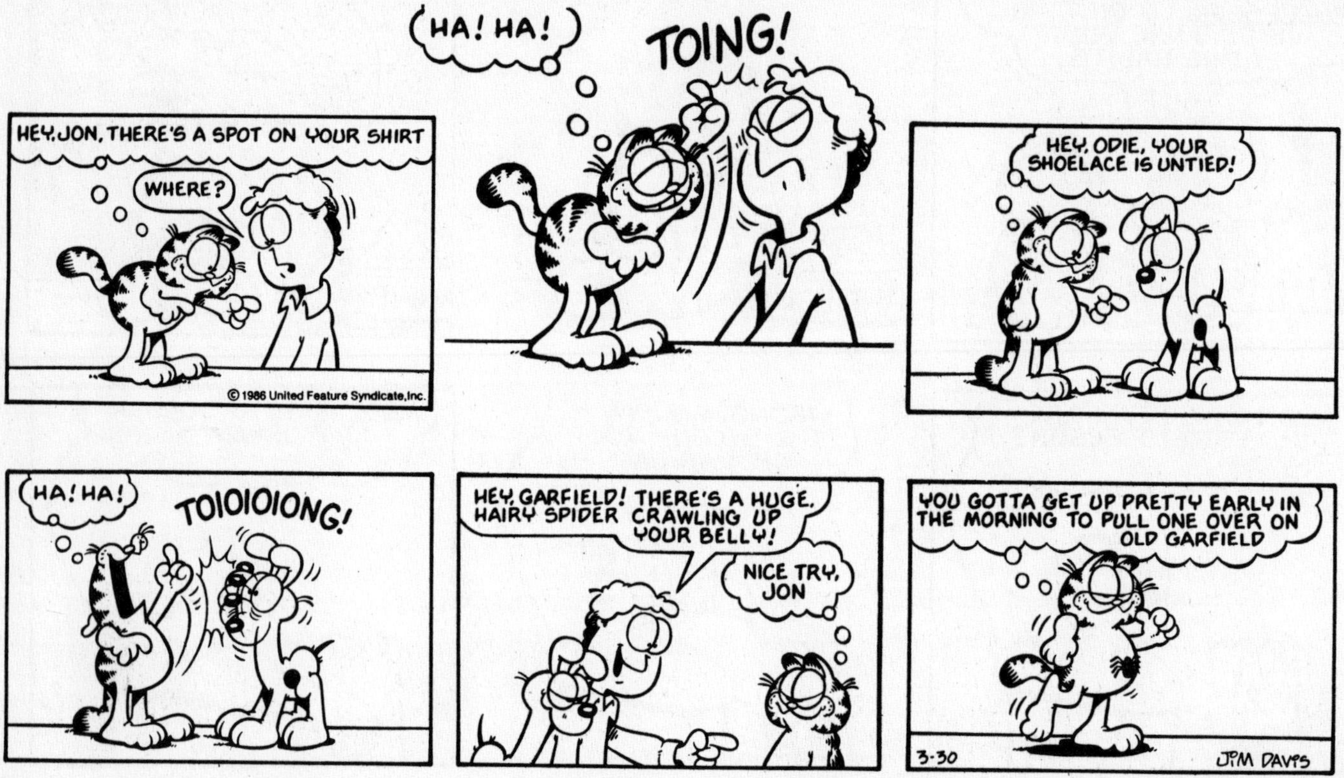
HEY, JON, THERE'S A SPOT ON YOUR SHIRT
WHERE?
HA! HA!
TOING!
© 1986 United Feature Syndicate, Inc.
HEY, ODIE, YOUR SHOELACE IS UNTIED!
HA! HA!
TOIOIOIONG!
HEY, GARFIELD! THERE'S A HUGE, HAIRY SPIDER CRAWLING UP YOUR BELLY!
NICE TRY, JON
YOU GOTTA GET UP PRETTY EARLY IN THE MORNING TO PULL ONE OVER ON OLD GARFIELD
3-30
JIM DAVIS

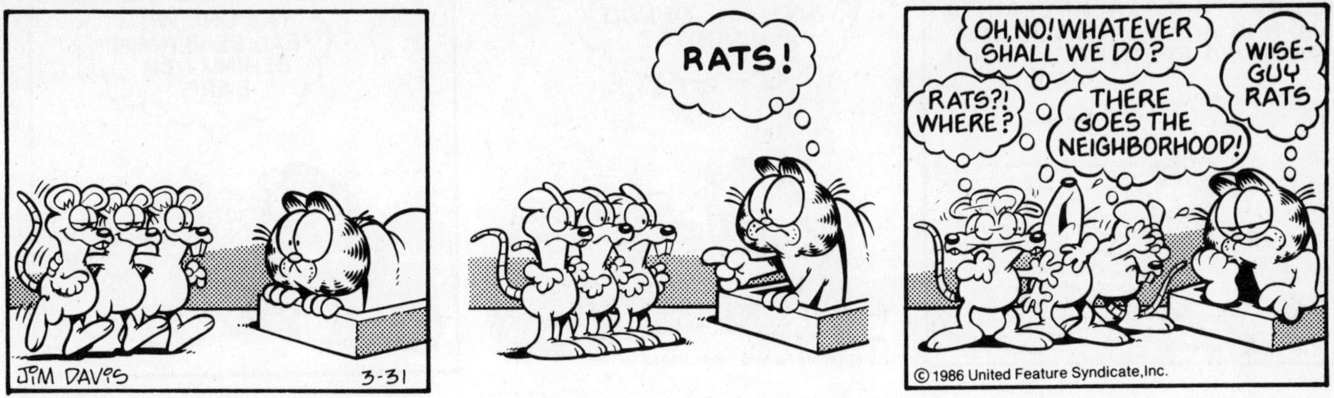
RATS!
RATS?! WHERE?
OH, NO! WHATEVER SHALL WE DO?
THERE GOES THE NEIGHBORHOOD!
WISE-GUY RATS
JIM DAVIS 3-31
© 1986 United Feature Syndicate, Inc.

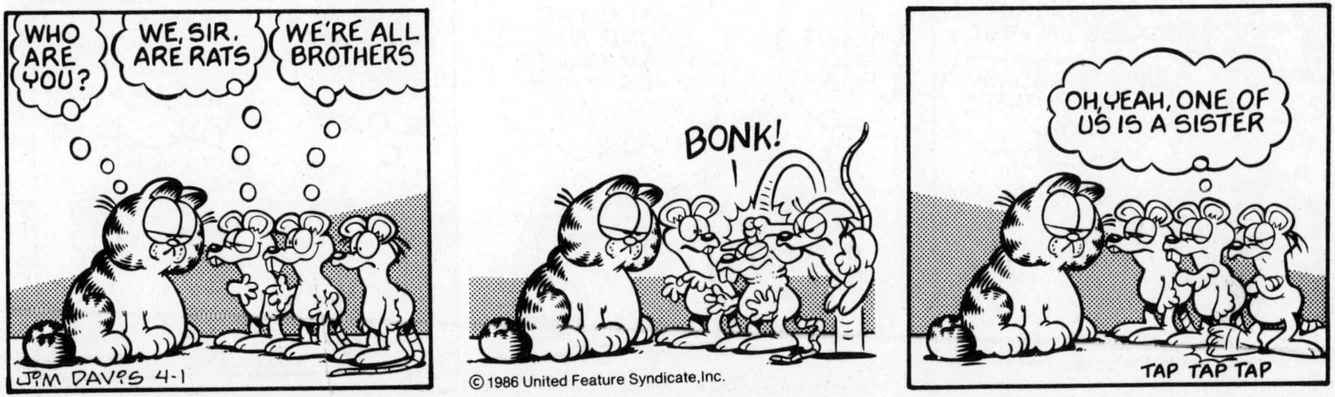
WHO ARE YOU?
WE, SIR, ARE RATS
WE'RE ALL BROTHERS
BONK!
OH, YEAH, ONE OF US IS A SISTER
TAP TAP TAP
JIM DAVIS 4-1
© 1986 United Feature Syndicate, Inc.

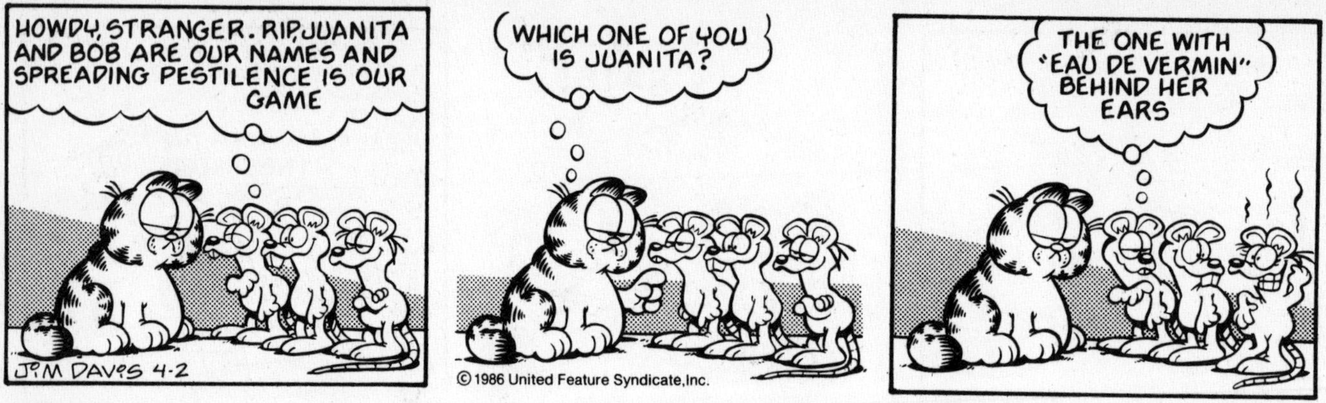
HOWDY, STRANGER. RIP, JUANITA AND BOB ARE OUR NAMES AND SPREADING PESTILENCE IS OUR GAME
JIM DAVIS 4-2
WHICH ONE OF YOU IS JUANITA?
© 1986 United Feature Syndicate, Inc.
THE ONE WITH "EAU DE VERMIN" BEHIND HER EARS

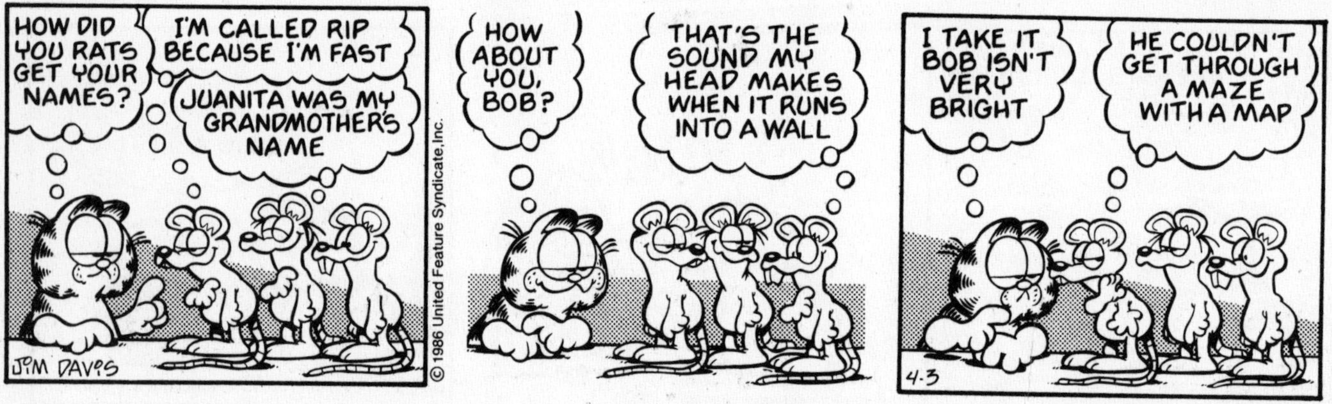
HOW DID YOU RATS GET YOUR NAMES?
I'M CALLED RIP BECAUSE I'M FAST
JUANITA WAS MY GRANDMOTHER'S NAME
JIM DAVIS
© 1986 United Feature Syndicate, Inc.
HOW ABOUT YOU, BOB?
THAT'S THE SOUND MY HEAD MAKES WHEN IT RUNS INTO A WALL
I TAKE IT BOB ISN'T VERY BRIGHT
HE COULDN'T GET THROUGH A MAZE WITH A MAP
4-3

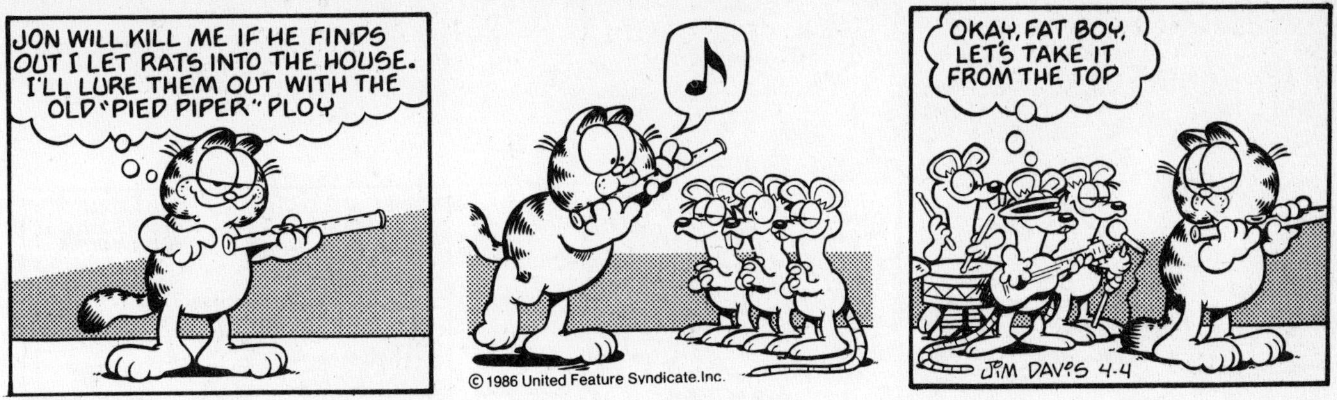
JON WILL KILL ME IF HE FINDS OUT I LET RATS INTO THE HOUSE. I'LL LURE THEM OUT WITH THE OLD "PIED PIPER" PLOY
♪
OKAY, FAT BOY, LET'S TAKE IT FROM THE TOP
© 1986 United Feature Syndicate.Inc.
JIM DAVIS 4-4

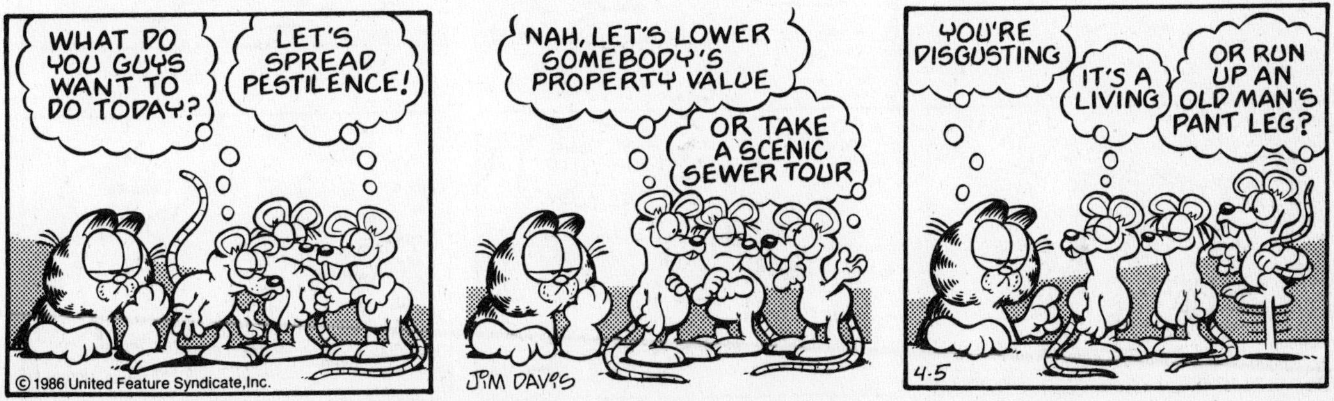
WHAT DO YOU GUYS WANT TO DO TODAY?
LET'S SPREAD PESTILENCE!
NAH, LET'S LOWER SOMEBODY'S PROPERTY VALUE
OR TAKE A SCENIC SEWER TOUR
YOU'RE DISGUSTING
IT'S A LIVING
OR RUN UP AN OLD MAN'S PANT LEG?
© 1986 United Feature Syndicate,Inc.
JIM DAVIS
4-5

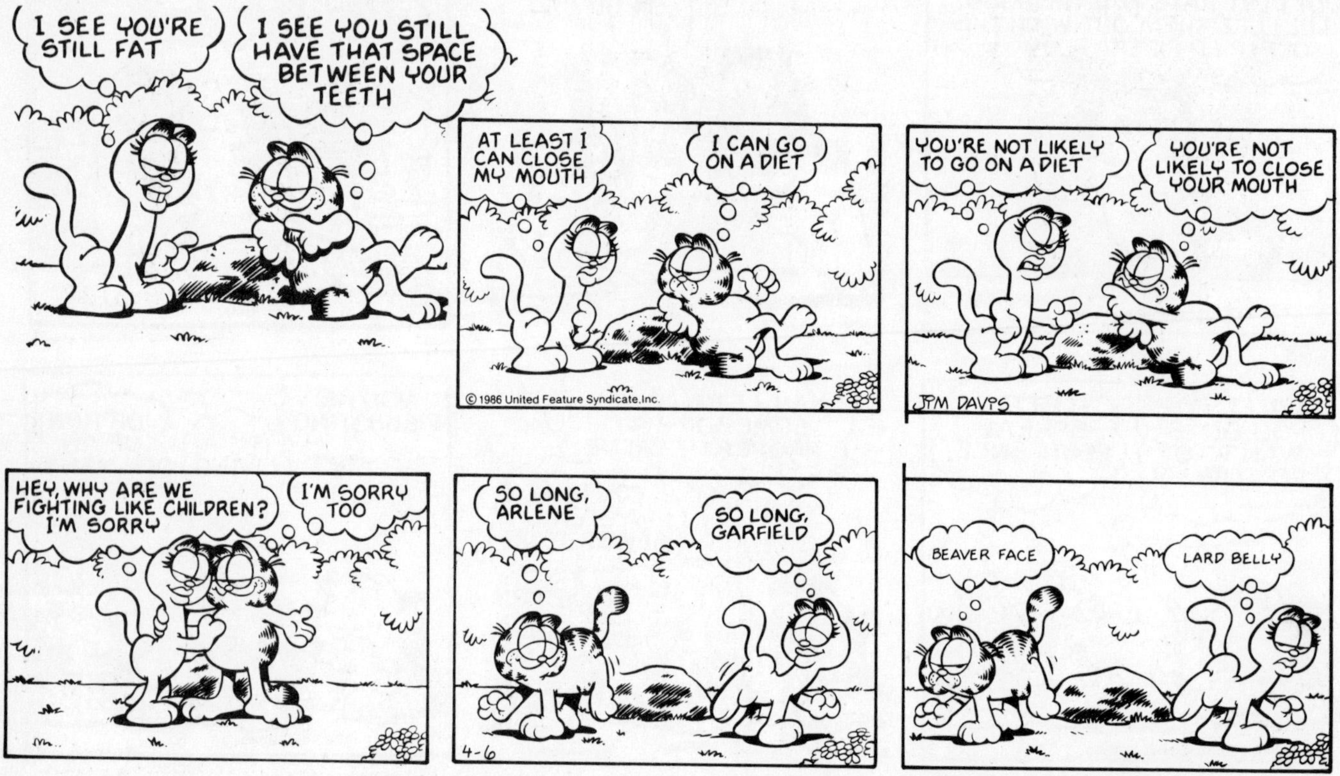
I SEE YOU'RE STILL FAT
I SEE YOU STILL HAVE THAT SPACE BETWEEN YOUR TEETH
AT LEAST I CAN CLOSE MY MOUTH
I CAN GO ON A DIET
© 1986 United Feature Syndicate, Inc.
YOU'RE NOT LIKELY TO GO ON A DIET
YOU'RE NOT LIKELY TO CLOSE YOUR MOUTH
JIM DAVIS
HEY, WHY ARE WE FIGHTING LIKE CHILDREN? I'M SORRY
I'M SORRY TOO
SO LONG, ARLENE
SO LONG, GARFIELD
4-6
BEAVER FACE
LARD BELLY

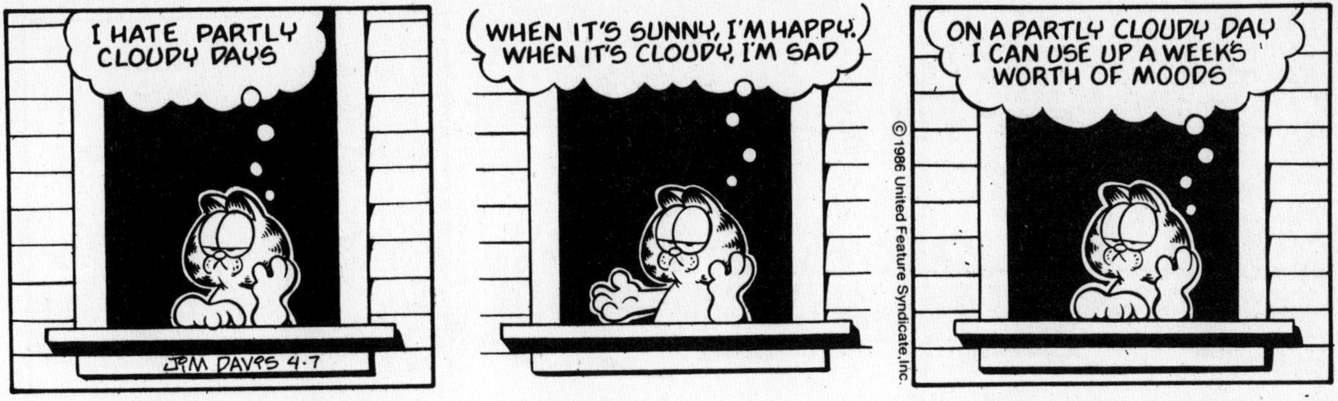
I HATE PARTLY CLOUDY DAYS
JIM DAVIS 4-7
WHEN IT'S SUNNY, I'M HAPPY. WHEN IT'S CLOUDY, I'M SAD
© 1986 United Feature Syndicate, Inc.
ON A PARTLY CLOUDY DAY I CAN USE UP A WEEK'S WORTH OF MOODS

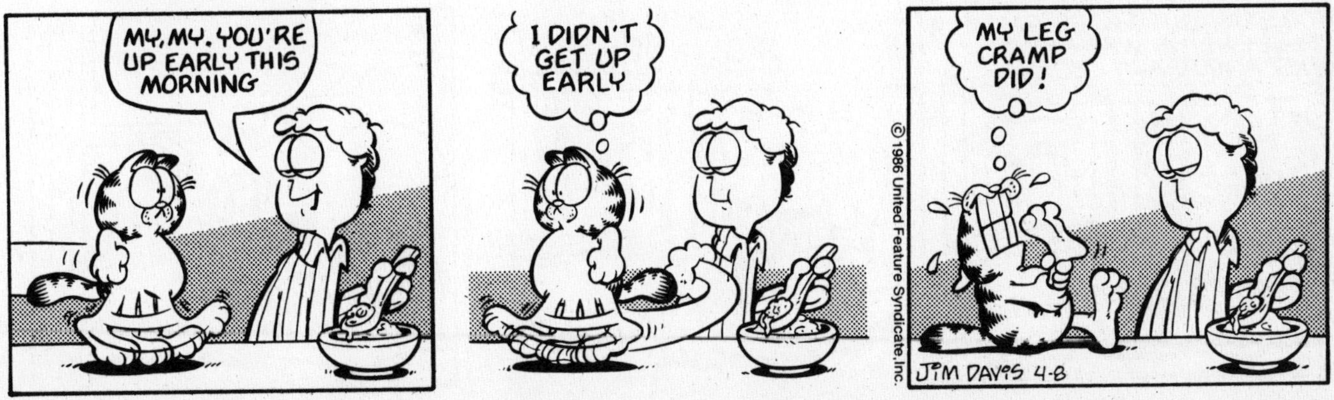
MY, MY. YOU'RE UP EARLY THIS MORNING
I DIDN'T GET UP EARLY
© 1986 United Feature Syndicate, Inc.
MY LEG CRAMP DID!
JIM DAVIS 4-8

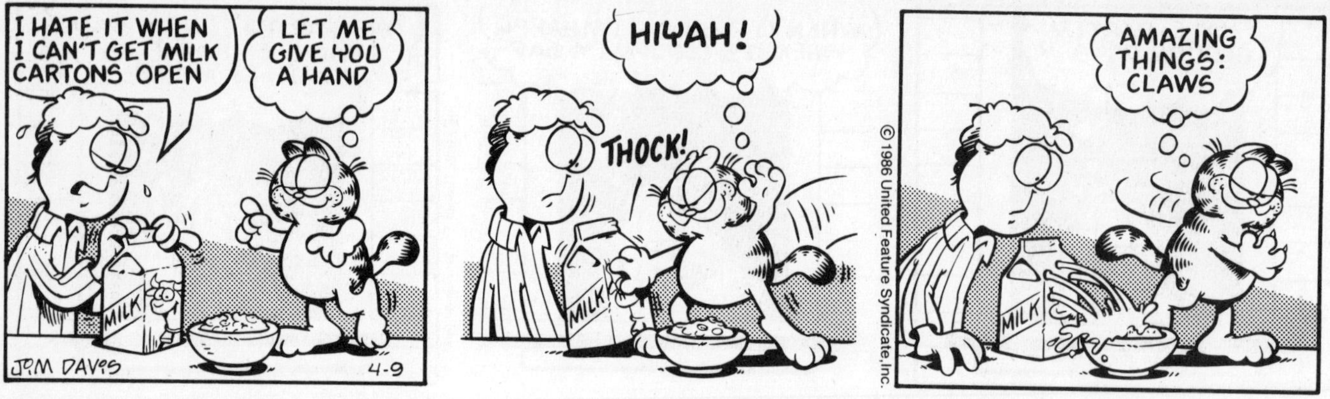
I HATE IT WHEN I CAN'T GET MILK CARTONS OPEN
LET ME GIVE YOU A HAND
MILK
JIM DAVIS
4-9
HIYAH!
THOCK!
MILK
© 1986 United Feature Syndicate, Inc.
AMAZING THINGS: CLAWS
MILK

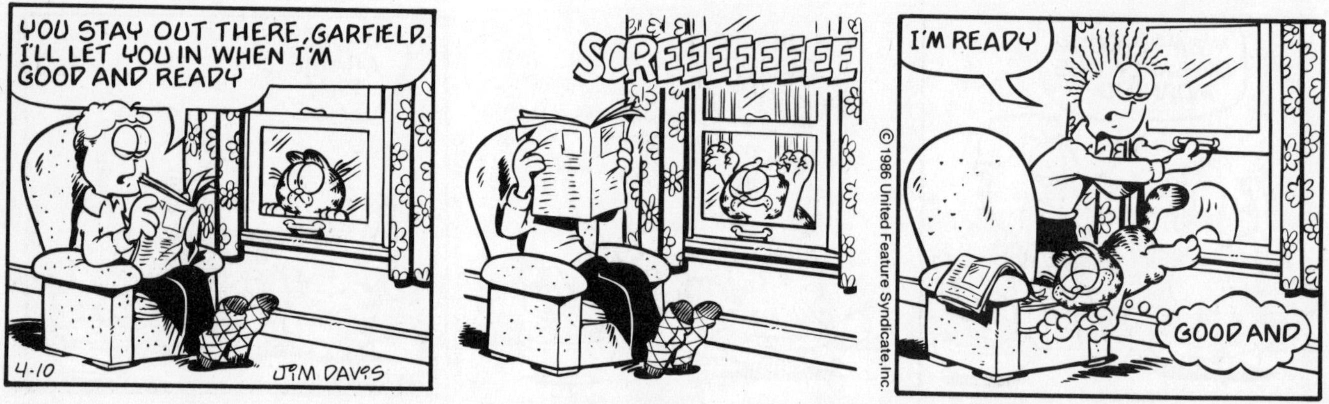
YOU STAY OUT THERE, GARFIELD. I'LL LET YOU IN WHEN I'M GOOD AND READY
4-10
JIM DAVIS
SCREEEEEEEEE
© 1986 United Feature Syndicate, Inc.
I'M READY
GOOD AND

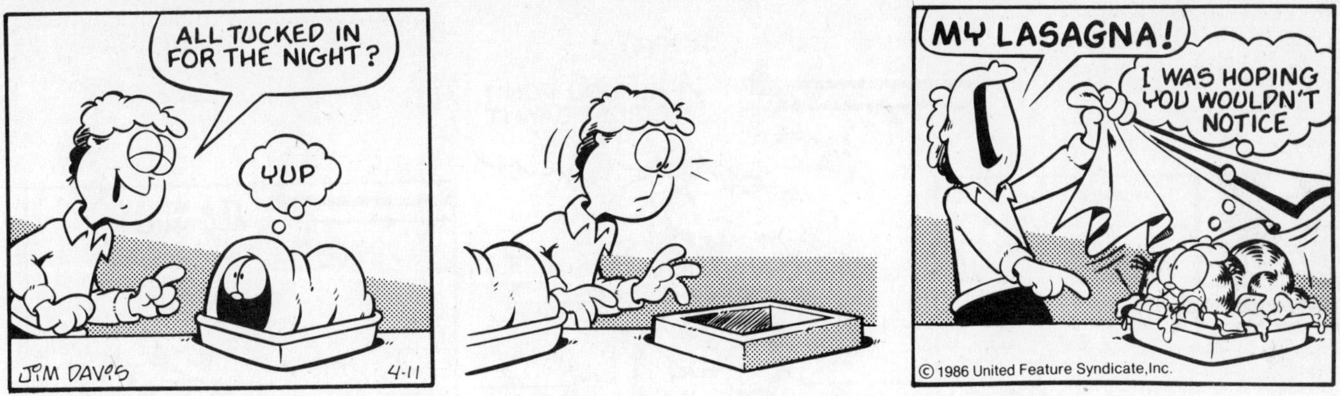
ALL TUCKED IN FOR THE NIGHT?
YUP
MY LASAGNA!
I WAS HOPING YOU WOULDN'T NOTICE
JIM DAVIS
4-11
© 1986 United Feature Syndicate, Inc.

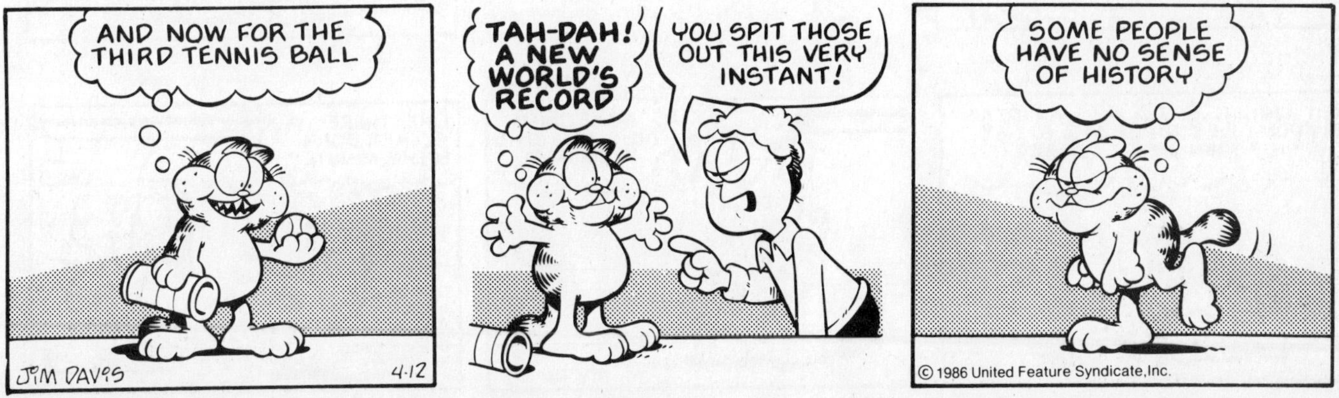
AND NOW FOR THE THIRD TENNIS BALL
TAH-DAH! A NEW WORLD'S RECORD
YOU SPIT THOSE OUT THIS VERY INSTANT!
SOME PEOPLE HAVE NO SENSE OF HISTORY
JIM DAVIS
4-12
© 1986 United Feature Syndicate, Inc.

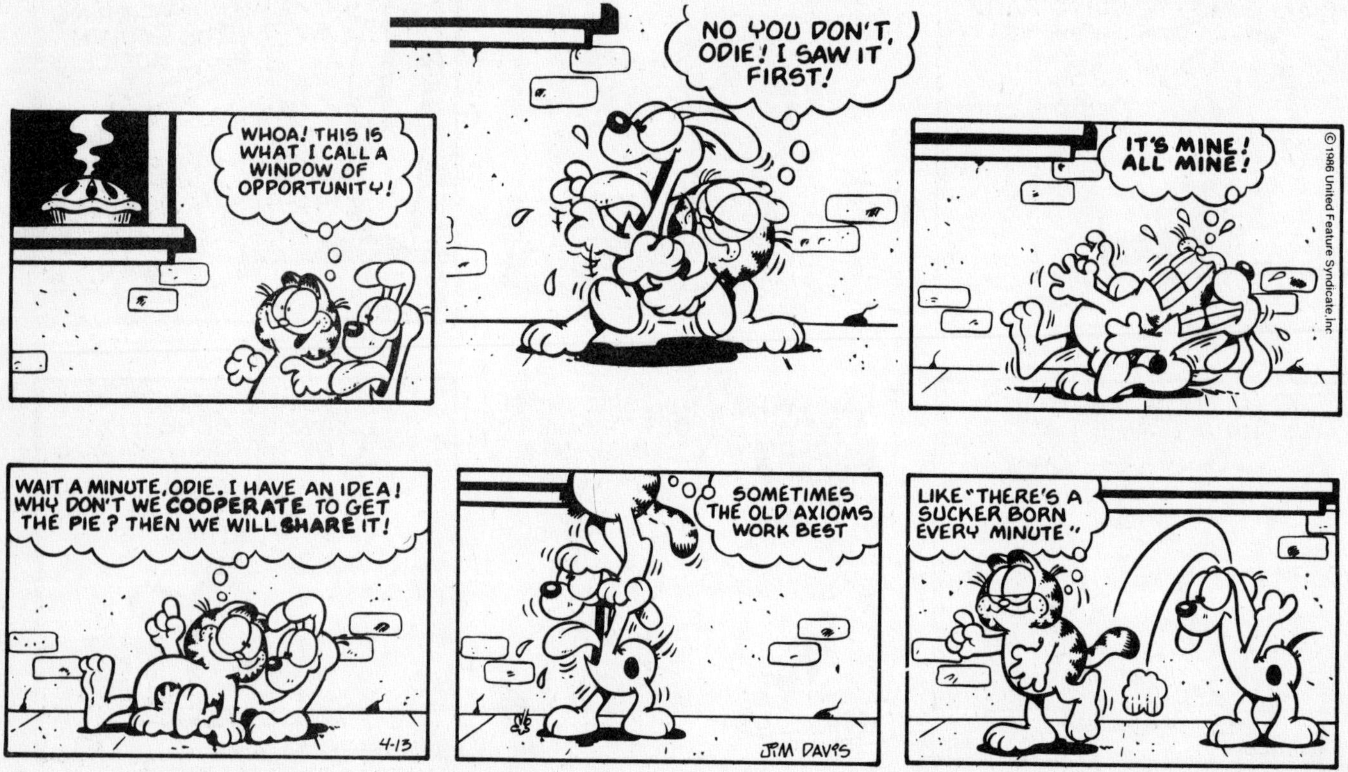

WHOA! THIS IS WHAT I CALL A WINDOW OF OPPORTUNITY!
NO YOU DON'T, ODIE! I SAW IT FIRST!
IT'S MINE! ALL MINE!
© 1986 United Feature Syndicate, Inc.
WAIT A MINUTE, ODIE. I HAVE AN IDEA! WHY DON'T WE COOPERATE TO GET THE PIE? THEN WE WILL SHARE IT!
4-13
SOMETIMES THE OLD AXIOMS WORK BEST
JIM DAVIS
LIKE "THERE'S A SUCKER BORN EVERY MINUTE"

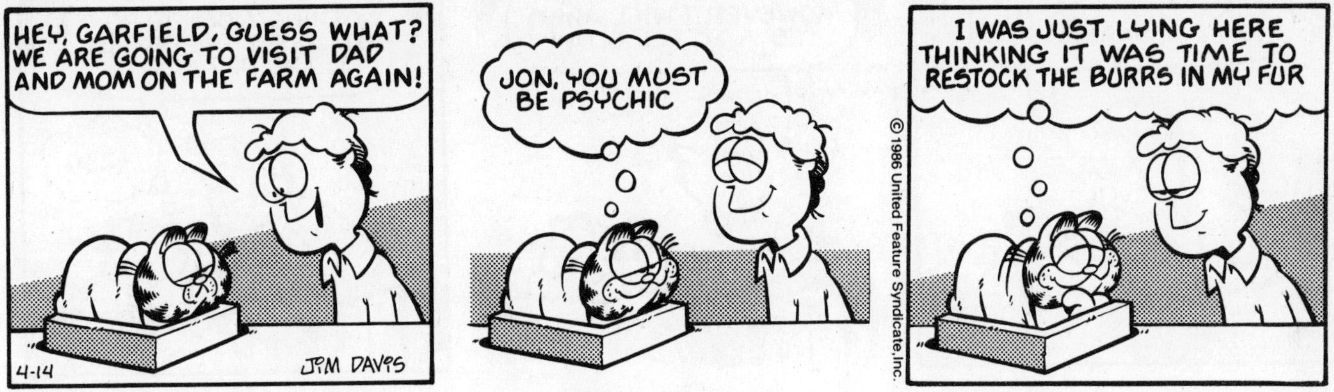
HEY, GARFIELD, GUESS WHAT? WE ARE GOING TO VISIT DAD AND MOM ON THE FARM AGAIN!
4-14
JIM DAVIS
JON, YOU MUST BE PSYCHIC
I WAS JUST LYING HERE THINKING IT WAS TIME TO RESTOCK THE BURRS IN MY FUR
© 1986 United Feature Syndicate, Inc.

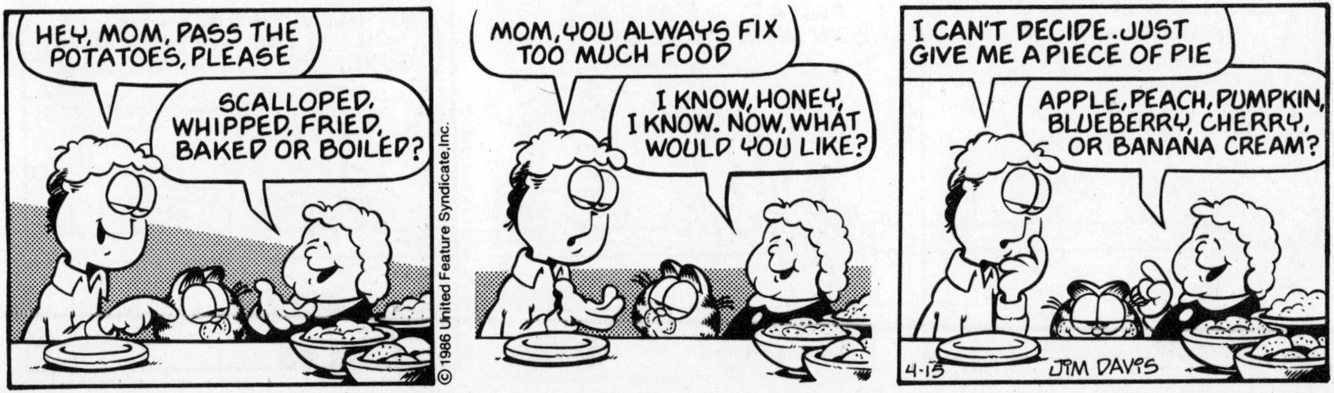
HEY, MOM, PASS THE POTATOES, PLEASE
SCALLOPED, WHIPPED, FRIED, BAKED OR BOILED?
© 1986 United Feature Syndicate, Inc.
MOM, YOU ALWAYS FIX TOO MUCH FOOD
I KNOW, HONEY, I KNOW. NOW, WHAT WOULD YOU LIKE?
I CAN'T DECIDE. JUST GIVE ME A PIECE OF PIE
APPLE, PEACH, PUMPKIN, BLUEBERRY, CHERRY, OR BANANA CREAM?
4-15
JIM DAVIS

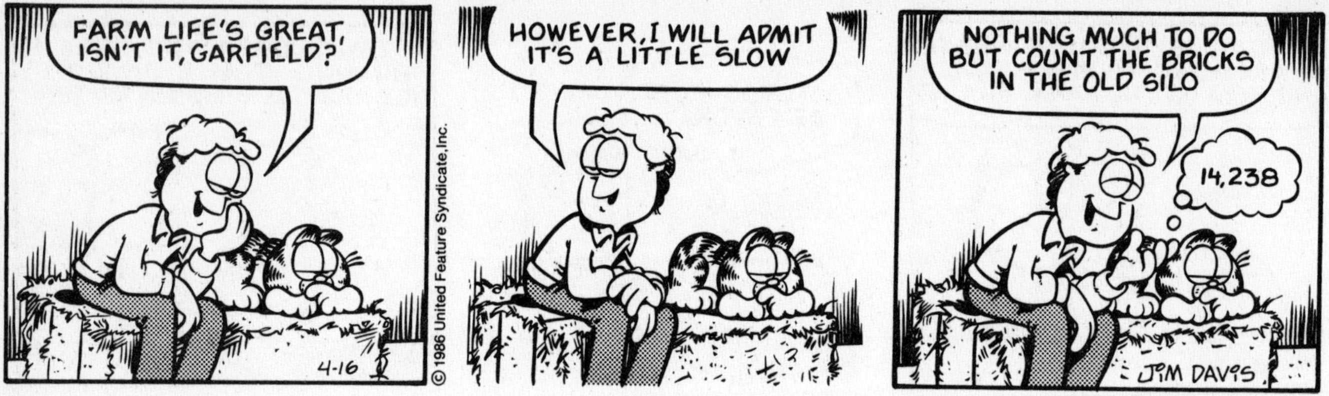
FARM LIFE'S GREAT, ISN'T IT, GARFIELD?
4-16
© 1986 United Feature Syndicate, Inc.
HOWEVER, I WILL ADMIT IT'S A LITTLE SLOW
NOTHING MUCH TO DO BUT COUNT THE BRICKS IN THE OLD SILO
14,238
JIM DAVIS

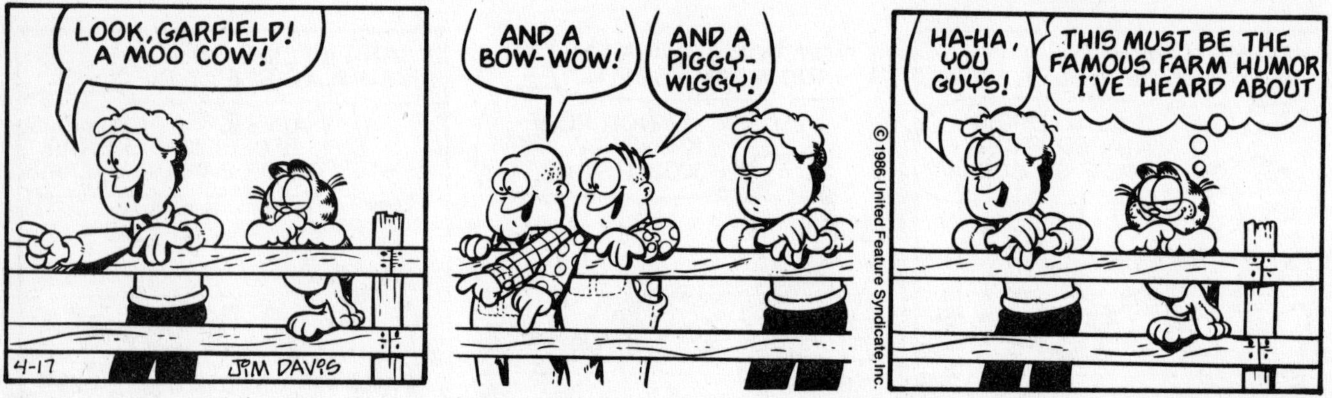
LOOK, GARFIELD! A MOO COW!
4-17
JIM DAVIS
AND A BOW-WOW!
AND A PIGGY-WIGGY!
© 1986 United Feature Syndicate, Inc.
HA-HA, YOU GUYS!
THIS MUST BE THE FAMOUS FARM HUMOR I'VE HEARD ABOUT

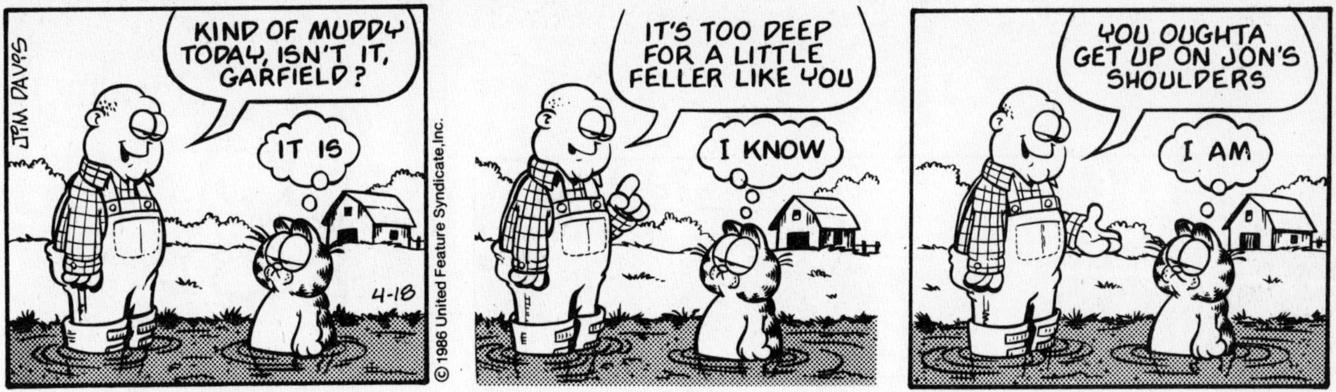
JIM DAVIS
KIND OF MUDDY TODAY, ISN'T IT, GARFIELD?
IT IS
4-18
© 1986 United Feature Syndicate, Inc.
IT'S TOO DEEP FOR A LITTLE FELLER LIKE YOU
I KNOW
YOU OUGHTA GET UP ON JON'S SHOULDERS
I AM

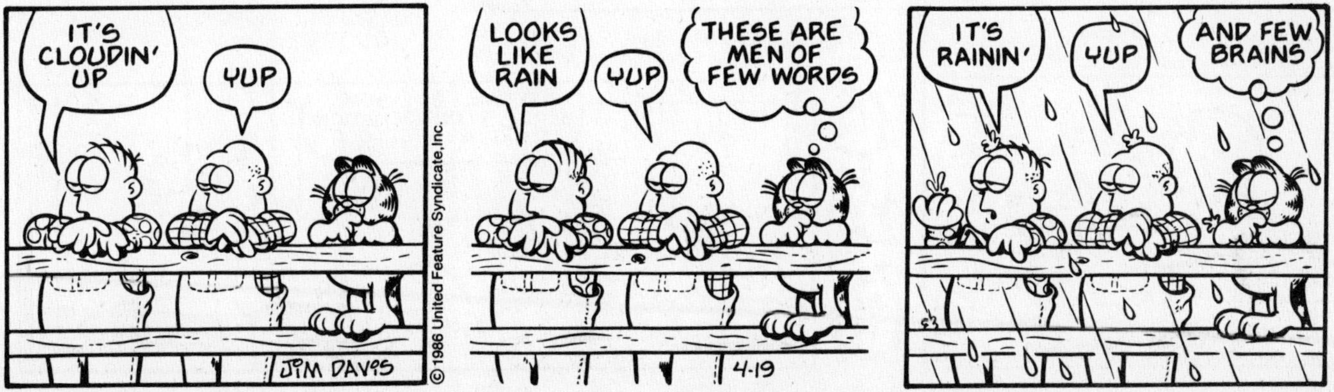
IT'S CLOUDIN' UP
YUP
JIM DAVIS
© 1986 United Feature Syndicate, Inc.
LOOKS LIKE RAIN
YUP
THESE ARE MEN OF FEW WORDS
4-19
IT'S RAININ'
YUP
AND FEW BRAINS

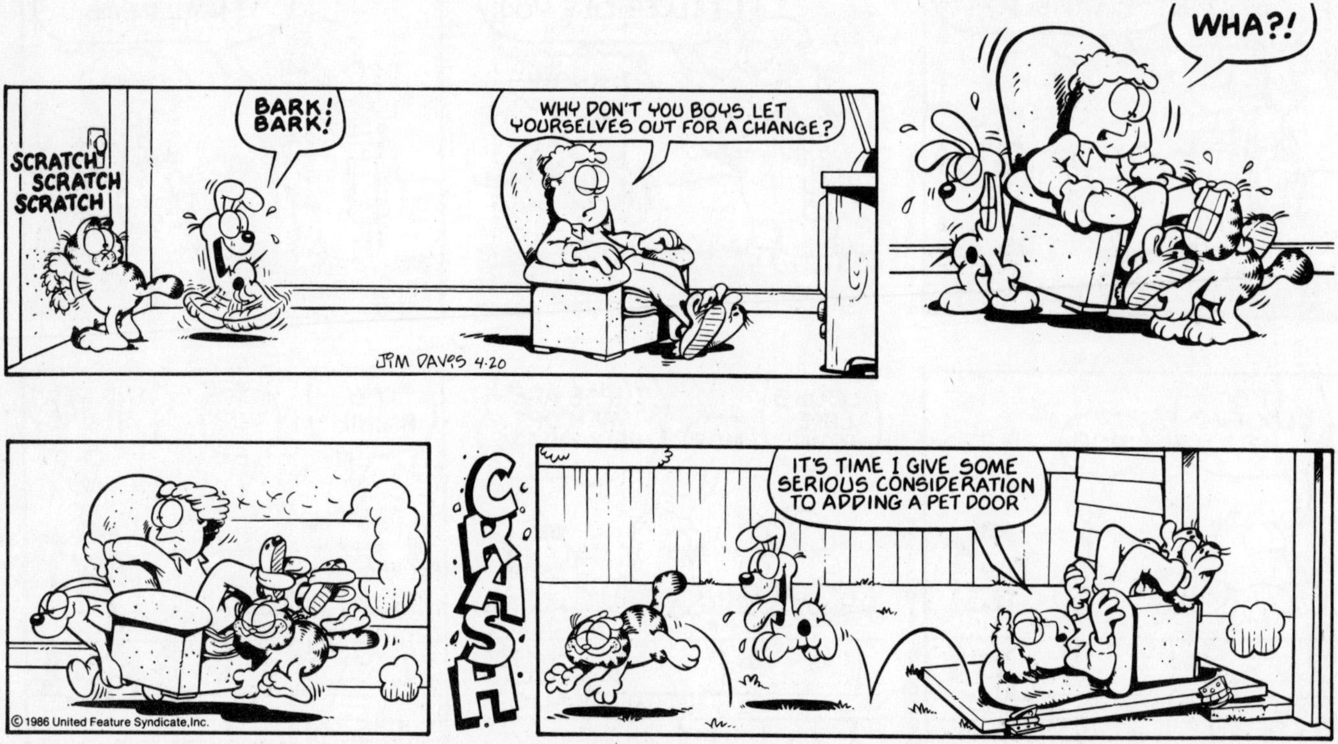

SCRATCH SCRATCH SCRATCH
BARK! BARK!
WHY DON'T YOU BOYS LET YOURSELVES OUT FOR A CHANGE?
JIM DAVIS 4-20
WHA?!
© 1986 United Feature Syndicate, Inc.
CRASH
IT'S TIME I GIVE SOME SERIOUS CONSIDERATION TO ADDING A PET DOOR

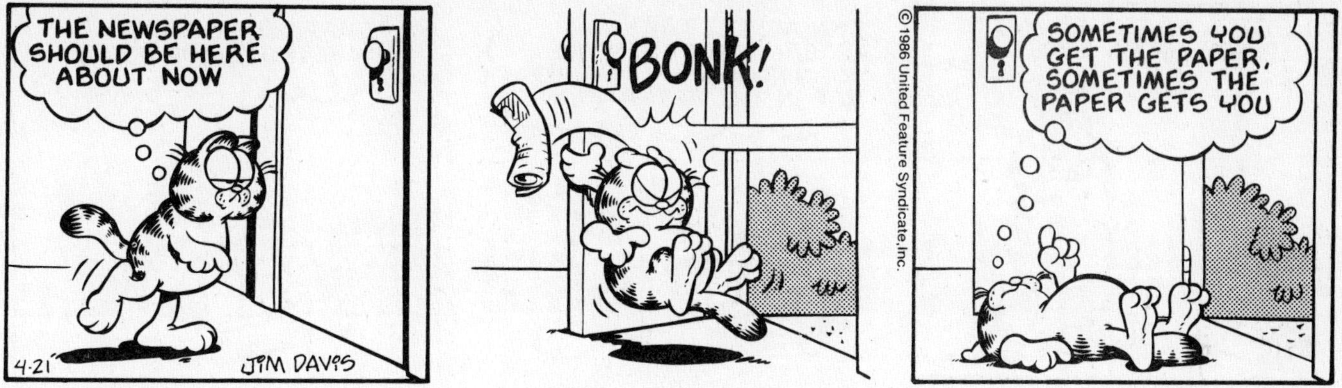
THE NEWSPAPER SHOULD BE HERE ABOUT NOW
4·21
JIM DAVIS
BONK!
© 1986 United Feature Syndicate,Inc.
SOMETIMES YOU GET THE PAPER, SOMETIMES THE PAPER GETS YOU

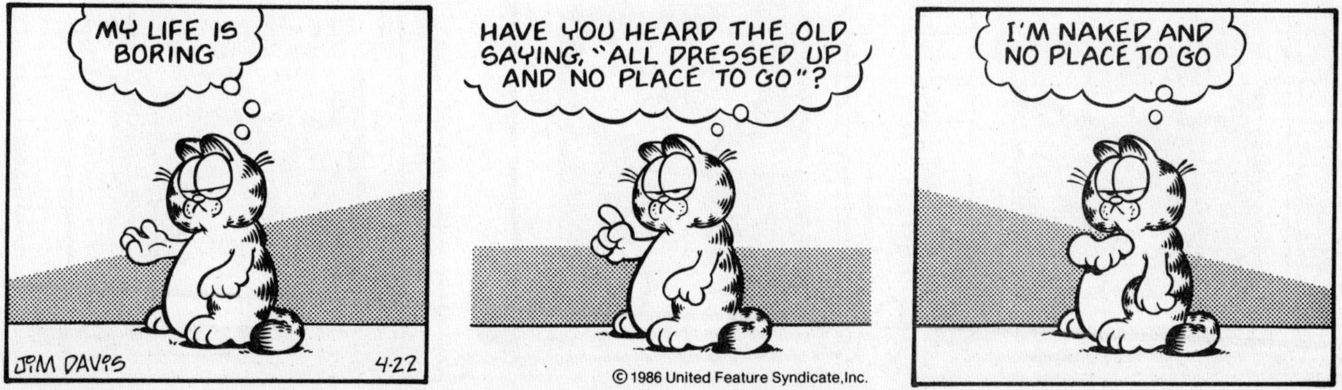
MY LIFE IS BORING
JIM DAVIS
4·22
HAVE YOU HEARD THE OLD SAYING, "ALL DRESSED UP AND NO PLACE TO GO"?
© 1986 United Feature Syndicate,Inc.
I'M NAKED AND NO PLACE TO GO

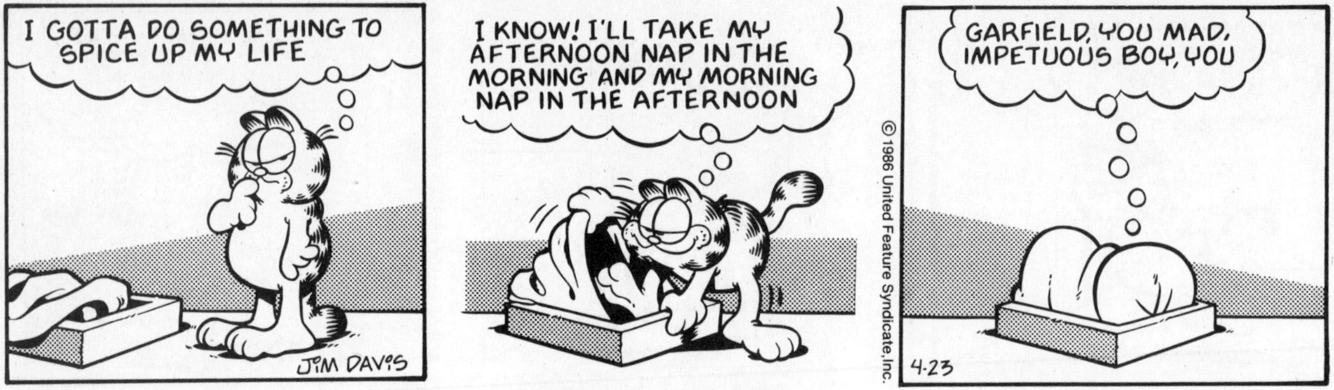
I GOTTA DO SOMETHING TO SPICE UP MY LIFE
JIM DAVIS
I KNOW! I'LL TAKE MY AFTERNOON NAP IN THE MORNING AND MY MORNING NAP IN THE AFTERNOON
© 1986 United Feature Syndicate, Inc.
GARFIELD, YOU MAD, IMPETUOUS BOY, YOU
4-23

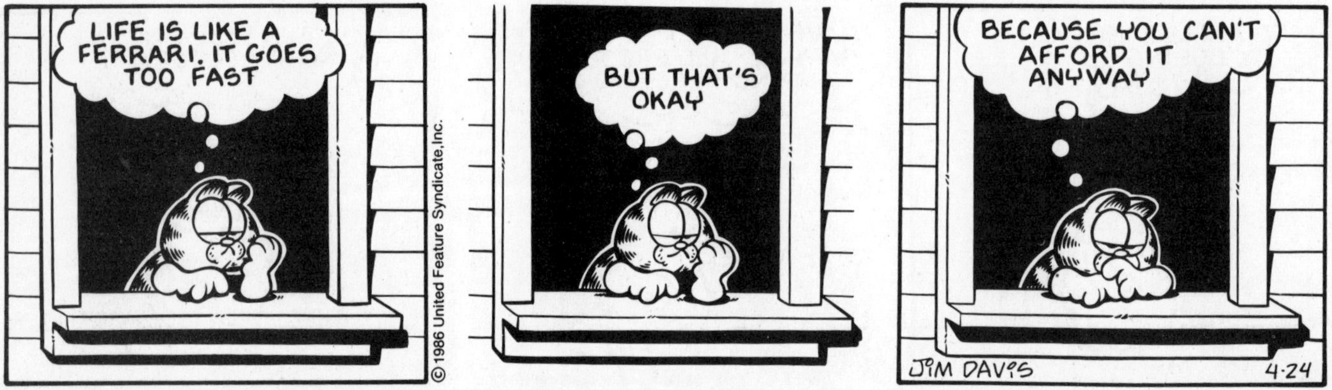
LIFE IS LIKE A FERRARI. IT GOES TOO FAST
© 1986 United Feature Syndicate, Inc.
BUT THAT'S OKAY
BECAUSE YOU CAN'T AFFORD IT ANYWAY
JIM DAVIS
4-24

I SHALL NOW MEDITATE IN ORDER TO ENRICH MY LIFE
4-25
JIM DAVIS
THERE IS NOTHING LIKE MEDITATION TO GET IN TOUCH WITH ONE'S SELF
© 1986 United Feature Syndicate, Inc.
SELF... IF YOU DON'T GET OUT OF THIS STUPID POSITION IN ABOUT THREE SECONDS, YOUR KNEECAPS ARE GOING TO FALL OFF!

LIFE IS LIKE A BIRDBATH. IT'S MADE OF CONCRETE, FILLED WITH WATER, AND UH... BIRDS LIKE TO SPLASH IN IT
BOY, THAT WAS DUMB. LIFE ISN'T ANYTHING LIKE A BIRDBATH
TAP TAP
© 1986 United Feature Syndicate, Inc.
LIFE... IS LIKE A SOCK MONKEY...
JIM DAVIS 4-26

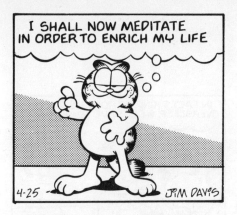

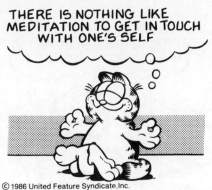

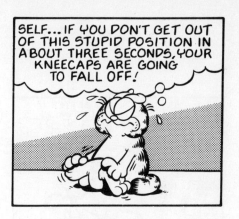

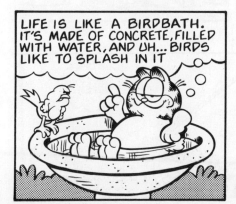

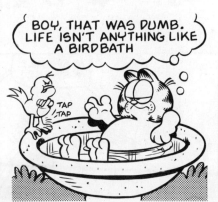

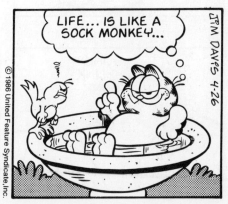

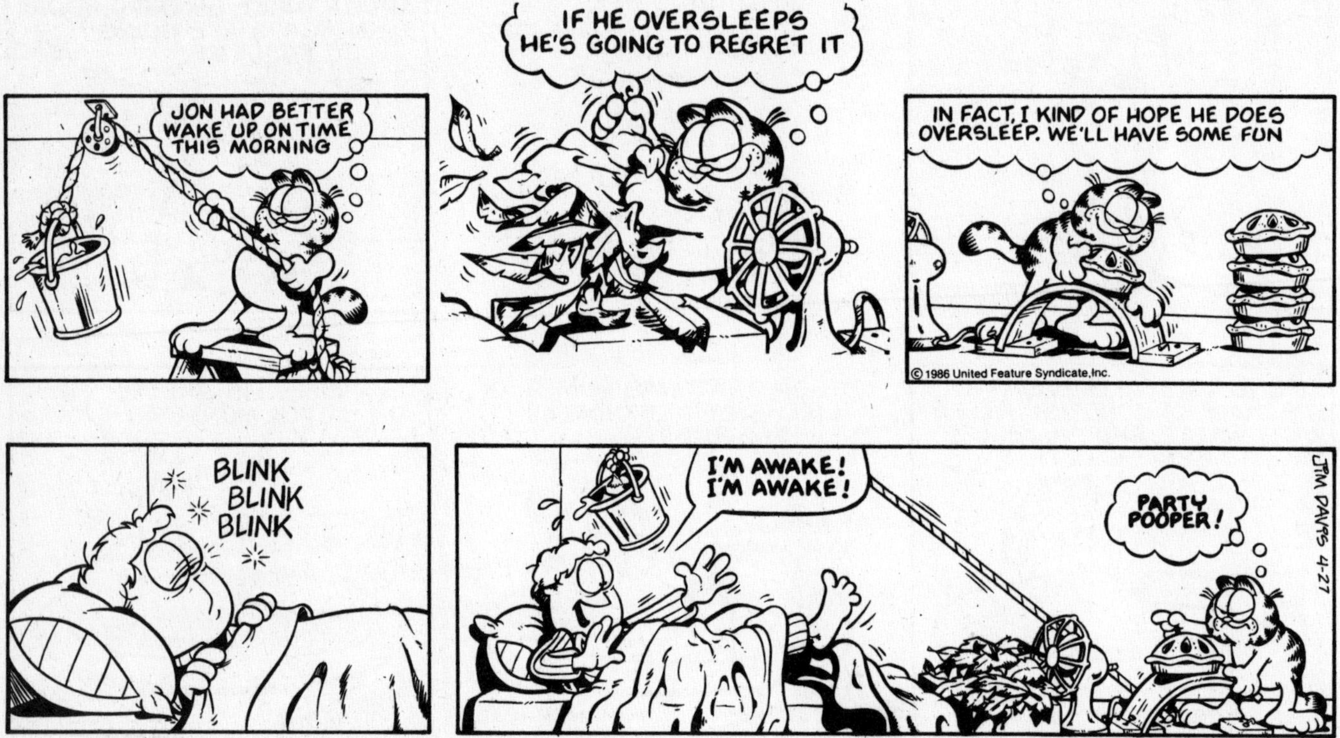

JON HAD BETTER WAKE UP ON TIME THIS MORNING
IF HE OVERSLEEPS HE'S GOING TO REGRET IT
IN FACT, I KIND OF HOPE HE DOES OVERSLEEP. WE'LL HAVE SOME FUN
© 1986 United Feature Syndicate, Inc.
BLINK BLINK BLINK
I'M AWAKE! I'M AWAKE!
PARTY POOPER!
JIM DAVIS 4-27

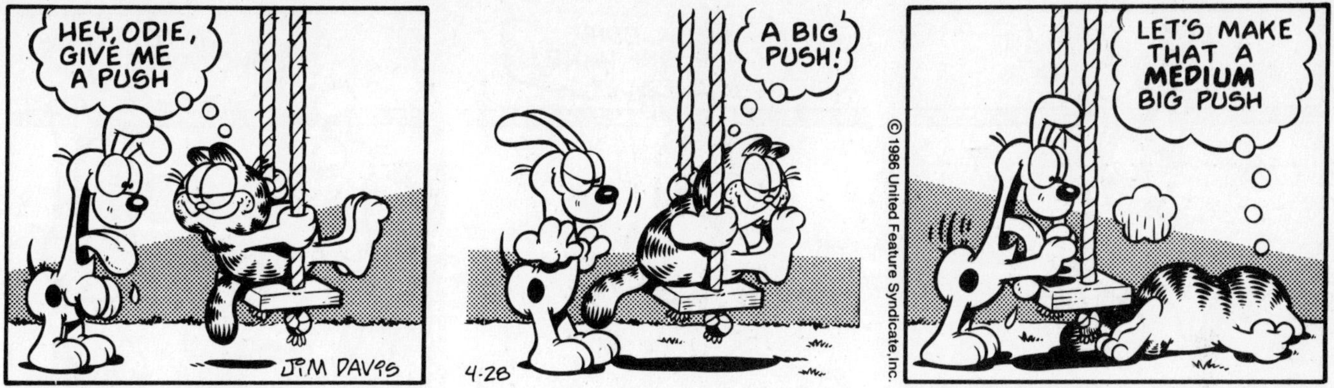
HEY, ODIE, GIVE ME A PUSH
JIM DAVIS
A BIG PUSH!
4-28
LET'S MAKE THAT A **MEDIUM** BIG PUSH


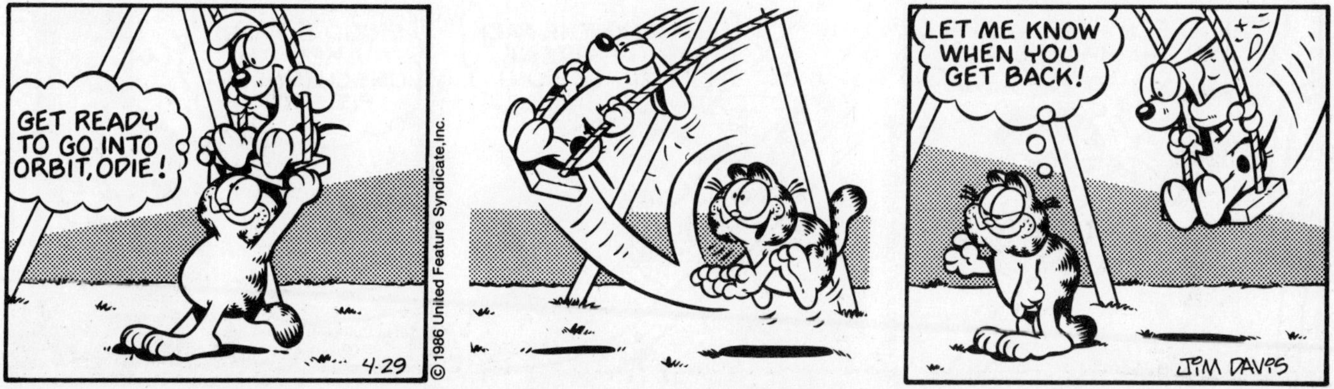
GET READY TO GO INTO ORBIT, ODIE!
4-29
LET ME KNOW WHEN YOU GET BACK!
JIM DAVIS

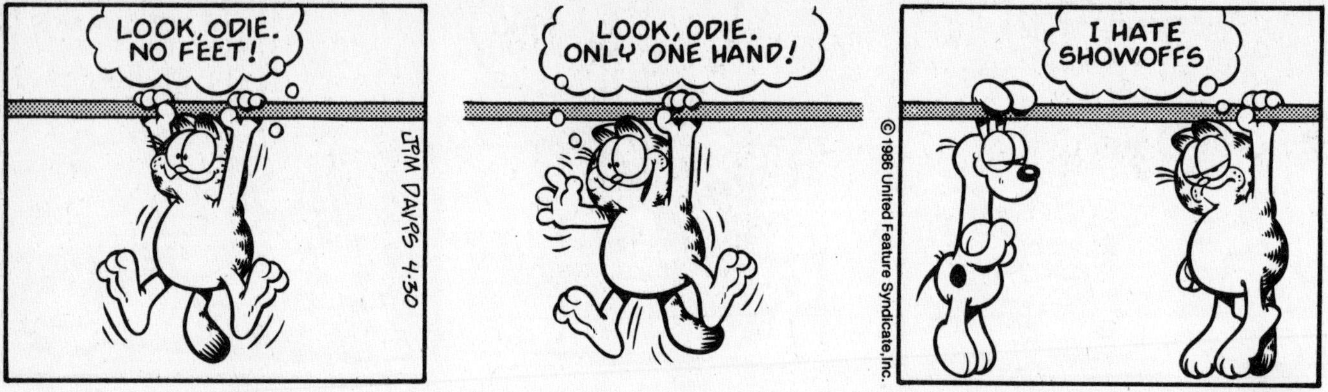
LOOK, ODIE. NO FEET!
JIM DAVIS 4-30
LOOK, ODIE. ONLY ONE HAND!
© 1986 United Feature Syndicate, Inc.
I HATE SHOWOFFS

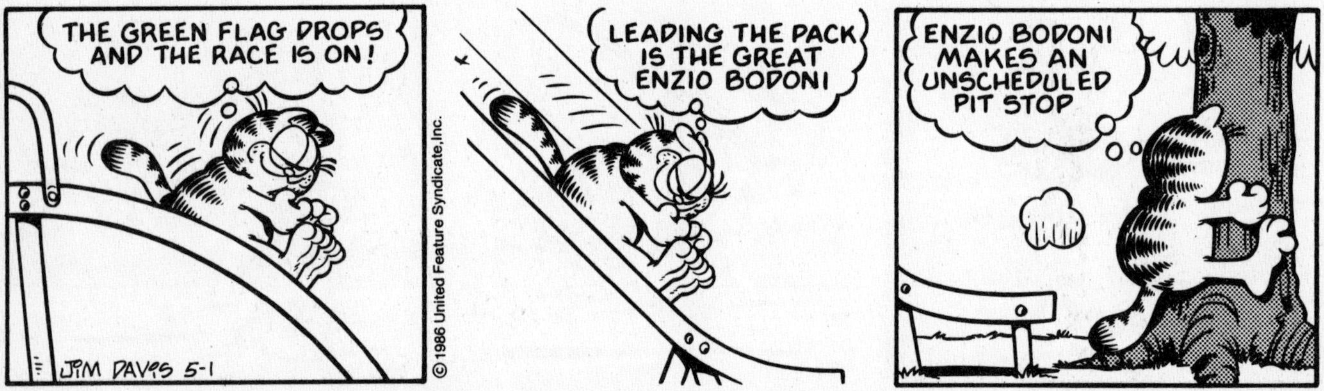
THE GREEN FLAG DROPS AND THE RACE IS ON!
JIM DAVIS 5-1
© 1986 United Feature Syndicate, Inc.
LEADING THE PACK IS THE GREAT ENZIO BODONI
ENZIO BODONI MAKES AN UNSCHEDULED PIT STOP

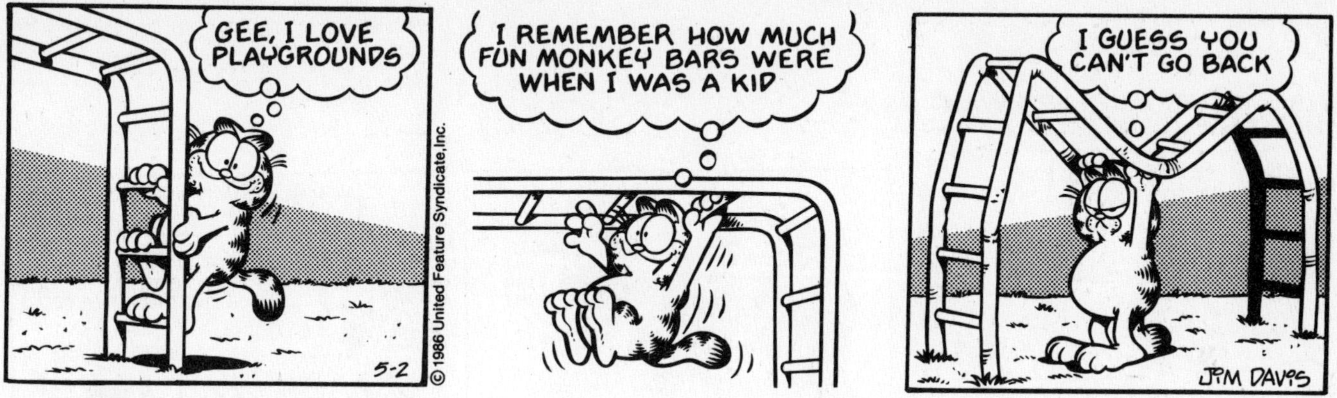
GEE, I LOVE PLAYGROUNDS
5-2
I REMEMBER HOW MUCH FUN MONKEY BARS WERE WHEN I WAS A KID
I GUESS YOU CAN'T GO BACK
JIM DAVIS
© 1986 United Feature Syndicate, Inc.

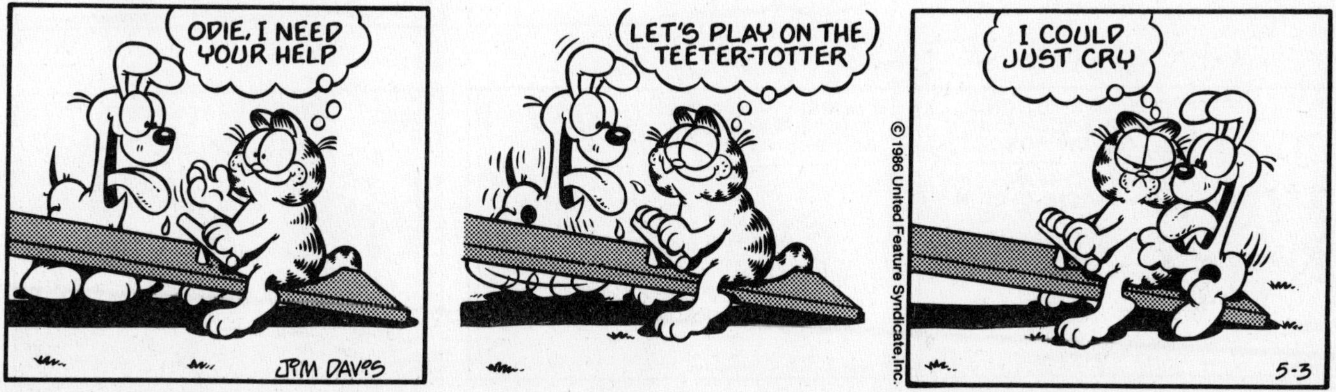
ODIE, I NEED YOUR HELP
JIM DAVIS
LET'S PLAY ON THE TEETER-TOTTER
I COULD JUST CRY
5-3
© 1986 United Feature Syndicate, Inc.

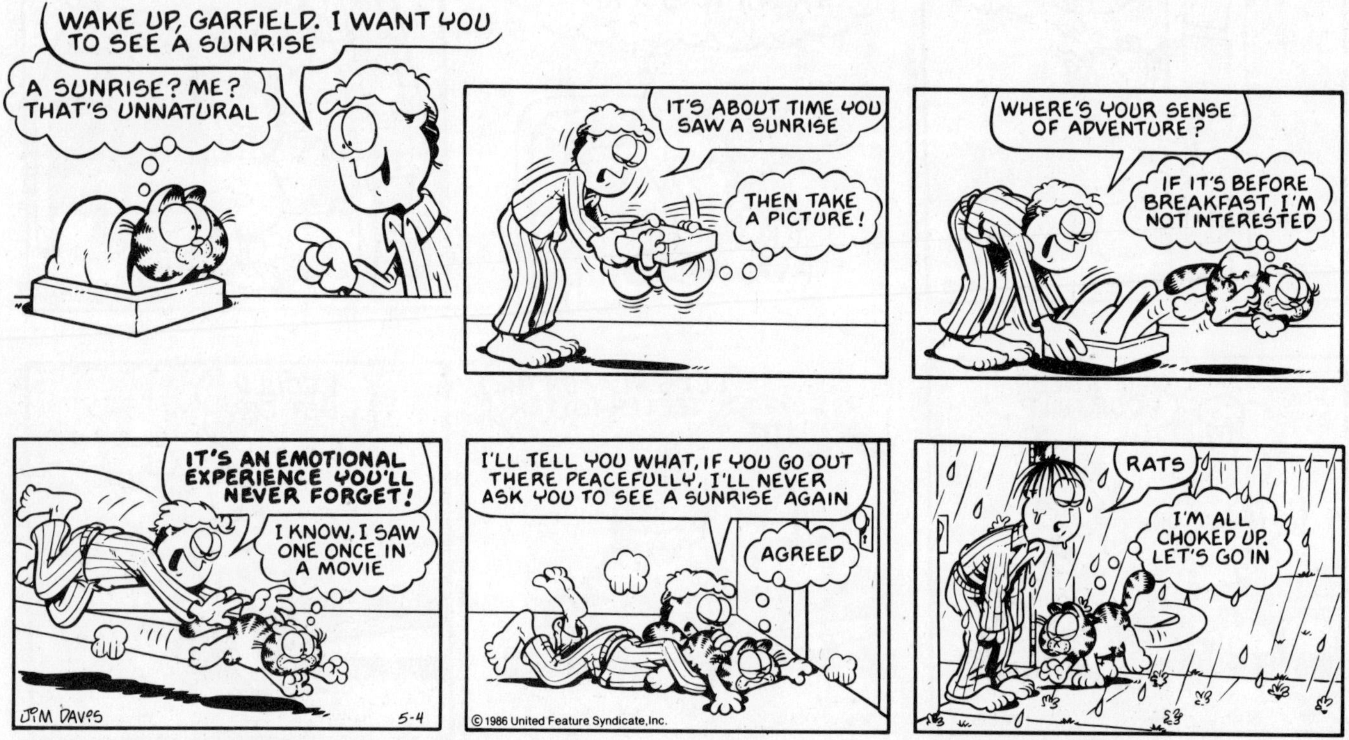
WAKE UP, GARFIELD. I WANT YOU TO SEE A SUNRISE
A SUNRISE? ME? THAT'S UNNATURAL
IT'S ABOUT TIME YOU SAW A SUNRISE
THEN TAKE A PICTURE!
WHERE'S YOUR SENSE OF ADVENTURE?
IF IT'S BEFORE BREAKFAST, I'M NOT INTERESTED
IT'S AN EMOTIONAL EXPERIENCE YOU'LL NEVER FORGET!
I KNOW. I SAW ONE ONCE IN A MOVIE
JIM DAVIS
5-4
I'LL TELL YOU WHAT, IF YOU GO OUT THERE PEACEFULLY, I'LL NEVER ASK YOU TO SEE A SUNRISE AGAIN
AGREED
© 1986 United Feature Syndicate, Inc.
RATS
I'M ALL CHOKED UP. LET'S GO IN

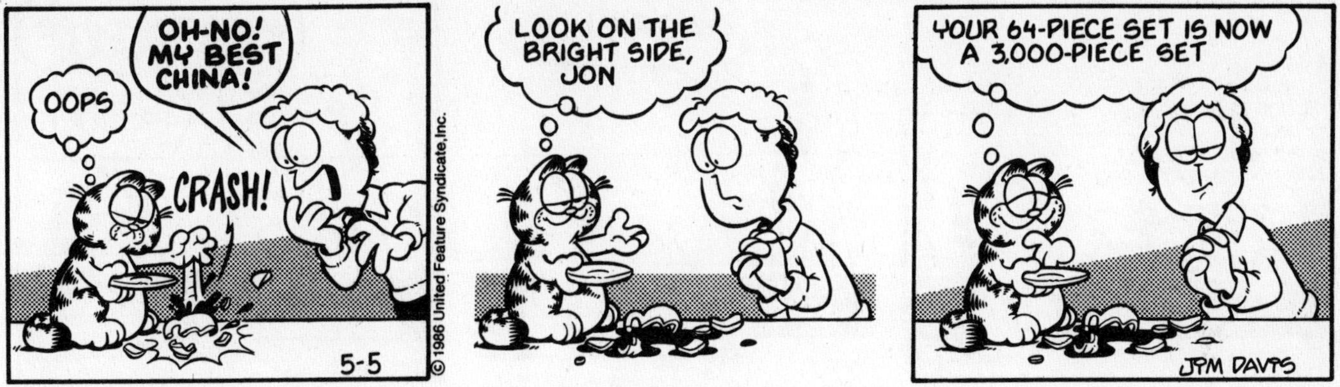
OOPS
OH-NO! MY BEST CHINA!
CRASH!
5-5
© 1986 United Feature Syndicate, Inc.
LOOK ON THE BRIGHT SIDE, JON
YOUR 64-PIECE SET IS NOW A 3,000-PIECE SET
JIM DAVIS

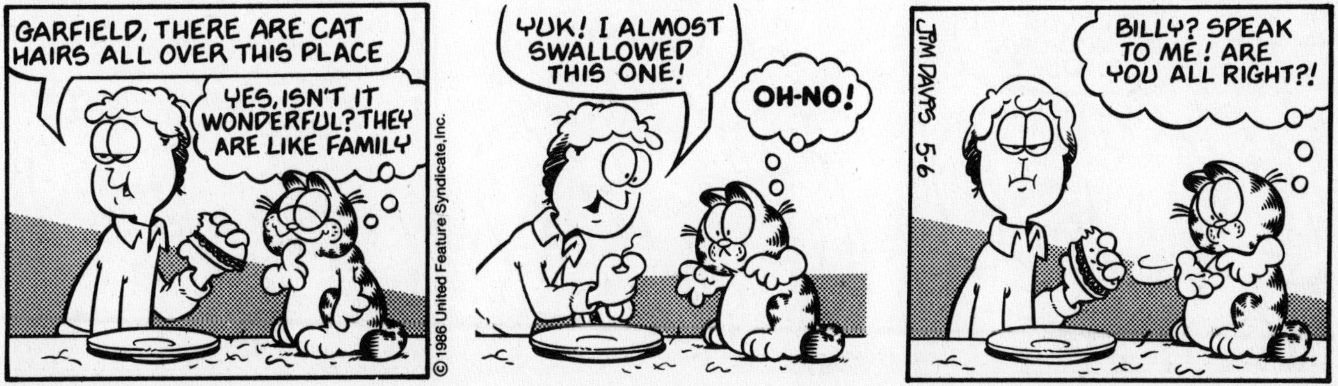
GARFIELD, THERE ARE CAT HAIRS ALL OVER THIS PLACE
YES, ISN'T IT WONDERFUL? THEY ARE LIKE FAMILY
© 1986 United Feature Syndicate, Inc.
YUK! I ALMOST SWALLOWED THIS ONE!
OH-NO!
JIM DAVIS 5-6
BILLY? SPEAK TO ME! ARE YOU ALL RIGHT?!

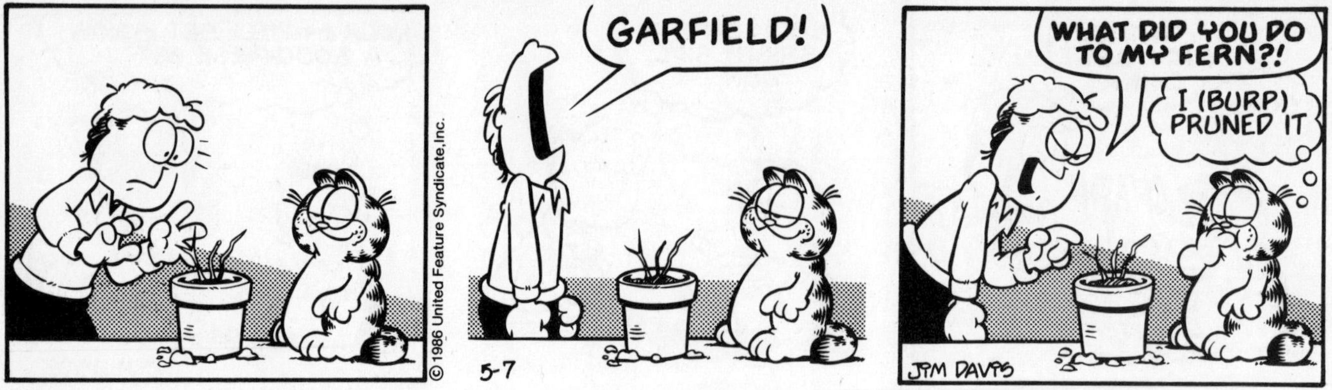
GARFIELD!
WHAT DID YOU DO TO MY FERN?!
I (BURP) PRUNED IT
© 1986 United Feature Syndicate, Inc.
5-7
JIM DAVIS

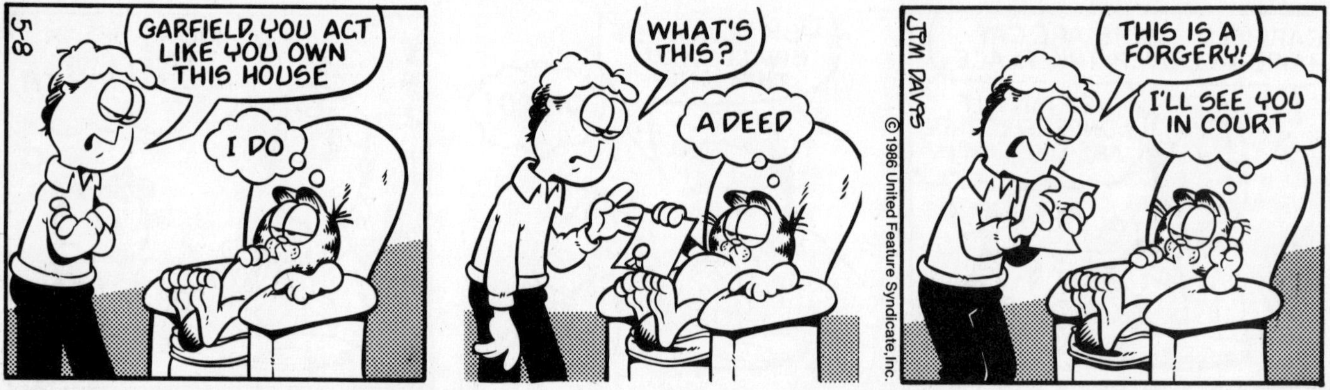
5-8
GARFIELD, YOU ACT LIKE YOU OWN THIS HOUSE
I DO
WHAT'S THIS?
A DEED
THIS IS A FORGERY!
I'LL SEE YOU IN COURT
JIM DAVIS
© 1986 United Feature Syndicate, Inc.

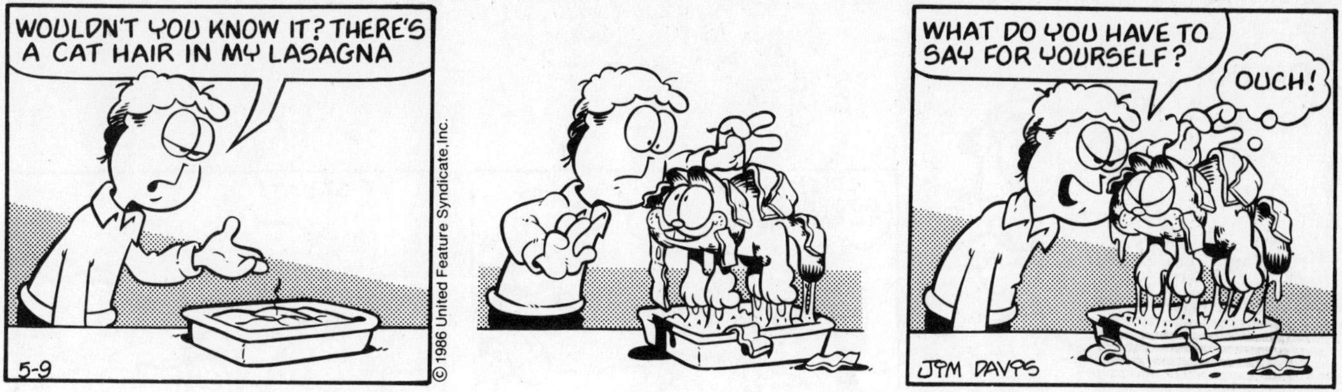
WOULDN'T YOU KNOW IT? THERE'S A CAT HAIR IN MY LASAGNA
5-9
© 1986 United Feature Syndicate, Inc.
WHAT DO YOU HAVE TO SAY FOR YOURSELF?
OUCH!
JIM DAVIS

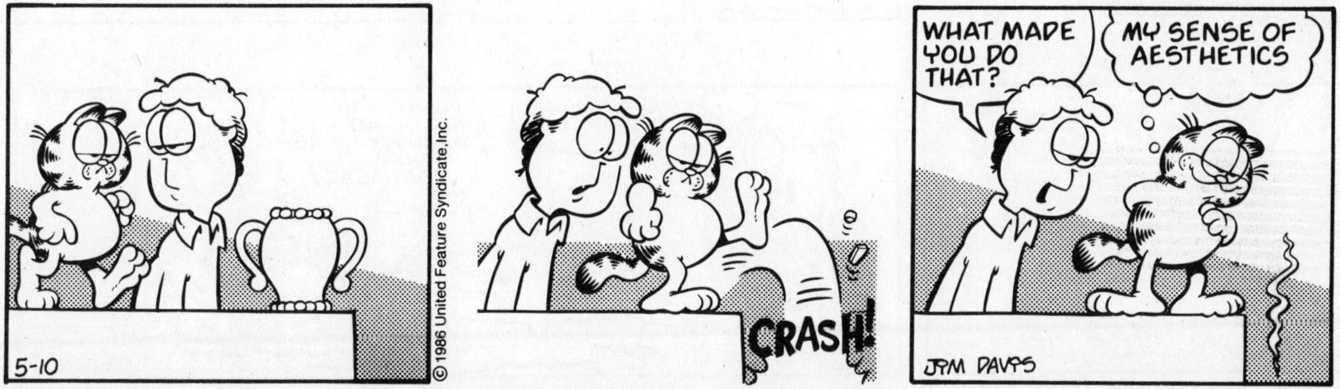
5-10
© 1986 United Feature Syndicate, Inc.
CRASH!
WHAT MADE YOU DO THAT?
MY SENSE OF AESTHETICS
JIM DAVIS

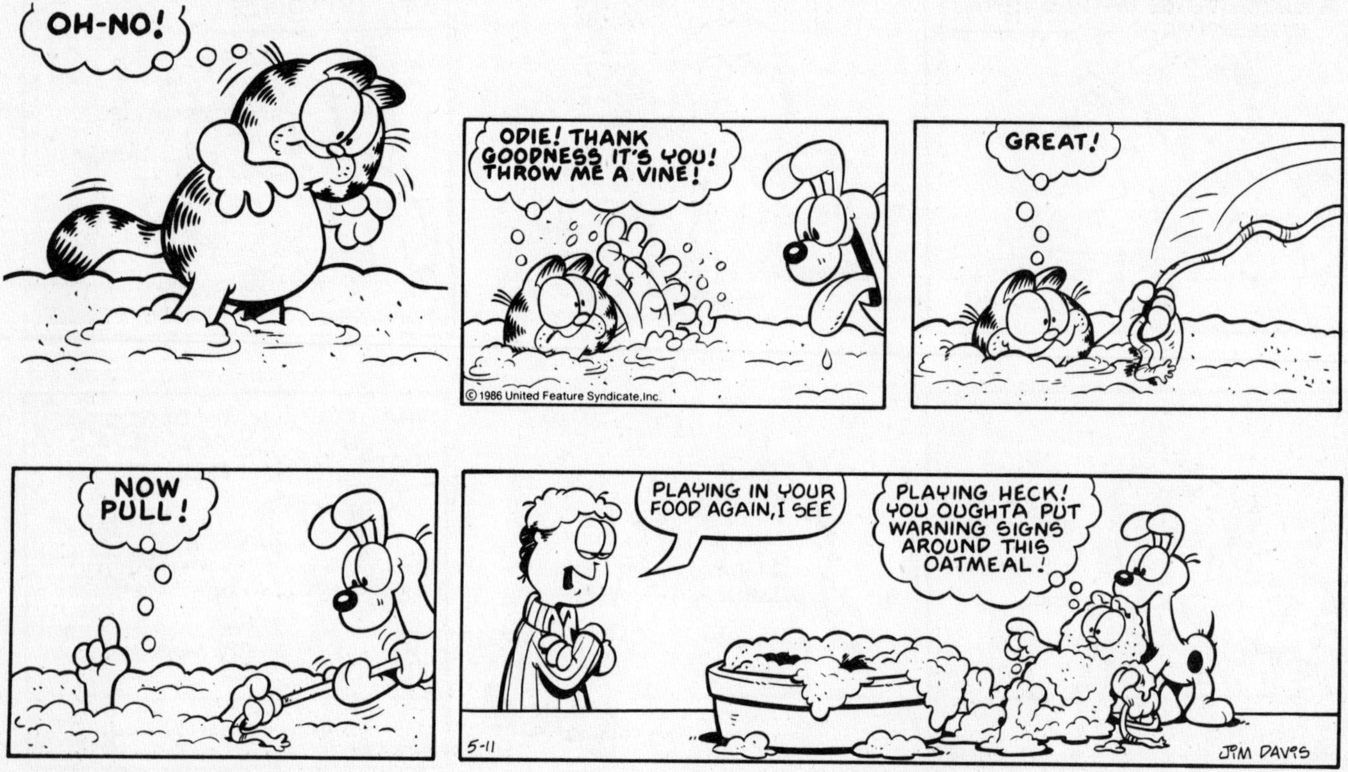
OH-NO!
ODIE! THANK GOODNESS IT'S YOU! THROW ME A VINE!
© 1986 United Feature Syndicate, Inc.
GREAT!
NOW PULL!
PLAYING IN YOUR FOOD AGAIN, I SEE
PLAYING HECK! YOU OUGHTA PUT WARNING SIGNS AROUND THIS OATMEAL!
5-11
JIM DAVIS

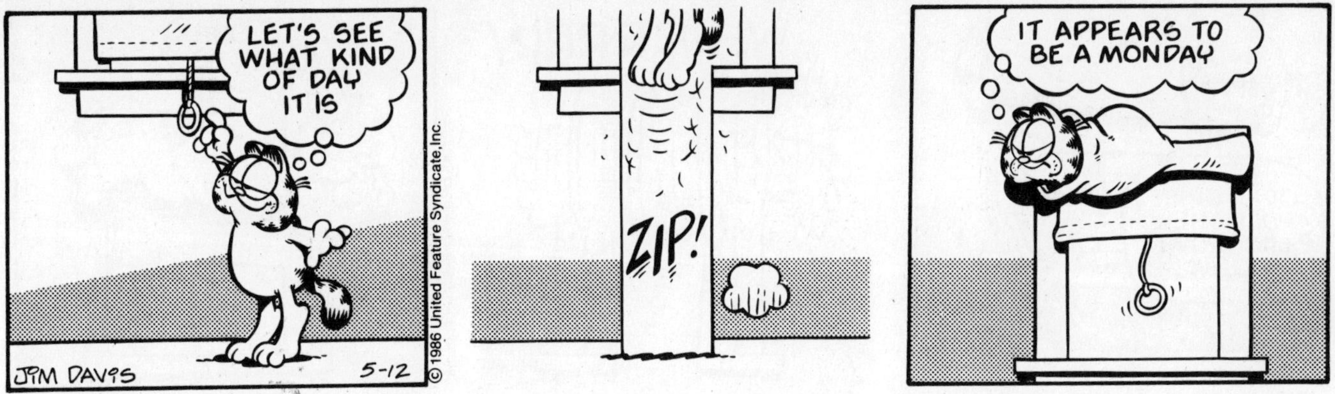
LET'S SEE WHAT KIND OF DAY IT IS
JIM DAVIS
5-12
© 1986 United Feature Syndicate, Inc.
ZIP!
IT APPEARS TO BE A MONDAY

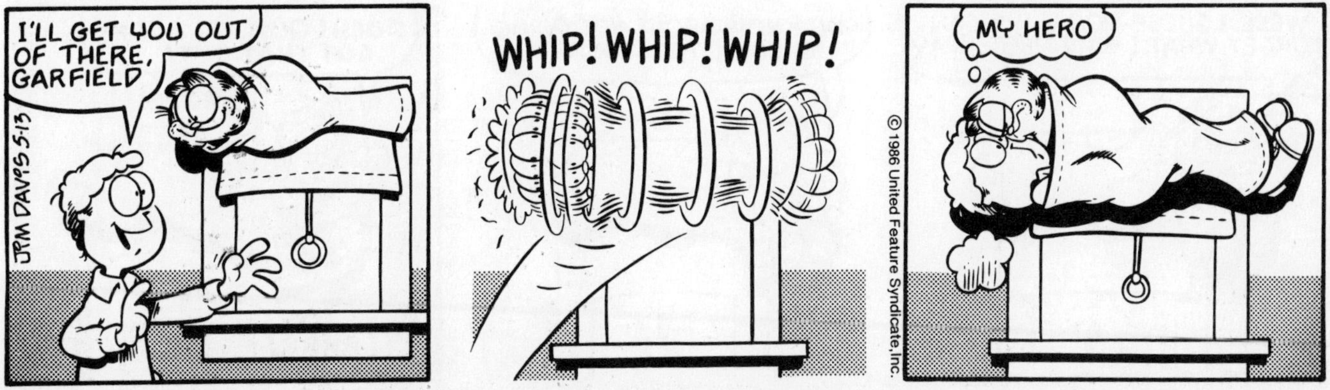
I'LL GET YOU OUT OF THERE, GARFIELD
JIM DAVIS 5-13
WHIP! WHIP! WHIP!
© 1986 United Feature Syndicate, Inc.
MY HERO

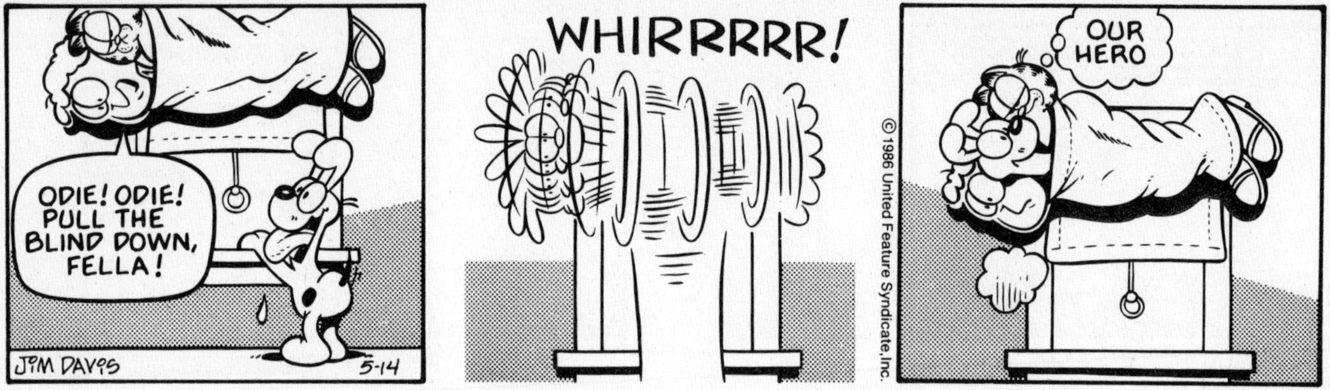
ODIE! ODIE! PULL THE BLIND DOWN, FELLA!
JIM DAVIS
5-14
WHIRRRRR!
OUR HERO
© 1986 United Feature Syndicate, Inc.

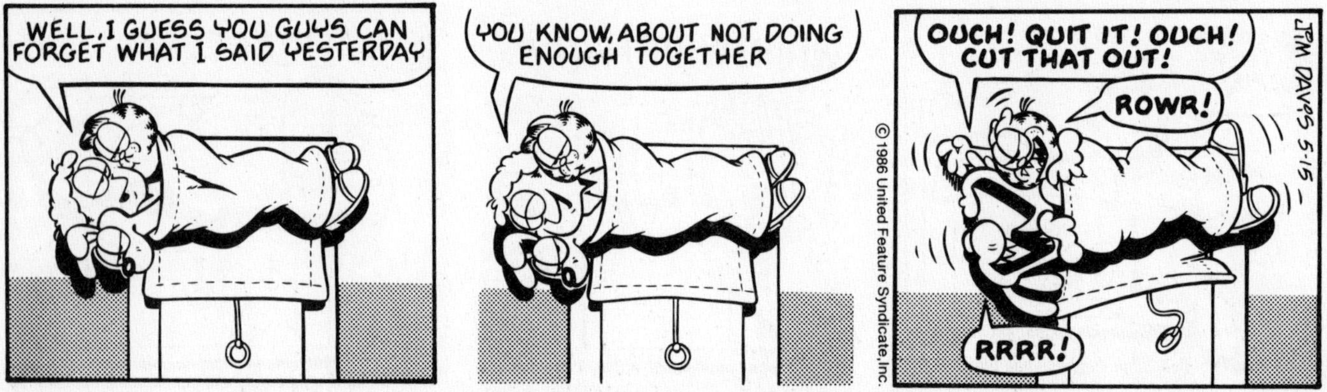
WELL, I GUESS YOU GUYS CAN FORGET WHAT I SAID YESTERDAY
YOU KNOW, ABOUT NOT DOING ENOUGH TOGETHER
OUCH! QUIT IT! OUCH! CUT THAT OUT!
ROWR!
RRRR!
JIM DAVIS 5-15
© 1986 United Feature Syndicate, Inc.

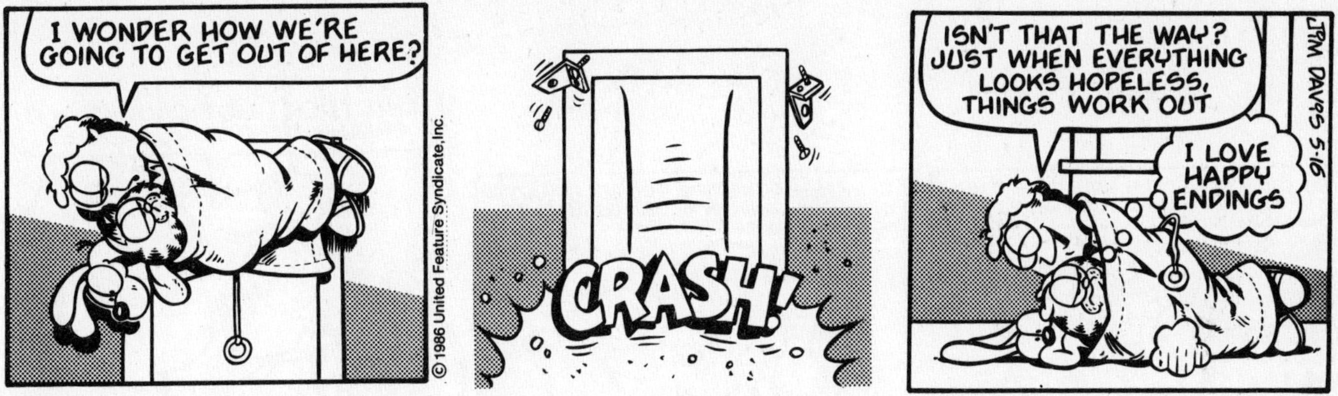
I WONDER HOW WE'RE GOING TO GET OUT OF HERE?
© 1986 United Feature Syndicate, Inc.
CRASH!
ISN'T THAT THE WAY? JUST WHEN EVERYTHING LOOKS HOPELESS, THINGS WORK OUT
I LOVE HAPPY ENDINGS
JIM DAVIS 5-16

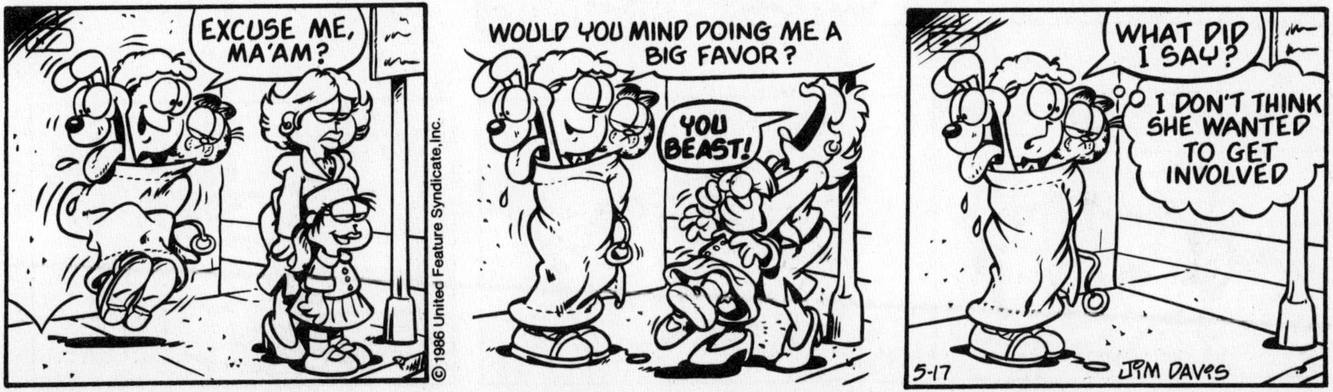
EXCUSE ME, MA'AM?
© 1986 United Feature Syndicate, Inc.
WOULD YOU MIND DOING ME A BIG FAVOR?
YOU BEAST!
WHAT DID I SAY?
I DON'T THINK SHE WANTED TO GET INVOLVED
5-17
JIM DAVIS

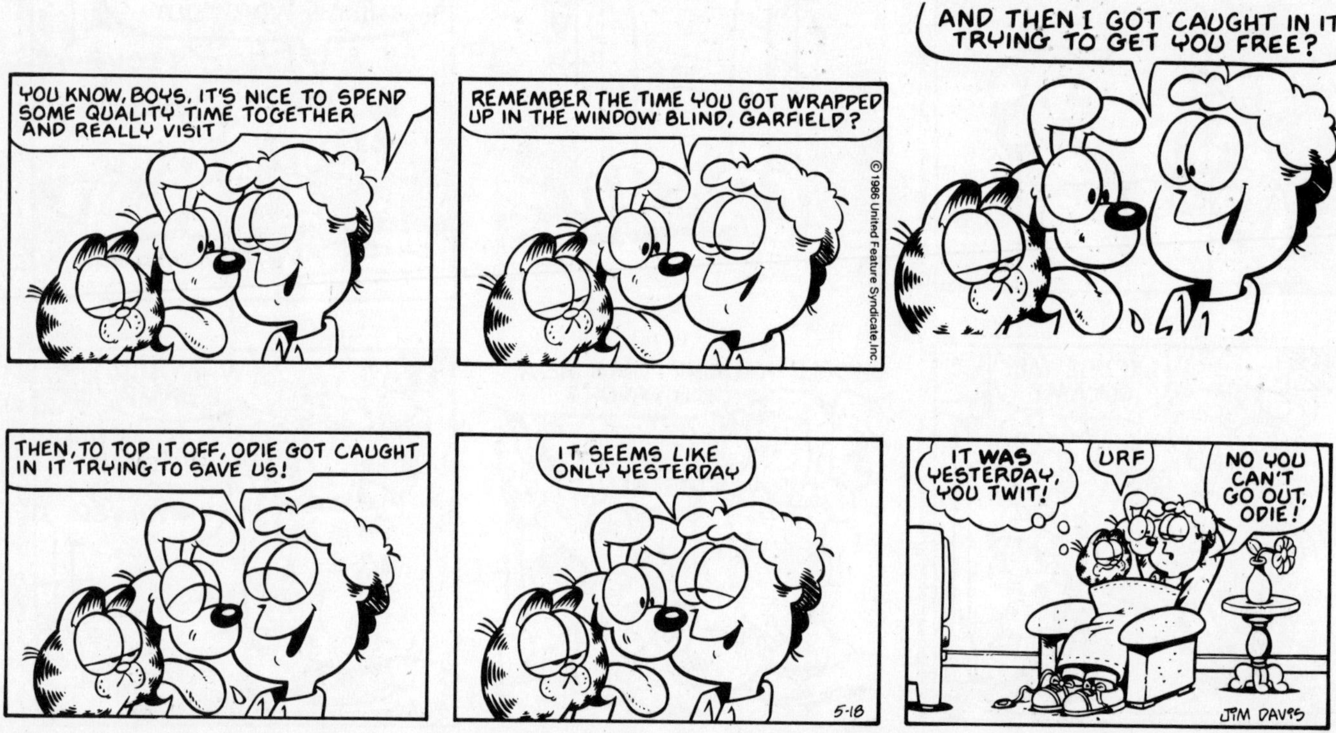
YOU KNOW, BOYS, IT'S NICE TO SPEND SOME QUALITY TIME TOGETHER AND REALLY VISIT
REMEMBER THE TIME YOU GOT WRAPPED UP IN THE WINDOW BLIND, GARFIELD?
© 1986 United Feature Syndicate, Inc.
AND THEN I GOT CAUGHT IN IT TRYING TO GET YOU FREE?
THEN, TO TOP IT OFF, ODIE GOT CAUGHT IN IT TRYING TO SAVE US!
IT SEEMS LIKE ONLY YESTERDAY
5-18
IT WAS YESTERDAY, YOU TWIT!
URF
NO YOU CAN'T GO OUT, ODIE!
JIM DAVIS

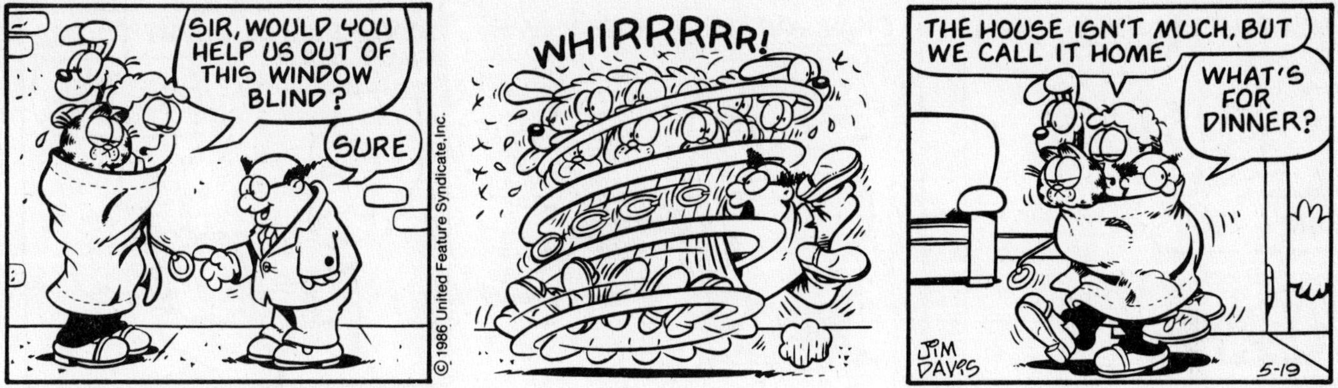
SIR, WOULD YOU HELP US OUT OF THIS WINDOW BLIND?
SURE
© 1986 United Feature Syndicate,Inc.
WHIRRRRR!
THE HOUSE ISN'T MUCH, BUT WE CALL IT HOME
WHAT'S FOR DINNER?
JIM DAVIS
5-19

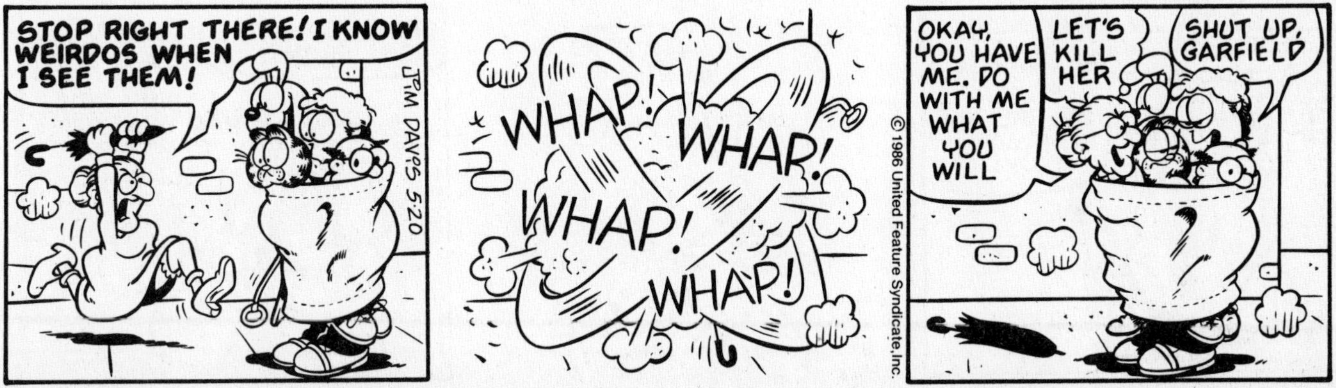
STOP RIGHT THERE! I KNOW WEIRDOS WHEN I SEE THEM!
JIM DAVIS 5-20
WHAP!
WHAP!
WHAP!
WHAP!
OKAY, YOU HAVE ME. DO WITH ME WHAT YOU WILL
LET'S KILL HER
SHUT UP, GARFIELD
© 1986 United Feature Syndicate,Inc.

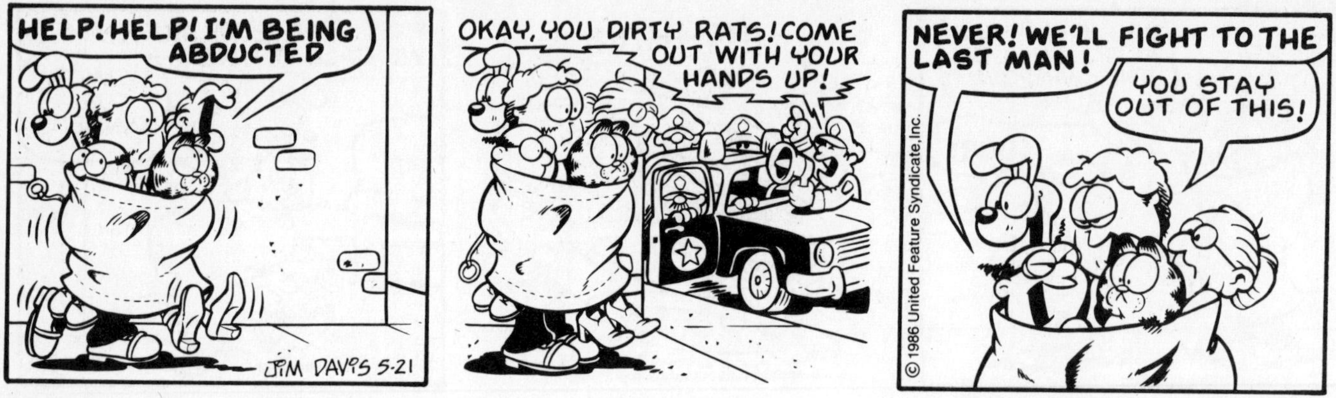
HELP! HELP! I'M BEING ABDUCTED
JIM DAVIS 5-21
OKAY, YOU DIRTY RATS! COME OUT WITH YOUR HANDS UP!
NEVER! WE'LL FIGHT TO THE LAST MAN!
YOU STAY OUT OF THIS!
© 1986 United Feature Syndicate, Inc.

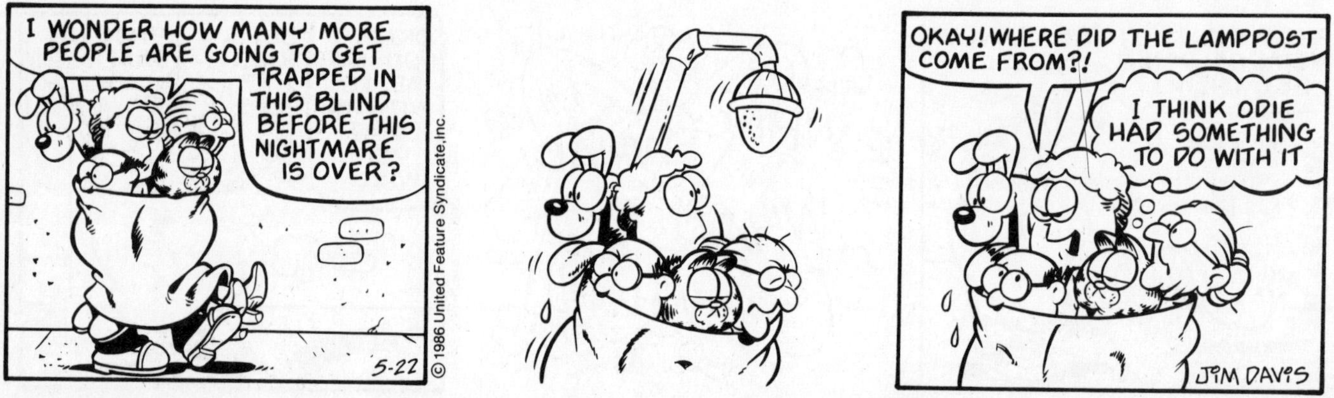
I WONDER HOW MANY MORE PEOPLE ARE GOING TO GET TRAPPED IN THIS BLIND BEFORE THIS NIGHTMARE IS OVER?
5-22
© 1986 United Feature Syndicate, Inc.
OKAY! WHERE DID THE LAMPPOST COME FROM?!
I THINK ODIE HAD SOMETHING TO DO WITH IT
JIM DAVIS

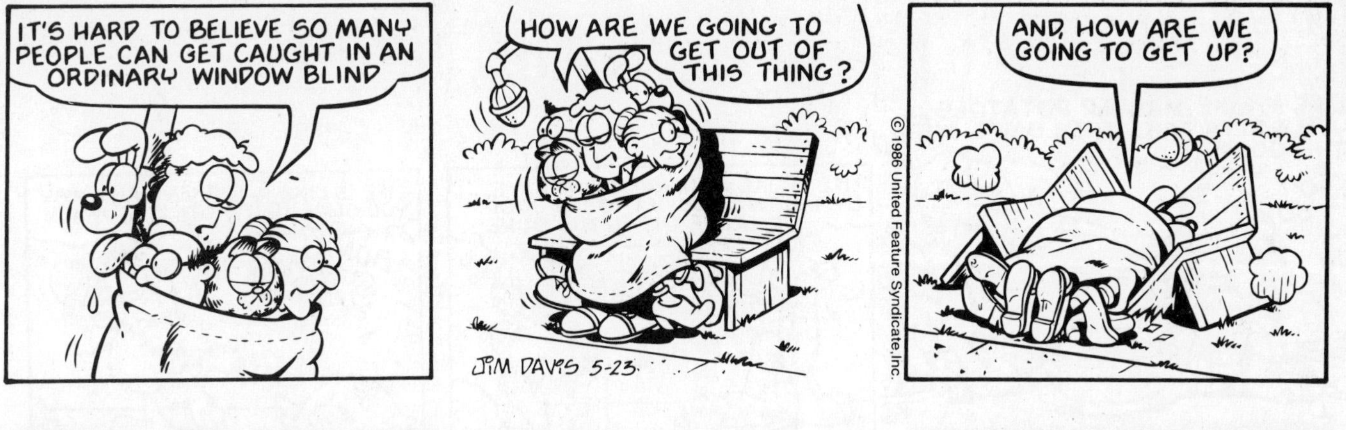
IT'S HARD TO BELIEVE SO MANY PEOPLE CAN GET CAUGHT IN AN ORDINARY WINDOW BLIND
HOW ARE WE GOING TO GET OUT OF THIS THING?
JIM DAVIS 5-23
© 1986 United Feature Syndicate, Inc.
AND, HOW ARE WE GOING TO GET UP?

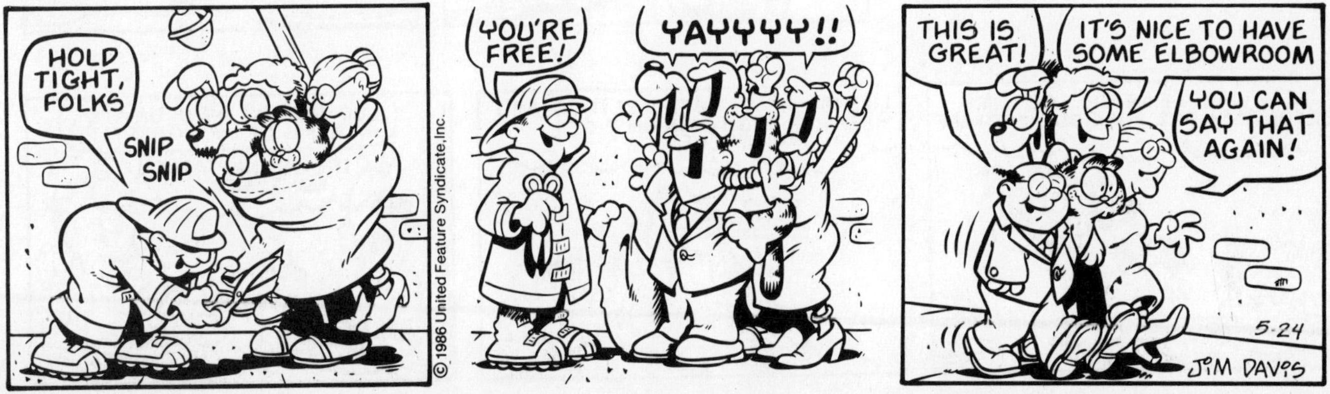
HOLD TIGHT, FOLKS
SNIP SNIP
© 1986 United Feature Syndicate, Inc.
YOU'RE FREE!
YAYYYY!!
THIS IS GREAT!
IT'S NICE TO HAVE SOME ELBOWROOM
YOU CAN SAY THAT AGAIN!
5-24
JIM DAVIS

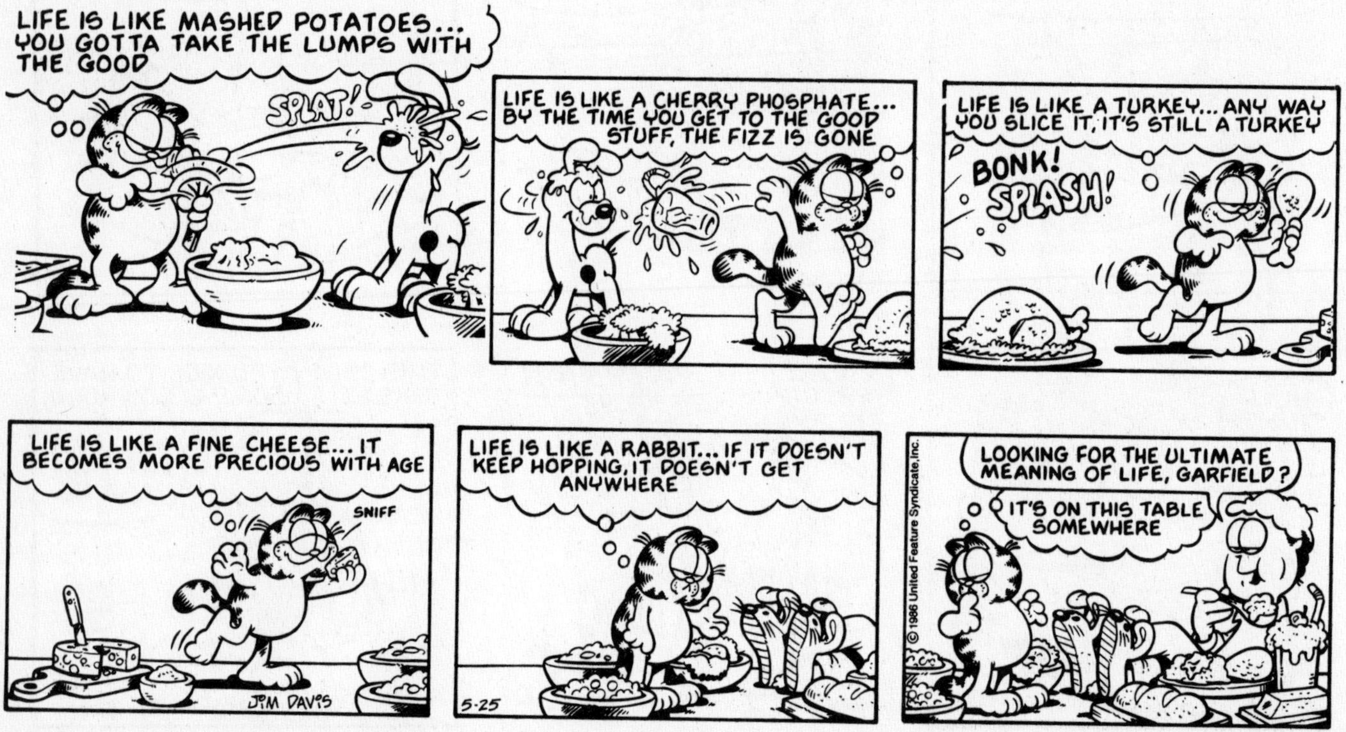
LIFE IS LIKE MASHED POTATOES... YOU GOTTA TAKE THE LUMPS WITH THE GOOD
SPLAT!
LIFE IS LIKE A CHERRY PHOSPHATE... BY THE TIME YOU GET TO THE GOOD STUFF, THE FIZZ IS GONE
LIFE IS LIKE A TURKEY... ANY WAY YOU SLICE IT, IT'S STILL A TURKEY
BONK!
SPLASH!
LIFE IS LIKE A FINE CHEESE... IT BECOMES MORE PRECIOUS WITH AGE
SNIFF
JIM DAVIS
LIFE IS LIKE A RABBIT... IF IT DOESN'T KEEP HOPPING, IT DOESN'T GET ANYWHERE
5-25
LOOKING FOR THE ULTIMATE MEANING OF LIFE, GARFIELD?
IT'S ON THIS TABLE SOMEWHERE
© 1986 United Feature Syndicate, Inc.

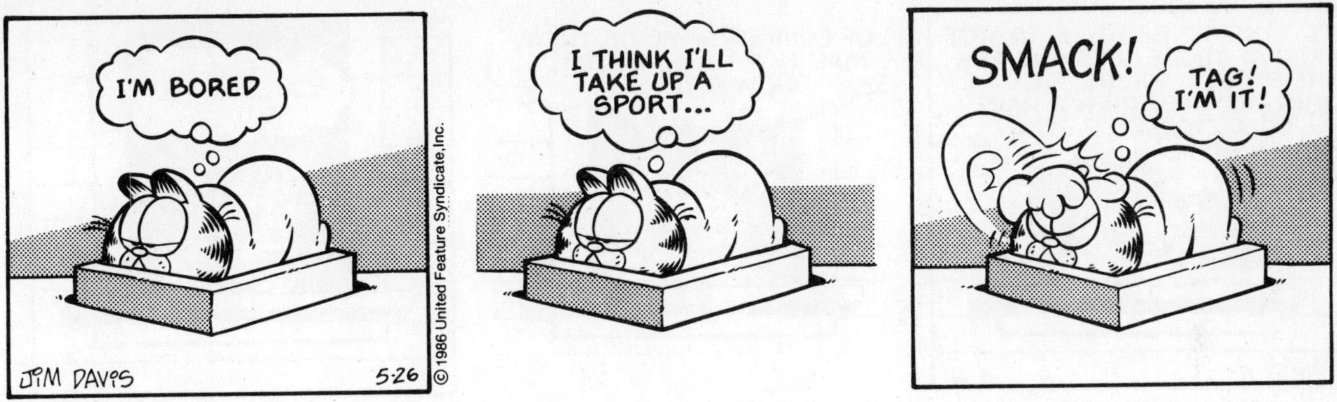
I'M BORED
JIM DAVIS
5-26
I THINK I'LL TAKE UP A SPORT...
SMACK!
TAG! I'M IT!


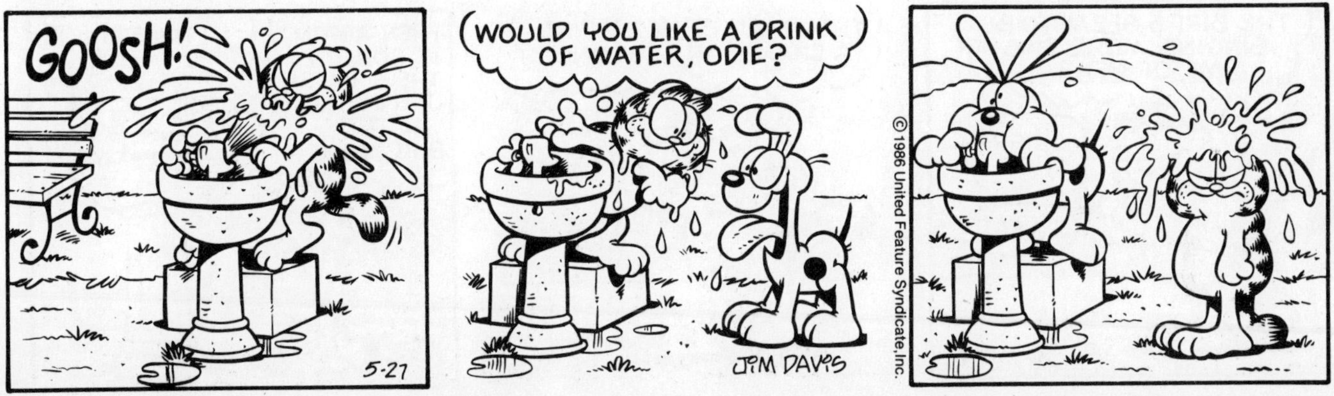
GOOSH!
5-27
WOULD YOU LIKE A DRINK OF WATER, ODIE?
JIM DAVIS

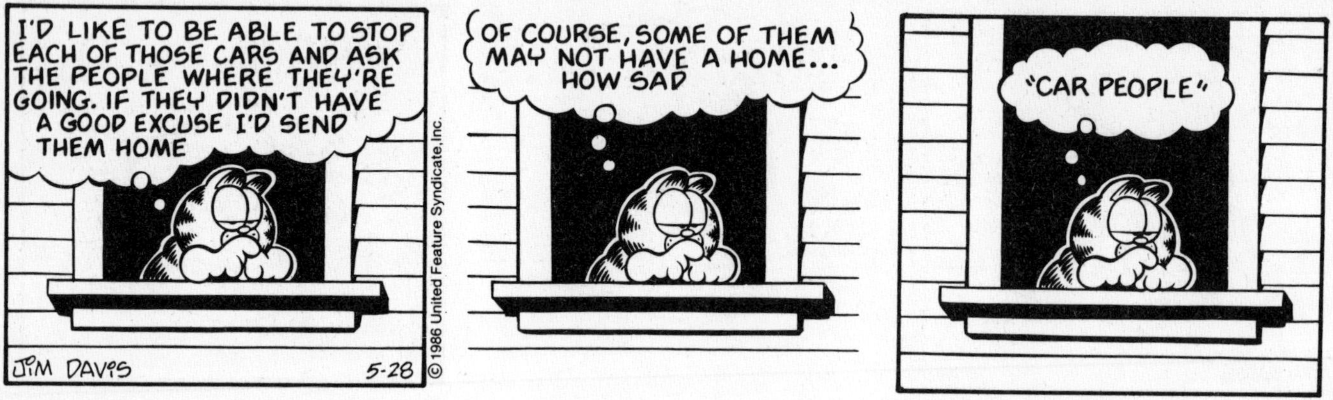
I'D LIKE TO BE ABLE TO STOP EACH OF THOSE CARS AND ASK THE PEOPLE WHERE THEY'RE GOING. IF THEY DIDN'T HAVE A GOOD EXCUSE I'D SEND THEM HOME
JIM DAVIS
5-28
© 1986 United Feature Syndicate, Inc.
OF COURSE, SOME OF THEM MAY NOT HAVE A HOME... HOW SAD
"CAR PEOPLE"

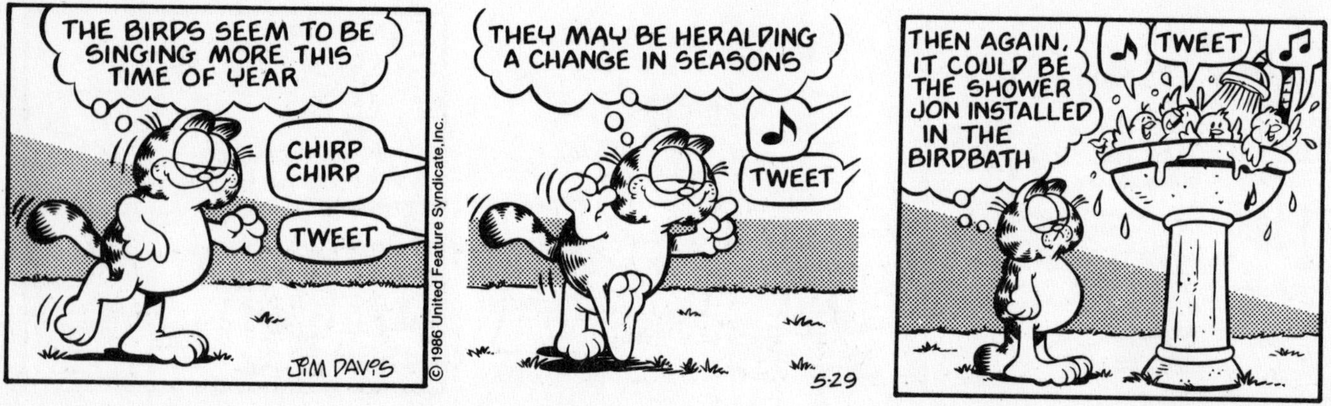
THE BIRDS SEEM TO BE SINGING MORE THIS TIME OF YEAR
CHIRP CHIRP
TWEET
JIM DAVIS
© 1986 United Feature Syndicate, Inc.
THEY MAY BE HERALDING A CHANGE IN SEASONS
TWEET
5-29
THEN AGAIN, IT COULD BE THE SHOWER JON INSTALLED IN THE BIRDBATH
TWEET

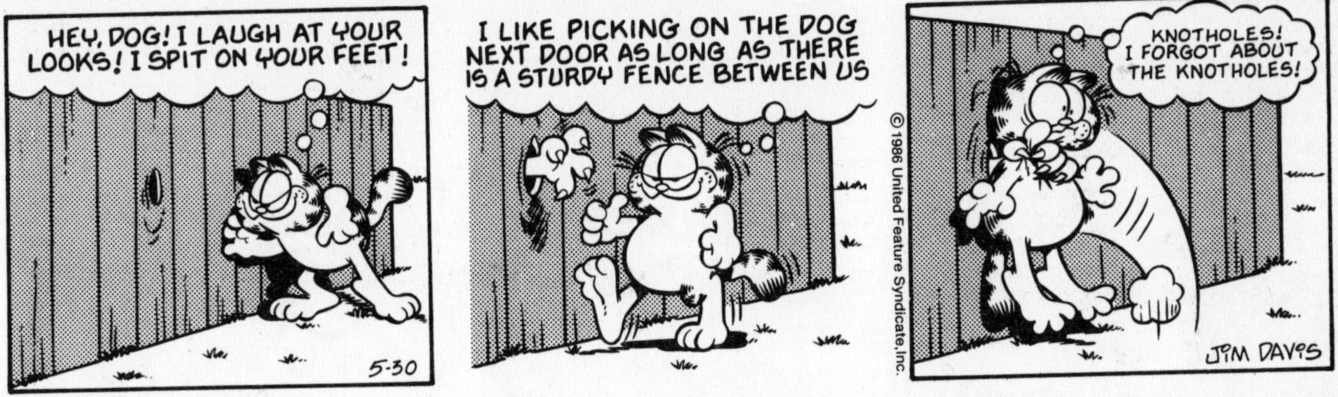
HEY, DOG! I LAUGH AT YOUR LOOKS! I SPIT ON YOUR FEET!
5-30
I LIKE PICKING ON THE DOG NEXT DOOR AS LONG AS THERE IS A STURDY FENCE BETWEEN US
© 1986 United Feature Syndicate, Inc.
KNOTHOLES! I FORGOT ABOUT THE KNOTHOLES!
JIM DAVIS

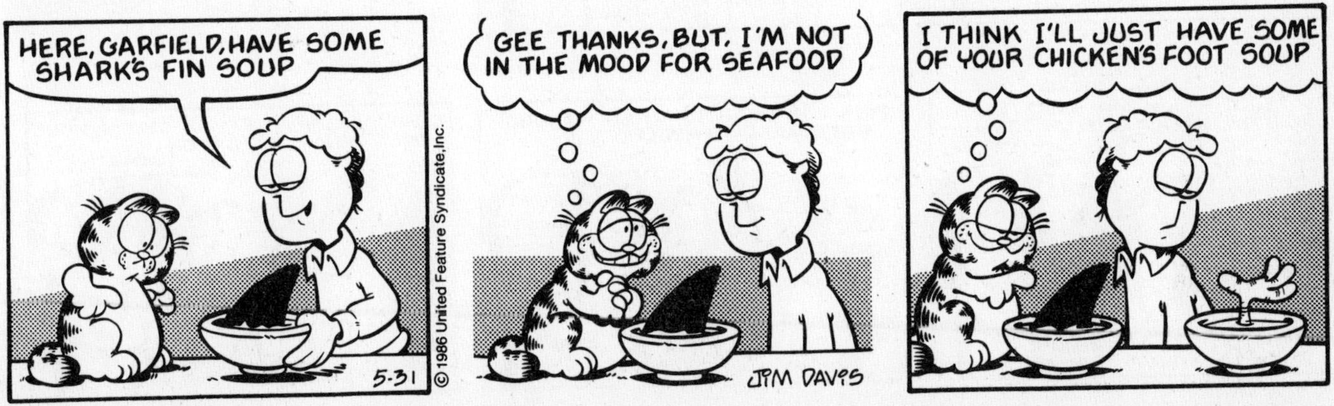
HERE, GARFIELD, HAVE SOME SHARK'S FIN SOUP
5-31
© 1986 United Feature Syndicate, Inc.
GEE THANKS, BUT, I'M NOT IN THE MOOD FOR SEAFOOD
JIM DAVIS
I THINK I'LL JUST HAVE SOME OF YOUR CHICKEN'S FOOT SOUP

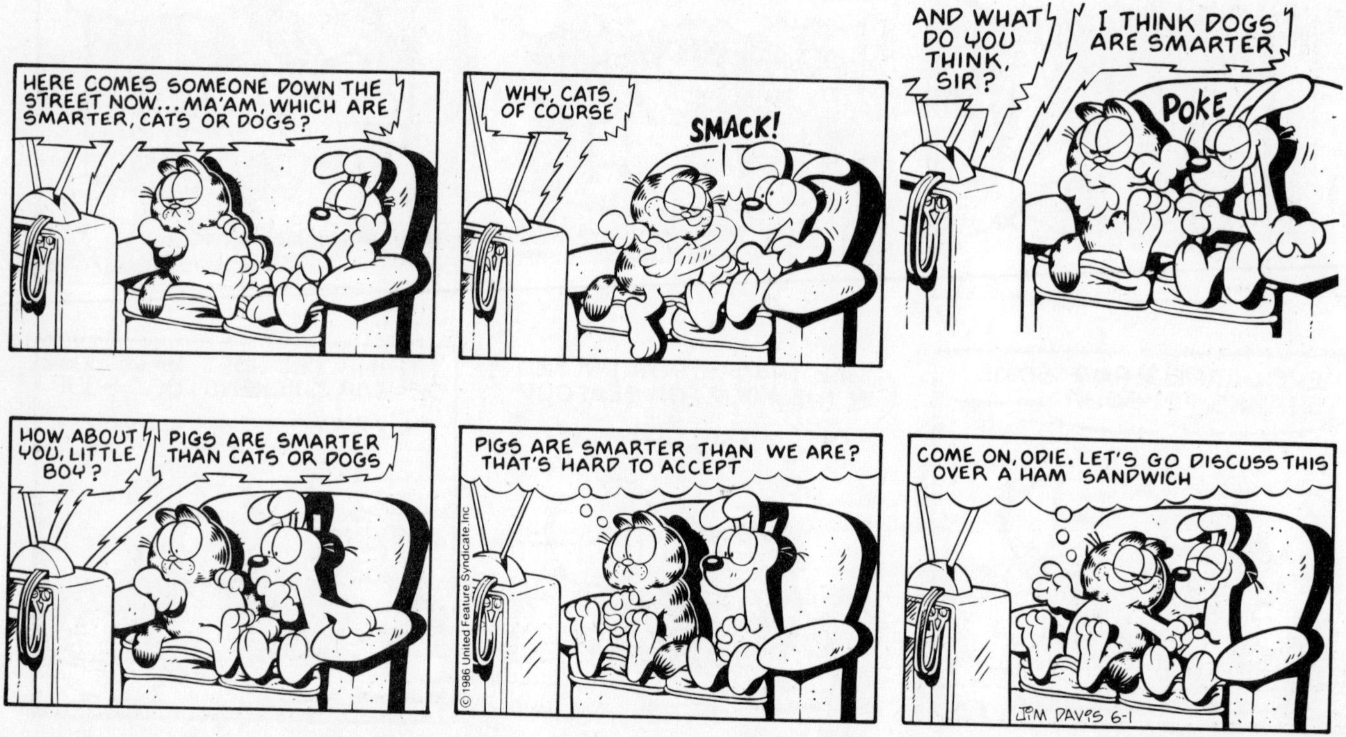
HERE COMES SOMEONE DOWN THE STREET NOW... MA'AM, WHICH ARE SMARTER, CATS OR DOGS?
WHY, CATS, OF COURSE
SMACK!
AND WHAT DO YOU THINK, SIR?
I THINK DOGS ARE SMARTER
POKE
HOW ABOUT YOU, LITTLE BOY?
PIGS ARE SMARTER THAN CATS OR DOGS
PIGS ARE SMARTER THAN WE ARE? THAT'S HARD TO ACCEPT
COME ON, ODIE. LET'S GO DISCUSS THIS OVER A HAM SANDWICH
© 1986 United Feature Syndicate, Inc
JIM DAVIS 6-1

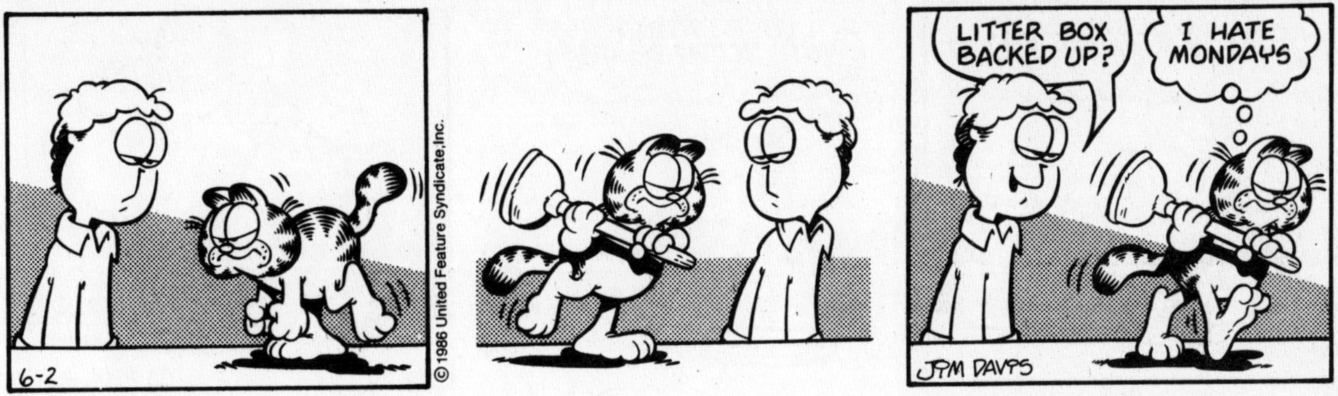
6-2
© 1986 United Feature Syndicate, Inc.
LITTER BOX BACKED UP?
I HATE MONDAYS
JIM DAVIS

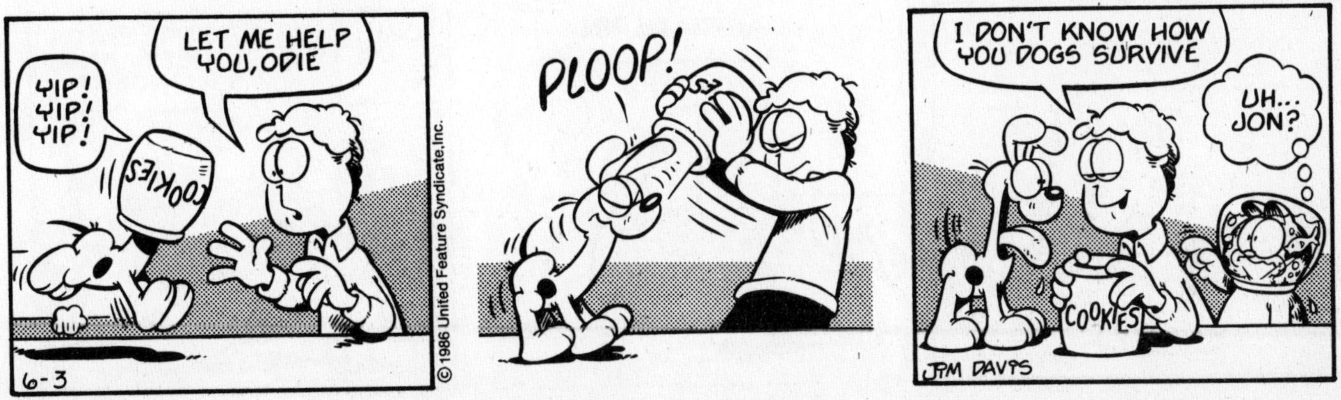
YIP! YIP! YIP!
LET ME HELP YOU, ODIE
COOKIES
6-3
© 1986 United Feature Syndicate, Inc.
PLOOP!
I DON'T KNOW HOW YOU DOGS SURVIVE
UH... JON?
COOKIES
JIM DAVIS

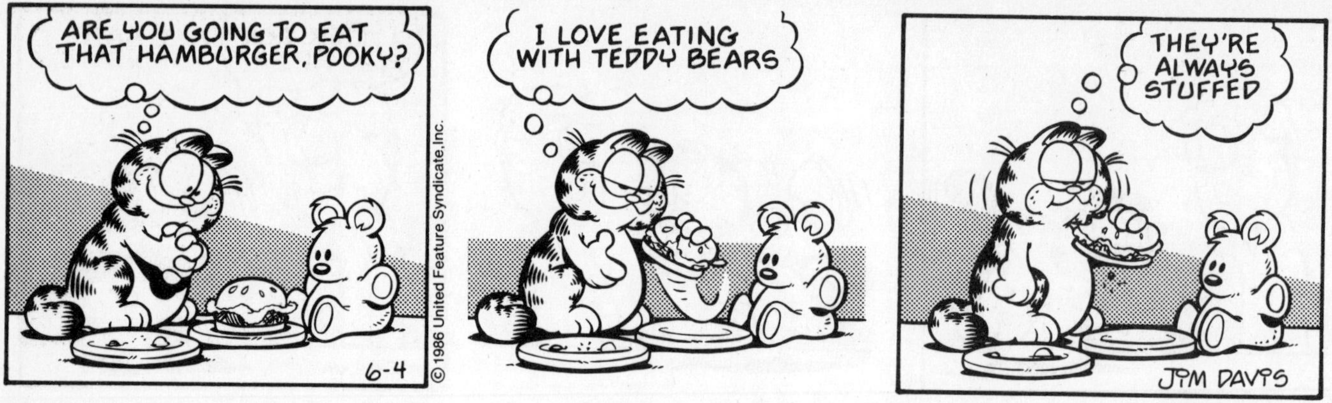
ARE YOU GOING TO EAT THAT HAMBURGER, POOKY?
6-4
© 1986 United Feature Syndicate,Inc.
I LOVE EATING WITH TEDDY BEARS
THEY'RE ALWAYS STUFFED
JIM DAVIS

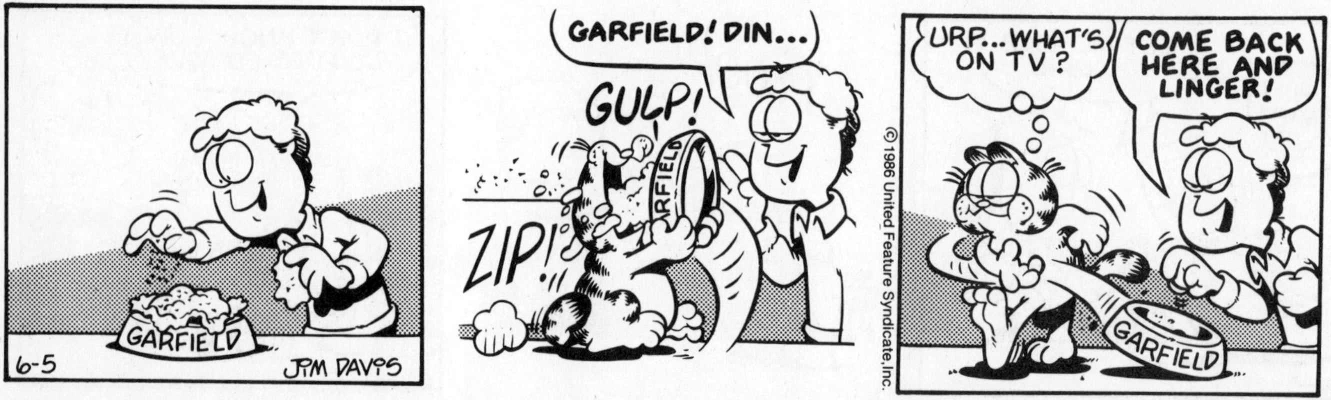
GARFIELD
6-5
JIM DAVIS
GARFIELD! DIN...
GULP!
ZIP!
GARFIELD
© 1986 United Feature Syndicate,Inc.
URP...WHAT'S ON TV?
COME BACK HERE AND LINGER!
GARFIELD

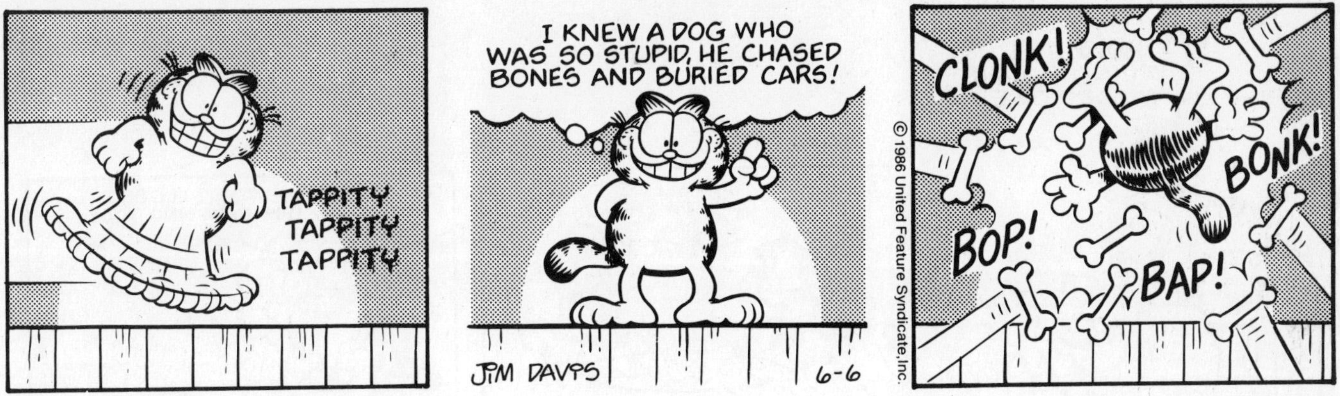
TAPPITY
TAPPITY
TAPPITY
I KNEW A DOG WHO WAS SO STUPID, HE CHASED BONES AND BURIED CARS!
JIM DAVIS
6-6
CLONK!
BONK!
BOP!
BAP!
© 1986 United Feature Syndicate, Inc.

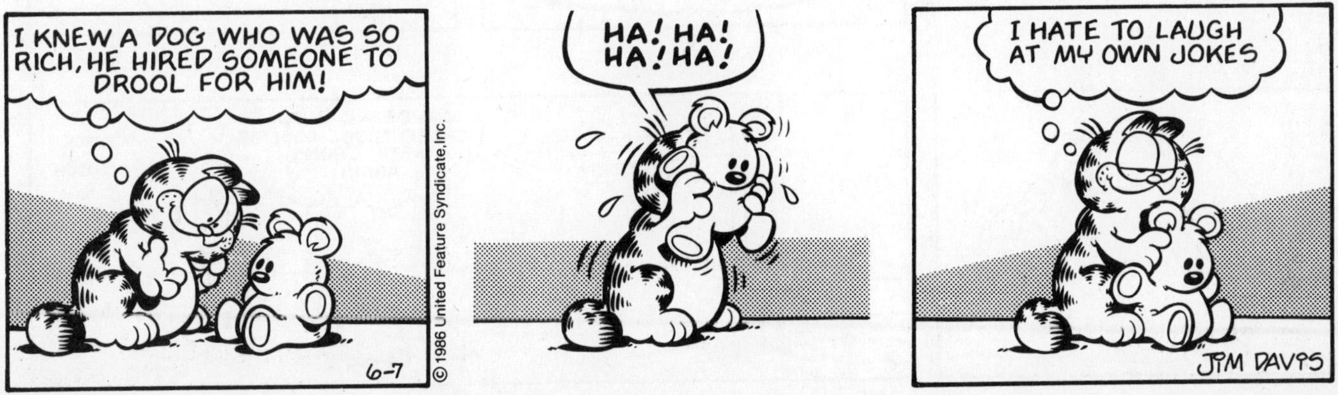
I KNEW A DOG WHO WAS SO RICH, HE HIRED SOMEONE TO DROOL FOR HIM!
6-7
© 1986 United Feature Syndicate, Inc.
HA! HA!
HA! HA!
I HATE TO LAUGH AT MY OWN JOKES
JIM DAVIS

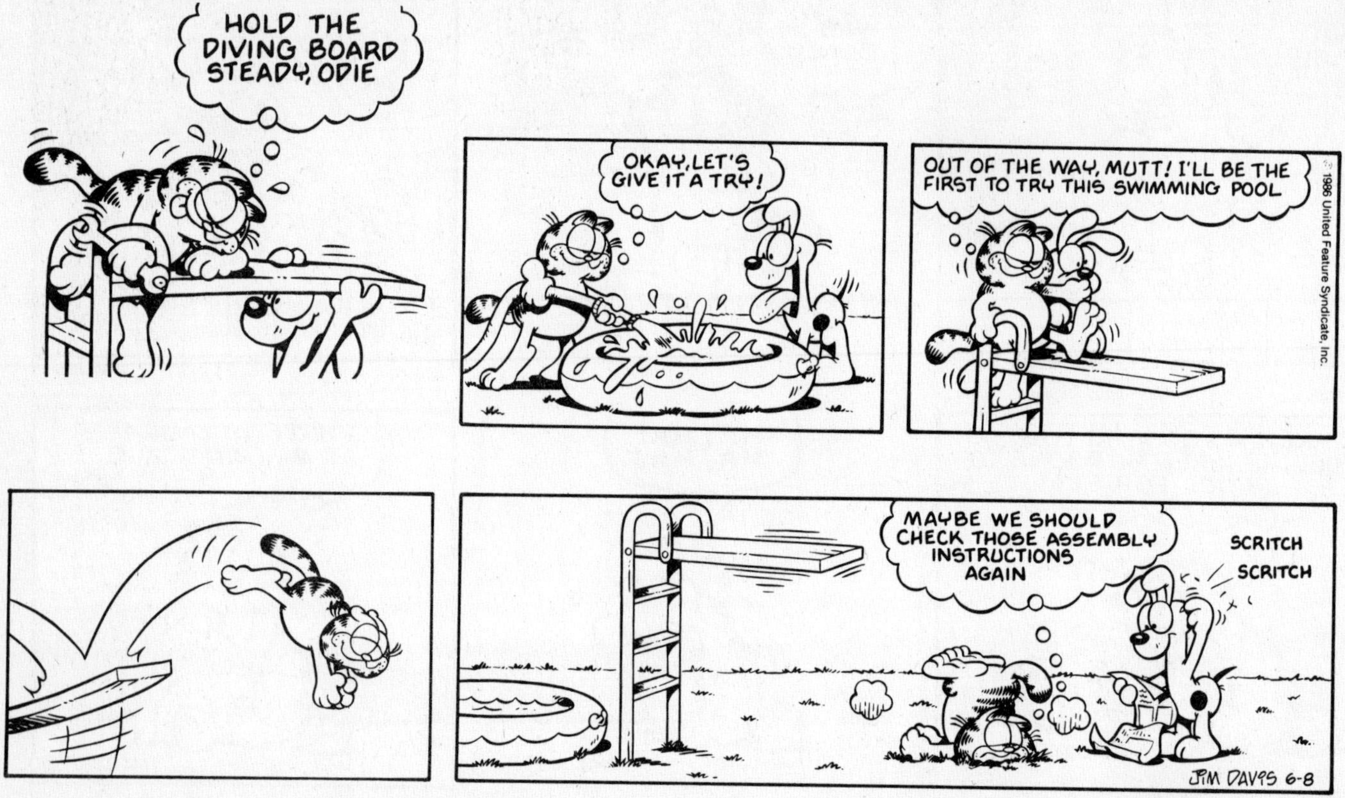
HOLD THE DIVING BOARD STEADY, ODIE
OKAY, LET'S GIVE IT A TRY!
OUT OF THE WAY, MUTT! I'LL BE THE FIRST TO TRY THIS SWIMMING POOL
© 1986 United Feature Syndicate, Inc.
MAYBE WE SHOULD CHECK THOSE ASSEMBLY INSTRUCTIONS AGAIN
SCRITCH
SCRITCH
JIM DAVIS 6-8

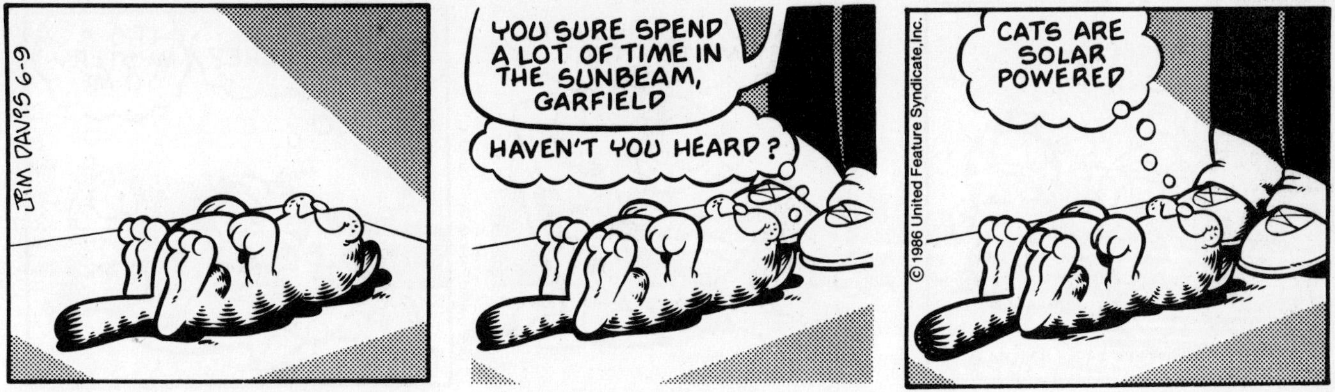
JIM DAVIS 6-9
YOU SURE SPEND A LOT OF TIME IN THE SUNBEAM, GARFIELD
HAVEN'T YOU HEARD?
© 1986 United Feature Syndicate, Inc.
CATS ARE SOLAR POWERED

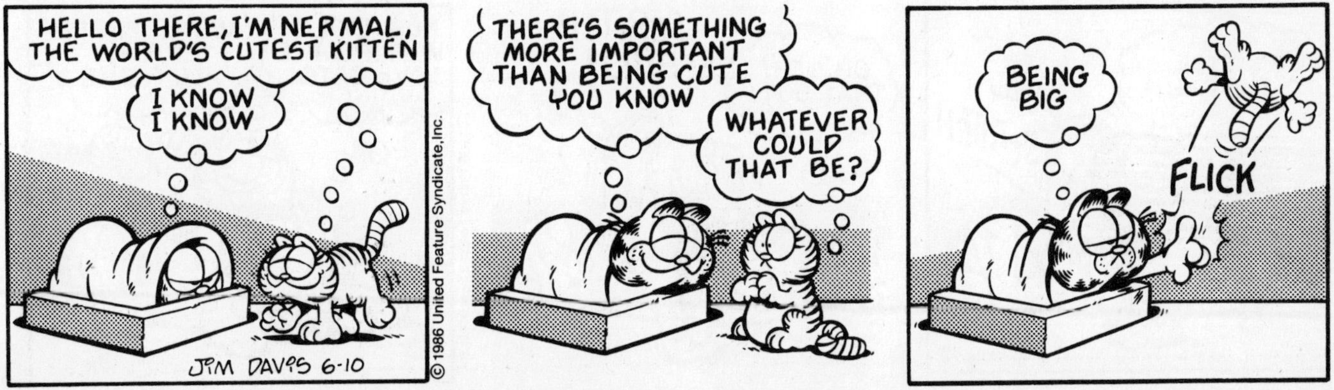
HELLO THERE, I'M NERMAL, THE WORLD'S CUTEST KITTEN
I KNOW I KNOW
JIM DAVIS 6-10
© 1986 United Feature Syndicate, Inc.
THERE'S SOMETHING MORE IMPORTANT THAN BEING CUTE YOU KNOW
WHATEVER COULD THAT BE?
BEING BIG
FLICK

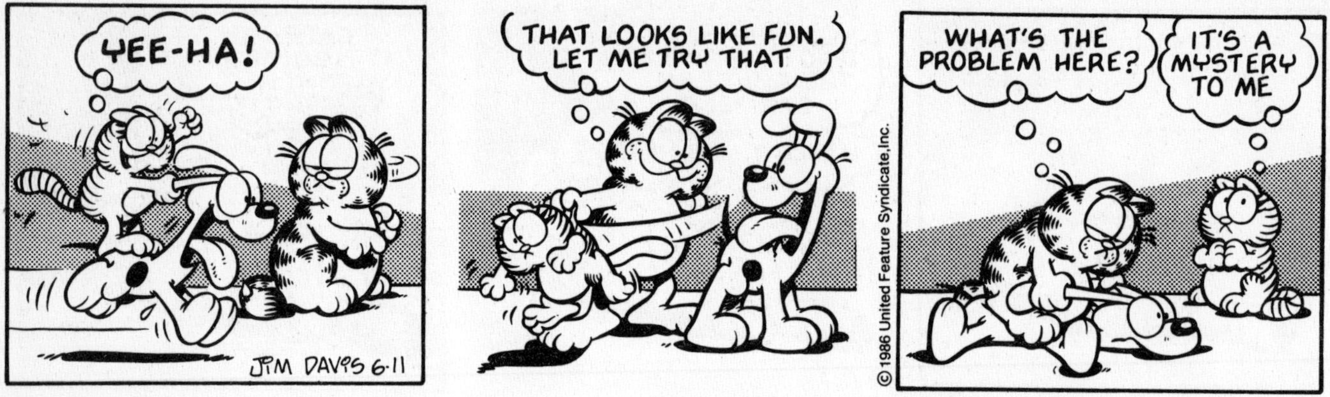
YEE-HA!
JIM DAVIS 6·11
THAT LOOKS LIKE FUN. LET ME TRY THAT
WHAT'S THE PROBLEM HERE?
IT'S A MYSTERY TO ME
© 1986 United Feature Syndicate, Inc.

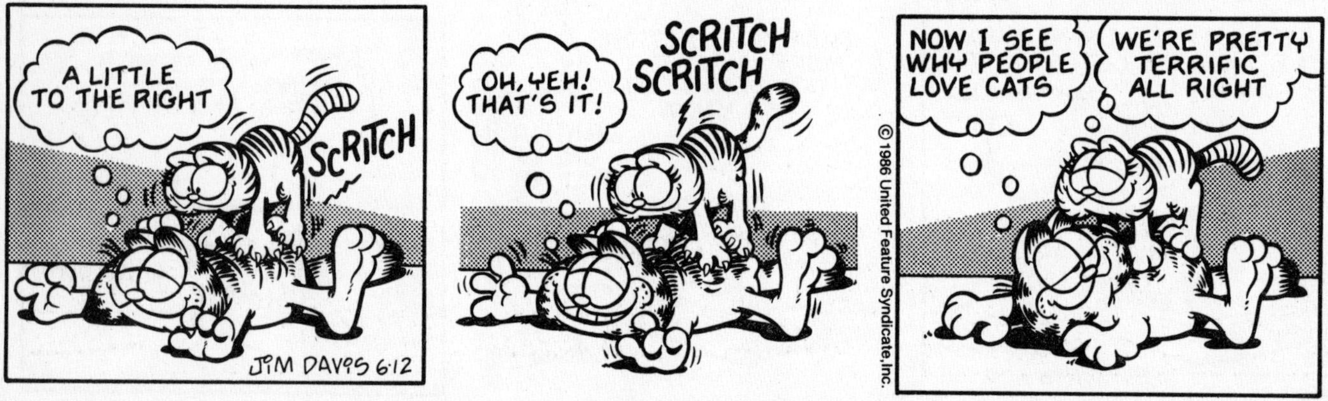
A LITTLE TO THE RIGHT
SCRITCH
JIM DAVIS 6·12
OH, YEH! THAT'S IT!
SCRITCH SCRITCH
NOW I SEE WHY PEOPLE LOVE CATS
WE'RE PRETTY TERRIFIC ALL RIGHT
© 1986 United Feature Syndicate, Inc.

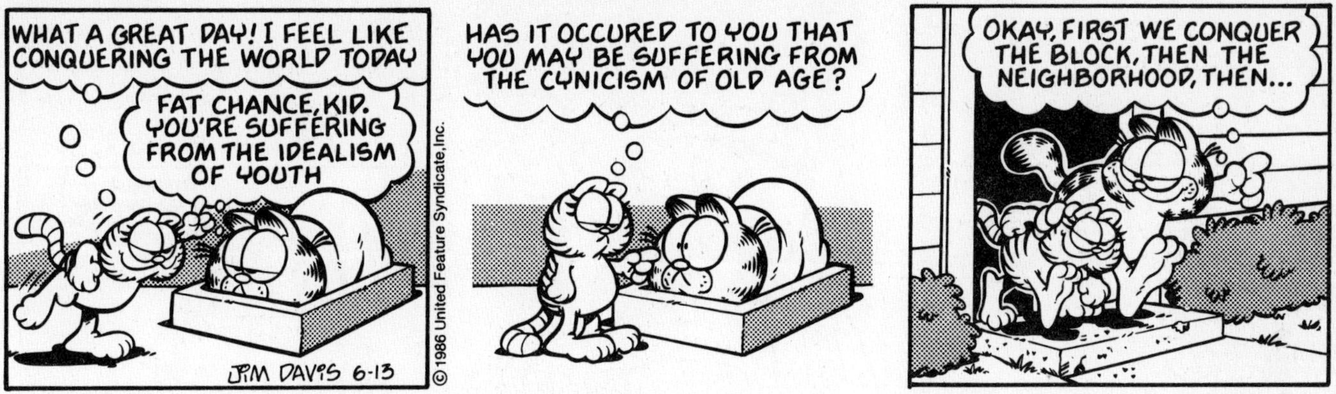
WHAT A GREAT DAY! I FEEL LIKE CONQUERING THE WORLD TODAY
FAT CHANCE, KID. YOU'RE SUFFERING FROM THE IDEALISM OF YOUTH
JIM DAVIS 6-13
© 1986 United Feature Syndicate, Inc.
HAS IT OCCURED TO YOU THAT YOU MAY BE SUFFERING FROM THE CYNICISM OF OLD AGE?
OKAY, FIRST WE CONQUER THE BLOCK, THEN THE NEIGHBORHOOD, THEN...

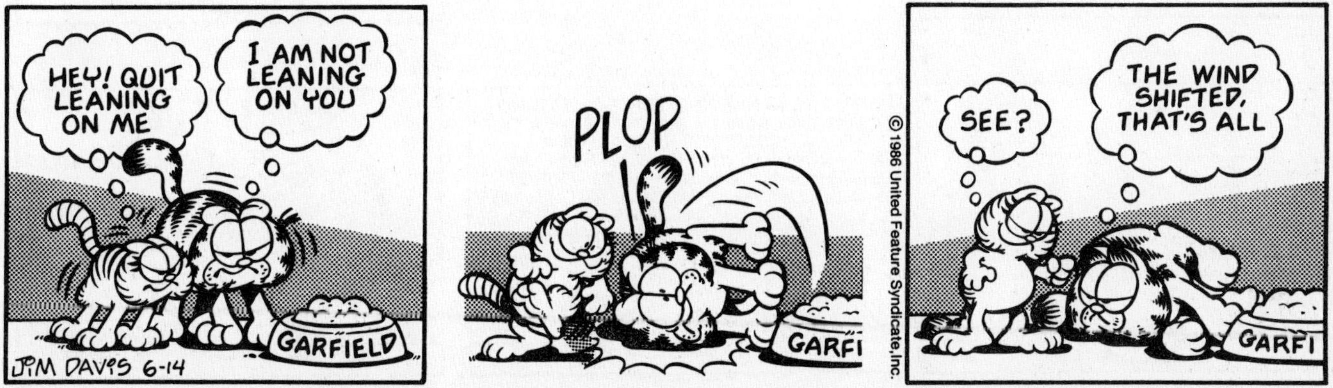
HEY! QUIT LEANING ON ME
I AM NOT LEANING ON YOU
GARFIELD
JIM DAVIS 6-14
PLOP
GARFI
© 1986 United Feature Syndicate, Inc.
SEE?
THE WIND SHIFTED, THAT'S ALL
GARFI

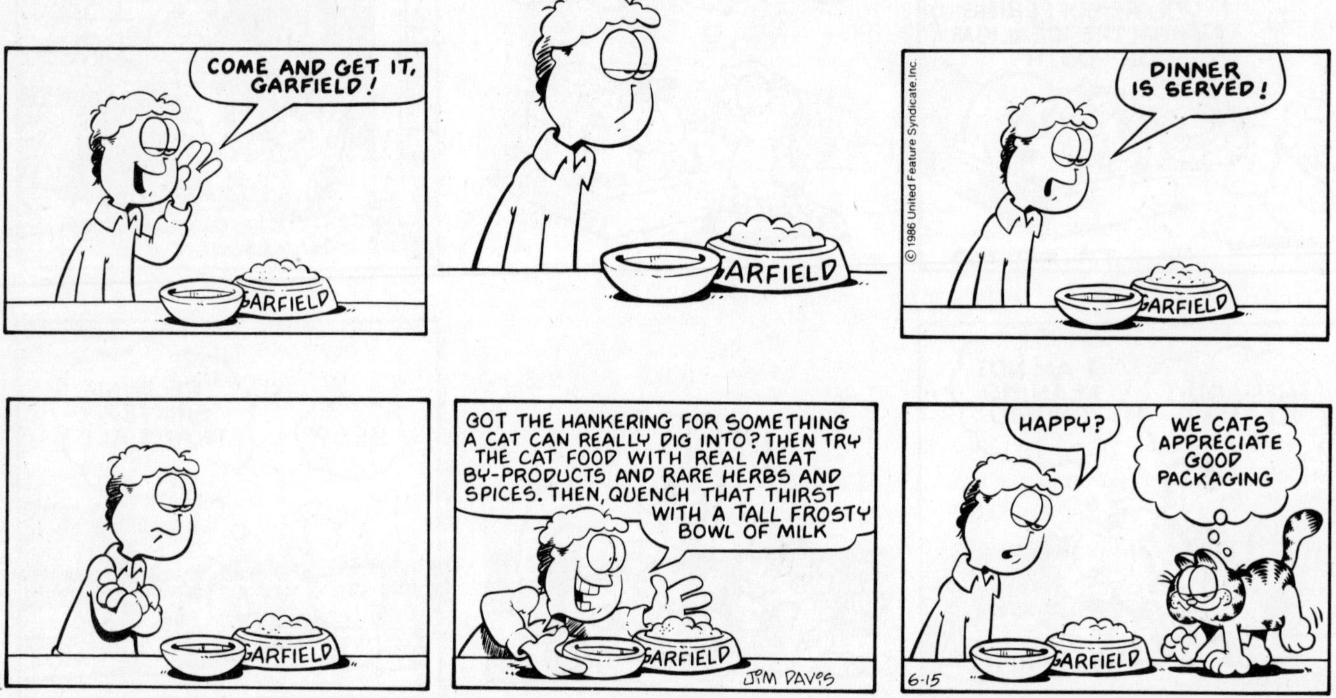
COME AND GET IT, GARFIELD!
GARFIELD
GARFIELD
© 1986 United Feature Syndicate, Inc.
DINNER IS SERVED!
GARFIELD
GARFIELD
GOT THE HANKERING FOR SOMETHING A CAT CAN REALLY DIG INTO? THEN TRY THE CAT FOOD WITH REAL MEAT BY-PRODUCTS AND RARE HERBS AND SPICES. THEN, QUENCH THAT THIRST WITH A TALL FROSTY BOWL OF MILK
GARFIELD
JIM DAVIS
HAPPY?
WE CATS APPRECIATE GOOD PACKAGING
GARFIELD
6-15

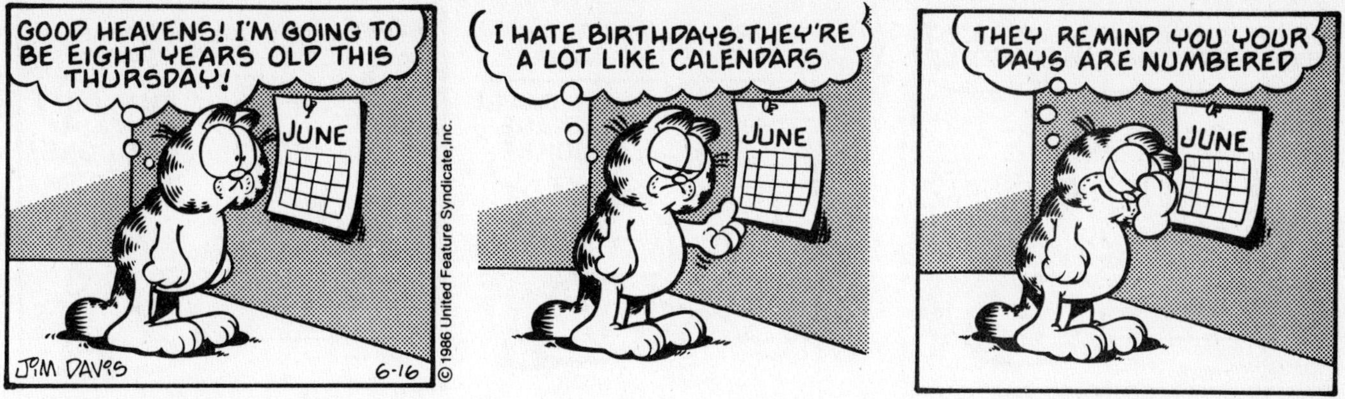
GOOD HEAVENS! I'M GOING TO BE EIGHT YEARS OLD THIS THURSDAY!
JUNE
JIM DAVIS
6-16
© 1986 United Feature Syndicate, Inc.
I HATE BIRTHDAYS. THEY'RE A LOT LIKE CALENDARS
JUNE
THEY REMIND YOU YOUR DAYS ARE NUMBERED
JUNE

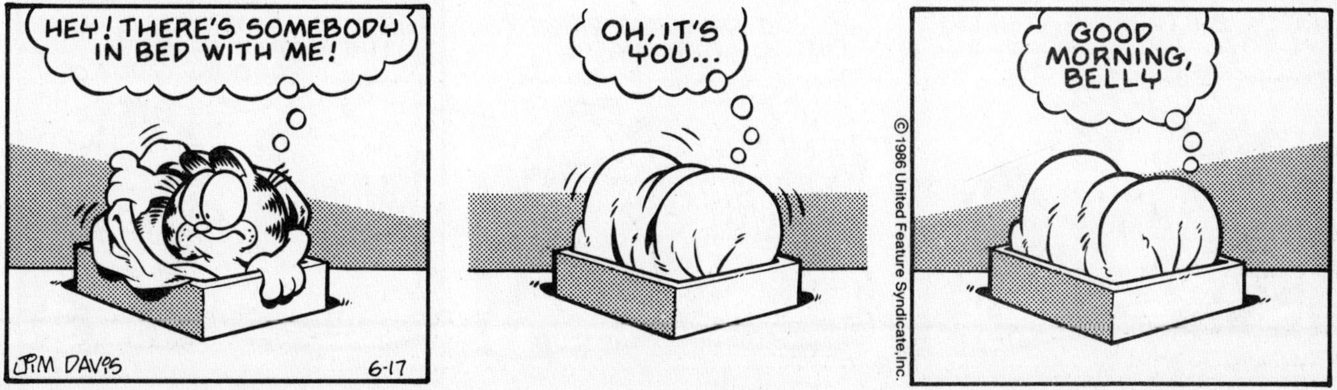
HEY! THERE'S SOMEBODY IN BED WITH ME!
JIM DAVIS
6-17
OH, IT'S YOU...
© 1986 United Feature Syndicate, Inc.
GOOD MORNING, BELLY

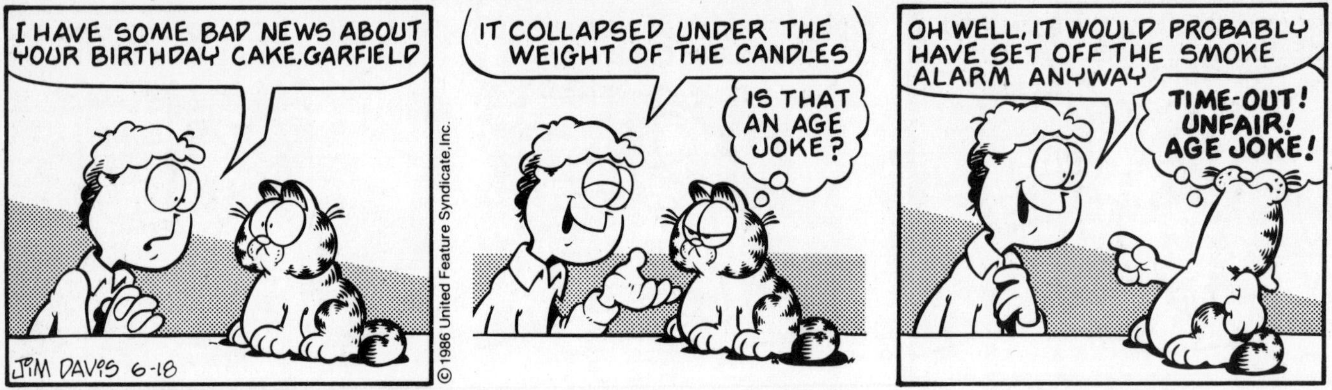
I HAVE SOME BAD NEWS ABOUT YOUR BIRTHDAY CAKE, GARFIELD
JIM DAVIS 6-18
IT COLLAPSED UNDER THE WEIGHT OF THE CANDLES
IS THAT AN AGE JOKE?
OH WELL, IT WOULD PROBABLY HAVE SET OFF THE SMOKE ALARM ANYWAY
TIME-OUT! UNFAIR! AGE JOKE!
© 1986 United Feature Syndicate, Inc.

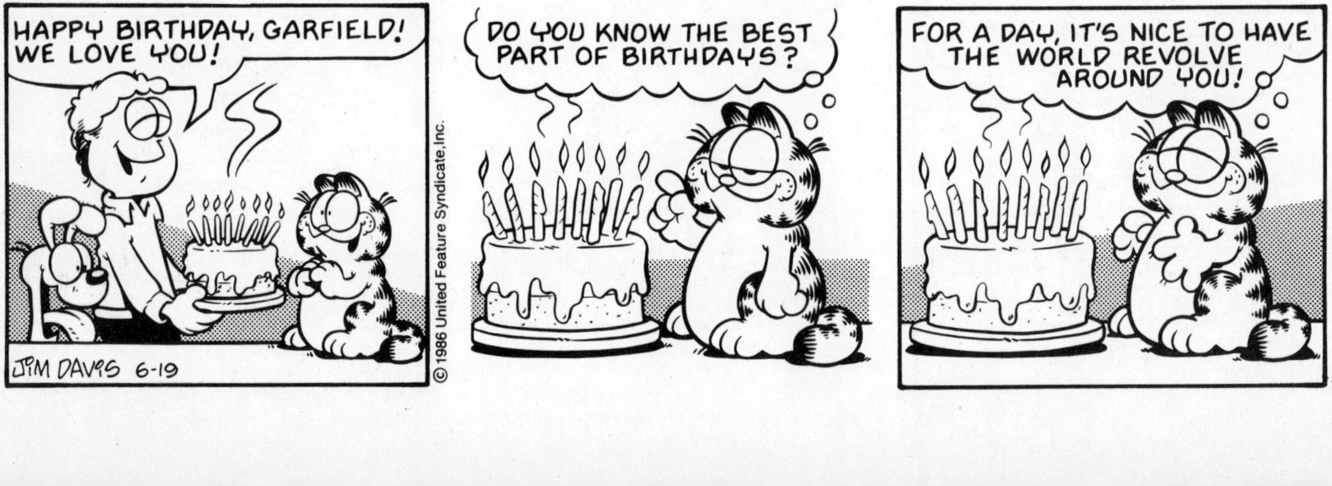
HAPPY BIRTHDAY, GARFIELD! WE LOVE YOU!
JIM DAVIS 6-19
DO YOU KNOW THE BEST PART OF BIRTHDAYS?
FOR A DAY, IT'S NICE TO HAVE THE WORLD REVOLVE AROUND YOU!
© 1986 United Feature Syndicate, Inc.

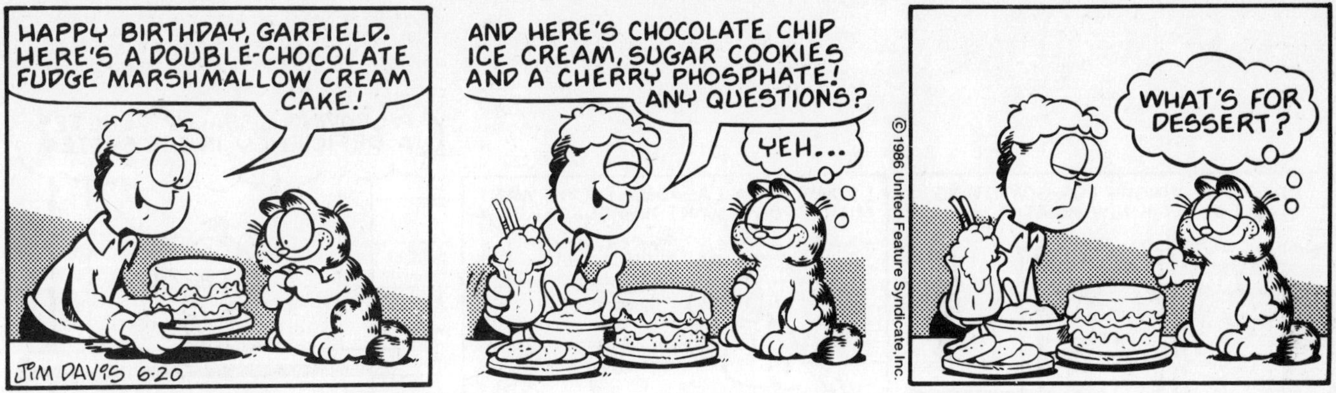
HAPPY BIRTHDAY, GARFIELD. HERE'S A DOUBLE-CHOCOLATE FUDGE MARSHMALLOW CREAM CAKE!
AND HERE'S CHOCOLATE CHIP ICE CREAM, SUGAR COOKIES AND A CHERRY PHOSPHATE! ANY QUESTIONS?
YEH...
WHAT'S FOR DESSERT?
JIM DAVIS 6-20


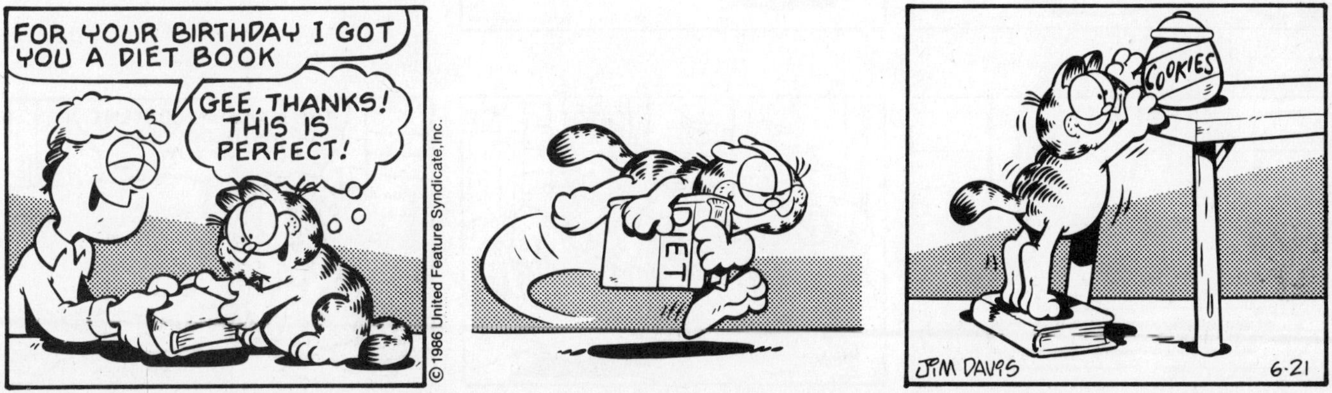
FOR YOUR BIRTHDAY I GOT YOU A DIET BOOK
GEE, THANKS! THIS IS PERFECT!
DIET
COOKIES
JIM DAVIS 6-21

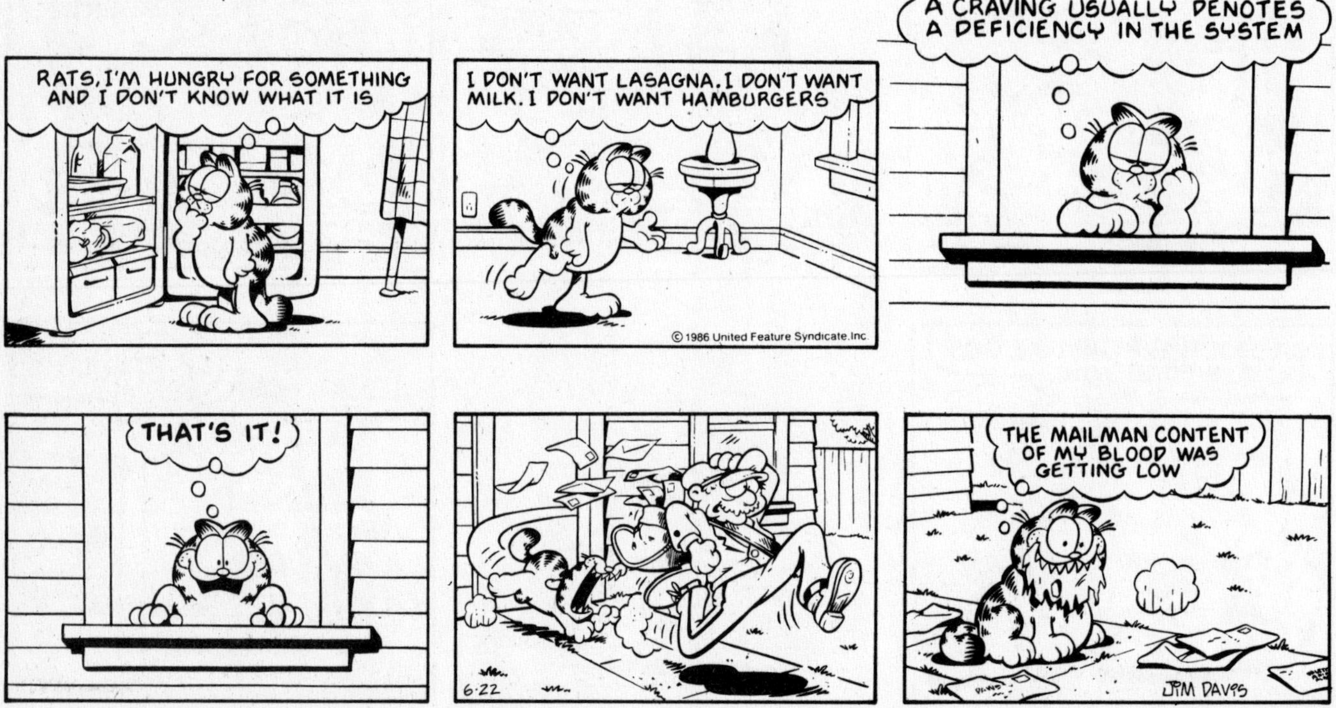
RATS, I'M HUNGRY FOR SOMETHING AND I DON'T KNOW WHAT IT IS
I DON'T WANT LASAGNA. I DON'T WANT MILK. I DON'T WANT HAMBURGERS
© 1986 United Feature Syndicate, Inc.
A CRAVING USUALLY DENOTES A DEFICIENCY IN THE SYSTEM
THAT'S IT!
6-22
THE MAILMAN CONTENT OF MY BLOOD WAS GETTING LOW
JIM DAVIS

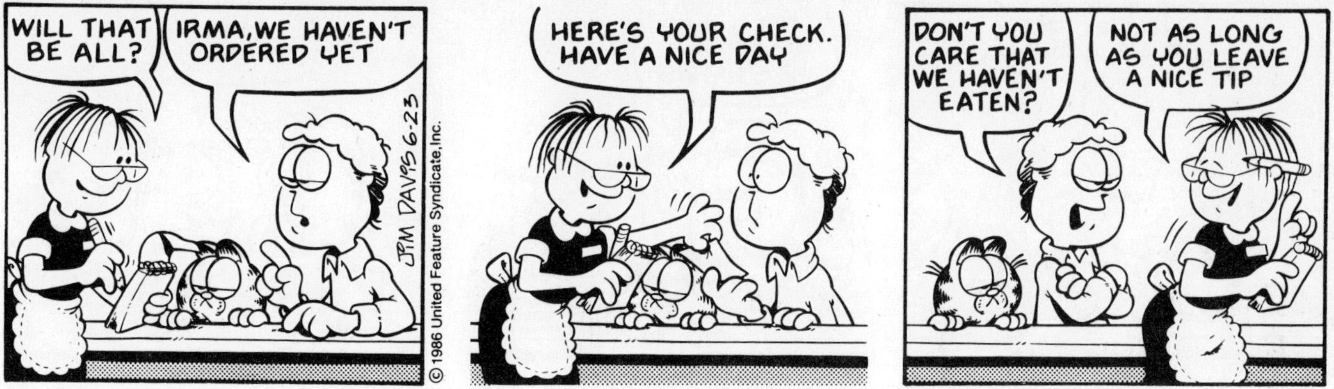
WILL THAT BE ALL?
IRMA, WE HAVEN'T ORDERED YET
JIM DAVIS 6-23
© 1986 United Feature Syndicate, Inc.
HERE'S YOUR CHECK. HAVE A NICE DAY
DON'T YOU CARE THAT WE HAVEN'T EATEN?
NOT AS LONG AS YOU LEAVE A NICE TIP

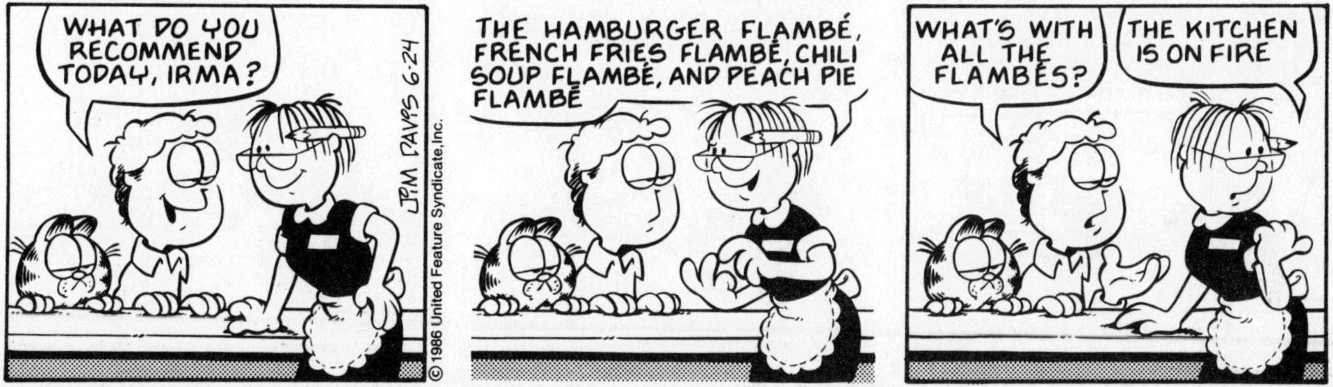
WHAT DO YOU RECOMMEND TODAY, IRMA?
JIM DAVIS 6-24
© 1986 United Feature Syndicate, Inc.
THE HAMBURGER FLAMBÉ, FRENCH FRIES FLAMBÉ, CHILI SOUP FLAMBÉ, AND PEACH PIE FLAMBÉ
WHAT'S WITH ALL THE FLAMBÉS?
THE KITCHEN IS ON FIRE

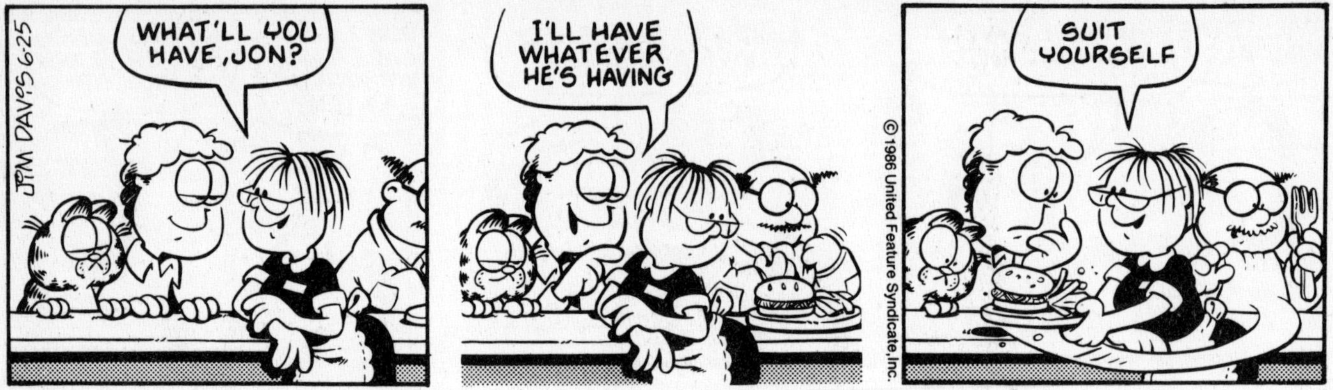
JIM DAVIS 6-25
WHAT'LL YOU HAVE, JON?
I'LL HAVE WHATEVER HE'S HAVING
SUIT YOURSELF
© 1986 United Feature Syndicate, Inc.

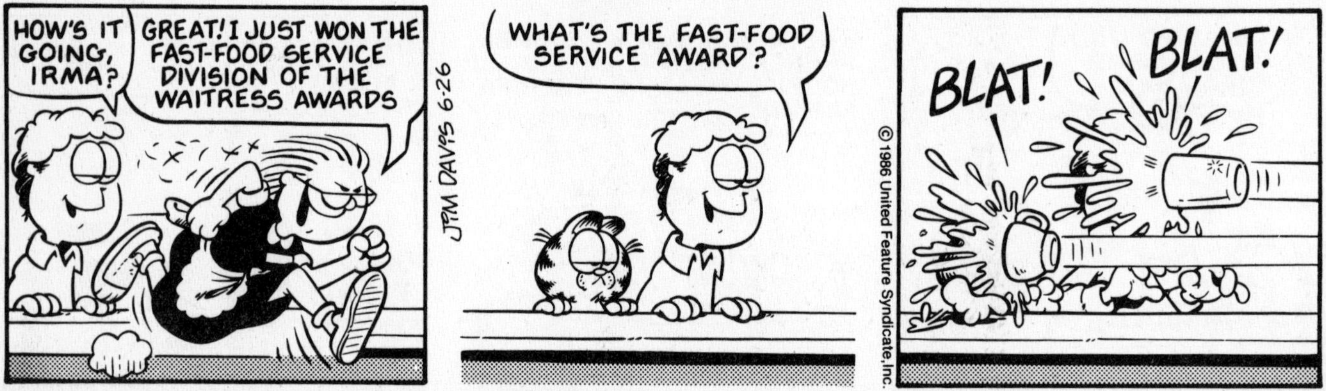
HOW'S IT GOING, IRMA?
GREAT! I JUST WON THE FAST-FOOD SERVICE DIVISION OF THE WAITRESS AWARDS
JIM DAVIS 6-26
WHAT'S THE FAST-FOOD SERVICE AWARD?
BLAT!
BLAT!
© 1986 United Feature Syndicate, Inc.

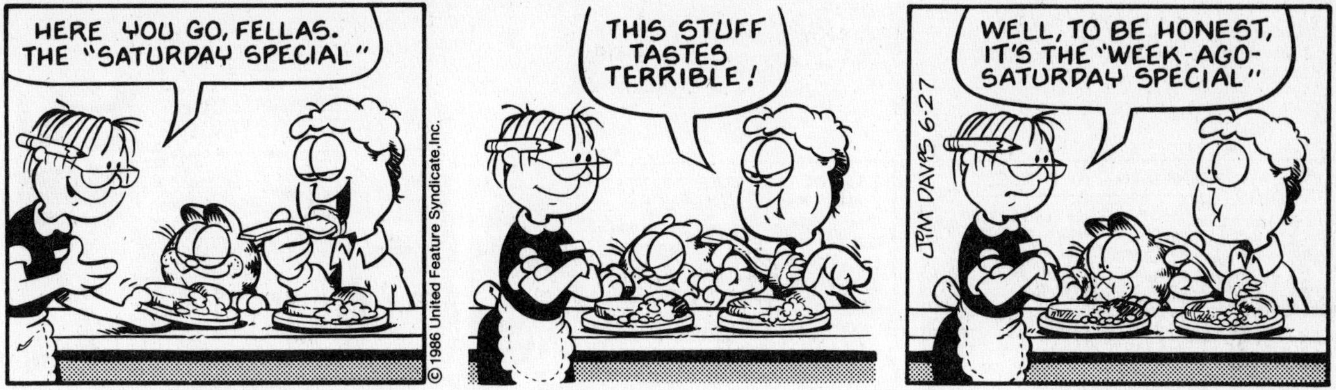
HERE YOU GO, FELLAS. THE "SATURDAY SPECIAL"
© 1986 United Feature Syndicate, Inc.
THIS STUFF TASTES TERRIBLE!
JIM DAVIS 6-27
WELL, TO BE HONEST, IT'S THE "WEEK-AGO-SATURDAY SPECIAL"

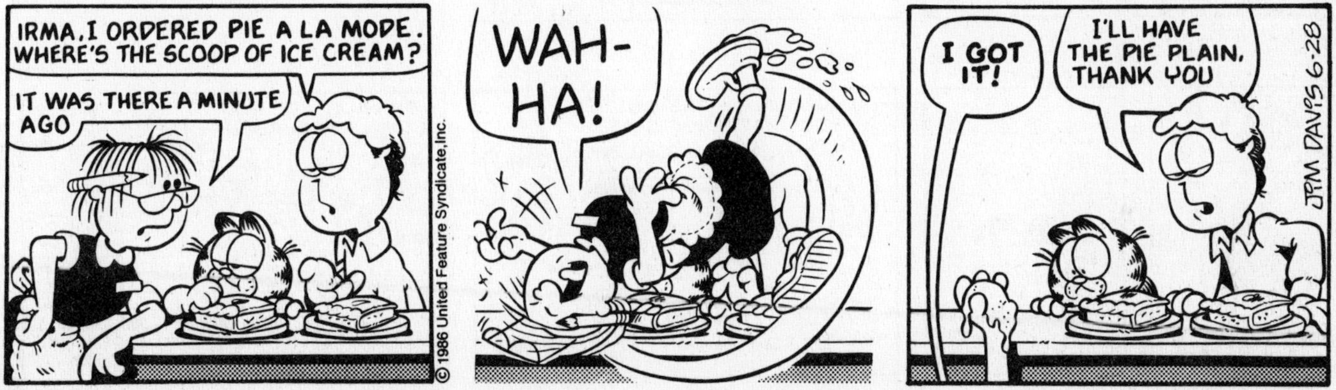
IRMA, I ORDERED PIE A LA MODE. WHERE'S THE SCOOP OF ICE CREAM?
IT WAS THERE A MINUTE AGO
© 1986 United Feature Syndicate, Inc.
WAH-HA!
I GOT IT!
I'LL HAVE THE PIE PLAIN, THANK YOU
JIM DAVIS 6-28

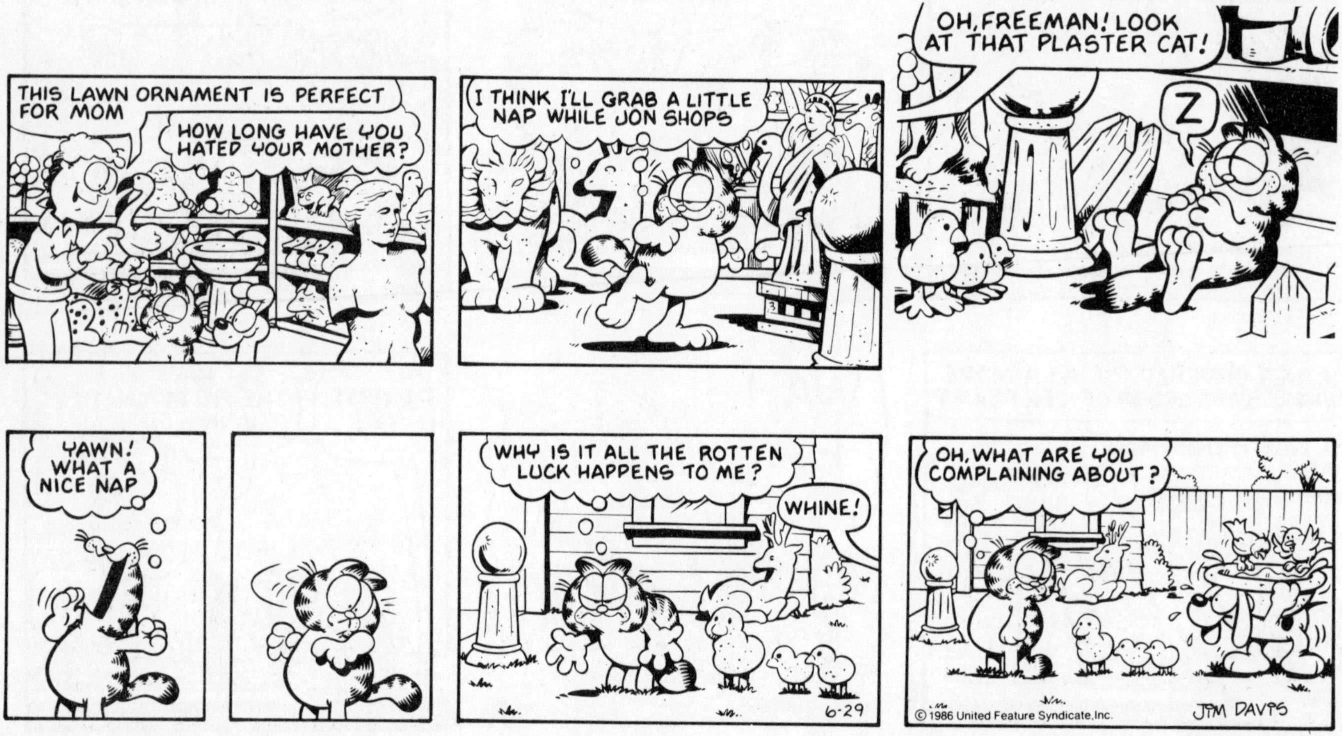
THIS LAWN ORNAMENT IS PERFECT FOR MOM
HOW LONG HAVE YOU HATED YOUR MOTHER?
I THINK I'LL GRAB A LITTLE NAP WHILE JON SHOPS
OH, FREEMAN! LOOK AT THAT PLASTER CAT!
Z
YAWN! WHAT A NICE NAP
WHY IS IT ALL THE ROTTEN LUCK HAPPENS TO ME?
WHINE!
6-29
OH, WHAT ARE YOU COMPLAINING ABOUT?
© 1986 United Feature Syndicate, Inc.
JIM DAVIS

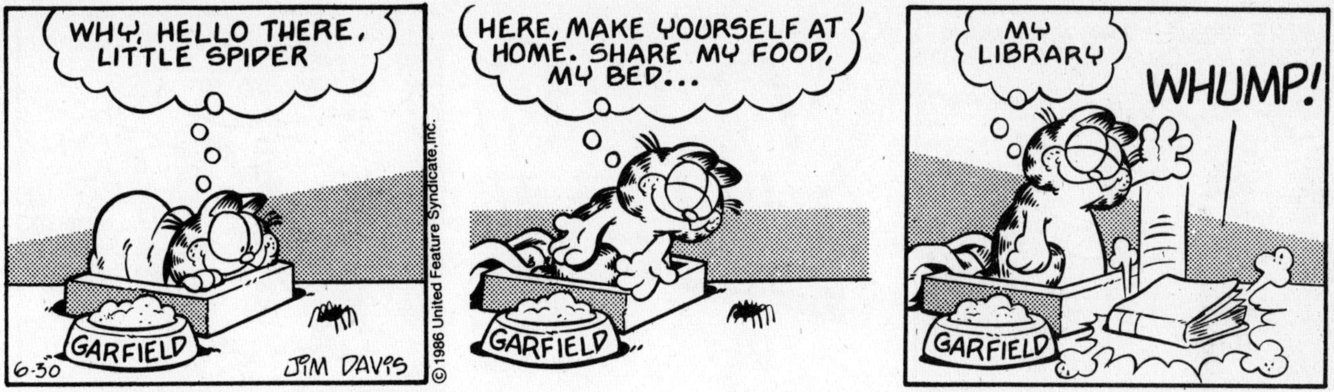
WHY, HELLO THERE, LITTLE SPIDER
GARFIELD
6-30
JIM DAVIS
© 1986 United Feature Syndicate, Inc.
HERE, MAKE YOURSELF AT HOME. SHARE MY FOOD, MY BED...
GARFIELD
MY LIBRARY
WHUMP!
GARFIELD

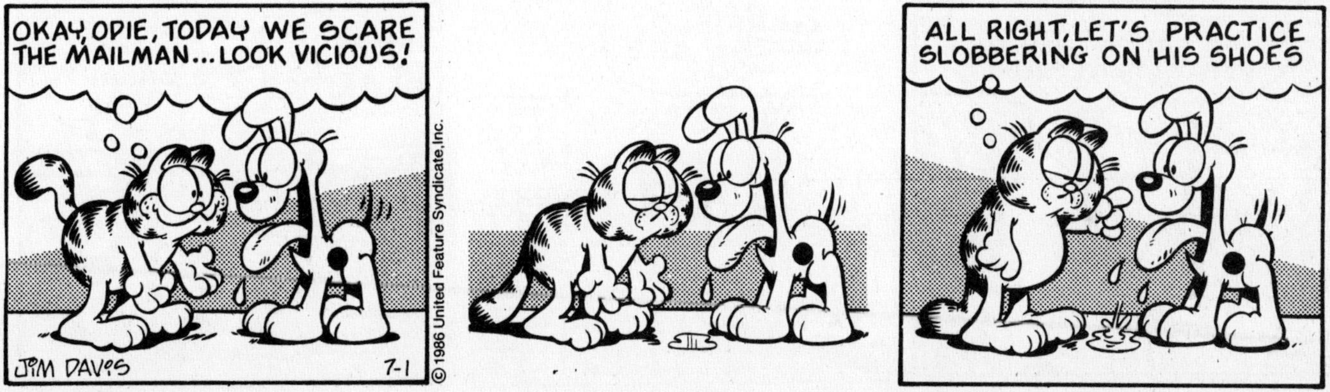
OKAY, ODIE, TODAY WE SCARE THE MAILMAN... LOOK VICIOUS!
JIM DAVIS
7-1
© 1986 United Feature Syndicate, Inc.
ALL RIGHT, LET'S PRACTICE SLOBBERING ON HIS SHOES

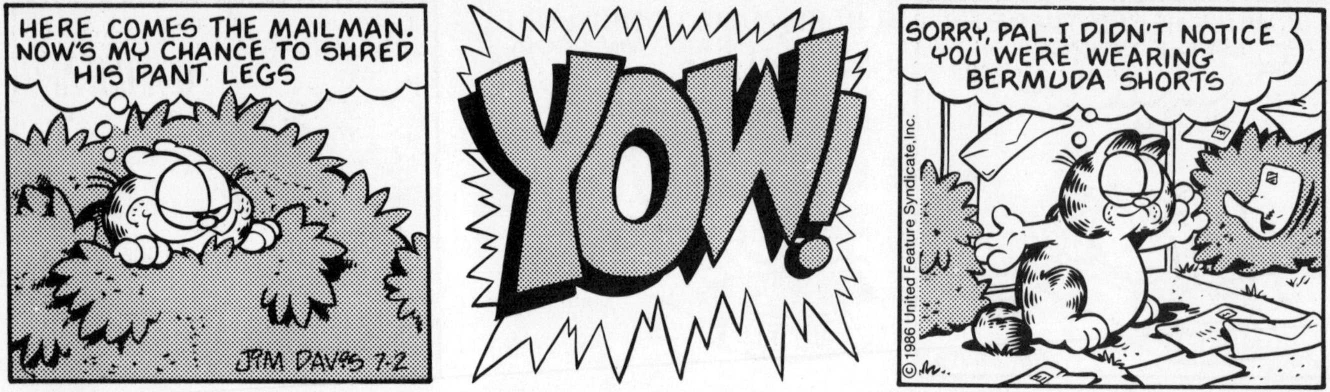
HERE COMES THE MAILMAN. NOW'S MY CHANCE TO SHRED HIS PANT LEGS
JIM DAVIS 7-2
YOW!
SORRY, PAL. I DIDN'T NOTICE YOU WERE WEARING BERMUDA SHORTS
© 1986 United Feature Syndicate, Inc.

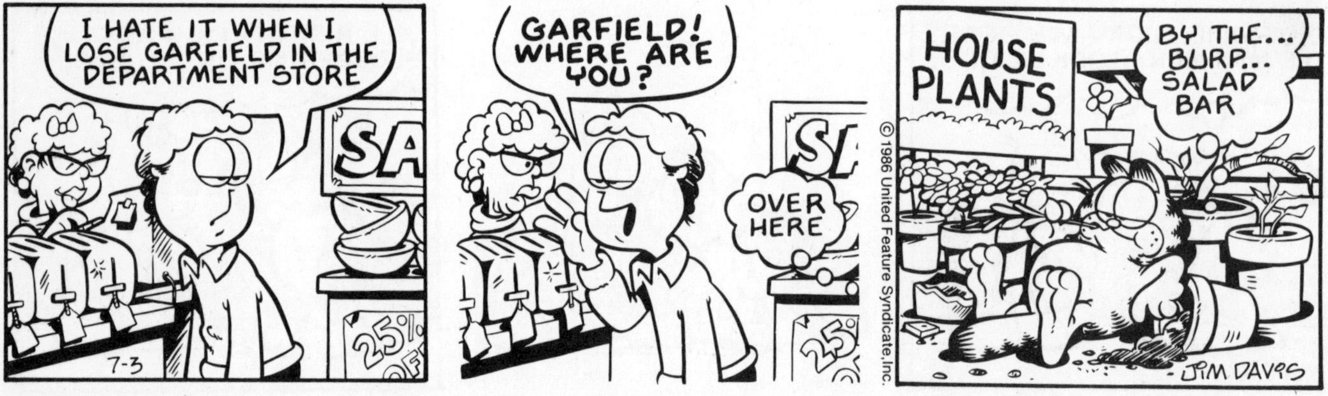
I HATE IT WHEN I LOSE GARFIELD IN THE DEPARTMENT STORE
7-3
GARFIELD! WHERE ARE YOU?
OVER HERE
HOUSE PLANTS
BY THE... BURP... SALAD BAR
JIM DAVIS
© 1986 United Feature Syndicate, Inc.

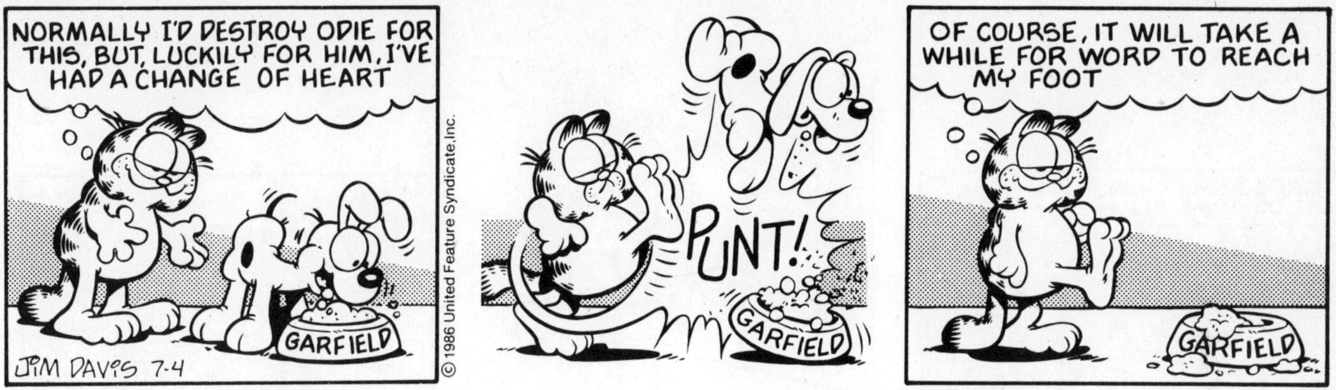
NORMALLY I'D DESTROY ODIE FOR THIS, BUT, LUCKILY FOR HIM, I'VE HAD A CHANGE OF HEART
GARFIELD
JIM DAVIS 7-4
© 1986 United Feature Syndicate, Inc.
PUNT!
GARFIELD
OF COURSE, IT WILL TAKE A WHILE FOR WORD TO REACH MY FOOT
GARFIELD

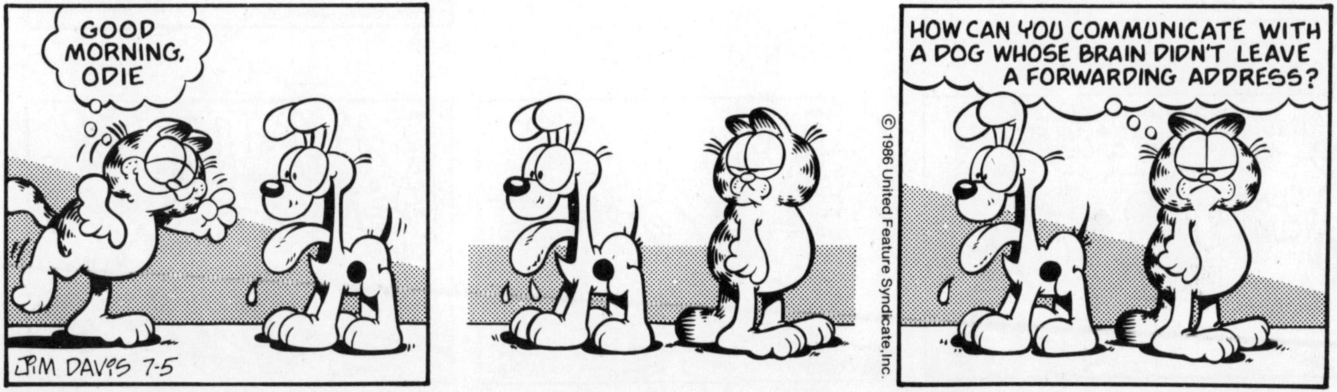
GOOD MORNING, ODIE
JIM DAVIS 7-5
© 1986 United Feature Syndicate, Inc.
HOW CAN YOU COMMUNICATE WITH A DOG WHOSE BRAIN DIDN'T LEAVE A FORWARDING ADDRESS?

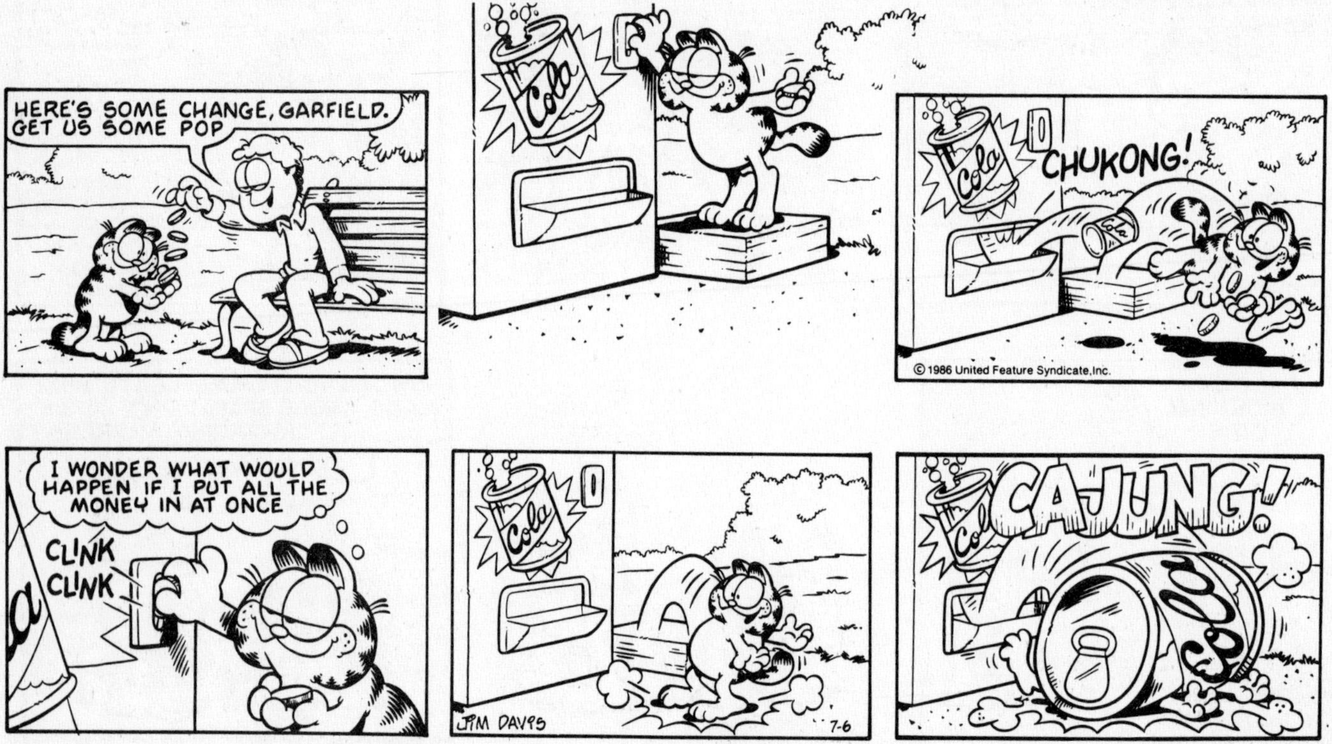
HERE'S SOME CHANGE, GARFIELD. GET US SOME POP
CHUKONG!
© 1986 United Feature Syndicate, Inc.
I WONDER WHAT WOULD HAPPEN IF I PUT ALL THE MONEY IN AT ONCE
CLINK
CLINK
JIM DAVIS
7-6
CAJUNG!

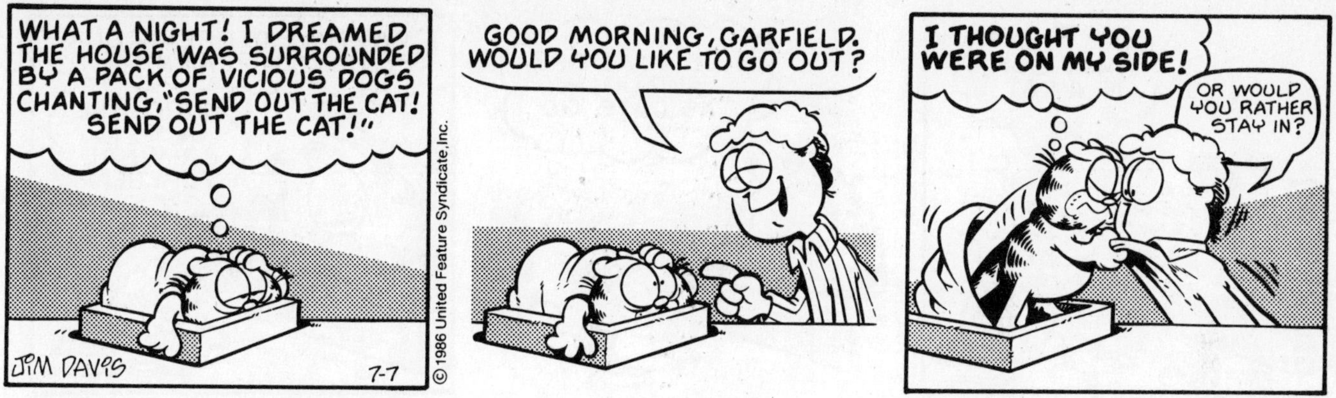
WHAT A NIGHT! I DREAMED THE HOUSE WAS SURROUNDED BY A PACK OF VICIOUS DOGS CHANTING, "SEND OUT THE CAT! SEND OUT THE CAT!"
JIM DAVIS 7-7
© 1986 United Feature Syndicate, Inc.
GOOD MORNING, GARFIELD. WOULD YOU LIKE TO GO OUT?
I THOUGHT YOU WERE ON MY SIDE!
OR WOULD YOU RATHER STAY IN?

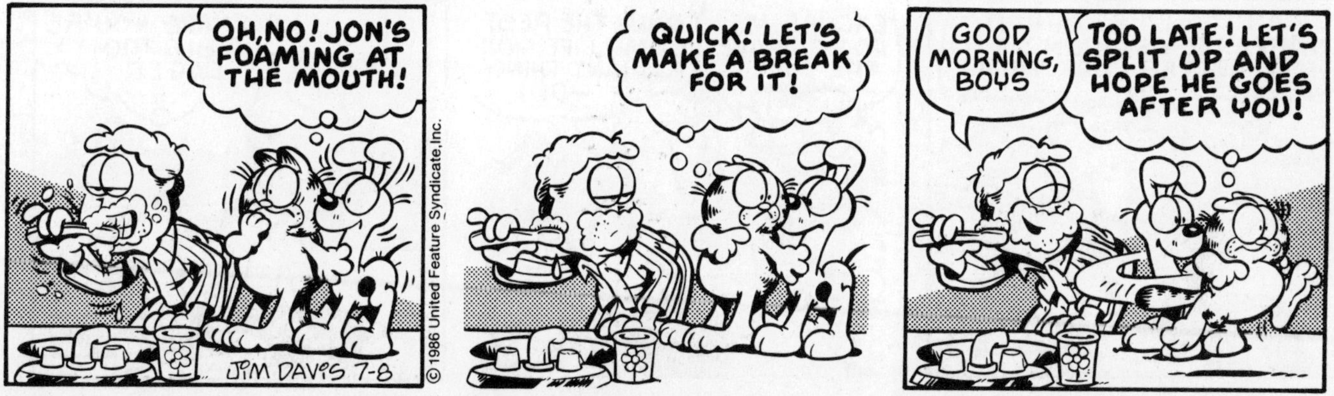
OH, NO! JON'S FOAMING AT THE MOUTH!
JIM DAVIS 7-8
© 1986 United Feature Syndicate, Inc.
QUICK! LET'S MAKE A BREAK FOR IT!
GOOD MORNING, BOYS
TOO LATE! LET'S SPLIT UP AND HOPE HE GOES AFTER YOU!

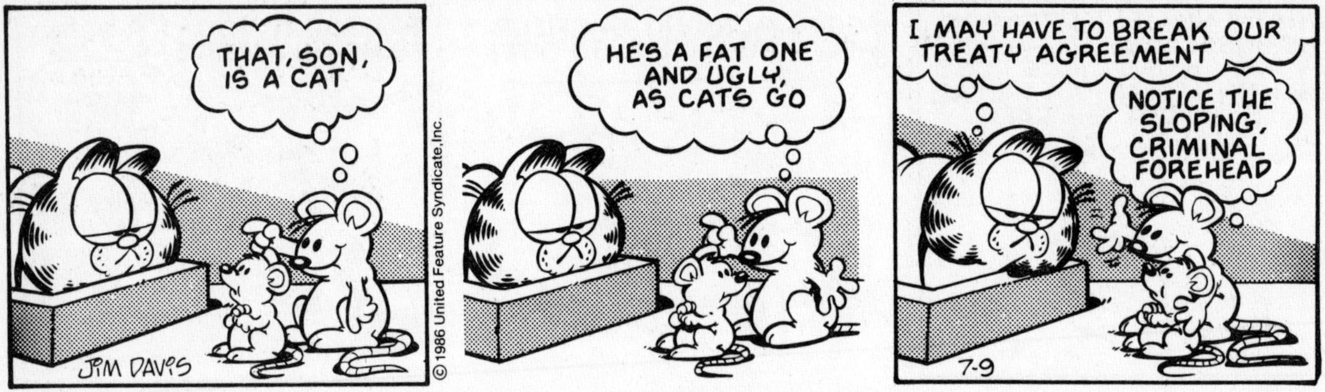
THAT, SON, IS A CAT
JIM DAVIS
© 1986 United Feature Syndicate, Inc.
HE'S A FAT ONE AND UGLY, AS CATS GO
I MAY HAVE TO BREAK OUR TREATY AGREEMENT
NOTICE THE SLOPING, CRIMINAL FOREHEAD
7-9

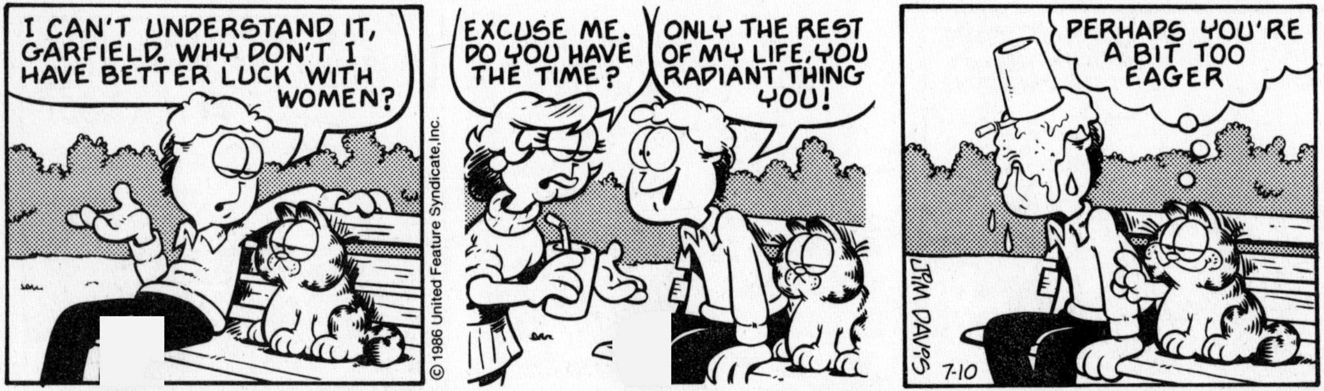
I CAN'T UNDERSTAND IT, GARFIELD. WHY DON'T I HAVE BETTER LUCK WITH WOMEN?
© 1986 United Feature Syndicate, Inc.
EXCUSE ME. DO YOU HAVE THE TIME?
ONLY THE REST OF MY LIFE, YOU RADIANT THING YOU!
PERHAPS YOU'RE A BIT TOO EAGER
JIM DAVIS
7-10

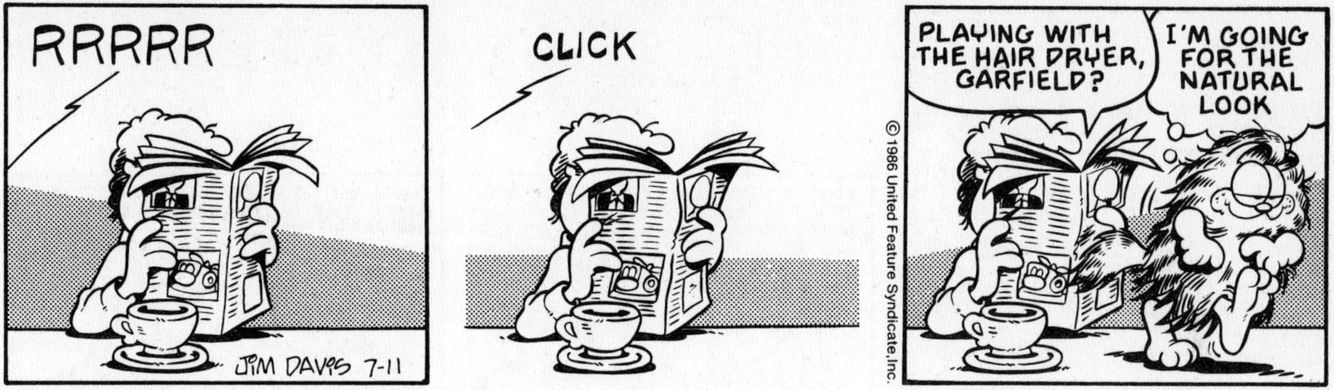
RRRRR
JIM DAVIS 7-11
CLICK
PLAYING WITH THE HAIR DRYER, GARFIELD?
I'M GOING FOR THE NATURAL LOOK
© 1986 United Feature Syndicate,Inc.

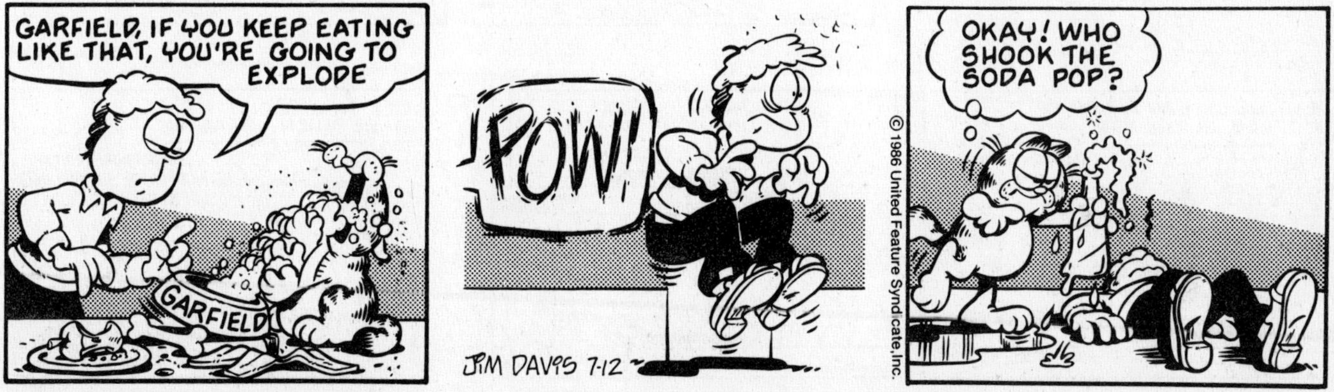
GARFIELD, IF YOU KEEP EATING LIKE THAT, YOU'RE GOING TO EXPLODE
GARFIELD
POW!
JIM DAVIS 7-12
OKAY! WHO SHOOK THE SODA POP?
© 1986 United Feature Syndicate,Inc.

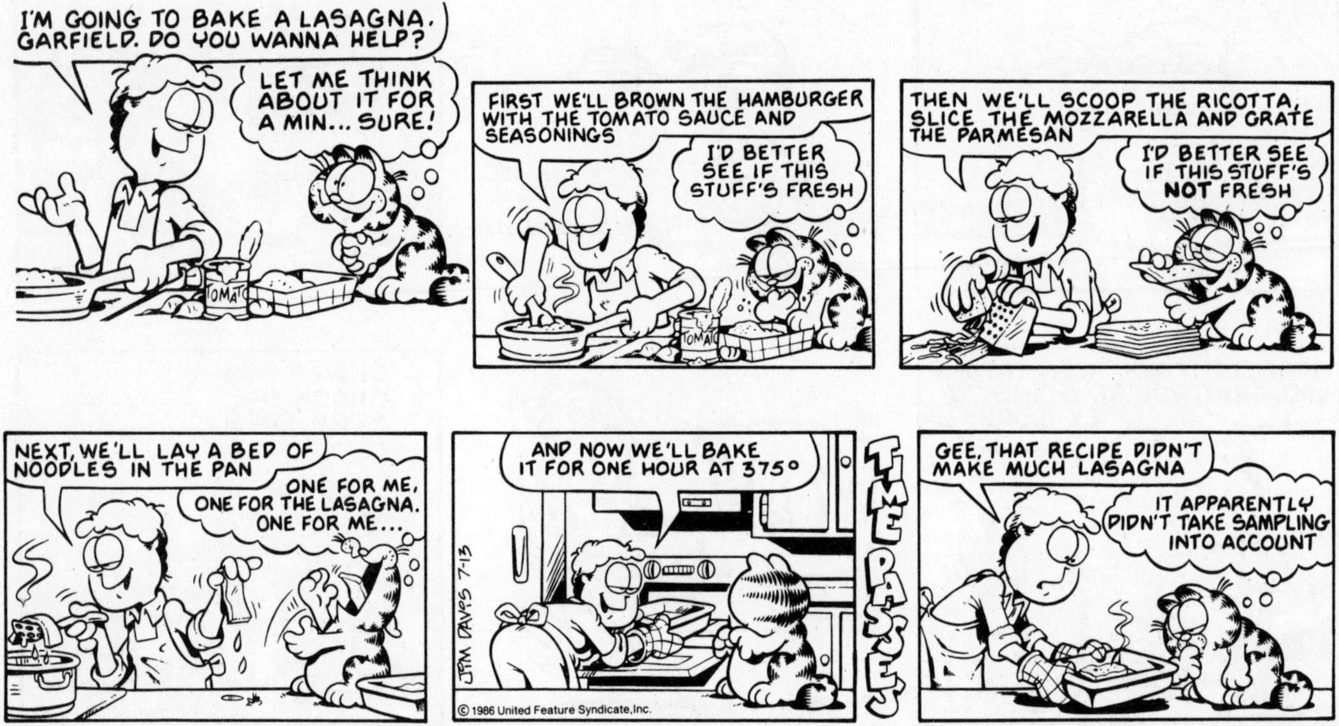
I'M GOING TO BAKE A LASAGNA, GARFIELD. DO YOU WANNA HELP?
LET ME THINK ABOUT IT FOR A MIN... SURE!
TOMATO
FIRST WE'LL BROWN THE HAMBURGER WITH THE TOMATO SAUCE AND SEASONINGS
I'D BETTER SEE IF THIS STUFF'S FRESH
TOMATO
THEN WE'LL SCOOP THE RICOTTA, SLICE THE MOZZARELLA AND GRATE THE PARMESAN
I'D BETTER SEE IF THIS STUFF'S **NOT** FRESH
NEXT, WE'LL LAY A BED OF NOODLES IN THE PAN
ONE FOR ME, ONE FOR THE LASAGNA. ONE FOR ME...
JIM DAVIS 7-13
AND NOW WE'LL BAKE IT FOR ONE HOUR AT 375°
© 1986 United Feature Syndicate, Inc.
TIME PASSES
GEE, THAT RECIPE DIDN'T MAKE MUCH LASAGNA
IT APPARENTLY DIDN'T TAKE SAMPLING INTO ACCOUNT

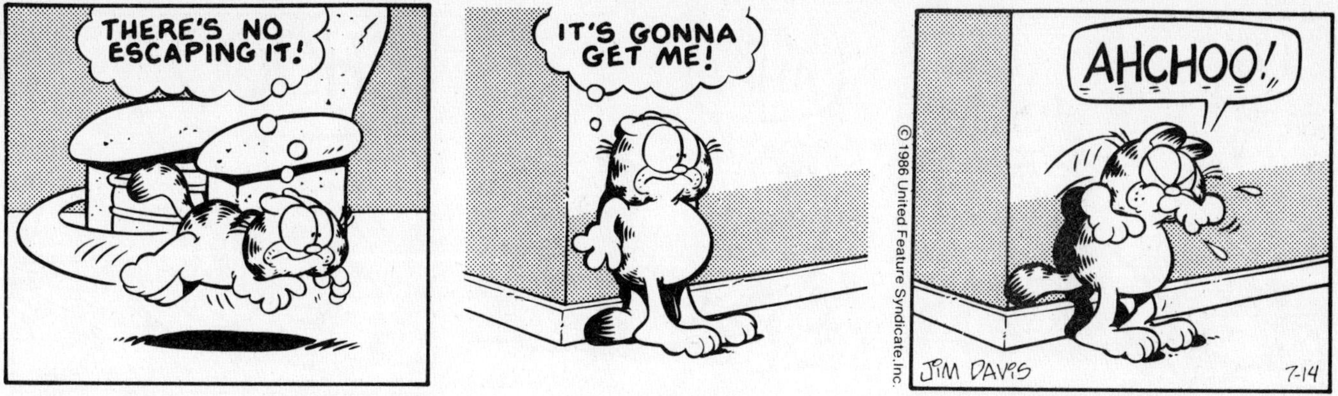
THERE'S NO ESCAPING IT!
IT'S GONNA GET ME!
AHCHOO!
© 1986 United Feature Syndicate, Inc.
JIM DAVIS
7-14

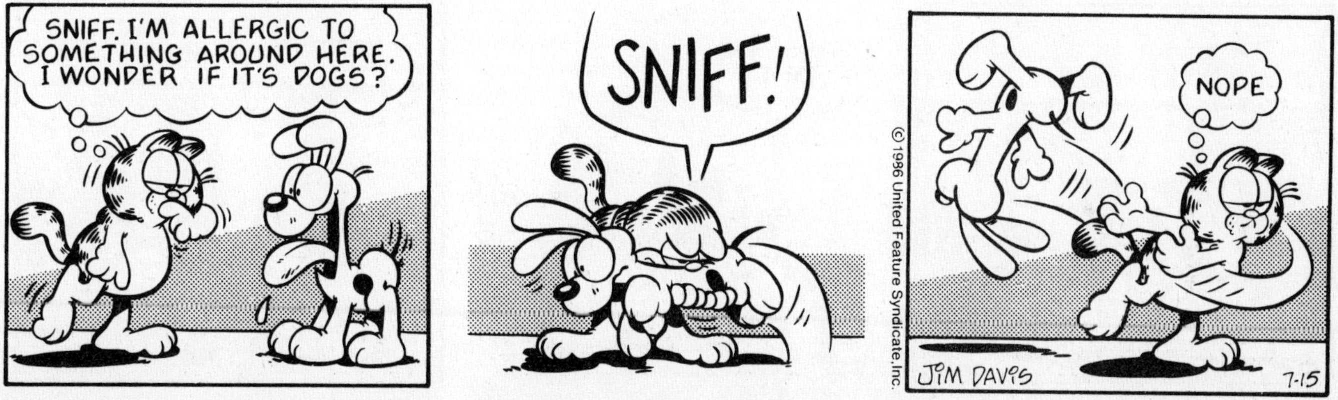
SNIFF. I'M ALLERGIC TO SOMETHING AROUND HERE. I WONDER IF IT'S DOGS?
SNIFF!
NOPE
© 1986 United Feature Syndicate, Inc.
JIM DAVIS
7-15

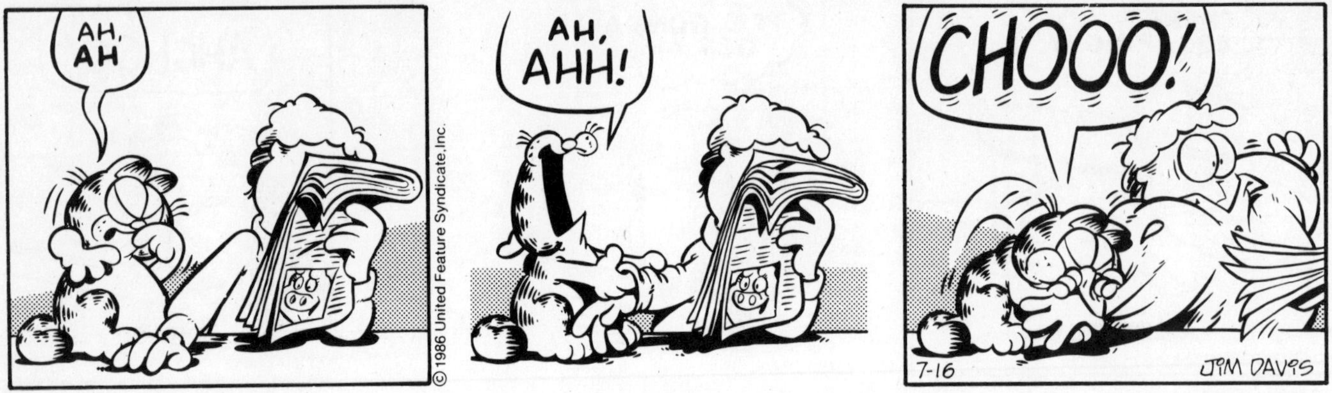
AH, AH
AH, AHH!
CHOOO!
© 1986 United Feature Syndicate, Inc.
7-16
JIM DAVIS

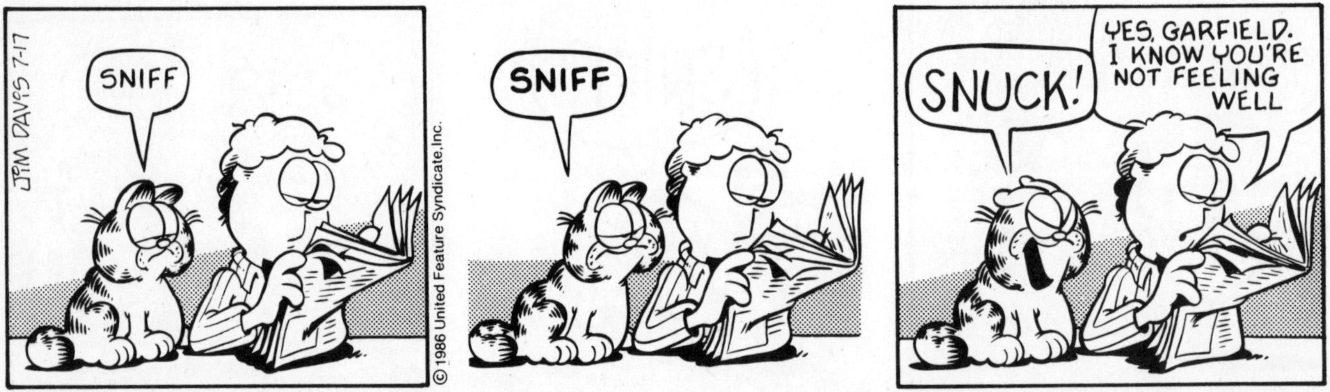
JIM DAVIS 7-17
SNIFF
SNIFF
SNUCK!
YES, GARFIELD. I KNOW YOU'RE NOT FEELING WELL
© 1986 United Feature Syndicate, Inc.

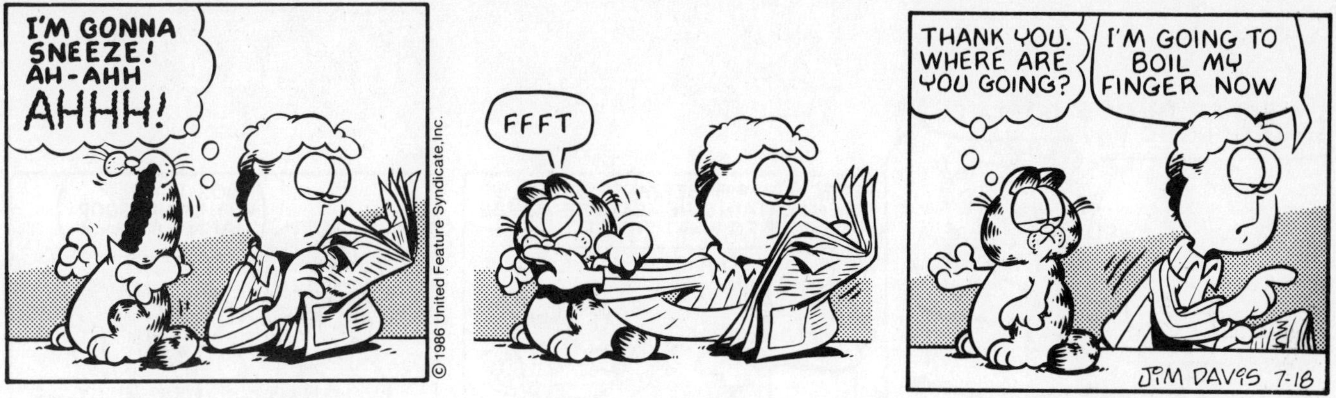
I'M GONNA SNEEZE! AH-AHH AHHH!
FFFT
THANK YOU. WHERE ARE YOU GOING?
I'M GOING TO BOIL MY FINGER NOW
JIM DAVIS 7-18
© 1986 United Feature Syndicate, Inc.

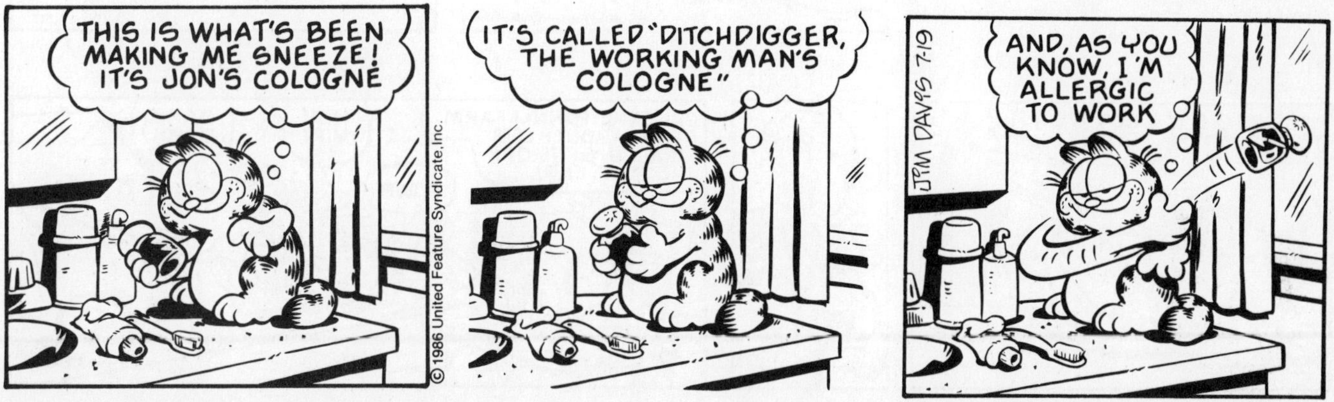
THIS IS WHAT'S BEEN MAKING ME SNEEZE! IT'S JON'S COLOGNE
IT'S CALLED "DITCHDIGGER, THE WORKING MAN'S COLOGNE"
AND, AS YOU KNOW, I'M ALLERGIC TO WORK
JIM DAVIS 7-19
© 1986 United Feature Syndicate, Inc.

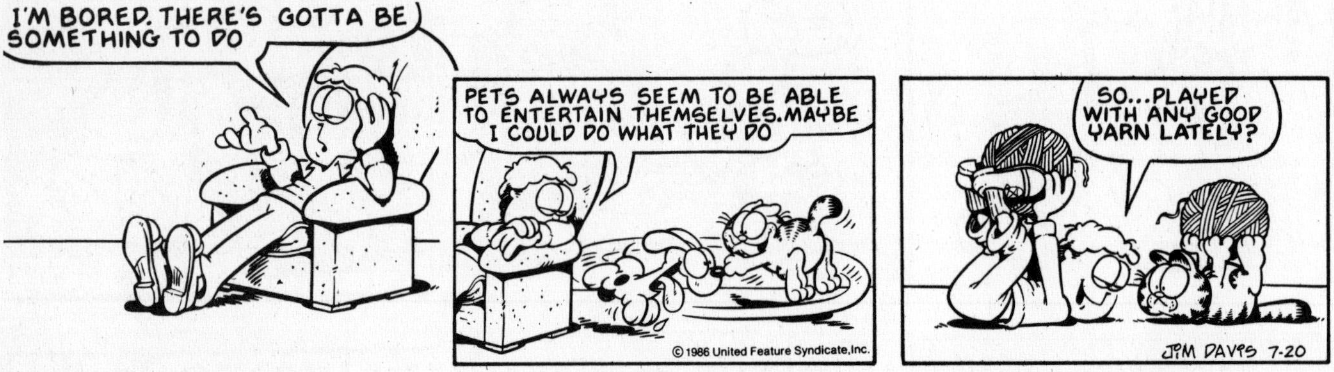
I'M BORED. THERE'S GOTTA BE SOMETHING TO DO
PETS ALWAYS SEEM TO BE ABLE TO ENTERTAIN THEMSELVES. MAYBE I COULD DO WHAT THEY DO
SO...PLAYED WITH ANY GOOD YARN LATELY?
© 1986 United Feature Syndicate, Inc.
JIM DAVIS 7-20

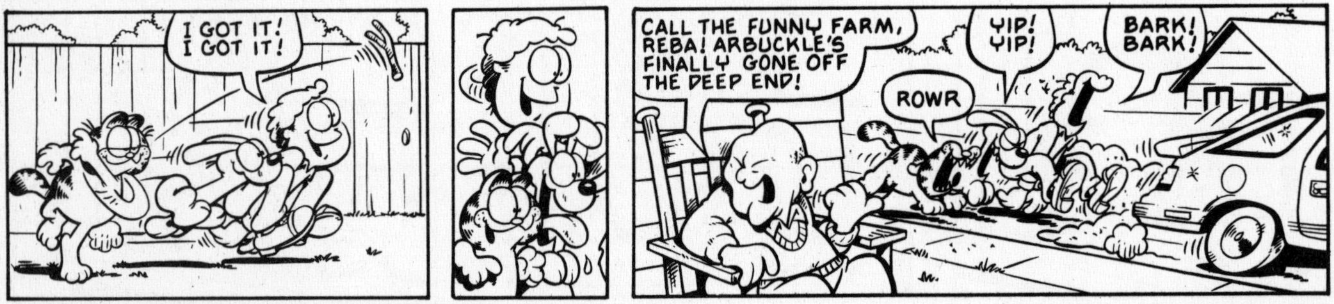
I GOT IT! I GOT IT!
CALL THE FUNNY FARM, REBA! ARBUCKLE'S FINALLY GONE OFF THE DEEP END!
ROWR
YIP! YIP!
BARK! BARK!

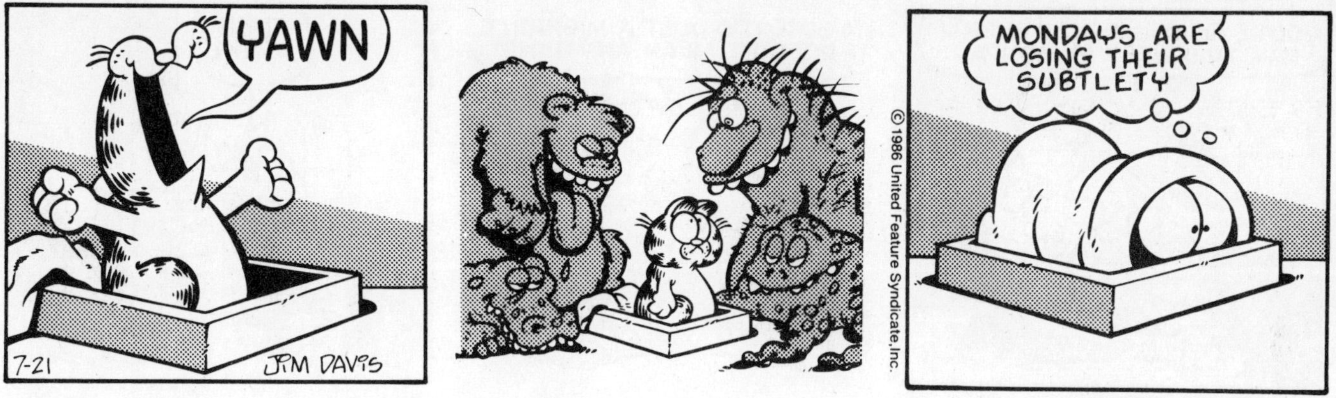
YAWN
7-21
JIM DAVIS
© 1986 United Feature Syndicate, Inc.
MONDAYS ARE LOSING THEIR SUBTLETY

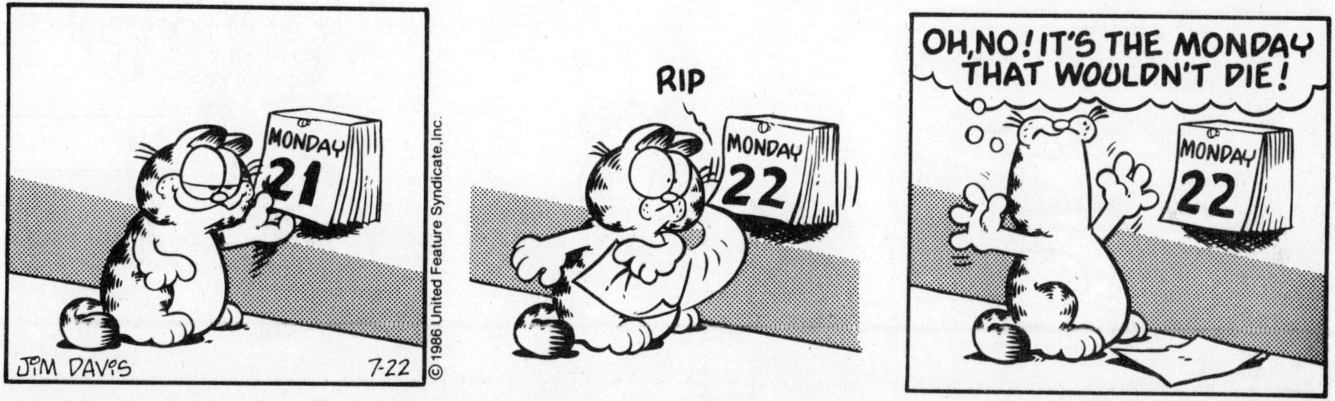
MONDAY
21
JIM DAVIS
7-22
© 1986 United Feature Syndicate, Inc.
RIP
MONDAY
22
OH, NO! IT'S THE MONDAY THAT WOULDN'T DIE!
MONDAY
22

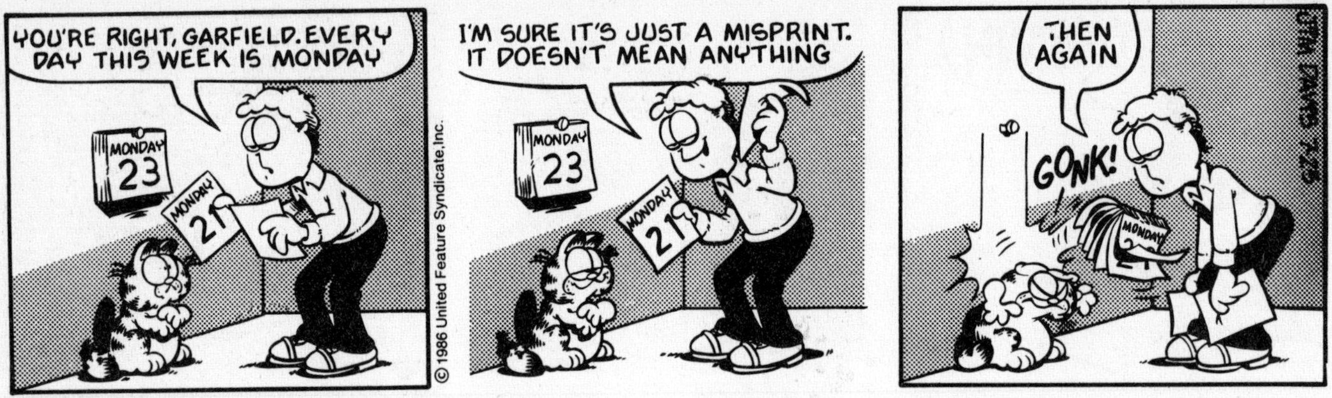
YOU'RE RIGHT, GARFIELD. EVERY DAY THIS WEEK IS MONDAY
MONDAY 23
MONDAY 21
© 1986 United Feature Syndicate, Inc.
I'M SURE IT'S JUST A MISPRINT. IT DOESN'T MEAN ANYTHING
MONDAY 23
MONDAY 21
THEN AGAIN
GONK!
MONDAY
JIM DAVIS 7-25

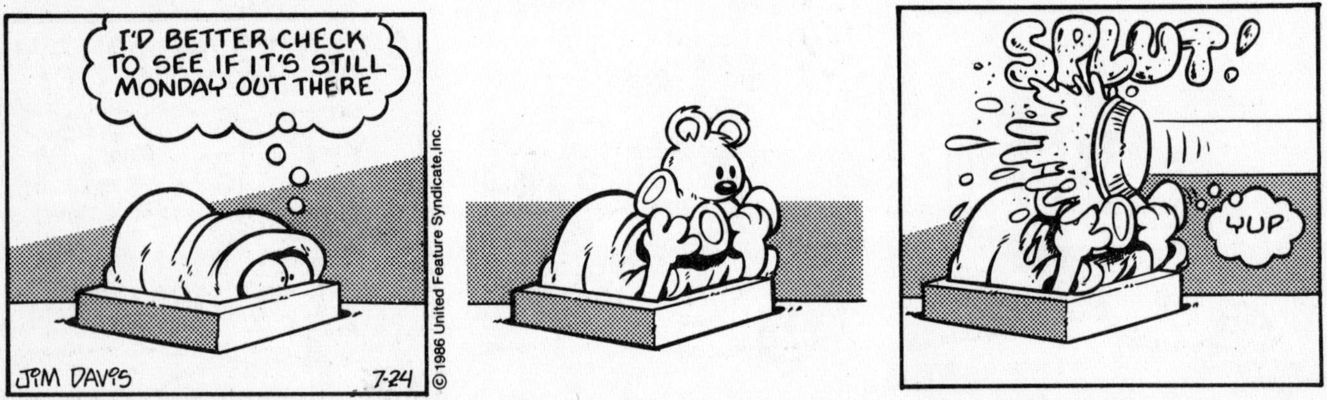
I'D BETTER CHECK TO SEE IF IT'S STILL MONDAY OUT THERE
JIM DAVIS
7-24
© 1986 United Feature Syndicate, Inc.
SPLUT!
YUP

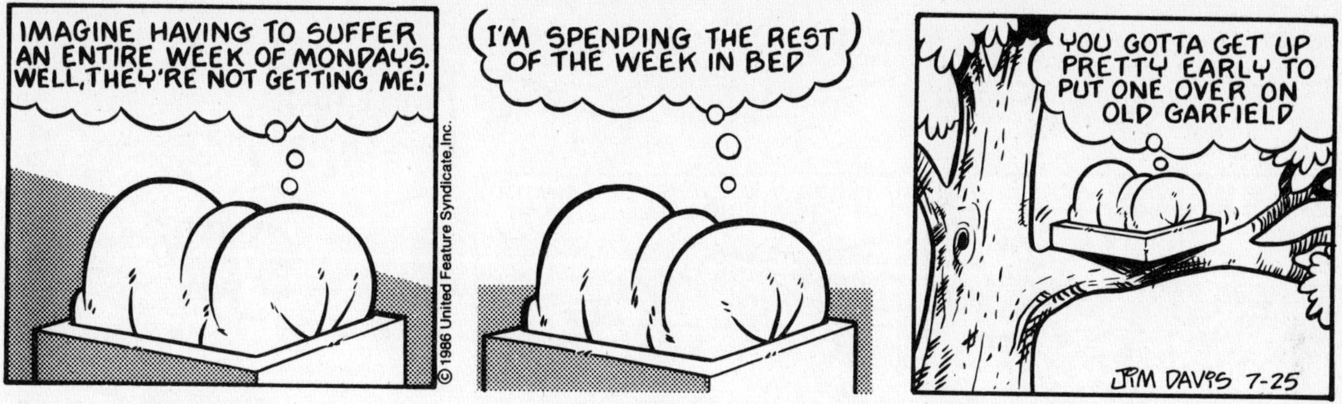
IMAGINE HAVING TO SUFFER AN ENTIRE WEEK OF MONDAYS. WELL, THEY'RE NOT GETTING ME!
I'M SPENDING THE REST OF THE WEEK IN BED
YOU GOTTA GET UP PRETTY EARLY TO PUT ONE OVER ON OLD GARFIELD
JIM DAVIS 7-25
© 1986 United Feature Syndicate, Inc.

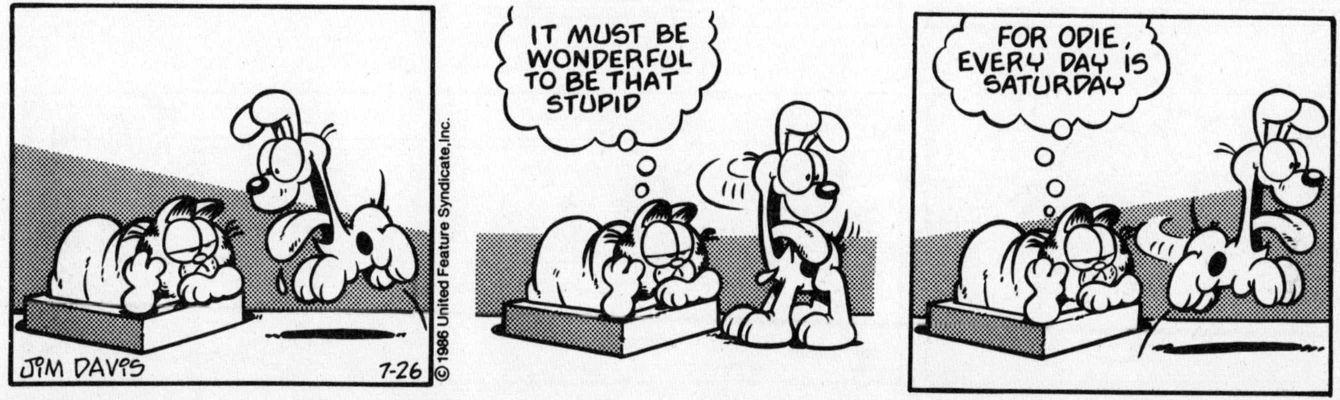
JIM DAVIS 7-26
© 1986 United Feature Syndicate, Inc.
IT MUST BE WONDERFUL TO BE THAT STUPID
FOR ODIE, EVERY DAY IS SATURDAY

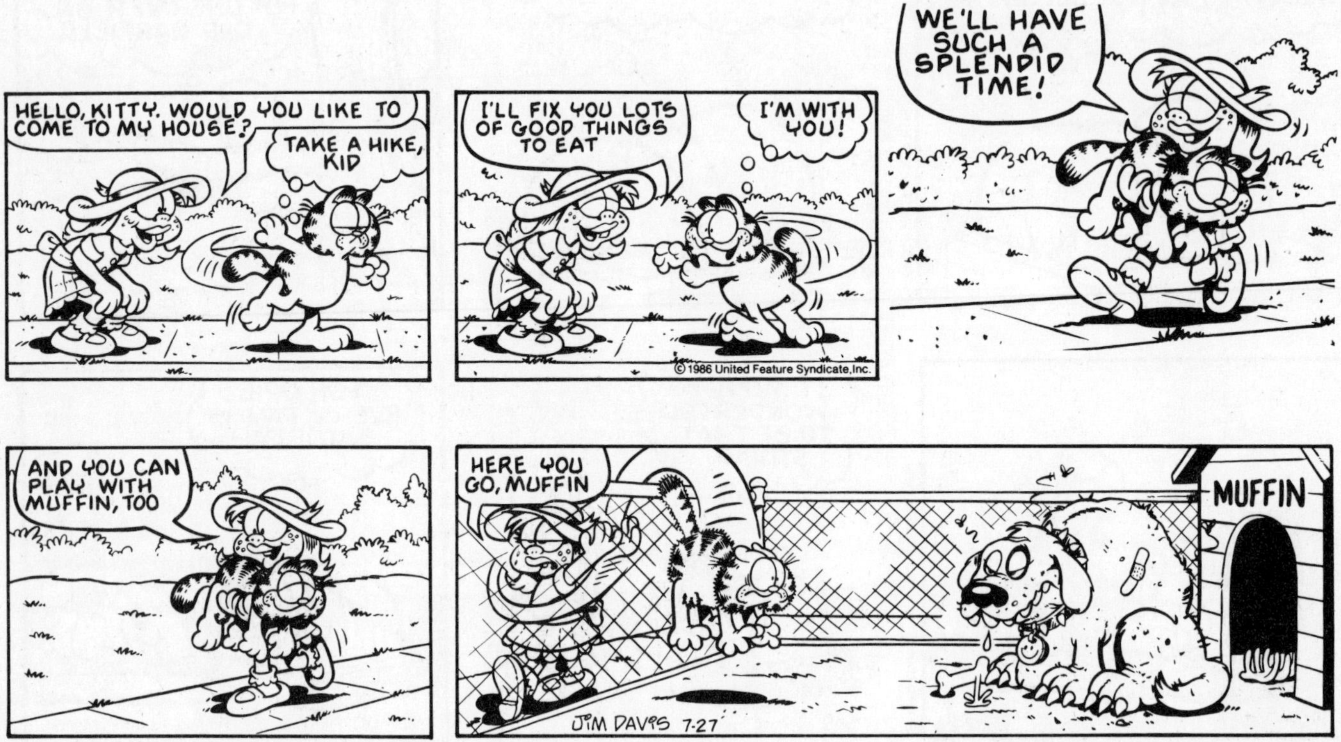
HELLO, KITTY. WOULD YOU LIKE TO COME TO MY HOUSE?
TAKE A HIKE, KID
I'LL FIX YOU LOTS OF GOOD THINGS TO EAT
I'M WITH YOU!
© 1986 United Feature Syndicate, Inc.
WE'LL HAVE SUCH A SPLENDID TIME!
AND YOU CAN PLAY WITH MUFFIN, TOO
HERE YOU GO, MUFFIN
MUFFIN
JIM DAVIS 7-27

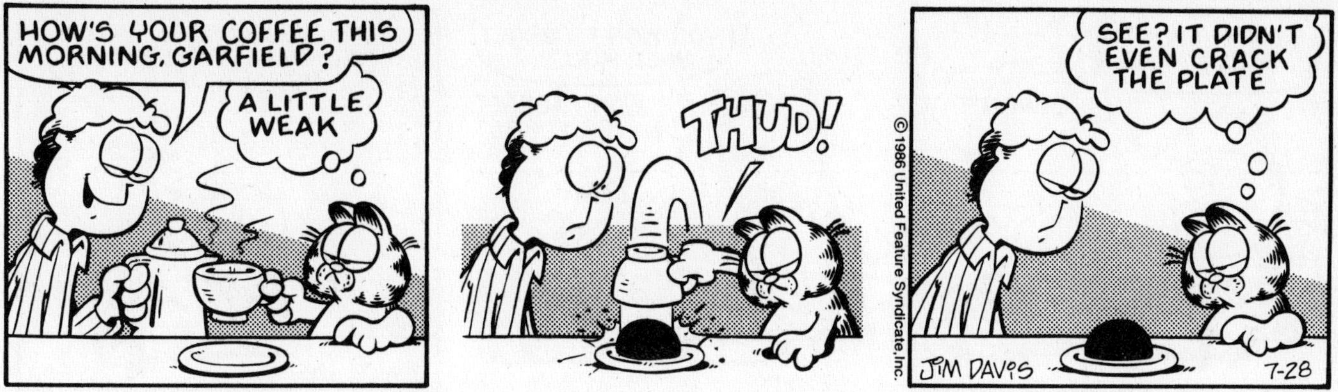
HOW'S YOUR COFFEE THIS MORNING, GARFIELD?
A LITTLE WEAK
THUD!
SEE? IT DIDN'T EVEN CRACK THE PLATE
© 1986 United Feature Syndicate, Inc.
JIM DAVIS
7-28

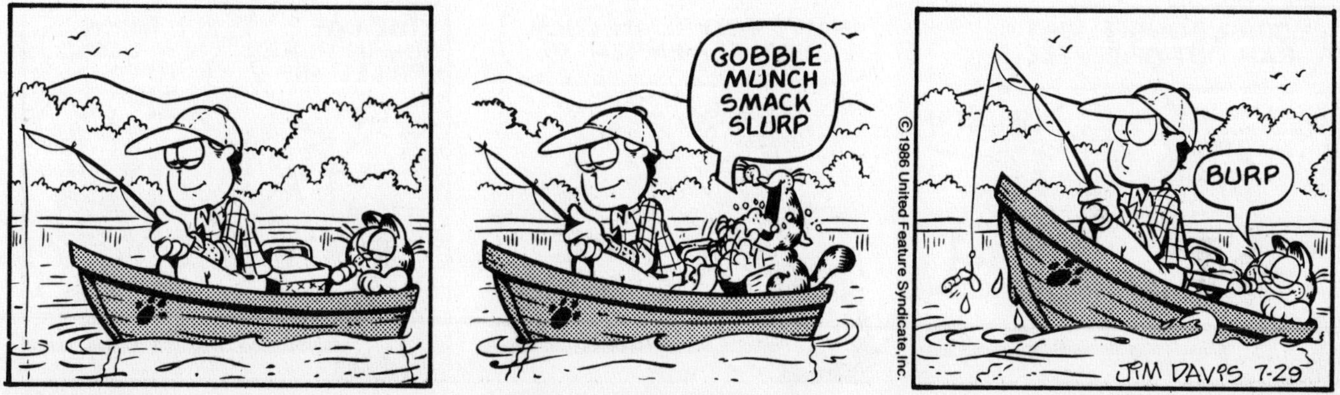
GOBBLE MUNCH SMACK SLURP
BURP
© 1986 United Feature Syndicate, Inc.
JIM DAVIS 7-29

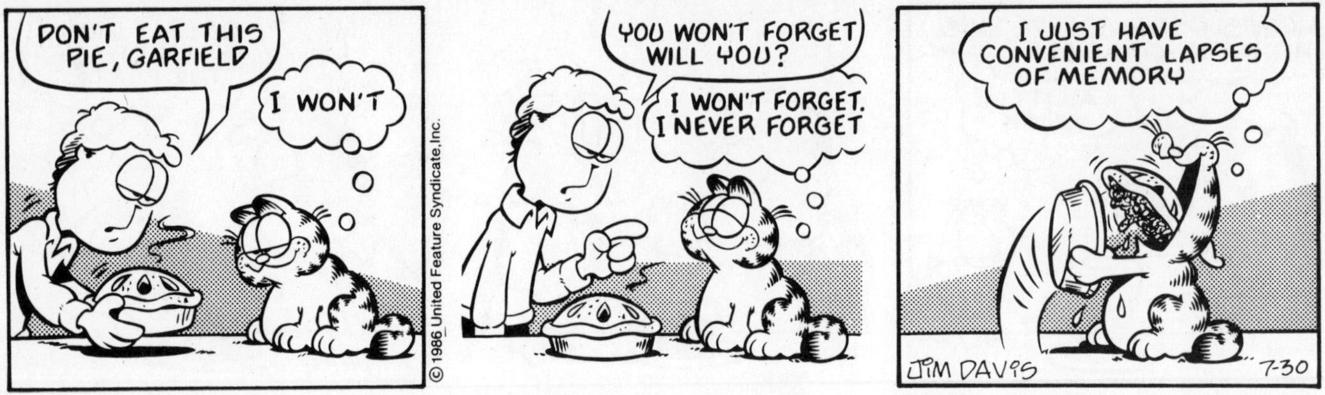
DON'T EAT THIS PIE, GARFIELD
I WON'T
© 1986 United Feature Syndicate, Inc.
YOU WON'T FORGET WILL YOU?
I WON'T FORGET. I NEVER FORGET
I JUST HAVE CONVENIENT LAPSES OF MEMORY
JIM DAVIS 7-30

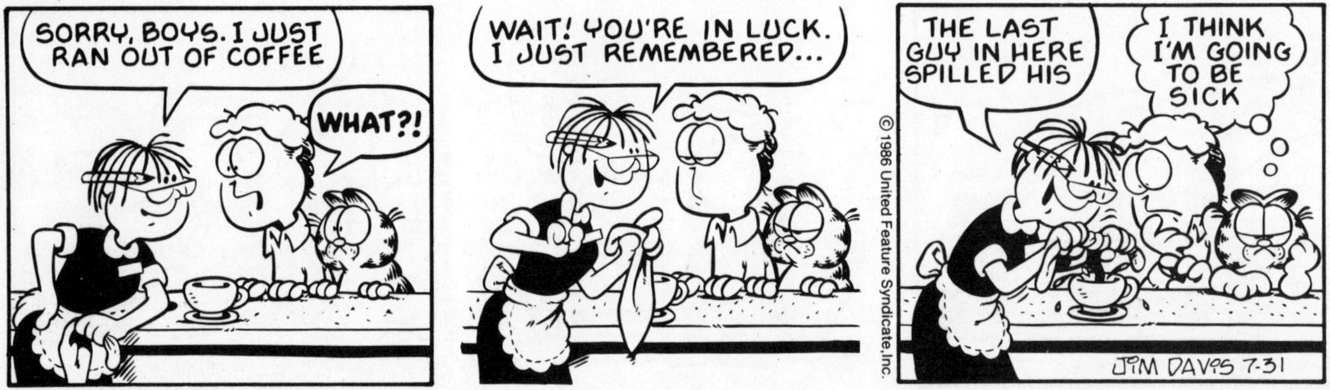
SORRY, BOYS. I JUST RAN OUT OF COFFEE
WHAT?!
WAIT! YOU'RE IN LUCK. I JUST REMEMBERED...
© 1986 United Feature Syndicate, Inc.
THE LAST GUY IN HERE SPILLED HIS
I THINK I'M GOING TO BE SICK
JIM DAVIS 7-31

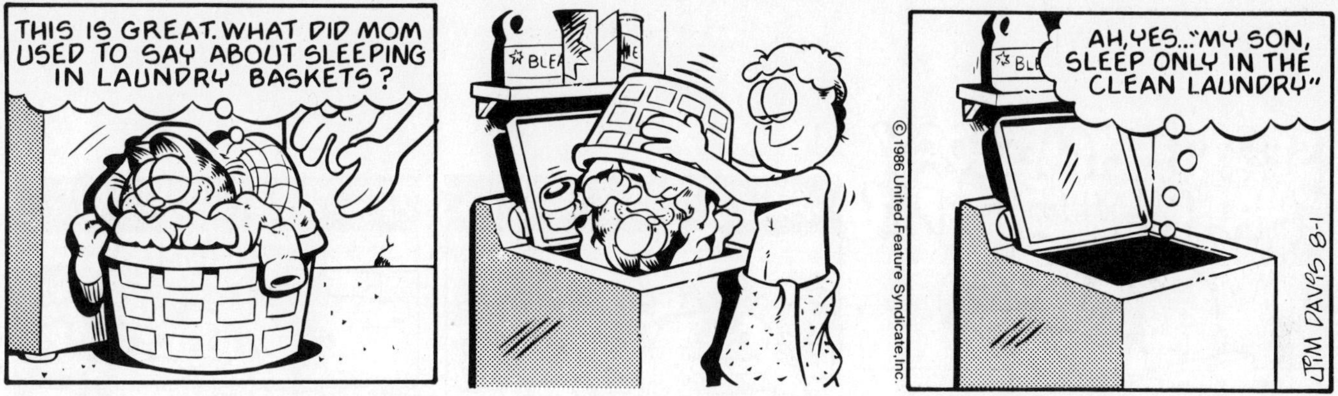
THIS IS GREAT. WHAT DID MOM USED TO SAY ABOUT SLEEPING IN LAUNDRY BASKETS?
AH, YES... "MY SON, SLEEP ONLY IN THE CLEAN LAUNDRY"
© 1986 United Feature Syndicate, Inc.
JIM DAVIS 8-1

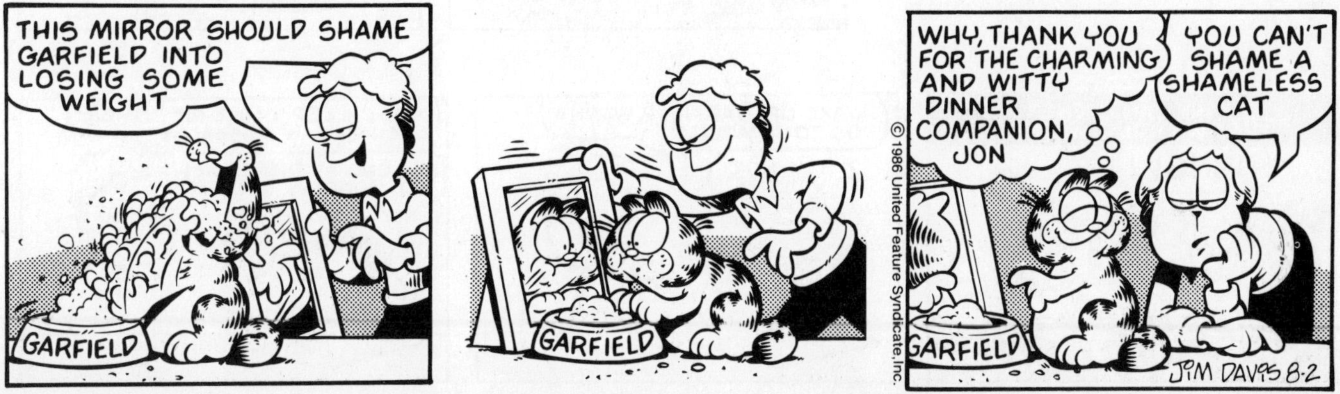
THIS MIRROR SHOULD SHAME GARFIELD INTO LOSING SOME WEIGHT
GARFIELD
GARFIELD
WHY, THANK YOU FOR THE CHARMING AND WITTY DINNER COMPANION, JON
YOU CAN'T SHAME A SHAMELESS CAT
GARFIELD
© 1986 United Feature Syndicate, Inc.
JIM DAVIS 8-2

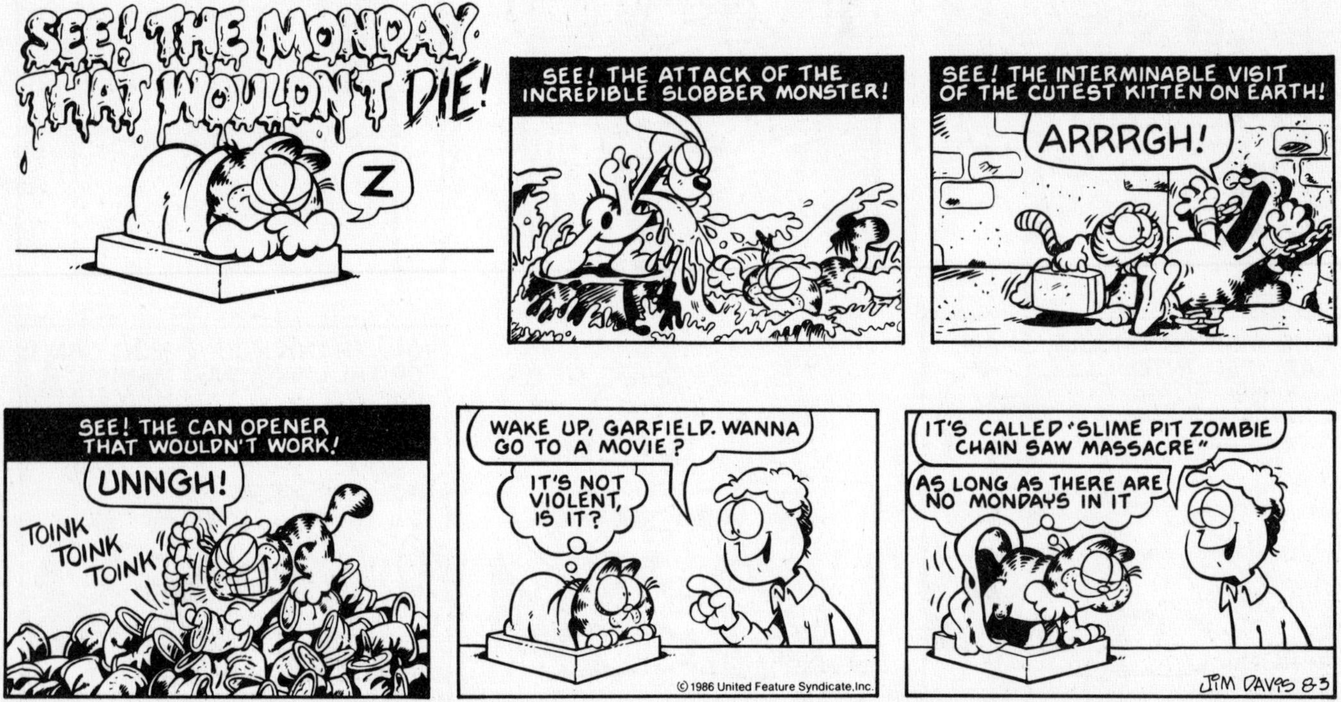

SEE! THE MONDAY THAT WOULDN'T DIE!
Z
SEE! THE ATTACK OF THE INCREDIBLE SLOBBER MONSTER!
SEE! THE INTERMINABLE VISIT OF THE CUTEST KITTEN ON EARTH!
ARRRGH!
SEE! THE CAN OPENER THAT WOULDN'T WORK!
UNNGH!
TOINK TOINK TOINK
WAKE UP, GARFIELD. WANNA GO TO A MOVIE?
IT'S NOT VIOLENT, IS IT?
IT'S CALLED "SLIME PIT ZOMBIE CHAIN SAW MASSACRE"
AS LONG AS THERE ARE NO MONDAYS IN IT
© 1986 United Feature Syndicate, Inc.
JIM DAVIS 8-3

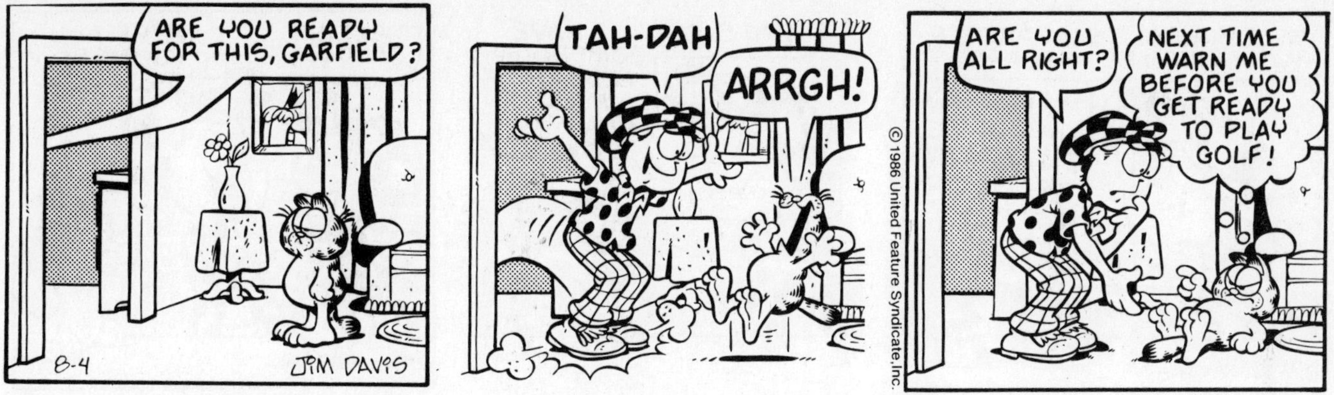
ARE YOU READY FOR THIS, GARFIELD?
8-4
JIM DAVIS
TAH-DAH
ARRGH!
ARE YOU ALL RIGHT?
NEXT TIME WARN ME BEFORE YOU GET READY TO PLAY GOLF!
© 1986 United Feature Syndicate, Inc.

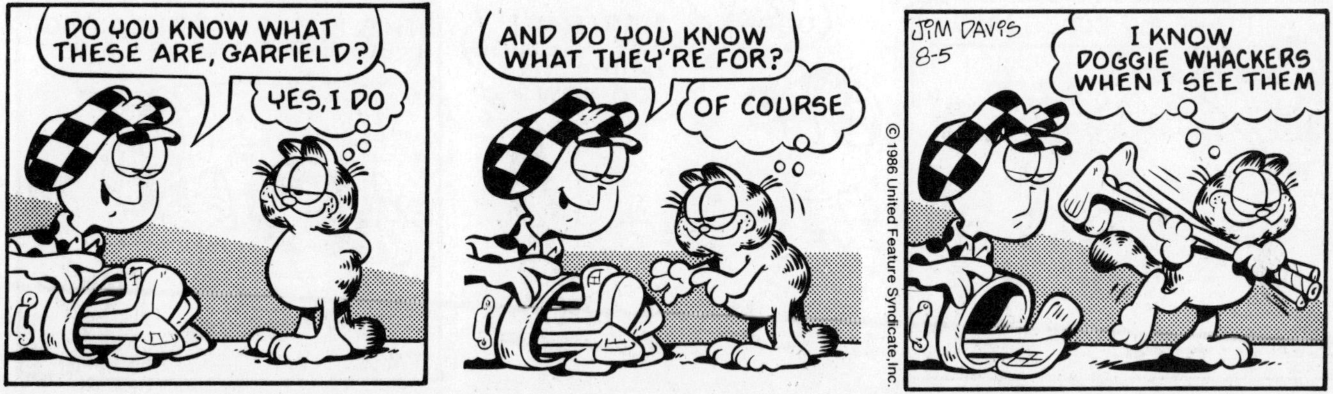
DO YOU KNOW WHAT THESE ARE, GARFIELD?
YES, I DO
AND DO YOU KNOW WHAT THEY'RE FOR?
OF COURSE
JIM DAVIS
8-5
I KNOW DOGGIE WHACKERS WHEN I SEE THEM
© 1986 United Feature Syndicate, Inc.

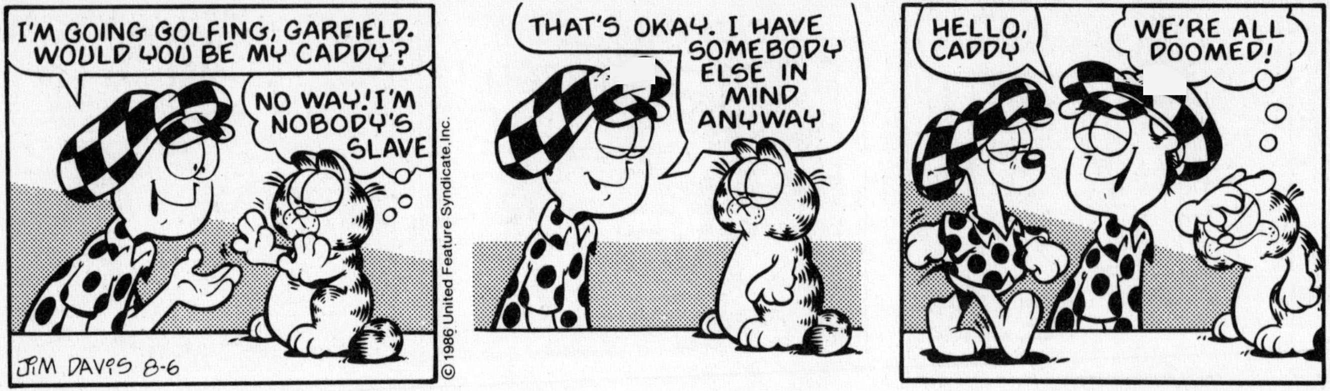
I'M GOING GOLFING, GARFIELD. WOULD YOU BE MY CADDY?
NO WAY! I'M NOBODY'S SLAVE
JIM DAVIS 8-6
© 1986 United Feature Syndicate, Inc.
THAT'S OKAY. I HAVE SOMEBODY ELSE IN MIND ANYWAY
HELLO, CADDY
WE'RE ALL DOOMED!

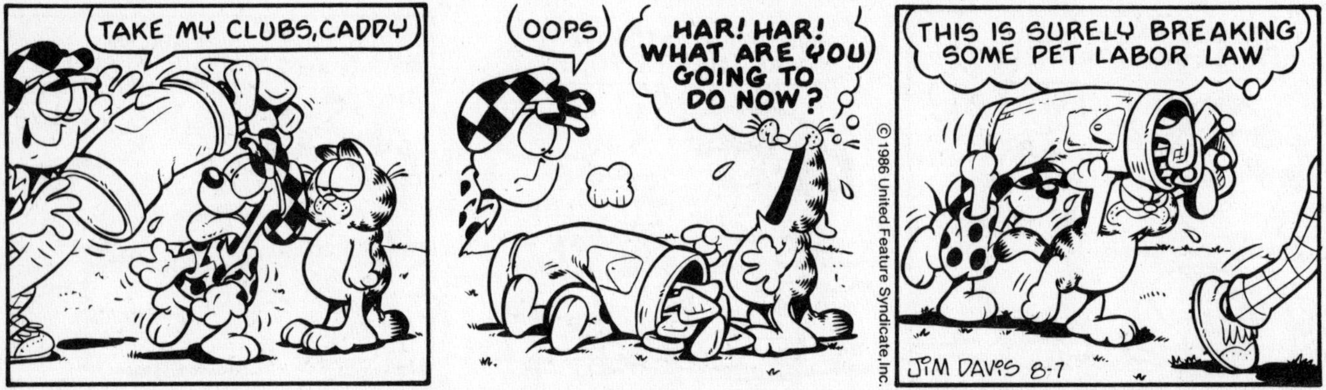
TAKE MY CLUBS, CADDY
OOPS
HAR! HAR! WHAT ARE YOU GOING TO DO NOW?
© 1986 United Feature Syndicate, Inc.
THIS IS SURELY BREAKING SOME PET LABOR LAW
JIM DAVIS 8-7

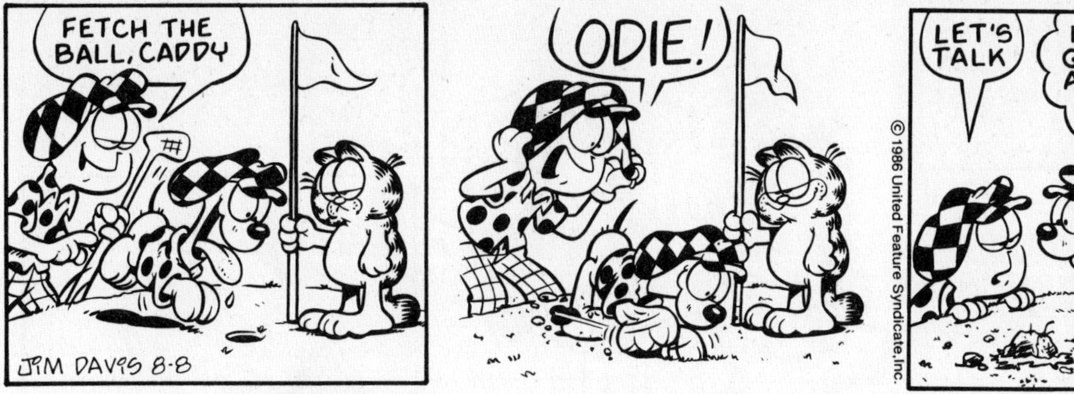
FETCH THE BALL, CADDY
JIM DAVIS 8-8
ODIE!
LET'S TALK
HERE COMES THE GROUNDS KEEPER, AND, YES, I BELIEVE HE'S CARRYING A GUN
© 1986 United Feature Syndicate, Inc.

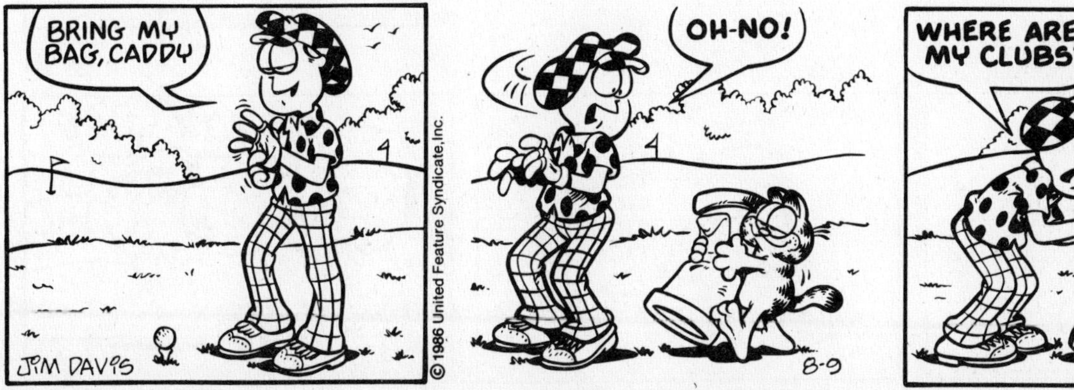
BRING MY BAG, CADDY
JIM DAVIS
© 1986 United Feature Syndicate, Inc.
OH-NO!
8-9
WHERE ARE MY CLUBS?!
BACK WHERE I DECIDED TO LIGHTEN THE LOAD

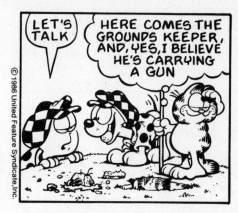

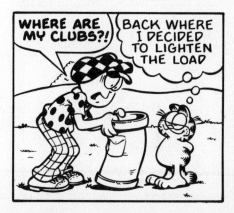

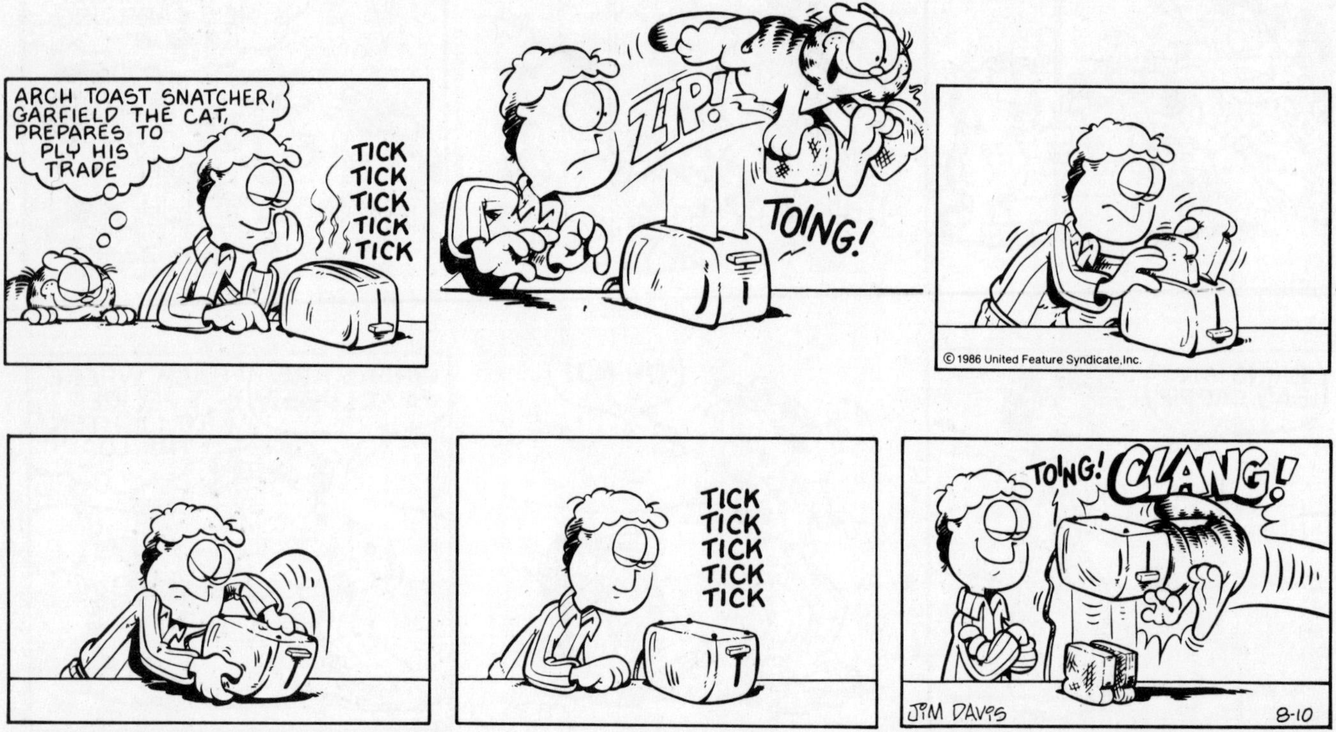
ARCH TOAST SNATCHER, GARFIELD THE CAT, PREPARES TO PLY HIS TRADE
TICK TICK TICK TICK TICK
ZIP!
TOING!
© 1986 United Feature Syndicate, Inc.
TICK TICK TICK TICK TICK
TOING!
CLANG!
JIM DAVIS
8-10

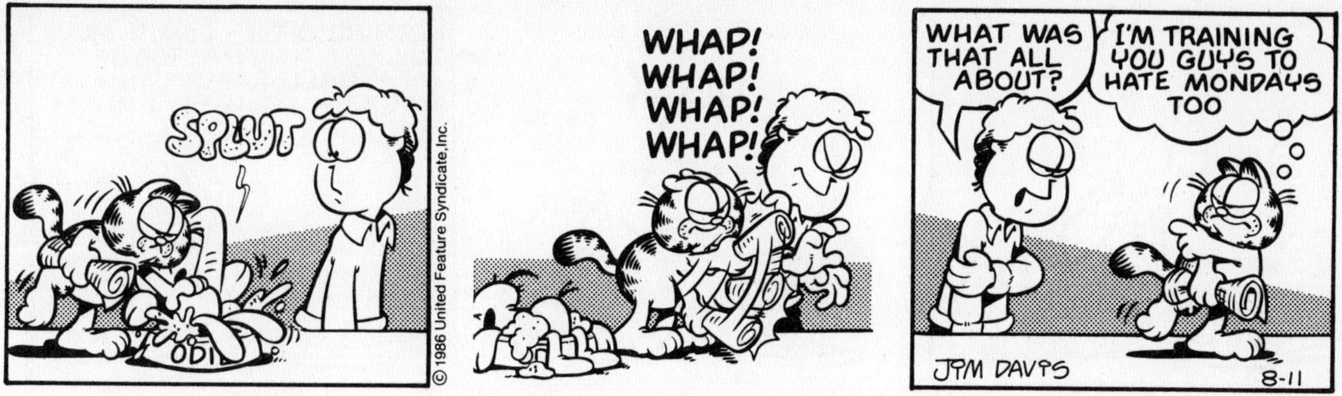
SPLUT
ODI
© 1986 United Feature Syndicate, Inc.
WHAP! WHAP! WHAP! WHAP!
WHAT WAS THAT ALL ABOUT?
I'M TRAINING YOU GUYS TO HATE MONDAYS TOO
JIM DAVIS
8-11

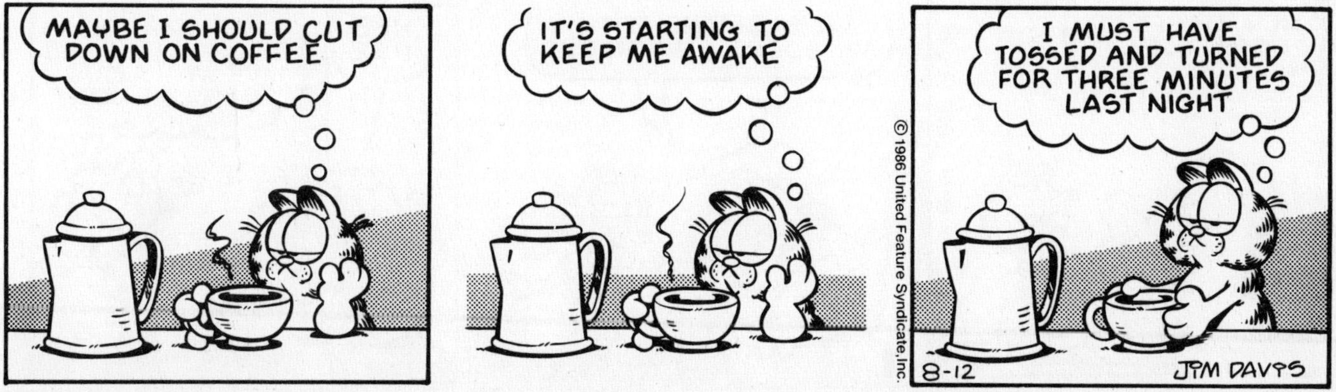
MAYBE I SHOULD CUT DOWN ON COFFEE
IT'S STARTING TO KEEP ME AWAKE
© 1986 United Feature Syndicate, Inc.
I MUST HAVE TOSSED AND TURNED FOR THREE MINUTES LAST NIGHT
8-12
JIM DAVIS

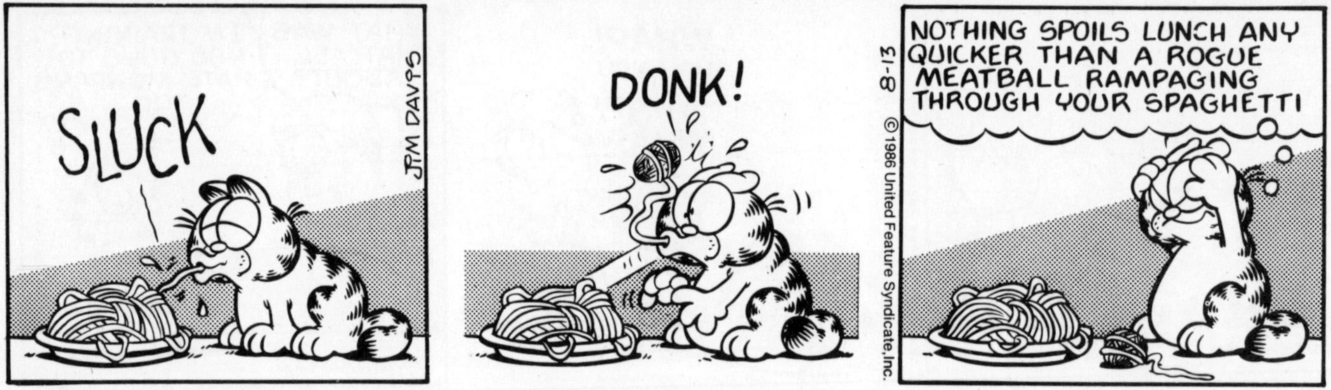
SLUCK
JIM DAVIS
DONK!
8-13
© 1986 United Feature Syndicate, Inc.
NOTHING SPOILS LUNCH ANY QUICKER THAN A ROGUE MEATBALL RAMPAGING THROUGH YOUR SPAGHETTI

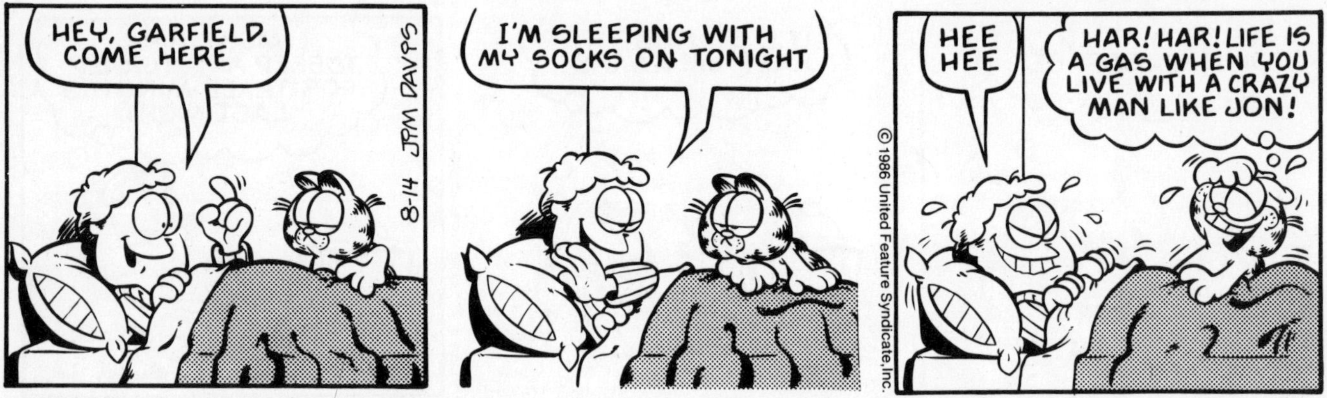
HEY, GARFIELD. COME HERE
JIM DAVIS
8-14
I'M SLEEPING WITH MY SOCKS ON TONIGHT
© 1986 United Feature Syndicate, Inc.
HEE HEE
HAR! HAR! LIFE IS A GAS WHEN YOU LIVE WITH A CRAZY MAN LIKE JON!

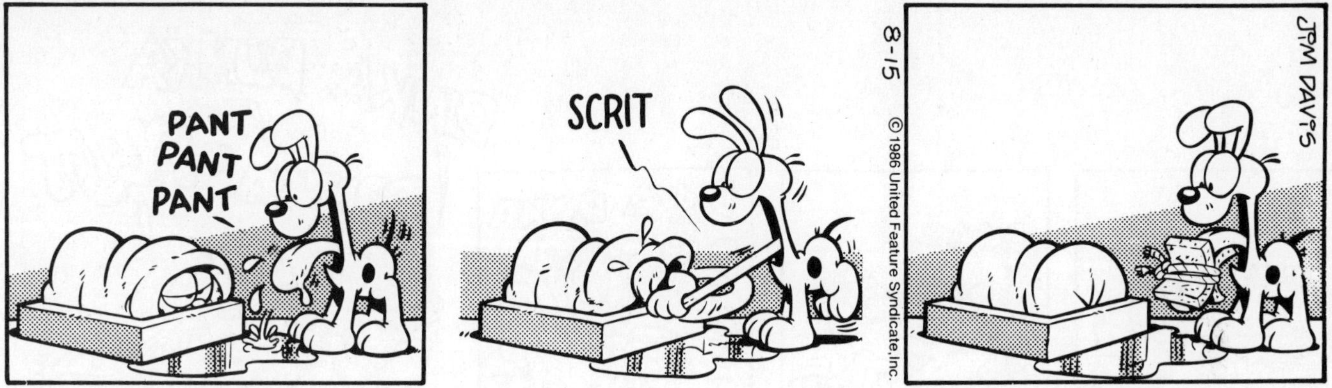
PANT
PANT
PANT
SCRIT
8-15
© 1986 United Feature Syndicate, Inc.
JIM DAVIS

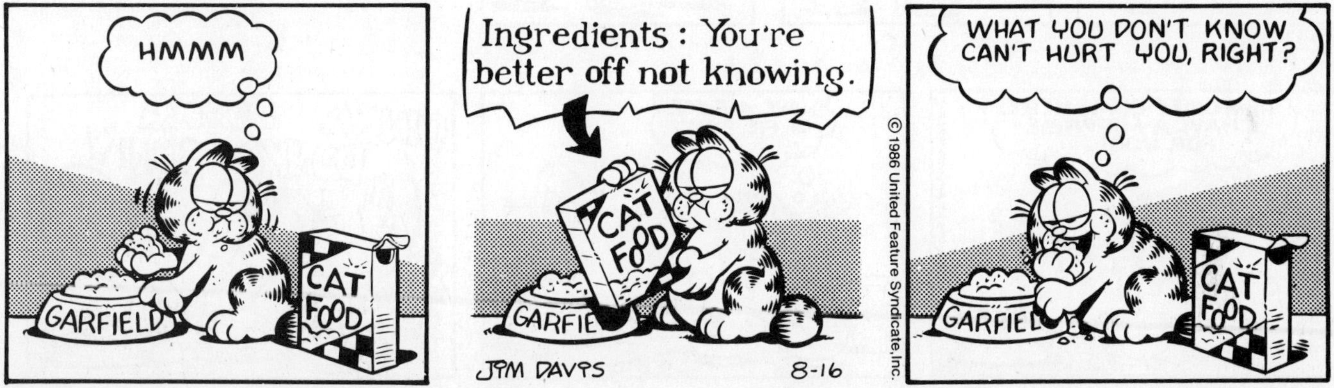
HMMM
GARFIELD
CAT FOOD
Ingredients: You're better off not knowing.
CAT FOOD
GARFIE
JIM DAVIS
8-16
© 1986 United Feature Syndicate, Inc.
WHAT YOU DON'T KNOW CAN'T HURT YOU, RIGHT?
GARFIEL
CAT FOOD

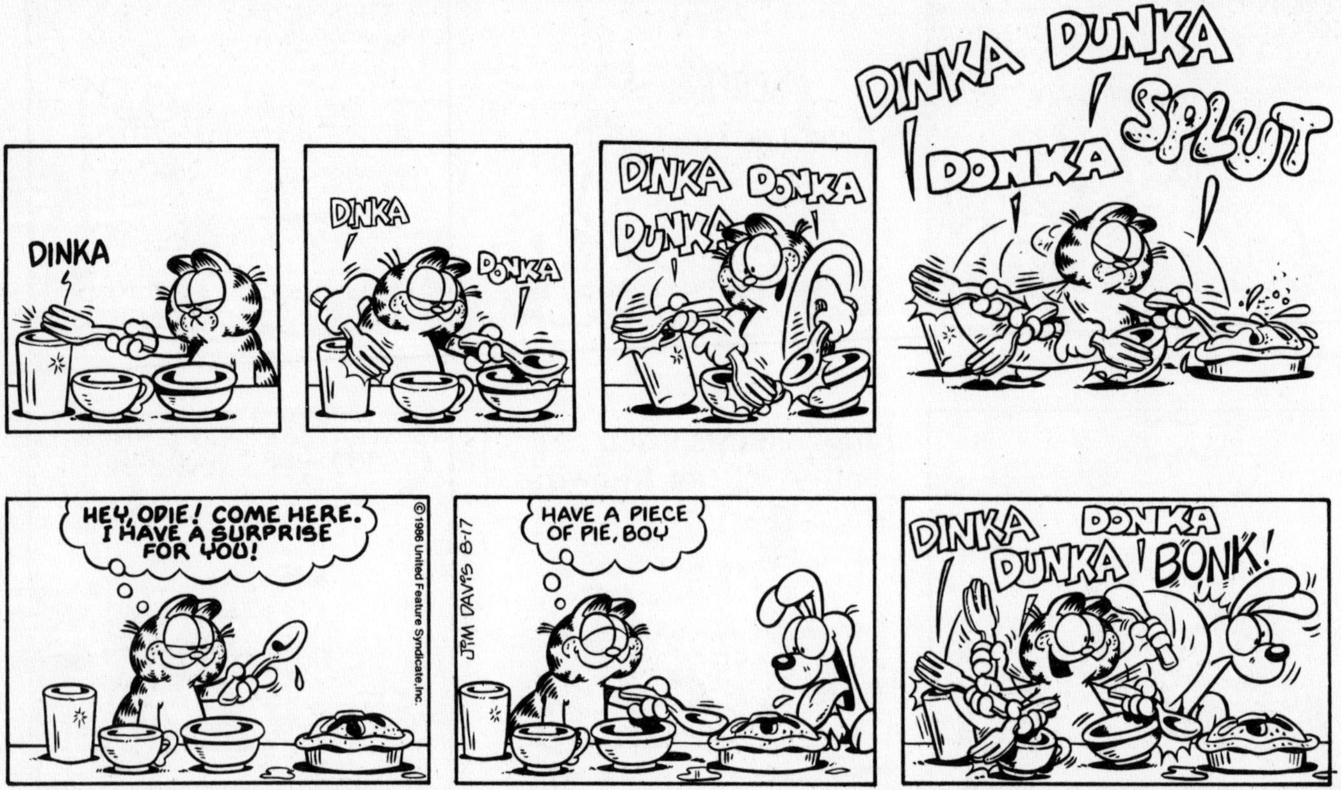
DINKA
DINKA
DONKA
DINKA
DONKA
DUNKA
DINKA
DUNKA
DONKA
SPLUT
HEY, ODIE! COME HERE. I HAVE A SURPRISE FOR YOU!
© 1986 United Feature Syndicate, Inc.
JIM DAVIS 8-17
HAVE A PIECE OF PIE, BOY
DINKA
DONKA
DUNKA
BONK!

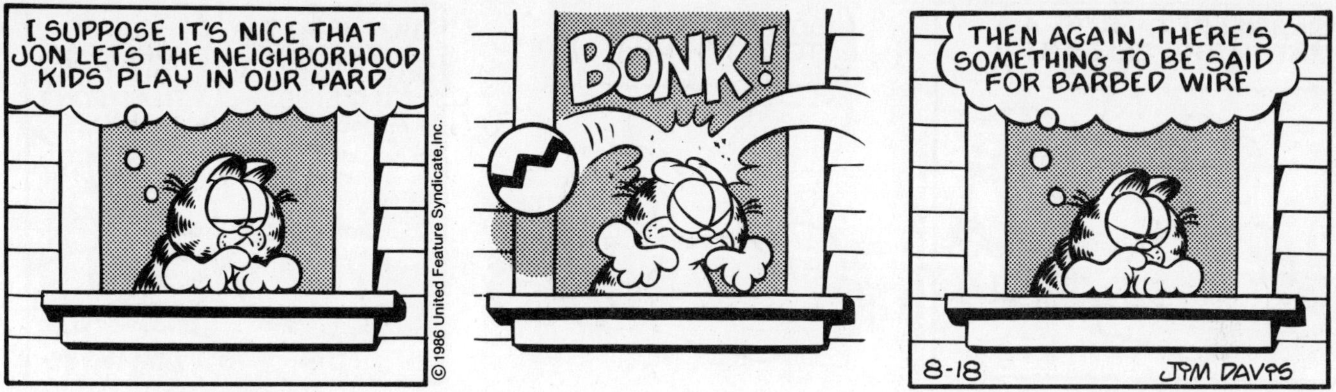
I SUPPOSE IT'S NICE THAT JON LETS THE NEIGHBORHOOD KIDS PLAY IN OUR YARD
© 1986 United Feature Syndicate, Inc.
BONK!
THEN AGAIN, THERE'S SOMETHING TO BE SAID FOR BARBED WIRE
8-18
JIM DAVIS

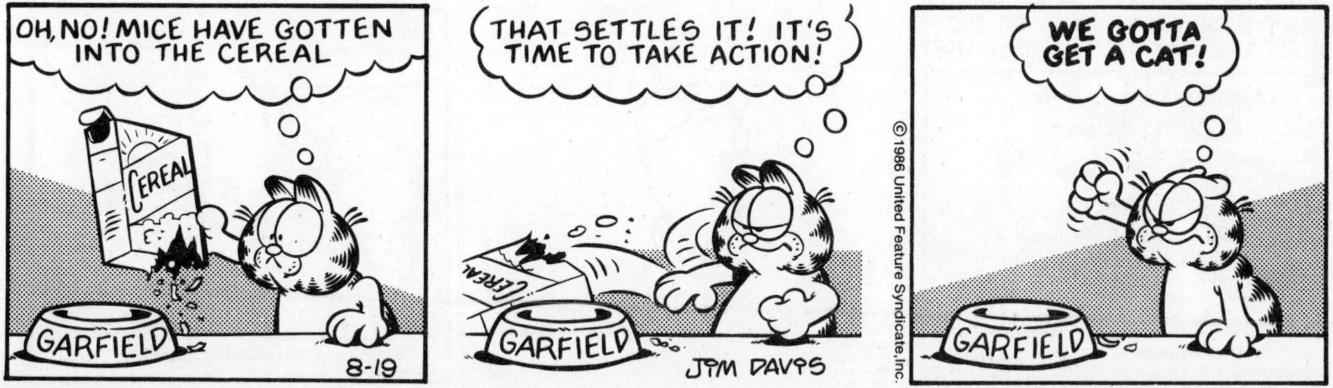
OH, NO! MICE HAVE GOTTEN INTO THE CEREAL
CEREAL
GARFIELD
8-19
THAT SETTLES IT! IT'S TIME TO TAKE ACTION!
CEREAL
GARFIELD
JIM DAVIS
© 1986 United Feature Syndicate, Inc.
WE GOTTA GET A CAT!
GARFIELD

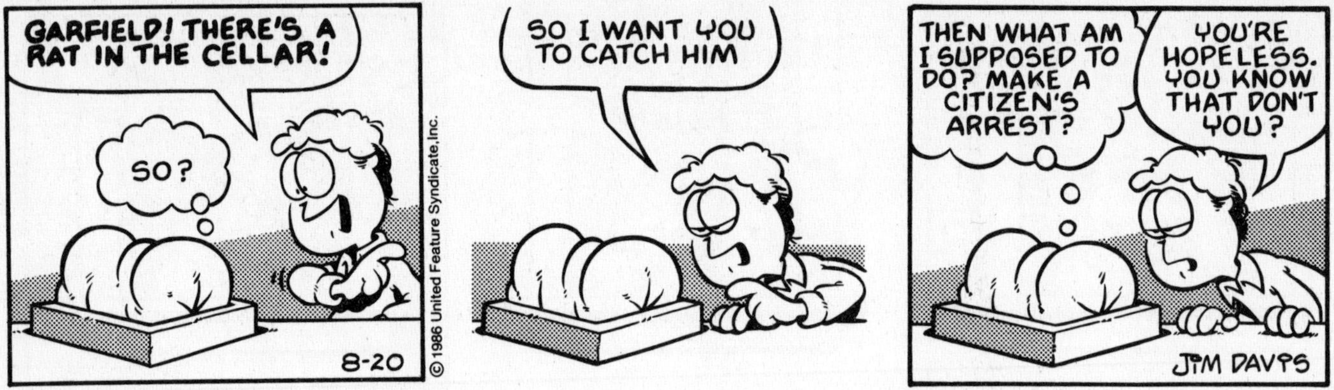
GARFIELD! THERE'S A RAT IN THE CELLAR!
SO?
SO I WANT YOU TO CATCH HIM
THEN WHAT AM I SUPPOSED TO DO? MAKE A CITIZEN'S ARREST?
YOU'RE HOPELESS. YOU KNOW THAT DON'T YOU?
8-20
JIM DAVIS



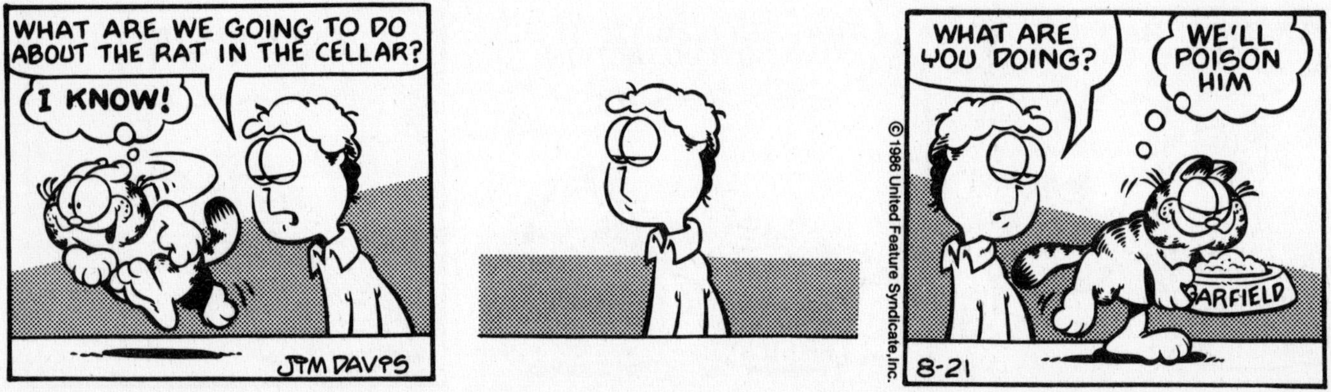
WHAT ARE WE GOING TO DO ABOUT THE RAT IN THE CELLAR?
I KNOW!
JIM DAVIS
WHAT ARE YOU DOING?
WE'LL POISON HIM
GARFIELD
8-21

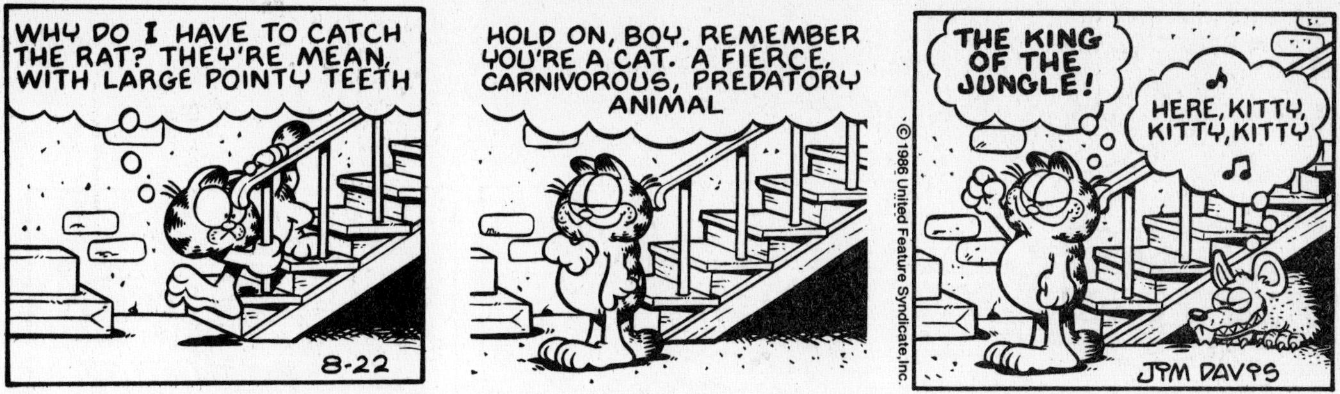
WHY DO I HAVE TO CATCH THE RAT? THEY'RE MEAN, WITH LARGE POINTY TEETH
8-22
HOLD ON, BOY. REMEMBER YOU'RE A CAT. A FIERCE, CARNIVOROUS, PREDATORY ANIMAL
THE KING OF THE JUNGLE!
HERE, KITTY, KITTY, KITTY
© 1986 United Feature Syndicate, Inc.
JIM DAVIS

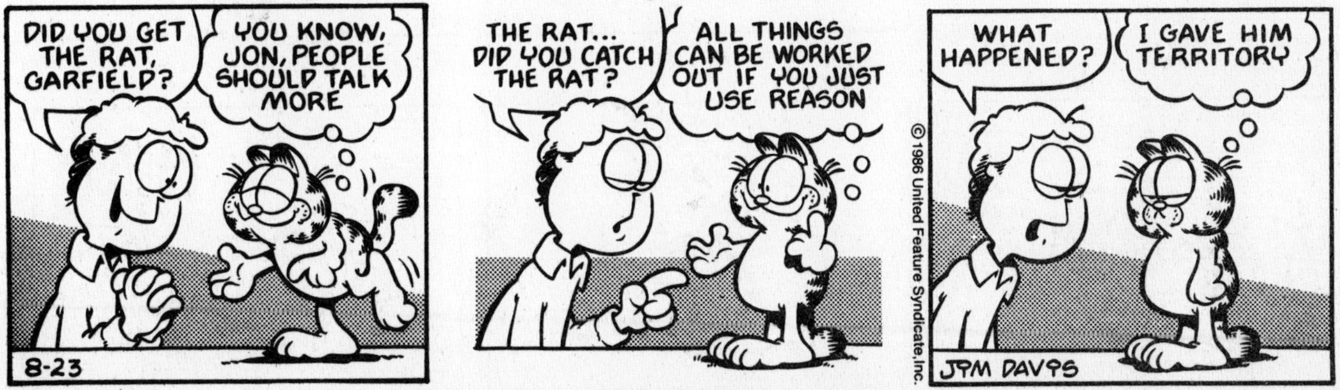
DID YOU GET THE RAT, GARFIELD?
YOU KNOW, JON, PEOPLE SHOULD TALK MORE
8-23
THE RAT... DID YOU CATCH THE RAT?
ALL THINGS CAN BE WORKED OUT IF YOU JUST USE REASON
WHAT HAPPENED?
I GAVE HIM TERRITORY
© 1986 United Feature Syndicate, Inc.
JIM DAVIS

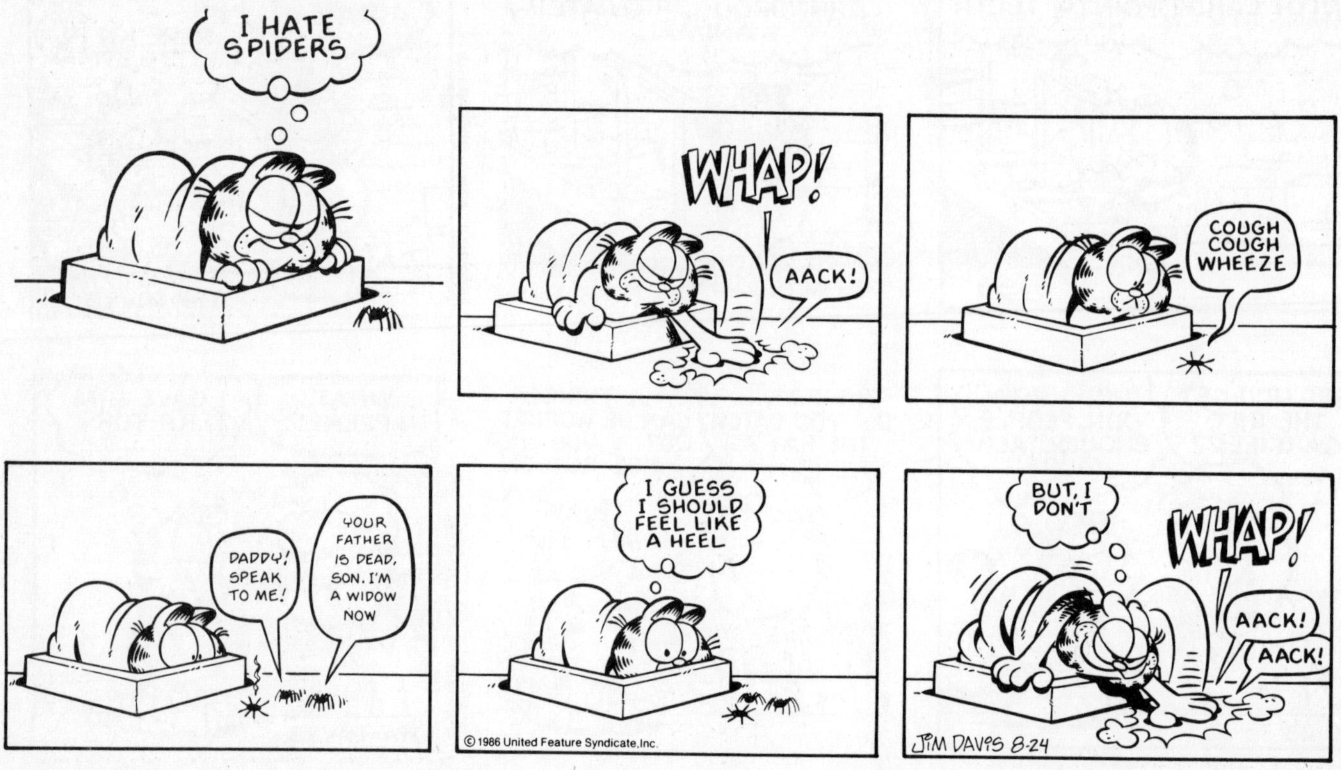
I HATE SPIDERS
WHAP!
AACK!
COUGH COUGH WHEEZE
DADDY! SPEAK TO ME!
YOUR FATHER IS DEAD, SON. I'M A WIDOW NOW
I GUESS I SHOULD FEEL LIKE A HEEL
BUT, I DON'T
WHAP!
AACK!
AACK!
© 1986 United Feature Syndicate, Inc.
JIM DAVIS 8-24

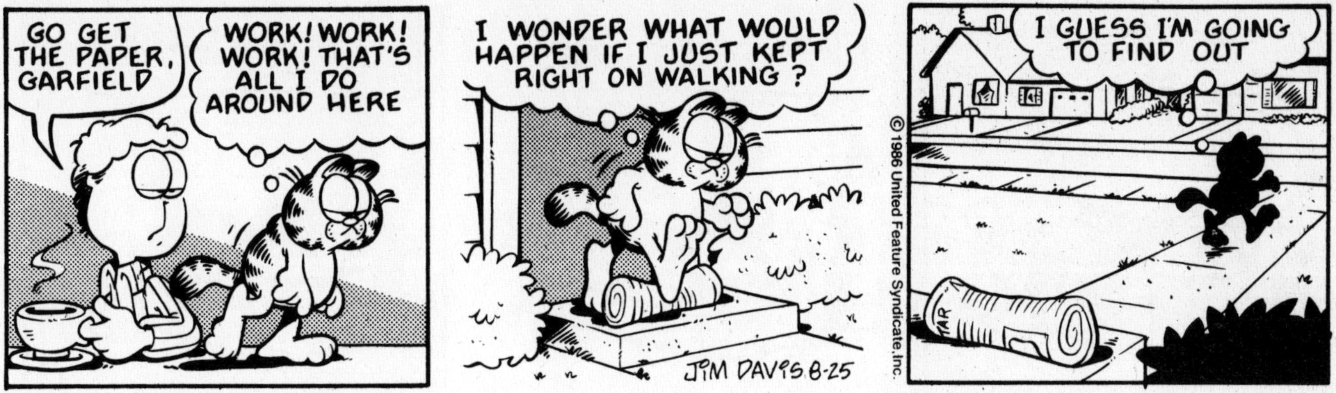
GO GET THE PAPER, GARFIELD
WORK! WORK! WORK! THAT'S ALL I DO AROUND HERE
I WONDER WHAT WOULD HAPPEN IF I JUST KEPT RIGHT ON WALKING ?
JIM DAVIS 8-25
I GUESS I'M GOING TO FIND OUT
© 1986 United Feature Syndicate, Inc.

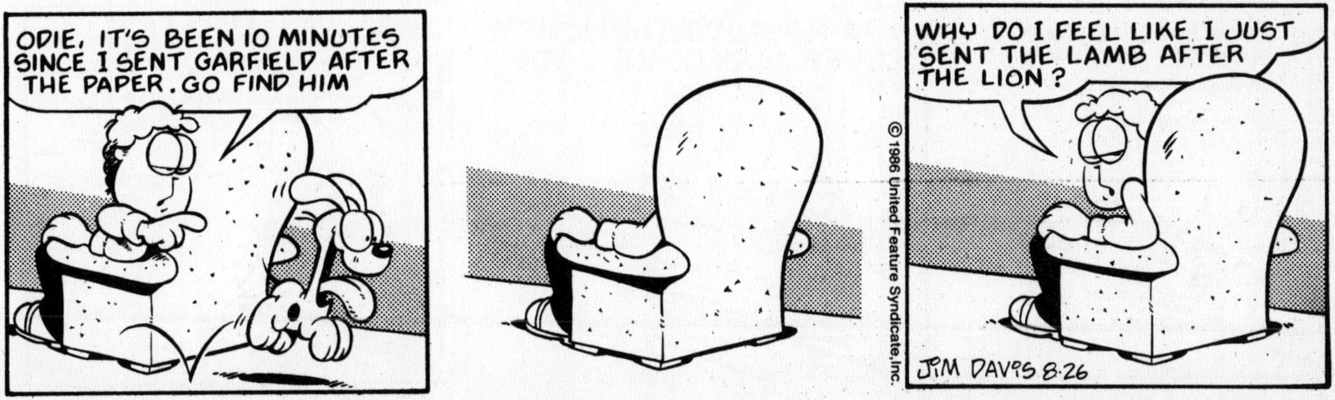
ODIE, IT'S BEEN 10 MINUTES SINCE I SENT GARFIELD AFTER THE PAPER. GO FIND HIM
WHY DO I FEEL LIKE I JUST SENT THE LAMB AFTER THE LION ?
JIM DAVIS 8-26
© 1986 United Feature Syndicate, Inc.

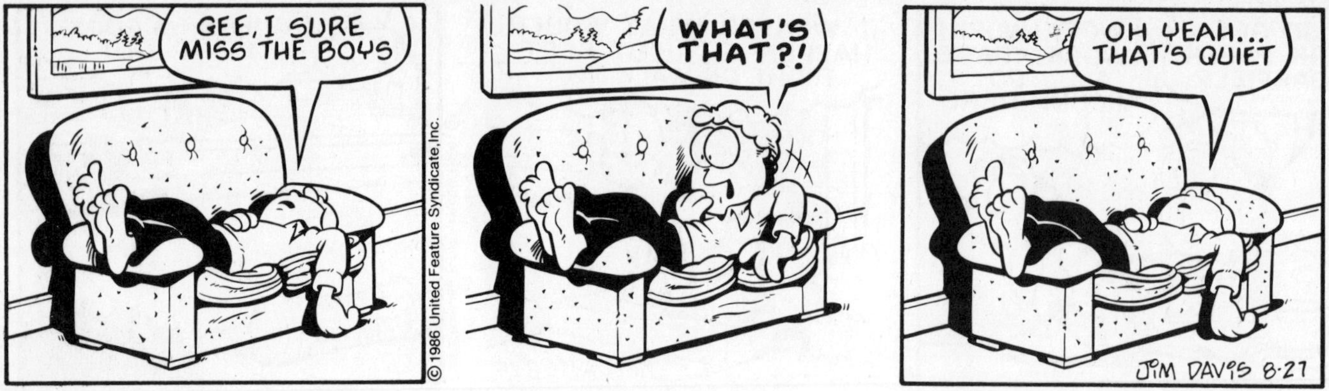
GEE, I SURE MISS THE BOYS
WHAT'S THAT?!
OH YEAH... THAT'S QUIET
JIM DAVIS 8·27
© 1986 United Feature Syndicate,Inc.

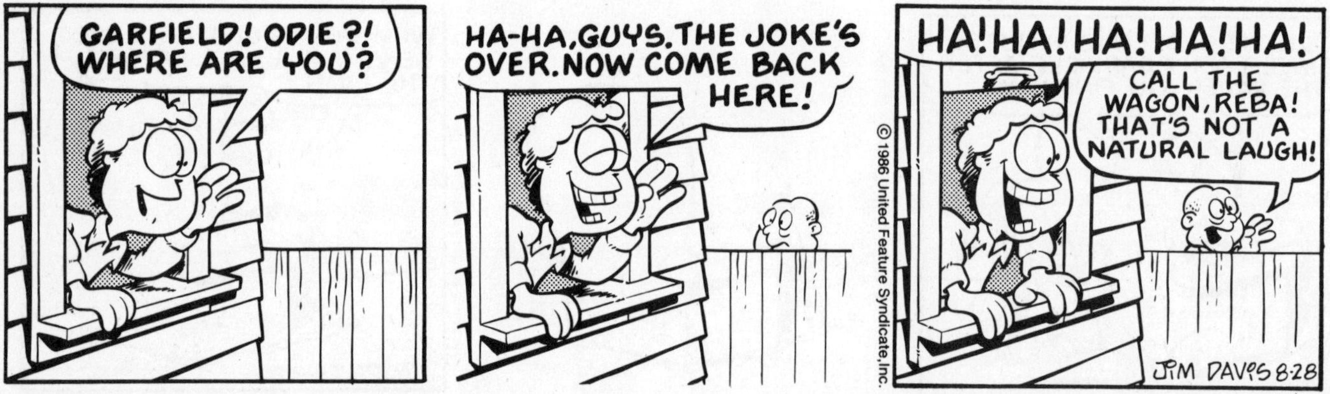
GARFIELD! ODIE?! WHERE ARE YOU?
HA-HA, GUYS. THE JOKE'S OVER. NOW COME BACK HERE!
HA! HA! HA! HA! HA!
CALL THE WAGON, REBA! THAT'S NOT A NATURAL LAUGH!
JIM DAVIS 8·28
© 1986 United Feature Syndicate,Inc.

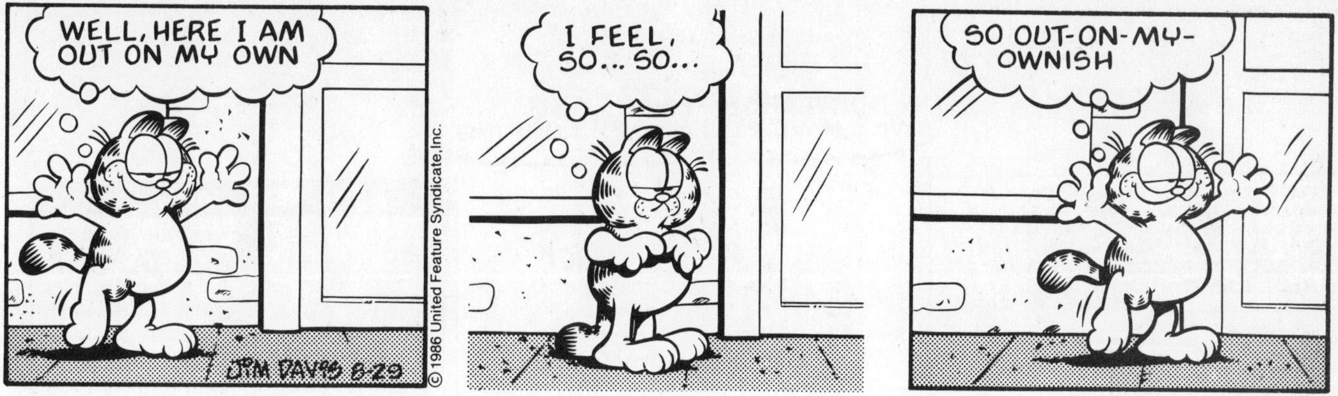
WELL, HERE I AM OUT ON MY OWN
JIM DAVIS 8-29
© 1986 United Feature Syndicate, Inc.
I FEEL, SO... SO...
SO OUT-ON-MY-OWNISH

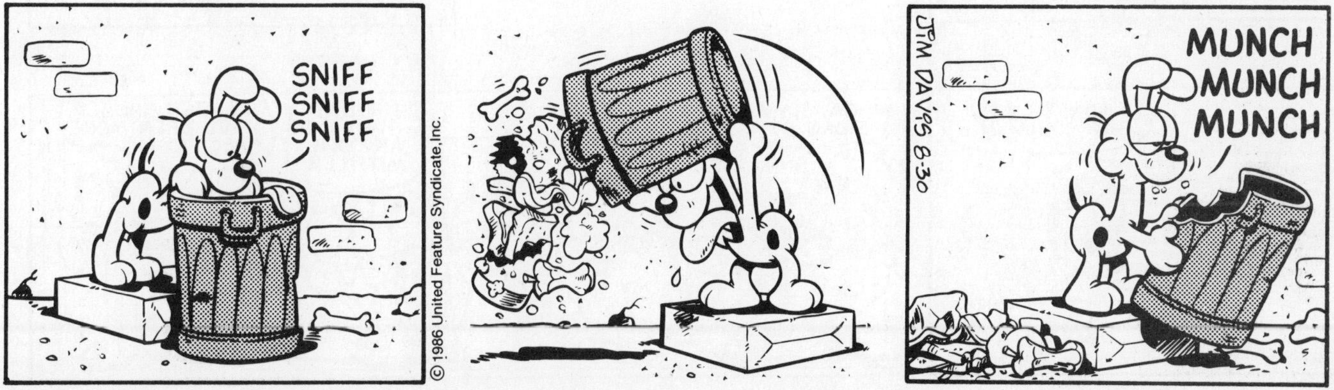
SNIFF SNIFF SNIFF
© 1986 United Feature Syndicate, Inc.
JIM DAVIS 8-30
MUNCH MUNCH MUNCH

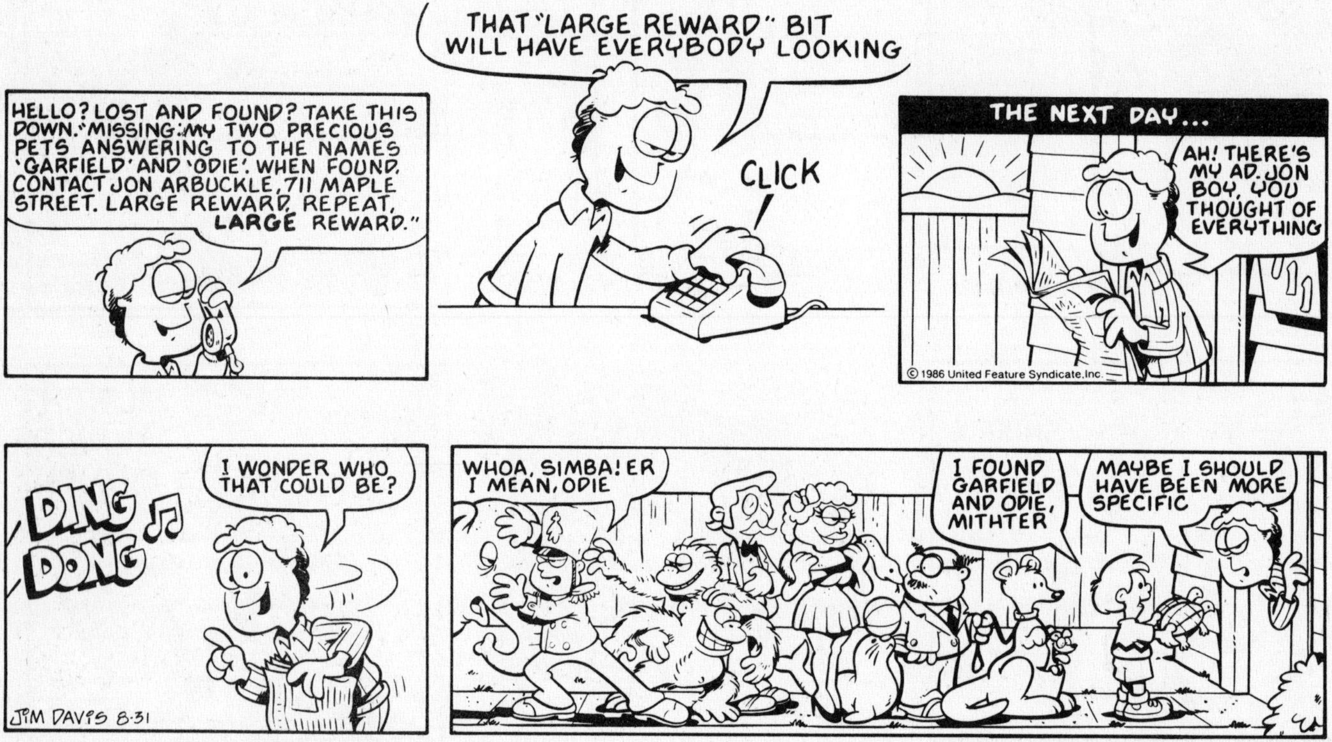
HELLO? LOST AND FOUND? TAKE THIS DOWN. "MISSING: MY TWO PRECIOUS PETS ANSWERING TO THE NAMES 'GARFIELD' AND 'ODIE'. WHEN FOUND, CONTACT JON ARBUCKLE, 711 MAPLE STREET. LARGE REWARD, REPEAT, LARGE REWARD."
THAT "LARGE REWARD" BIT WILL HAVE EVERYBODY LOOKING
CLICK
THE NEXT DAY...
AH! THERE'S MY AD. JON BOY, YOU THOUGHT OF EVERYTHING
© 1986 United Feature Syndicate, Inc.
DING DONG
I WONDER WHO THAT COULD BE?
JIM DAVIS 8-31
WHOA, SIMBA! ER I MEAN, ODIE
I FOUND GARFIELD AND ODIE, MITHTER
MAYBE I SHOULD HAVE BEEN MORE SPECIFIC

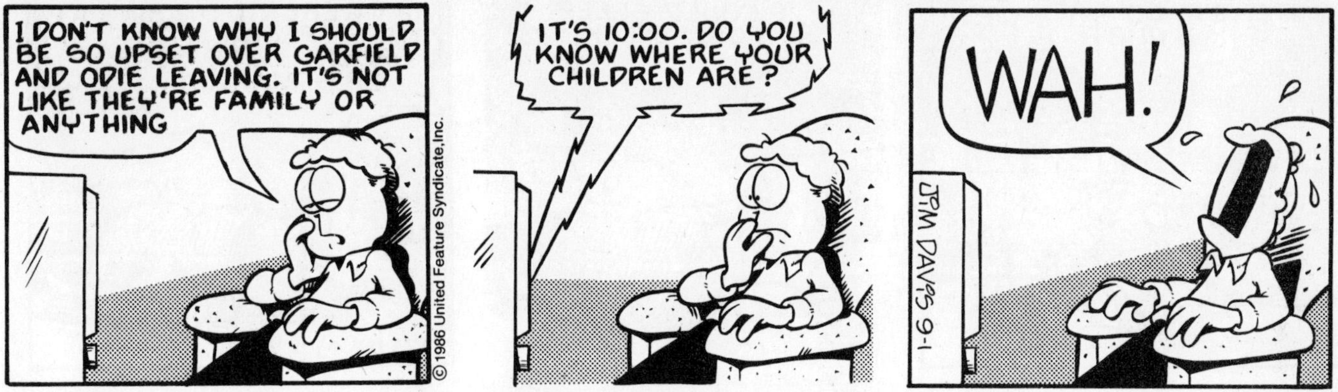
I DON'T KNOW WHY I SHOULD BE SO UPSET OVER GARFIELD AND ODIE LEAVING. IT'S NOT LIKE THEY'RE FAMILY OR ANYTHING
© 1986 United Feature Syndicate, Inc.
IT'S 10:00. DO YOU KNOW WHERE YOUR CHILDREN ARE?
WAH!
JIM DAVIS 9-1

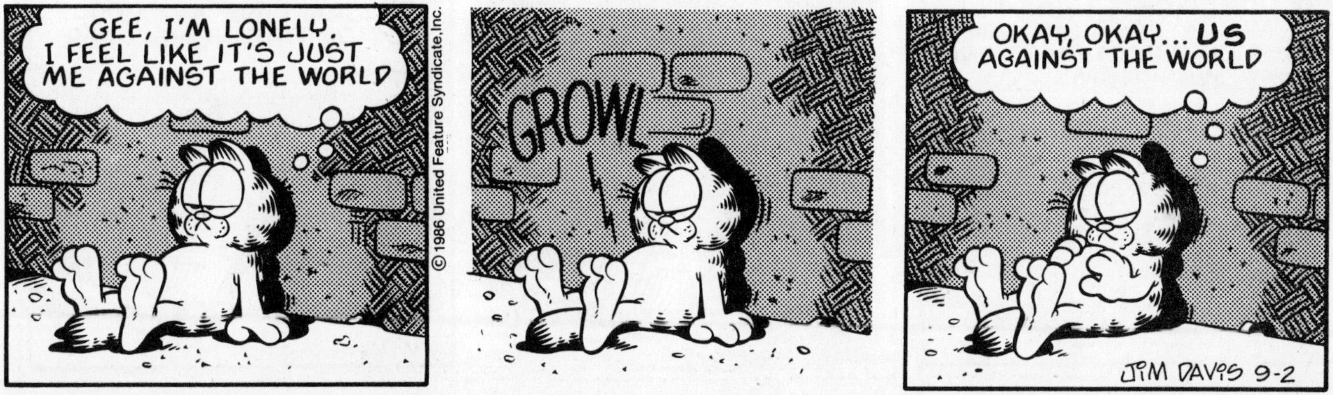
GEE, I'M LONELY. I FEEL LIKE IT'S JUST ME AGAINST THE WORLD
© 1986 United Feature Syndicate, Inc.
GROWL
OKAY, OKAY... **US** AGAINST THE WORLD
JIM DAVIS 9-2

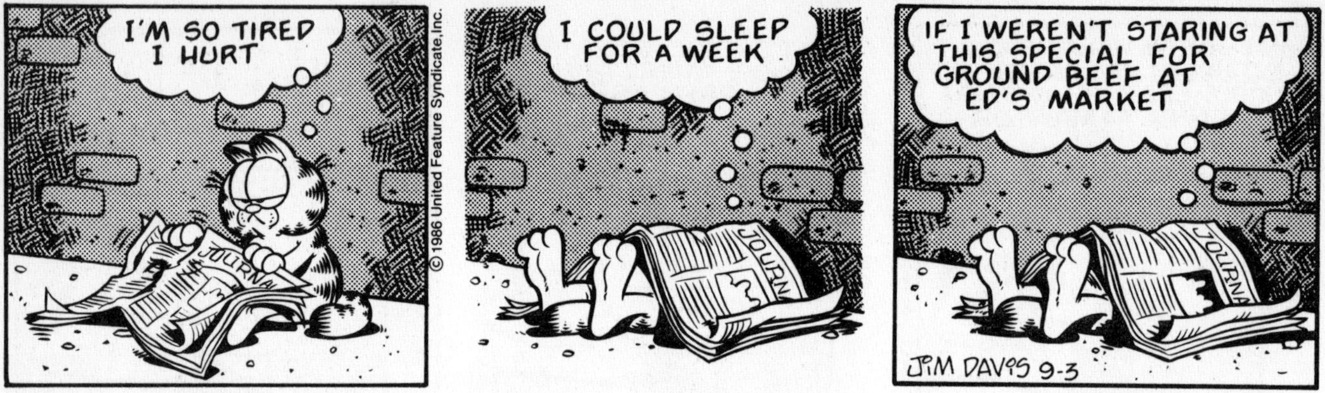
I'M SO TIRED I HURT
© 1986 United Feature Syndicate,Inc.
I COULD SLEEP FOR A WEEK
IF I WEREN'T STARING AT THIS SPECIAL FOR GROUND BEEF AT ED'S MARKET
JIM DAVIS 9-3

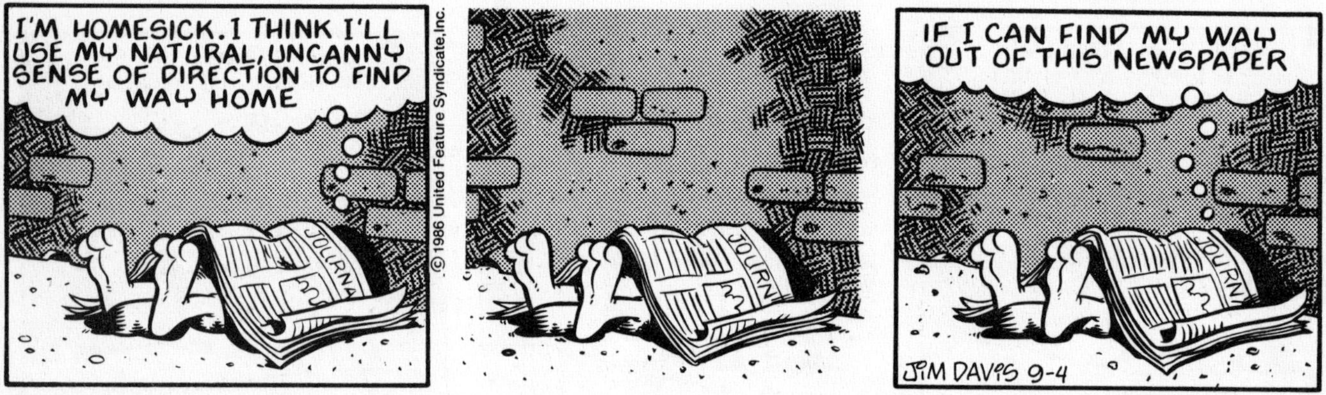
I'M HOMESICK. I THINK I'LL USE MY NATURAL, UNCANNY SENSE OF DIRECTION TO FIND MY WAY HOME
© 1986 United Feature Syndicate,Inc.
IF I CAN FIND MY WAY OUT OF THIS NEWSPAPER
JIM DAVIS 9-4

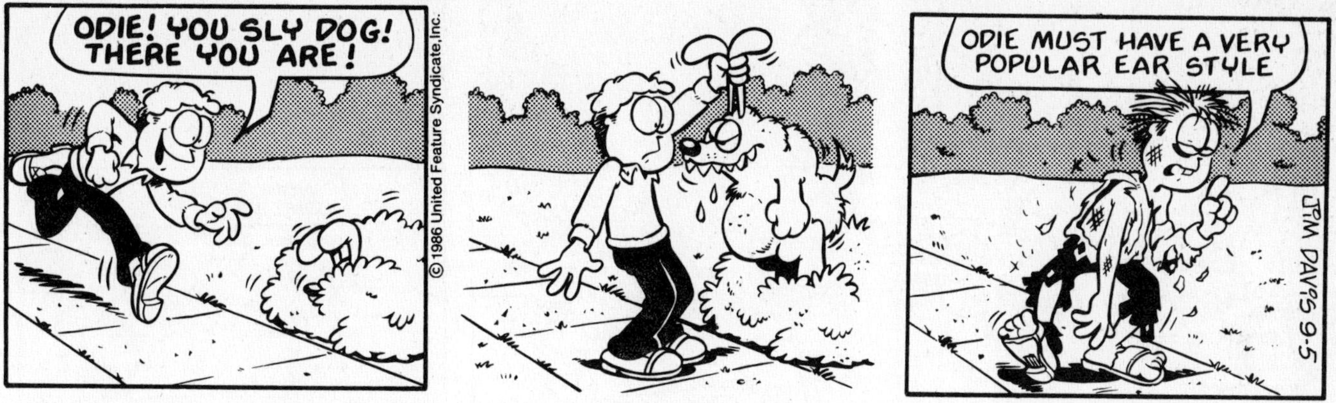
ODIE! YOU SLY DOG! THERE YOU ARE!
ODIE MUST HAVE A VERY POPULAR EAR STYLE
© 1986 United Feature Syndicate, Inc.
JIM DAVIS 9-5

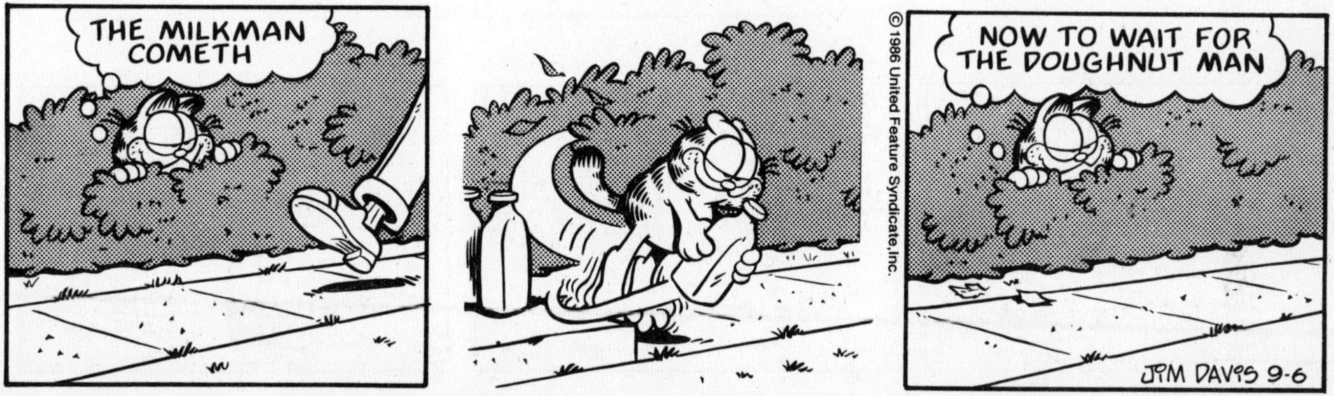
THE MILKMAN COMETH
NOW TO WAIT FOR THE DOUGHNUT MAN
© 1986 United Feature Syndicate, Inc.
JIM DAVIS 9-6

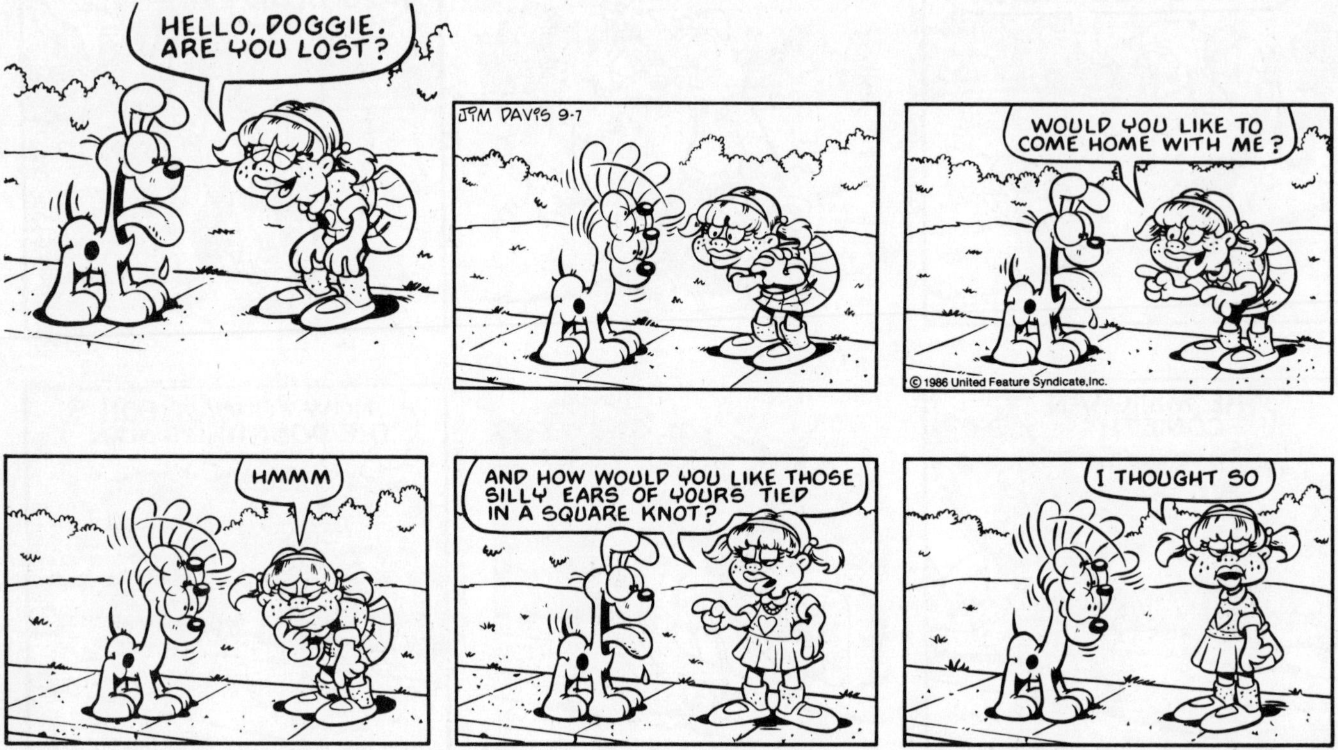
HELLO, DOGGIE. ARE YOU LOST?
JIM DAVIS 9-7
WOULD YOU LIKE TO COME HOME WITH ME?
© 1986 United Feature Syndicate, Inc.
HMMM
AND HOW WOULD YOU LIKE THOSE SILLY EARS OF YOURS TIED IN A SQUARE KNOT?
I THOUGHT SO

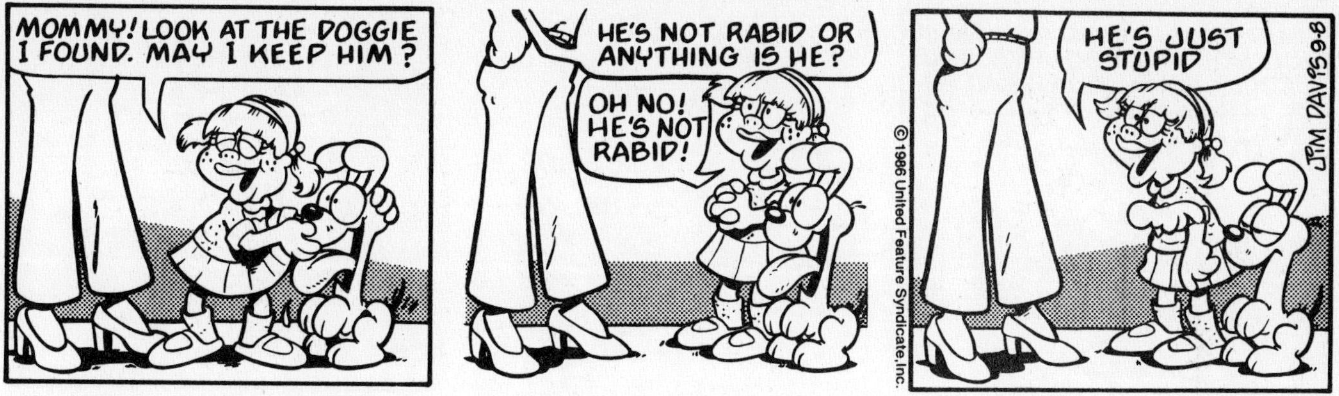
MOMMY! LOOK AT THE DOGGIE I FOUND. MAY I KEEP HIM?
HE'S NOT RABID OR ANYTHING IS HE?
OH NO! HE'S NOT RABID!
HE'S JUST STUPID
JIM DAVIS 9-8
© 1986 United Feature Syndicate, Inc.

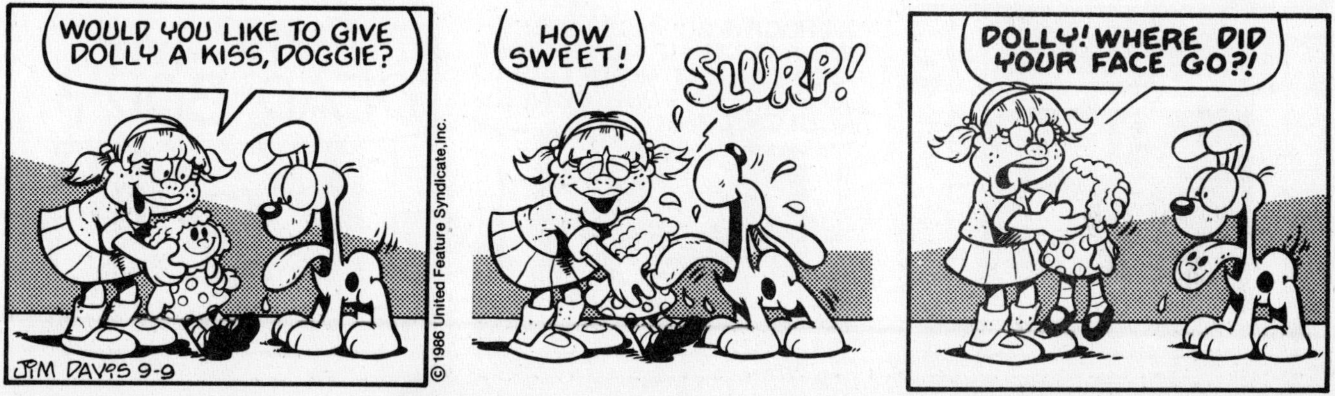
WOULD YOU LIKE TO GIVE DOLLY A KISS, DOGGIE?
JIM DAVIS 9-9
© 1986 United Feature Syndicate, Inc.
HOW SWEET!
SLURP!
DOLLY! WHERE DID YOUR FACE GO?!

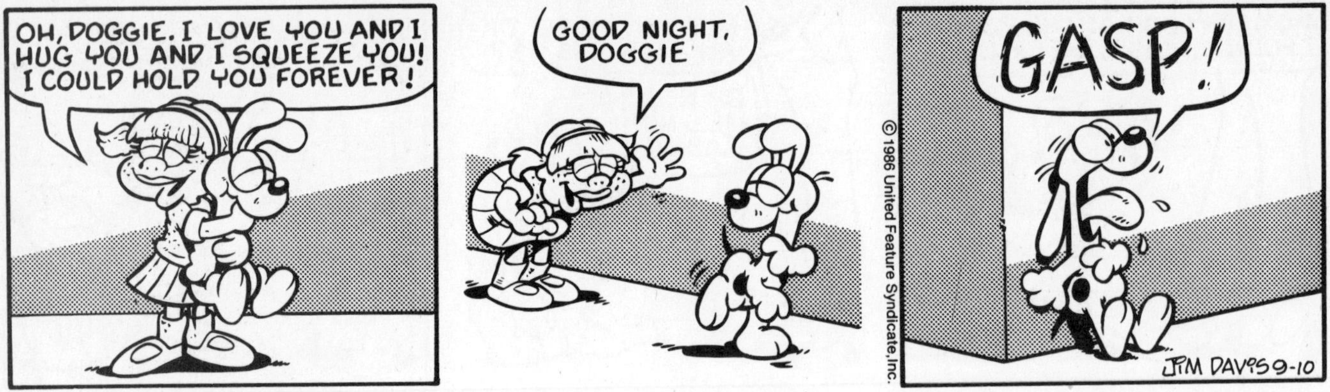
OH, DOGGIE. I LOVE YOU AND I HUG YOU AND I SQUEEZE YOU! I COULD HOLD YOU FOREVER!
GOOD NIGHT, DOGGIE
GASP!
JIM DAVIS 9-10



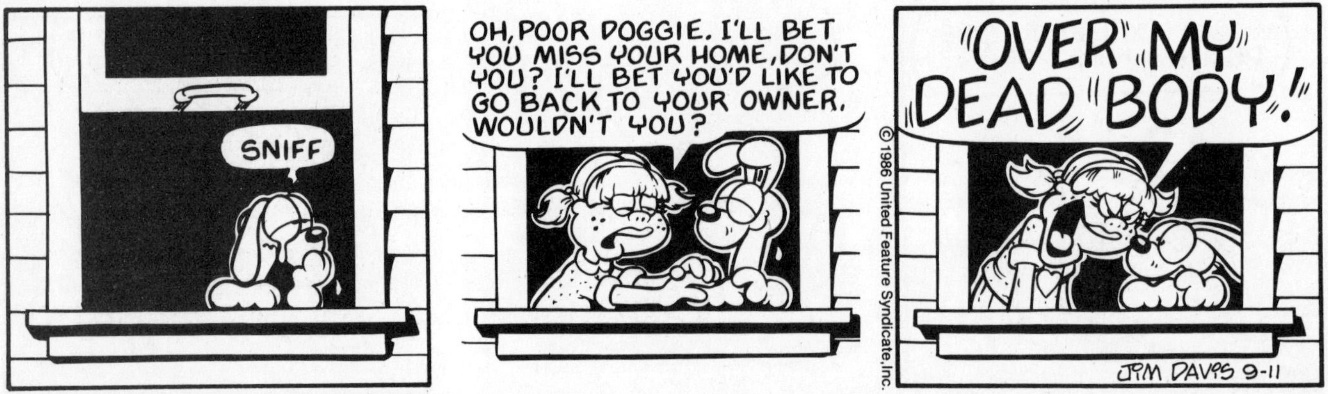
SNIFF
OH, POOR DOGGIE. I'LL BET YOU MISS YOUR HOME, DON'T YOU? I'LL BET YOU'D LIKE TO GO BACK TO YOUR OWNER, WOULDN'T YOU?
OVER MY DEAD BODY!
JIM DAVIS 9-11

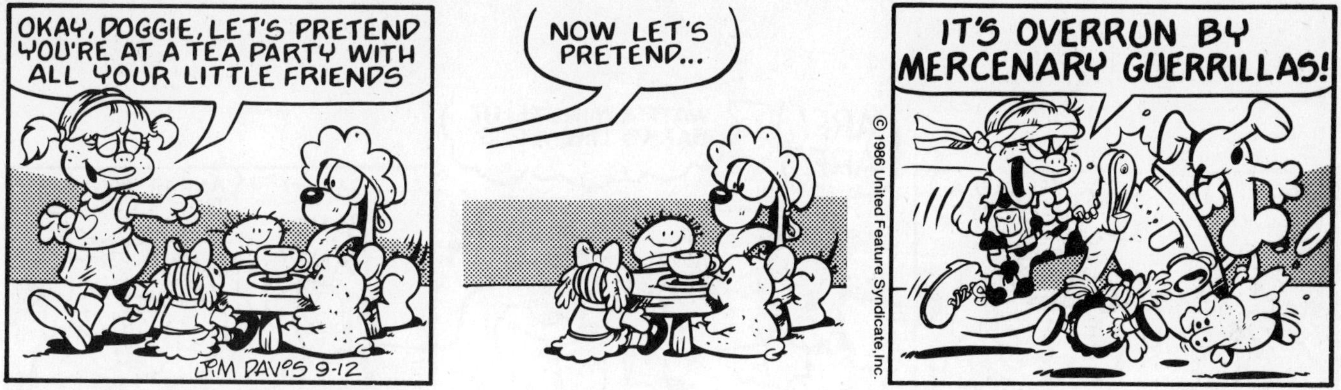
OKAY, DOGGIE, LET'S PRETEND YOU'RE AT A TEA PARTY WITH ALL YOUR LITTLE FRIENDS
JIM DAVIS 9-12
NOW LET'S PRETEND...
IT'S OVERRUN BY MERCENARY GUERRILLAS!


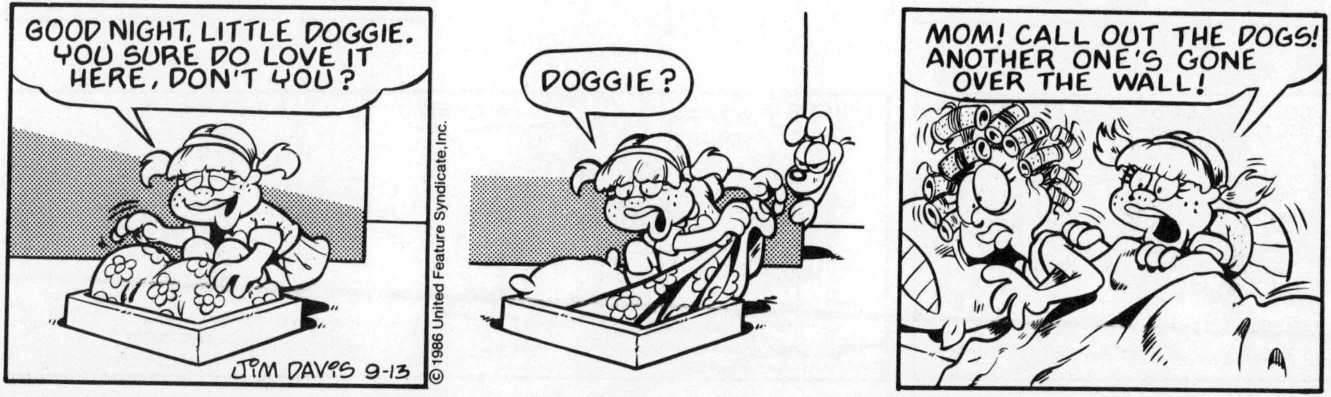
GOOD NIGHT, LITTLE DOGGIE. YOU SURE DO LOVE IT HERE, DON'T YOU?
JIM DAVIS 9-13
DOGGIE?
MOM! CALL OUT THE DOGS! ANOTHER ONE'S GONE OVER THE WALL!

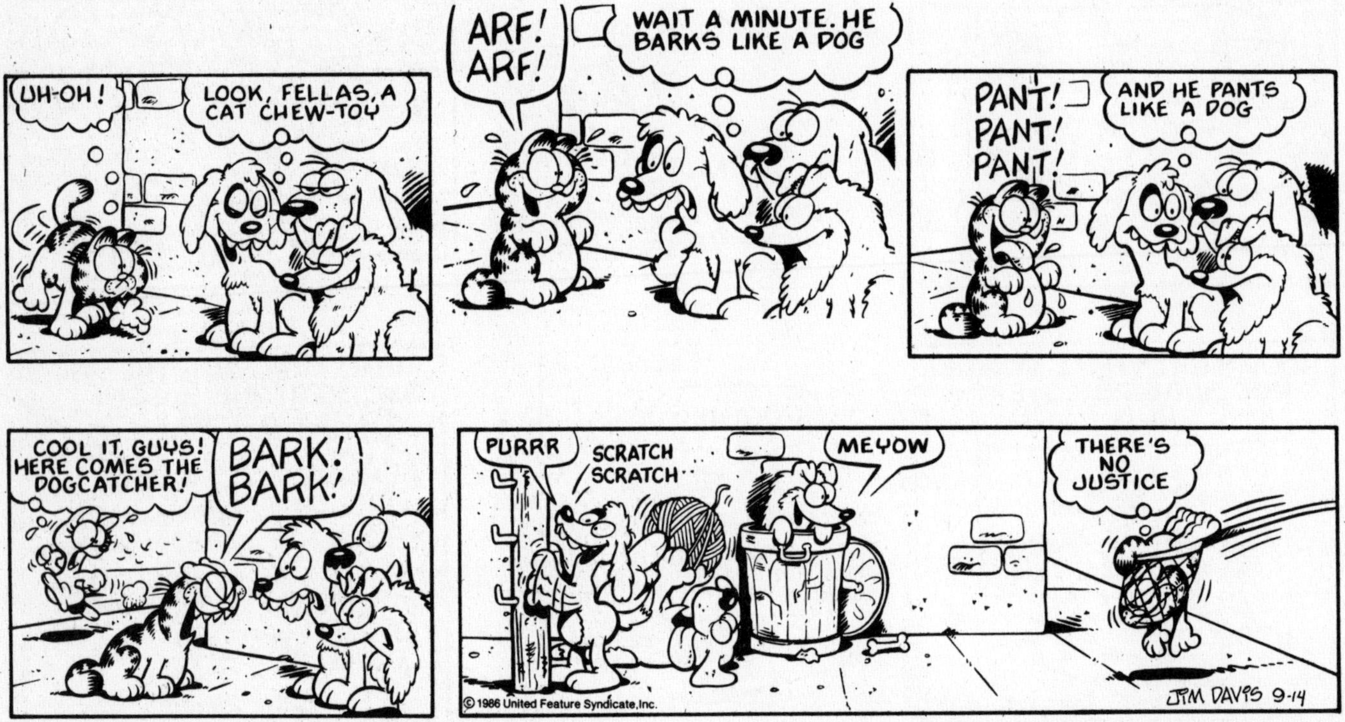
UH-OH!
LOOK, FELLAS, A CAT CHEW-TOY
ARF! ARF!
WAIT A MINUTE. HE BARKS LIKE A DOG
PANT! PANT! PANT!
AND HE PANTS LIKE A DOG
COOL IT, GUYS! HERE COMES THE DOGCATCHER!
BARK! BARK!
PURRR
SCRATCH SCRATCH
MEYOW
THERE'S NO JUSTICE
JIM DAVIS 9-14
© 1986 United Feature Syndicate, Inc.

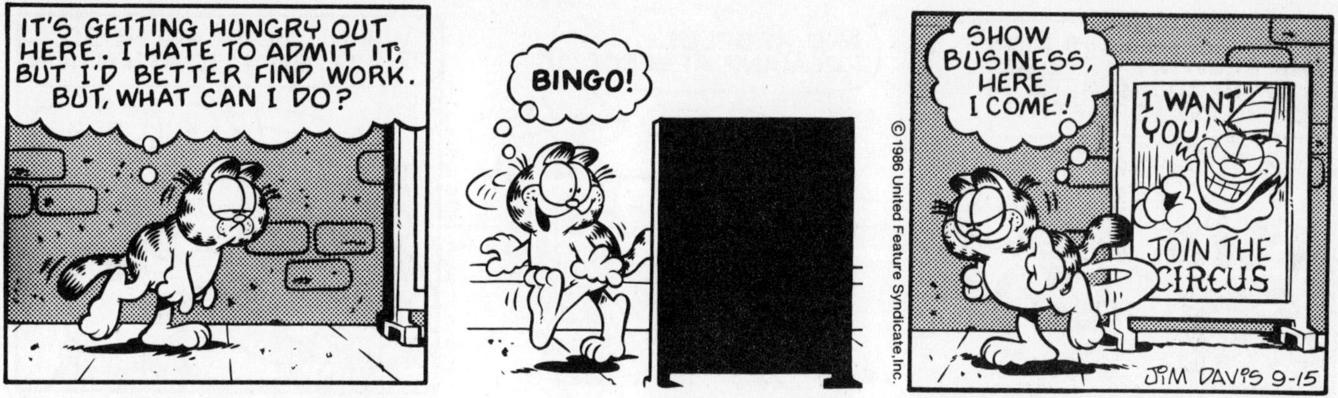
IT'S GETTING HUNGRY OUT HERE. I HATE TO ADMIT IT, BUT I'D BETTER FIND WORK. BUT, WHAT CAN I DO?
BINGO!
SHOW BUSINESS, HERE I COME!
I WANT YOU!
JOIN THE CIRCUS
JIM DAVIS 9-15
© 1986 United Feature Syndicate, Inc.

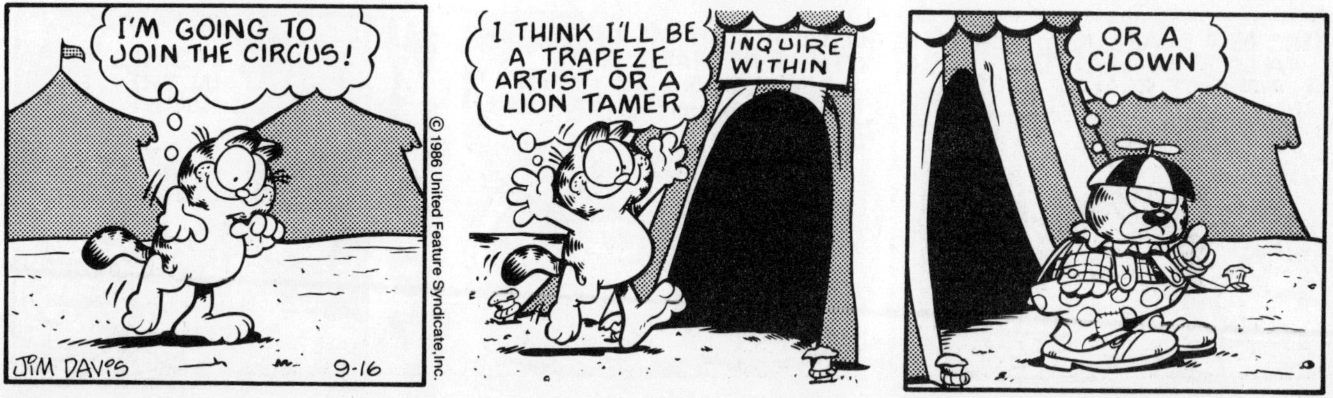
I'M GOING TO JOIN THE CIRCUS!
JIM DAVIS 9-16
© 1986 United Feature Syndicate, Inc.
I THINK I'LL BE A TRAPEZE ARTIST OR A LION TAMER
INQUIRE WITHIN
OR A CLOWN

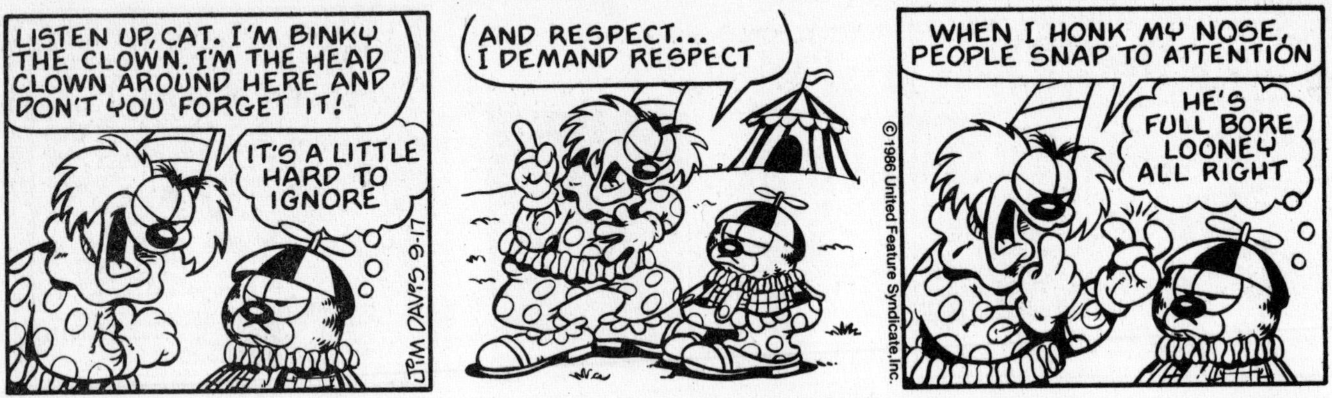
LISTEN UP, CAT. I'M BINKY THE CLOWN. I'M THE HEAD CLOWN AROUND HERE AND DON'T YOU FORGET IT!
IT'S A LITTLE HARD TO IGNORE
JIM DAVIS 9-17
AND RESPECT... I DEMAND RESPECT
© 1986 United Feature Syndicate, Inc.
WHEN I HONK MY NOSE, PEOPLE SNAP TO ATTENTION
HE'S FULL BORE LOONEY ALL RIGHT

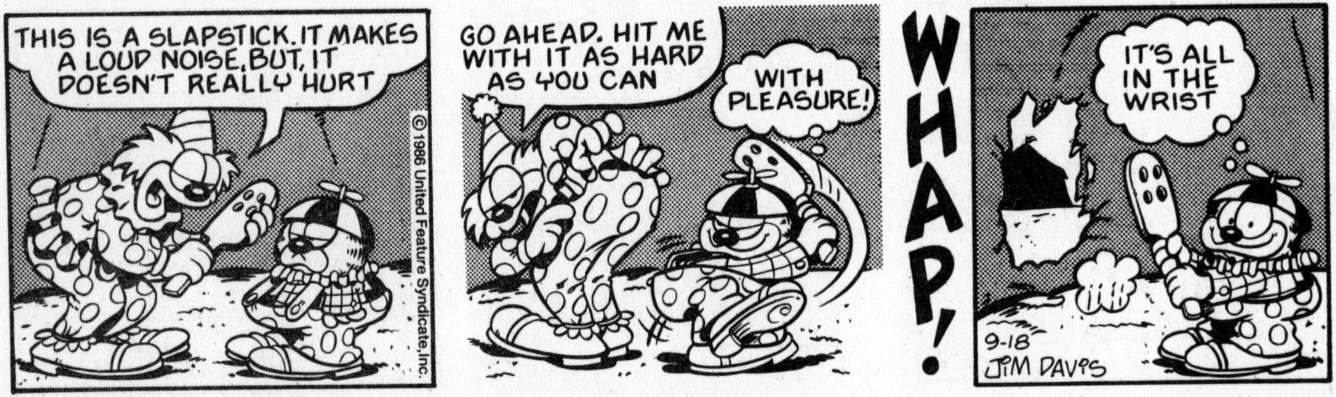
THIS IS A SLAPSTICK. IT MAKES A LOUD NOISE, BUT, IT DOESN'T REALLY HURT
© 1986 United Feature Syndicate, Inc.
GO AHEAD. HIT ME WITH IT AS HARD AS YOU CAN
WITH PLEASURE!
WHAP!
IT'S ALL IN THE WRIST
9-18
JIM DAVIS

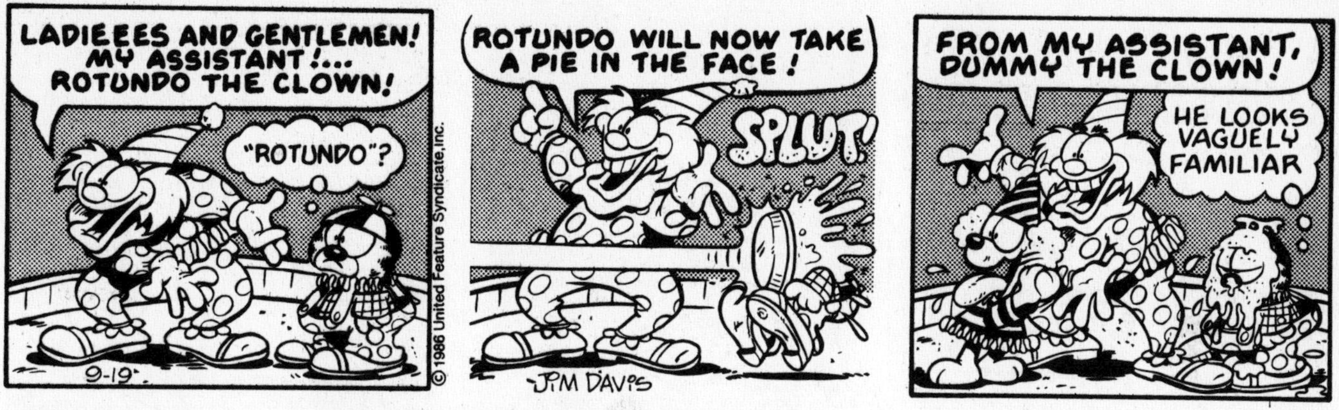
LADIEEES AND GENTLEMEN! MY ASSISTANT!... ROTUNDO THE CLOWN!
"ROTUNDO"?
9-19
© 1986 United Feature Syndicate,Inc.
ROTUNDO WILL NOW TAKE A PIE IN THE FACE!
SPLUT!
JIM DAVIS
FROM MY ASSISTANT, DUMMY THE CLOWN!
HE LOOKS VAGUELY FAMILIAR

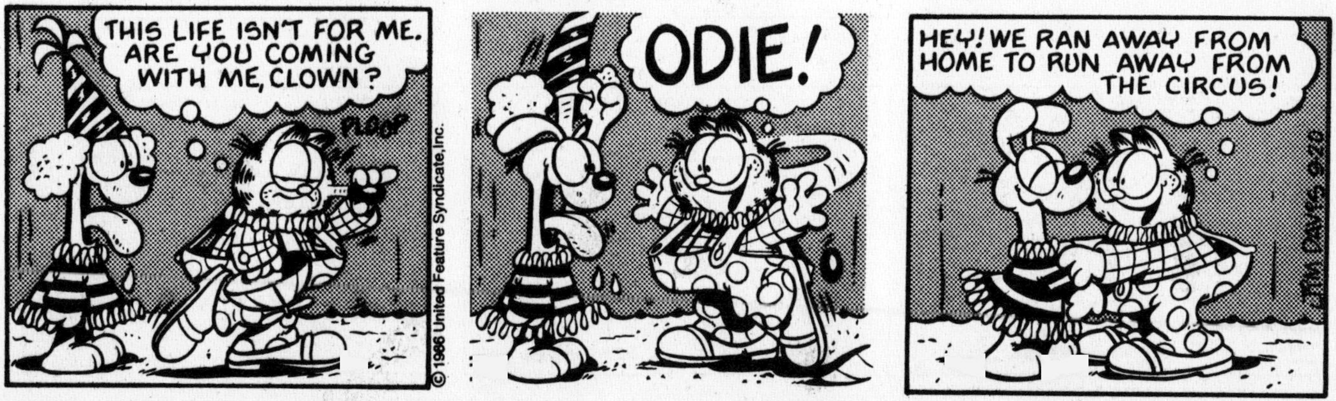
THIS LIFE ISN'T FOR ME. ARE YOU COMING WITH ME, CLOWN?
PLOOP
© 1986 United Feature Syndicate,Inc.
ODIE!
HEY! WE RAN AWAY FROM HOME TO RUN AWAY FROM THE CIRCUS!
JIM DAVIS 9-20

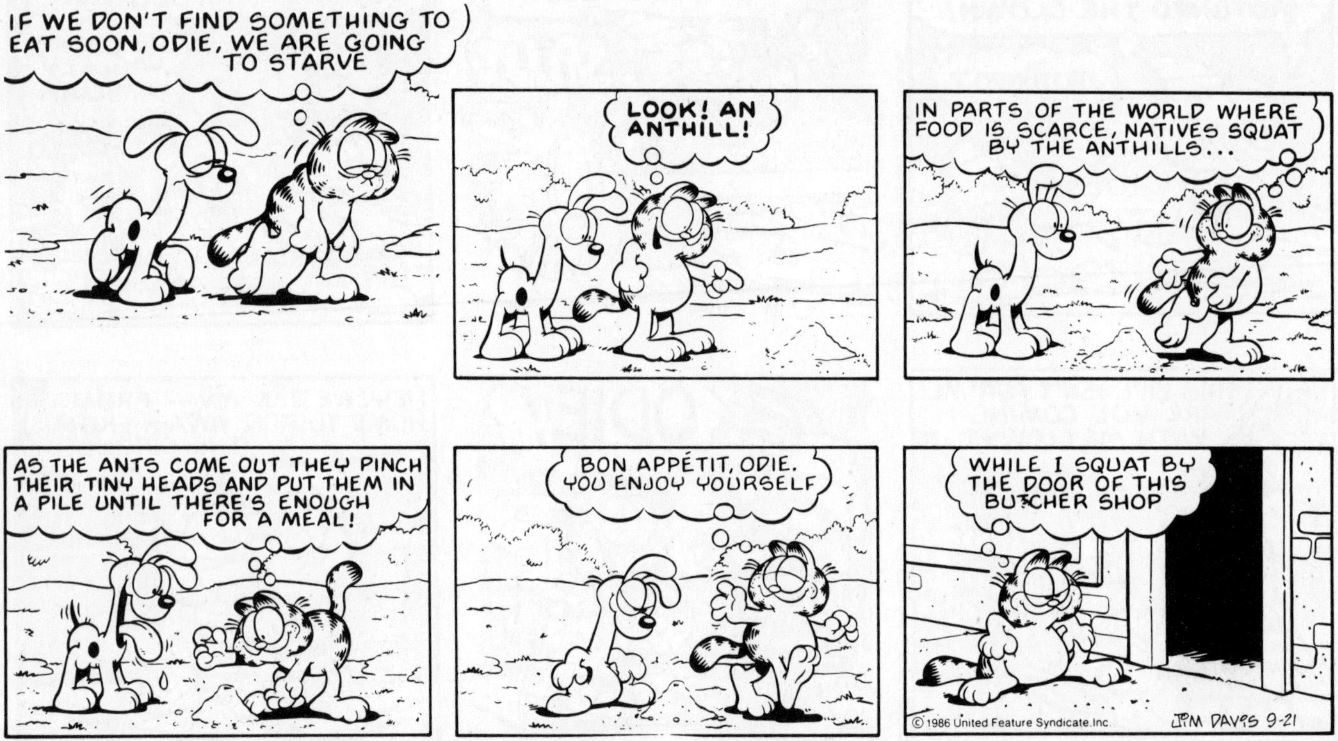
IF WE DON'T FIND SOMETHING TO EAT SOON, ODIE, WE ARE GOING TO STARVE
LOOK! AN ANTHILL!
IN PARTS OF THE WORLD WHERE FOOD IS SCARCE, NATIVES SQUAT BY THE ANTHILLS...
AS THE ANTS COME OUT THEY PINCH THEIR TINY HEADS AND PUT THEM IN A PILE UNTIL THERE'S ENOUGH FOR A MEAL!
BON APPÉTIT, ODIE. YOU ENJOY YOURSELF
WHILE I SQUAT BY THE DOOR OF THIS BUTCHER SHOP
© 1986 United Feature Syndicate, Inc.
JIM DAVIS 9-21

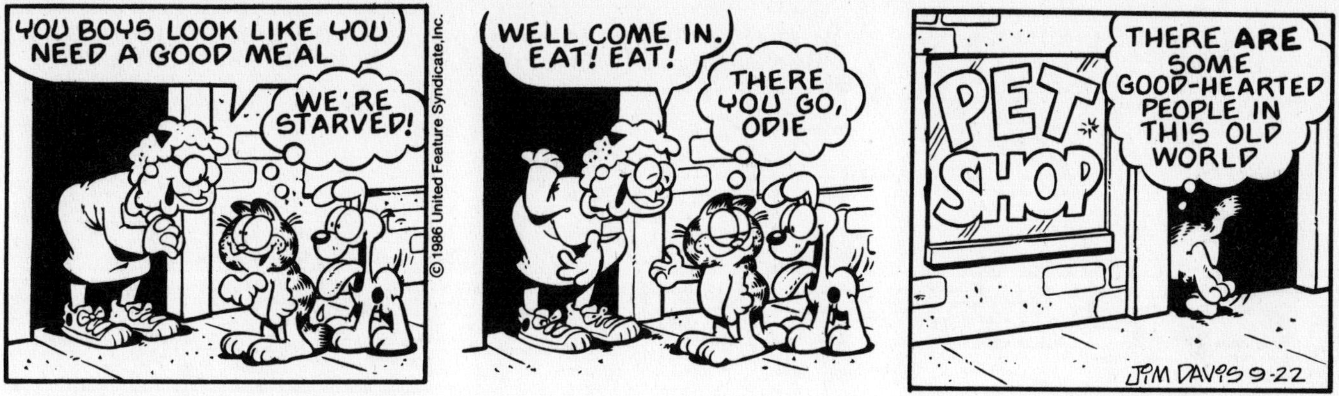

YOU BOYS LOOK LIKE YOU NEED A GOOD MEAL
WE'RE STARVED!
© 1986 United Feature Syndicate, Inc.
WELL COME IN. EAT! EAT!
THERE YOU GO, ODIE
PET SHOP
THERE ARE SOME GOOD-HEARTED PEOPLE IN THIS OLD WORLD
JIM DAVIS 9-22


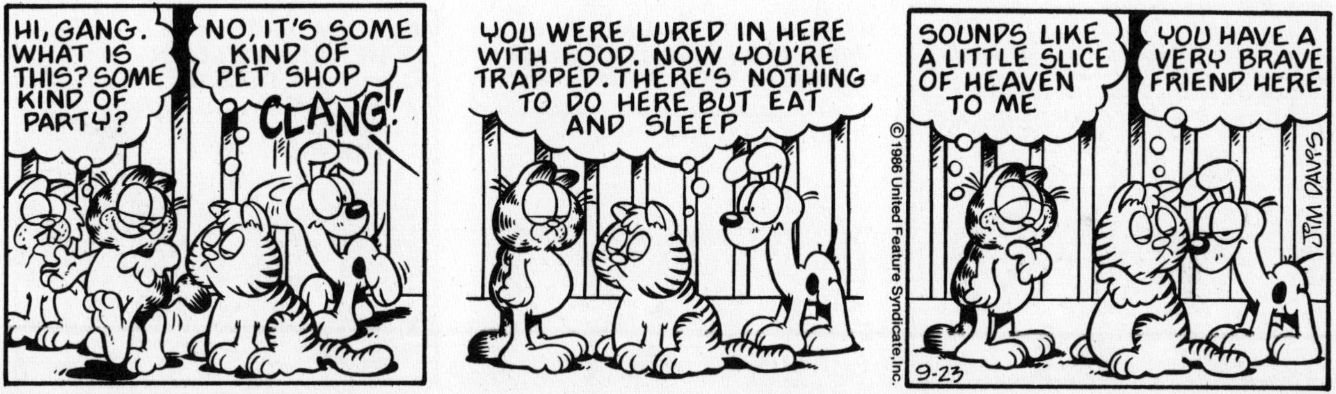

HI, GANG. WHAT IS THIS? SOME KIND OF PARTY?
NO, IT'S SOME KIND OF PET SHOP
CLANG!
YOU WERE LURED IN HERE WITH FOOD. NOW YOU'RE TRAPPED. THERE'S NOTHING TO DO HERE BUT EAT AND SLEEP
© 1986 United Feature Syndicate, Inc.
SOUNDS LIKE A LITTLE SLICE OF HEAVEN TO ME
YOU HAVE A VERY BRAVE FRIEND HERE
JIM DAVIS
9-23

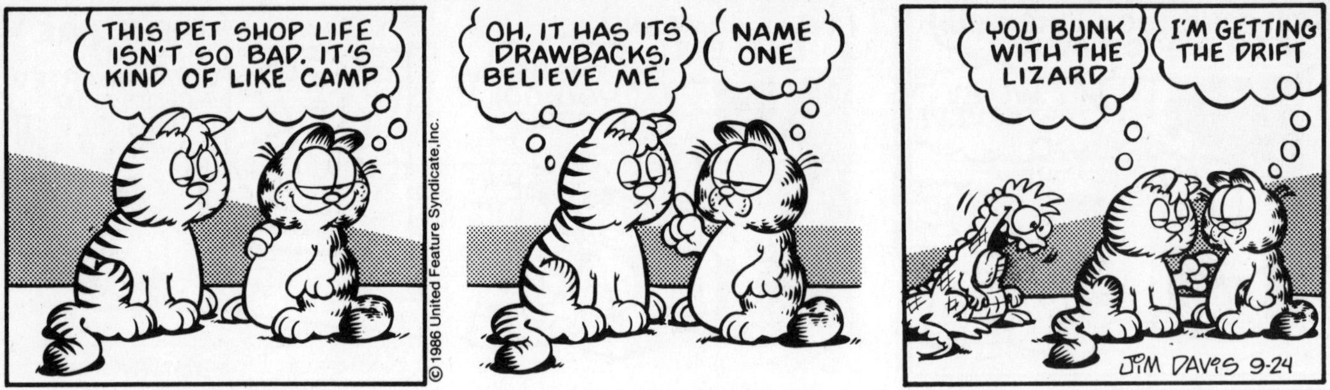
THIS PET SHOP LIFE ISN'T SO BAD. IT'S KIND OF LIKE CAMP
© 1986 United Feature Syndicate, Inc.
OH, IT HAS ITS DRAWBACKS, BELIEVE ME
NAME ONE
YOU BUNK WITH THE LIZARD
I'M GETTING THE DRIFT
JIM DAVIS 9-24

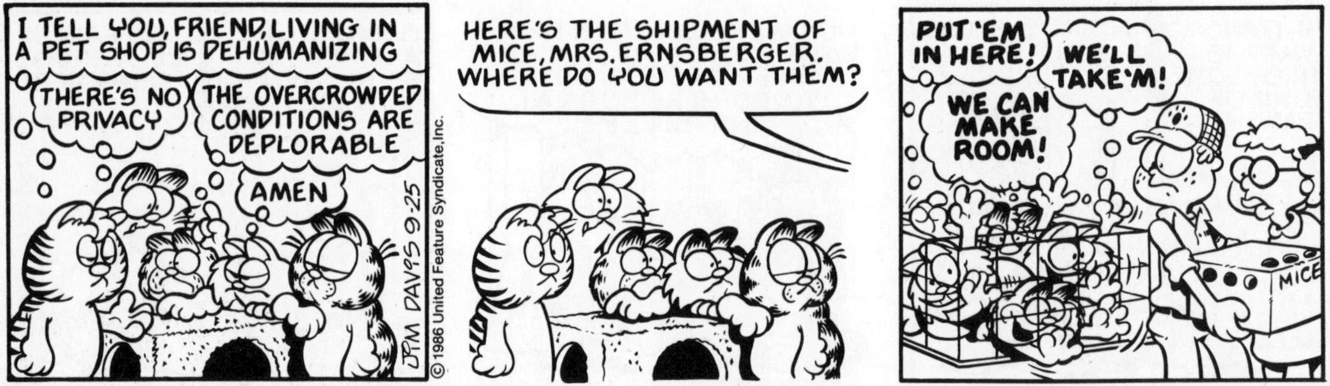
I TELL YOU, FRIEND, LIVING IN A PET SHOP IS DEHUMANIZING
THERE'S NO PRIVACY
THE OVERCROWDED CONDITIONS ARE DEPLORABLE
AMEN
JIM DAVIS 9-25
© 1986 United Feature Syndicate, Inc.
HERE'S THE SHIPMENT OF MICE, MRS. ERNSBERGER. WHERE DO YOU WANT THEM?
PUT 'EM IN HERE!
WE'LL TAKE 'M!
WE CAN MAKE ROOM!
MICE

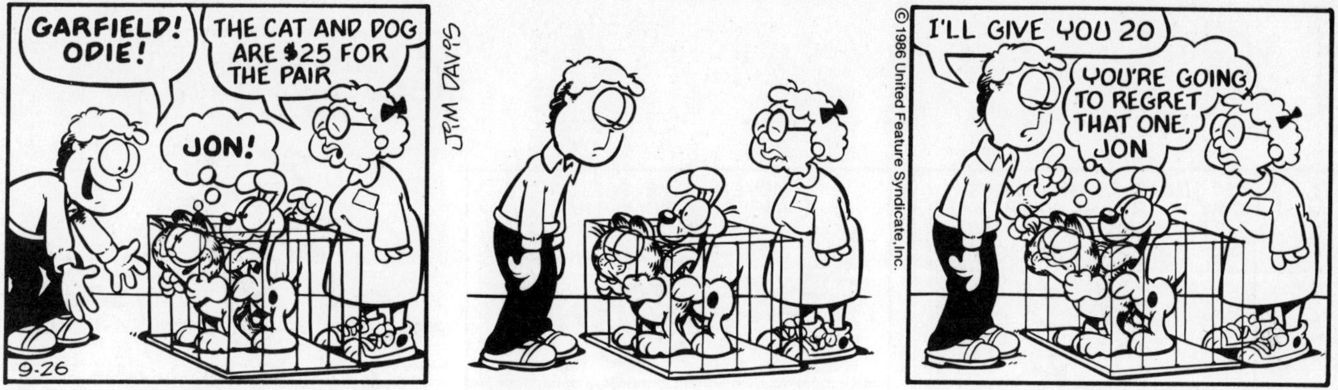
GARFIELD! ODIE!
THE CAT AND DOG ARE $25 FOR THE PAIR
JON!
JIM DAVIS
9-26
© 1986 United Feature Syndicate,Inc.
I'LL GIVE YOU 20
YOU'RE GOING TO REGRET THAT ONE, JON

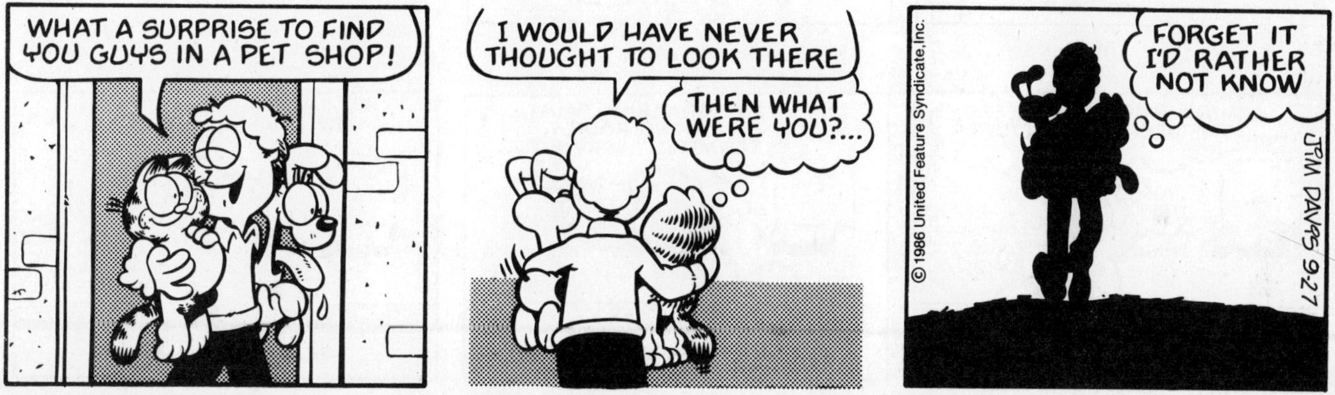
WHAT A SURPRISE TO FIND YOU GUYS IN A PET SHOP!
I WOULD HAVE NEVER THOUGHT TO LOOK THERE
THEN WHAT WERE YOU?...
© 1986 United Feature Syndicate,Inc.
FORGET IT I'D RATHER NOT KNOW
JIM DAVIS 9-27

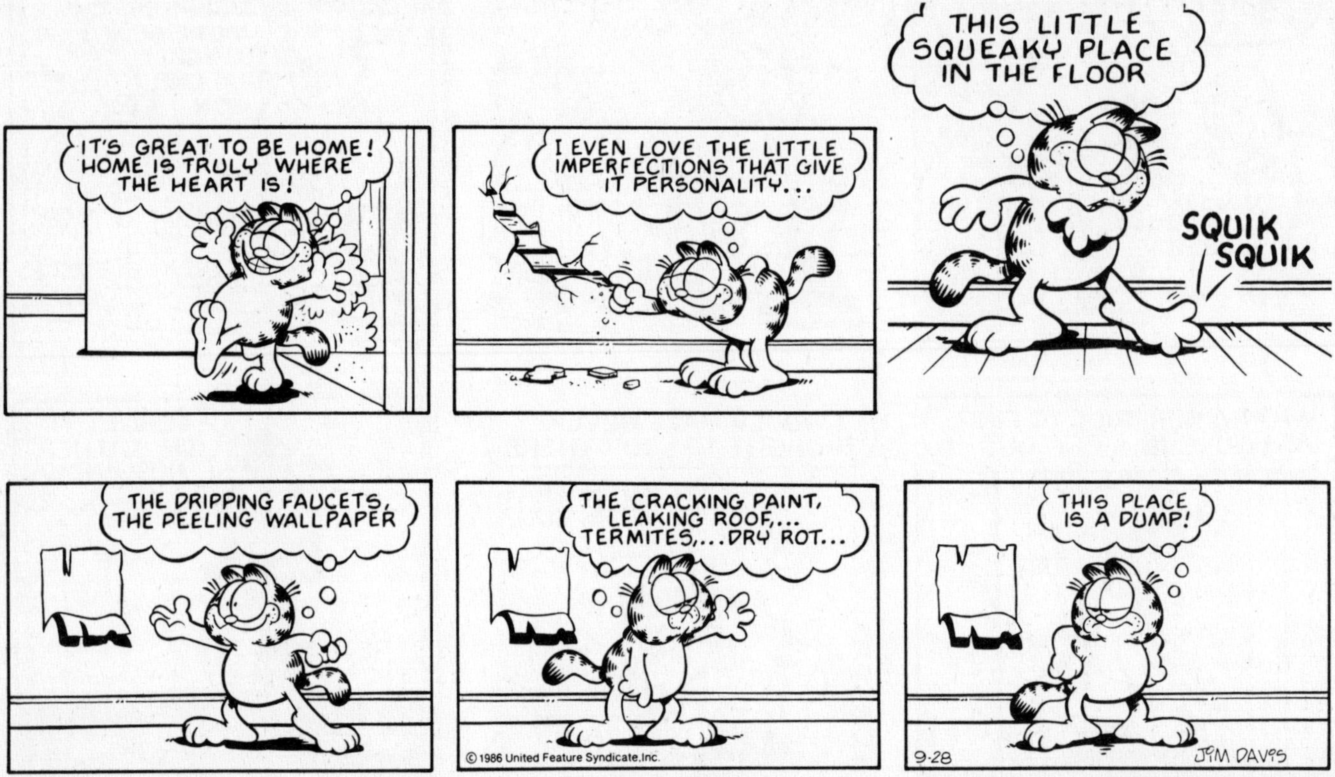
IT'S GREAT TO BE HOME! HOME IS TRULY WHERE THE HEART IS!
I EVEN LOVE THE LITTLE IMPERFECTIONS THAT GIVE IT PERSONALITY...
THIS LITTLE SQUEAKY PLACE IN THE FLOOR
SQUIK SQUIK
THE DRIPPING FAUCETS, THE PEELING WALLPAPER
THE CRACKING PAINT, LEAKING ROOF,... TERMITES,... DRY ROT...
THIS PLACE IS A DUMP!
© 1986 United Feature Syndicate, Inc.
9-28
JIM DAVIS

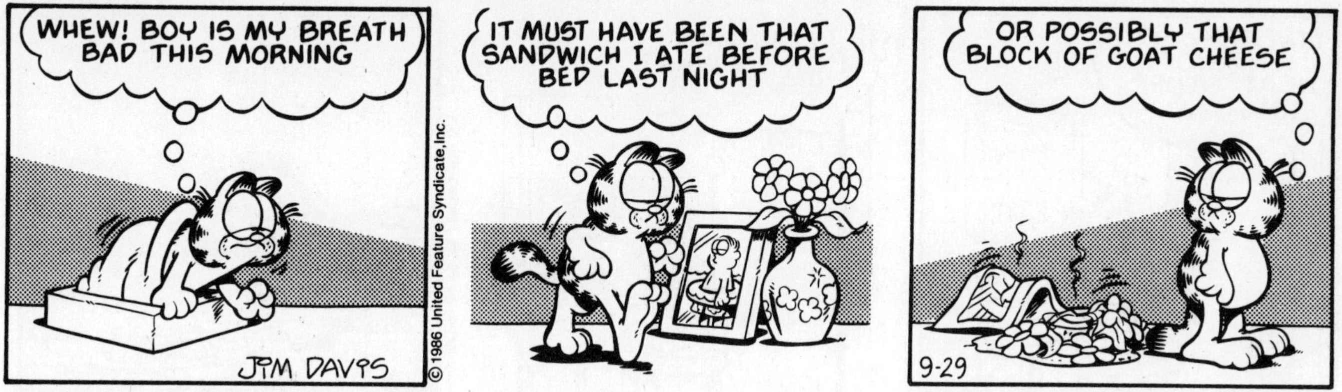
WHEW! BOY IS MY BREATH BAD THIS MORNING
JIM DAVIS
© 1986 United Feature Syndicate, Inc.
IT MUST HAVE BEEN THAT SANDWICH I ATE BEFORE BED LAST NIGHT
OR POSSIBLY THAT BLOCK OF GOAT CHEESE
9-29

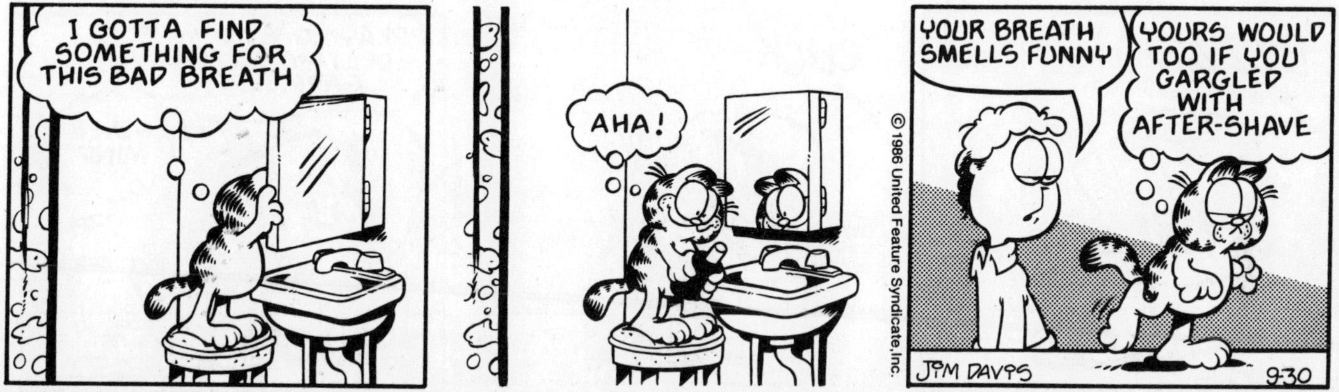
I GOTTA FIND SOMETHING FOR THIS BAD BREATH
AHA!
© 1986 United Feature Syndicate, Inc.
YOUR BREATH SMELLS FUNNY
YOURS WOULD TOO IF YOU GARGLED WITH AFTER-SHAVE
JIM DAVIS
9-30

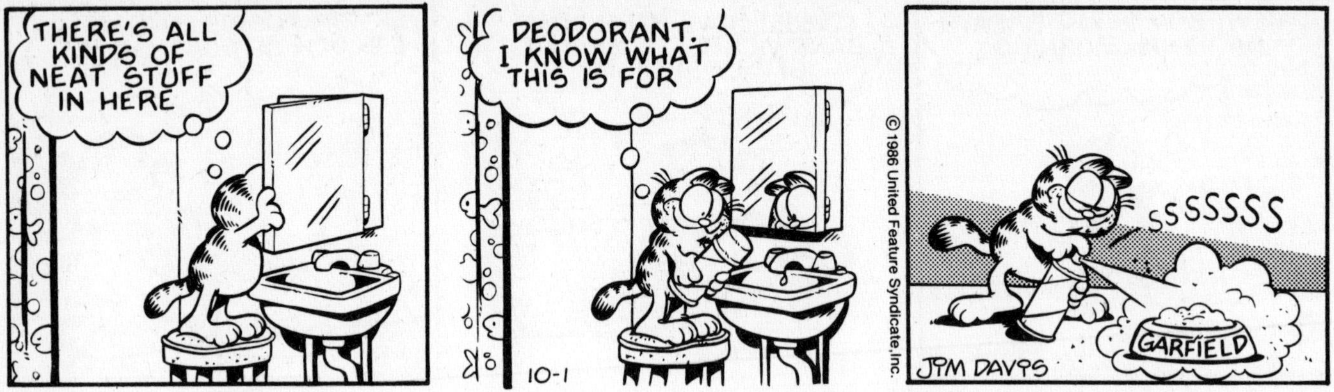
THERE'S ALL KINDS OF NEAT STUFF IN HERE
DEODORANT. I KNOW WHAT THIS IS FOR
10-1
SSSSSSS
GARFIELD
JIM DAVIS
© 1986 United Feature Syndicate,Inc.

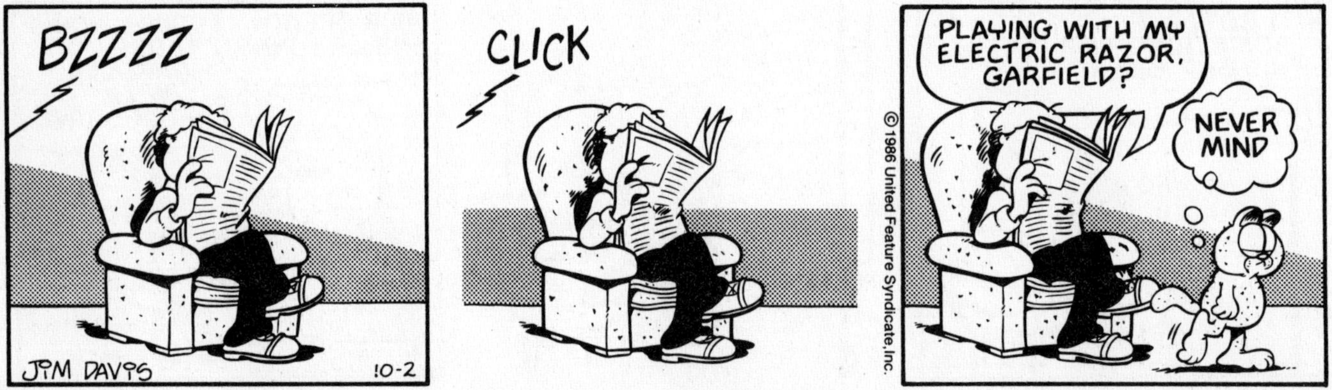
BZZZZ
JIM DAVIS
10-2
CLICK
PLAYING WITH MY ELECTRIC RAZOR, GARFIELD?
NEVER MIND
© 1986 United Feature Syndicate,Inc.

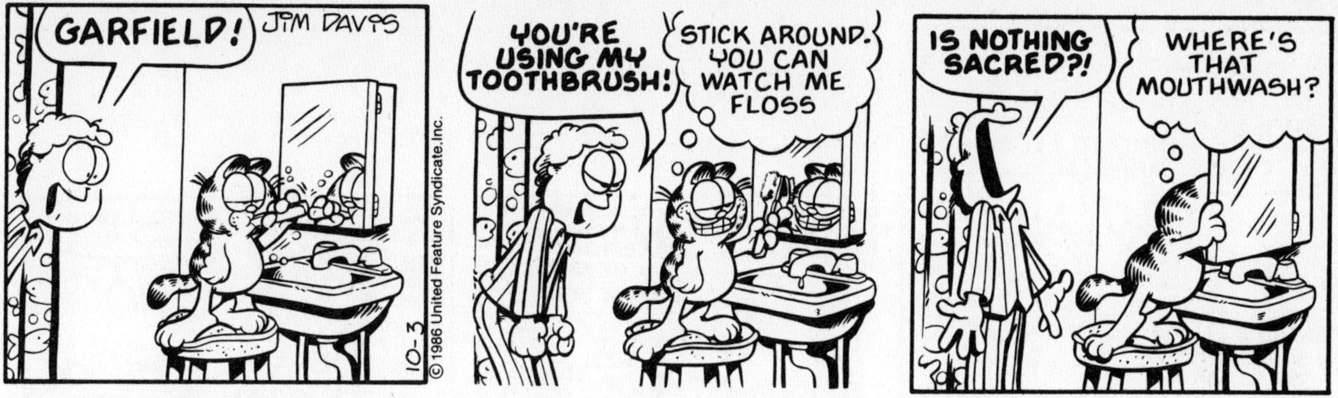
GARFIELD!
JIM DAVIS
10-3
© 1986 United Feature Syndicate, Inc.
YOU'RE USING MY TOOTHBRUSH!
STICK AROUND. YOU CAN WATCH ME FLOSS
IS NOTHING SACRED?!
WHERE'S THAT MOUTHWASH?

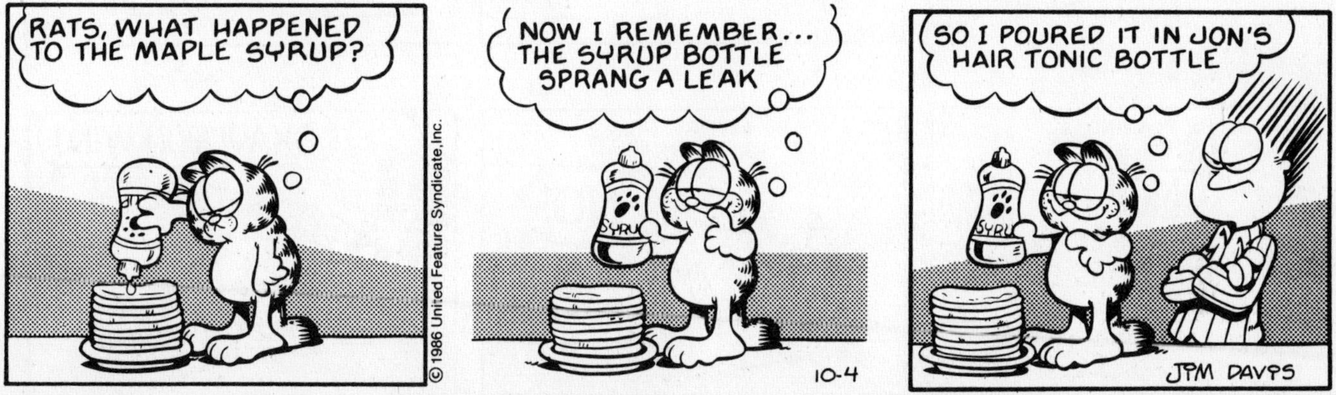
RATS, WHAT HAPPENED TO THE MAPLE SYRUP?
© 1986 United Feature Syndicate, Inc.
NOW I REMEMBER... THE SYRUP BOTTLE SPRANG A LEAK
SYRU
10-4
SO I POURED IT IN JON'S HAIR TONIC BOTTLE
SYRU
JIM DAVIS

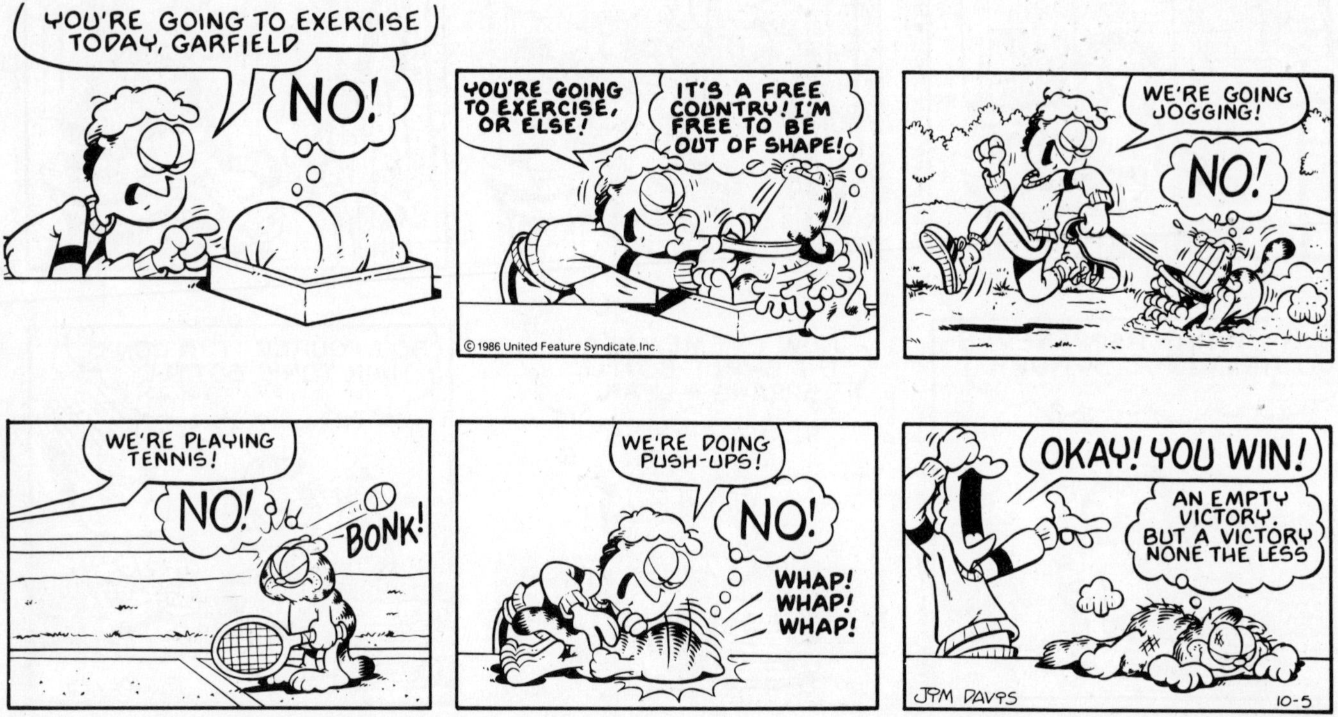
YOU'RE GOING TO EXERCISE TODAY, GARFIELD
NO!
YOU'RE GOING TO EXERCISE, OR ELSE!
IT'S A FREE COUNTRY! I'M FREE TO BE OUT OF SHAPE!
© 1986 United Feature Syndicate, Inc.
WE'RE GOING JOGGING!
NO!
WE'RE PLAYING TENNIS!
NO!
BONK!
WE'RE DOING PUSH-UPS!
NO!
WHAP! WHAP! WHAP!
OKAY! YOU WIN!
AN EMPTY VICTORY. BUT A VICTORY NONE THE LESS
JIM DAVIS
10-5

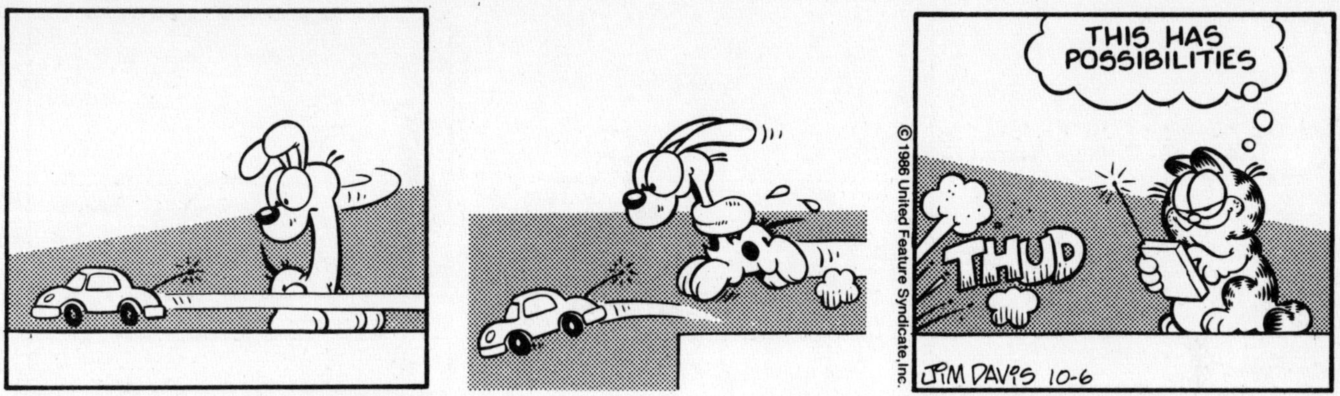
THUD
THIS HAS POSSIBILITIES
© 1986 United Feature Syndicate, Inc.
JIM DAVIS 10-6

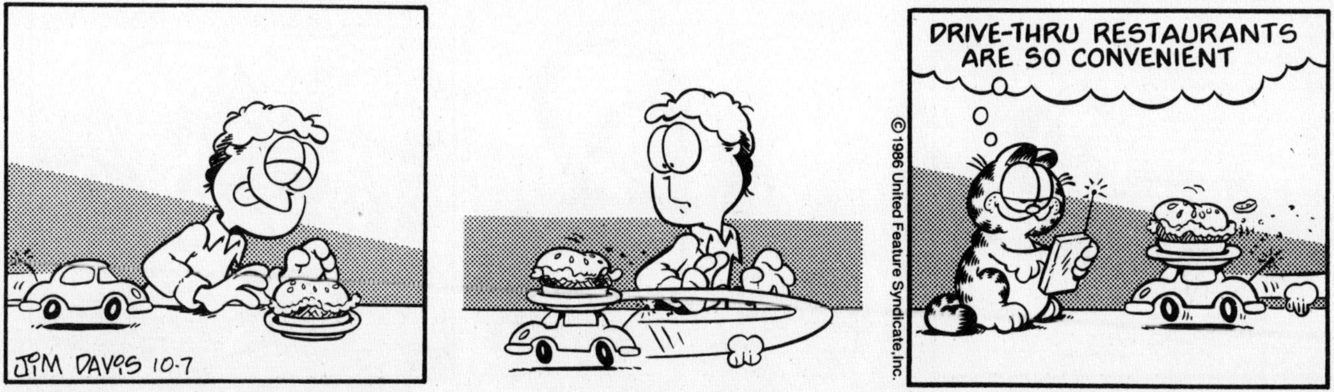
JIM DAVIS 10-7
DRIVE-THRU RESTAURANTS ARE SO CONVENIENT
© 1986 United Feature Syndicate, Inc.

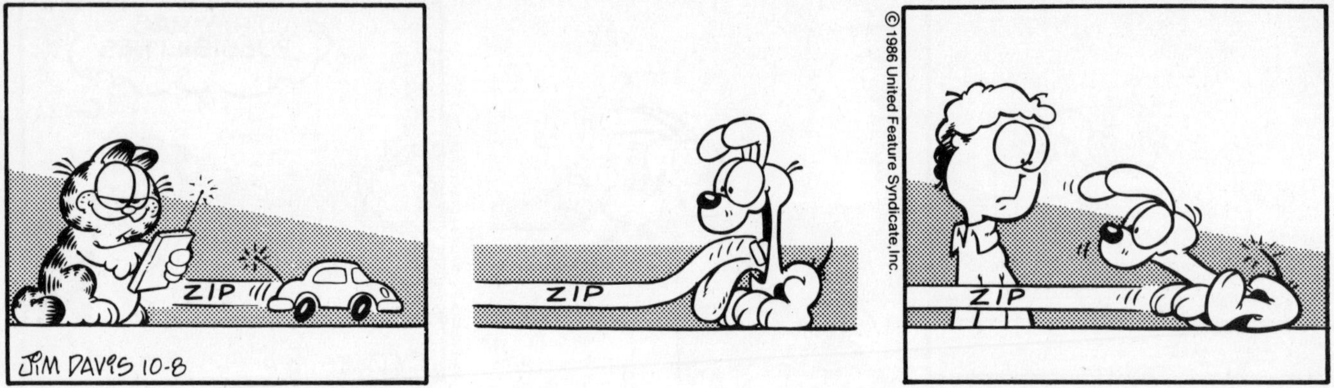
ZIP
JIM DAVIS 10-8
ZIP
© 1986 United Feature Syndicate, Inc.
ZIP

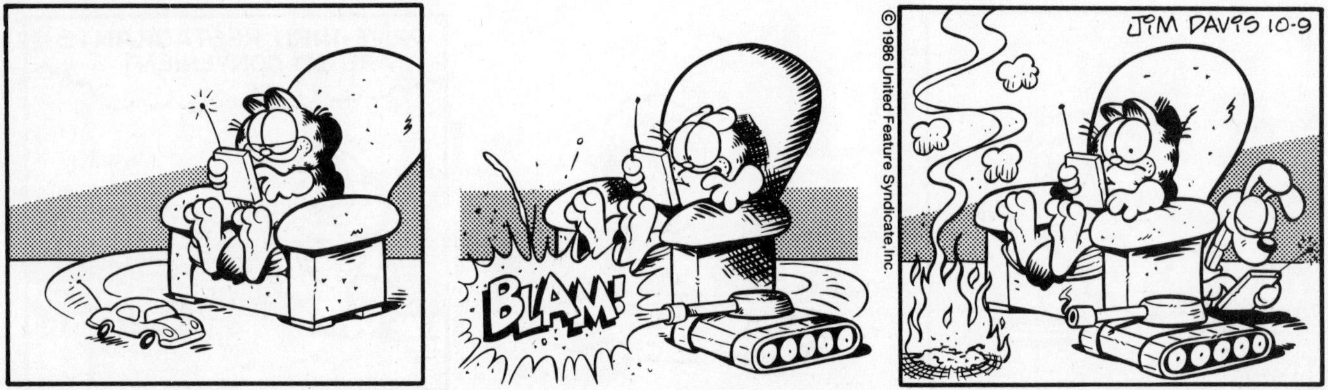
BLAM!
© 1986 United Feature Syndicate, Inc.
JIM DAVIS 10-9

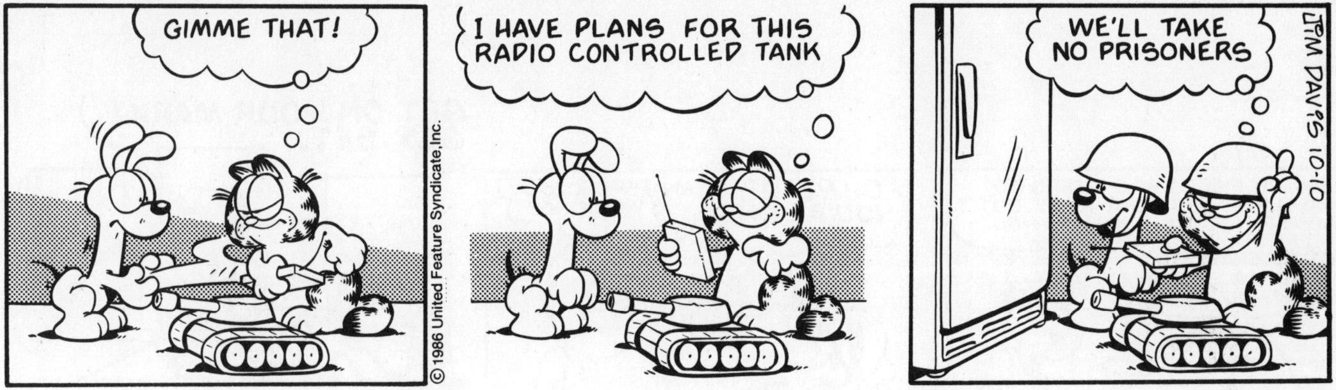
GIMME THAT!
I HAVE PLANS FOR THIS RADIO CONTROLLED TANK
WE'LL TAKE NO PRISONERS
JIM DAVIS 10-10
© 1986 United Feature Syndicate, Inc.

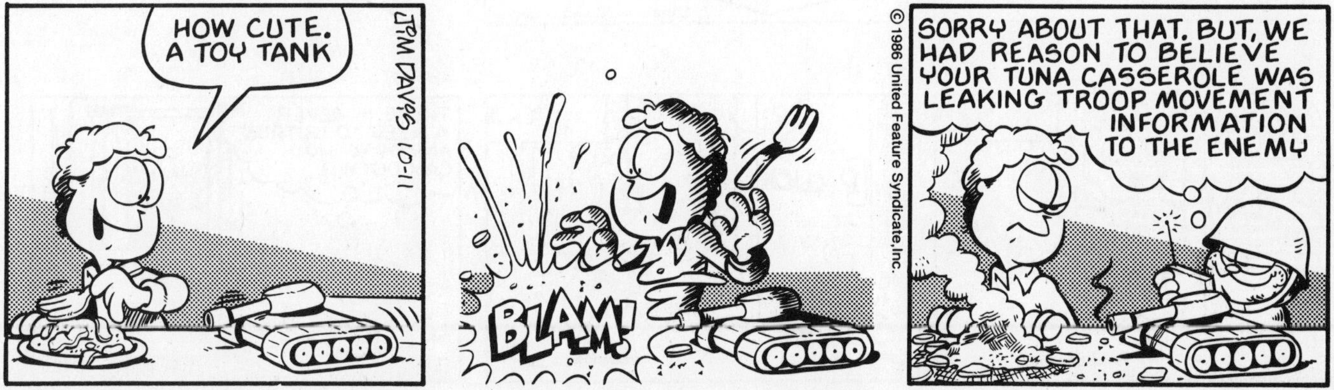
HOW CUTE. A TOY TANK
JIM DAVIS 10-11
BLAM!
SORRY ABOUT THAT. BUT, WE HAD REASON TO BELIEVE YOUR TUNA CASSEROLE WAS LEAKING TROOP MOVEMENT INFORMATION TO THE ENEMY
© 1986 United Feature Syndicate, Inc.

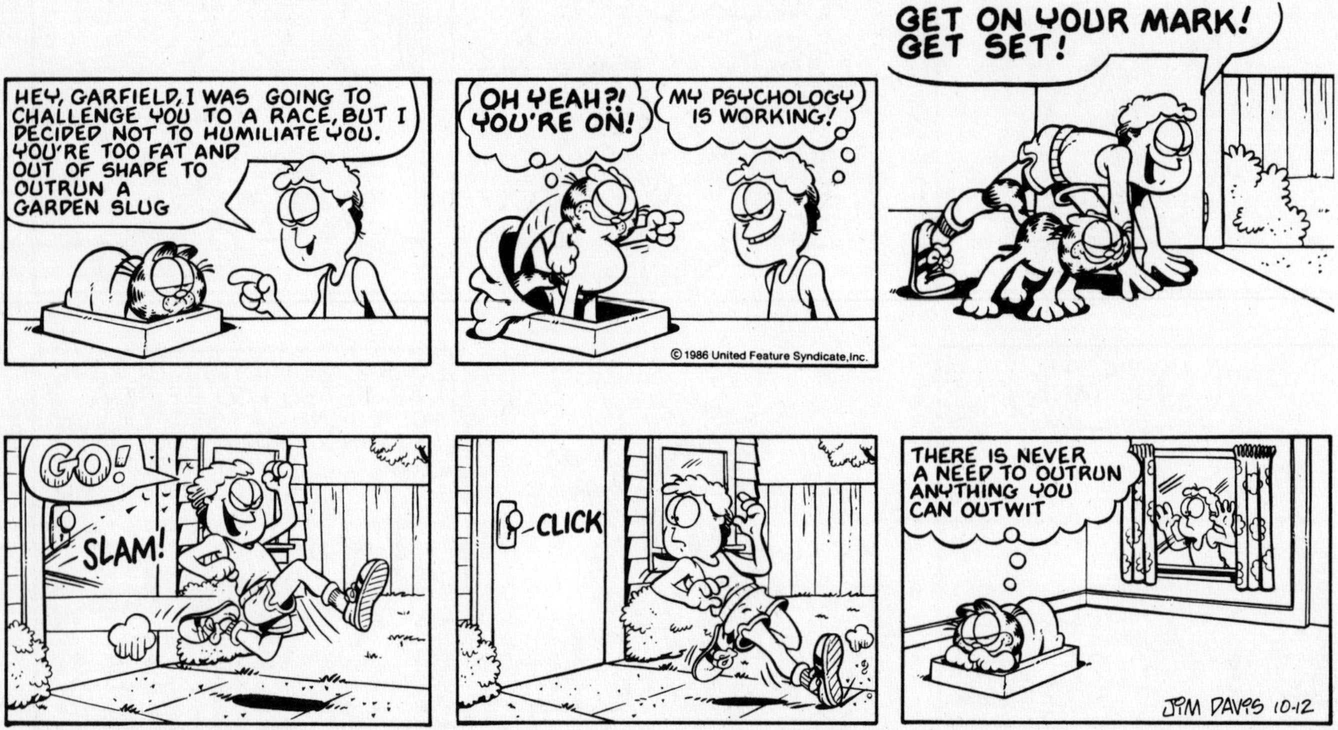
HEY, GARFIELD, I WAS GOING TO CHALLENGE YOU TO A RACE, BUT I DECIDED NOT TO HUMILIATE YOU. YOU'RE TOO FAT AND OUT OF SHAPE TO OUTRUN A GARDEN SLUG
OH YEAH?! YOU'RE ON!
MY PSYCHOLOGY IS WORKING!
© 1986 United Feature Syndicate, Inc.
GET ON YOUR MARK! GET SET!
GO!
SLAM!
CLICK
THERE IS NEVER A NEED TO OUTRUN ANYTHING YOU CAN OUTWIT
JIM DAVIS 10-12

# Garfield world-wide

BY: JiM DAViS

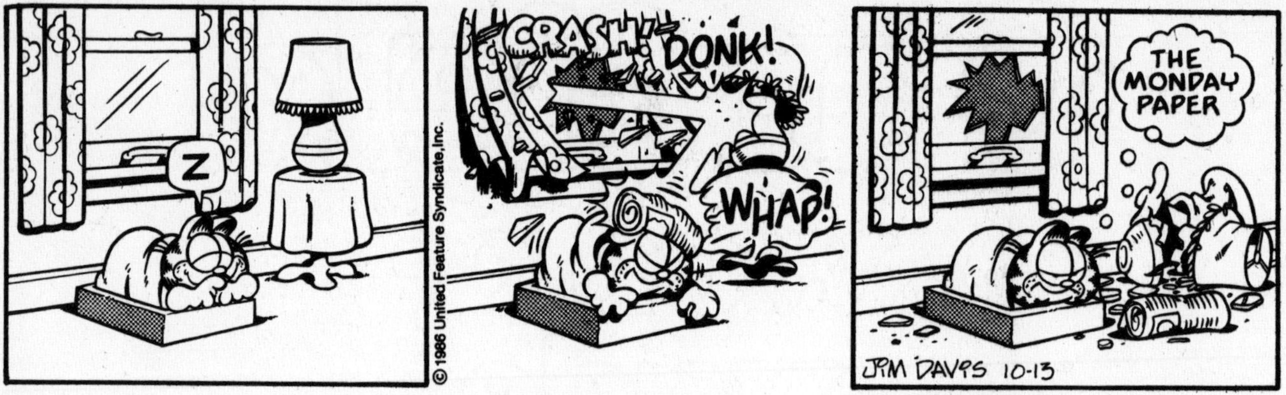
Z
CRASH!
DONK!
WHAP!
© 1986 United Feature Syndicate, Inc.
THE MONDAY PAPER
JIM DAVIS 10-13

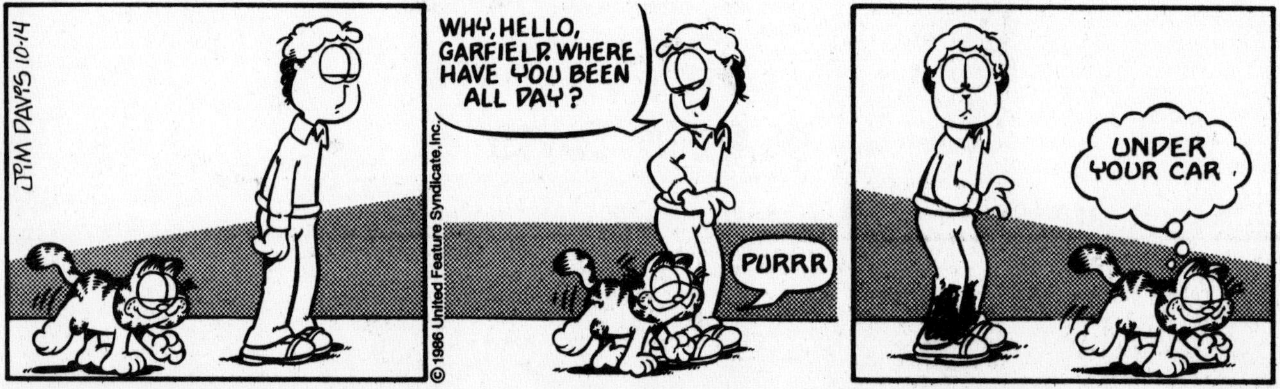
JIM DAVIS 10-14
© 1986 United Feature Syndicate, Inc.
WHY, HELLO, GARFIELD. WHERE HAVE YOU BEEN ALL DAY?
PURRR
UNDER YOUR CAR

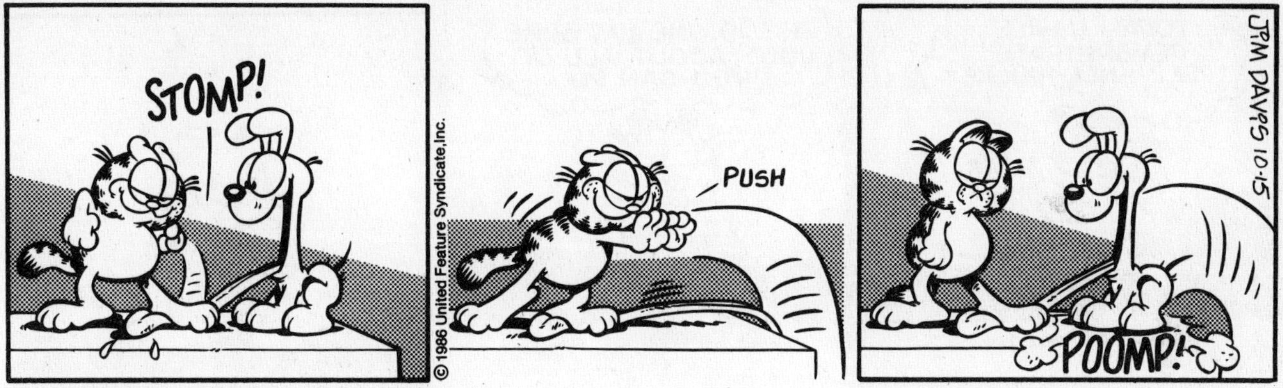
STOMP!
© 1986 United Feature Syndicate, Inc.
PUSH
JIM DAVIS 10-15
POOMP!

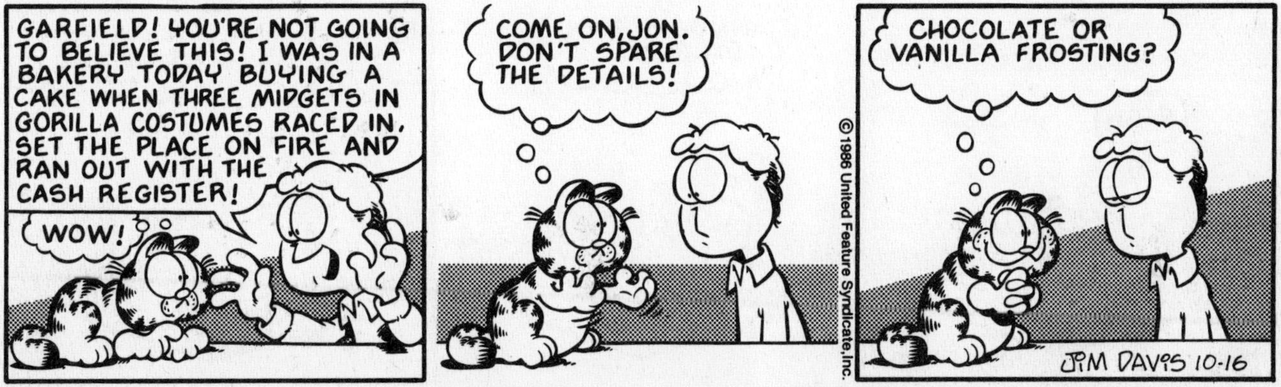
GARFIELD! YOU'RE NOT GOING TO BELIEVE THIS! I WAS IN A BAKERY TODAY BUYING A CAKE WHEN THREE MIDGETS IN GORILLA COSTUMES RACED IN, SET THE PLACE ON FIRE AND RAN OUT WITH THE CASH REGISTER!
WOW!
COME ON, JON. DON'T SPARE THE DETAILS!
© 1986 United Feature Syndicate, Inc.
CHOCOLATE OR VANILLA FROSTING?
JIM DAVIS 10-16

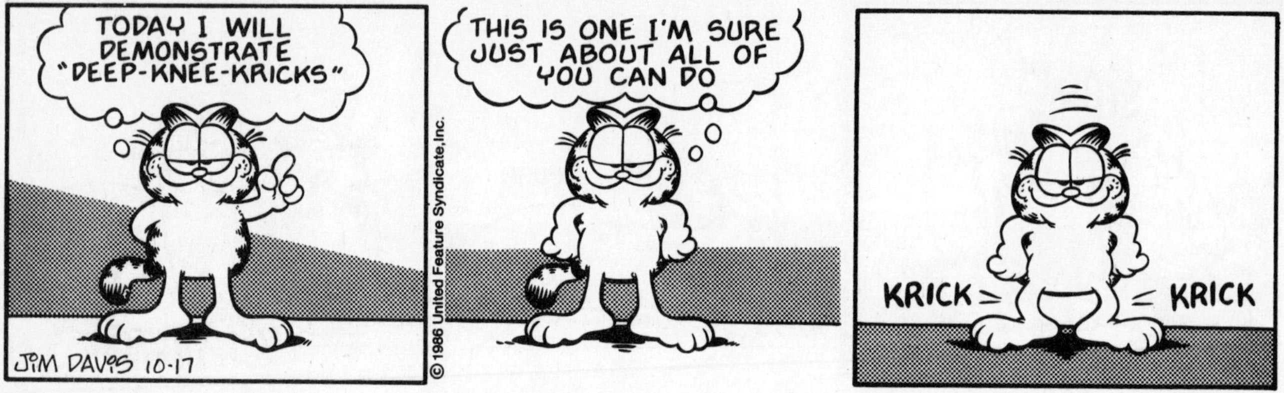
TODAY I WILL DEMONSTRATE "DEEP-KNEE-KRICKS"
THIS IS ONE I'M SURE JUST ABOUT ALL OF YOU CAN DO
KRICK
KRICK
JIM DAVIS 10-17
© 1986 United Feature Syndicate, Inc.

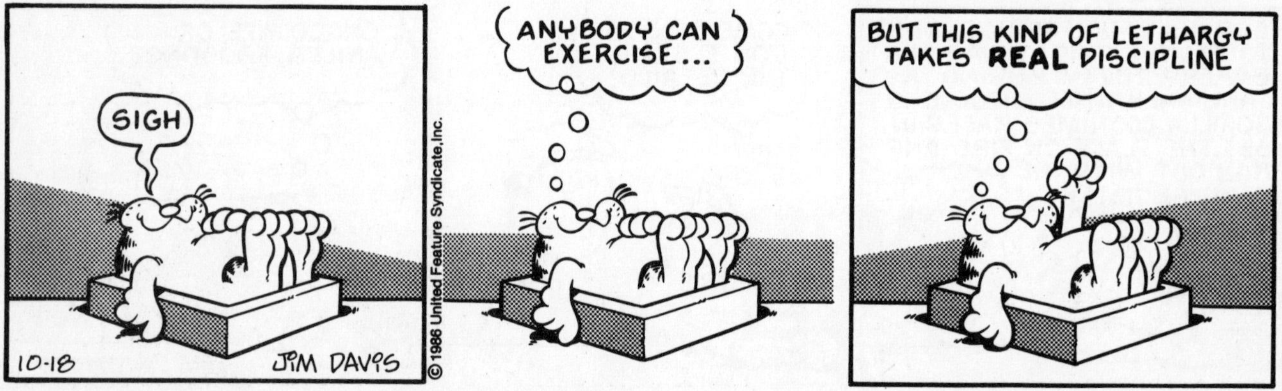
SIGH
ANYBODY CAN EXERCISE...
BUT THIS KIND OF LETHARGY TAKES **REAL** DISCIPLINE
10-18 JIM DAVIS
© 1986 United Feature Syndicate, Inc.

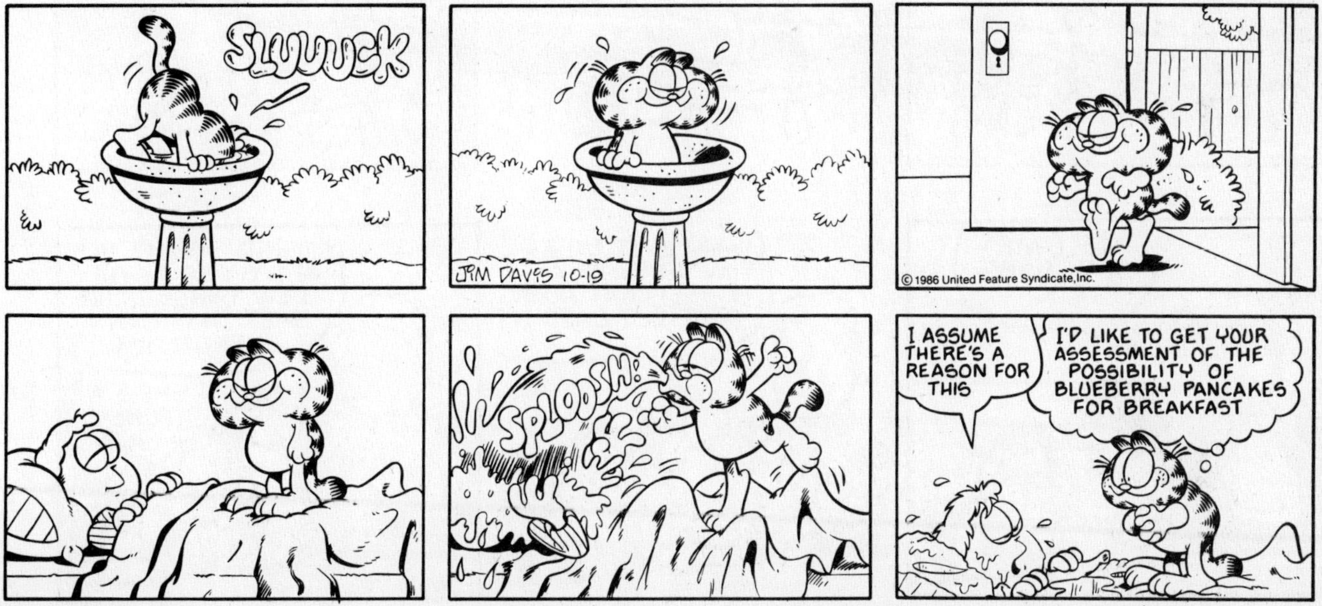
SLUUUCK
JIM DAVIS 10-19
© 1986 United Feature Syndicate, Inc.
SPLOOSH!
I ASSUME THERE'S A REASON FOR THIS
I'D LIKE TO GET YOUR ASSESSMENT OF THE POSSIBILITY OF BLUEBERRY PANCAKES FOR BREAKFAST

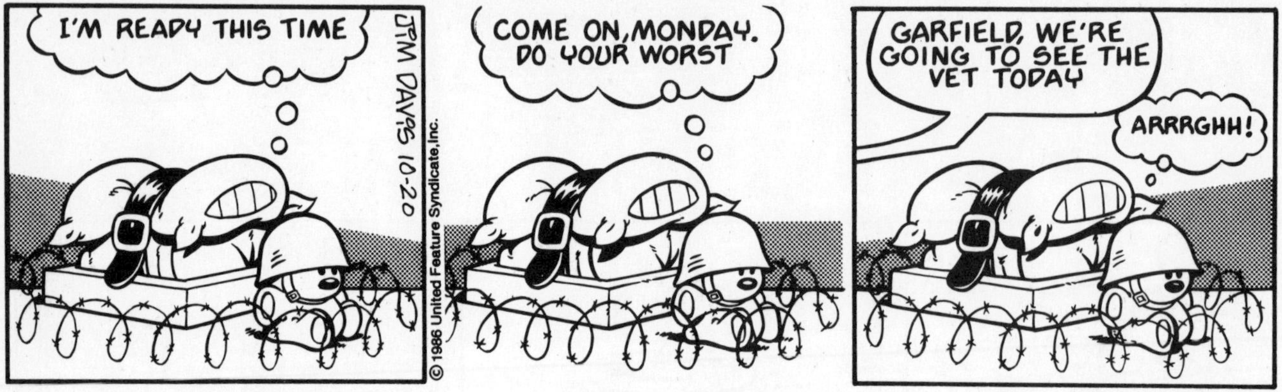
I'M READY THIS TIME
JIM DAVIS 10-20
© 1986 United Feature Syndicate, Inc.
COME ON, MONDAY. DO YOUR WORST
GARFIELD, WE'RE GOING TO SEE THE VET TODAY
ARRRGHH!

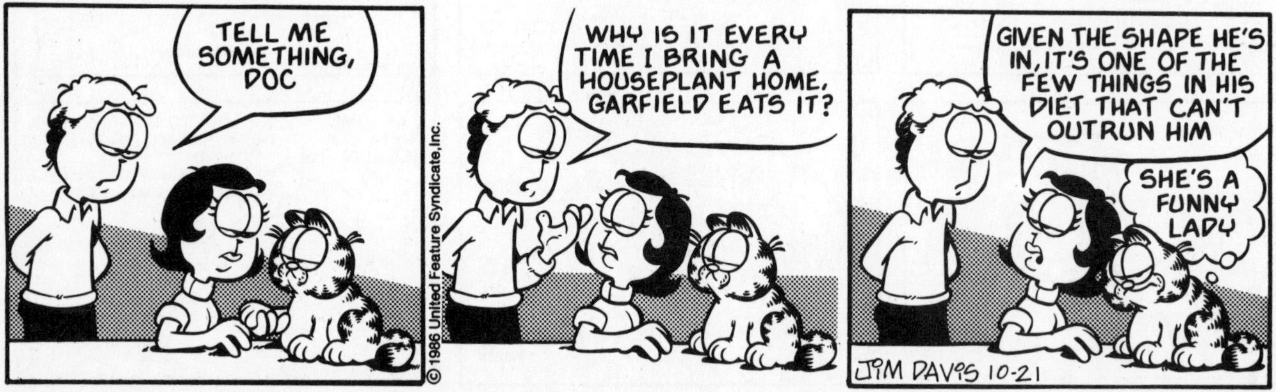
TELL ME SOMETHING, DOC
© 1986 United Feature Syndicate, Inc.
WHY IS IT EVERY TIME I BRING A HOUSEPLANT HOME, GARFIELD EATS IT?
GIVEN THE SHAPE HE'S IN, IT'S ONE OF THE FEW THINGS IN HIS DIET THAT CAN'T OUTRUN HIM
SHE'S A FUNNY LADY
JIM DAVIS 10-21

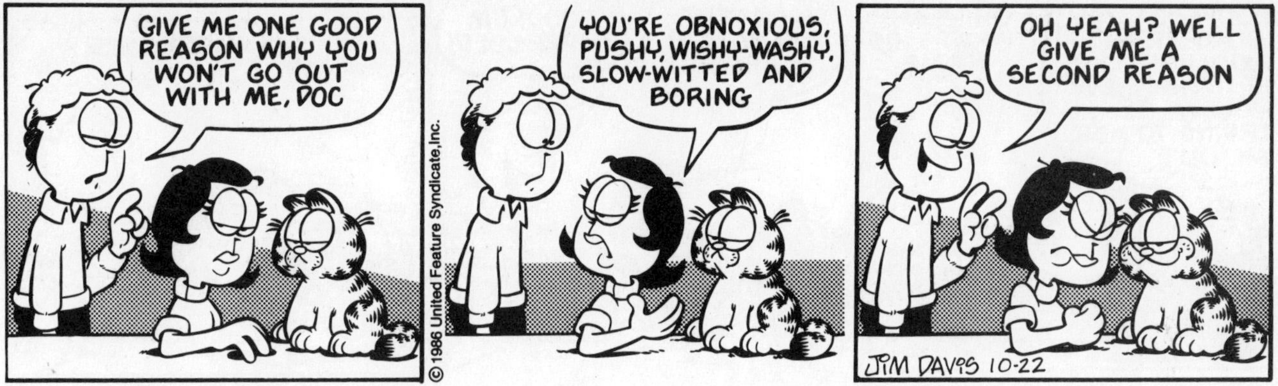
GIVE ME ONE GOOD REASON WHY YOU WON'T GO OUT WITH ME, DOC
YOU'RE OBNOXIOUS, PUSHY, WISHY-WASHY, SLOW-WITTED AND BORING
OH YEAH? WELL GIVE ME A SECOND REASON
© 1986 United Feature Syndicate, Inc.
JIM DAVIS 10-22

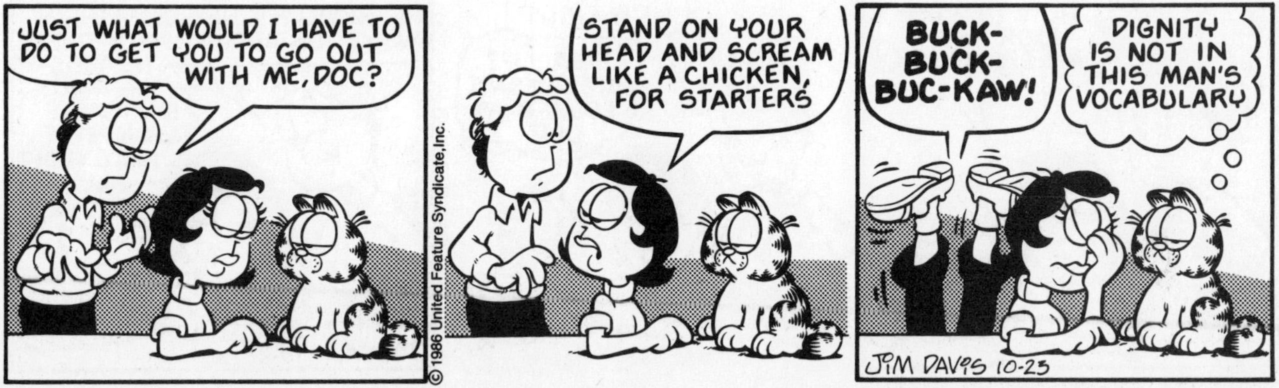
JUST WHAT WOULD I HAVE TO DO TO GET YOU TO GO OUT WITH ME, DOC?
STAND ON YOUR HEAD AND SCREAM LIKE A CHICKEN, FOR STARTERS
BUCK-BUCK-BUC-KAW!
DIGNITY IS NOT IN THIS MAN'S VOCABULARY
© 1986 United Feature Syndicate, Inc.
JIM DAVIS 10-23

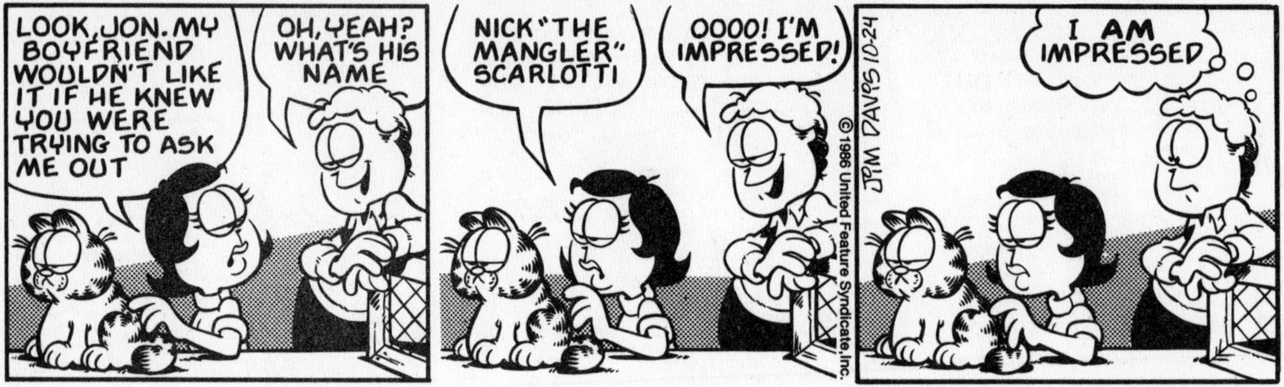
LOOK, JON. MY BOYFRIEND WOULDN'T LIKE IT IF HE KNEW YOU WERE TRYING TO ASK ME OUT
OH, YEAH? WHAT'S HIS NAME
NICK "THE MANGLER" SCARLOTTI
OOOO! I'M IMPRESSED!
© 1986 United Feature Syndicate, Inc.
JIM DAVIS 10-24
I AM IMPRESSED

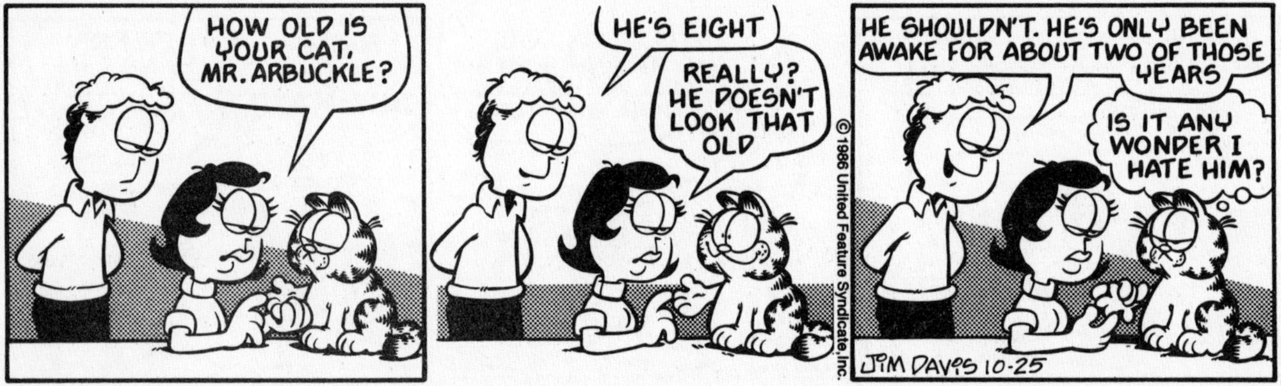
HOW OLD IS YOUR CAT, MR. ARBUCKLE?
HE'S EIGHT
REALLY? HE DOESN'T LOOK THAT OLD
© 1986 United Feature Syndicate, Inc.
HE SHOULDN'T. HE'S ONLY BEEN AWAKE FOR ABOUT TWO OF THOSE YEARS
IS IT ANY WONDER I HATE HIM?
JIM DAVIS 10-25

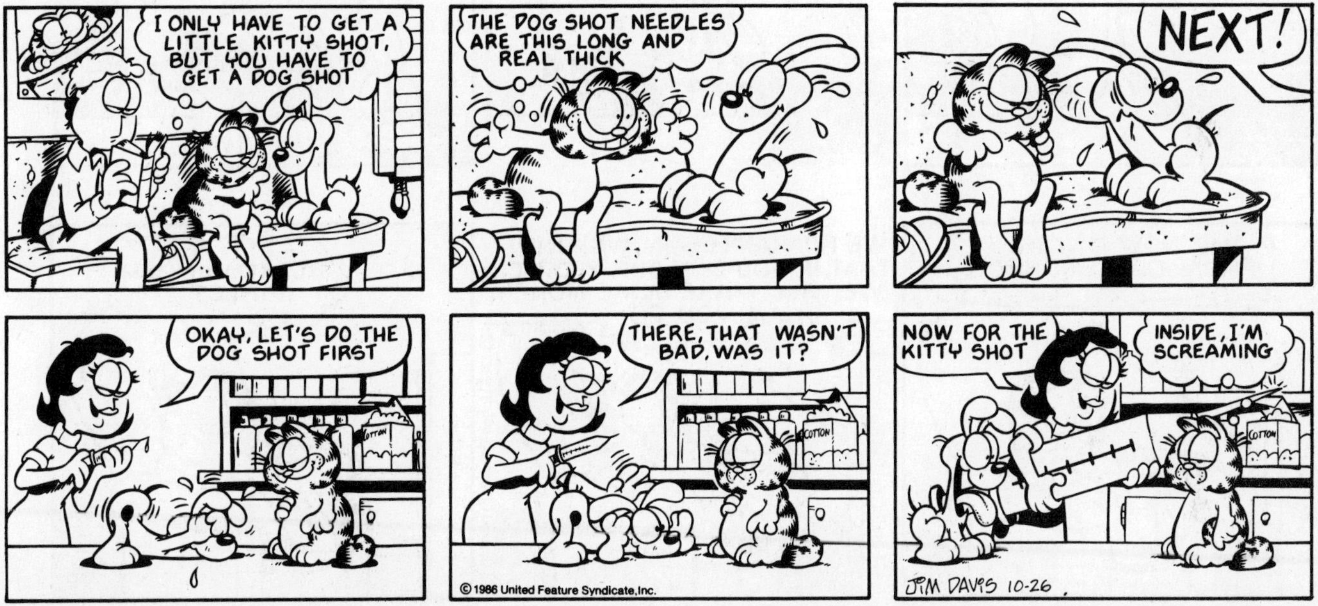
I ONLY HAVE TO GET A LITTLE KITTY SHOT, BUT YOU HAVE TO GET A DOG SHOT
THE DOG SHOT NEEDLES ARE THIS LONG AND REAL THICK
NEXT!
OKAY, LET'S DO THE DOG SHOT FIRST
COTTON
THERE, THAT WASN'T BAD, WAS IT?
COTTON
© 1986 United Feature Syndicate, Inc.
NOW FOR THE KITTY SHOT
INSIDE, I'M SCREAMING
COTTON
JIM DAVIS 10-26

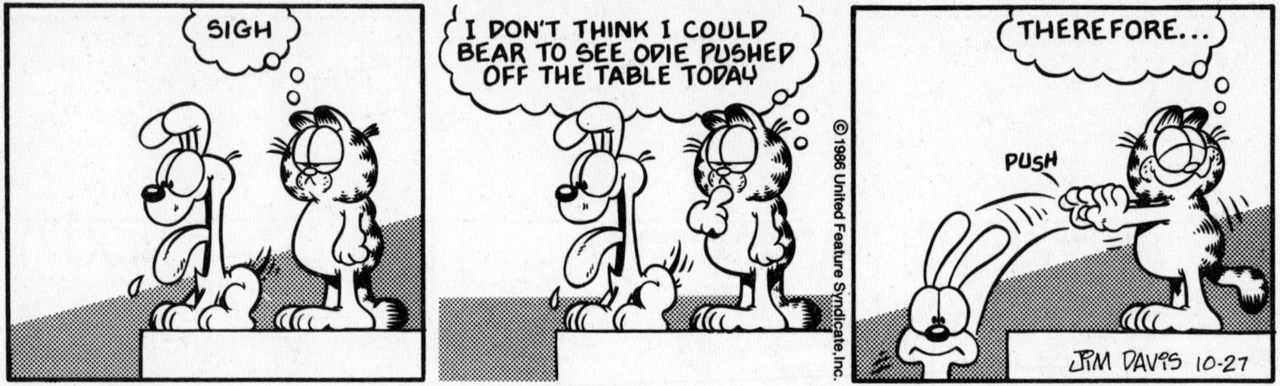
SIGH
I DON'T THINK I COULD BEAR TO SEE ODIE PUSHED OFF THE TABLE TODAY
THEREFORE...
PUSH
JIM DAVIS 10-27
© 1986 United Feature Syndicate, Inc.

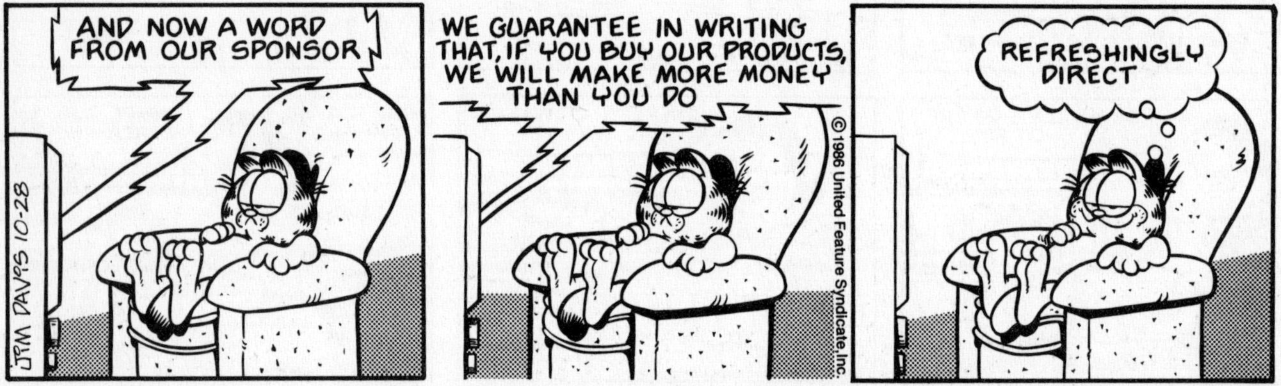
AND NOW A WORD FROM OUR SPONSOR
WE GUARANTEE IN WRITING THAT, IF YOU BUY OUR PRODUCTS, WE WILL MAKE MORE MONEY THAN YOU DO
REFRESHINGLY DIRECT
JIM DAVIS 10-28
© 1986 United Feature Syndicate, Inc.

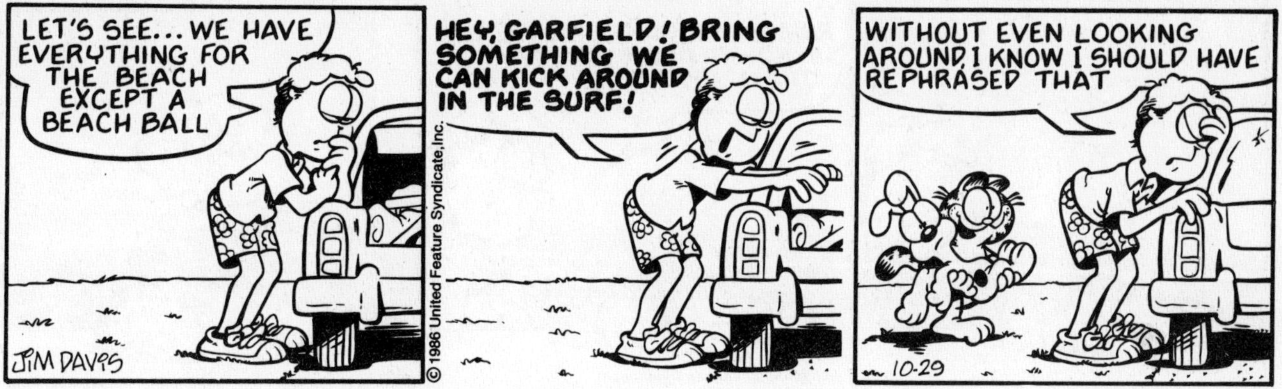
LET'S SEE... WE HAVE EVERYTHING FOR THE BEACH EXCEPT A BEACH BALL
JIM DAVIS
© 1986 United Feature Syndicate, Inc.
HEY, GARFIELD! BRING SOMETHING WE CAN KICK AROUND IN THE SURF!
WITHOUT EVEN LOOKING AROUND, I KNOW I SHOULD HAVE REPHRASED THAT
10-29

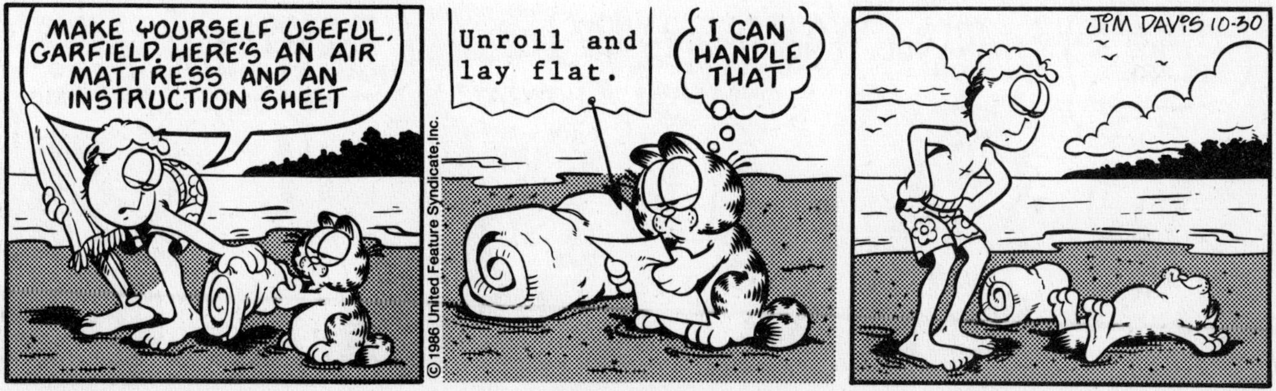
MAKE YOURSELF USEFUL, GARFIELD. HERE'S AN AIR MATTRESS AND AN INSTRUCTION SHEET
© 1986 United Feature Syndicate, Inc.
Unroll and lay flat.
I CAN HANDLE THAT
JIM DAVIS 10-30

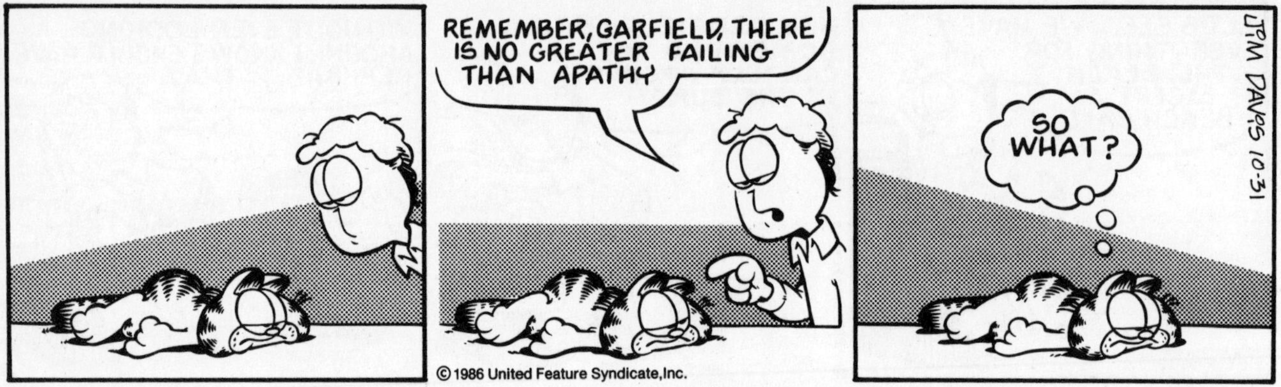
REMEMBER, GARFIELD, THERE IS NO GREATER FAILING THAN APATHY
SO WHAT?
JIM DAVIS 10-31
© 1986 United Feature Syndicate, Inc.

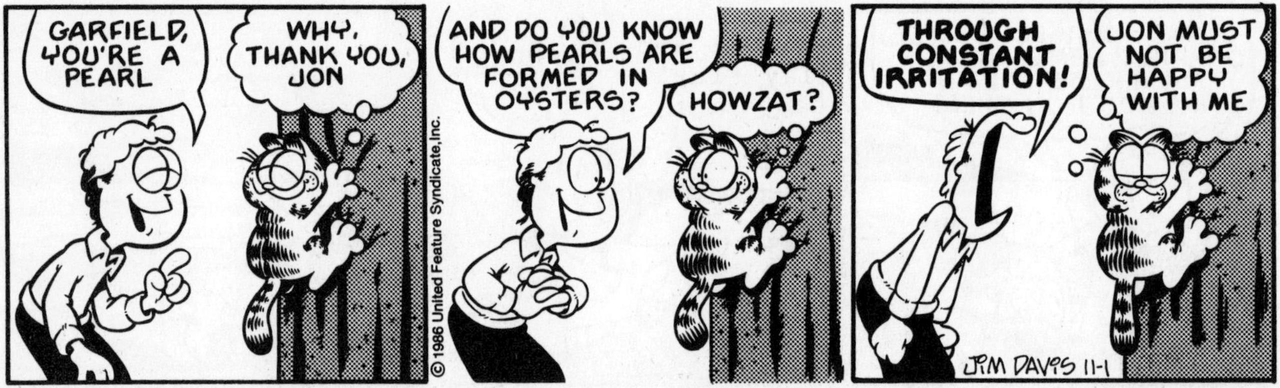
GARFIELD, YOU'RE A PEARL
WHY, THANK YOU, JON
© 1986 United Feature Syndicate, Inc.
AND DO YOU KNOW HOW PEARLS ARE FORMED IN OYSTERS?
HOWZAT?
THROUGH CONSTANT IRRITATION!
JON MUST NOT BE HAPPY WITH ME
JIM DAVIS 11-1

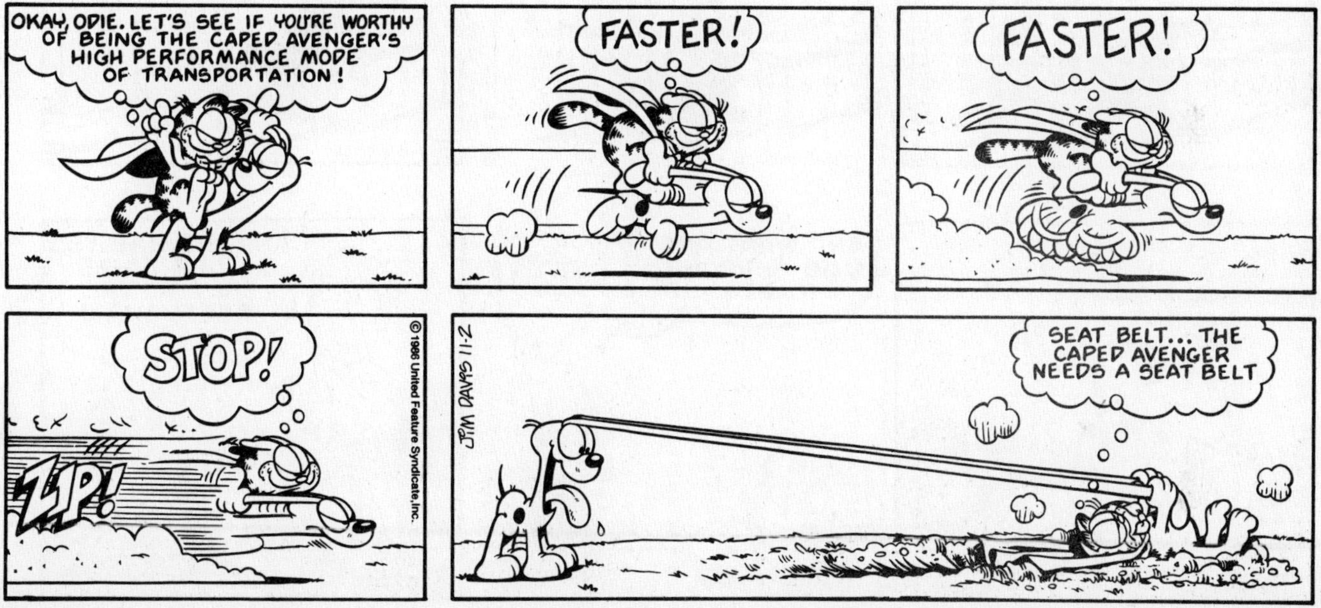

OKAY, ODIE. LET'S SEE IF YOU'RE WORTHY OF BEING THE CAPED AVENGER'S HIGH PERFORMANCE MODE OF TRANSPORTATION!
FASTER!
FASTER!
STOP!
ZIP!
© 1986 United Feature Syndicate, Inc.
JIM DAVIS 11-2
SEAT BELT... THE CAPED AVENGER NEEDS A SEAT BELT

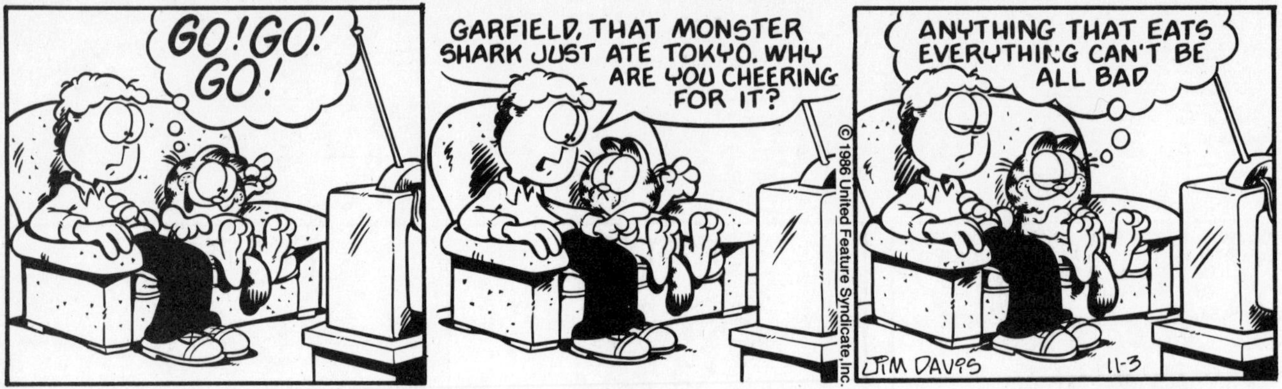
GO! GO! GO!
GARFIELD, THAT MONSTER SHARK JUST ATE TOKYO. WHY ARE YOU CHEERING FOR IT?
© 1986 United Feature Syndicate, Inc.
ANYTHING THAT EATS EVERYTHING CAN'T BE ALL BAD
JIM DAVIS 11-3

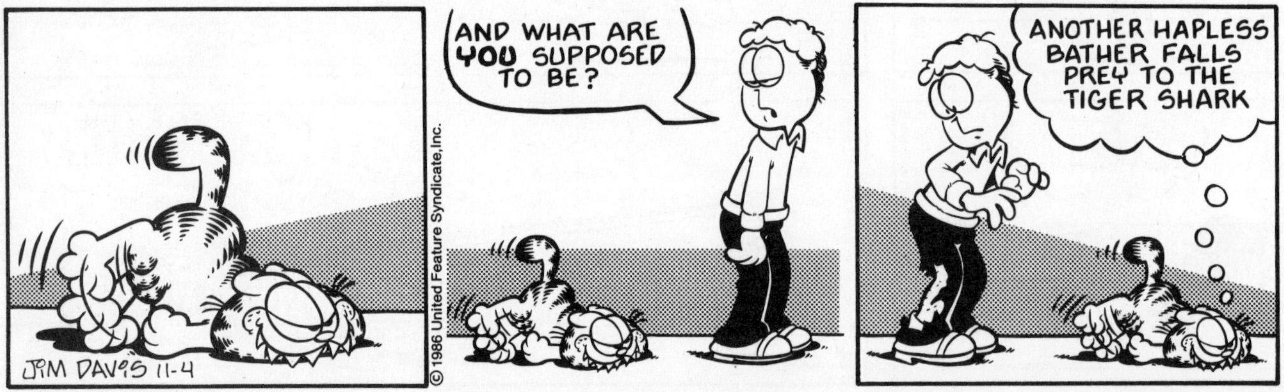
JIM DAVIS 11-4
© 1986 United Feature Syndicate, Inc.
AND WHAT ARE YOU SUPPOSED TO BE?
ANOTHER HAPLESS BATHER FALLS PREY TO THE TIGER SHARK

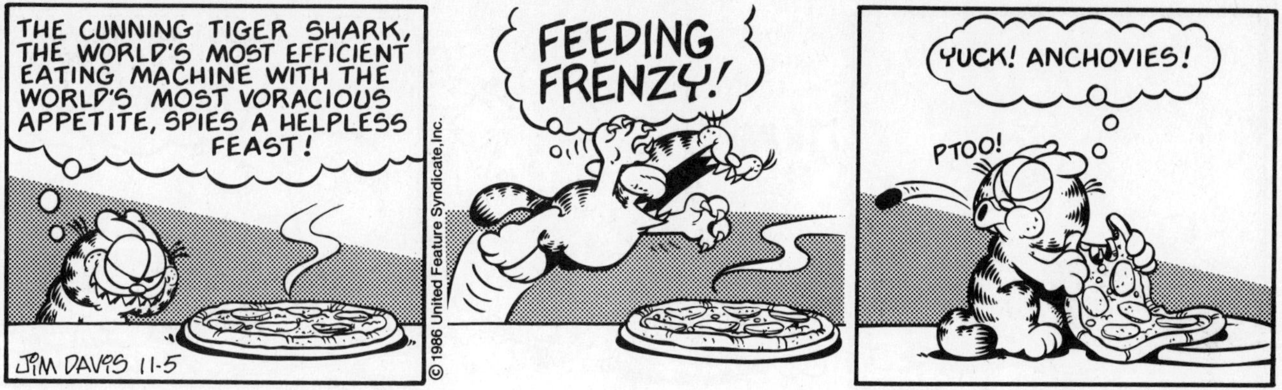
THE CUNNING TIGER SHARK, THE WORLD'S MOST EFFICIENT EATING MACHINE WITH THE WORLD'S MOST VORACIOUS APPETITE, SPIES A HELPLESS FEAST!
JIM DAVIS 11-5
© 1986 United Feature Syndicate, Inc.
FEEDING FRENZY!
YUCK! ANCHOVIES!
PTOO!

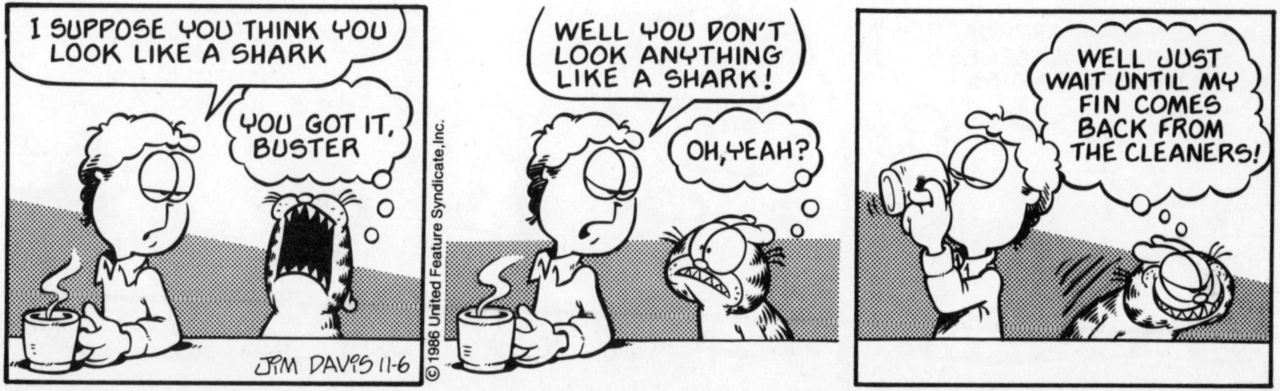
I SUPPOSE YOU THINK YOU LOOK LIKE A SHARK
YOU GOT IT, BUSTER
JIM DAVIS 11-6
© 1986 United Feature Syndicate, Inc.
WELL YOU DON'T LOOK ANYTHING LIKE A SHARK!
OH, YEAH?
WELL JUST WAIT UNTIL MY FIN COMES BACK FROM THE CLEANERS!

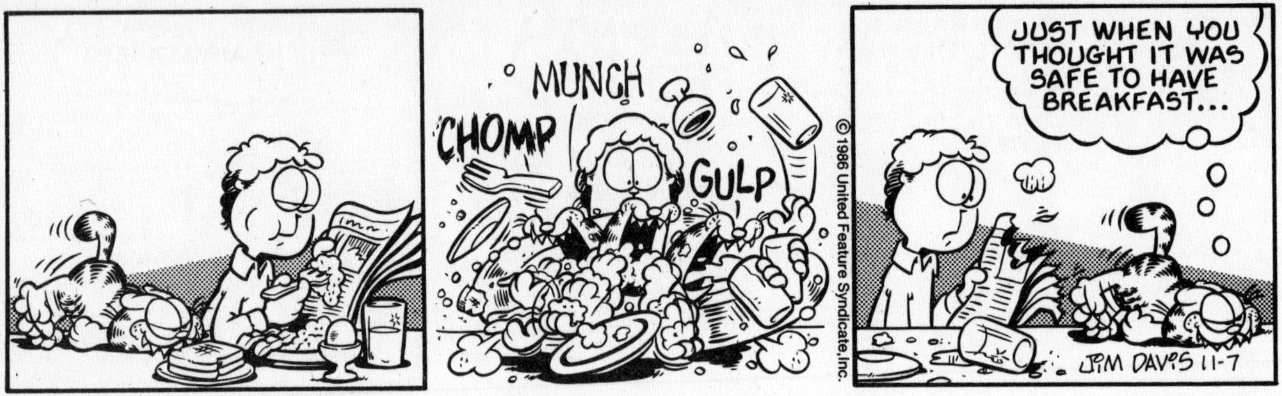
CHOMP
MUNCH
GULP
© 1986 United Feature Syndicate, Inc.
JUST WHEN YOU THOUGHT IT WAS SAFE TO HAVE BREAKFAST...
JIM DAVIS 11-7

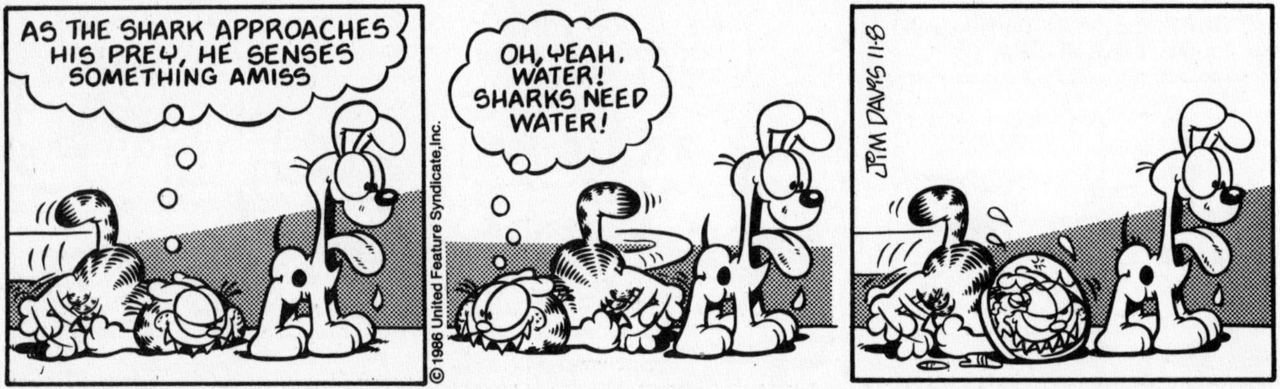
AS THE SHARK APPROACHES HIS PREY, HE SENSES SOMETHING AMISS
© 1986 United Feature Syndicate, Inc.
OH, YEAH. WATER! SHARKS NEED WATER!
JIM DAVIS 11-8

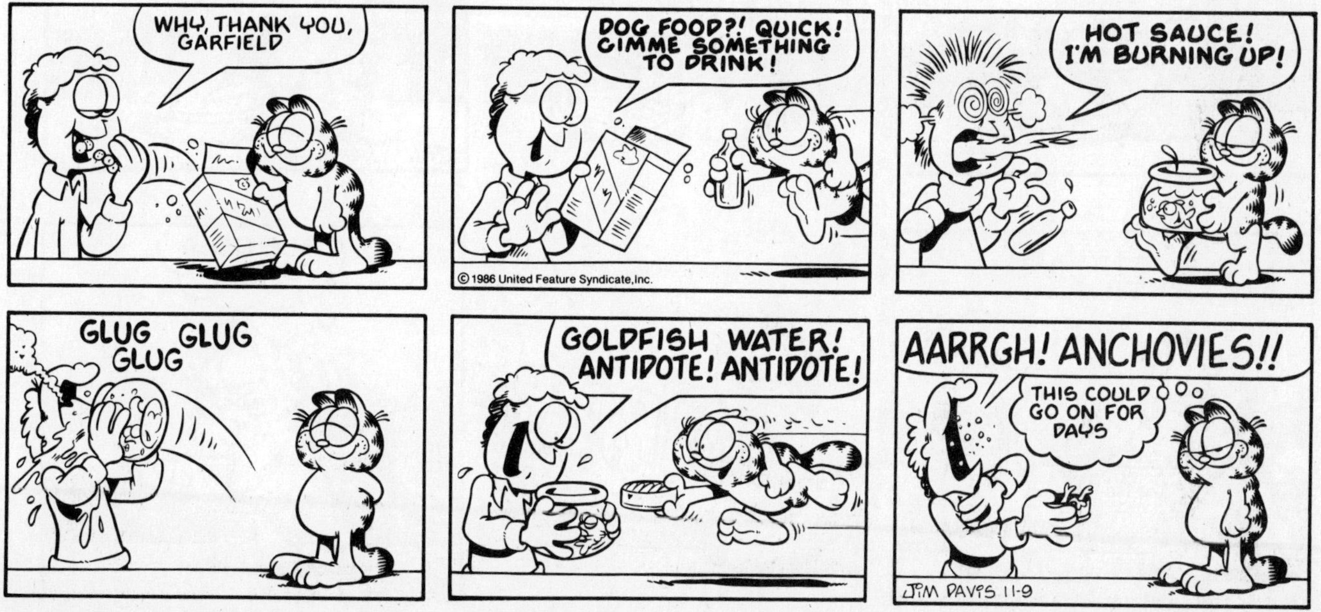
WHY, THANK YOU, GARFIELD
DOG FOOD?! QUICK! GIMME SOMETHING TO DRINK!
© 1986 United Feature Syndicate, Inc.
HOT SAUCE! I'M BURNING UP!
GLUG GLUG GLUG
GOLDFISH WATER! ANTIDOTE! ANTIDOTE!
AARRGH! ANCHOVIES!!
THIS COULD GO ON FOR DAYS
JIM DAVIS 11-9

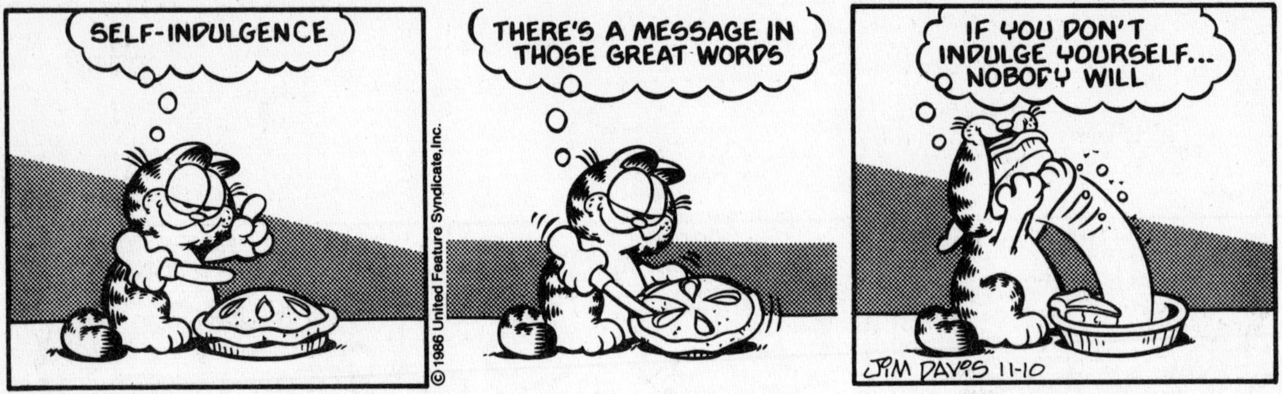
SELF-INDULGENCE
THERE'S A MESSAGE IN THOSE GREAT WORDS
IF YOU DON'T INDULGE YOURSELF... NOBODY WILL
© 1986 United Feature Syndicate, Inc.
JIM DAVIS 11-10

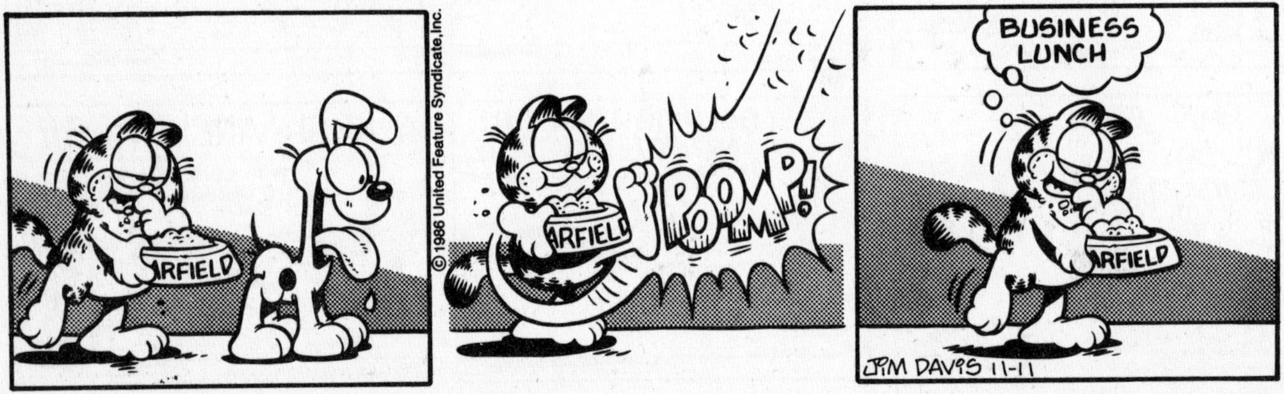
GARFIELD
POMP!
BUSINESS LUNCH
© 1986 United Feature Syndicate, Inc.
JIM DAVIS 11-11

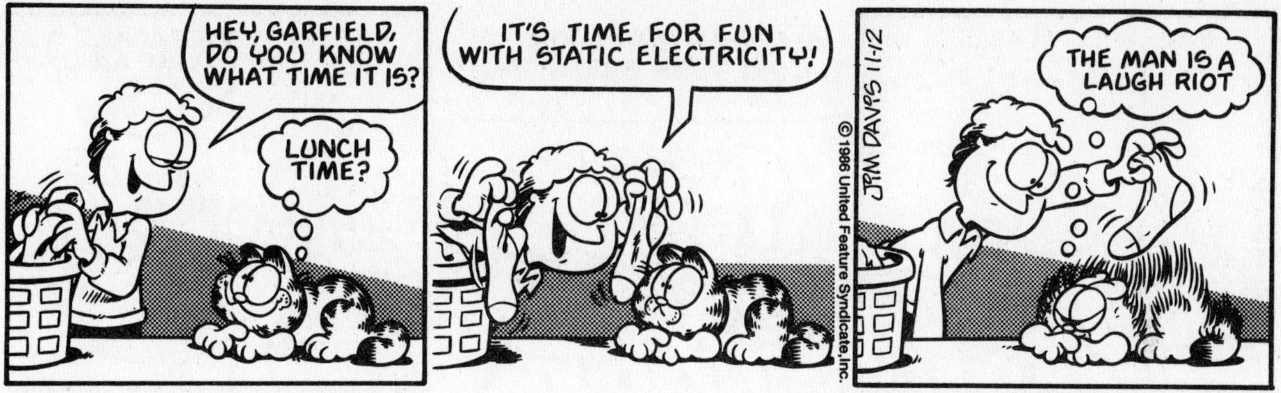
HEY, GARFIELD, DO YOU KNOW WHAT TIME IT IS?
LUNCH TIME?
IT'S TIME FOR FUN WITH STATIC ELECTRICITY!
© 1986 United Feature Syndicate, Inc.
JIM DAVIS 11-12
THE MAN IS A LAUGH RIOT

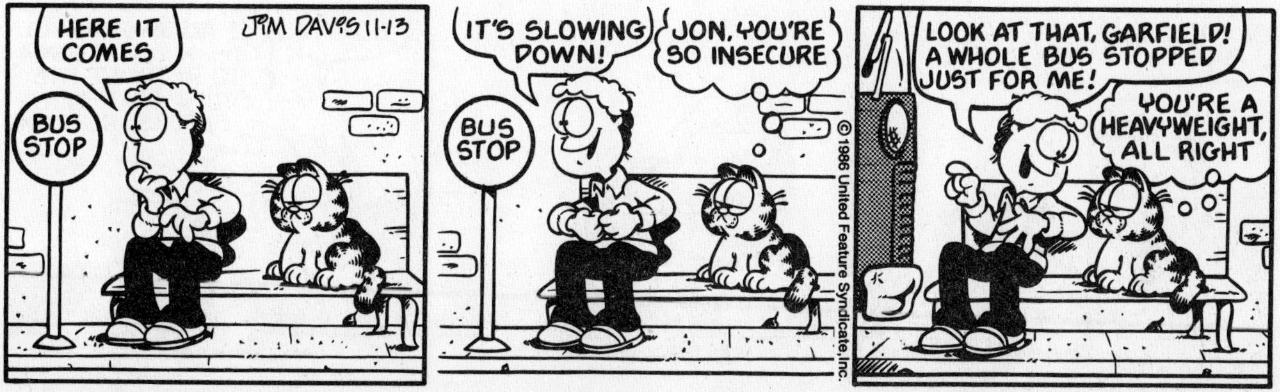
HERE IT COMES
JIM DAVIS 11-13
BUS STOP
IT'S SLOWING DOWN!
JON, YOU'RE SO INSECURE
BUS STOP
© 1986 United Feature Syndicate, Inc.
LOOK AT THAT, GARFIELD! A WHOLE BUS STOPPED JUST FOR ME!
YOU'RE A HEAVYWEIGHT, ALL RIGHT

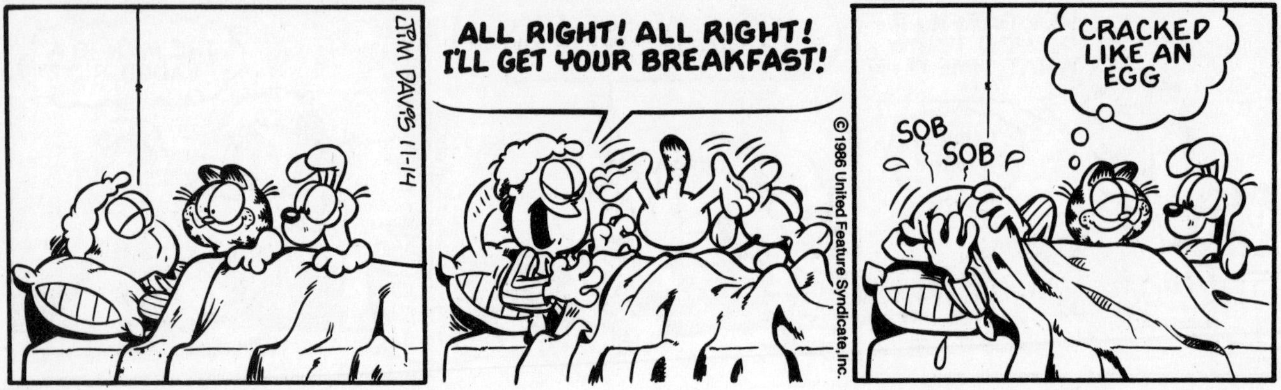
JIM DAVIS 11-14
ALL RIGHT! ALL RIGHT! I'LL GET YOUR BREAKFAST!
© 1986 United Feature Syndicate, Inc.
SOB
SOB
CRACKED LIKE AN EGG

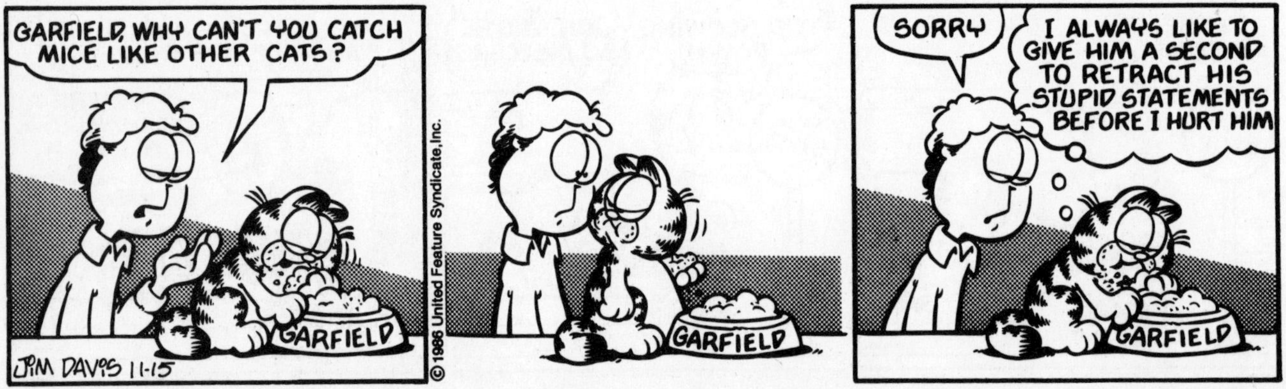
GARFIELD, WHY CAN'T YOU CATCH MICE LIKE OTHER CATS?
GARFIELD
JIM DAVIS 11-15
© 1986 United Feature Syndicate, Inc.
GARFIELD
SORRY
I ALWAYS LIKE TO GIVE HIM A SECOND TO RETRACT HIS STUPID STATEMENTS BEFORE I HURT HIM
GARFIELD

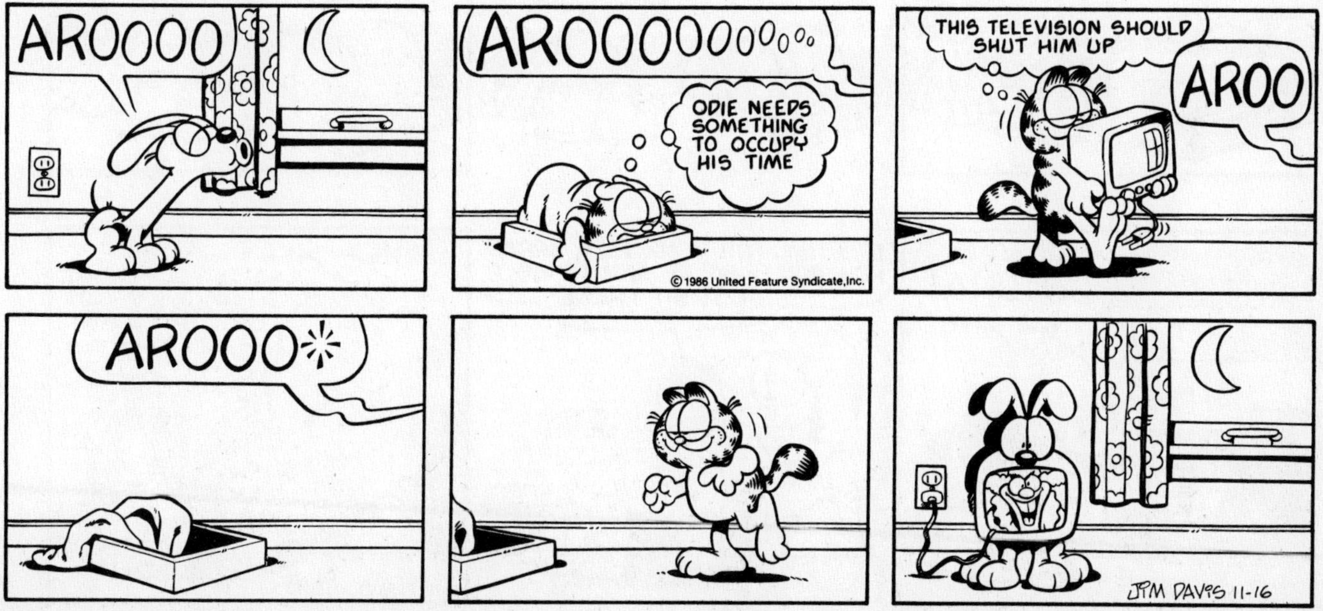
AROOOO
AROOOOOOOooo
ODIE NEEDS SOMETHING TO OCCUPY HIS TIME
© 1986 United Feature Syndicate, Inc.
THIS TELEVISION SHOULD SHUT HIM UP
AROO
AROOO
JIM DAVIS 11-16

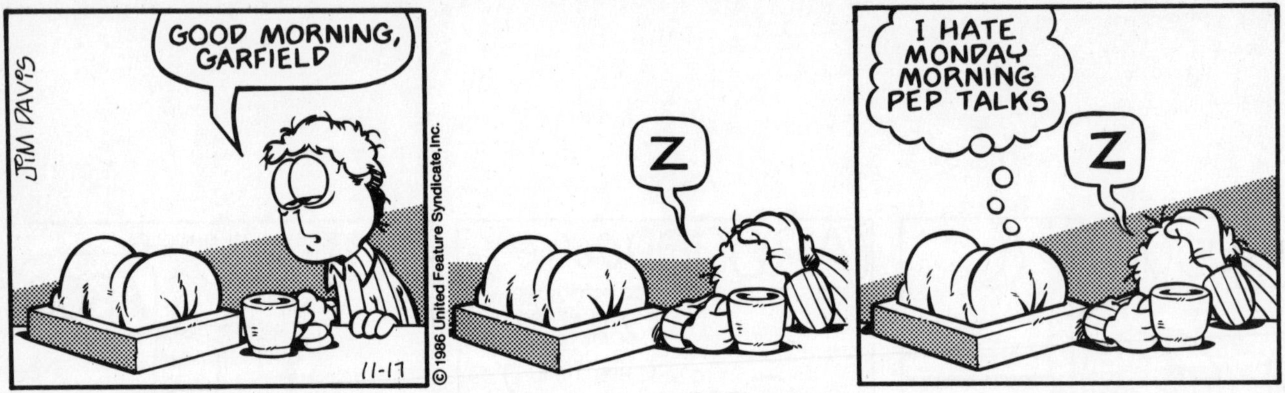
GOOD MORNING, GARFIELD
JIM DAVIS
11-17
© 1986 United Feature Syndicate, Inc.
Z
I HATE MONDAY MORNING PEP TALKS
Z

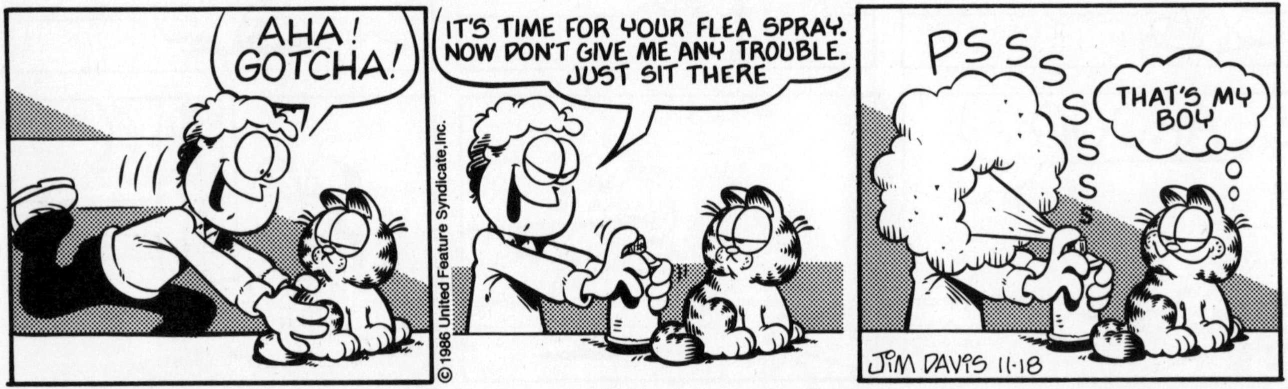
AHA! GOTCHA!
© 1986 United Feature Syndicate, Inc.
IT'S TIME FOR YOUR FLEA SPRAY. NOW DON'T GIVE ME ANY TROUBLE. JUST SIT THERE
PSSSSSSSS
THAT'S MY BOY
JIM DAVIS 11-18

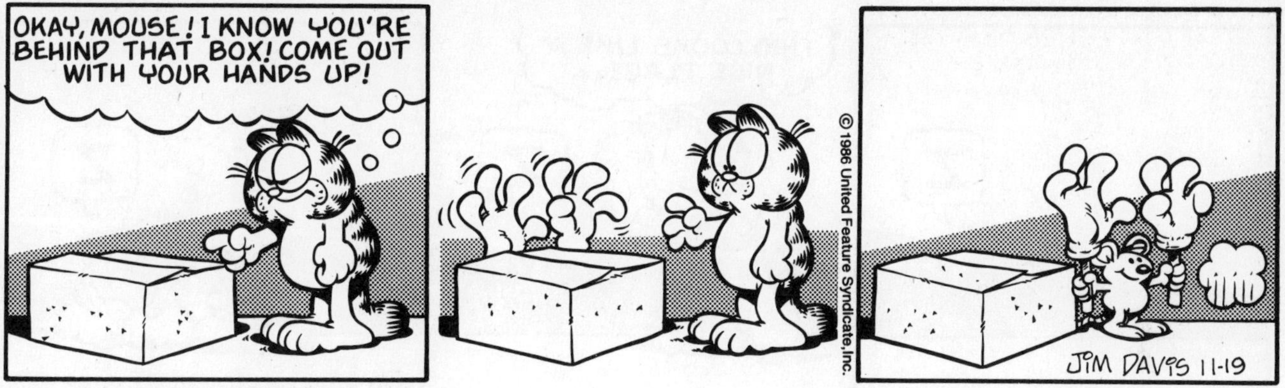
OKAY, MOUSE! I KNOW YOU'RE BEHIND THAT BOX! COME OUT WITH YOUR HANDS UP!
© 1986 United Feature Syndicate, Inc.
JIM DAVIS 11-19

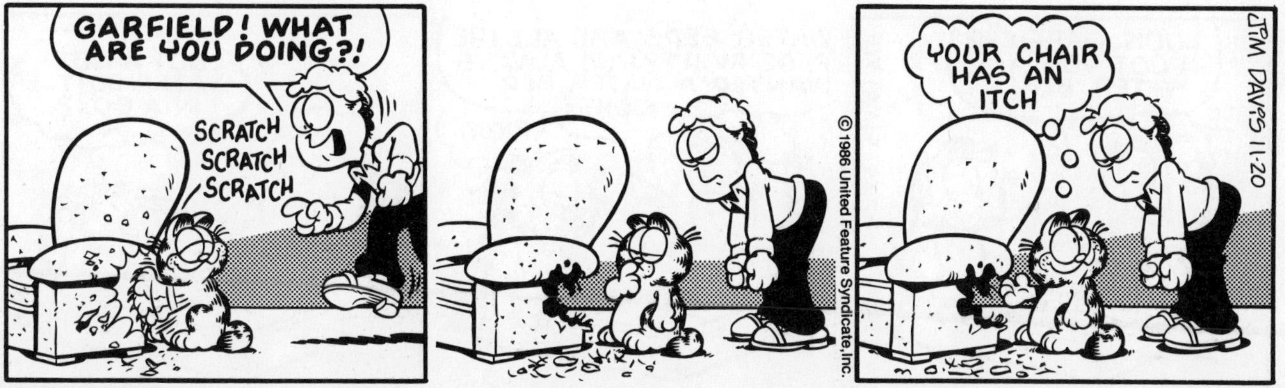
GARFIELD! WHAT ARE YOU DOING?!
SCRATCH
SCRATCH
SCRATCH
© 1986 United Feature Syndicate, Inc.
YOUR CHAIR HAS AN ITCH
JIM DAVIS 11-20

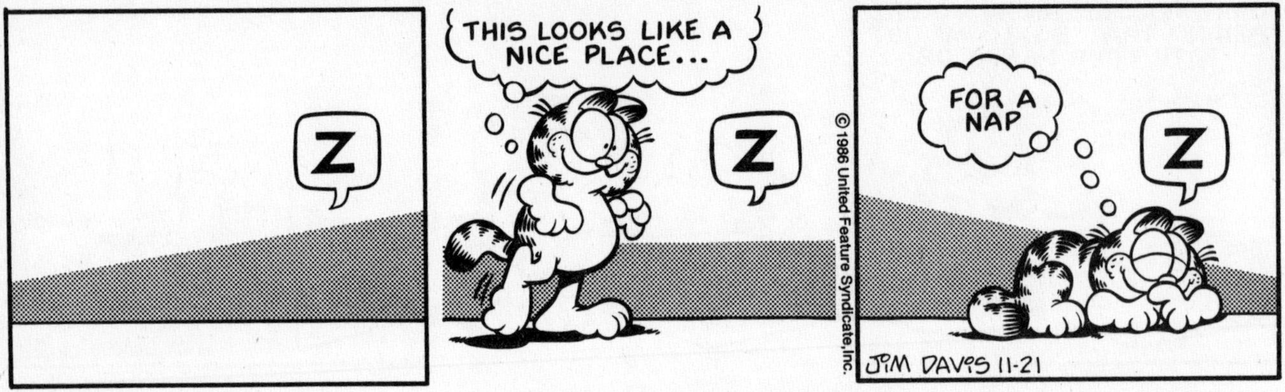
Z
THIS LOOKS LIKE A NICE PLACE...
Z
© 1986 United Feature Syndicate, Inc.
FOR A NAP
Z
JIM DAVIS 11-21

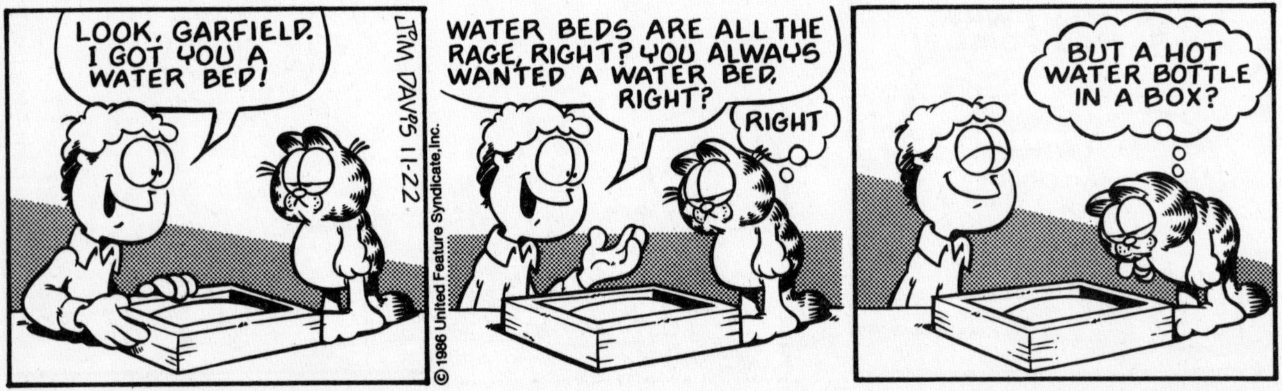
LOOK, GARFIELD. I GOT YOU A WATER BED!
JIM DAVIS 11-22
© 1986 United Feature Syndicate, Inc.
WATER BEDS ARE ALL THE RAGE, RIGHT? YOU ALWAYS WANTED A WATER BED, RIGHT?
RIGHT
BUT A HOT WATER BOTTLE IN A BOX?

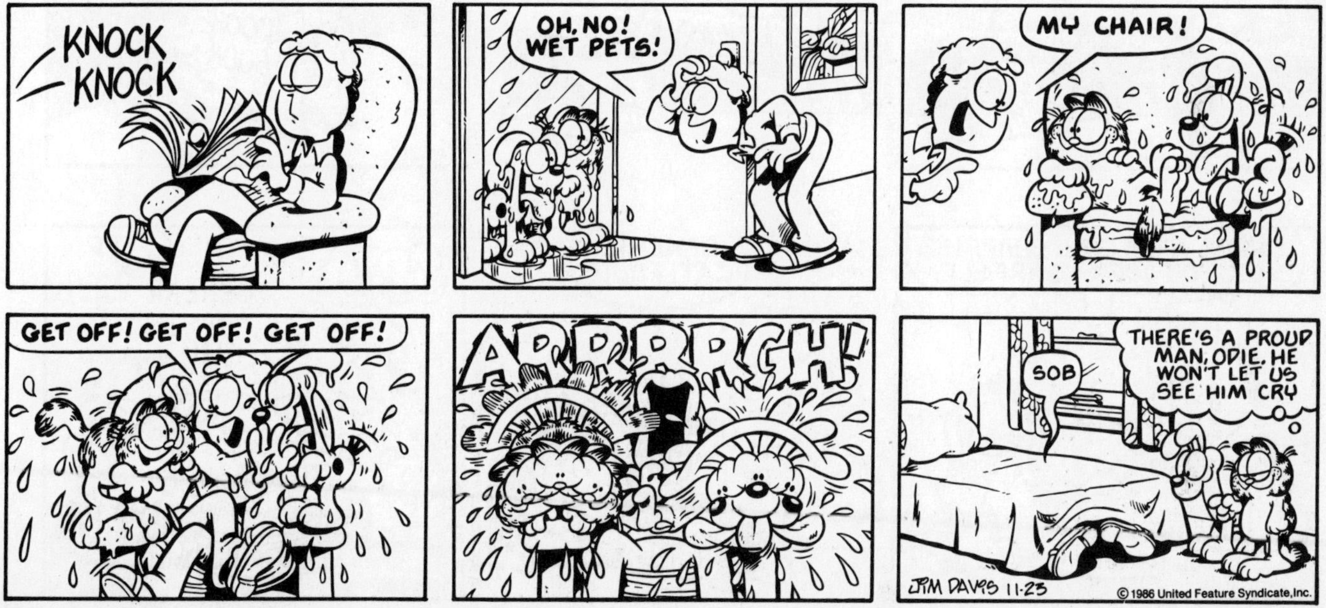
KNOCK
KNOCK
OH, NO! WET PETS!
MY CHAIR!
GET OFF! GET OFF! GET OFF!
ARRRRGH!
SOB
THERE'S A PROUD MAN, ODIE. HE WON'T LET US SEE HIM CRY
JIM DAVIS 11-23
© 1986 United Feature Syndicate, Inc.

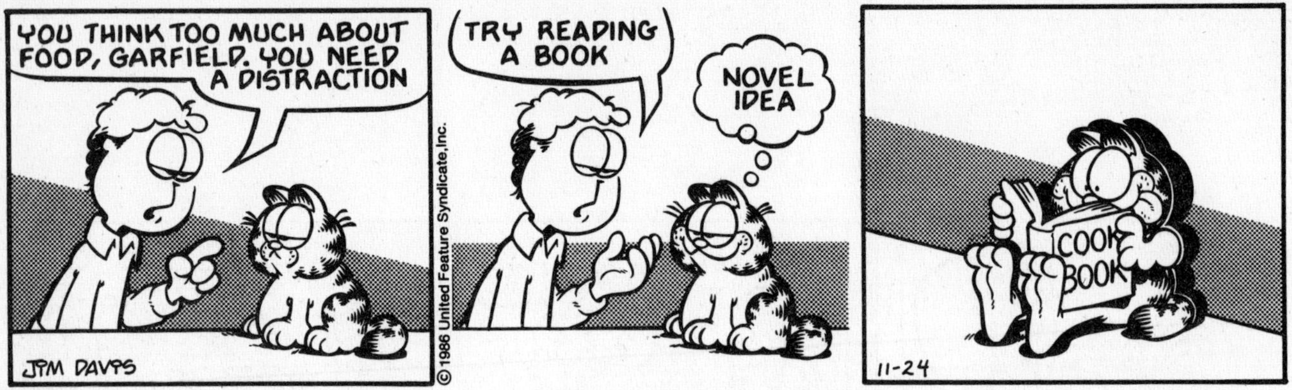
YOU THINK TOO MUCH ABOUT FOOD, GARFIELD. YOU NEED A DISTRACTION
JIM DAVIS
© 1986 United Feature Syndicate, Inc.
TRY READING A BOOK
NOVEL IDEA
COOK BOOK
11-24

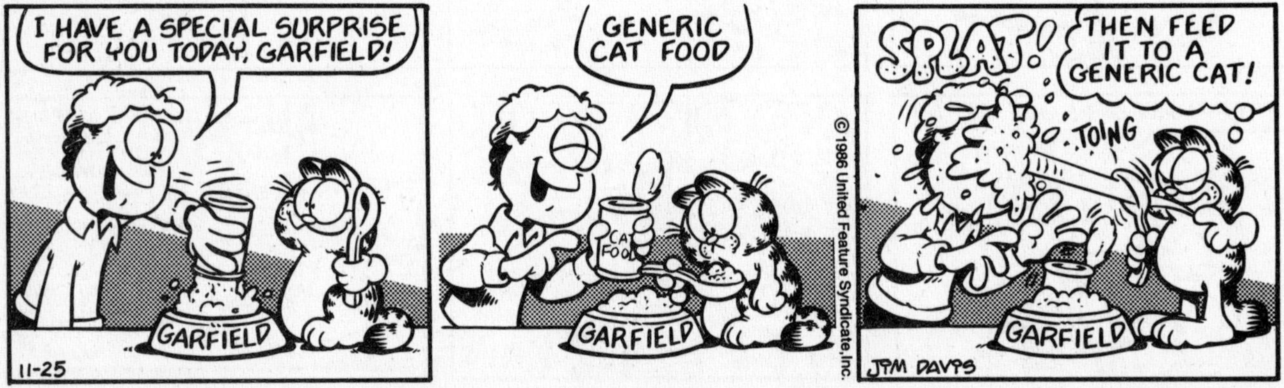
I HAVE A SPECIAL SURPRISE FOR YOU TODAY, GARFIELD!
GARFIELD
11-25
GENERIC CAT FOOD
CAT FOOD
GARFIELD
© 1986 United Feature Syndicate, Inc.
SPLAT!
THEN FEED IT TO A GENERIC CAT!
TOING
GARFIELD
JIM DAVIS

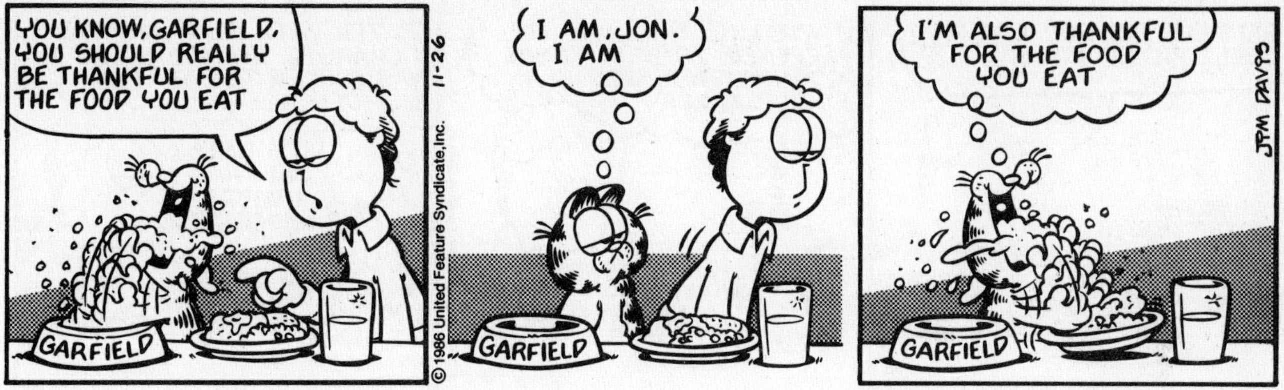
YOU KNOW, GARFIELD, YOU SHOULD REALLY BE THANKFUL FOR THE FOOD YOU EAT
11-26
© 1986 United Feature Syndicate, Inc.
I AM, JON. I AM
I'M ALSO THANKFUL FOR THE FOOD YOU EAT
GARFIELD
JPM DAVPS

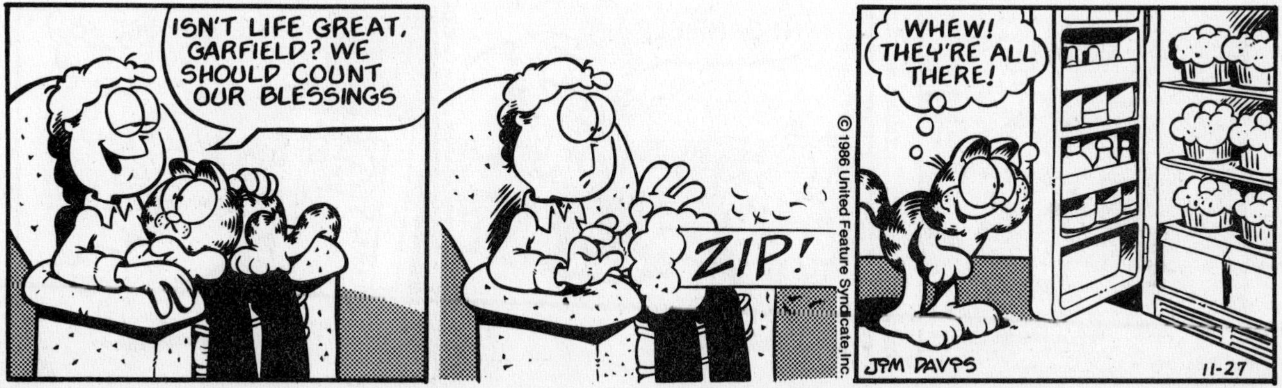
ISN'T LIFE GREAT, GARFIELD? WE SHOULD COUNT OUR BLESSINGS
ZIP!
© 1986 United Feature Syndicate, Inc.
WHEW! THEY'RE ALL THERE!
JPM DAVPS
11-27

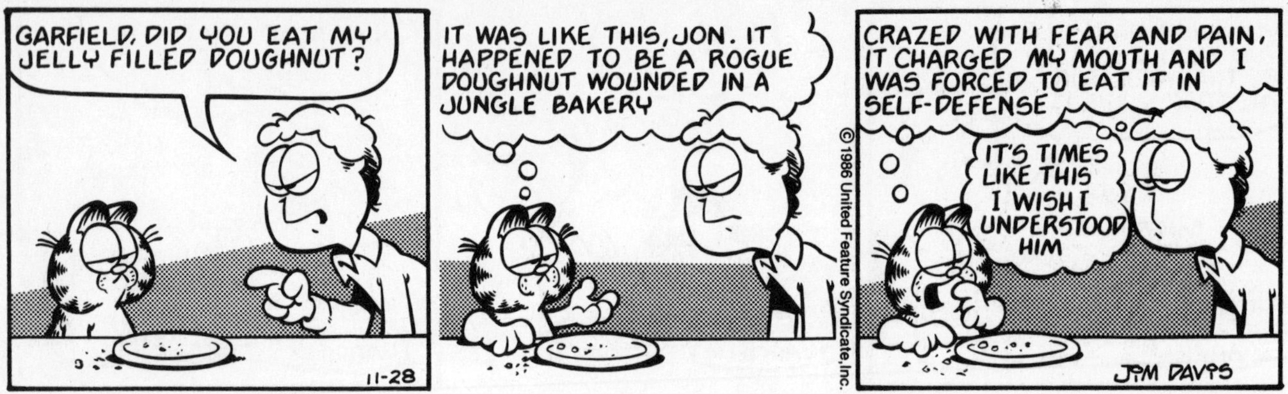
GARFIELD, DID YOU EAT MY JELLY FILLED DOUGHNUT?
11-28
IT WAS LIKE THIS, JON. IT HAPPENED TO BE A ROGUE DOUGHNUT WOUNDED IN A JUNGLE BAKERY
© 1986 United Feature Syndicate, Inc.
CRAZED WITH FEAR AND PAIN, IT CHARGED MY MOUTH AND I WAS FORCED TO EAT IT IN SELF-DEFENSE
IT'S TIMES LIKE THIS I WISH I UNDERSTOOD HIM
JIM DAVIS

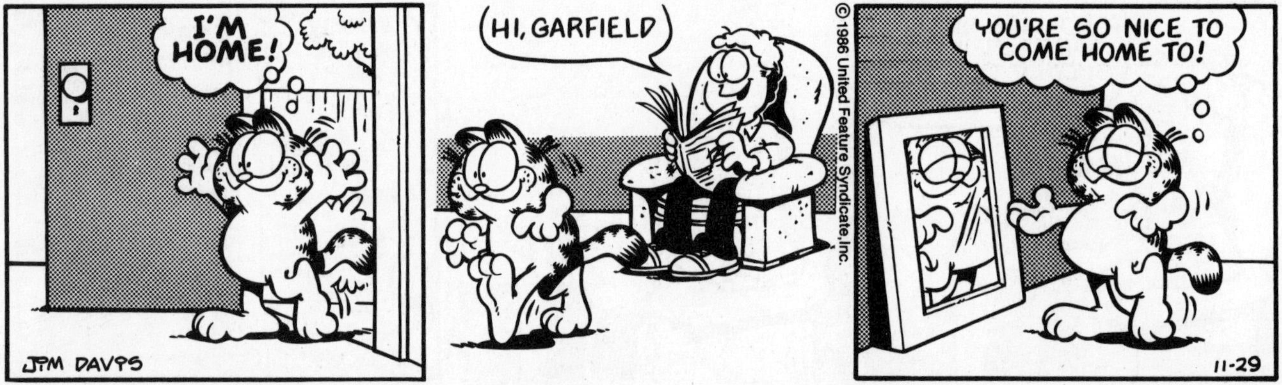
I'M HOME!
JIM DAVIS
HI, GARFIELD
© 1986 United Feature Syndicate, Inc.
YOU'RE SO NICE TO COME HOME TO!
11-29

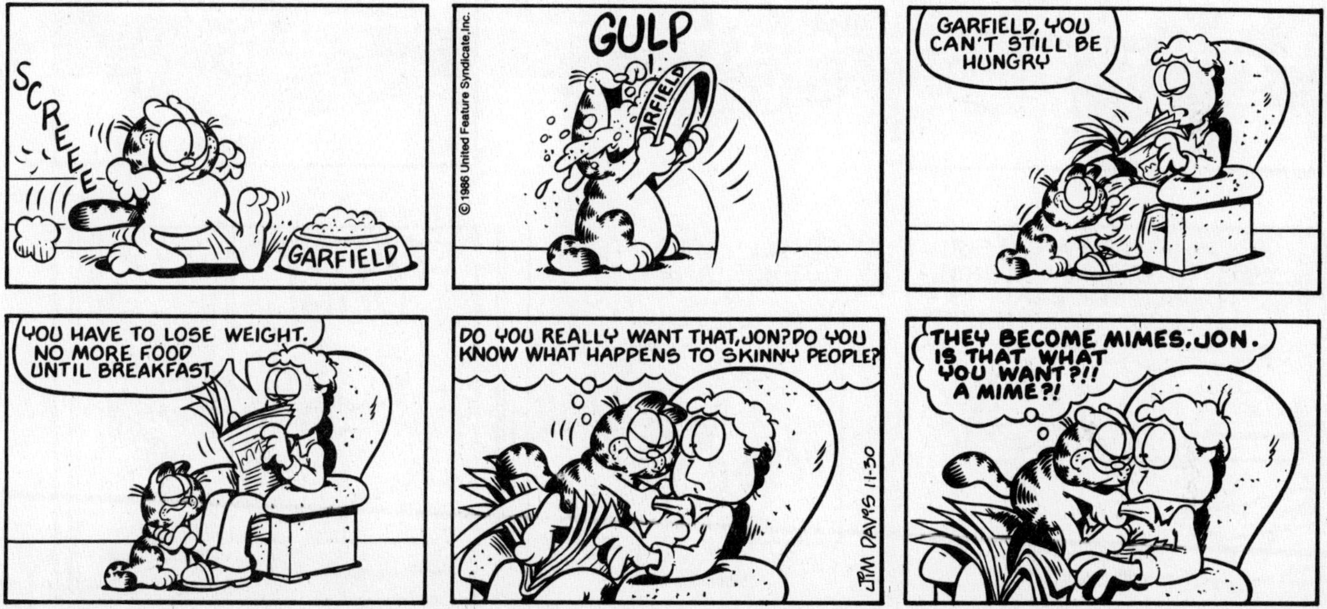
SCREEEE
GARFIELD
GULP
GARFIELD
© 1986 United Feature Syndicate, Inc.
GARFIELD, YOU CAN'T STILL BE HUNGRY
YOU HAVE TO LOSE WEIGHT. NO MORE FOOD UNTIL BREAKFAST
DO YOU REALLY WANT THAT, JON? DO YOU KNOW WHAT HAPPENS TO SKINNY PEOPLE?
JIM DAVIS 11-30
THEY BECOME MIMES, JON. IS THAT WHAT YOU WANT?!! A MIME?!

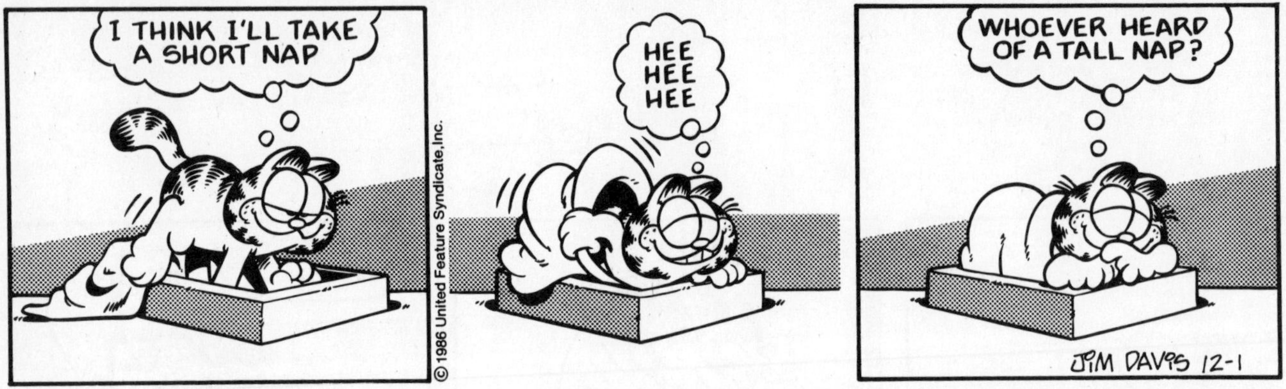
I THINK I'LL TAKE A SHORT NAP
HEE HEE HEE
WHOEVER HEARD OF A TALL NAP?
© 1986 United Feature Syndicate, Inc.
JIM DAVIS 12-1

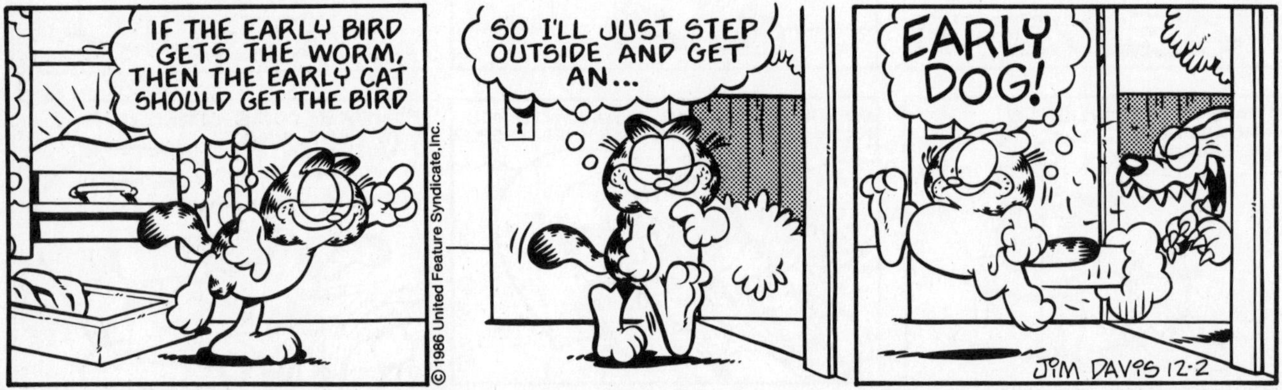
IF THE EARLY BIRD GETS THE WORM, THEN THE EARLY CAT SHOULD GET THE BIRD
SO I'LL JUST STEP OUTSIDE AND GET AN...
EARLY DOG!
© 1986 United Feature Syndicate, Inc.
JIM DAVIS 12-2

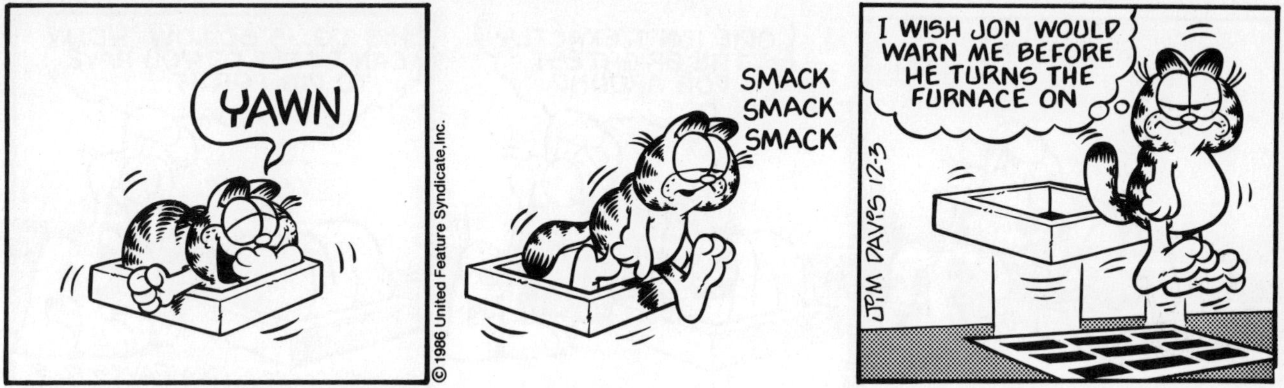

YAWN
SMACK SMACK SMACK
I WISH JON WOULD WARN ME BEFORE HE TURNS THE FURNACE ON
JIM DAVIS 12-3




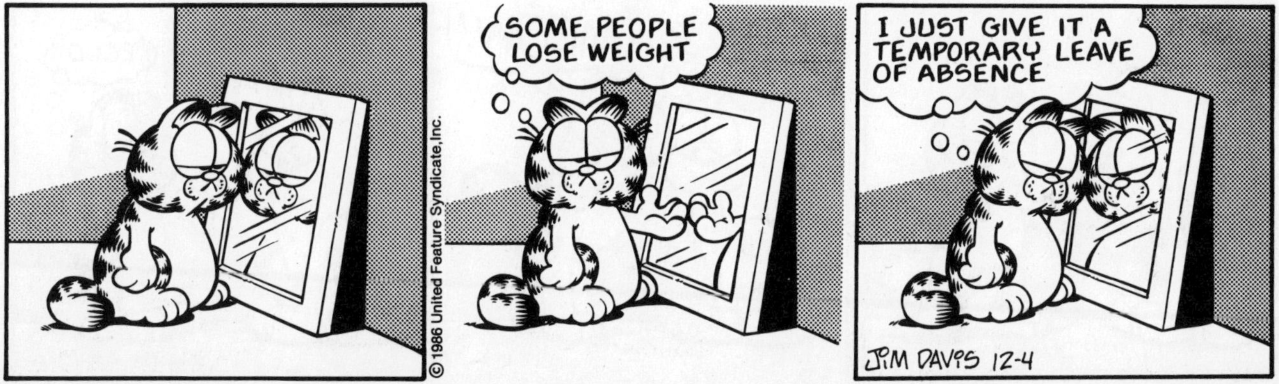

SOME PEOPLE LOSE WEIGHT
I JUST GIVE IT A TEMPORARY LEAVE OF ABSENCE
JIM DAVIS 12-4

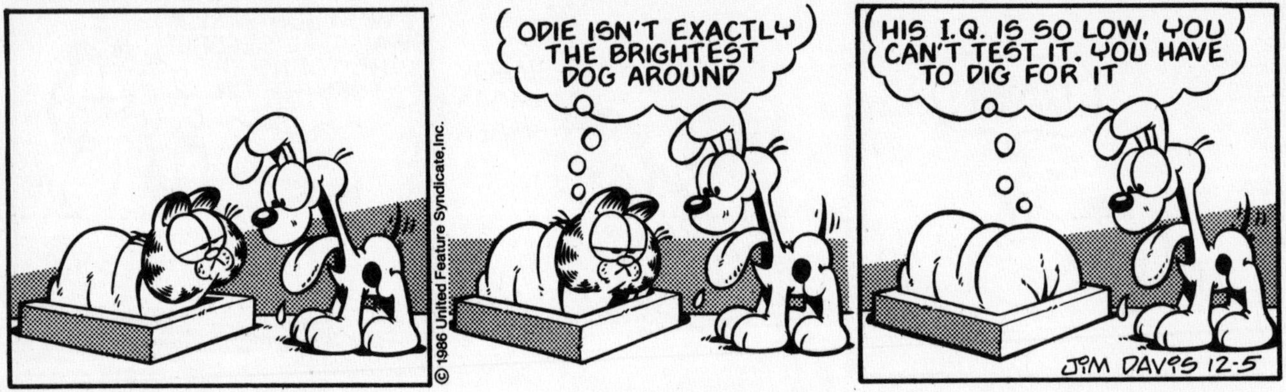
ODIE ISN'T EXACTLY THE BRIGHTEST DOG AROUND
HIS I.Q. IS SO LOW, YOU CAN'T TEST IT. YOU HAVE TO DIG FOR IT
© 1986 United Feature Syndicate, Inc.
JIM DAVIS 12-5

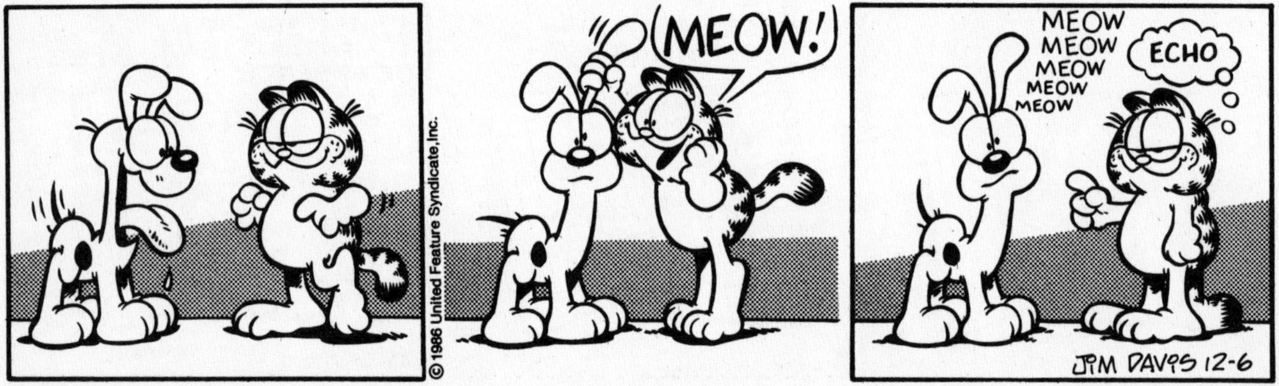
MEOW!
MEOW MEOW MEOW MEOW MEOW
ECHO
© 1986 United Feature Syndicate, Inc.
JIM DAVIS 12-6

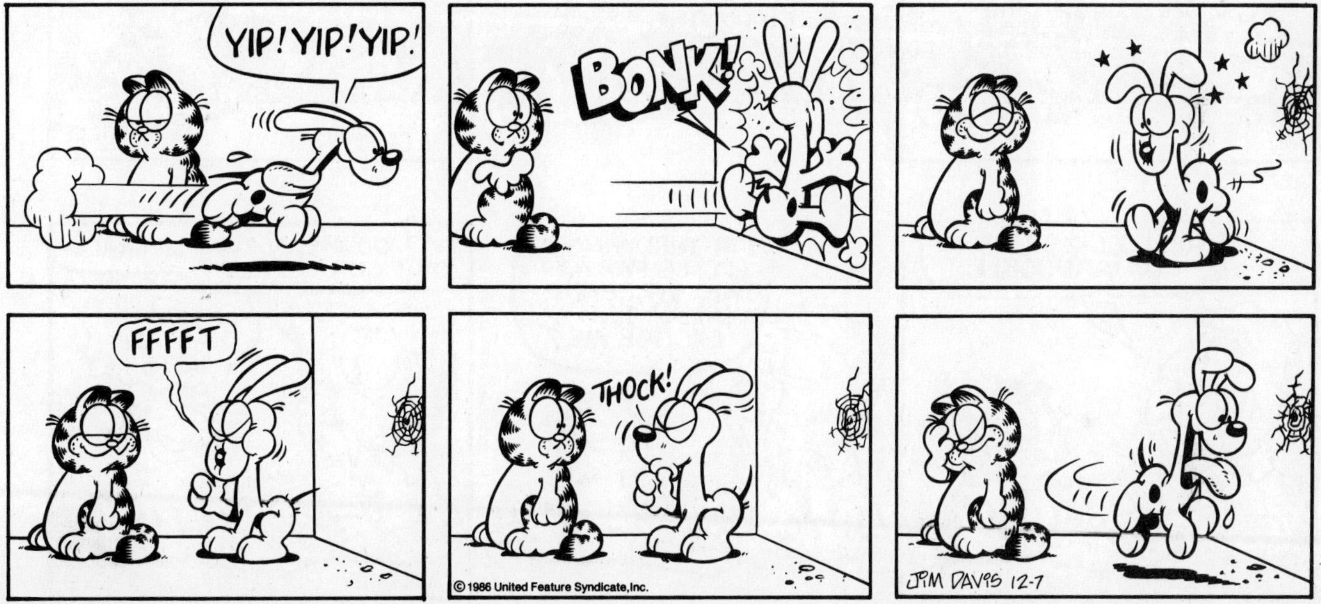
YIP! YIP! YIP!
BONK!
FFFFT
THOCK!
© 1986 United Feature Syndicate, Inc.
JIM DAVIS 12-7

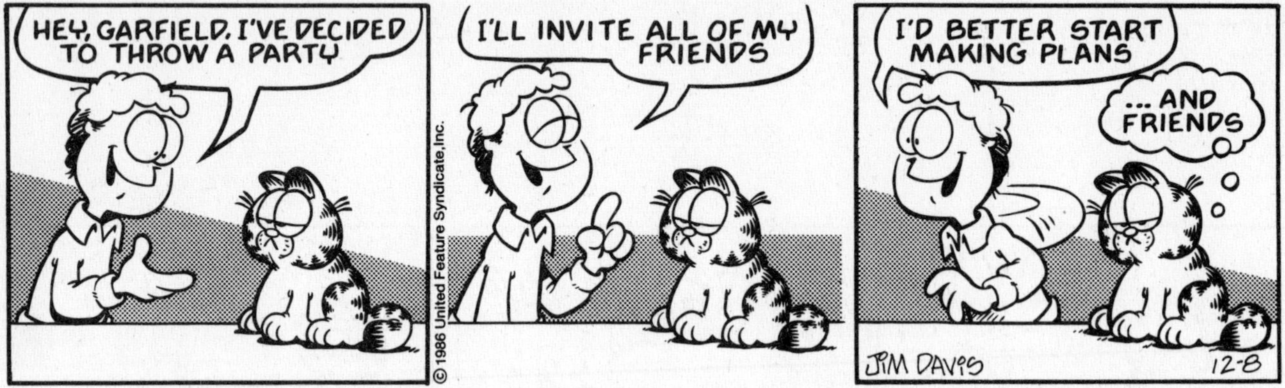
HEY, GARFIELD. I'VE DECIDED TO THROW A PARTY
© 1986 United Feature Syndicate, Inc.
I'LL INVITE ALL OF MY FRIENDS
I'D BETTER START MAKING PLANS
... AND FRIENDS
JIM DAVIS
12-8

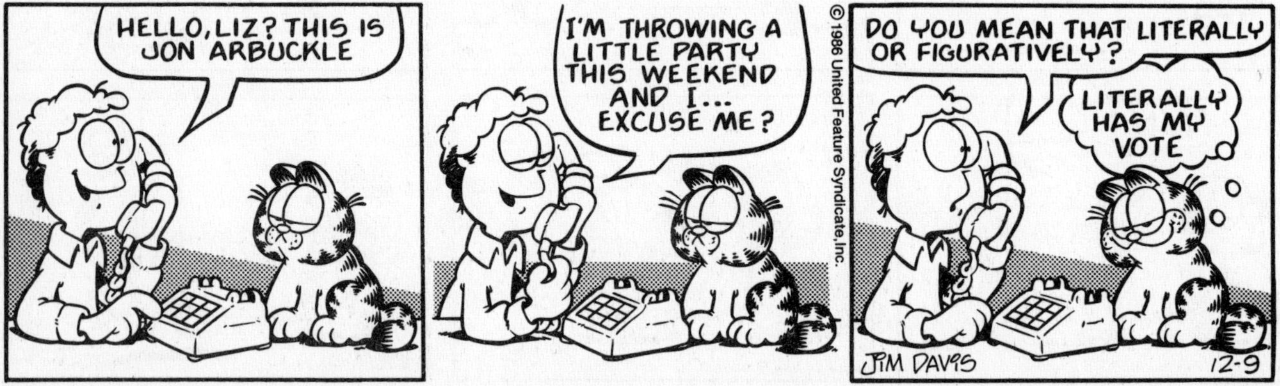
HELLO, LIZ? THIS IS JON ARBUCKLE
I'M THROWING A LITTLE PARTY THIS WEEKEND AND I... EXCUSE ME?
© 1986 United Feature Syndicate, Inc.
DO YOU MEAN THAT LITERALLY OR FIGURATIVELY?
LITERALLY HAS MY VOTE
JIM DAVIS
12-9

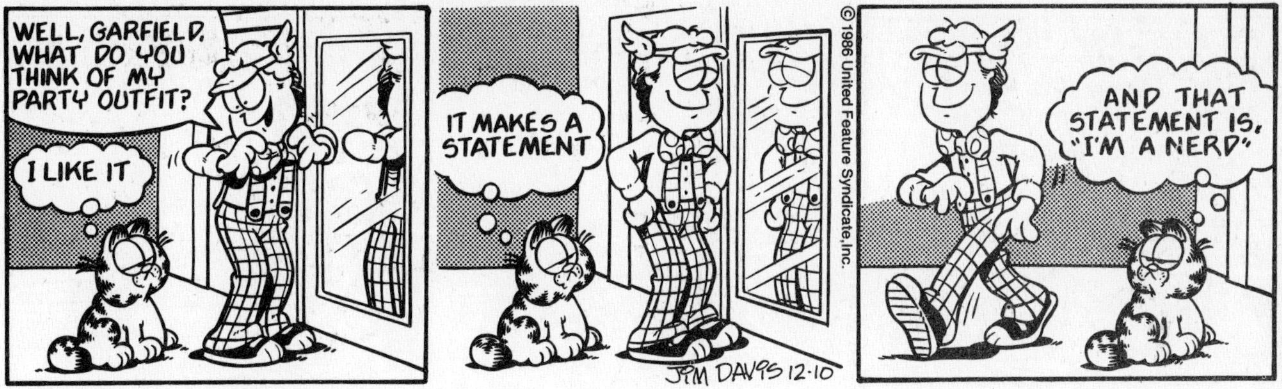
WELL, GARFIELD. WHAT DO YOU THINK OF MY PARTY OUTFIT?
I LIKE IT
IT MAKES A STATEMENT
AND THAT STATEMENT IS, "I'M A NERD"
© 1986 United Feature Syndicate, Inc.
JIM DAVIS 12-10

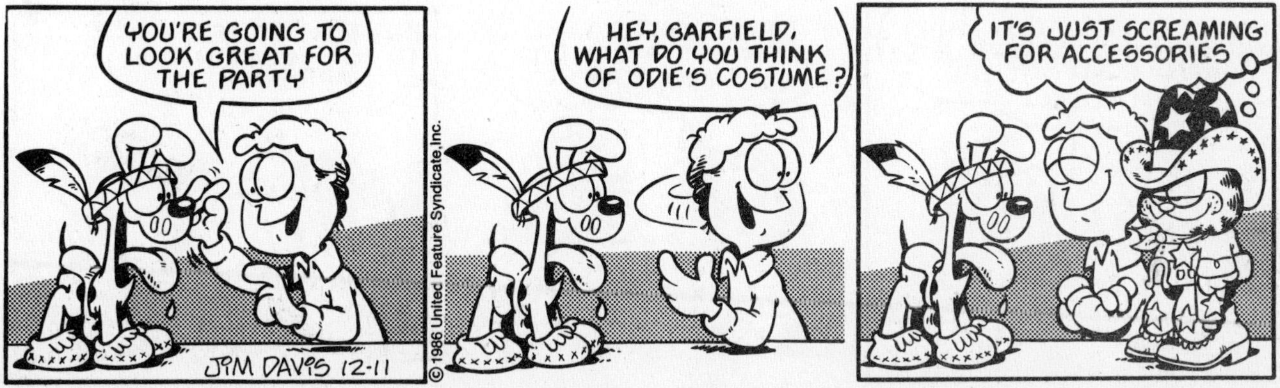
YOU'RE GOING TO LOOK GREAT FOR THE PARTY
HEY, GARFIELD, WHAT DO YOU THINK OF ODIE'S COSTUME?
IT'S JUST SCREAMING FOR ACCESSORIES
© 1986 United Feature Syndicate, Inc.
JIM DAVIS 12-11

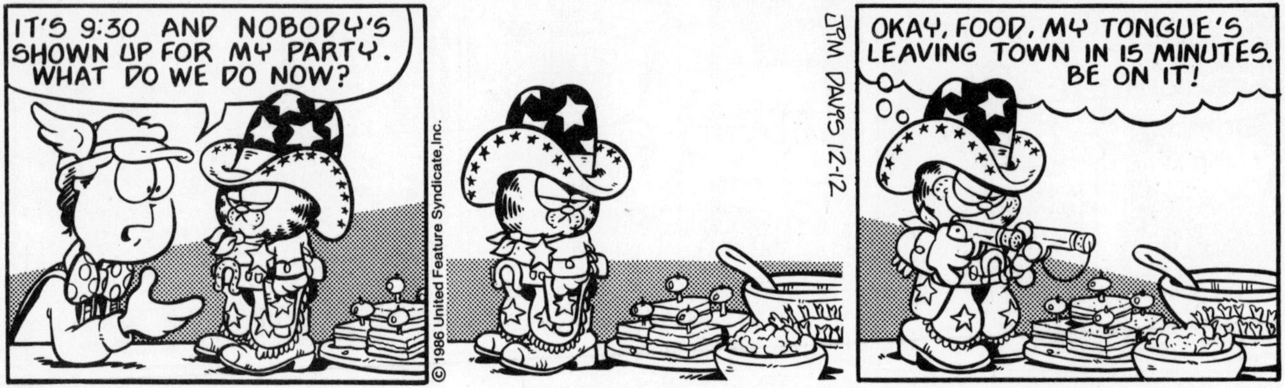
IT'S 9:30 AND NOBODY'S SHOWN UP FOR MY PARTY. WHAT DO WE DO NOW?
OKAY, FOOD, MY TONGUE'S LEAVING TOWN IN 15 MINUTES. BE ON IT!
JIM DAVIS 12-12
© 1986 United Feature Syndicate, Inc.

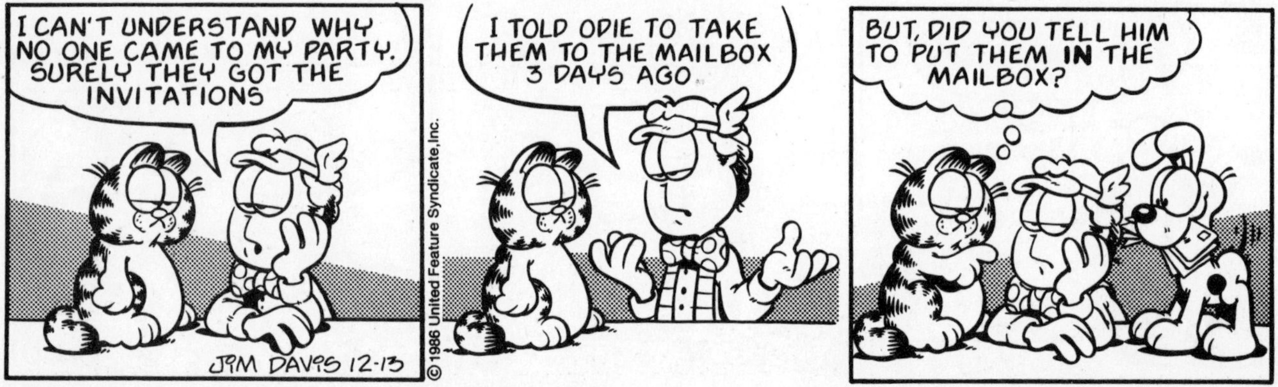
I CAN'T UNDERSTAND WHY NO ONE CAME TO MY PARTY. SURELY THEY GOT THE INVITATIONS
I TOLD ODIE TO TAKE THEM TO THE MAILBOX 3 DAYS AGO
BUT, DID YOU TELL HIM TO PUT THEM **IN** THE MAILBOX?
JIM DAVIS 12-13
© 1986 United Feature Syndicate, Inc.

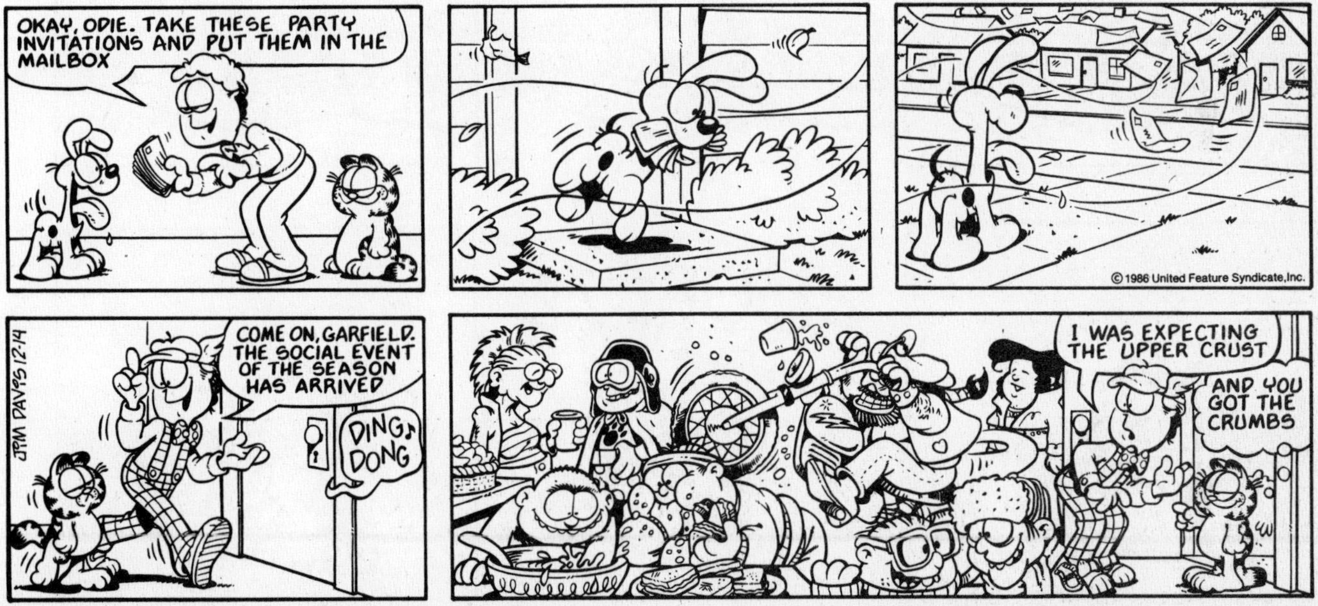

OKAY, ODIE. TAKE THESE PARTY INVITATIONS AND PUT THEM IN THE MAILBOX
© 1986 United Feature Syndicate, Inc.
JIM DAVIS 12·14
COME ON, GARFIELD. THE SOCIAL EVENT OF THE SEASON HAS ARRIVED
DING DONG
I WAS EXPECTING THE UPPER CRUST
AND YOU GOT THE CRUMBS

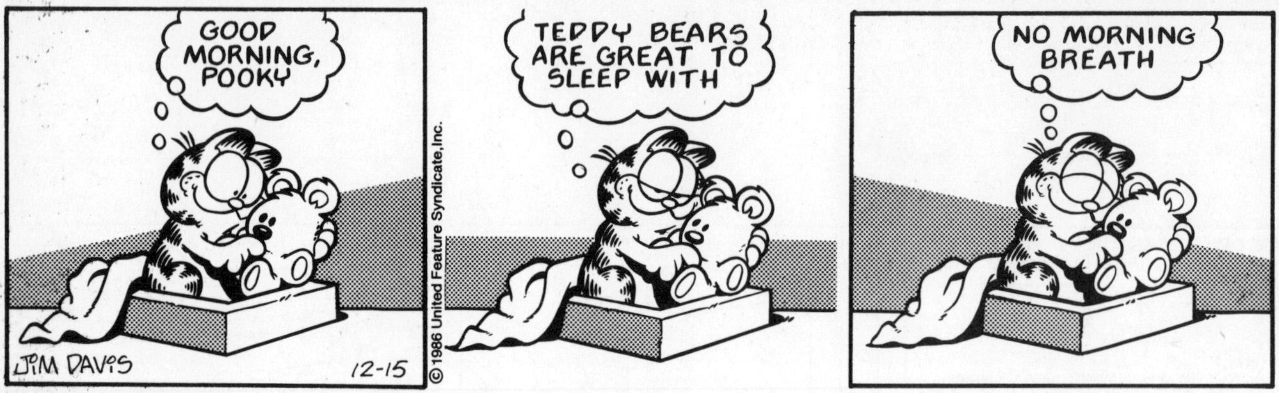
GOOD MORNING, POOKY
TEDDY BEARS ARE GREAT TO SLEEP WITH
NO MORNING BREATH
JIM DAVIS
12-15
© 1986 United Feature Syndicate, Inc.

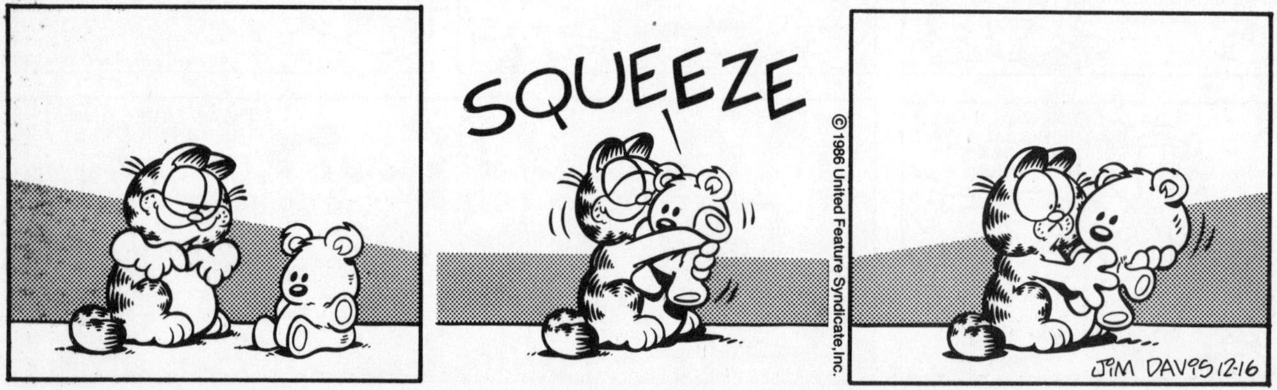
SQUEEZE
© 1986 United Feature Syndicate, Inc.
JIM DAVIS 12-16

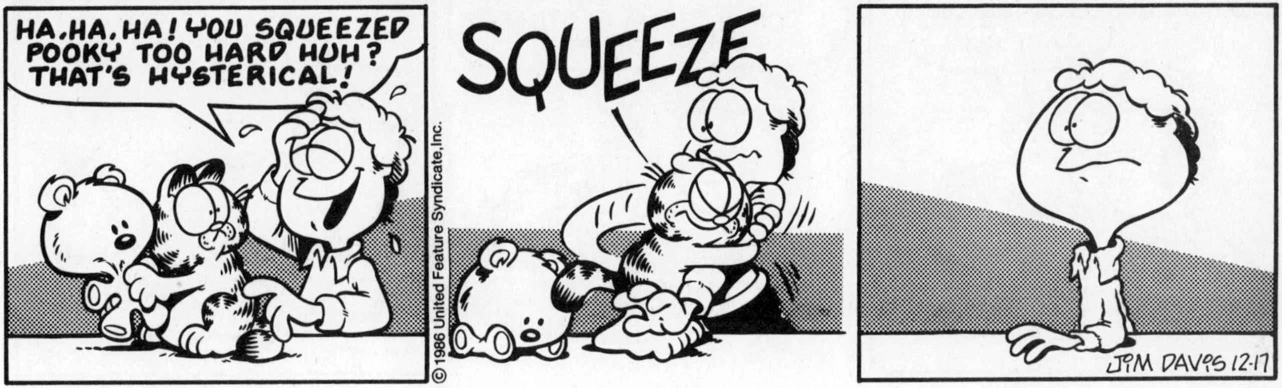
HA, HA, HA! YOU SQUEEZED POOKY TOO HARD HUH? THAT'S HYSTERICAL!
© 1986 United Feature Syndicate, Inc.
SQUEEZE
JIM DAVIS 12-17

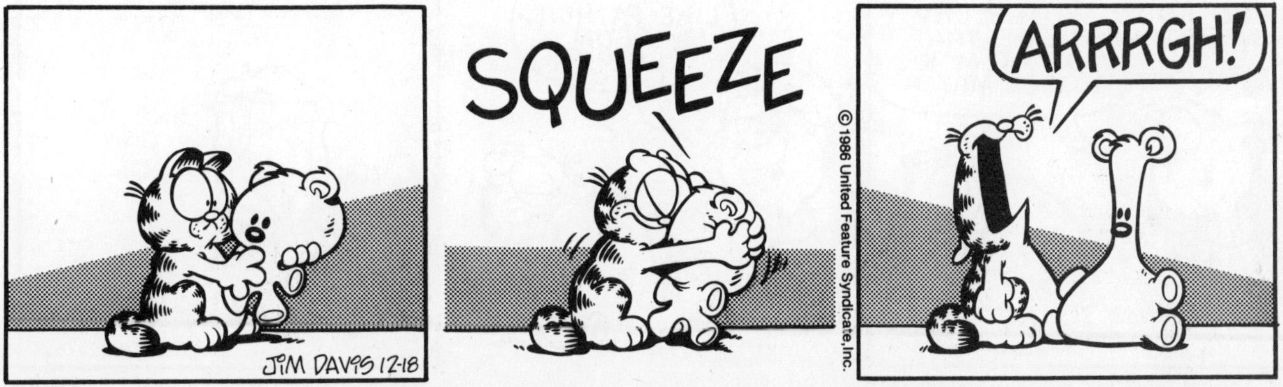
JIM DAVIS 12-18
SQUEEZE
© 1986 United Feature Syndicate, Inc.
ARRRGH!

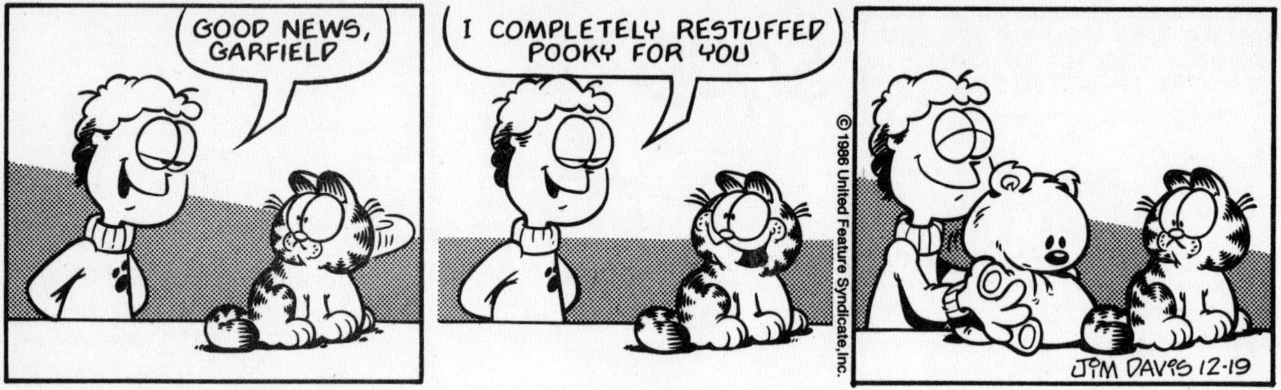
GOOD NEWS, GARFIELD
I COMPLETELY RESTUFFED POOKY FOR YOU
© 1986 United Feature Syndicate, Inc.
JIM DAVIS 12-19

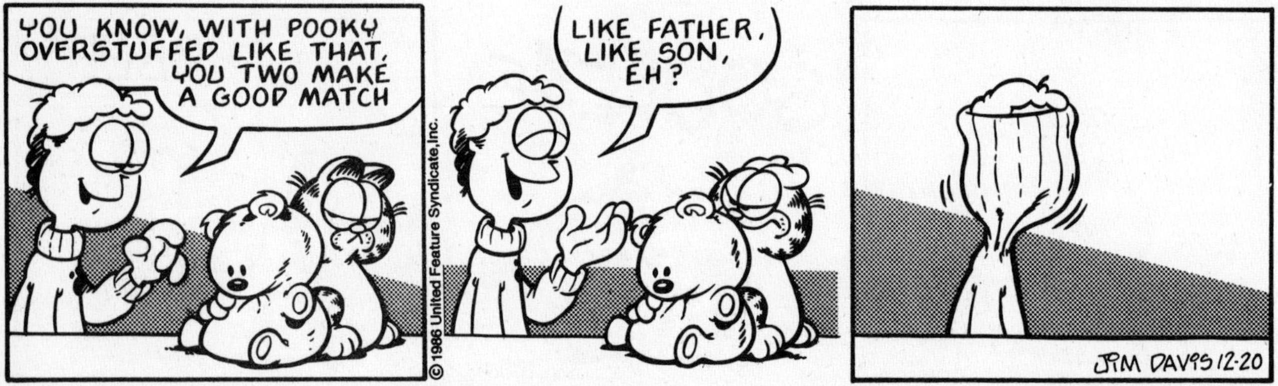
YOU KNOW, WITH POOKY OVERSTUFFED LIKE THAT, YOU TWO MAKE A GOOD MATCH
© 1986 United Feature Syndicate, Inc.
LIKE FATHER, LIKE SON, EH?
JIM DAVIS 12-20

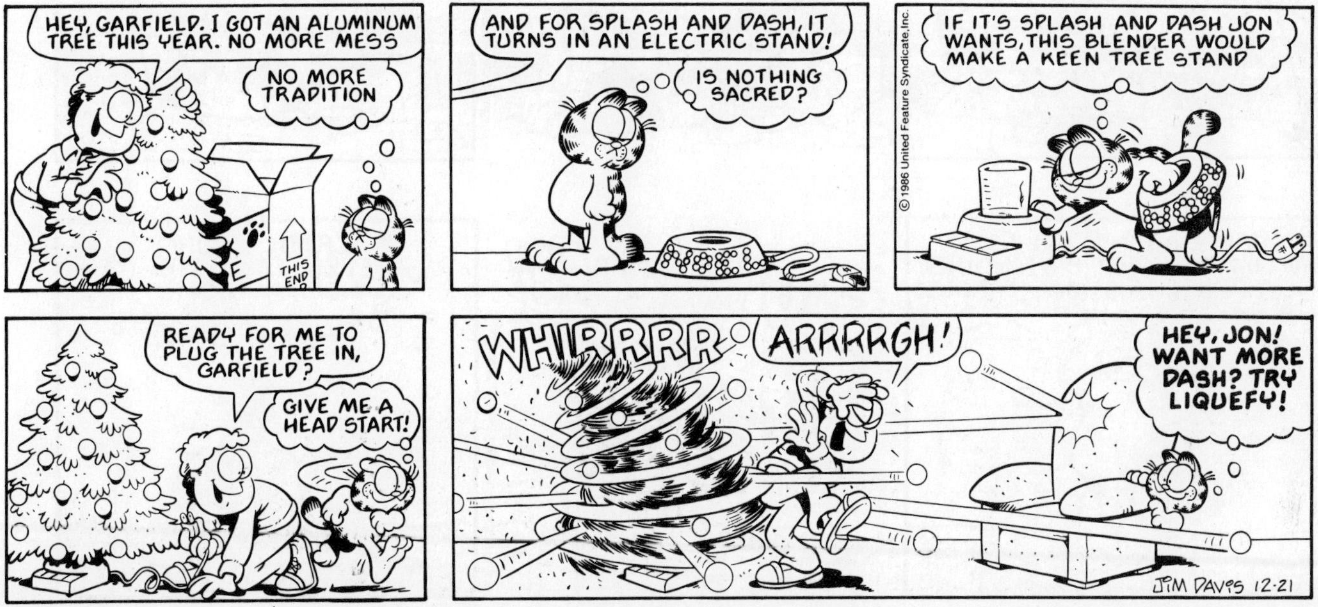

HEY, GARFIELD. I GOT AN ALUMINUM TREE THIS YEAR. NO MORE MESS
NO MORE TRADITION
THIS END
AND FOR SPLASH AND DASH, IT TURNS IN AN ELECTRIC STAND!
IS NOTHING SACRED?
© 1986 United Feature Syndicate, Inc.
IF IT'S SPLASH AND DASH JON WANTS, THIS BLENDER WOULD MAKE A KEEN TREE STAND
READY FOR ME TO PLUG THE TREE IN, GARFIELD?
GIVE ME A HEAD START!
WHIRRRR
ARRRRGH!
HEY, JON! WANT MORE DASH? TRY LIQUEFY!
JIM DAVIS 12-21

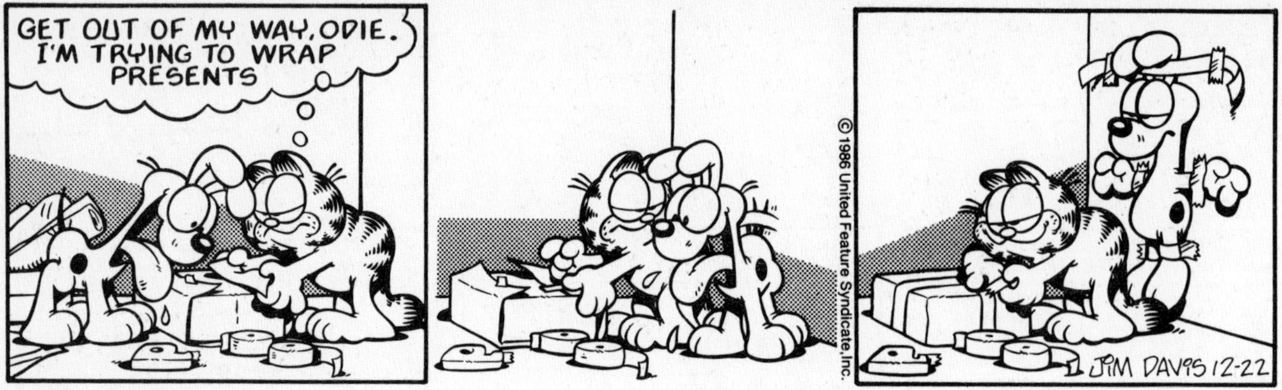
GET OUT OF MY WAY, ODIE. I'M TRYING TO WRAP PRESENTS
© 1986 United Feature Syndicate, Inc.
JIM DAVIS 12-22

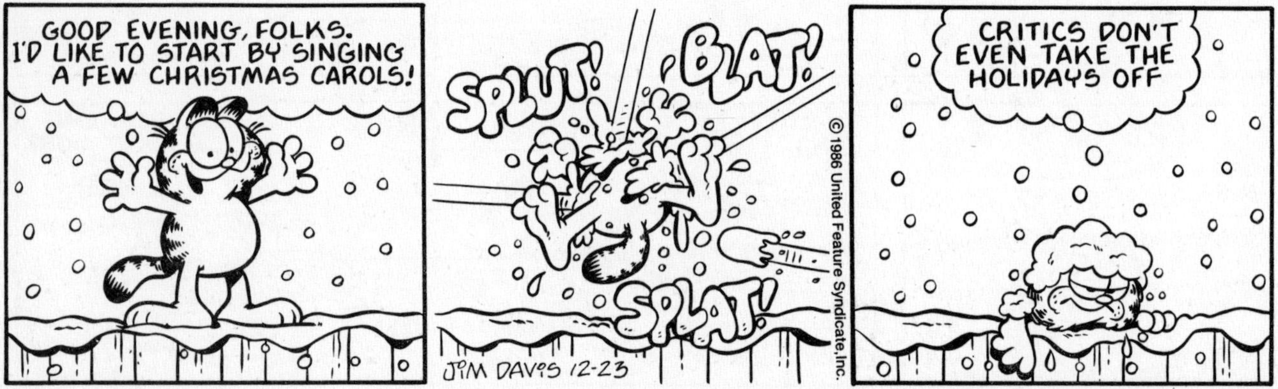
GOOD EVENING, FOLKS. I'D LIKE TO START BY SINGING A FEW CHRISTMAS CAROLS!
SPLUT!
BLAT!
SPLAT!
JIM DAVIS 12-23
© 1986 United Feature Syndicate, Inc.
CRITICS DON'T EVEN TAKE THE HOLIDAYS OFF

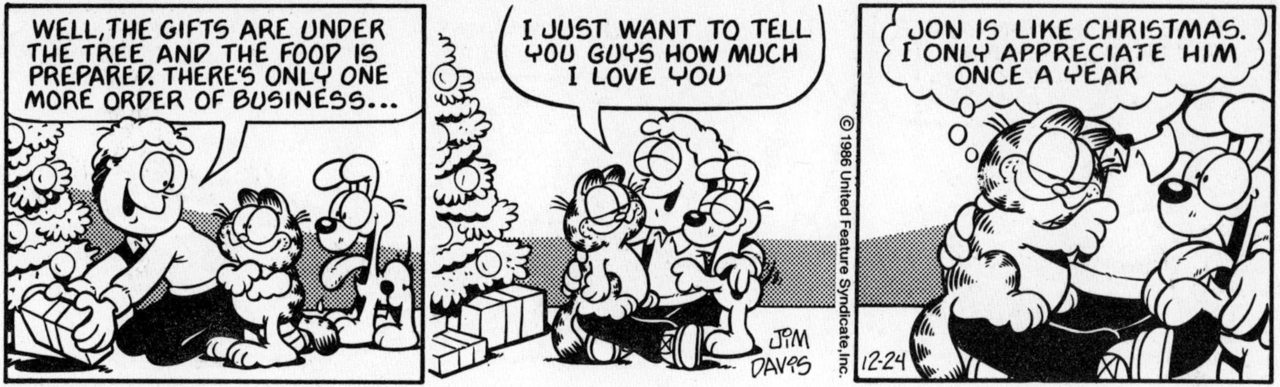
WELL, THE GIFTS ARE UNDER THE TREE AND THE FOOD IS PREPARED. THERE'S ONLY ONE MORE ORDER OF BUSINESS...
I JUST WANT TO TELL YOU GUYS HOW MUCH I LOVE YOU
JIM DAVIS
© 1986 United Feature Syndicate, Inc.
12-24
JON IS LIKE CHRISTMAS. I ONLY APPRECIATE HIM ONCE A YEAR

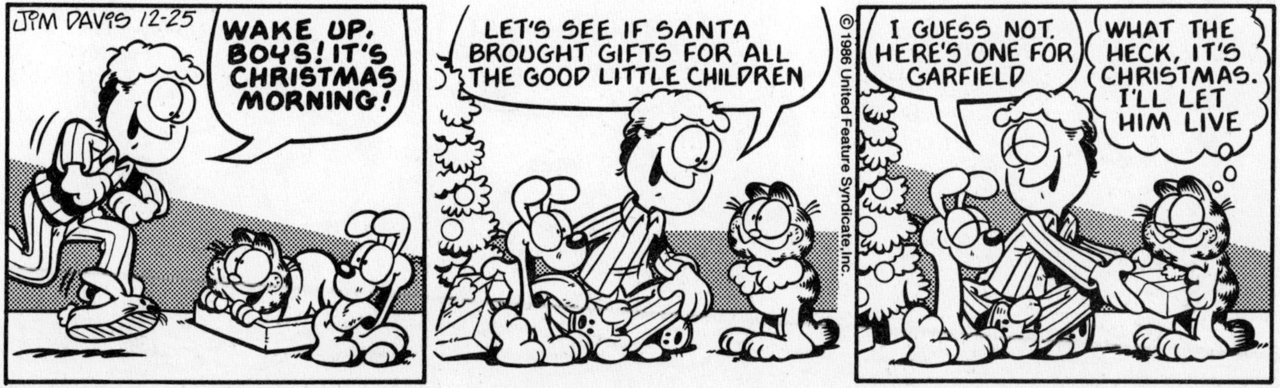
JIM DAVIS 12-25
WAKE UP, BOYS! IT'S CHRISTMAS MORNING!
LET'S SEE IF SANTA BROUGHT GIFTS FOR ALL THE GOOD LITTLE CHILDREN
© 1986 United Feature Syndicate, Inc.
I GUESS NOT. HERE'S ONE FOR GARFIELD
WHAT THE HECK, IT'S CHRISTMAS. I'LL LET HIM LIVE

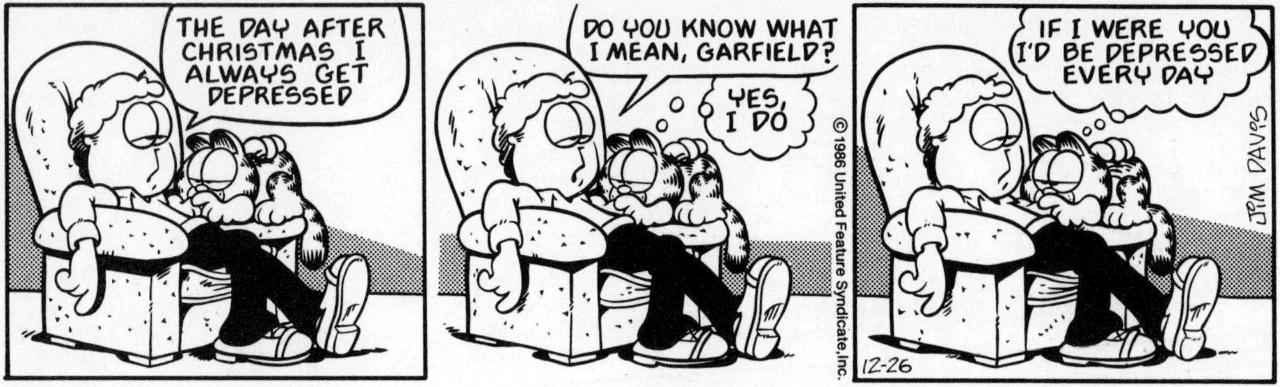
THE DAY AFTER CHRISTMAS I ALWAYS GET DEPRESSED
DO YOU KNOW WHAT I MEAN, GARFIELD?
YES, I DO
© 1986 United Feature Syndicate,Inc.
IF I WERE YOU I'D BE DEPRESSED EVERY DAY
JIM DAVIS
12-26

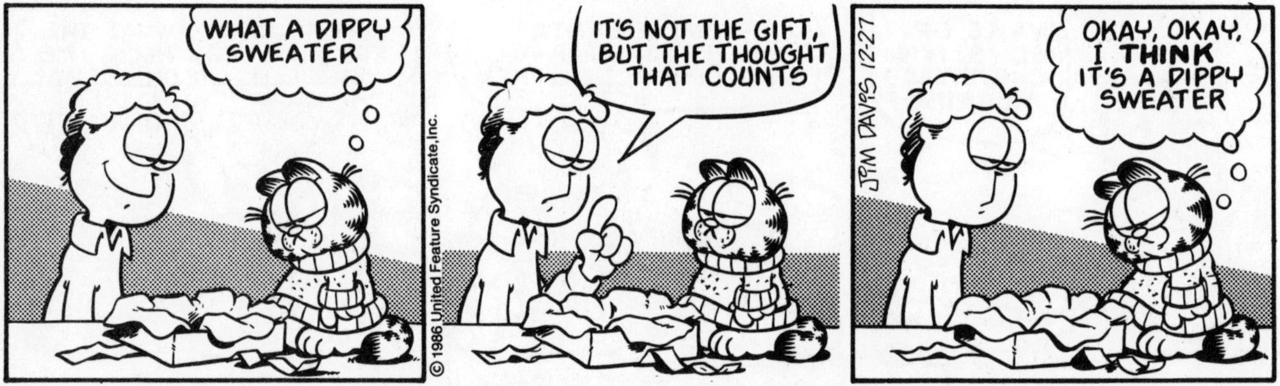
WHAT A DIPPY SWEATER
© 1986 United Feature Syndicate,Inc.
IT'S NOT THE GIFT, BUT THE THOUGHT THAT COUNTS
JIM DAVIS 12-27
OKAY, OKAY, I **THINK** IT'S A DIPPY SWEATER

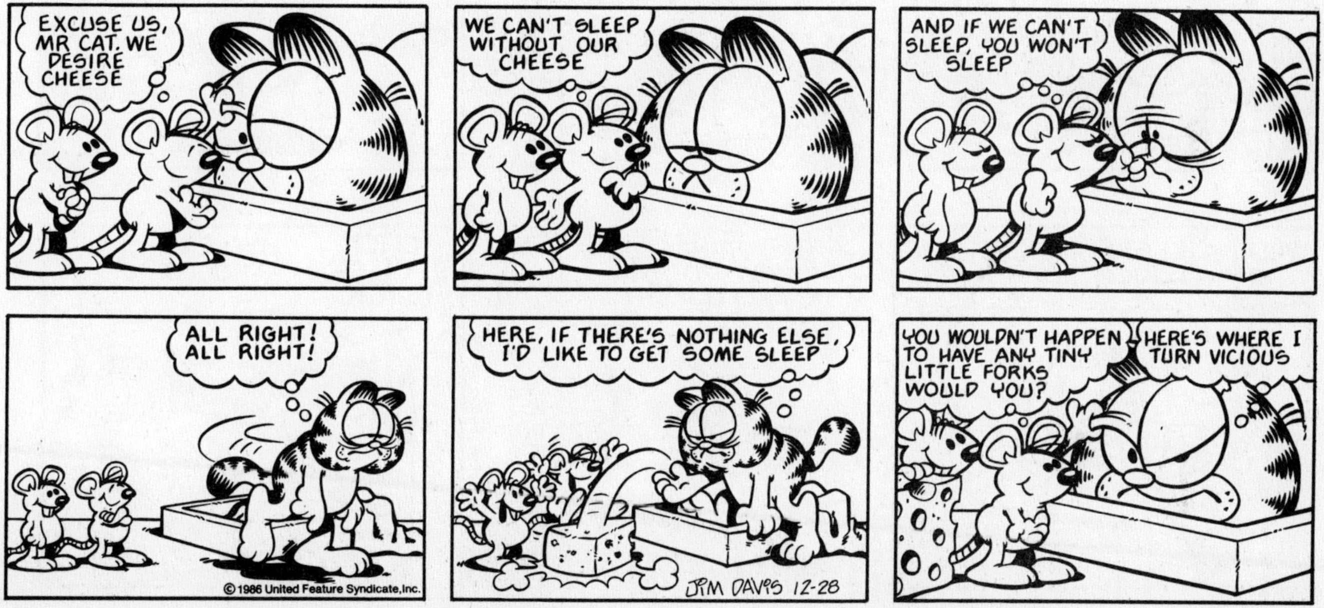

EXCUSE US, MR CAT. WE DESIRE CHEESE
WE CAN'T SLEEP WITHOUT OUR CHEESE
AND IF WE CAN'T SLEEP, YOU WON'T SLEEP
ALL RIGHT! ALL RIGHT!
© 1986 United Feature Syndicate, Inc.
HERE, IF THERE'S NOTHING ELSE, I'D LIKE TO GET SOME SLEEP
JIM DAVIS 12-28
YOU WOULDN'T HAPPEN TO HAVE ANY TINY LITTLE FORKS WOULD YOU?
HERE'S WHERE I TURN VICIOUS

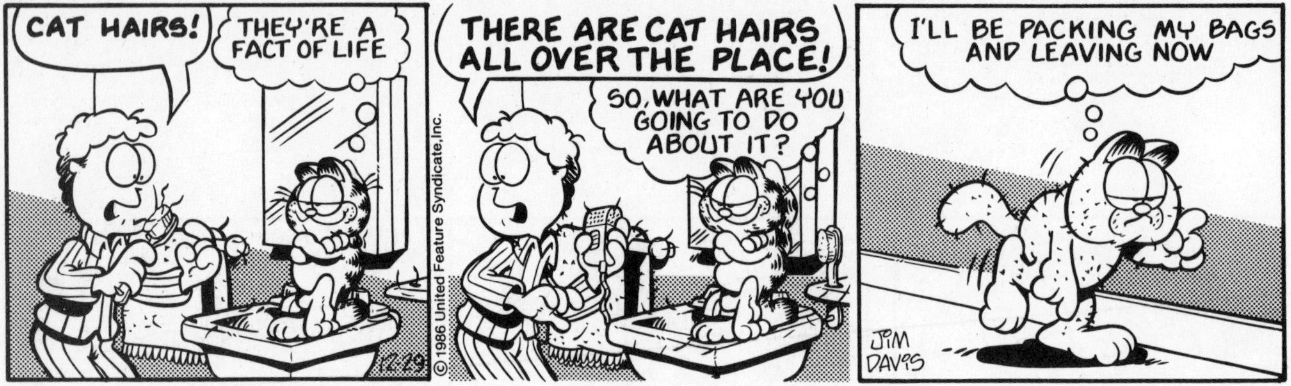
CAT HAIRS!
THEY'RE A FACT OF LIFE
12-29
© 1986 United Feature Syndicate, Inc.
THERE ARE CAT HAIRS ALL OVER THE PLACE!
SO, WHAT ARE YOU GOING TO DO ABOUT IT?
I'LL BE PACKING MY BAGS AND LEAVING NOW
JIM DAVIS

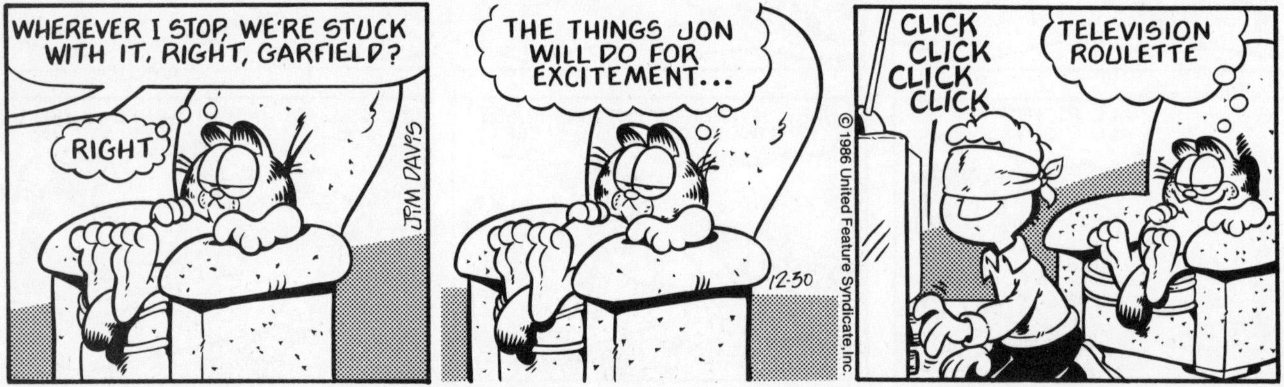
WHEREVER I STOP, WE'RE STUCK WITH IT, RIGHT, GARFIELD?
RIGHT
JIM DAVIS
THE THINGS JON WILL DO FOR EXCITEMENT...
12-30
© 1986 United Feature Syndicate, Inc.
CLICK
CLICK
CLICK
CLICK
TELEVISION ROULETTE

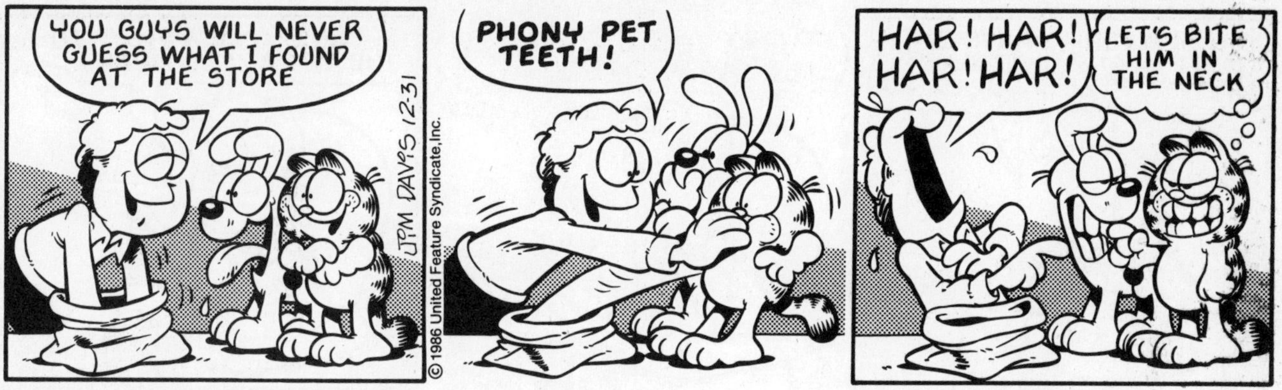
YOU GUYS WILL NEVER GUESS WHAT I FOUND AT THE STORE
JIM DAVIS 12-31
© 1986 United Feature Syndicate, Inc.
PHONY PET TEETH!
HAR! HAR! HAR! HAR!
LET'S BITE HIM IN THE NECK

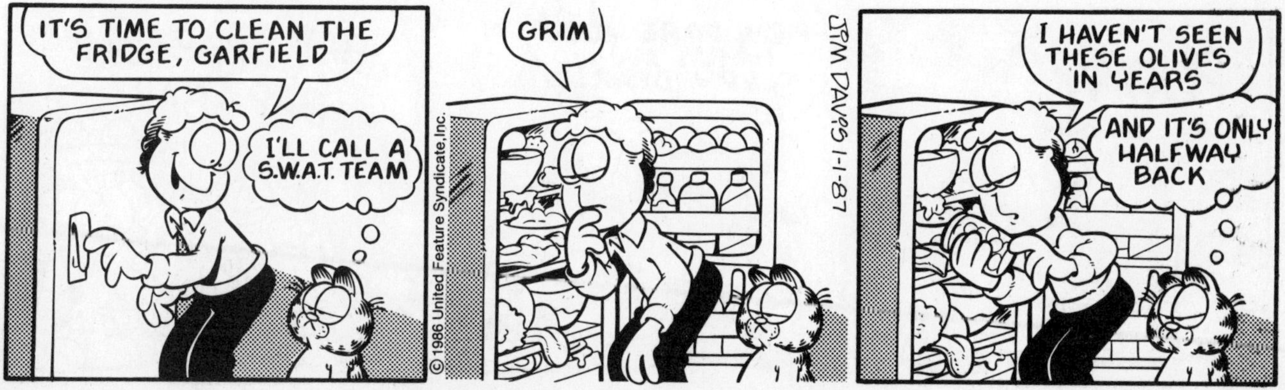
IT'S TIME TO CLEAN THE FRIDGE, GARFIELD
I'LL CALL A S.W.A.T. TEAM
© 1986 United Feature Syndicate, Inc.
GRIM
JIM DAVIS 1-1-87
I HAVEN'T SEEN THESE OLIVES IN YEARS
AND IT'S ONLY HALFWAY BACK

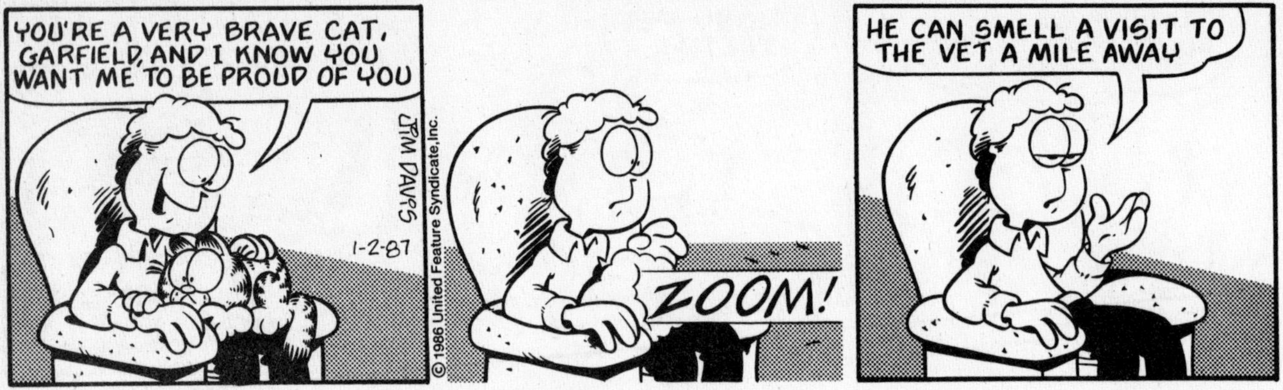
YOU'RE A VERY BRAVE CAT, GARFIELD, AND I KNOW YOU WANT ME TO BE PROUD OF YOU
JIM DAVIS 1-2-87
© 1986 United Feature Syndicate, Inc.
ZOOM!
HE CAN SMELL A VISIT TO THE VET A MILE AWAY

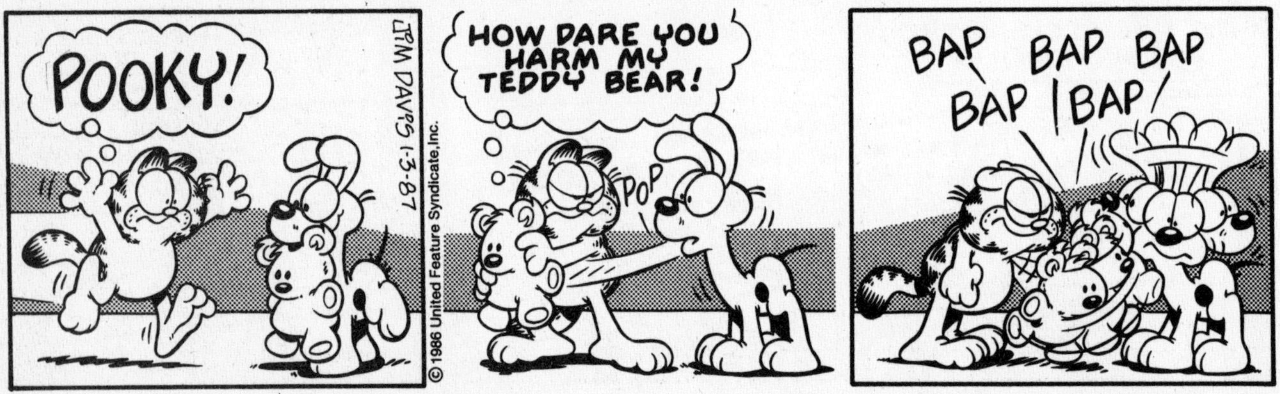
POOKY!
JIM DAVIS 1-3-87
© 1986 United Feature Syndicate, Inc.
HOW DARE YOU HARM MY TEDDY BEAR!
POP
BAP BAP BAP BAP BAP BAP

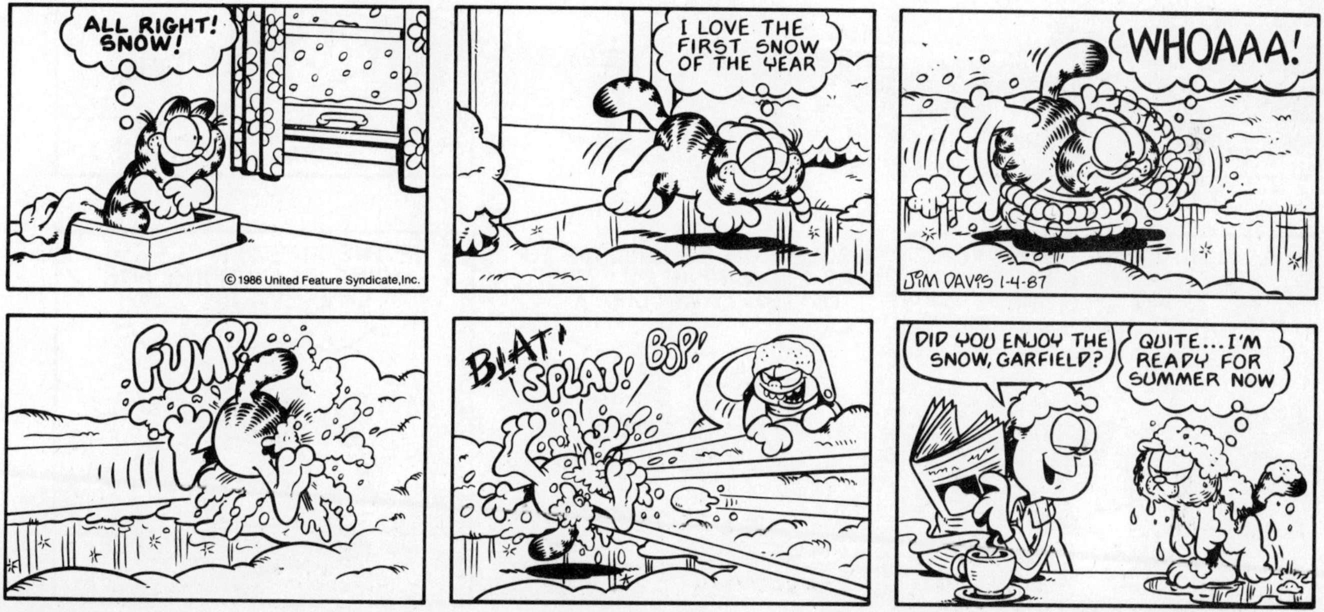

ALL RIGHT! SNOW!
© 1986 United Feature Syndicate, Inc.
I LOVE THE FIRST SNOW OF THE YEAR
WHOAAA!
JIM DAVIS 1-4-87
FUMP!
BLAT!
SPLAT!
BOP!
DID YOU ENJOY THE SNOW, GARFIELD?
QUITE... I'M READY FOR SUMMER NOW

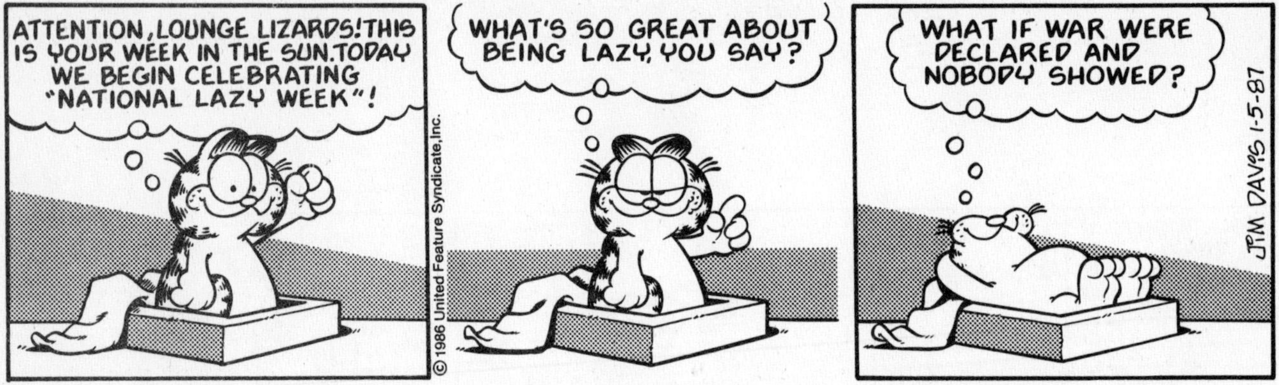
ATTENTION, LOUNGE LIZARDS! THIS IS YOUR WEEK IN THE SUN. TODAY WE BEGIN CELEBRATING "NATIONAL LAZY WEEK"!
WHAT'S SO GREAT ABOUT BEING LAZY, YOU SAY?
WHAT IF WAR WERE DECLARED AND NOBODY SHOWED?
JIM DAVIS 1-5-87
© 1986 United Feature Syndicate, Inc.

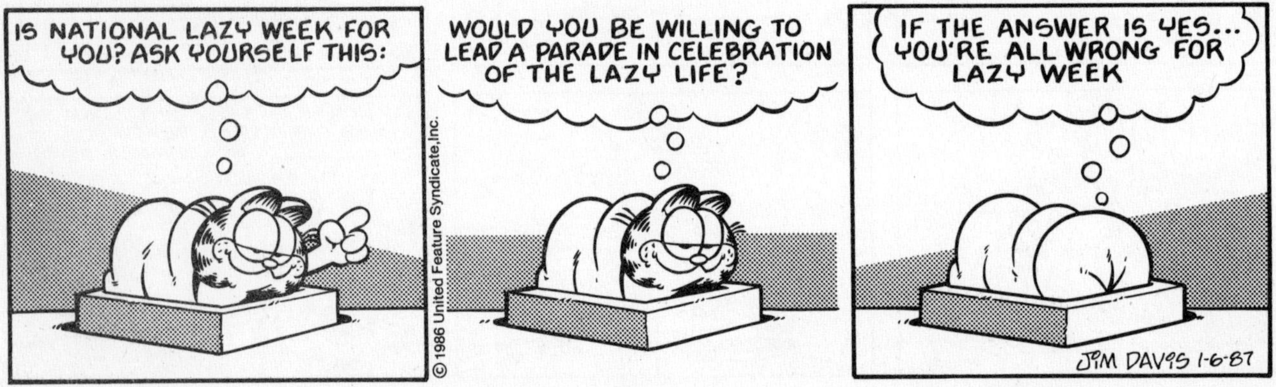
IS NATIONAL LAZY WEEK FOR YOU? ASK YOURSELF THIS:
WOULD YOU BE WILLING TO LEAD A PARADE IN CELEBRATION OF THE LAZY LIFE?
IF THE ANSWER IS YES... YOU'RE ALL WRONG FOR LAZY WEEK
JIM DAVIS 1-6-87
© 1986 United Feature Syndicate, Inc.

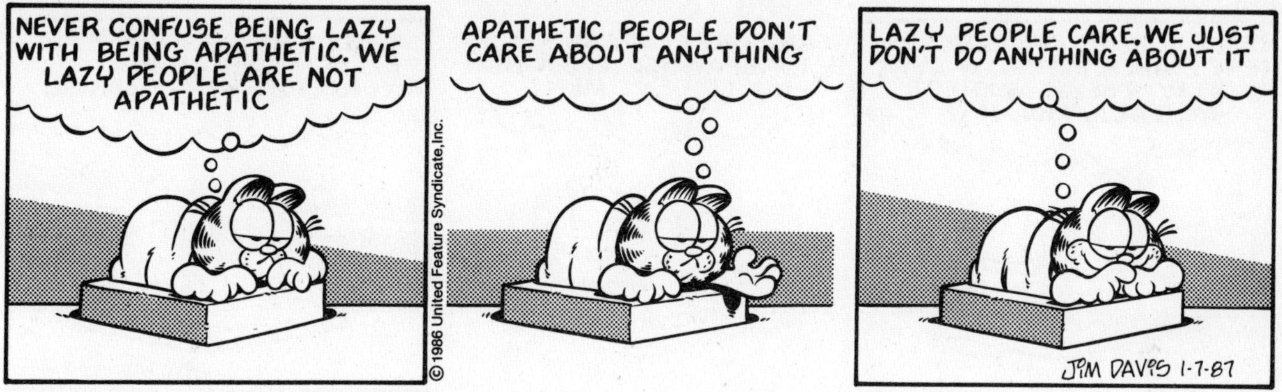
NEVER CONFUSE BEING LAZY WITH BEING APATHETIC. WE LAZY PEOPLE ARE NOT APATHETIC
APATHETIC PEOPLE DON'T CARE ABOUT ANYTHING
LAZY PEOPLE CARE. WE JUST DON'T DO ANYTHING ABOUT IT
© 1986 United Feature Syndicate, Inc.
JIM DAVIS 1-7-87

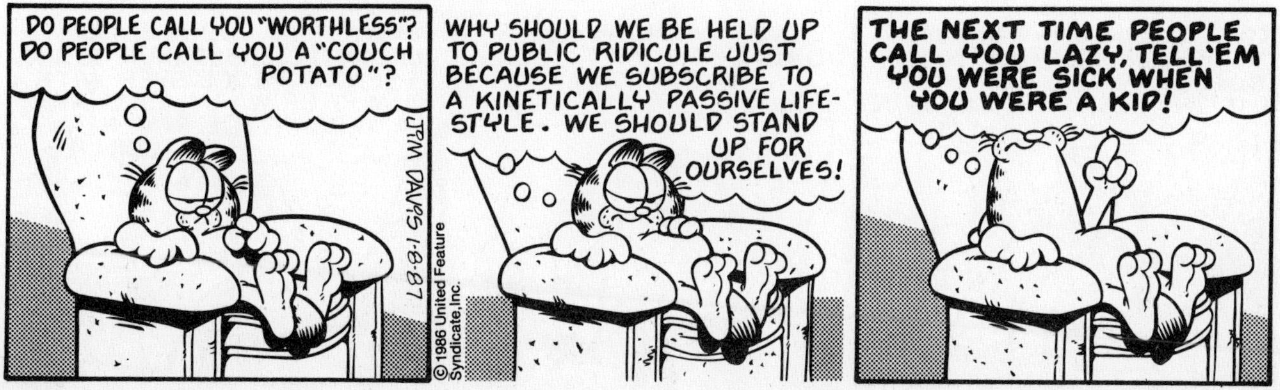
DO PEOPLE CALL YOU "WORTHLESS"? DO PEOPLE CALL YOU A "COUCH POTATO"?
JIM DAVIS 1-8-87
© 1986 United Feature Syndicate, Inc.
WHY SHOULD WE BE HELD UP TO PUBLIC RIDICULE JUST BECAUSE WE SUBSCRIBE TO A KINETICALLY PASSIVE LIFE-STYLE. WE SHOULD STAND UP FOR OURSELVES!
THE NEXT TIME PEOPLE CALL YOU LAZY, TELL 'EM YOU WERE SICK WHEN YOU WERE A KID!

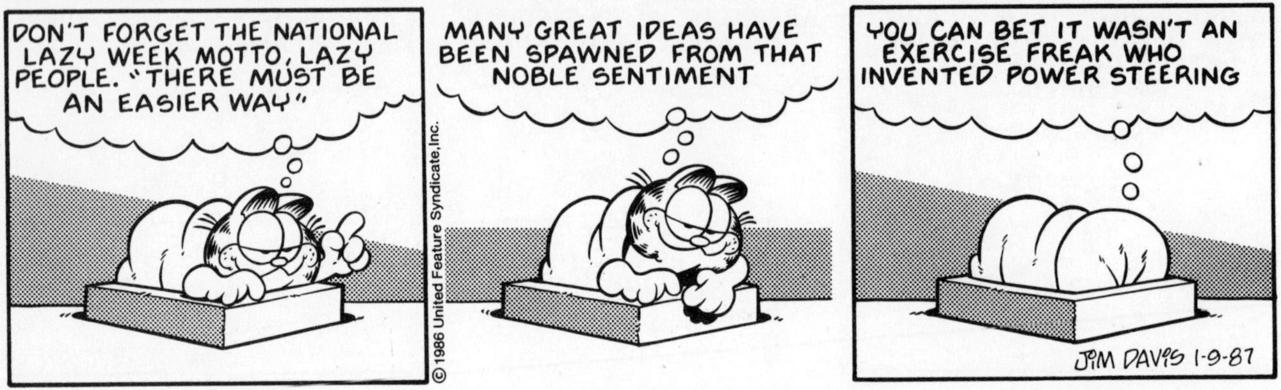

DON'T FORGET THE NATIONAL LAZY WEEK MOTTO, LAZY PEOPLE. "THERE MUST BE AN EASIER WAY"
© 1986 United Feature Syndicate, Inc.
MANY GREAT IDEAS HAVE BEEN SPAWNED FROM THAT NOBLE SENTIMENT
YOU CAN BET IT WASN'T AN EXERCISE FREAK WHO INVENTED POWER STEERING
JIM DAVIS 1-9-87


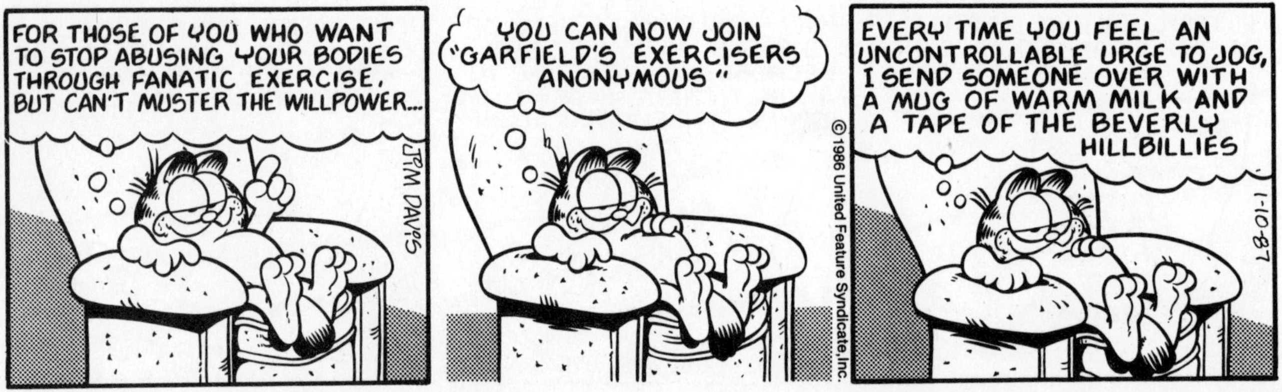

FOR THOSE OF YOU WHO WANT TO STOP ABUSING YOUR BODIES THROUGH FANATIC EXERCISE, BUT CAN'T MUSTER THE WILLPOWER...
JIM DAVIS
YOU CAN NOW JOIN "GARFIELD'S EXERCISERS ANONYMOUS"
© 1986 United Feature Syndicate, Inc.
EVERY TIME YOU FEEL AN UNCONTROLLABLE URGE TO JOG, I SEND SOMEONE OVER WITH A MUG OF WARM MILK AND A TAPE OF THE BEVERLY HILLBILLIES
1-10-87

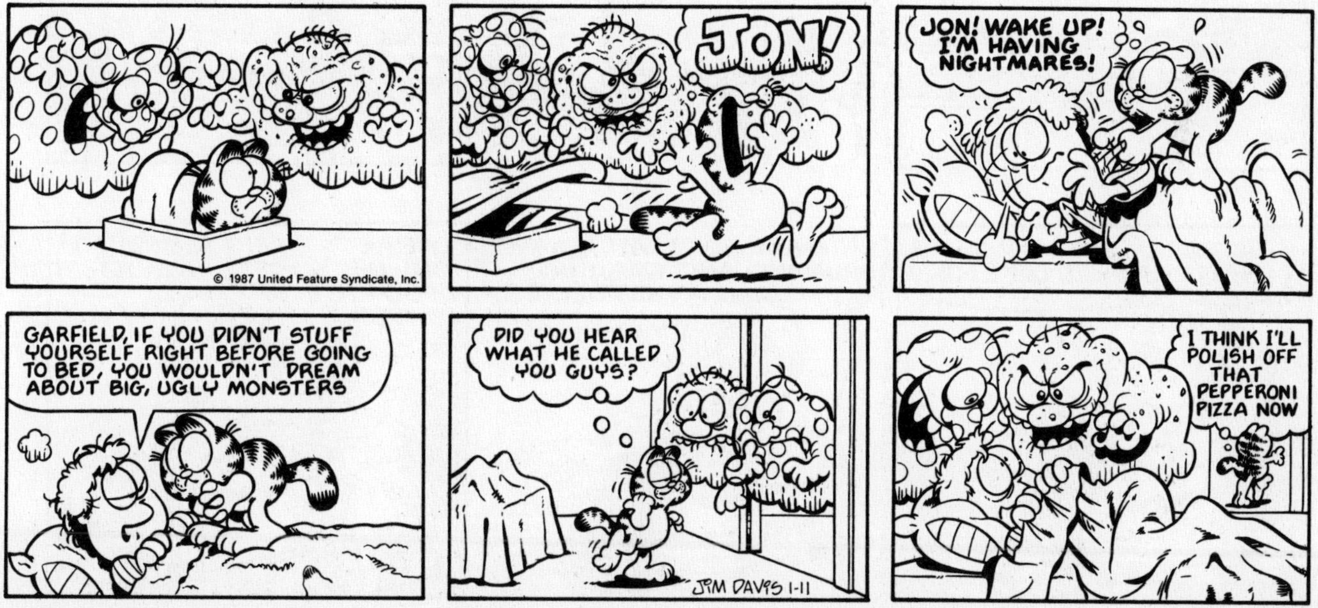

© 1987 United Feature Syndicate, Inc.
JON!
JON! WAKE UP! I'M HAVING NIGHTMARES!
GARFIELD, IF YOU DIDN'T STUFF YOURSELF RIGHT BEFORE GOING TO BED, YOU WOULDN'T DREAM ABOUT BIG, UGLY MONSTERS
DID YOU HEAR WHAT HE CALLED YOU GUYS?
JIM DAVIS 1-11
I THINK I'LL POLISH OFF THAT PEPPERONI PIZZA NOW

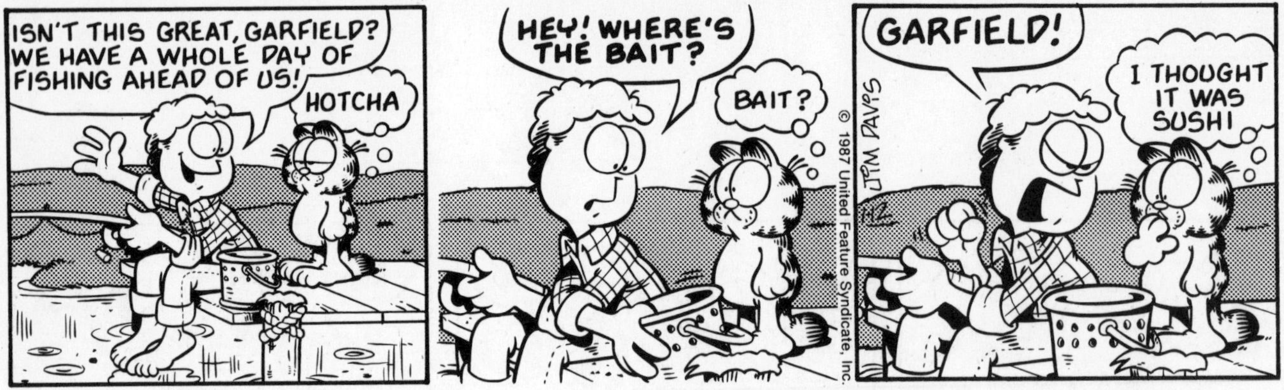
ISN'T THIS GREAT, GARFIELD? WE HAVE A WHOLE DAY OF FISHING AHEAD OF US!
HOTCHA
HEY! WHERE'S THE BAIT?
BAIT?
© 1987 United Feature Syndicate, Inc.
JIM DAVIS 1-12
GARFIELD!
I THOUGHT IT WAS SUSHI

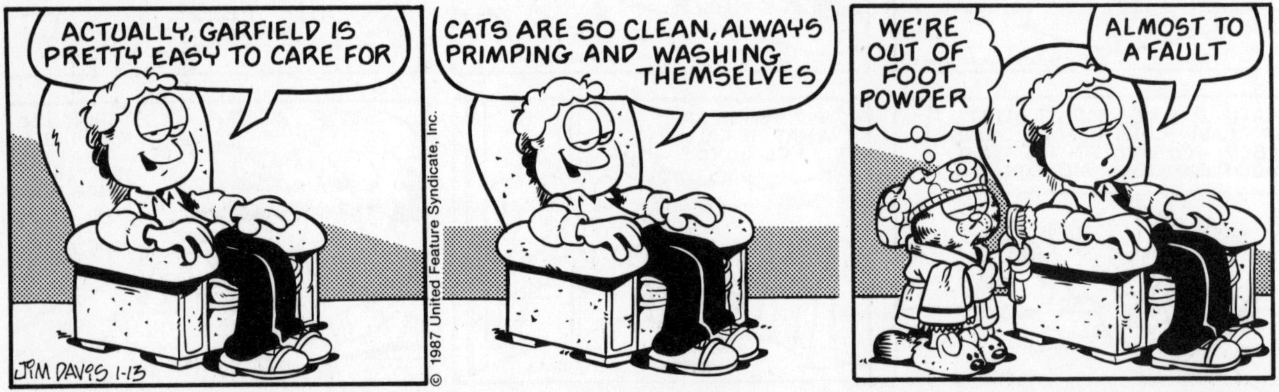
ACTUALLY, GARFIELD IS PRETTY EASY TO CARE FOR
JIM DAVIS 1-13
© 1987 United Feature Syndicate, Inc.
CATS ARE SO CLEAN, ALWAYS PRIMPING AND WASHING THEMSELVES
WE'RE OUT OF FOOT POWDER
ALMOST TO A FAULT

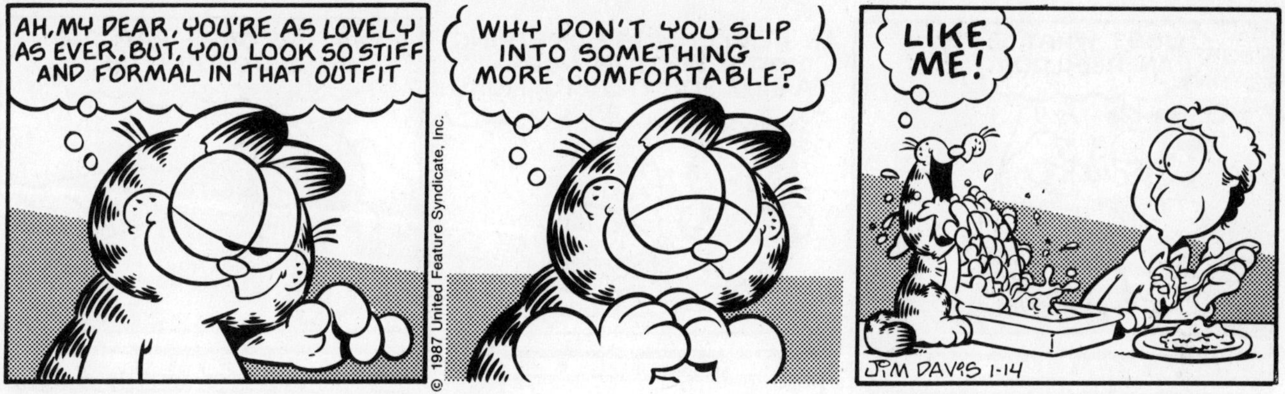
AH, MY DEAR, YOU'RE AS LOVELY AS EVER. BUT, YOU LOOK SO STIFF AND FORMAL IN THAT OUTFIT
WHY DON'T YOU SLIP INTO SOMETHING MORE COMFORTABLE?
LIKE ME!
JIM DAVIS 1-14
© 1987 United Feature Syndicate, Inc.

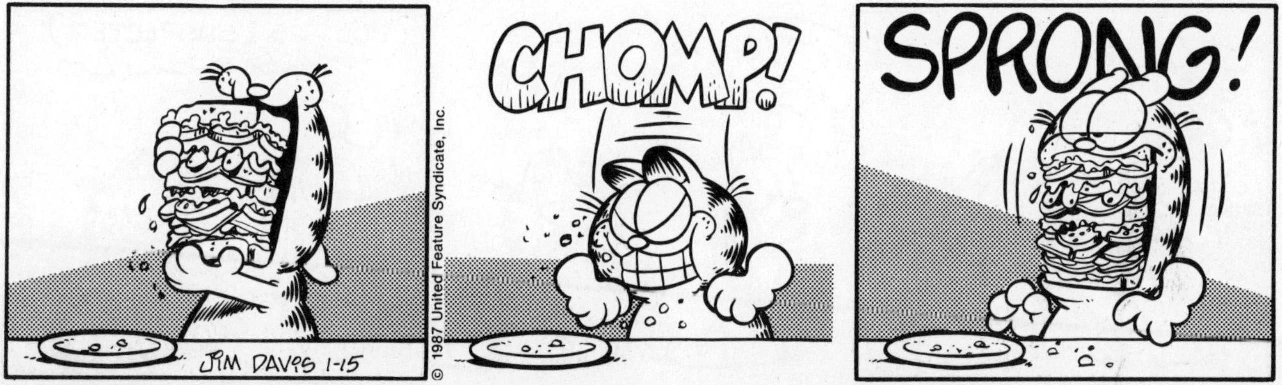
JIM DAVIS 1-15
CHOMP!
SPRONG!
© 1987 United Feature Syndicate, Inc.

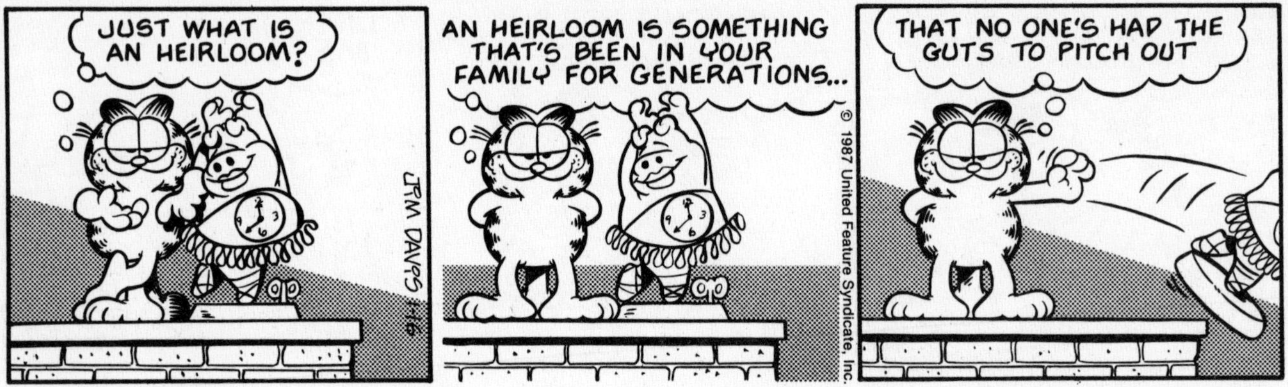
JUST WHAT IS AN HEIRLOOM?
AN HEIRLOOM IS SOMETHING THAT'S BEEN IN YOUR FAMILY FOR GENERATIONS...
THAT NO ONE'S HAD THE GUTS TO PITCH OUT
JIM DAVIS 1-16
© 1987 United Feature Syndicate, Inc.

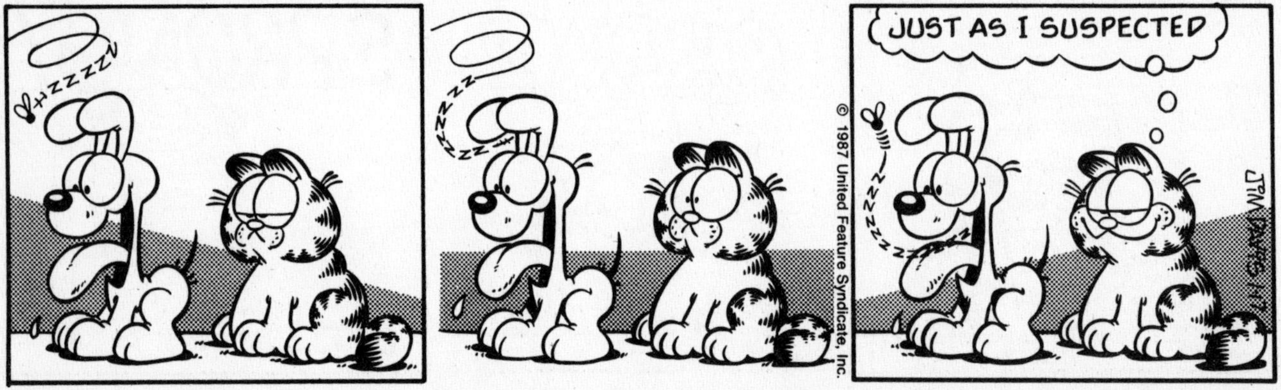
ZZZZZ
ZZZZZZZ
ZZZZZZZZ
JUST AS I SUSPECTED
JIM DAVIS 1-17
© 1987 United Feature Syndicate, Inc.

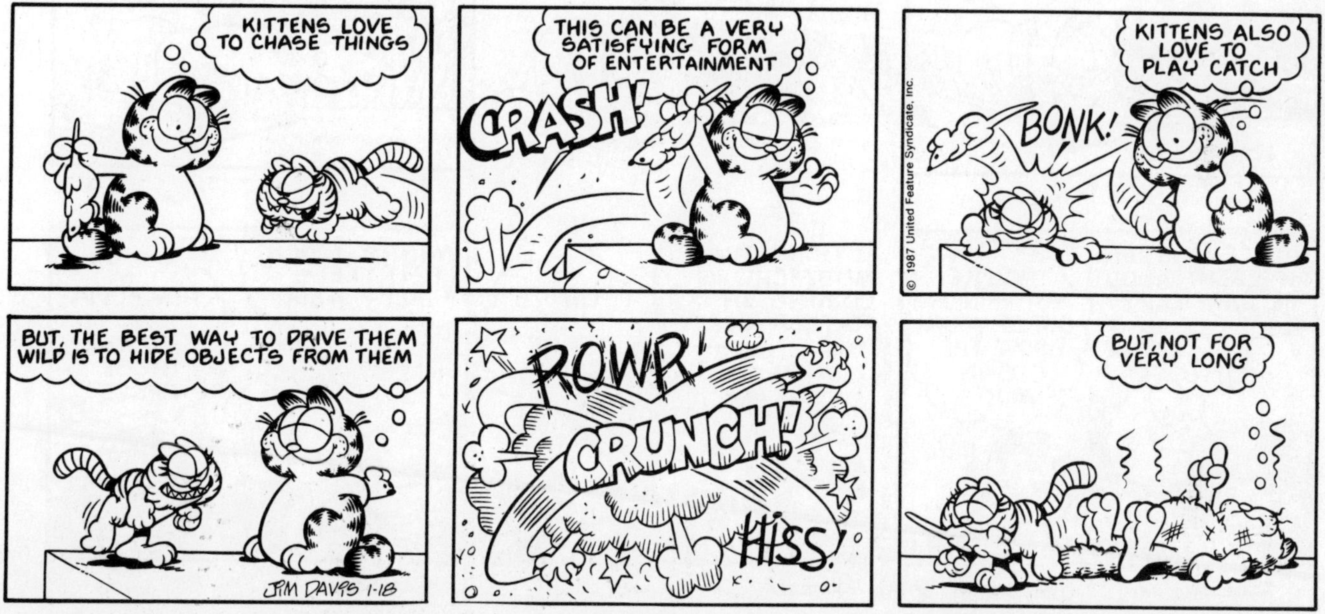
KITTENS LOVE TO CHASE THINGS
THIS CAN BE A VERY SATISFYING FORM OF ENTERTAINMENT
CRASH!
KITTENS ALSO LOVE TO PLAY CATCH
BONK!
© 1987 United Feature Syndicate, Inc.
BUT, THE BEST WAY TO DRIVE THEM WILD IS TO HIDE OBJECTS FROM THEM
JIM DAVIS 1-18
ROWR!
CRUNCH!
HISS!
BUT, NOT FOR VERY LONG

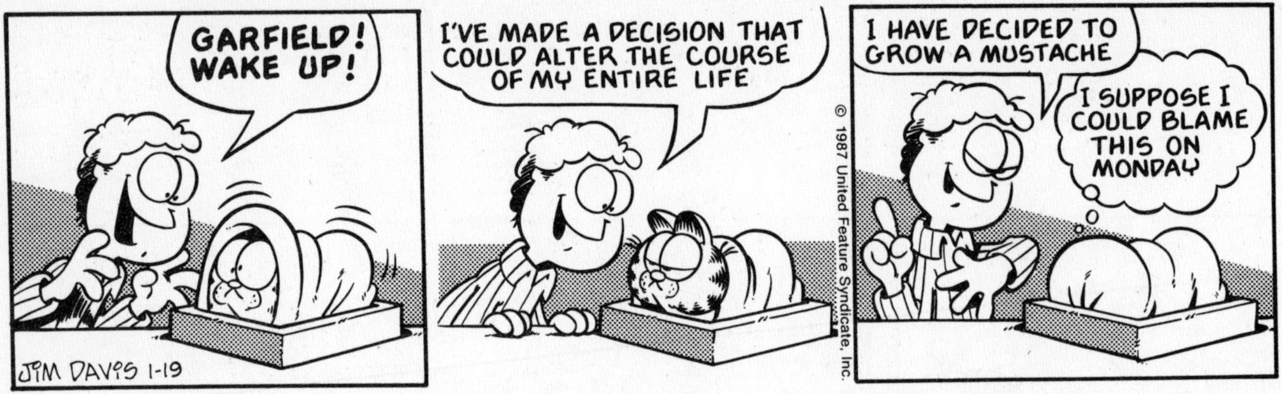
GARFIELD! WAKE UP!
JIM DAVIS 1-19
I'VE MADE A DECISION THAT COULD ALTER THE COURSE OF MY ENTIRE LIFE
© 1987 United Feature Syndicate, Inc.
I HAVE DECIDED TO GROW A MUSTACHE
I SUPPOSE I COULD BLAME THIS ON MONDAY

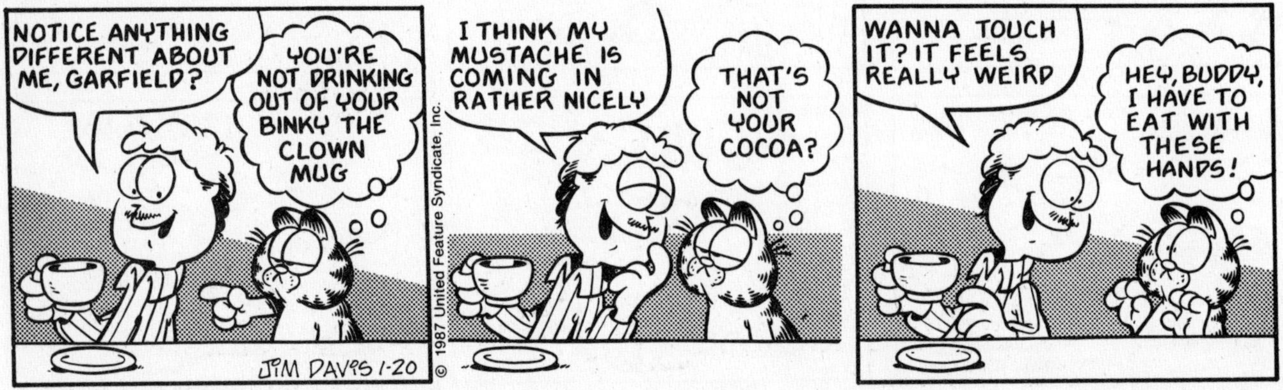
NOTICE ANYTHING DIFFERENT ABOUT ME, GARFIELD?
YOU'RE NOT DRINKING OUT OF YOUR BINKY THE CLOWN MUG
JIM DAVIS 1-20
© 1987 United Feature Syndicate, Inc.
I THINK MY MUSTACHE IS COMING IN RATHER NICELY
THAT'S NOT YOUR COCOA?
WANNA TOUCH IT? IT FEELS REALLY WEIRD
HEY, BUDDY, I HAVE TO EAT WITH THESE HANDS!

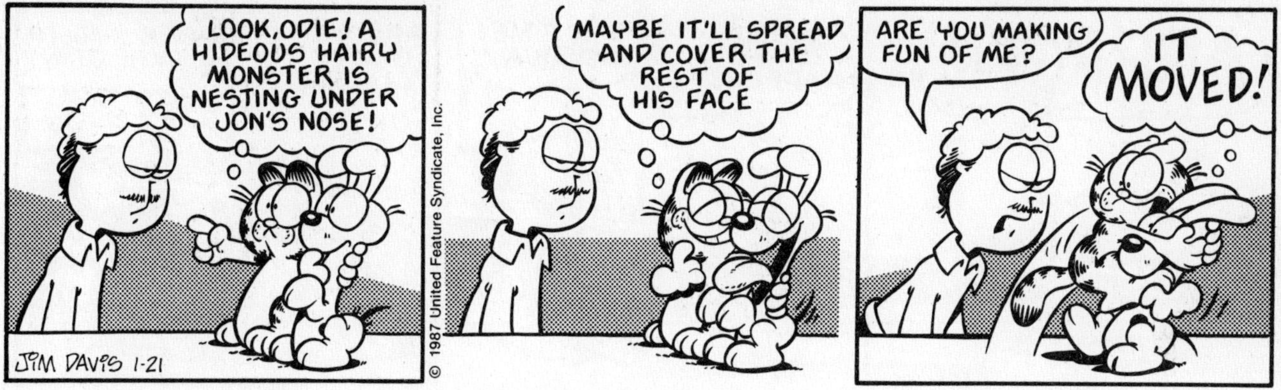

LOOK, ODIE! A HIDEOUS HAIRY MONSTER IS NESTING UNDER JON'S NOSE!
JIM DAVIS 1-21
© 1987 United Feature Syndicate, Inc.
MAYBE IT'LL SPREAD AND COVER THE REST OF HIS FACE
ARE YOU MAKING FUN OF ME?
IT MOVED!


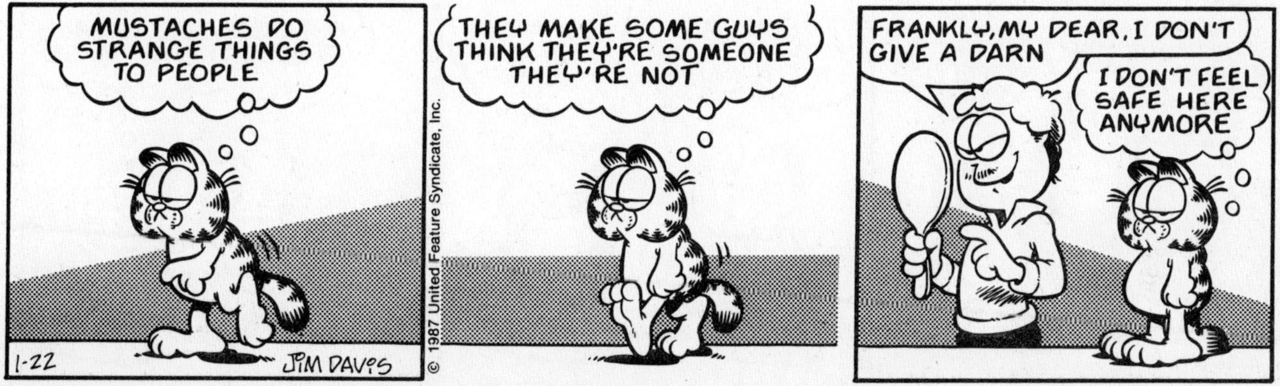

MUSTACHES DO STRANGE THINGS TO PEOPLE
1-22
JIM DAVIS
© 1987 United Feature Syndicate, Inc.
THEY MAKE SOME GUYS THINK THEY'RE SOMEONE THEY'RE NOT
FRANKLY, MY DEAR, I DON'T GIVE A DARN
I DON'T FEEL SAFE HERE ANYMORE

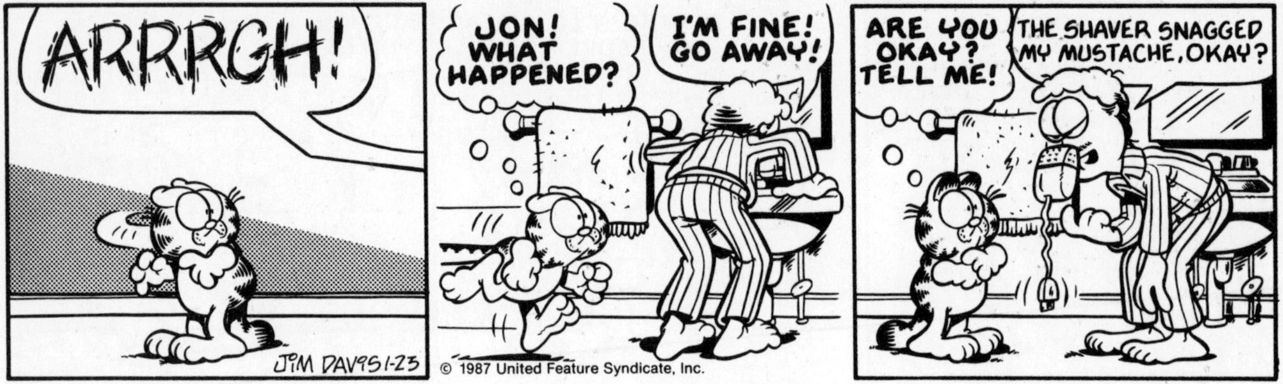
ARRRGH!
JIM DAVIS 1-23
JON! WHAT HAPPENED?
I'M FINE! GO AWAY!
© 1987 United Feature Syndicate, Inc.
ARE YOU OKAY? TELL ME!
THE SHAVER SNAGGED MY MUSTACHE, OKAY?

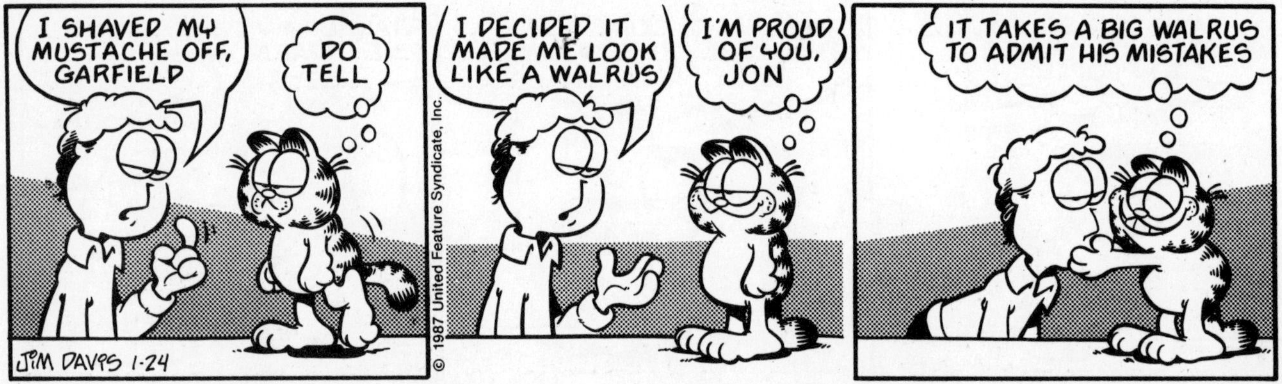
I SHAVED MY MUSTACHE OFF, GARFIELD
DO TELL
JIM DAVIS 1-24
© 1987 United Feature Syndicate, Inc.
I DECIDED IT MADE ME LOOK LIKE A WALRUS
I'M PROUD OF YOU, JON
IT TAKES A BIG WALRUS TO ADMIT HIS MISTAKES

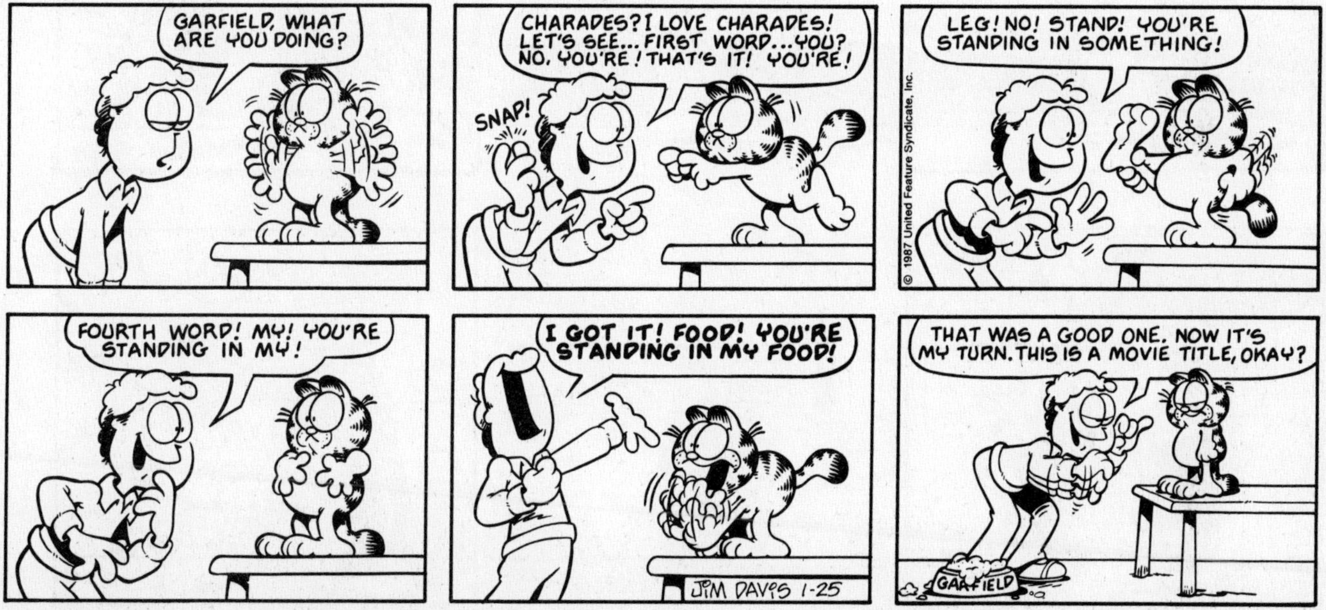
GARFIELD, WHAT ARE YOU DOING?
CHARADES? I LOVE CHARADES! LET'S SEE... FIRST WORD... YOU? NO, YOU'RE! THAT'S IT! YOU'RE!
SNAP!
LEG! NO! STAND! YOU'RE STANDING IN SOMETHING!
© 1987 United Feature Syndicate, Inc.
FOURTH WORD! MY! YOU'RE STANDING IN MY!
I GOT IT! FOOD! YOU'RE STANDING IN MY FOOD!
JIM DAVIS 1-25
THAT WAS A GOOD ONE. NOW IT'S MY TURN. THIS IS A MOVIE TITLE, OKAY?
GARFIELD

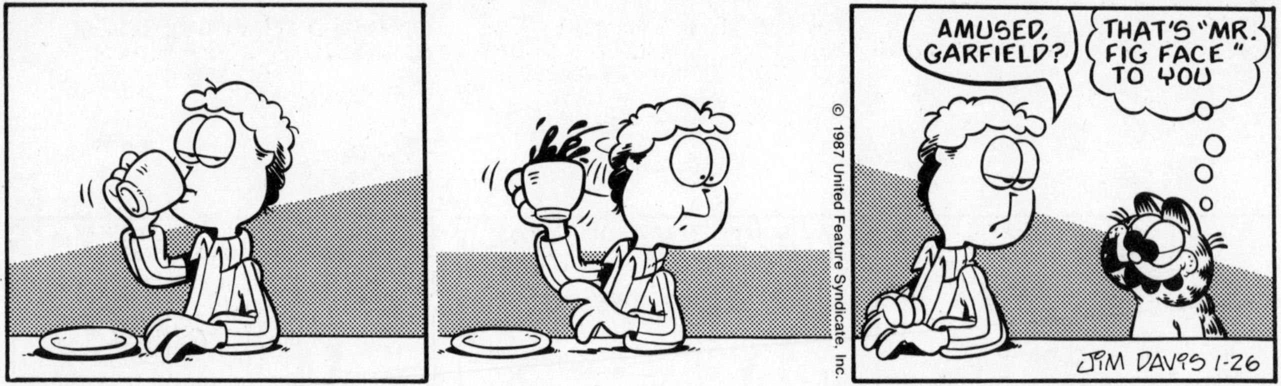
AMUSED, GARFIELD?
THAT'S "MR. FIG FACE" TO YOU
JIM DAVIS 1-26
© 1987 United Feature Syndicate, Inc.

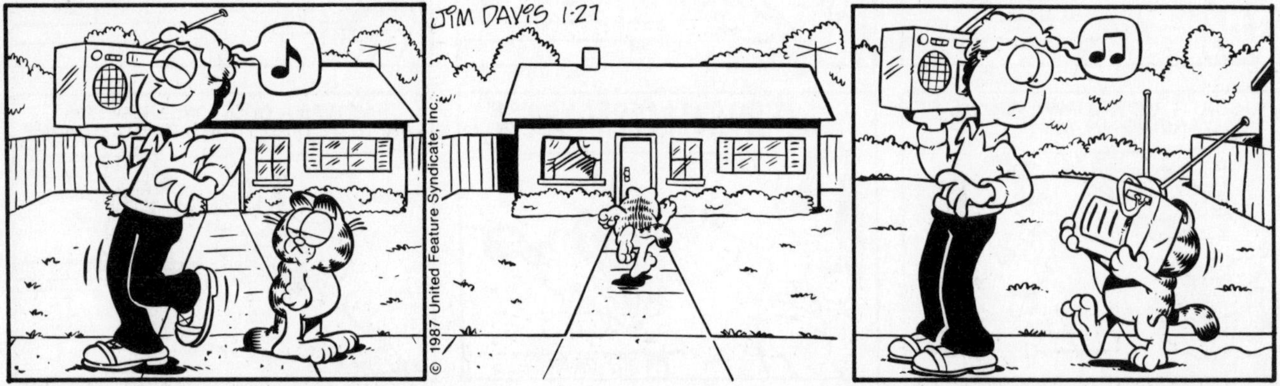
JIM DAVIS 1-27
© 1987 United Feature Syndicate, Inc.

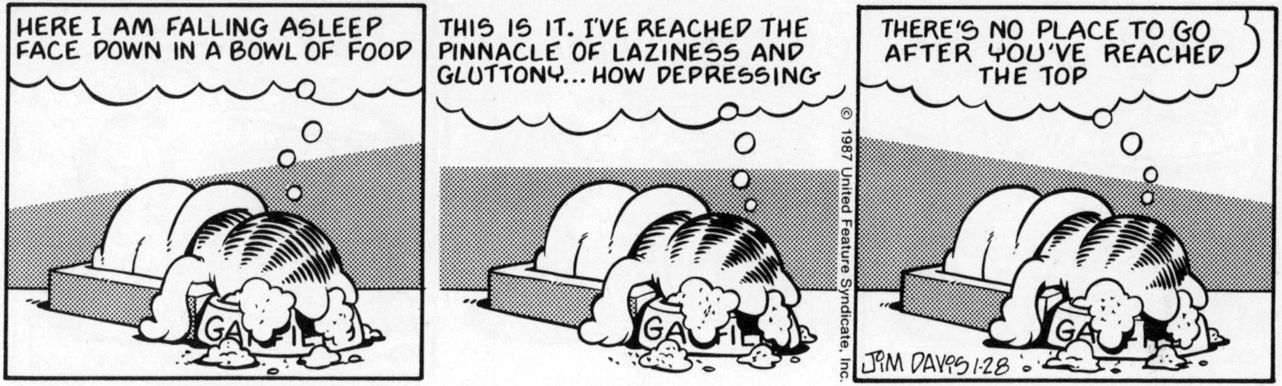
HERE I AM FALLING ASLEEP FACE DOWN IN A BOWL OF FOOD
THIS IS IT. I'VE REACHED THE PINNACLE OF LAZINESS AND GLUTTONY... HOW DEPRESSING
THERE'S NO PLACE TO GO AFTER YOU'VE REACHED THE TOP
GARFIELD
JIM DAVIS 1-28


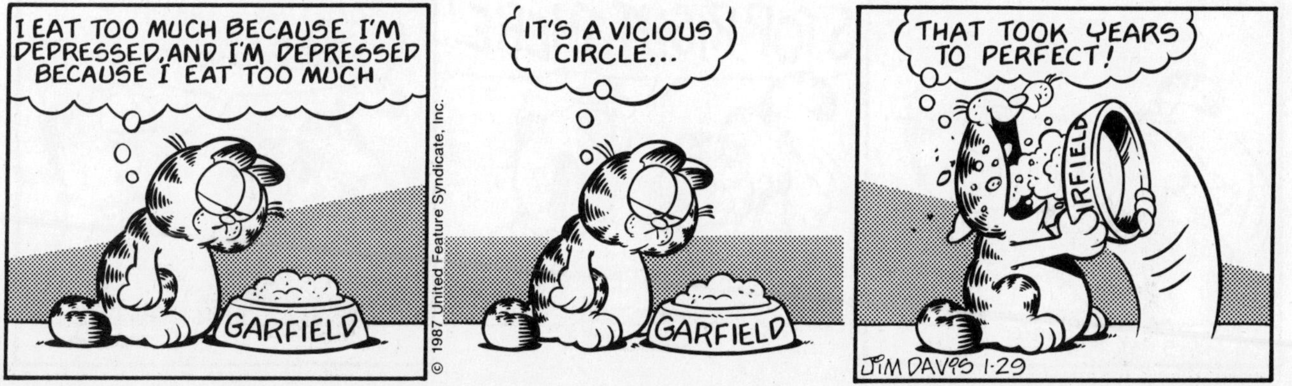
I EAT TOO MUCH BECAUSE I'M DEPRESSED, AND I'M DEPRESSED BECAUSE I EAT TOO MUCH
GARFIELD
IT'S A VICIOUS CIRCLE...
GARFIELD
THAT TOOK YEARS TO PERFECT!
GARFIELD
JIM DAVIS 1-29

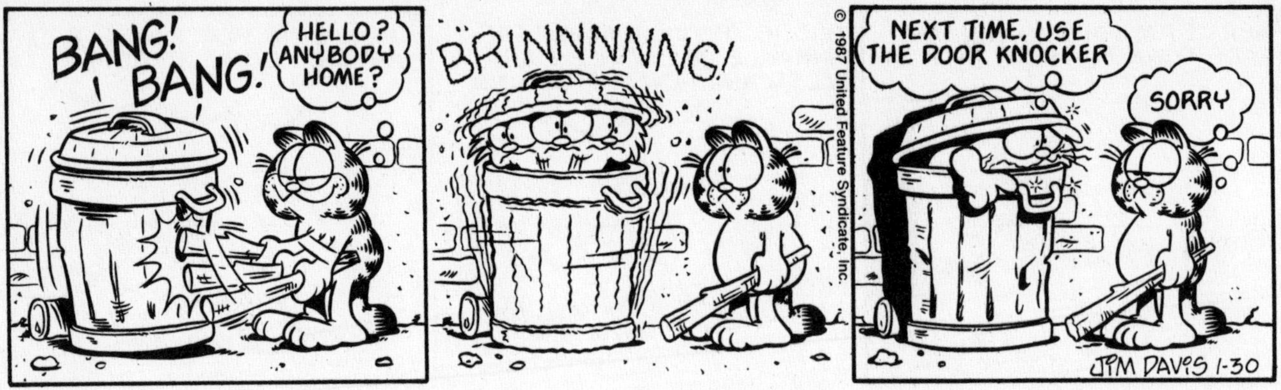
BANG! BANG!
HELLO? ANYBODY HOME?
BRINNNNNNG!
© 1987 United Feature Syndicate, Inc.
NEXT TIME, USE THE DOOR KNOCKER
SORRY
JIM DAVIS 1-30

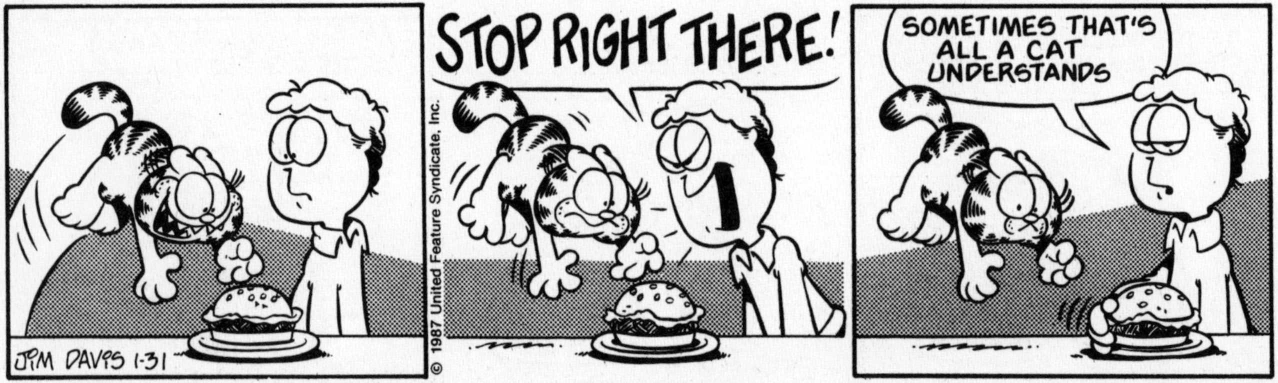
JIM DAVIS 1-31
© 1987 United Feature Syndicate, Inc.
STOP RIGHT THERE!
SOMETIMES THAT'S ALL A CAT UNDERSTANDS

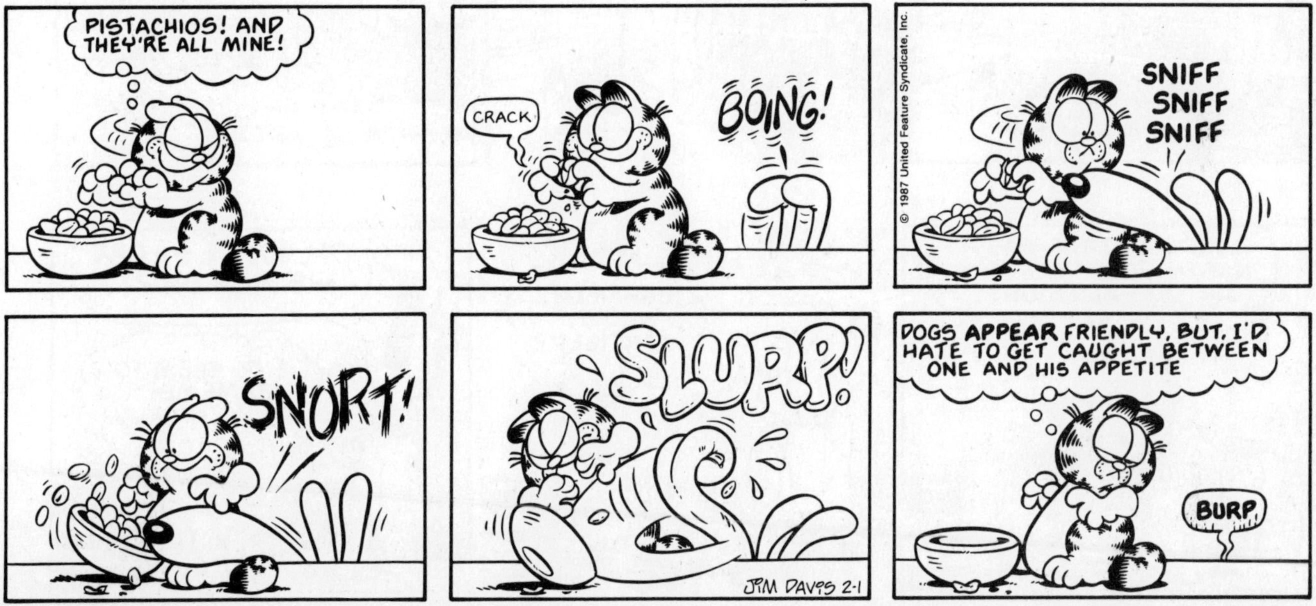

PISTACHIOS! AND THEY'RE ALL MINE!
CRACK
BOING!
© 1987 United Feature Syndicate, Inc.
SNIFF SNIFF SNIFF
SNORT!
SLURP!
JIM DAVIS 2-1
DOGS APPEAR FRIENDLY, BUT, I'D HATE TO GET CAUGHT BETWEEN ONE AND HIS APPETITE
BURP

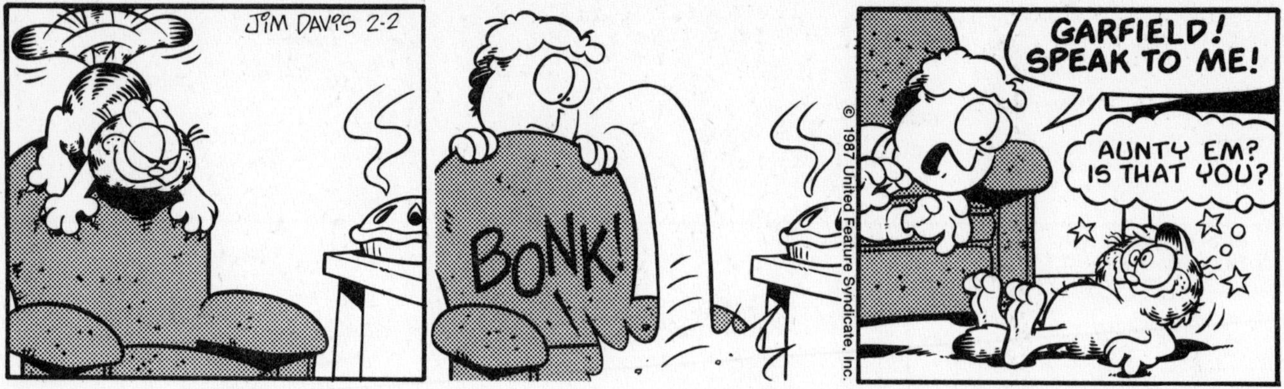
JIM DAVIS 2-2
BONK!
© 1987 United Feature Syndicate, Inc.
GARFIELD! SPEAK TO ME!
AUNTY EM? IS THAT YOU?

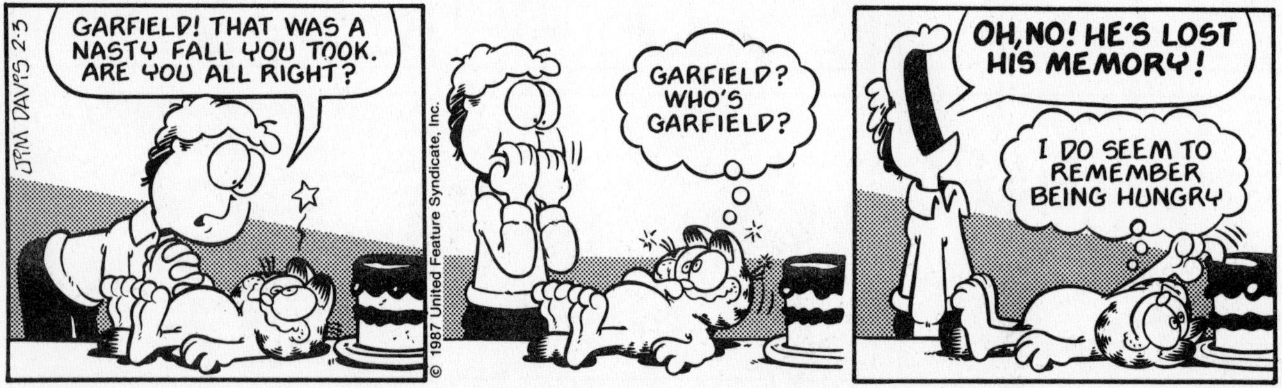
JIM DAVIS 2-3
GARFIELD! THAT WAS A NASTY FALL YOU TOOK. ARE YOU ALL RIGHT?
© 1987 United Feature Syndicate, Inc.
GARFIELD? WHO'S GARFIELD?
OH, NO! HE'S LOST HIS MEMORY!
I DO SEEM TO REMEMBER BEING HUNGRY

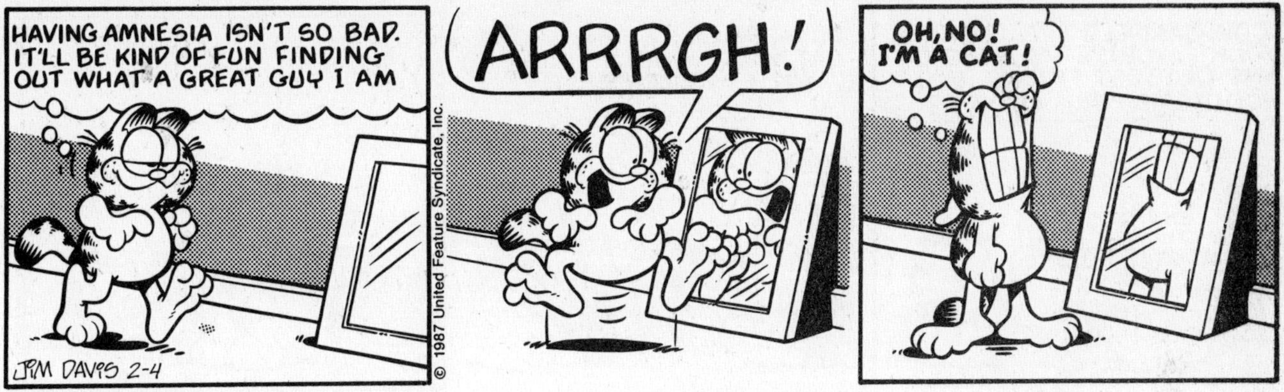
HAVING AMNESIA ISN'T SO BAD. IT'LL BE KIND OF FUN FINDING OUT WHAT A GREAT GUY I AM
JIM DAVIS 2-4
© 1987 United Feature Syndicate, Inc.
ARRRGH!
OH, NO! I'M A CAT!

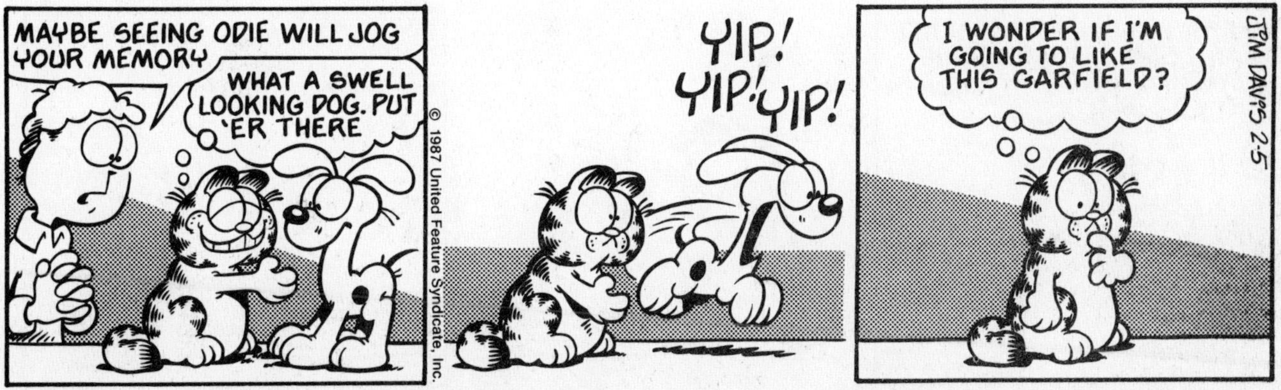
MAYBE SEEING ODIE WILL JOG YOUR MEMORY
WHAT A SWELL LOOKING DOG. PUT 'ER THERE
© 1987 United Feature Syndicate, Inc.
YIP! YIP! YIP!
I WONDER IF I'M GOING TO LIKE THIS GARFIELD?
JIM DAVIS 2-5

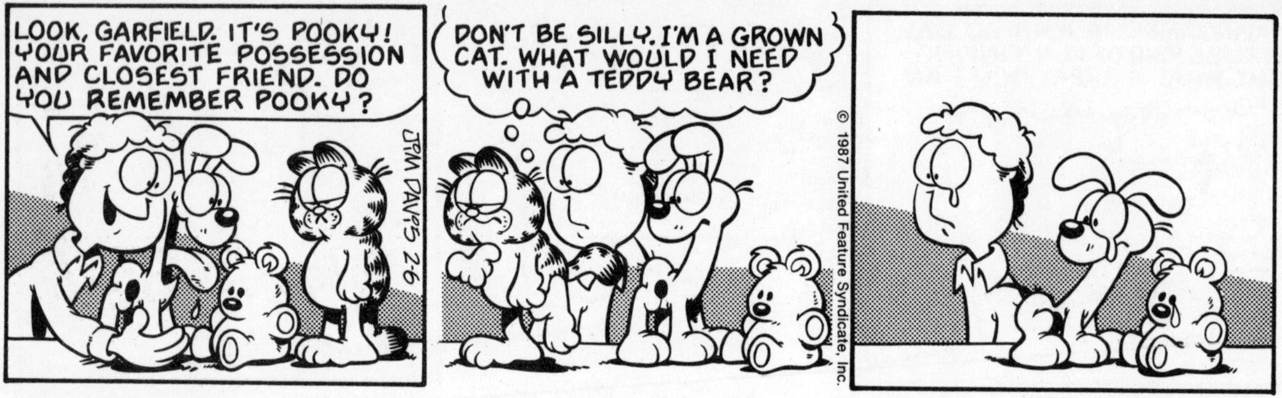
LOOK, GARFIELD. IT'S POOKY! YOUR FAVORITE POSSESSION AND CLOSEST FRIEND. DO YOU REMEMBER POOKY?
JIM DAVIS 2-6
DON'T BE SILLY. I'M A GROWN CAT. WHAT WOULD I NEED WITH A TEDDY BEAR?
© 1987 United Feature Syndicate, Inc.

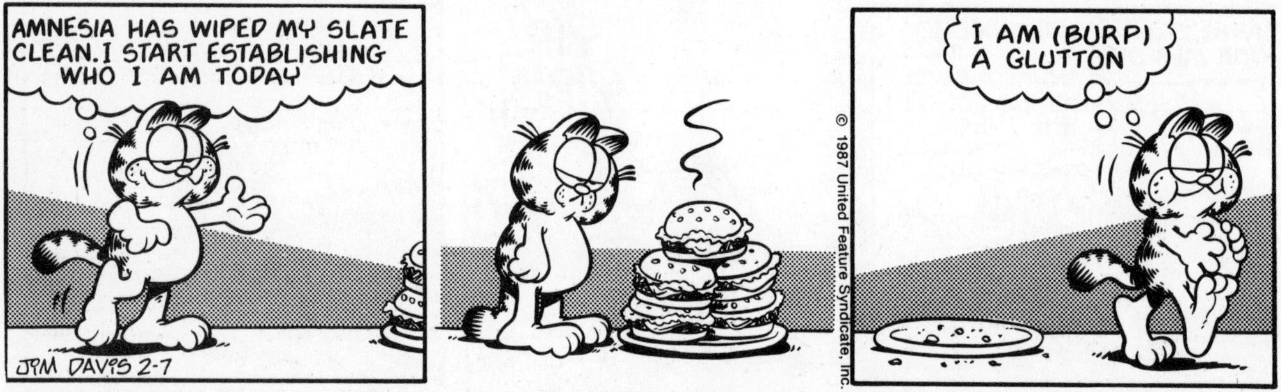
AMNESIA HAS WIPED MY SLATE CLEAN. I START ESTABLISHING WHO I AM TODAY
JIM DAVIS 2-7
© 1987 United Feature Syndicate, Inc.
I AM (BURP) A GLUTTON

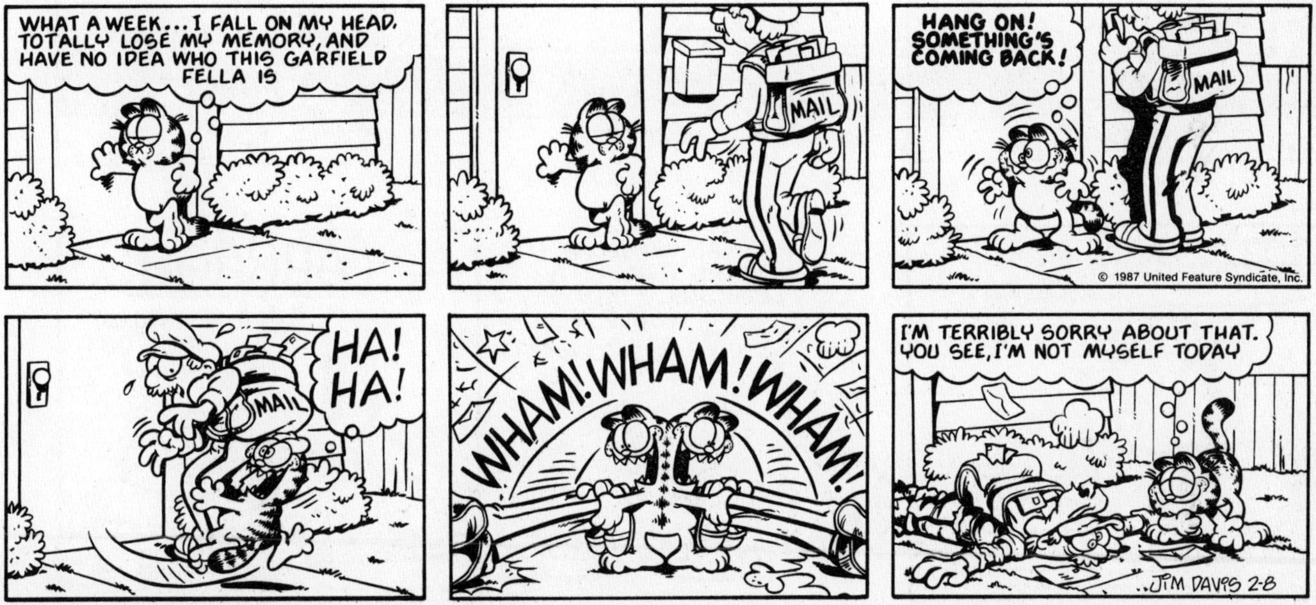
WHAT A WEEK... I FALL ON MY HEAD, TOTALLY LOSE MY MEMORY, AND HAVE NO IDEA WHO THIS GARFIELD FELLA IS
MAIL
HANG ON! SOMETHING'S COMING BACK!
MAIL
© 1987 United Feature Syndicate, Inc.
MAIL
HA! HA!
WHAM! WHAM! WHAM!
I'M TERRIBLY SORRY ABOUT THAT. YOU SEE, I'M NOT MYSELF TODAY
JIM DAVIS 2-8

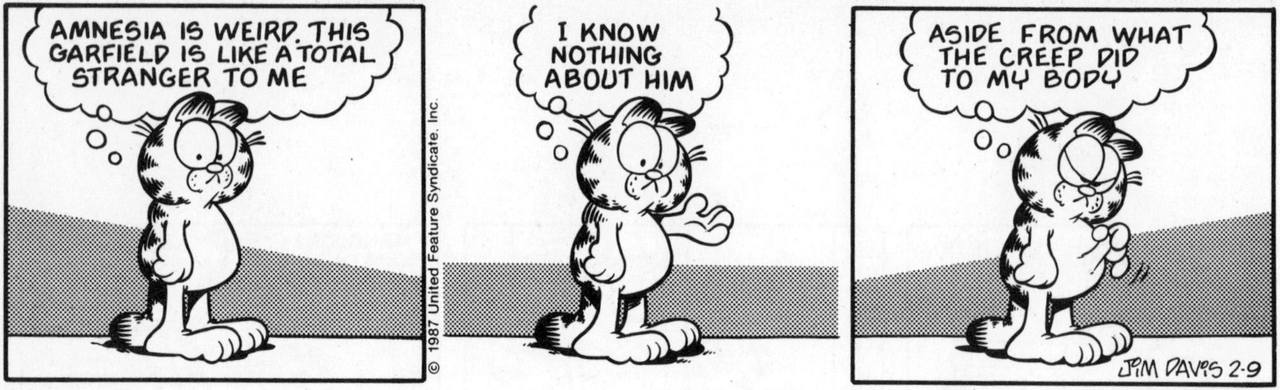
AMNESIA IS WEIRD. THIS GARFIELD IS LIKE A TOTAL STRANGER TO ME
© 1987 United Feature Syndicate, Inc.
I KNOW NOTHING ABOUT HIM
ASIDE FROM WHAT THE CREEP DID TO MY BODY
JIM DAVIS 2-9

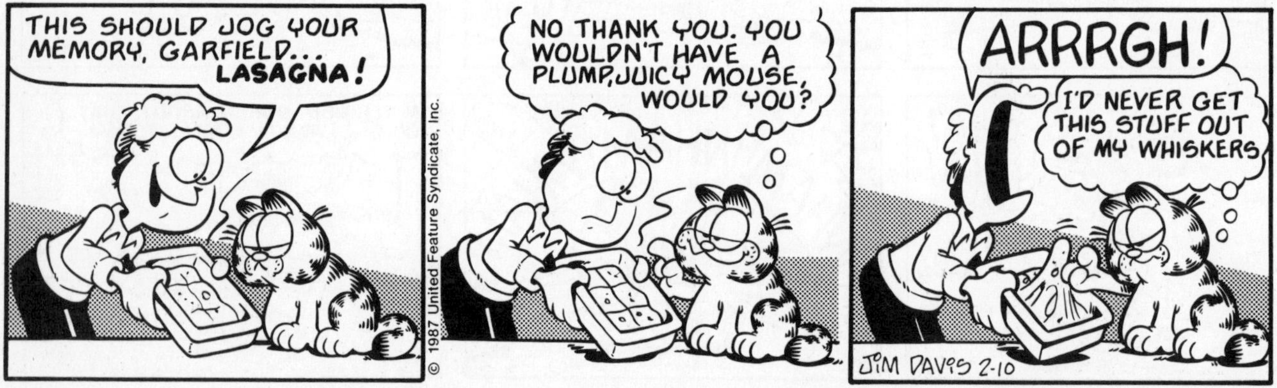
THIS SHOULD JOG YOUR MEMORY, GARFIELD... **LASAGNA!**
© 1987 United Feature Syndicate, Inc.
NO THANK YOU. YOU WOULDN'T HAVE A PLUMP, JUICY MOUSE, WOULD YOU?
ARRRGH!
I'D NEVER GET THIS STUFF OUT OF MY WHISKERS
JIM DAVIS 2-10

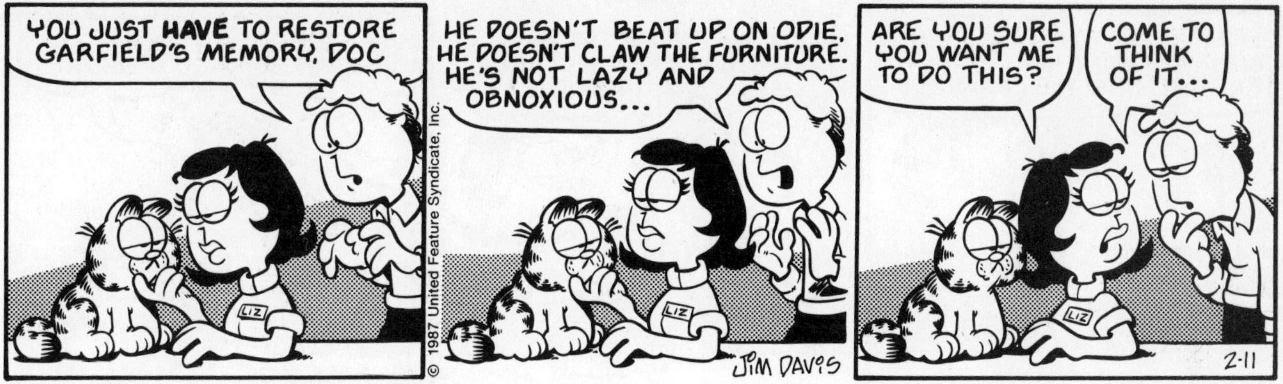
YOU JUST **HAVE** TO RESTORE GARFIELD'S MEMORY, DOC
HE DOESN'T BEAT UP ON ODIE. HE DOESN'T CLAW THE FURNITURE. HE'S NOT LAZY AND OBNOXIOUS...
ARE YOU SURE YOU WANT ME TO DO THIS?
COME TO THINK OF IT...
LIZ
JIM DAVIS
2-11


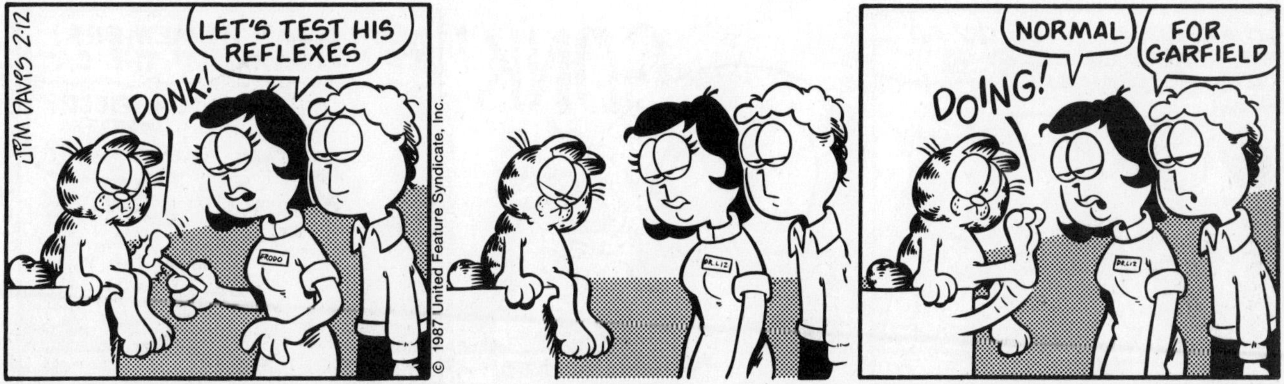
JIM DAVIS 2-12
LET'S TEST HIS REFLEXES
DONK!
NORMAL
FOR GARFIELD
DOING!

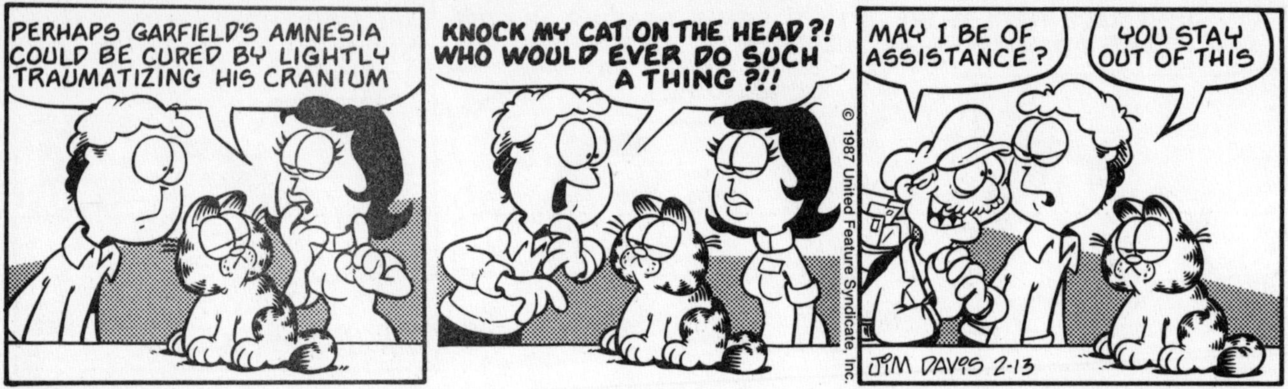
PERHAPS GARFIELD'S AMNESIA COULD BE CURED BY LIGHTLY TRAUMATIZING HIS CRANIUM
KNOCK MY CAT ON THE HEAD ?! WHO WOULD EVER DO SUCH A THING ?!!
MAY I BE OF ASSISTANCE ?
YOU STAY OUT OF THIS
JIM DAVIS 2-13
© 1987 United Feature Syndicate, Inc.

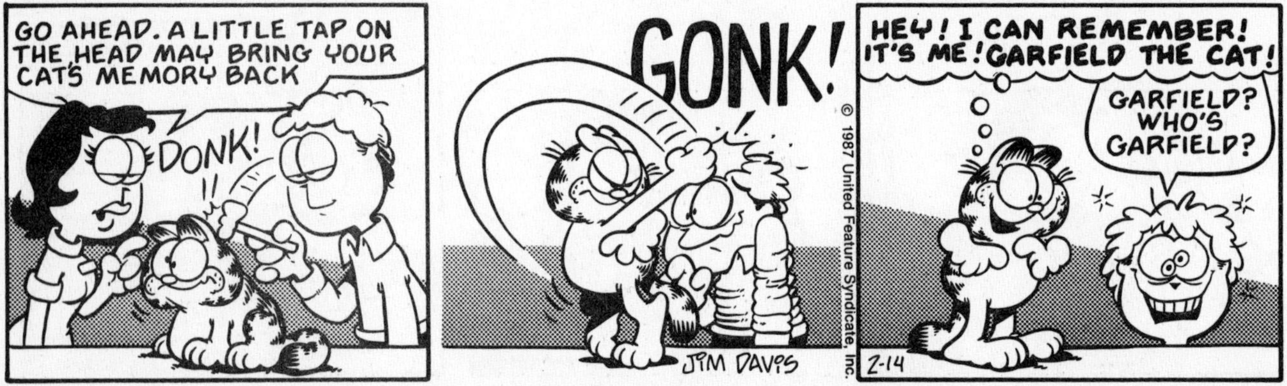
GO AHEAD. A LITTLE TAP ON THE HEAD MAY BRING YOUR CAT'S MEMORY BACK
DONK!
GONK!
HEY! I CAN REMEMBER! IT'S ME! GARFIELD THE CAT!
GARFIELD? WHO'S GARFIELD?
JIM DAVIS
2-14
© 1987 United Feature Syndicate, Inc.

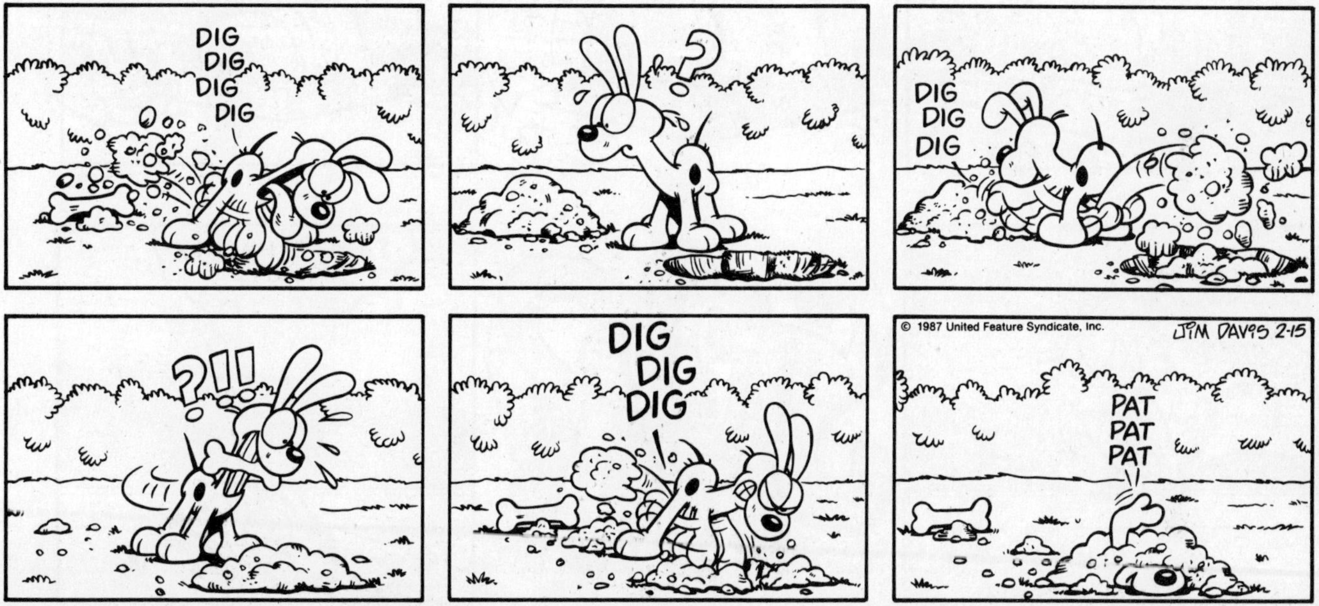
DIG
DIG
DIG
DIG
?
DIG
DIG
DIG
?!!
DIG
DIG
DIG
© 1987 United Feature Syndicate, Inc.
JIM DAVIS 2-15
PAT
PAT
PAT

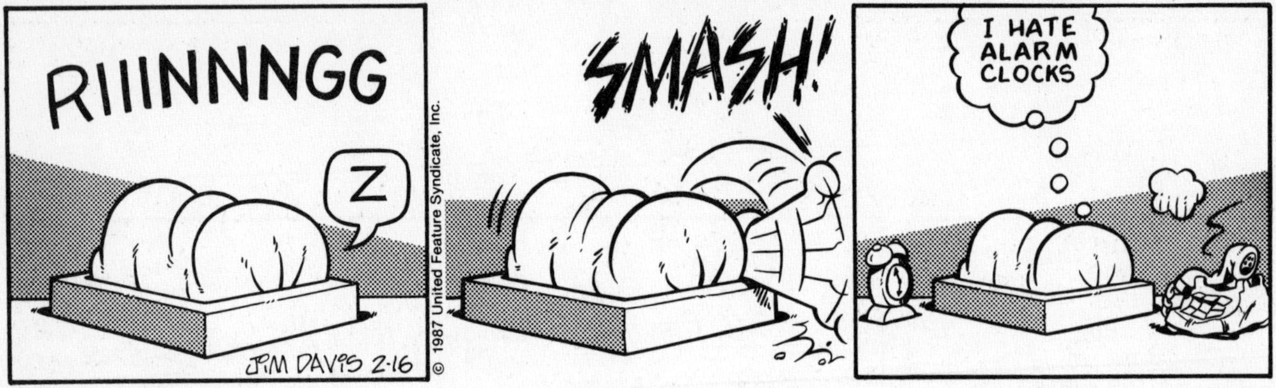
RIIINNNGG
Z
JIM DAVIS 2-16
© 1987 United Feature Syndicate, Inc.
SMASH!
I HATE ALARM CLOCKS

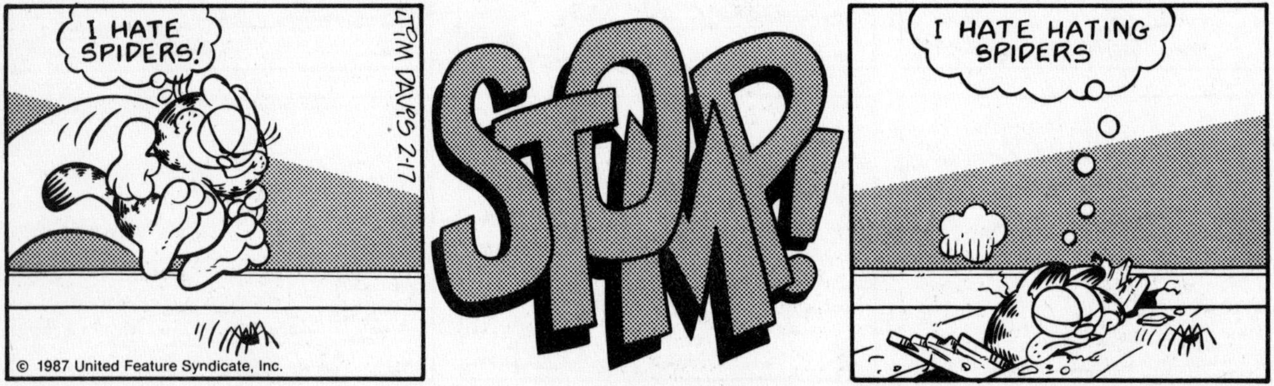
I HATE SPIDERS!
JIM DAVIS 2-17
© 1987 United Feature Syndicate, Inc.
STOMP!
I HATE HATING SPIDERS

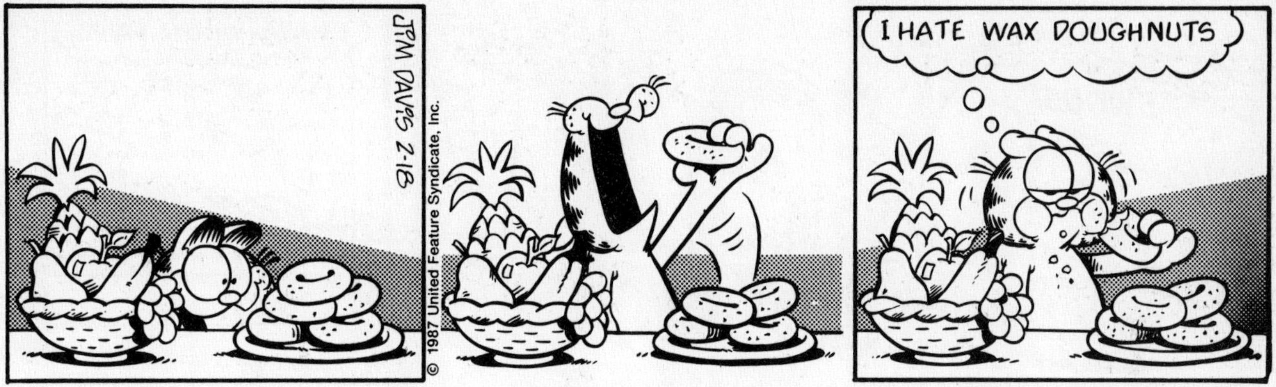
JIM DAVIS 2-18
© 1987 United Feature Syndicate, Inc.
I HATE WAX DOUGHNUTS

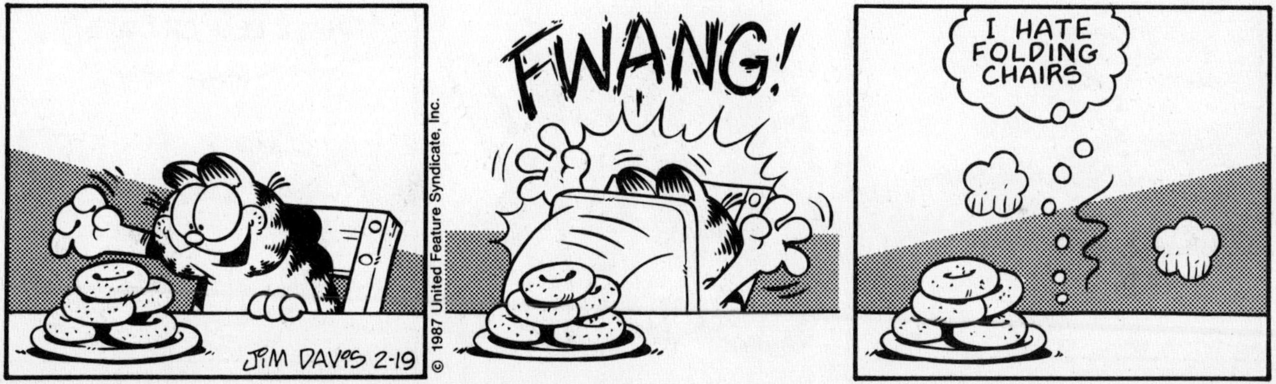
JIM DAVIS 2-19
© 1987 United Feature Syndicate, Inc.
FWANG!
I HATE FOLDING CHAIRS

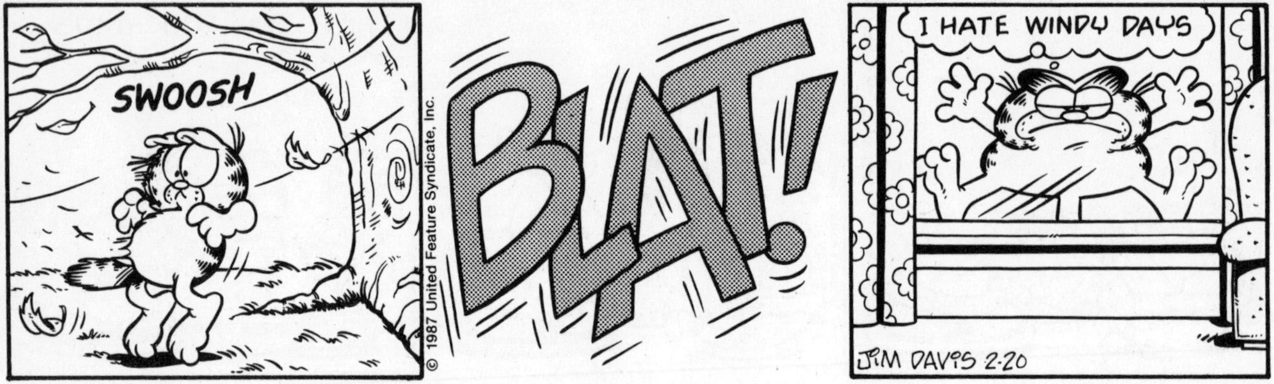
SWOOSH
© 1987 United Feature Syndicate, Inc.
BLAT!
I HATE WINDY DAYS
JIM DAVIS 2-20

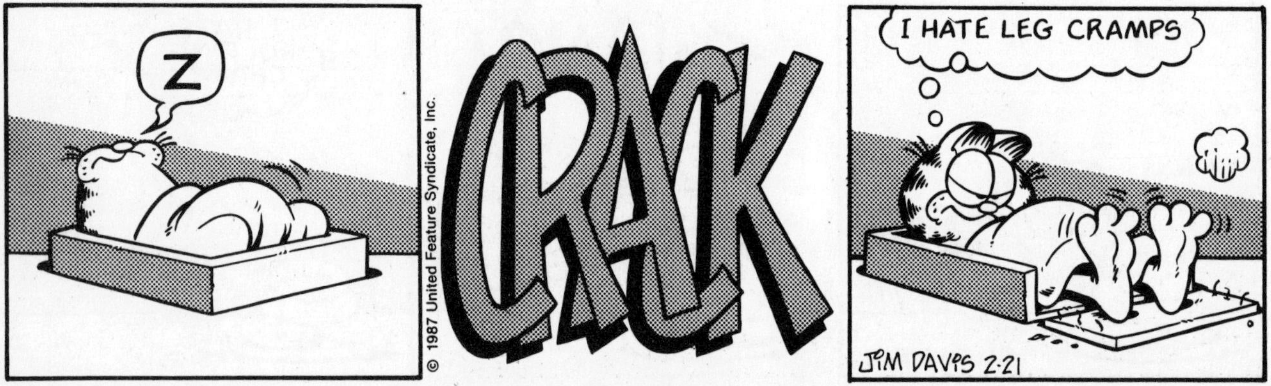
Z
© 1987 United Feature Syndicate, Inc.
CRACK
I HATE LEG CRAMPS
JIM DAVIS 2-21

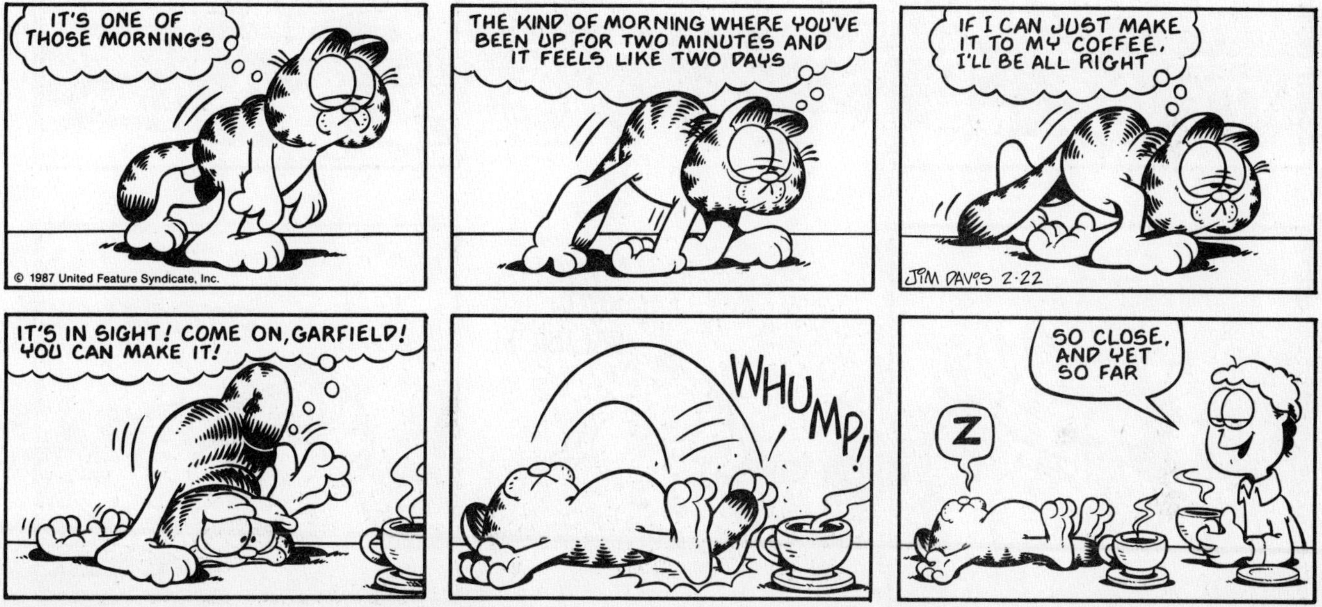
IT'S ONE OF THOSE MORNINGS
© 1987 United Feature Syndicate, Inc.
THE KIND OF MORNING WHERE YOU'VE BEEN UP FOR TWO MINUTES AND IT FEELS LIKE TWO DAYS
IF I CAN JUST MAKE IT TO MY COFFEE, I'LL BE ALL RIGHT
JIM DAVIS 2·22
IT'S IN SIGHT! COME ON, GARFIELD! YOU CAN MAKE IT!
WHUMP!
Z
SO CLOSE, AND YET SO FAR

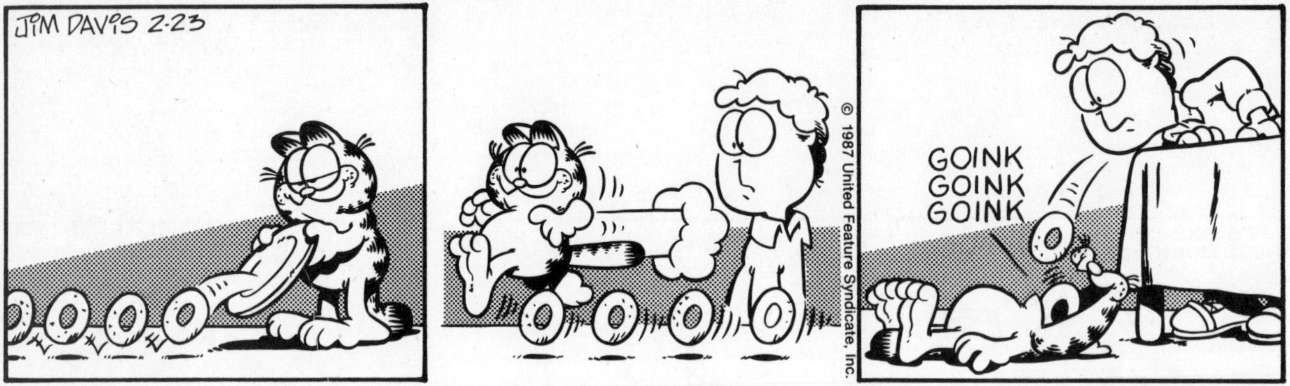
JIM DAVIS 2-23
© 1987 United Feature Syndicate, Inc.
GOINK
GOINK
GOINK

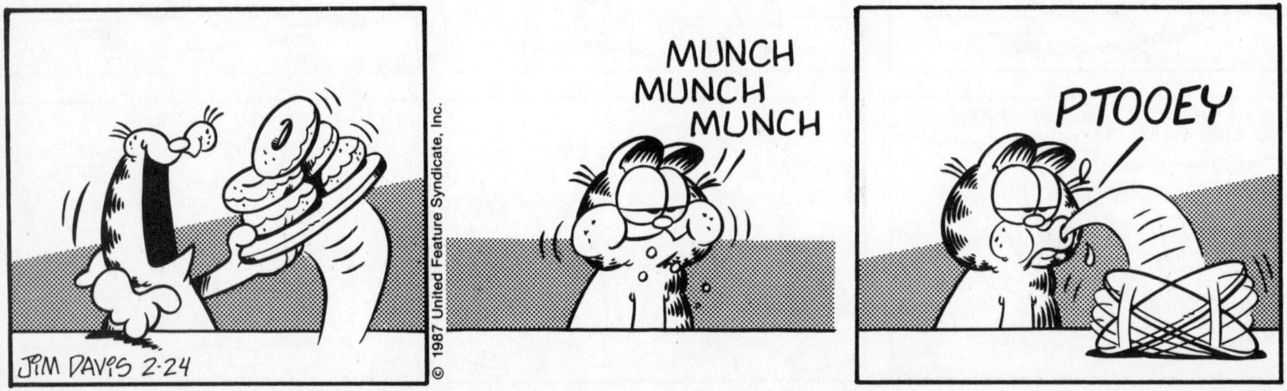
JIM DAVIS 2-24
© 1987 United Feature Syndicate, Inc.
MUNCH
MUNCH
MUNCH
PTOOEY

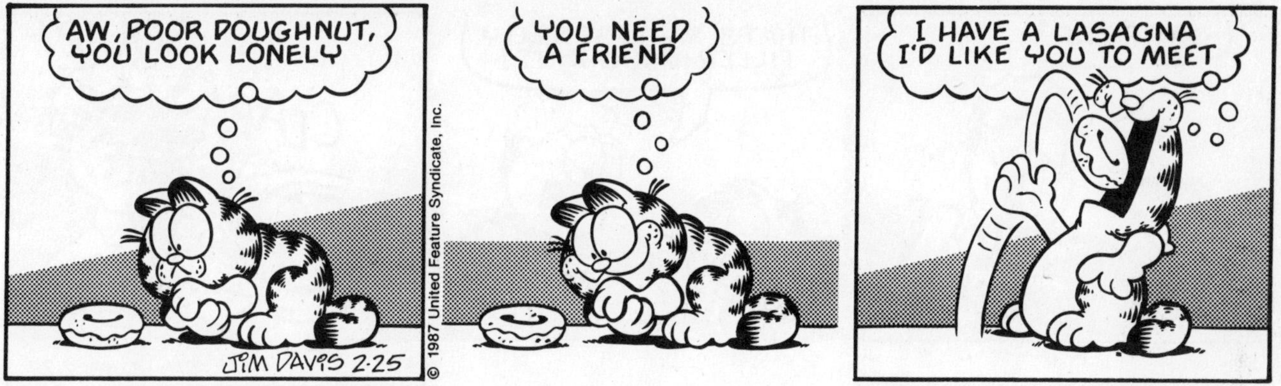
AW, POOR DOUGHNUT, YOU LOOK LONELY
YOU NEED A FRIEND
I HAVE A LASAGNA I'D LIKE YOU TO MEET
JIM DAVIS 2-25


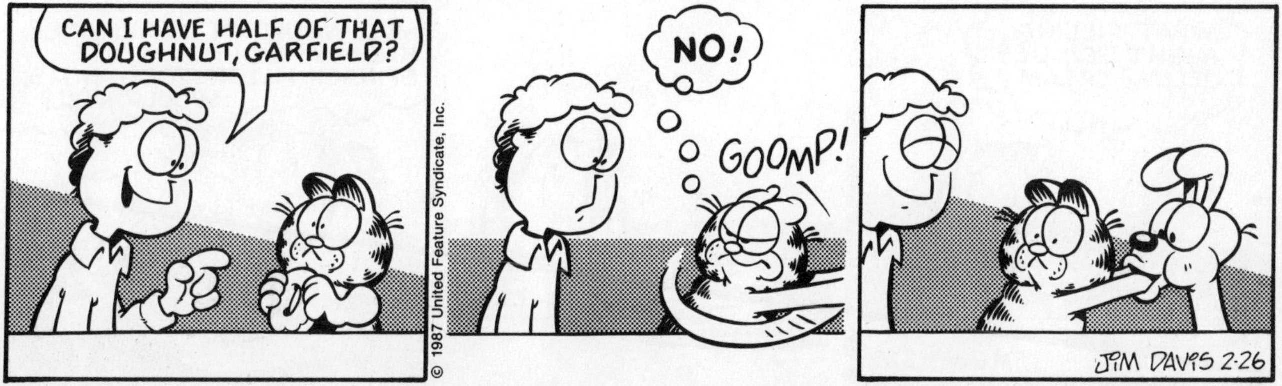
CAN I HAVE HALF OF THAT DOUGHNUT, GARFIELD?
NO!
GOOMP!
JIM DAVIS 2-26

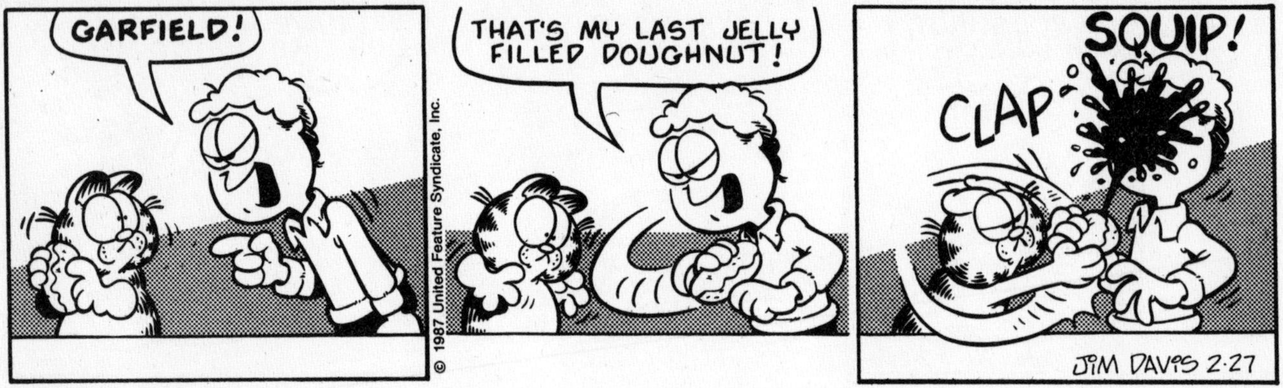
GARFIELD!
THAT'S MY LAST JELLY FILLED DOUGHNUT!
© 1987 United Feature Syndicate, Inc.
CLAP
SQUIP!
JIM DAVIS 2·27

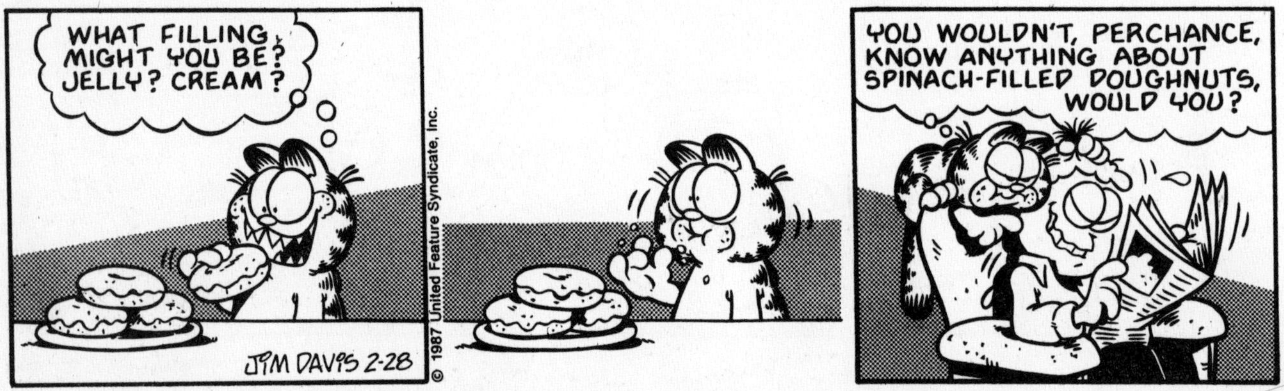
WHAT FILLING MIGHT YOU BE? JELLY? CREAM?
JIM DAVIS 2-28
© 1987 United Feature Syndicate, Inc.
YOU WOULDN'T, PERCHANCE, KNOW ANYTHING ABOUT SPINACH-FILLED DOUGHNUTS, WOULD YOU?

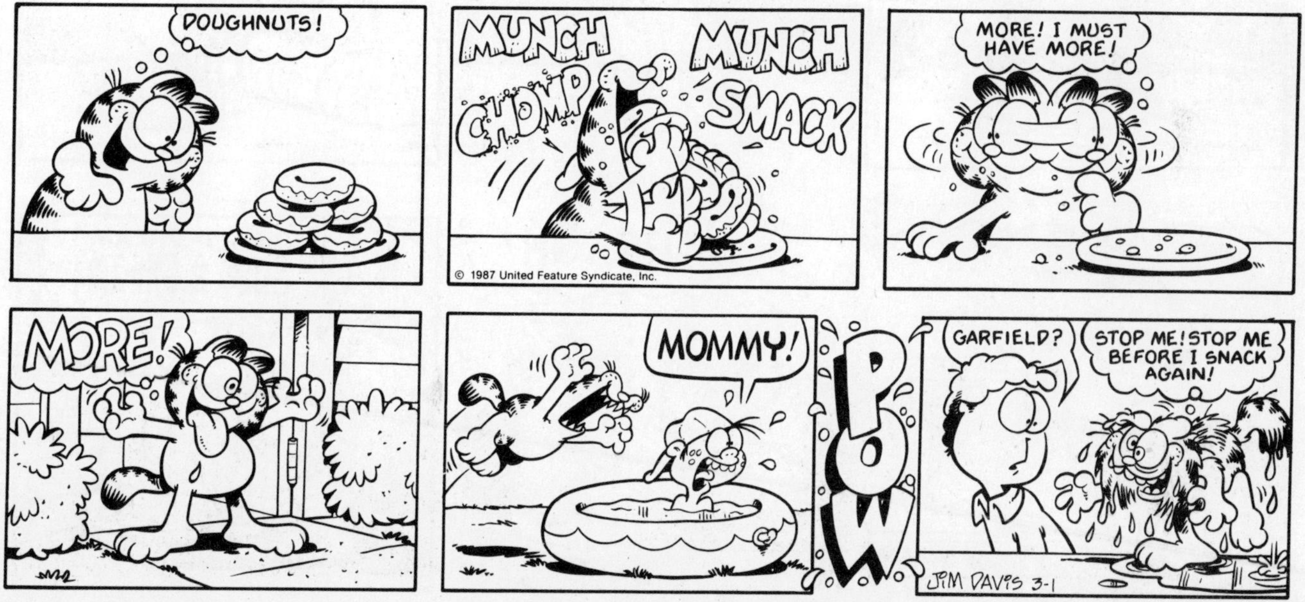

DOUGHNUTS!
MUNCH
CHOMP
MUNCH
SMACK
© 1987 United Feature Syndicate, Inc.
MORE! I MUST HAVE MORE!
MORE!
MOMMY!
POW
GARFIELD?
STOP ME! STOP ME BEFORE I SNACK AGAIN!
JIM DAVIS 3-1

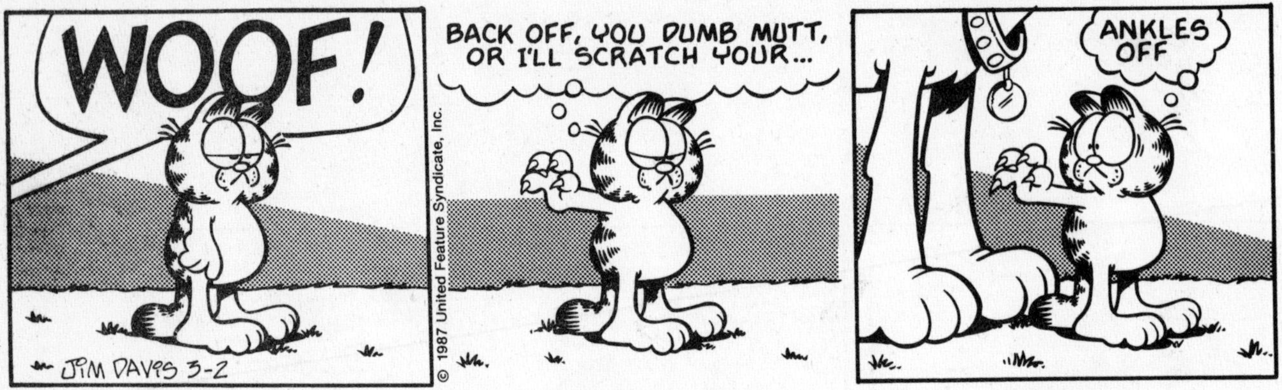
WOOF!
JIM DAVIS 3-2
BACK OFF, YOU DUMB MUTT, OR I'LL SCRATCH YOUR...
© 1987 United Feature Syndicate, Inc.
ANKLES OFF

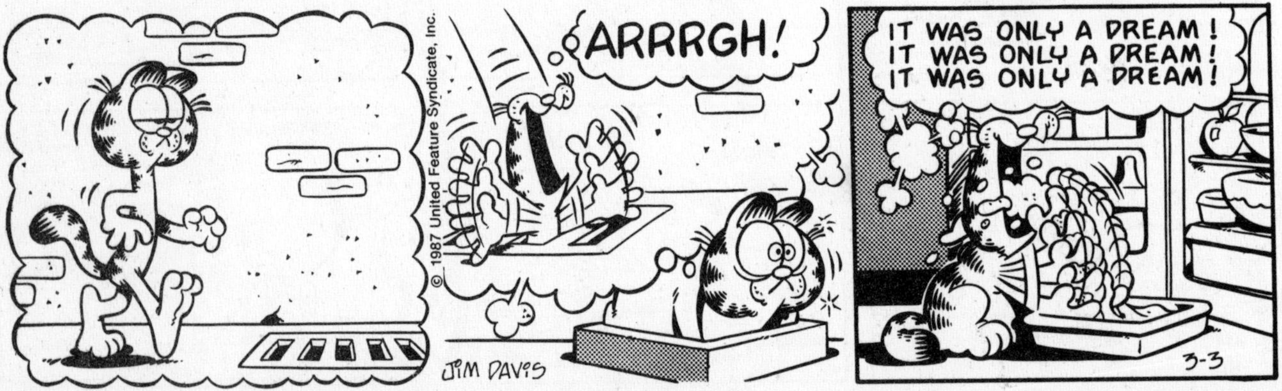
© 1987 United Feature Syndicate, Inc.
ARRRGH!
JIM DAVIS
IT WAS ONLY A DREAM!
IT WAS ONLY A DREAM!
IT WAS ONLY A DREAM!
3-3

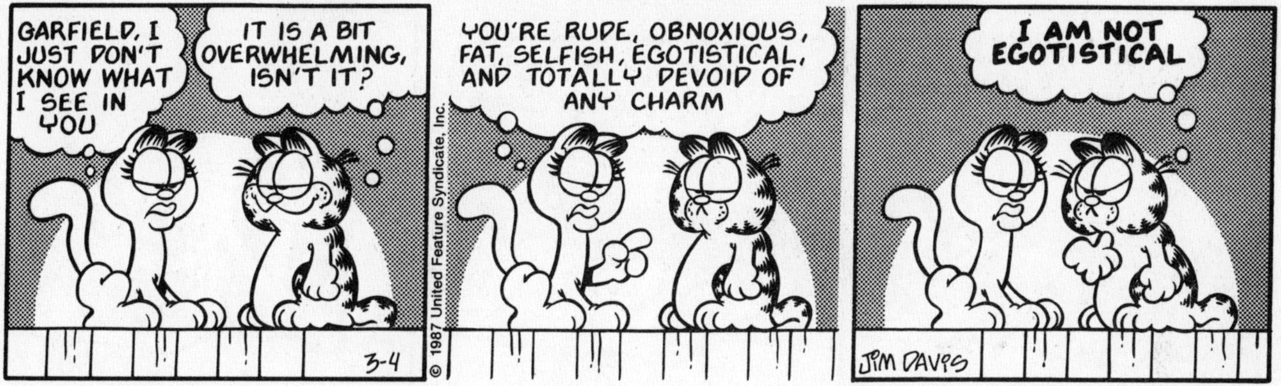
GARFIELD, I JUST DON'T KNOW WHAT I SEE IN YOU
IT IS A BIT OVERWHELMING, ISN'T IT?
YOU'RE RUDE, OBNOXIOUS, FAT, SELFISH, EGOTISTICAL, AND TOTALLY DEVOID OF ANY CHARM
I AM NOT EGOTISTICAL
3-4
© 1987 United Feature Syndicate, Inc.
JIM DAVIS

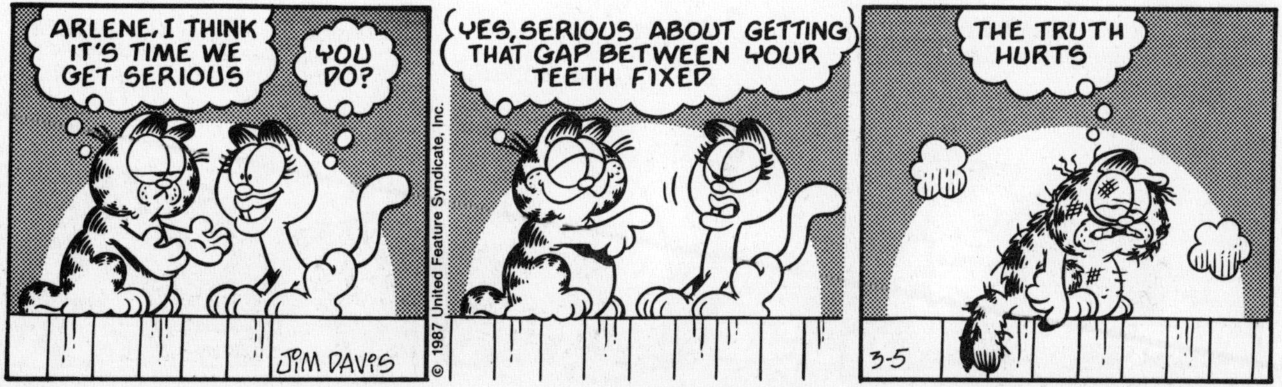
ARLENE, I THINK IT'S TIME WE GET SERIOUS
YOU DO?
JIM DAVIS
© 1987 United Feature Syndicate, Inc.
YES, SERIOUS ABOUT GETTING THAT GAP BETWEEN YOUR TEETH FIXED
THE TRUTH HURTS
3-5

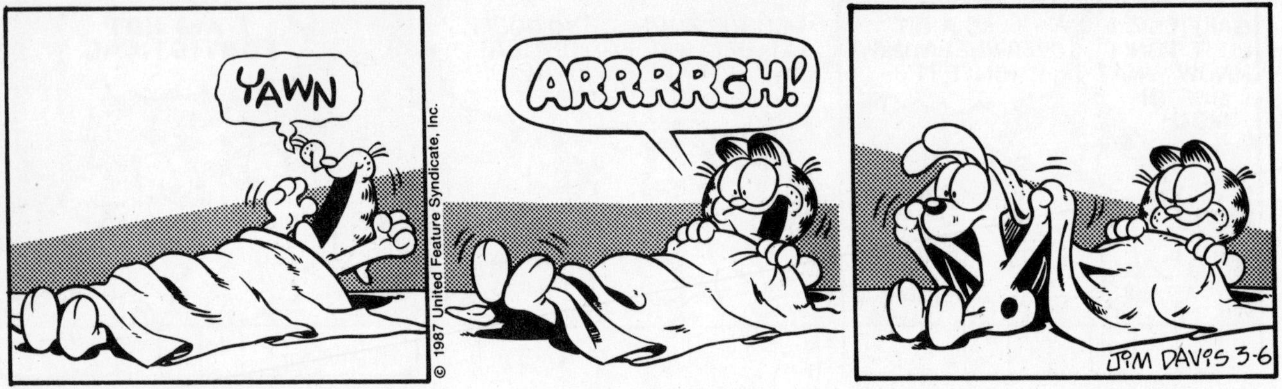
YAWN
ARRRRGH!
© 1987 United Feature Syndicate, Inc.
JIM DAVIS 3-6

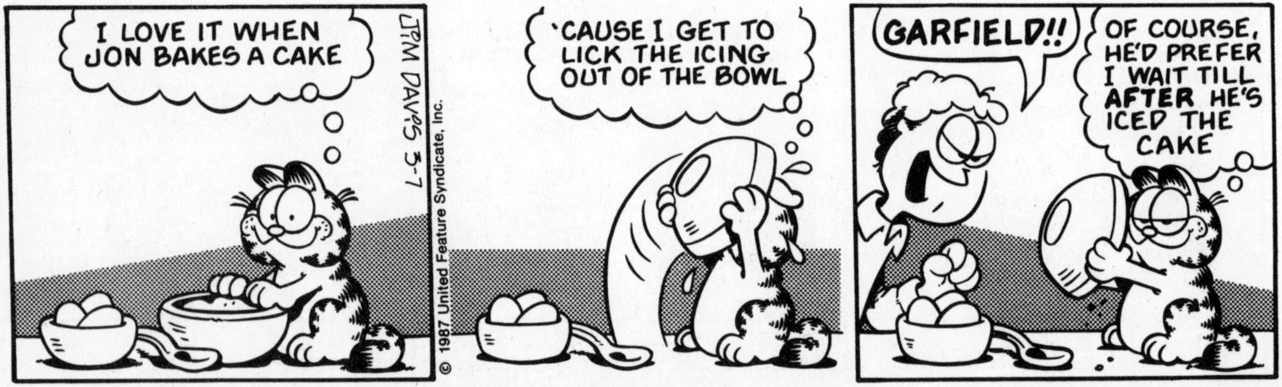
I LOVE IT WHEN JON BAKES A CAKE
JIM DAVIS 3-7
© 1987 United Feature Syndicate, Inc.
'CAUSE I GET TO LICK THE ICING OUT OF THE BOWL
GARFIELD!!
OF COURSE, HE'D PREFER I WAIT TILL AFTER HE'S ICED THE CAKE

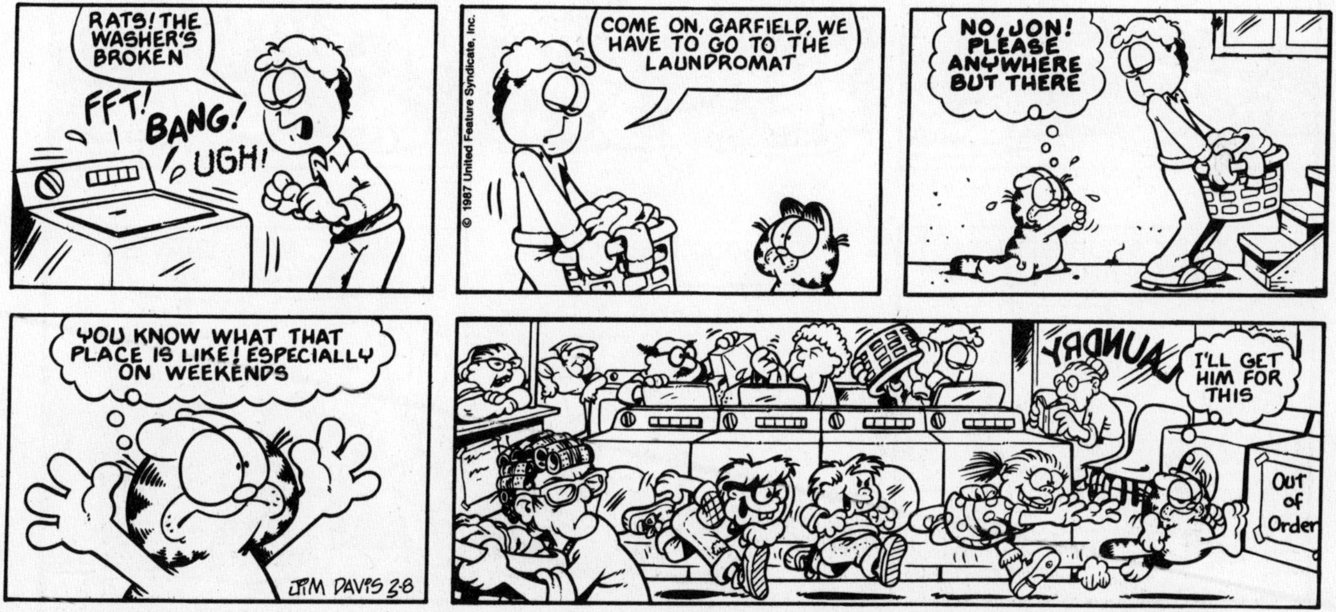
RATS! THE WASHER'S BROKEN
FFT!
BANG!
UGH!
© 1987 United Feature Syndicate, Inc.
COME ON, GARFIELD, WE HAVE TO GO TO THE LAUNDROMAT
NO, JON! PLEASE ANYWHERE BUT THERE
YOU KNOW WHAT THAT PLACE IS LIKE! ESPECIALLY ON WEEKENDS
JIM DAVIS 3-8
LAUNDRY
I'LL GET HIM FOR THIS
Out of Order

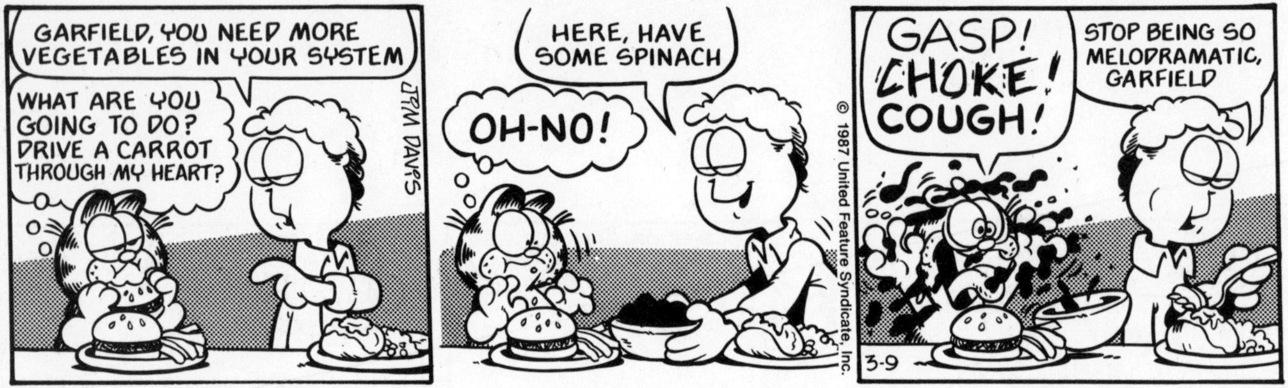
GARFIELD, YOU NEED MORE VEGETABLES IN YOUR SYSTEM
WHAT ARE YOU GOING TO DO? DRIVE A CARROT THROUGH MY HEART?
JIM DAVIS
HERE, HAVE SOME SPINACH
OH-NO!
© 1987 United Feature Syndicate, Inc.
GASP! CHOKE! COUGH!
STOP BEING SO MELODRAMATIC, GARFIELD
3-9

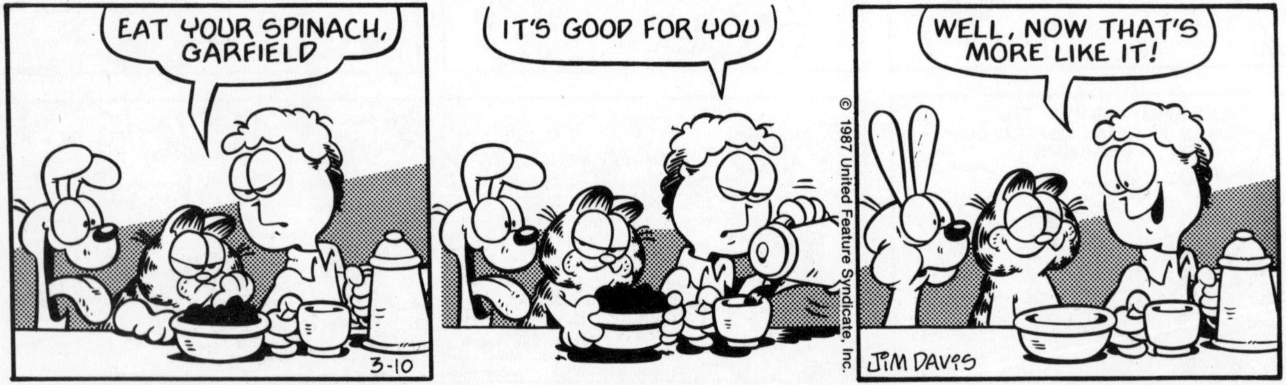
EAT YOUR SPINACH, GARFIELD
3-10
IT'S GOOD FOR YOU
© 1987 United Feature Syndicate, Inc.
WELL, NOW THAT'S MORE LIKE IT!
JIM DAVIS

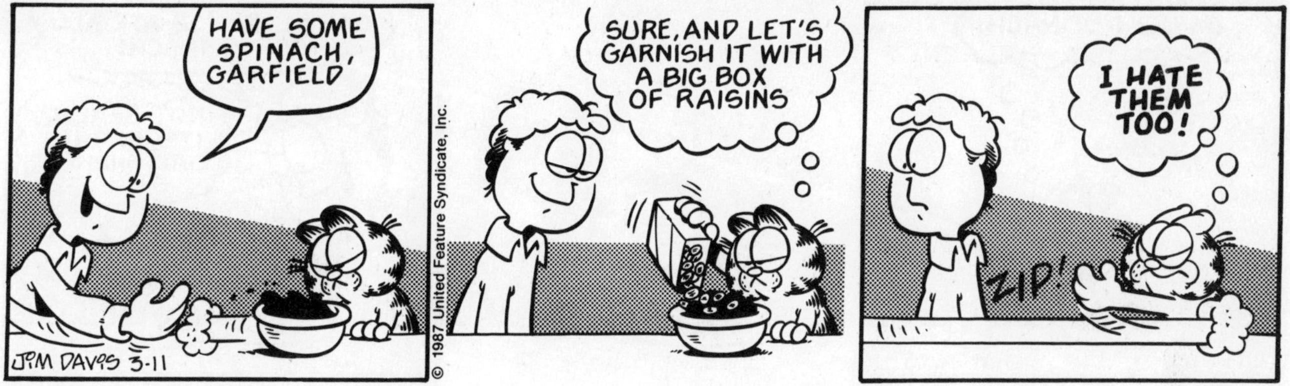
HAVE SOME SPINACH, GARFIELD
JIM DAVIS 3-11
© 1987 United Feature Syndicate, Inc.
SURE, AND LET'S GARNISH IT WITH A BIG BOX OF RAISINS
ZIP!
I HATE THEM TOO!

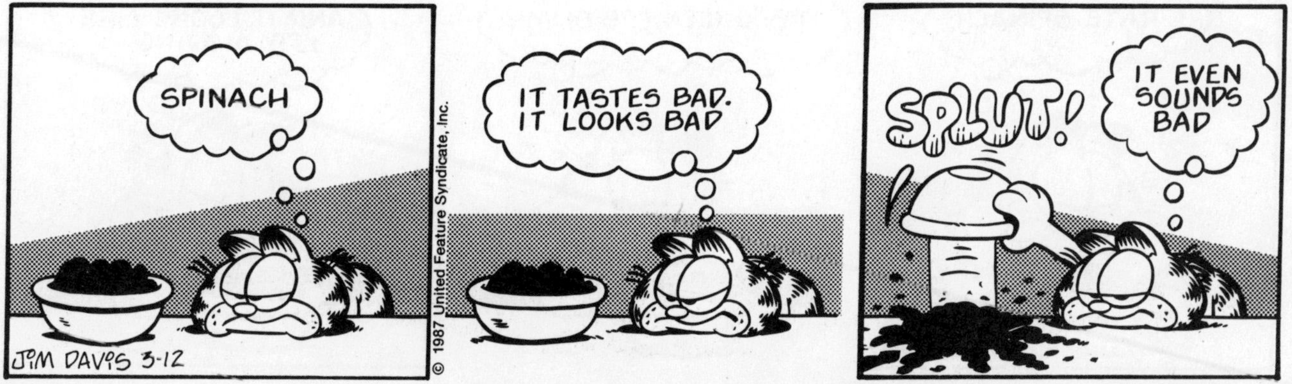
SPINACH
JIM DAVIS 3-12
© 1987 United Feature Syndicate, Inc.
IT TASTES BAD. IT LOOKS BAD
SPLUT!
IT EVEN SOUNDS BAD

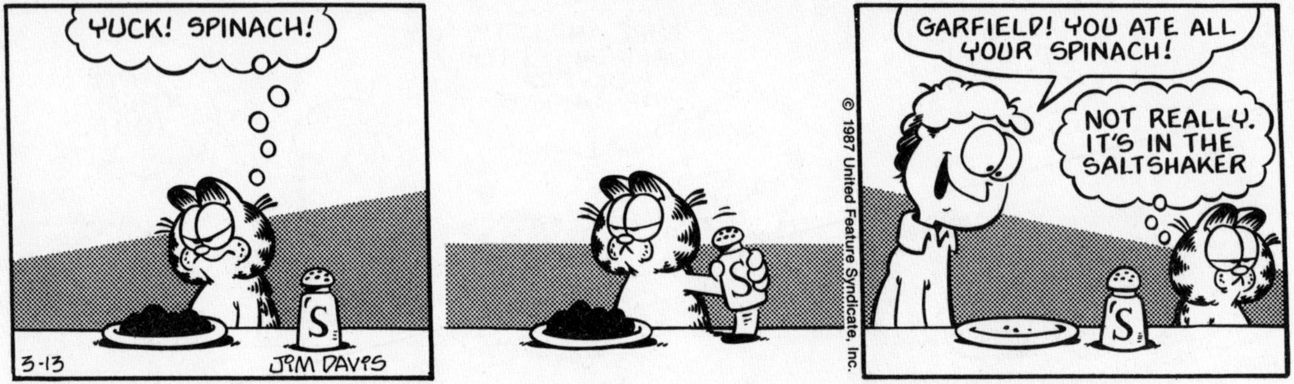
YUCK! SPINACH!
3-13
JIM DAVIS
© 1987 United Feature Syndicate, Inc.
GARFIELD! YOU ATE ALL YOUR SPINACH!
NOT REALLY. IT'S IN THE SALTSHAKER

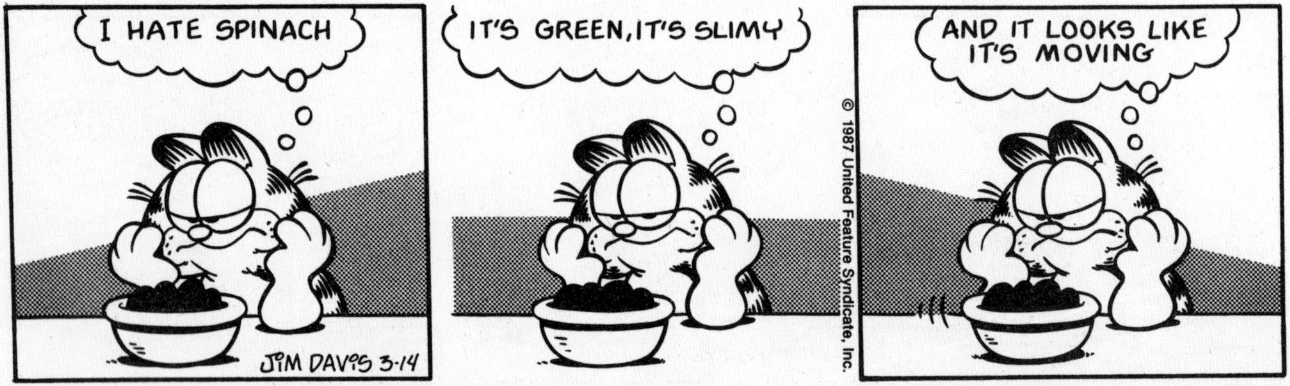
I HATE SPINACH
JIM DAVIS 3-14
IT'S GREEN, IT'S SLIMY
© 1987 United Feature Syndicate, Inc.
AND IT LOOKS LIKE IT'S MOVING

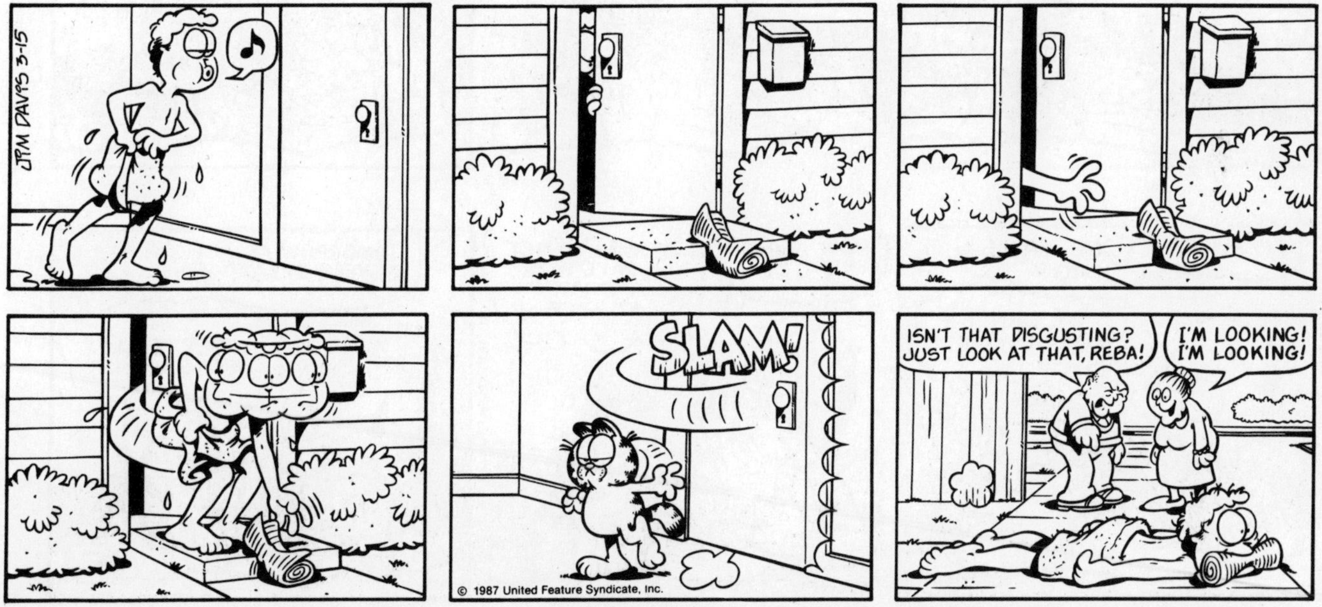
JIM DAVIS 3-15
SLAM!
© 1987 United Feature Syndicate, Inc.
ISN'T THAT DISGUSTING? JUST LOOK AT THAT, REBA!
I'M LOOKING! I'M LOOKING!

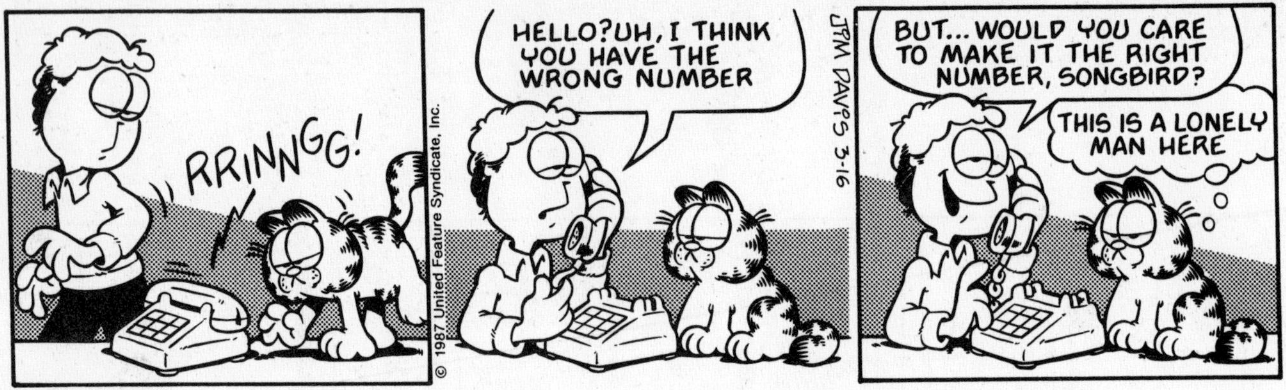
RRINNGG!
© 1987 United Feature Syndicate, Inc.
HELLO? UH, I THINK YOU HAVE THE WRONG NUMBER
JIM DAVIS 3-16
BUT... WOULD YOU CARE TO MAKE IT THE RIGHT NUMBER, SONGBIRD?
THIS IS A LONELY MAN HERE

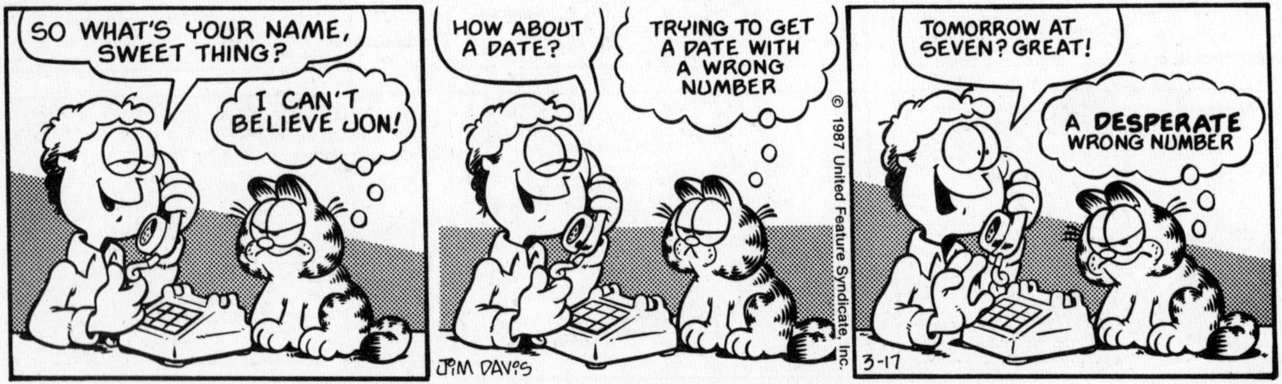
SO WHAT'S YOUR NAME, SWEET THING?
I CAN'T BELIEVE JON!
HOW ABOUT A DATE?
TRYING TO GET A DATE WITH A WRONG NUMBER
JIM DAVIS
© 1987 United Feature Syndicate, Inc.
TOMORROW AT SEVEN? GREAT!
A **DESPERATE** WRONG NUMBER
3-17

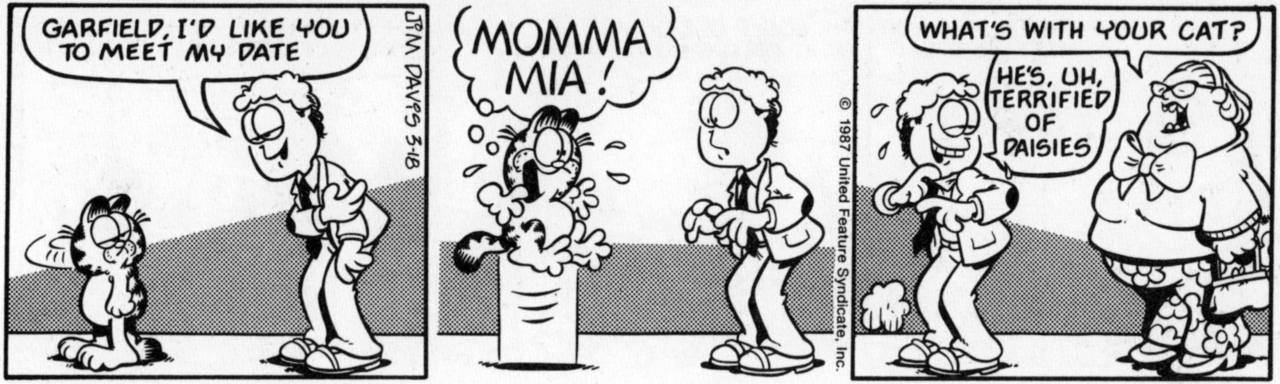

GARFIELD, I'D LIKE YOU TO MEET MY DATE
JIM DAVIS 3-18
MOMMA MIA!
WHAT'S WITH YOUR CAT?
HE'S, UH, TERRIFIED OF DAISIES
© 1987 United Feature Syndicate, Inc.


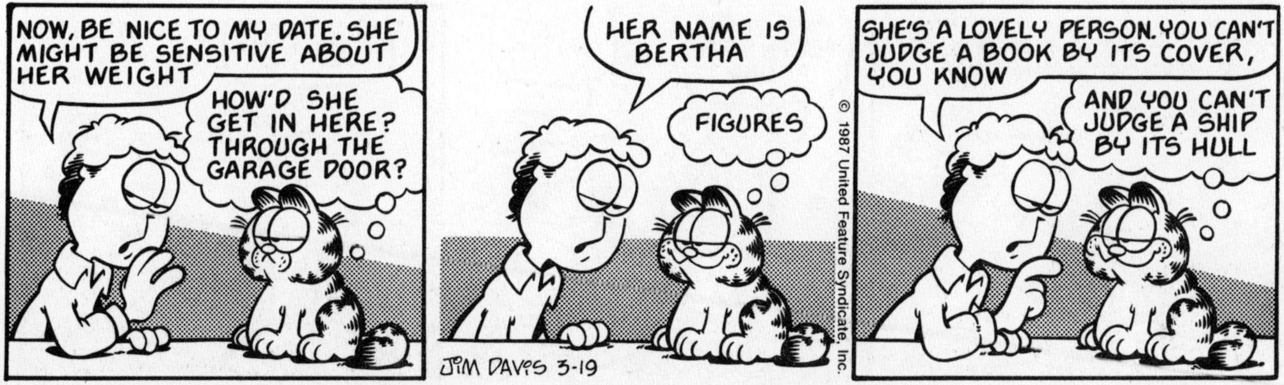

NOW, BE NICE TO MY DATE. SHE MIGHT BE SENSITIVE ABOUT HER WEIGHT
HOW'D SHE GET IN HERE? THROUGH THE GARAGE DOOR?
HER NAME IS BERTHA
FIGURES
JIM DAVIS 3-19
SHE'S A LOVELY PERSON. YOU CAN'T JUDGE A BOOK BY ITS COVER, YOU KNOW
AND YOU CAN'T JUDGE A SHIP BY ITS HULL
© 1987 United Feature Syndicate, Inc.

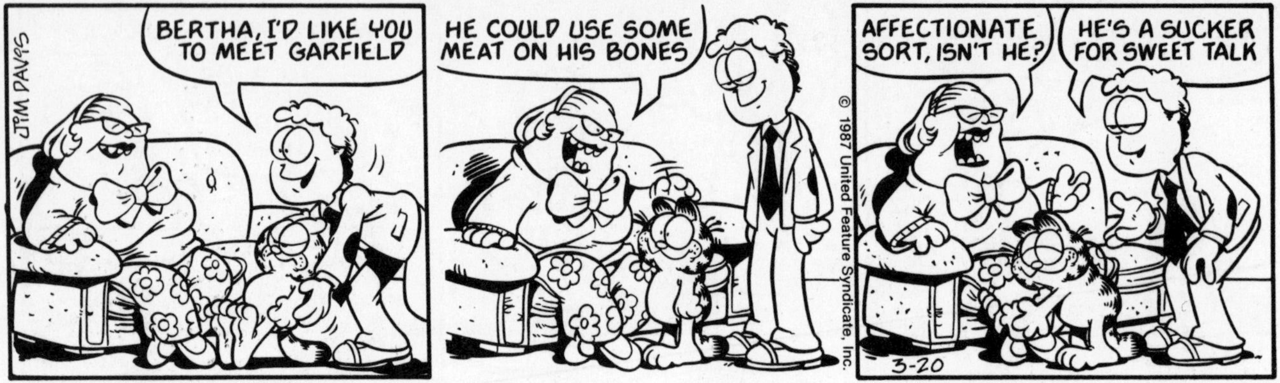
JIM DAVIS
BERTHA, I'D LIKE YOU TO MEET GARFIELD
HE COULD USE SOME MEAT ON HIS BONES
© 1987 United Feature Syndicate, Inc.
AFFECTIONATE SORT, ISN'T HE?
HE'S A SUCKER FOR SWEET TALK
3-20

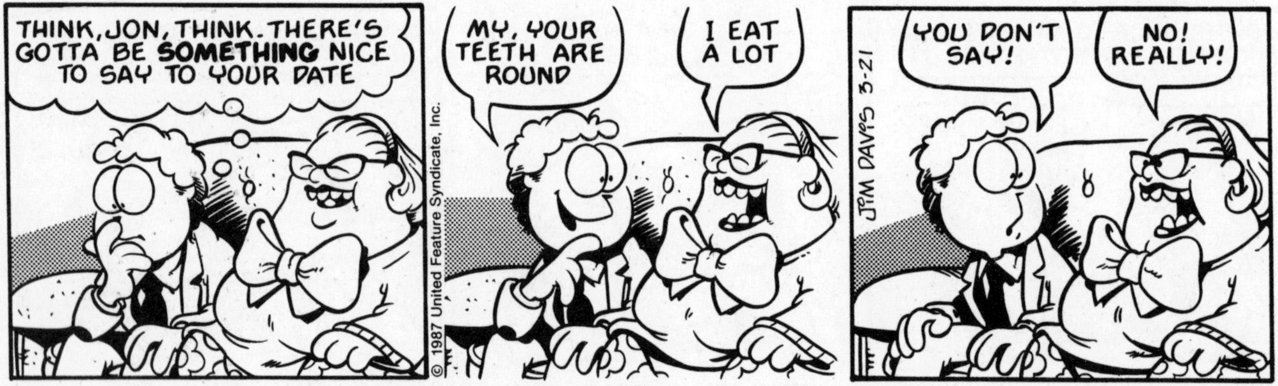
THINK, JON, THINK. THERE'S GOTTA BE **SOMETHING** NICE TO SAY TO YOUR DATE
© 1987 United Feature Syndicate, Inc.
MY, YOUR TEETH ARE ROUND
I EAT A LOT
JIM DAVIS 3-21
YOU DON'T SAY!
NO! REALLY!

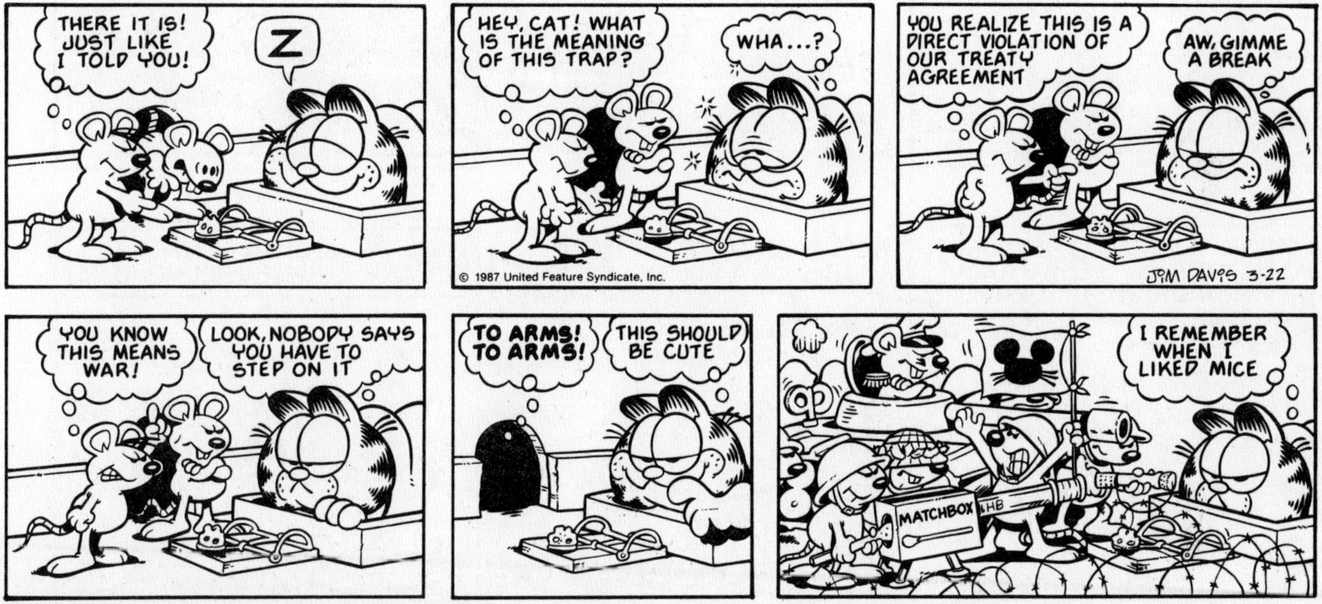
THERE IT IS! JUST LIKE I TOLD YOU!
Z
HEY, CAT! WHAT IS THE MEANING OF THIS TRAP?
WHA...?
© 1987 United Feature Syndicate, Inc.
YOU REALIZE THIS IS A DIRECT VIOLATION OF OUR TREATY AGREEMENT
AW, GIMME A BREAK
JIM DAVIS 3-22
YOU KNOW THIS MEANS WAR!
LOOK, NOBODY SAYS YOU HAVE TO STEP ON IT
TO ARMS! TO ARMS!
THIS SHOULD BE CUTE
MATCHBOX
HB
I REMEMBER WHEN I LIKED MICE

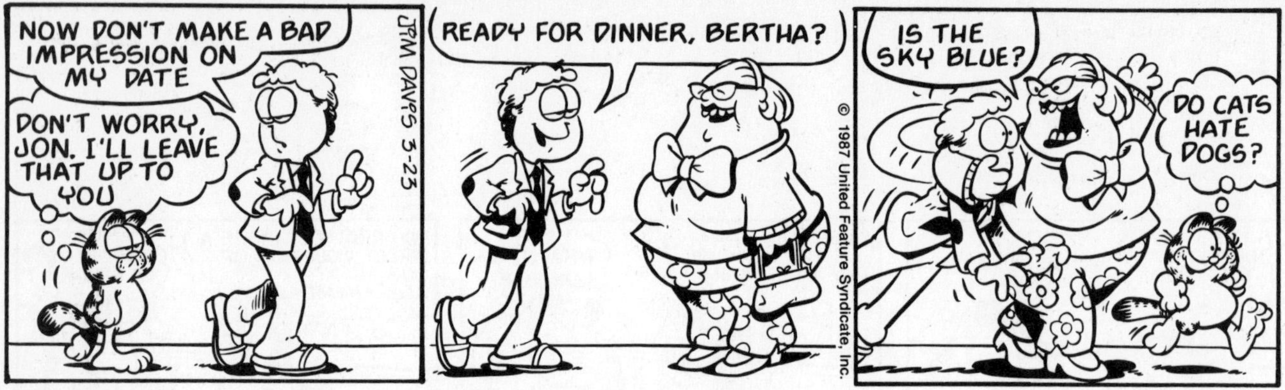
NOW DON'T MAKE A BAD IMPRESSION ON MY DATE
DON'T WORRY, JON. I'LL LEAVE THAT UP TO YOU
JIM DAVIS 3-23
READY FOR DINNER, BERTHA?
© 1987 United Feature Syndicate, Inc.
IS THE SKY BLUE?
DO CATS HATE DOGS?

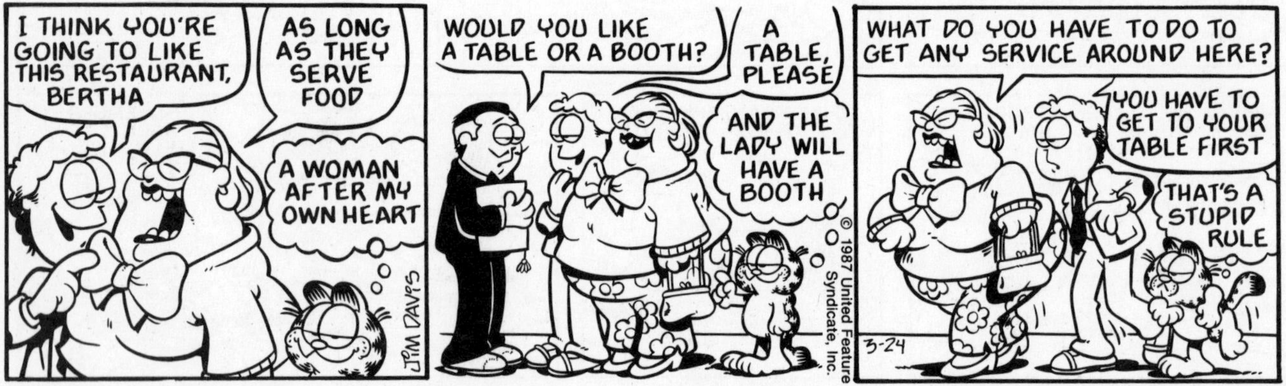
I THINK YOU'RE GOING TO LIKE THIS RESTAURANT, BERTHA
AS LONG AS THEY SERVE FOOD
A WOMAN AFTER MY OWN HEART
JIM DAVIS
WOULD YOU LIKE A TABLE OR A BOOTH?
A TABLE, PLEASE
AND THE LADY WILL HAVE A BOOTH
© 1987 United Feature Syndicate, Inc.
WHAT DO YOU HAVE TO DO TO GET ANY SERVICE AROUND HERE?
YOU HAVE TO GET TO YOUR TABLE FIRST
THAT'S A STUPID RULE
3-24

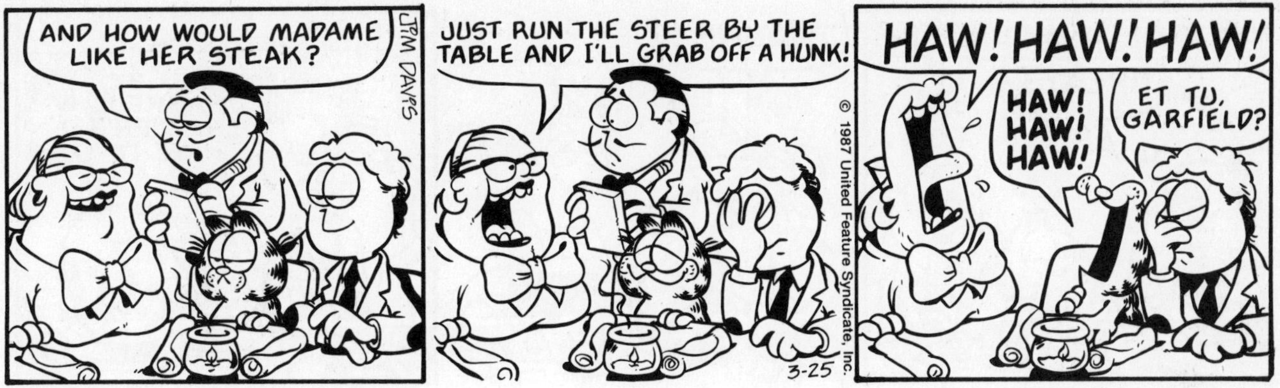
AND HOW WOULD MADAME LIKE HER STEAK?
JIM DAVIS
JUST RUN THE STEER BY THE TABLE AND I'LL GRAB OFF A HUNK!
© 1987 United Feature Syndicate, Inc.
3-25
HAW! HAW! HAW!
HAW! HAW! HAW!
ET TU, GARFIELD?

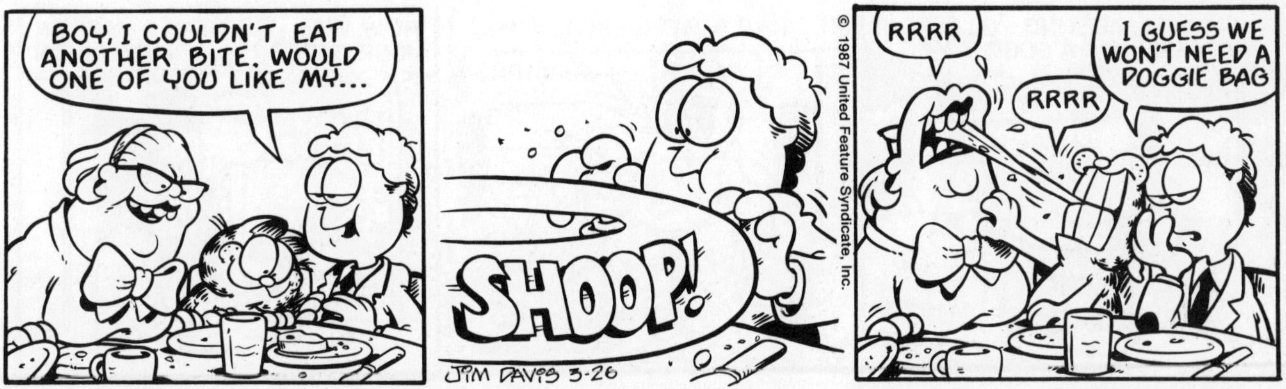
BOY, I COULDN'T EAT ANOTHER BITE. WOULD ONE OF YOU LIKE MY...
SHOOP!
JIM DAVIS 3-26
© 1987 United Feature Syndicate, Inc.
RRRR
RRRR
I GUESS WE WON'T NEED A DOGGIE BAG

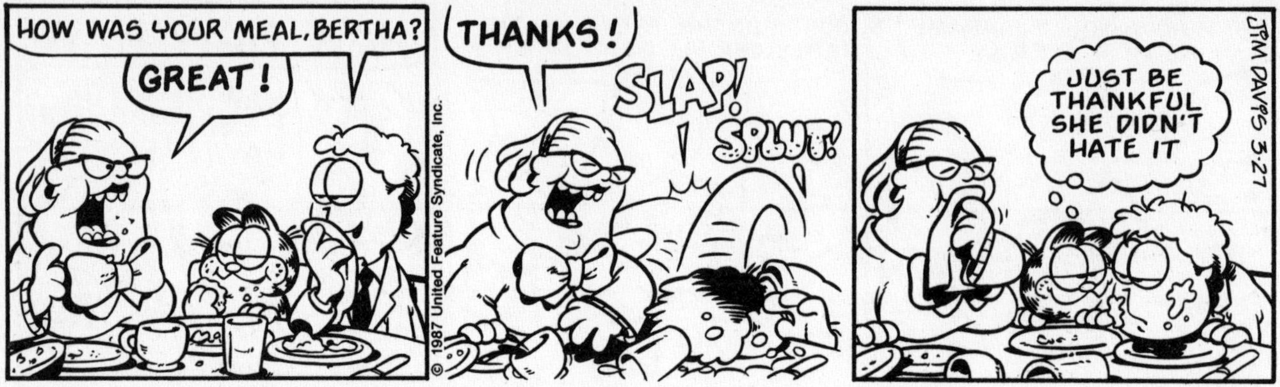
HOW WAS YOUR MEAL, BERTHA?
GREAT!
THANKS!
SLAP!
SPLUT!
JUST BE THANKFUL SHE DIDN'T HATE IT
JIM DAVIS 3-27
© 1987 United Feature Syndicate, Inc.

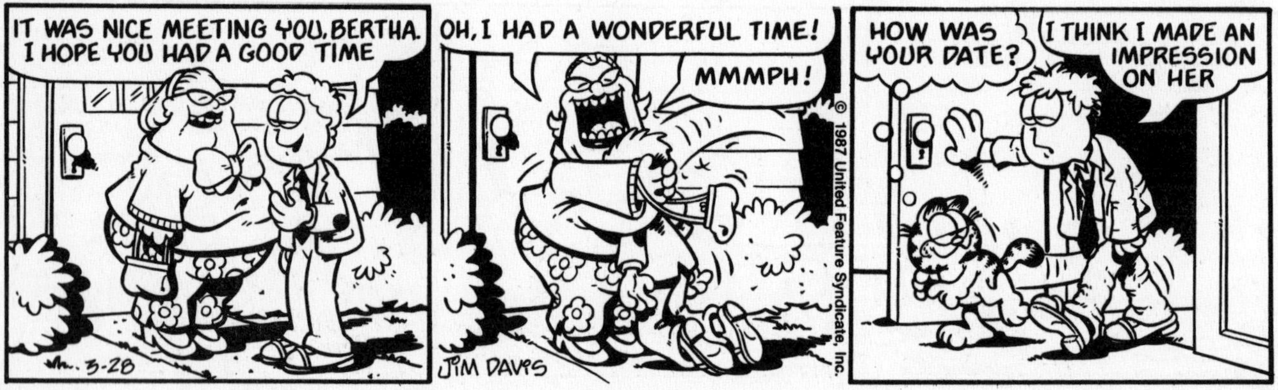
IT WAS NICE MEETING YOU, BERTHA. I HOPE YOU HAD A GOOD TIME
OH, I HAD A WONDERFUL TIME!
MMMPH!
HOW WAS YOUR DATE?
I THINK I MADE AN IMPRESSION ON HER
3-28
JIM DAVIS
© 1987 United Feature Syndicate, Inc.

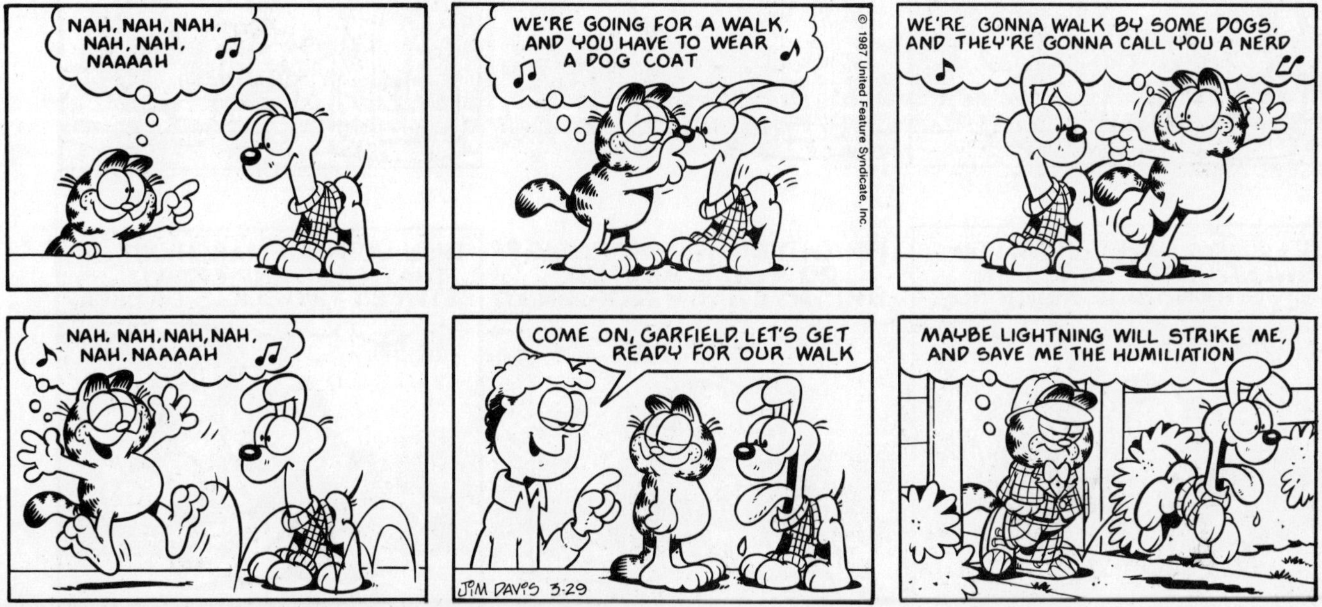
NAH, NAH, NAH, NAH, NAH, NAAAAH
WE'RE GOING FOR A WALK, AND YOU HAVE TO WEAR A DOG COAT
© 1987 United Feature Syndicate, Inc.
WE'RE GONNA WALK BY SOME DOGS, AND THEY'RE GONNA CALL YOU A NERD
NAH, NAH, NAH, NAH, NAH, NAAAAH
COME ON, GARFIELD. LET'S GET READY FOR OUR WALK
JIM DAVIS 3-29
MAYBE LIGHTNING WILL STRIKE ME, AND SAVE ME THE HUMILIATION

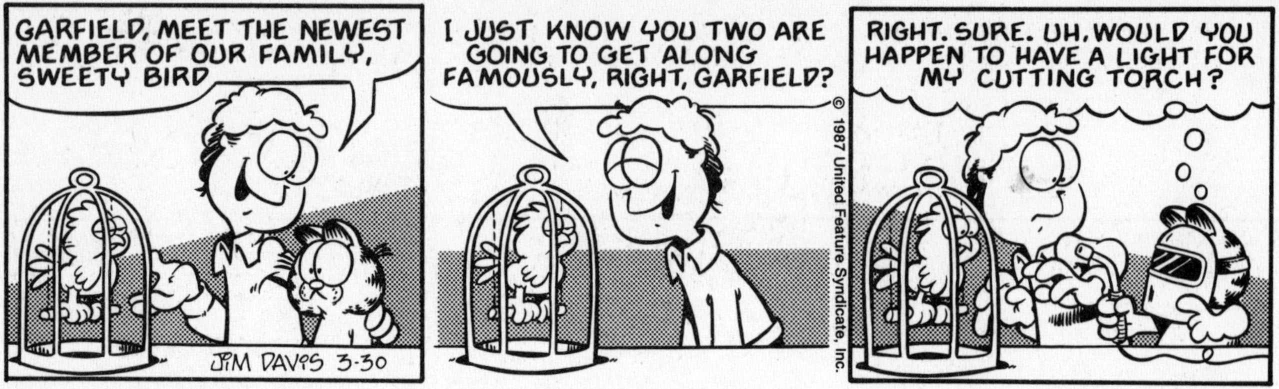
GARFIELD, MEET THE NEWEST MEMBER OF OUR FAMILY, SWEETY BIRD
JIM DAVIS 3-30
I JUST KNOW YOU TWO ARE GOING TO GET ALONG FAMOUSLY, RIGHT, GARFIELD?
© 1987 United Feature Syndicate, Inc.
RIGHT. SURE. UH, WOULD YOU HAPPEN TO HAVE A LIGHT FOR MY CUTTING TORCH?

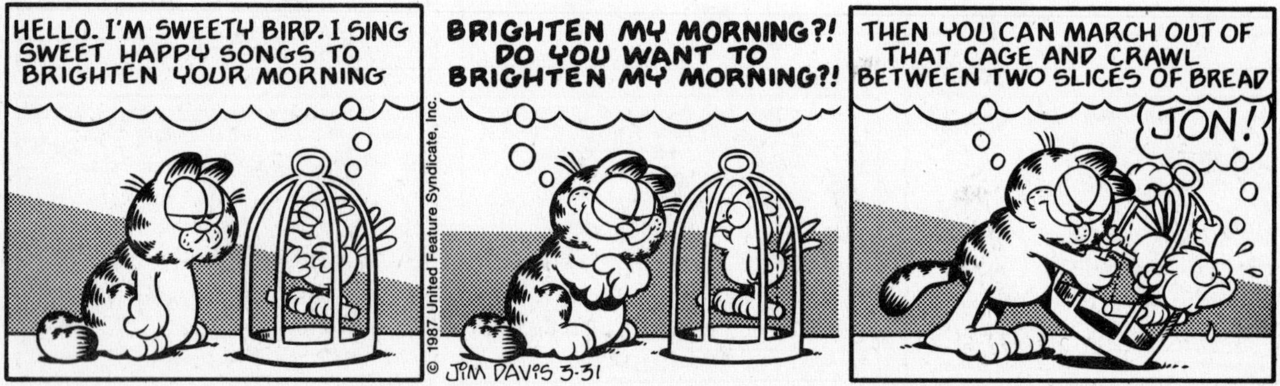
HELLO. I'M SWEETY BIRD. I SING SWEET HAPPY SONGS TO BRIGHTEN YOUR MORNING
© 1987 United Feature Syndicate, Inc.
BRIGHTEN MY MORNING?! DO YOU WANT TO BRIGHTEN MY MORNING?!
JIM DAVIS 3-31
THEN YOU CAN MARCH OUT OF THAT CAGE AND CRAWL BETWEEN TWO SLICES OF BREAD
JON!

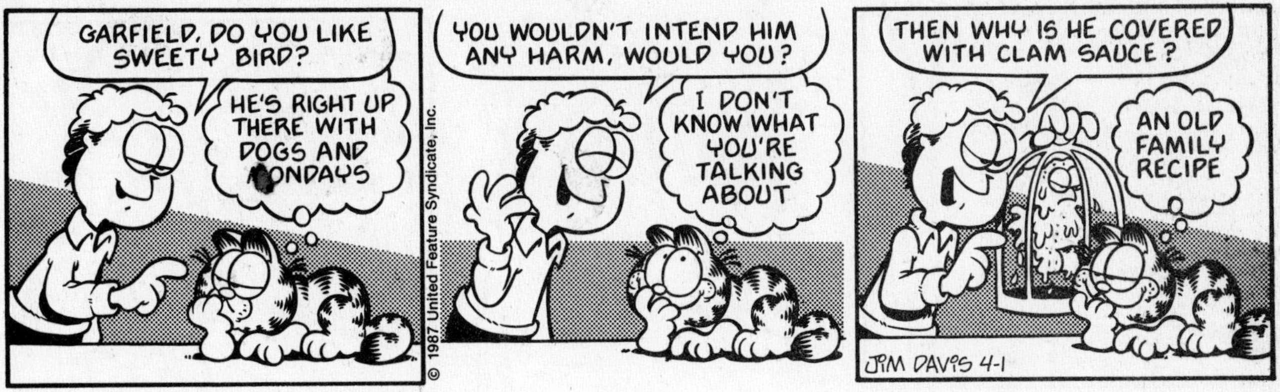

GARFIELD, DO YOU LIKE SWEETY BIRD?
HE'S RIGHT UP THERE WITH DOGS AND MONDAYS
© 1987 United Feature Syndicate, Inc.
YOU WOULDN'T INTEND HIM ANY HARM, WOULD YOU?
I DON'T KNOW WHAT YOU'RE TALKING ABOUT
THEN WHY IS HE COVERED WITH CLAM SAUCE?
AN OLD FAMILY RECIPE
JIM DAVIS 4-1


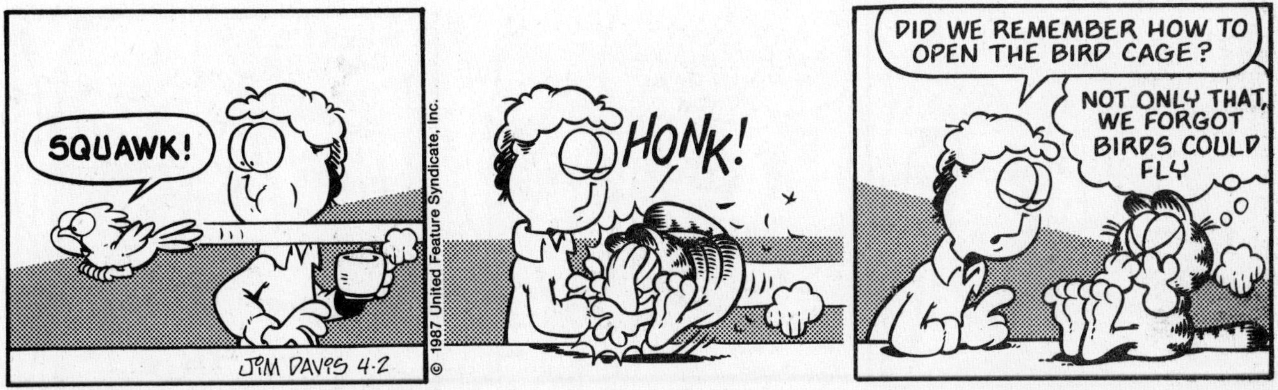

SQUAWK!
JIM DAVIS 4-2
© 1987 United Feature Syndicate, Inc.
HONK!
DID WE REMEMBER HOW TO OPEN THE BIRD CAGE?
NOT ONLY THAT, WE FORGOT BIRDS COULD FLY

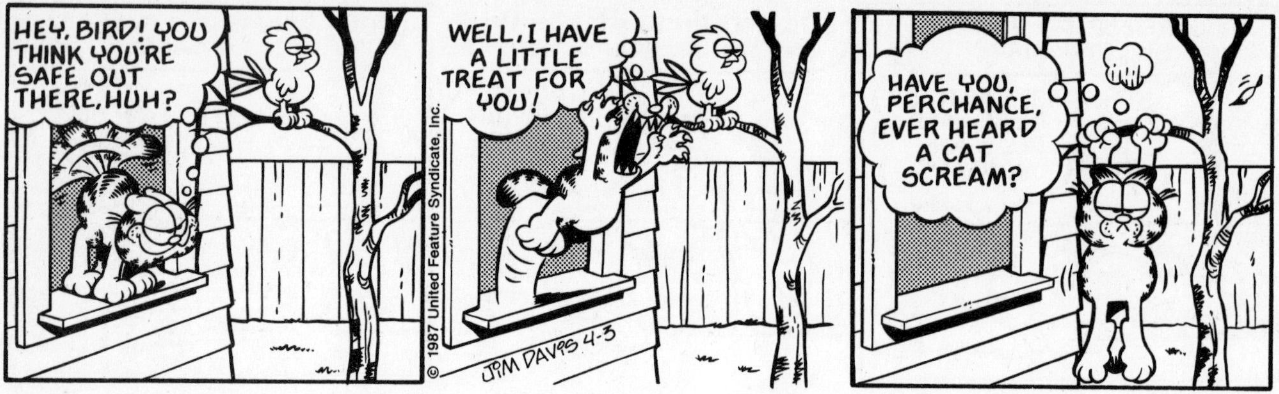
HEY, BIRD! YOU THINK YOU'RE SAFE OUT THERE, HUH?
WELL, I HAVE A LITTLE TREAT FOR YOU!
© 1987 United Feature Syndicate, Inc.
JIM DAVIS 4-3
HAVE YOU, PERCHANCE, EVER HEARD A CAT SCREAM?

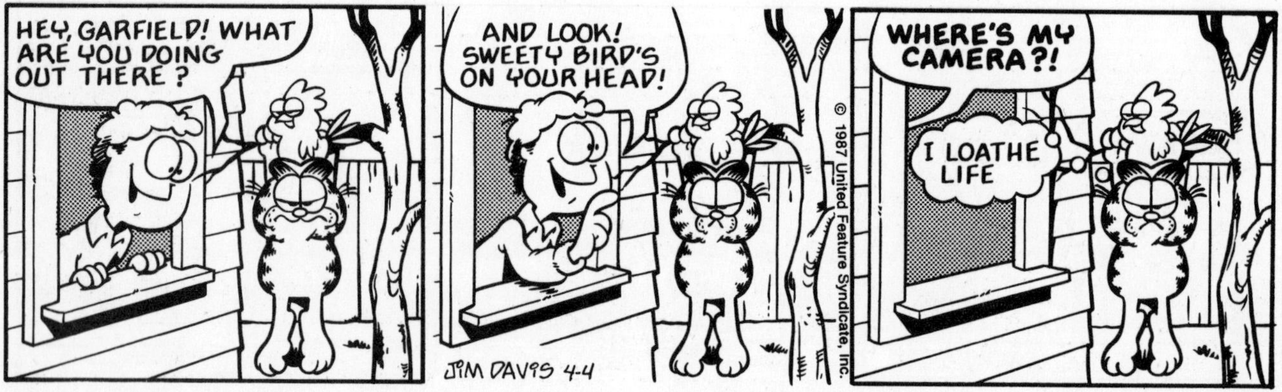
HEY, GARFIELD! WHAT ARE YOU DOING OUT THERE?
AND LOOK! SWEETY BIRD'S ON YOUR HEAD!
JIM DAVIS 4-4
© 1987 United Feature Syndicate, Inc.
WHERE'S MY CAMERA?!
I LOATHE LIFE

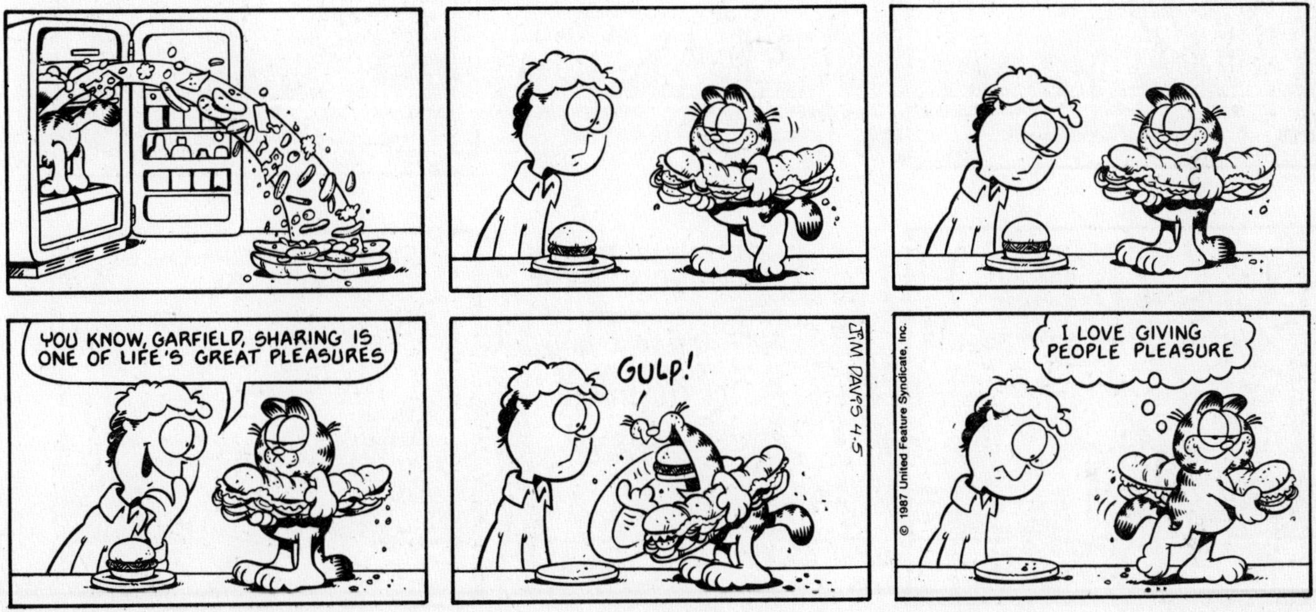
YOU KNOW, GARFIELD, SHARING IS ONE OF LIFE'S GREAT PLEASURES
JIM DAVIS 4-5
© 1987 United Feature Syndicate, Inc.
GULP!
I LOVE GIVING PEOPLE PLEASURE

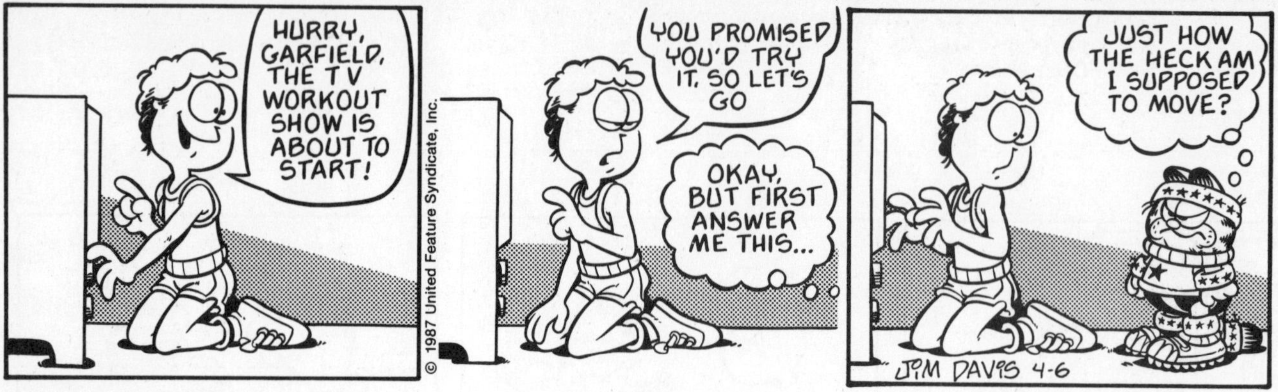
HURRY, GARFIELD, THE T V WORKOUT SHOW IS ABOUT TO START!
© 1987 United Feature Syndicate, Inc.
YOU PROMISED YOU'D TRY IT, SO LET'S GO
OKAY, BUT FIRST ANSWER ME THIS...
JUST HOW THE HECK AM I SUPPOSED TO MOVE?
JIM DAVIS 4-6

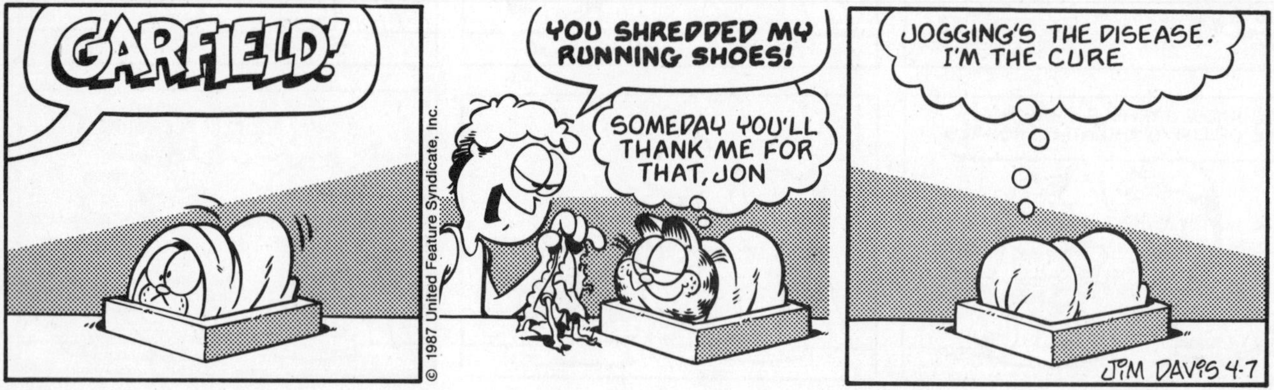
GARFIELD!
© 1987 United Feature Syndicate, Inc.
YOU SHREDDED MY RUNNING SHOES!
SOMEDAY YOU'LL THANK ME FOR THAT, JON
JOGGING'S THE DISEASE. I'M THE CURE
JIM DAVIS 4-7

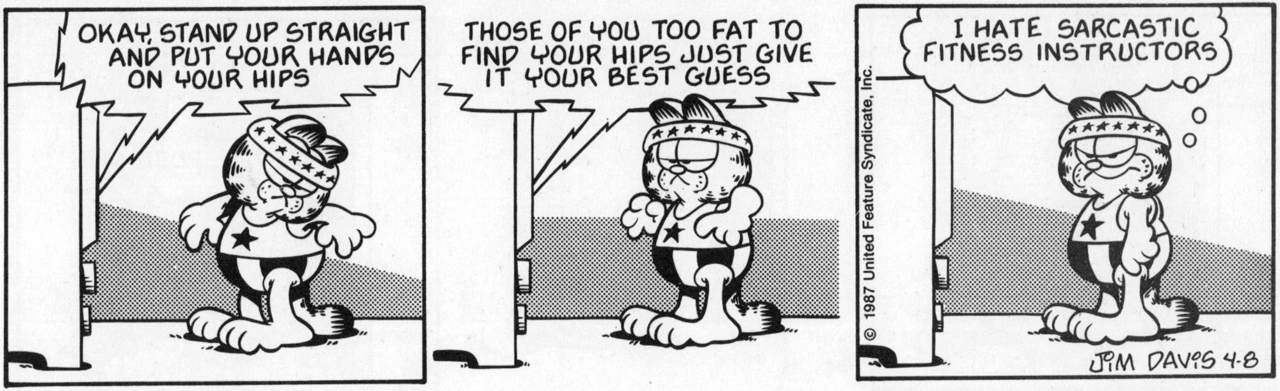
OKAY, STAND UP STRAIGHT AND PUT YOUR HANDS ON YOUR HIPS
THOSE OF YOU TOO FAT TO FIND YOUR HIPS JUST GIVE IT YOUR BEST GUESS
I HATE SARCASTIC FITNESS INSTRUCTORS
© 1987 United Feature Syndicate, Inc.
JIM DAVIS 4-8

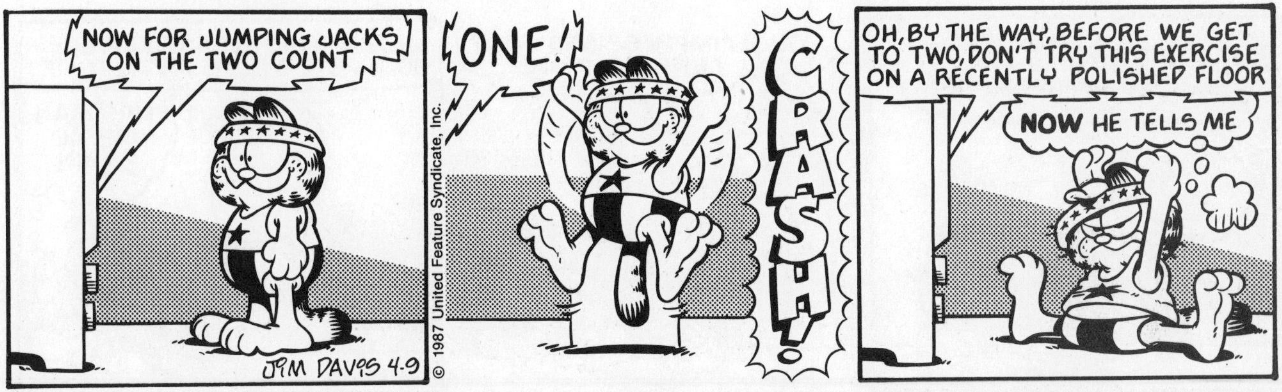
NOW FOR JUMPING JACKS ON THE TWO COUNT
JIM DAVIS 4-9
© 1987 United Feature Syndicate, Inc.
ONE!
CRASH!
OH, BY THE WAY, BEFORE WE GET TO TWO, DON'T TRY THIS EXERCISE ON A RECENTLY POLISHED FLOOR
NOW HE TELLS ME

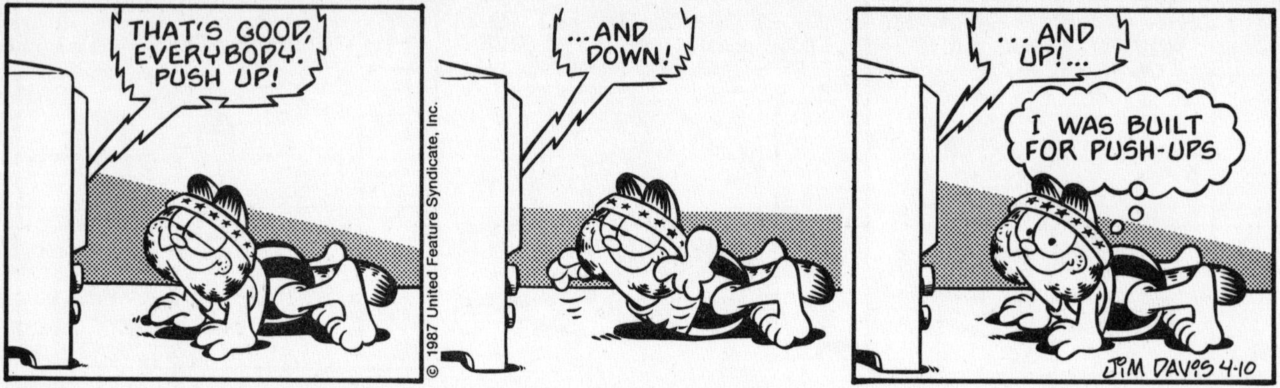
THAT'S GOOD, EVERYBODY. PUSH UP!
...AND DOWN!
...AND UP!...
I WAS BUILT FOR PUSH-UPS
JIM DAVIS 4-10



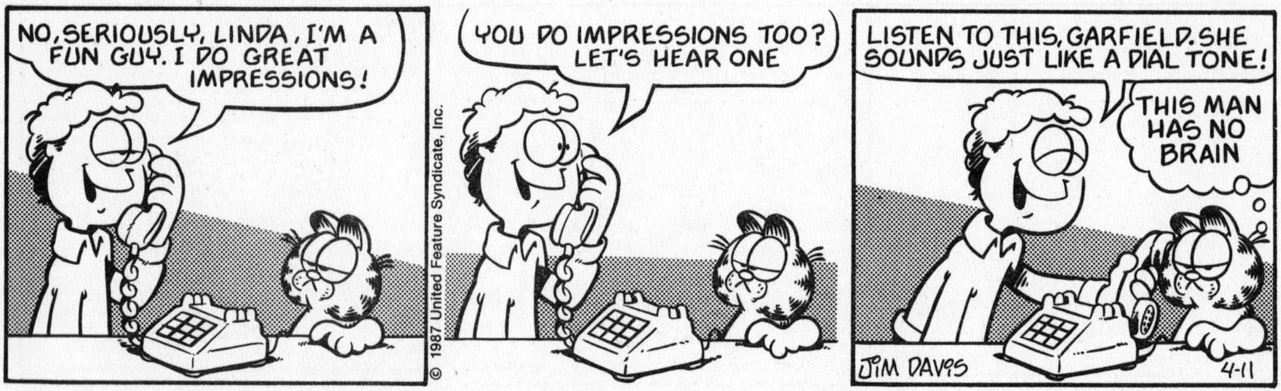
NO, SERIOUSLY, LINDA, I'M A FUN GUY. I DO GREAT IMPRESSIONS!
YOU DO IMPRESSIONS TOO? LET'S HEAR ONE
LISTEN TO THIS, GARFIELD. SHE SOUNDS JUST LIKE A DIAL TONE!
THIS MAN HAS NO BRAIN
JIM DAVIS
4-11

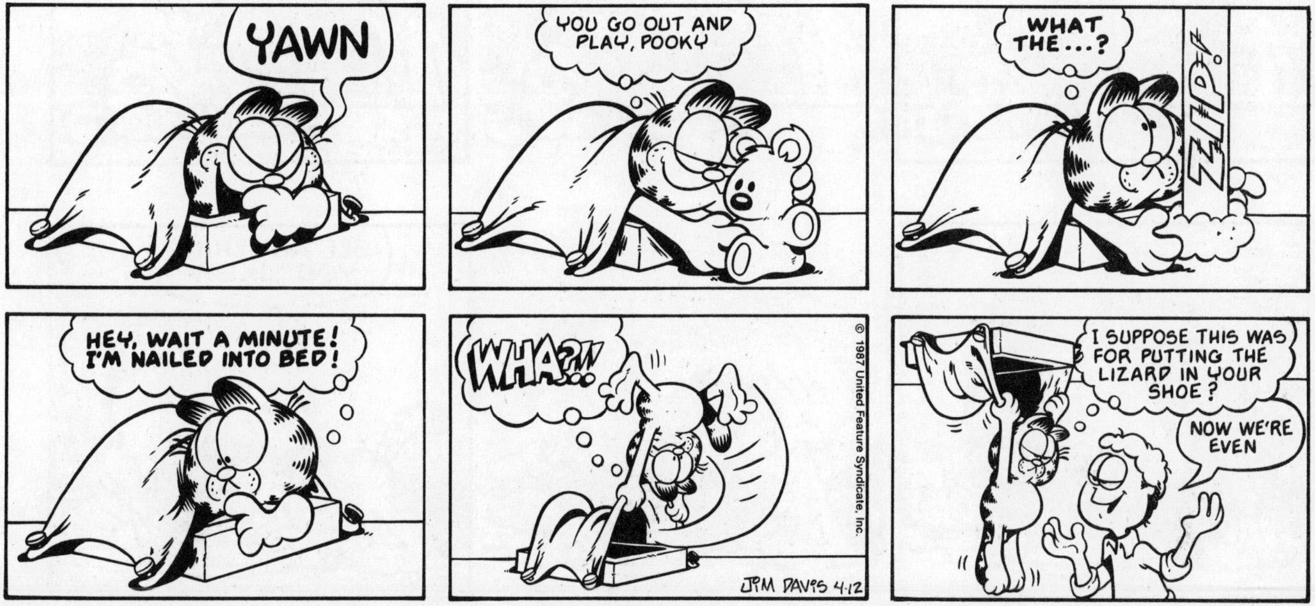
YAWN
YOU GO OUT AND PLAY, POOKY
WHAT THE...?
ZIP!
HEY, WAIT A MINUTE! I'M NAILED INTO BED!
WHA?!!
© 1987 United Feature Syndicate, Inc.
JIM DAVIS 4-12
I SUPPOSE THIS WAS FOR PUTTING THE LIZARD IN YOUR SHOE?
NOW WE'RE EVEN

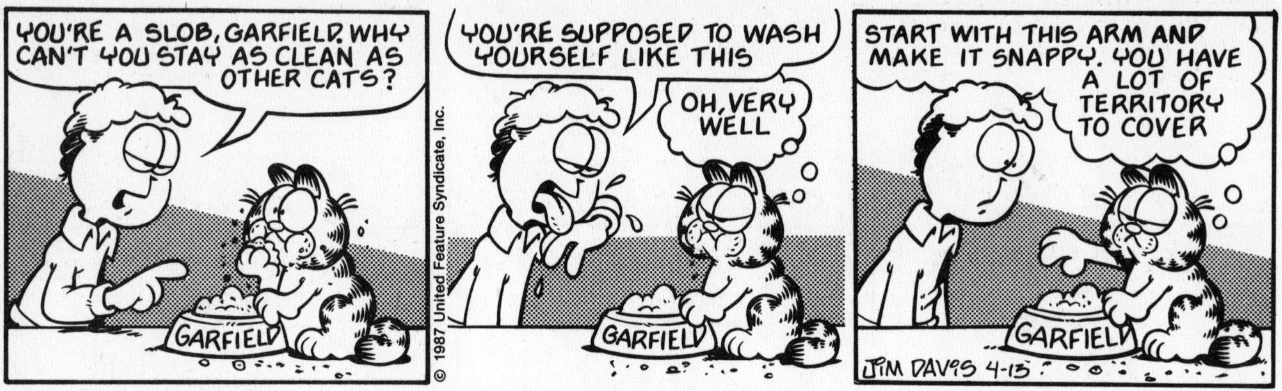
YOU'RE A SLOB, GARFIELD. WHY CAN'T YOU STAY AS CLEAN AS OTHER CATS?
GARFIELD
© 1987 United Feature Syndicate, Inc.
YOU'RE SUPPOSED TO WASH YOURSELF LIKE THIS
OH, VERY WELL
GARFIELD
START WITH THIS ARM AND MAKE IT SNAPPY. YOU HAVE A LOT OF TERRITORY TO COVER
GARFIELD
JIM DAVIS 4-13

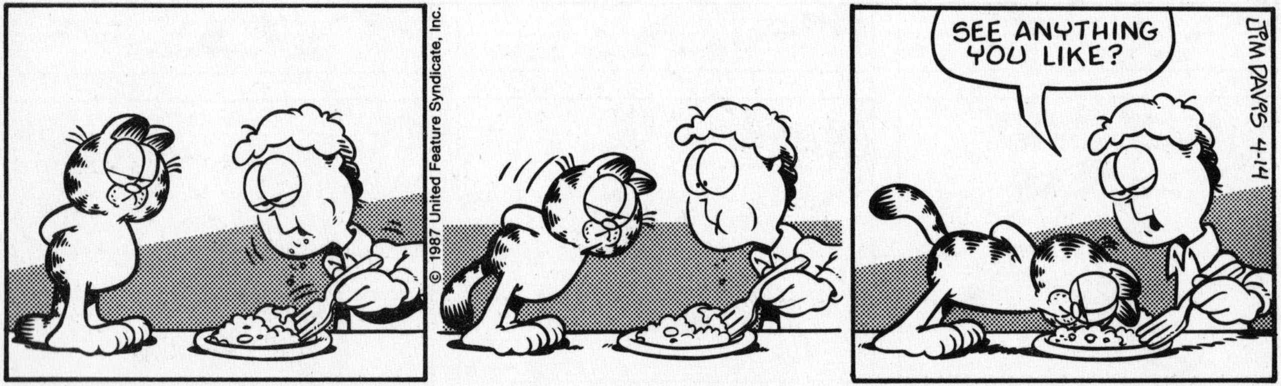
© 1987 United Feature Syndicate, Inc.
SEE ANYTHING YOU LIKE?
JIM DAVIS 4-14

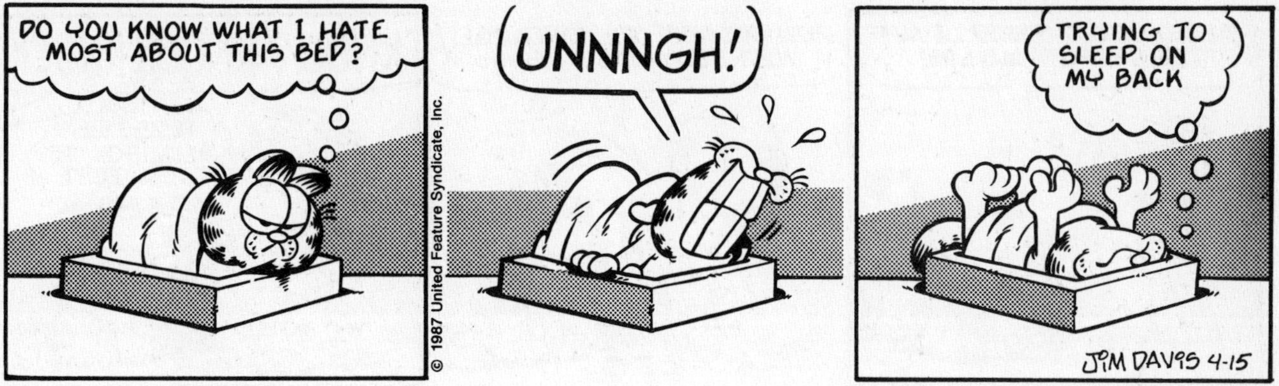
DO YOU KNOW WHAT I HATE MOST ABOUT THIS BED?
UNNNGH!
TRYING TO SLEEP ON MY BACK
JIM DAVIS 4-15
© 1987 United Feature Syndicate, Inc.

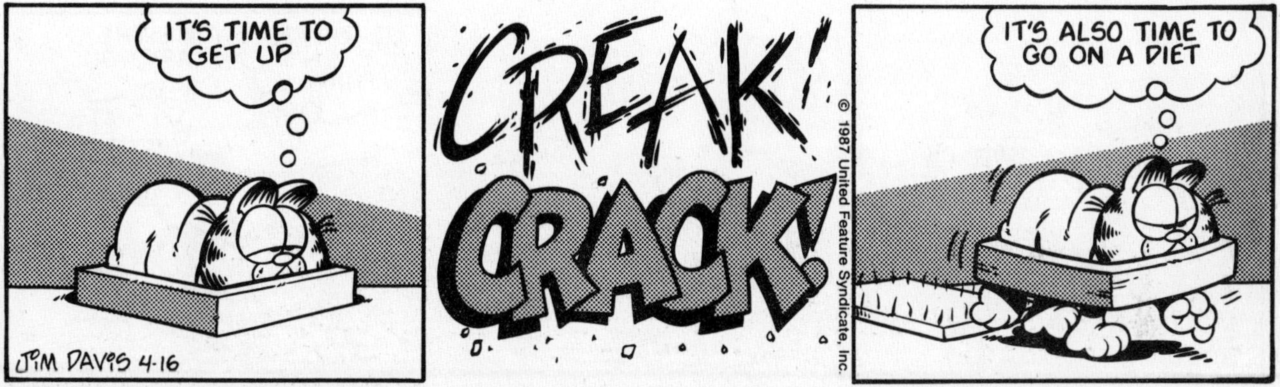
IT'S TIME TO GET UP
JIM DAVIS 4-16
CREAK!
CRACK!
IT'S ALSO TIME TO GO ON A DIET
© 1987 United Feature Syndicate, Inc.

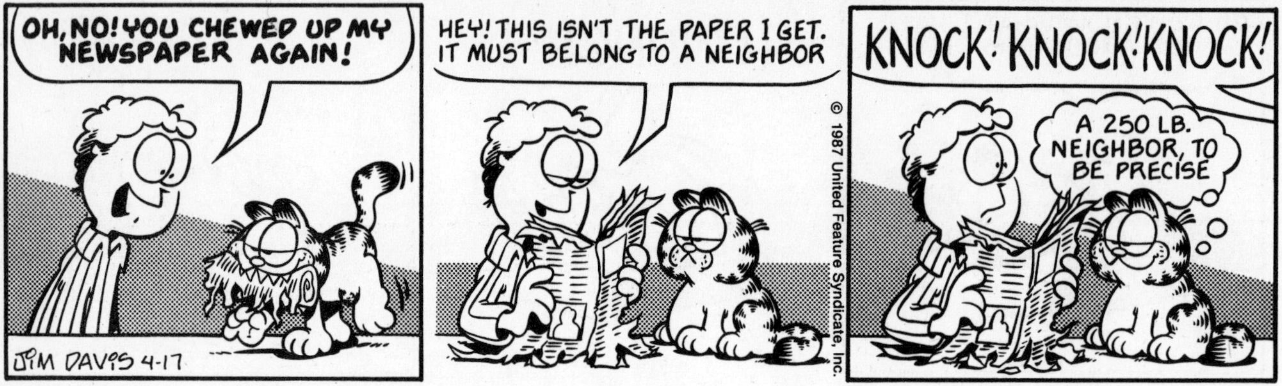
OH, NO! YOU CHEWED UP MY NEWSPAPER AGAIN!
JIM DAVIS 4-17
HEY! THIS ISN'T THE PAPER I GET. IT MUST BELONG TO A NEIGHBOR
© 1987 United Feature Syndicate, Inc.
KNOCK! KNOCK! KNOCK!
A 250 LB. NEIGHBOR, TO BE PRECISE

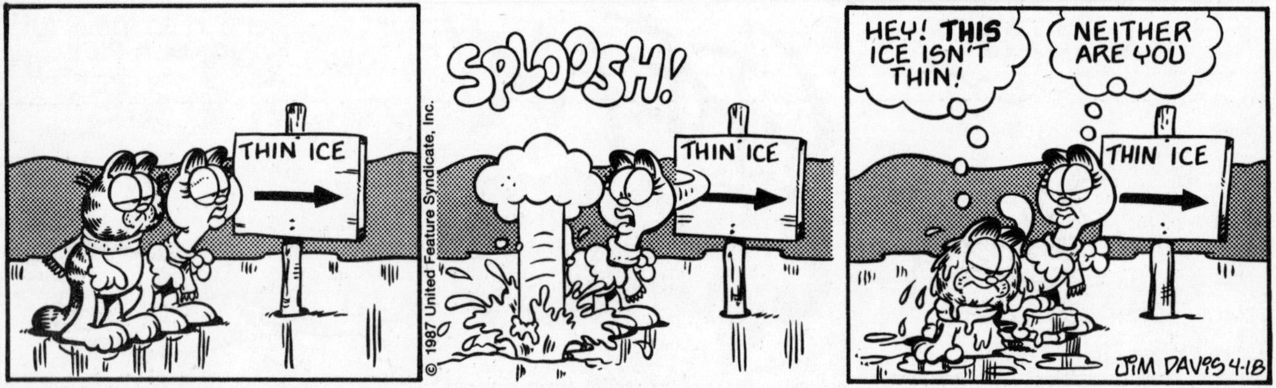
THIN ICE
SPLOOSH!
THIN ICE
© 1987 United Feature Syndicate, Inc.
HEY! THIS ICE ISN'T THIN!
NEITHER ARE YOU
THIN ICE
JIM DAVIS 4-18

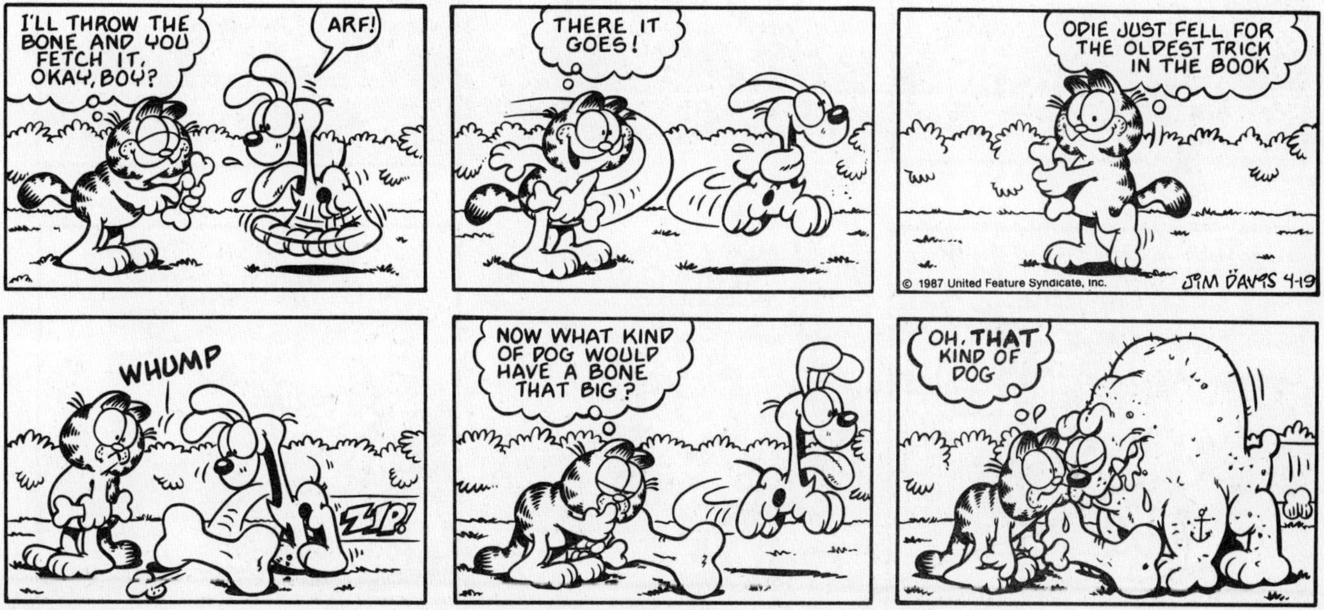
I'LL THROW THE BONE AND YOU FETCH IT, OKAY, BOY?
ARF!
THERE IT GOES!
ODIE JUST FELL FOR THE OLDEST TRICK IN THE BOOK
© 1987 United Feature Syndicate, Inc.
JIM DAVIS 4-19
WHUMP
ZIP!
NOW WHAT KIND OF DOG WOULD HAVE A BONE THAT BIG?
OH, THAT KIND OF DOG

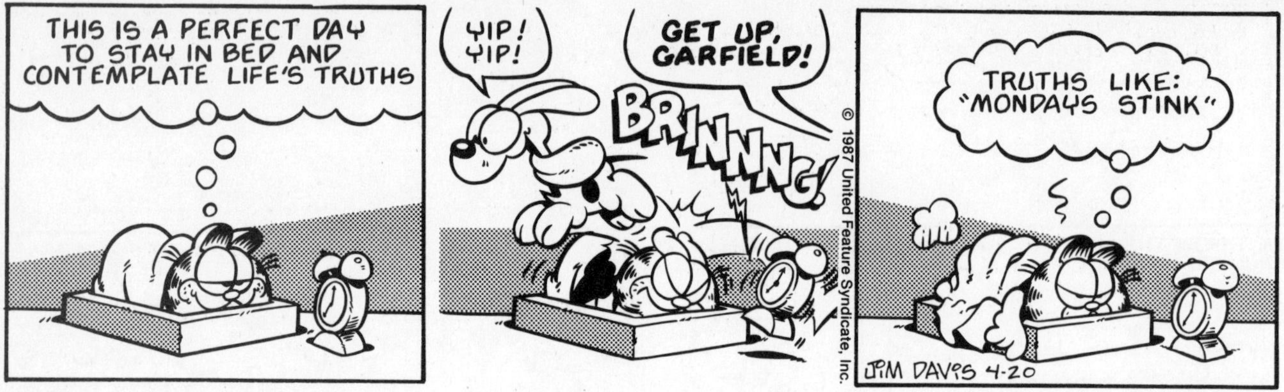
THIS IS A PERFECT DAY TO STAY IN BED AND CONTEMPLATE LIFE'S TRUTHS
YIP! YIP!
GET UP, GARFIELD!
BRINNNNG!
TRUTHS LIKE: "MONDAYS STINK"
JIM DAVIS 4-20
© 1987 United Feature Syndicate, Inc.

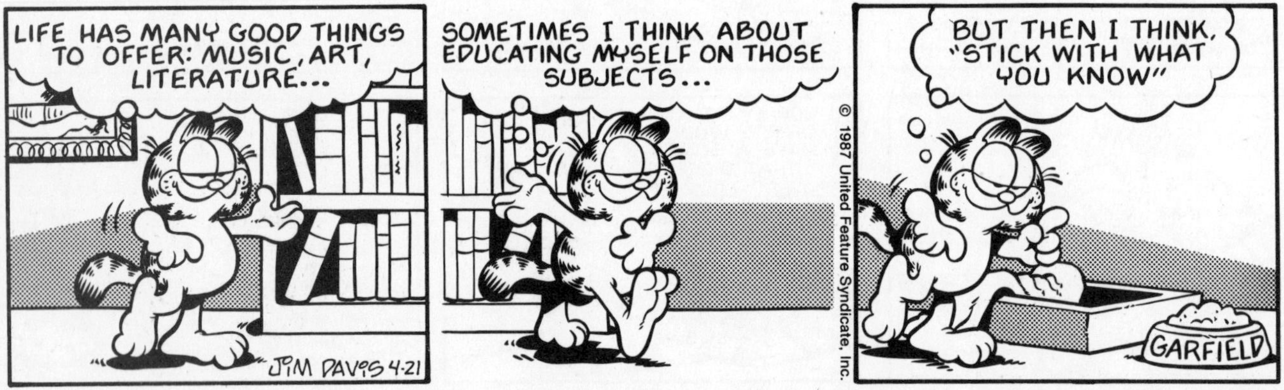
LIFE HAS MANY GOOD THINGS TO OFFER: MUSIC, ART, LITERATURE...
JIM DAVIS 4-21
SOMETIMES I THINK ABOUT EDUCATING MYSELF ON THOSE SUBJECTS...
BUT THEN I THINK, "STICK WITH WHAT YOU KNOW"
GARFIELD
© 1987 United Feature Syndicate, Inc.

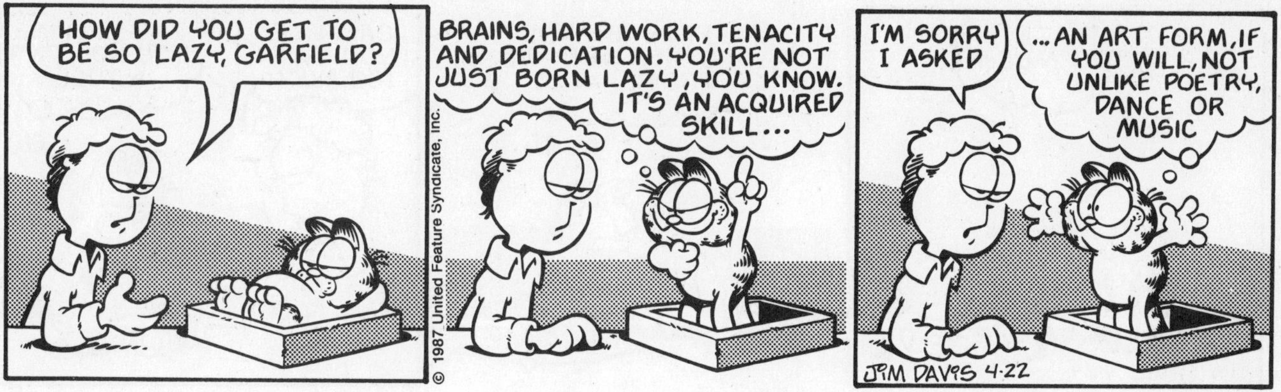
HOW DID YOU GET TO BE SO LAZY, GARFIELD?
BRAINS, HARD WORK, TENACITY AND DEDICATION. YOU'RE NOT JUST BORN LAZY, YOU KNOW. IT'S AN ACQUIRED SKILL...
I'M SORRY I ASKED
...AN ART FORM, IF YOU WILL, NOT UNLIKE POETRY, DANCE OR MUSIC
© 1987 United Feature Syndicate, Inc.
JIM DAVIS 4-22

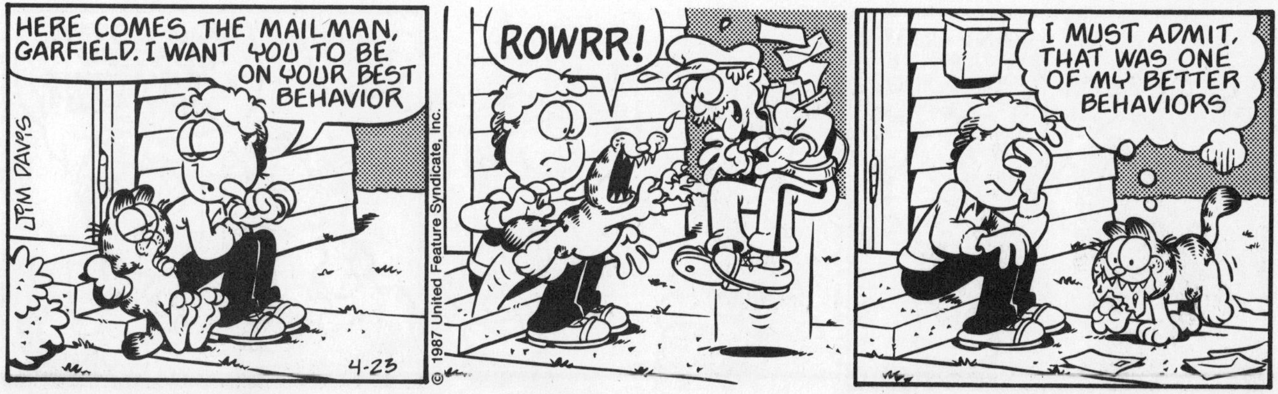
HERE COMES THE MAILMAN, GARFIELD. I WANT YOU TO BE ON YOUR BEST BEHAVIOR
JIM DAVIS
4-23
ROWRR!
© 1987 United Feature Syndicate, Inc.
I MUST ADMIT, THAT WAS ONE OF MY BETTER BEHAVIORS

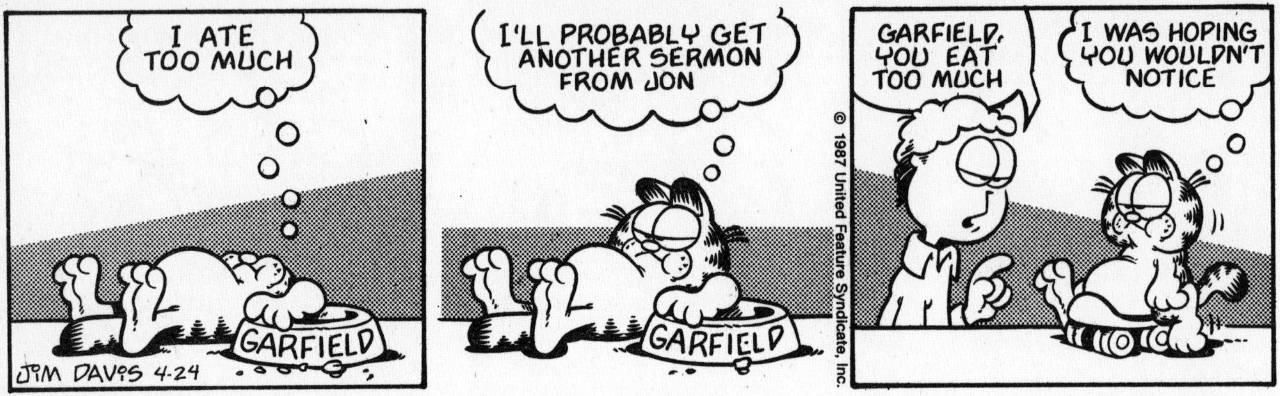
I ATE TOO MUCH
GARFIELD
JIM DAVIS 4-24
I'LL PROBABLY GET ANOTHER SERMON FROM JON
GARFIELD
© 1987 United Feature Syndicate, Inc.
GARFIELD, YOU EAT TOO MUCH
I WAS HOPING YOU WOULDN'T NOTICE

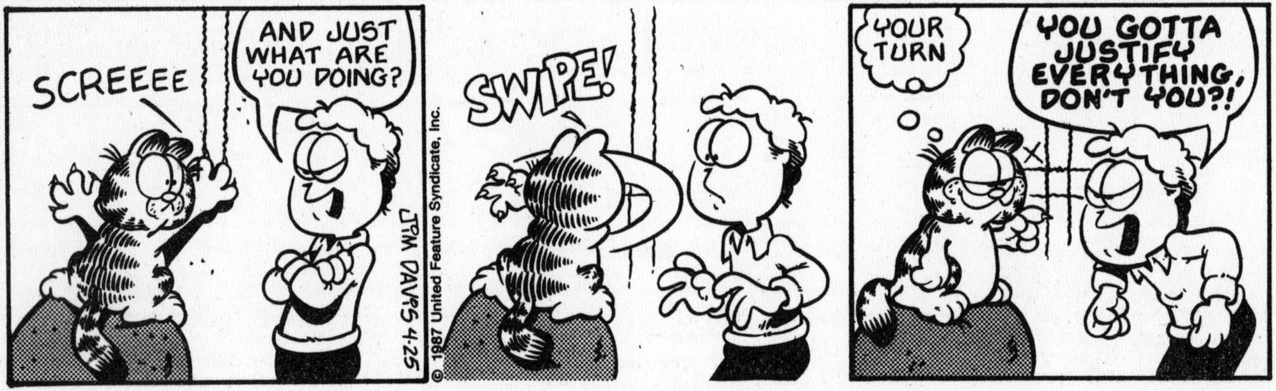
SCREEEEE
AND JUST WHAT ARE YOU DOING?
JIM DAVIS 4-25
© 1987 United Feature Syndicate, Inc.
SWIPE!
YOUR TURN
YOU GOTTA JUSTIFY EVERYTHING, DON'T YOU?!

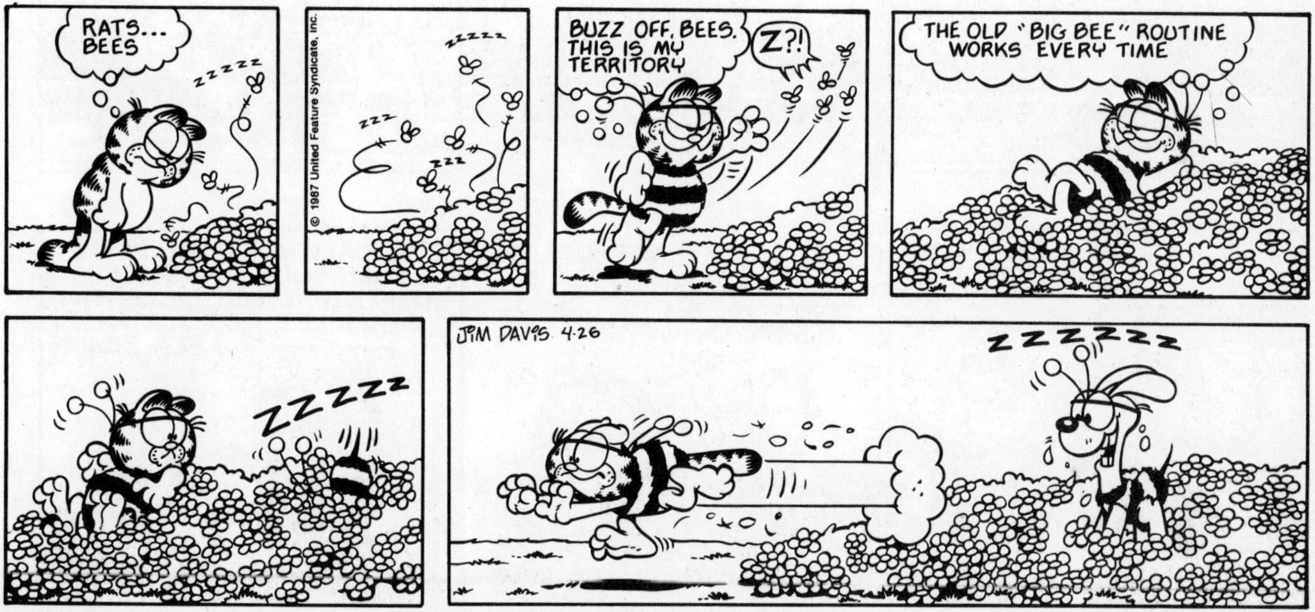
RATS... BEES
ZZZZZ
© 1987 United Feature Syndicate, Inc.
ZZZZZ
ZZZ
ZZZ
BUZZ OFF, BEES. THIS IS MY TERRITORY
Z?!
THE OLD "BIG BEE" ROUTINE WORKS EVERY TIME
ZZZZZ
JIM DAVIS 4-26
ZZZZZZZ

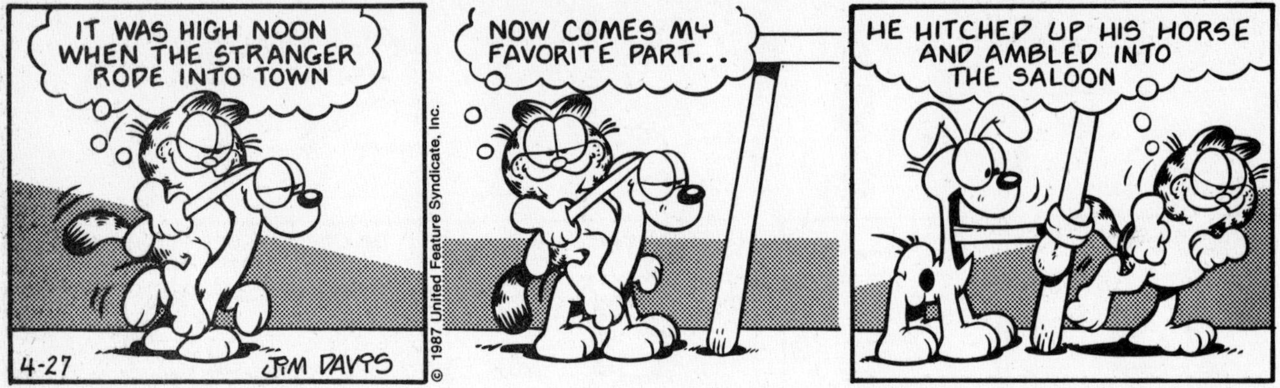
IT WAS HIGH NOON WHEN THE STRANGER RODE INTO TOWN
NOW COMES MY FAVORITE PART...
HE HITCHED UP HIS HORSE AND AMBLED INTO THE SALOON
4-27
JIM DAVIS
© 1987 United Feature Syndicate, Inc.

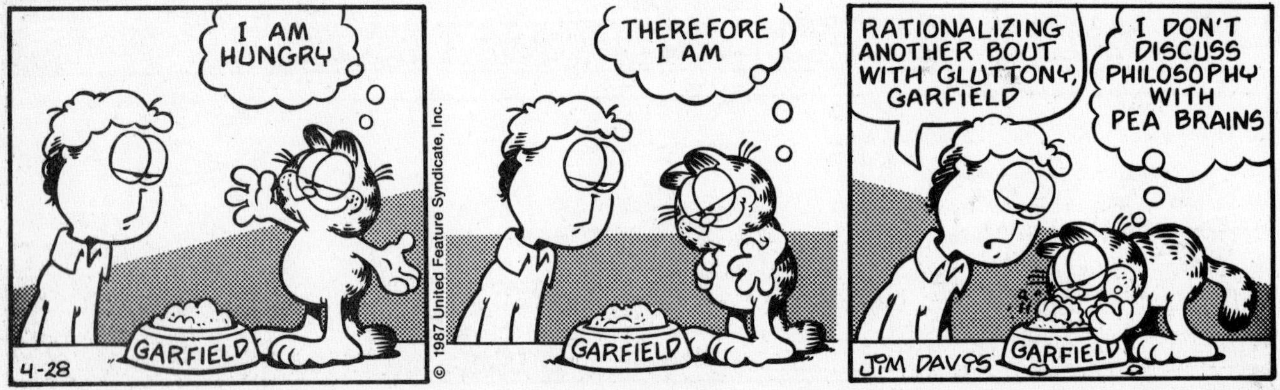
I AM HUNGRY
THEREFORE I AM
RATIONALIZING ANOTHER BOUT WITH GLUTTONY, GARFIELD
I DON'T DISCUSS PHILOSOPHY WITH PEA BRAINS
GARFIELD
GARFIELD
GARFIELD
4-28
JIM DAVIS
© 1987 United Feature Syndicate, Inc.

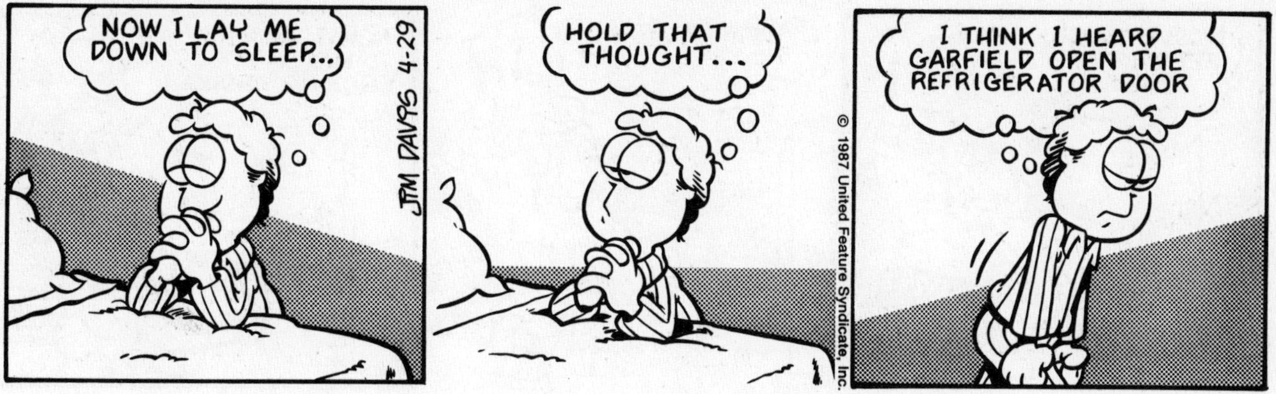
NOW I LAY ME DOWN TO SLEEP...
JIM DAVIS 4-29
HOLD THAT THOUGHT...
© 1987 United Feature Syndicate, Inc.
I THINK I HEARD GARFIELD OPEN THE REFRIGERATOR DOOR

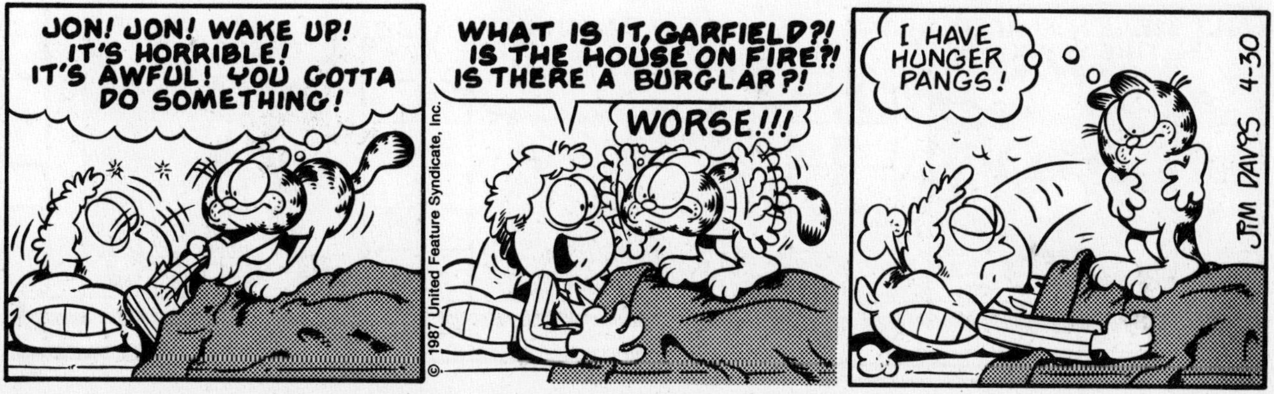
JON! JON! WAKE UP! IT'S HORRIBLE! IT'S AWFUL! YOU GOTTA DO SOMETHING!
© 1987 United Feature Syndicate, Inc.
WHAT IS IT, GARFIELD?! IS THE HOUSE ON FIRE?! IS THERE A BURGLAR?!
WORSE!!!
I HAVE HUNGER PANGS!
JIM DAVIS 4-30

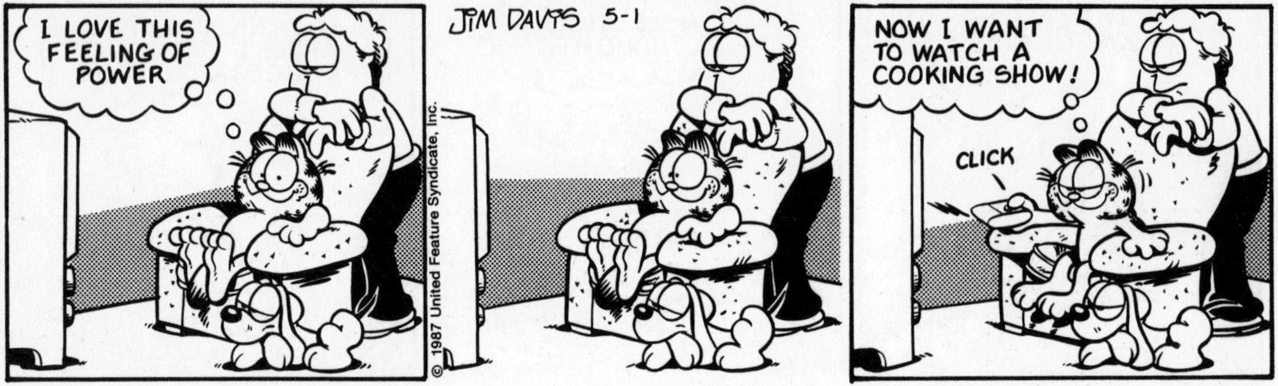
JIM DAVIS 5-1
I LOVE THIS FEELING OF POWER
NOW I WANT TO WATCH A COOKING SHOW!
CLICK
© 1987 United Feature Syndicate, Inc.

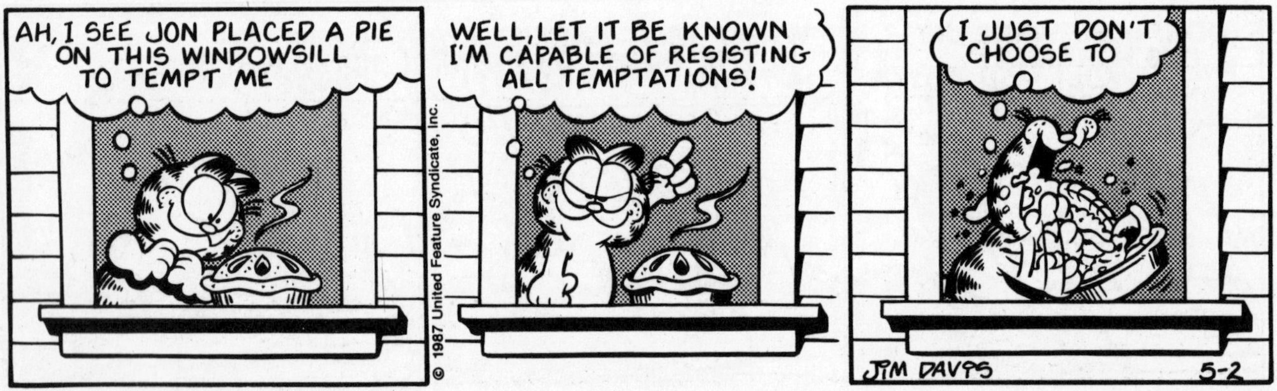
AH, I SEE JON PLACED A PIE ON THIS WINDOWSILL TO TEMPT ME
WELL, LET IT BE KNOWN I'M CAPABLE OF RESISTING ALL TEMPTATIONS!
I JUST DON'T CHOOSE TO
JIM DAVIS 5-2
© 1987 United Feature Syndicate, Inc.

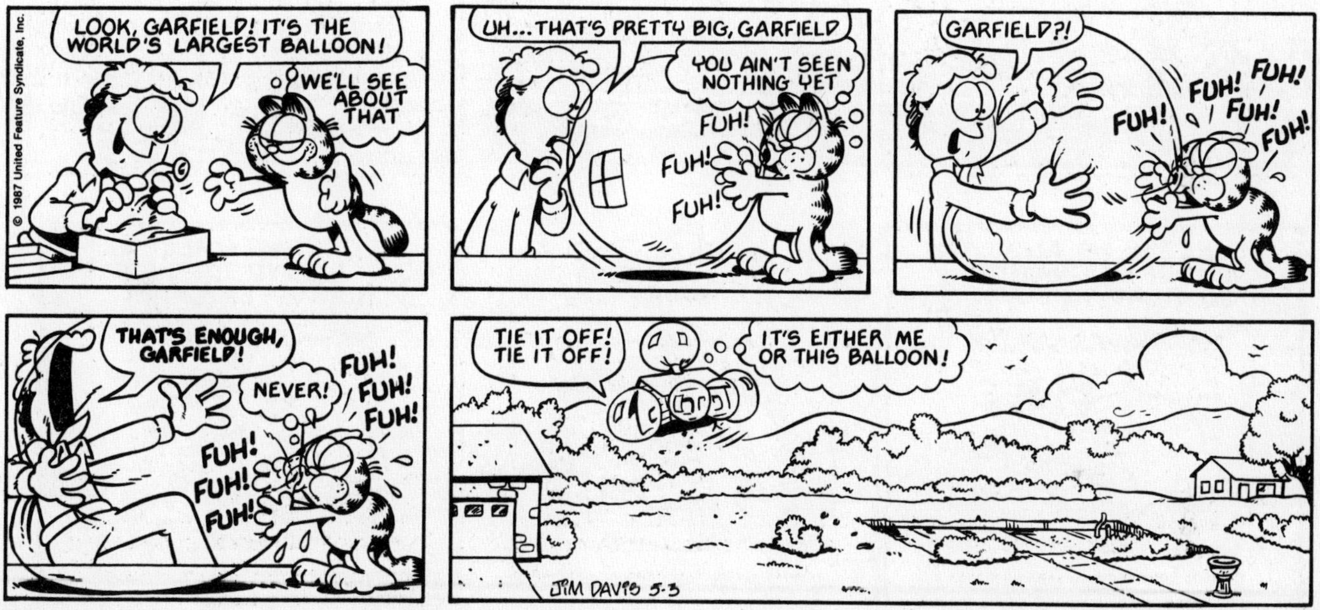
© 1987 United Feature Syndicate, Inc.
LOOK, GARFIELD! IT'S THE WORLD'S LARGEST BALLOON!
WE'LL SEE ABOUT THAT
UH... THAT'S PRETTY BIG, GARFIELD
YOU AIN'T SEEN NOTHING YET
FUH!
FUH!
FUH!
GARFIELD?!
FUH!
FUH!
FUH!
FUH!
FUH!
THAT'S ENOUGH, GARFIELD!
NEVER!
FUH!
FUH!
FUH!
FUH!
FUH!
FUH!
TIE IT OFF! TIE IT OFF!
IT'S EITHER ME OR THIS BALLOON!
JIM DAVIS 5-3

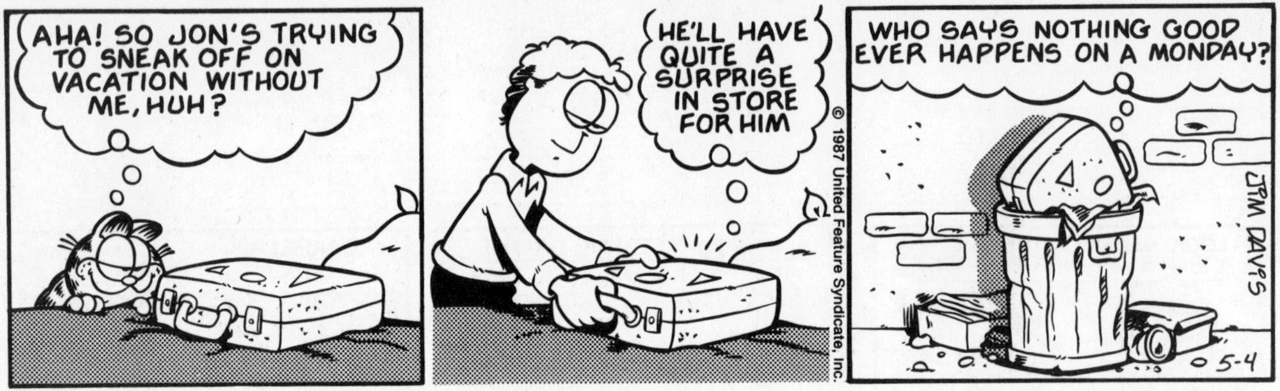
AHA! SO JON'S TRYING TO SNEAK OFF ON VACATION WITHOUT ME, HUH?
HE'LL HAVE QUITE A SURPRISE IN STORE FOR HIM
© 1987 United Feature Syndicate, Inc.
WHO SAYS NOTHING GOOD EVER HAPPENS ON A MONDAY?
JIM DAVIS
5-4

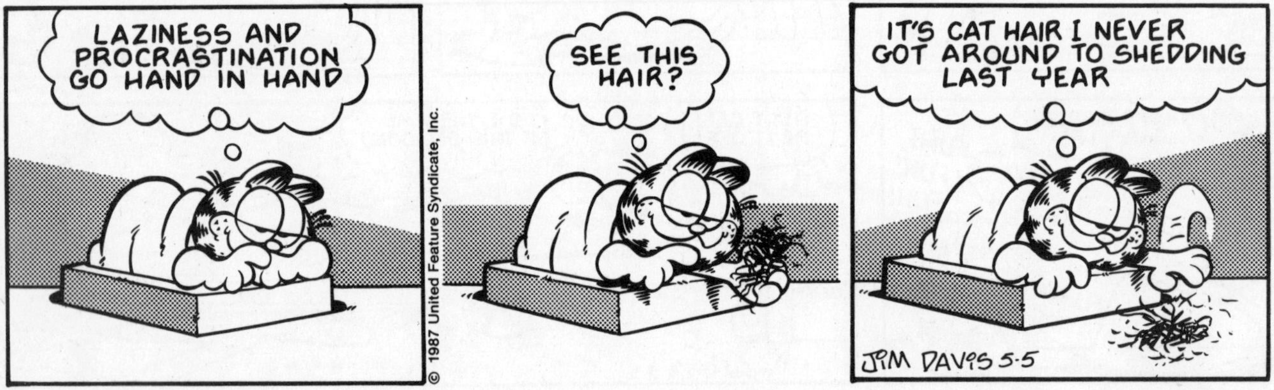
LAZINESS AND PROCRASTINATION GO HAND IN HAND
© 1987 United Feature Syndicate, Inc.
SEE THIS HAIR?
IT'S CAT HAIR I NEVER GOT AROUND TO SHEDDING LAST YEAR
JIM DAVIS 5-5

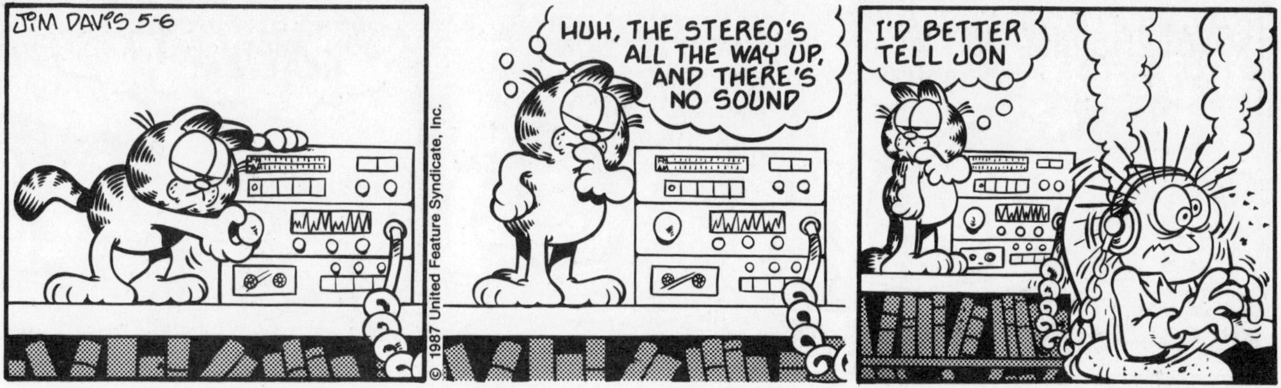
JIM DAVIS 5-6
© 1987 United Feature Syndicate, Inc.
HUH, THE STEREO'S ALL THE WAY UP, AND THERE'S NO SOUND
I'D BETTER TELL JON

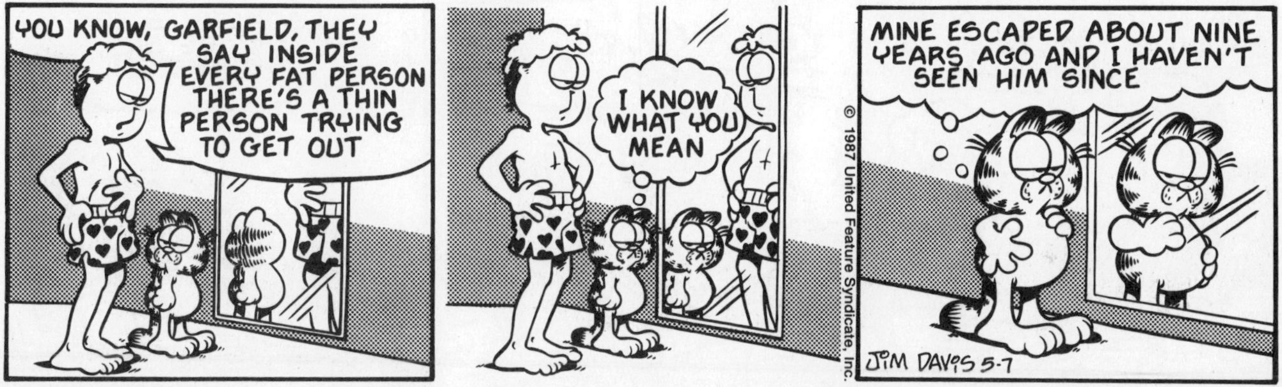
YOU KNOW, GARFIELD, THEY SAY INSIDE EVERY FAT PERSON THERE'S A THIN PERSON TRYING TO GET OUT
I KNOW WHAT YOU MEAN
© 1987 United Feature Syndicate, Inc.
MINE ESCAPED ABOUT NINE YEARS AGO AND I HAVEN'T SEEN HIM SINCE
JIM DAVIS 5-7

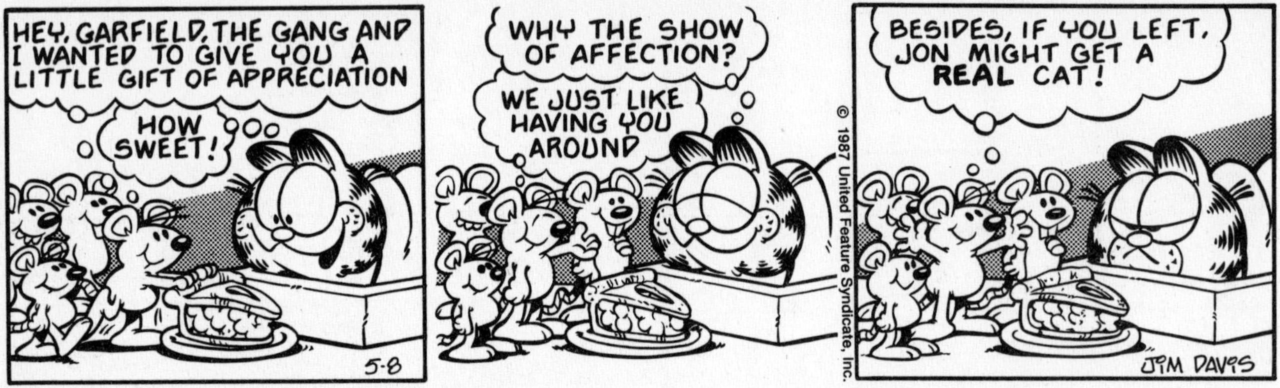
HEY, GARFIELD, THE GANG AND I WANTED TO GIVE YOU A LITTLE GIFT OF APPRECIATION
HOW SWEET!
5-8
WHY THE SHOW OF AFFECTION?
WE JUST LIKE HAVING YOU AROUND
© 1987 United Feature Syndicate, Inc.
BESIDES, IF YOU LEFT, JON MIGHT GET A **REAL** CAT!
JIM DAVIS

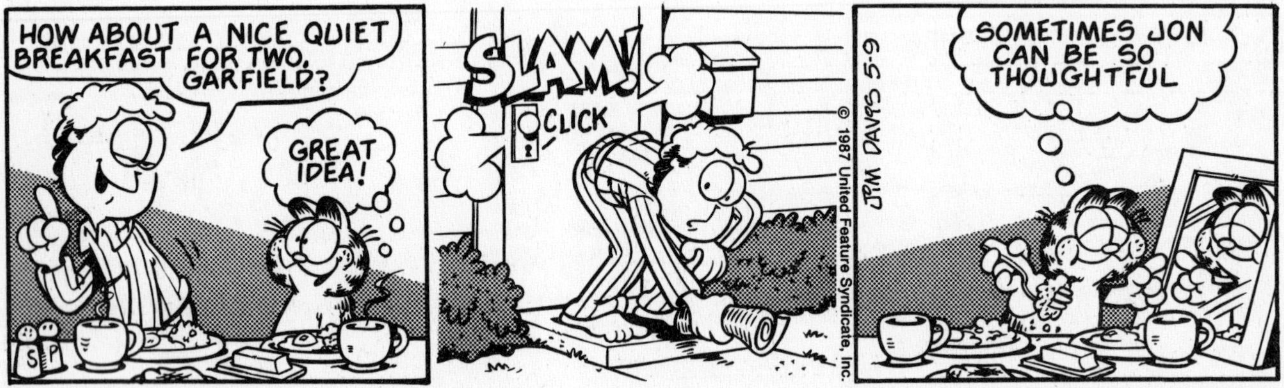
HOW ABOUT A NICE QUIET BREAKFAST FOR TWO, GARFIELD?
GREAT IDEA!
S
P
SLAM!
CLICK
© 1987 United Feature Syndicate, Inc.
JIM DAVIS 5-9
SOMETIMES JON CAN BE SO THOUGHTFUL

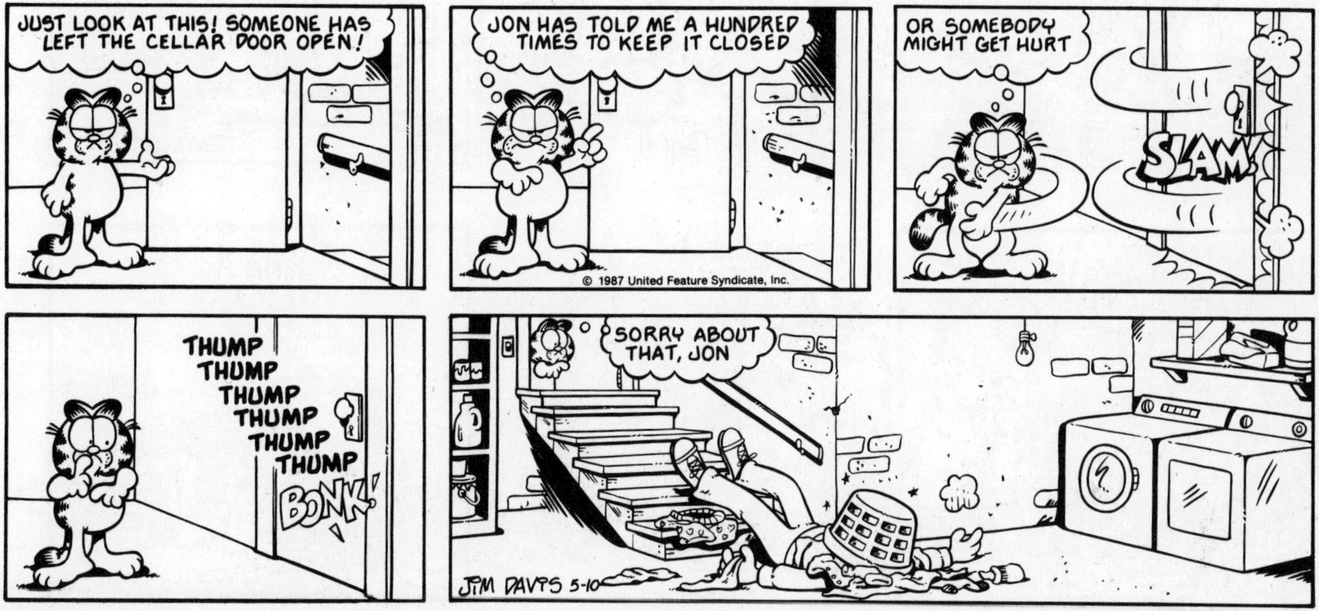

JUST LOOK AT THIS! SOMEONE HAS LEFT THE CELLAR DOOR OPEN!
JON HAS TOLD ME A HUNDRED TIMES TO KEEP IT CLOSED
© 1987 United Feature Syndicate, Inc.
OR SOMEBODY MIGHT GET HURT
SLAM!
THUMP THUMP THUMP THUMP THUMP THUMP
BONK!
SORRY ABOUT THAT, JON
JIM DAVIS 5-10

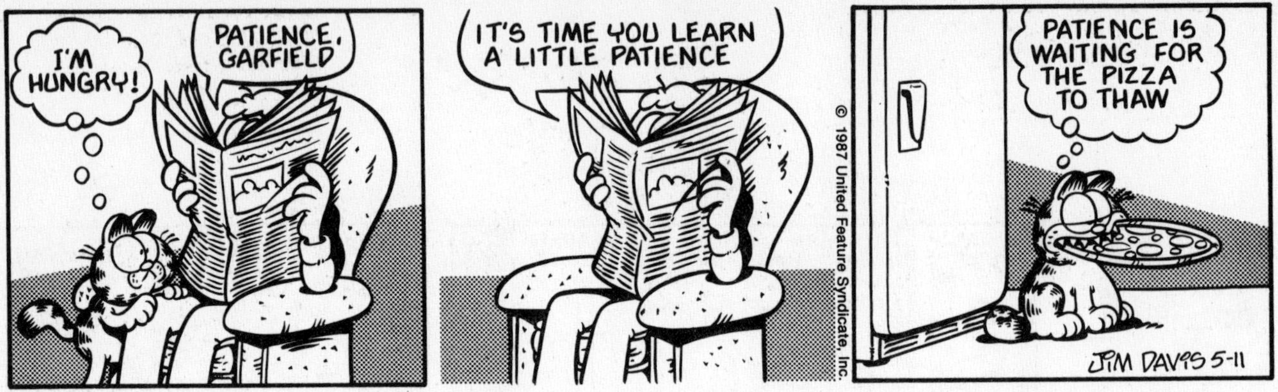
I'M HUNGRY!
PATIENCE, GARFIELD
IT'S TIME YOU LEARN A LITTLE PATIENCE
PATIENCE IS WAITING FOR THE PIZZA TO THAW
JIM DAVIS 5-11
© 1987 United Feature Syndicate, Inc.

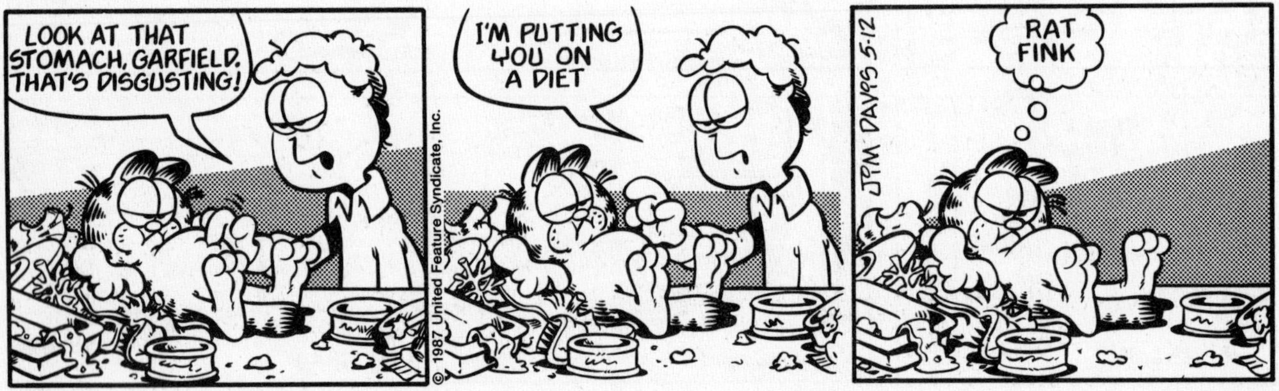
LOOK AT THAT STOMACH, GARFIELD. THAT'S DISGUSTING!
I'M PUTTING YOU ON A DIET
RAT FINK
JIM DAVIS 5-12
© 1987 United Feature Syndicate, Inc.

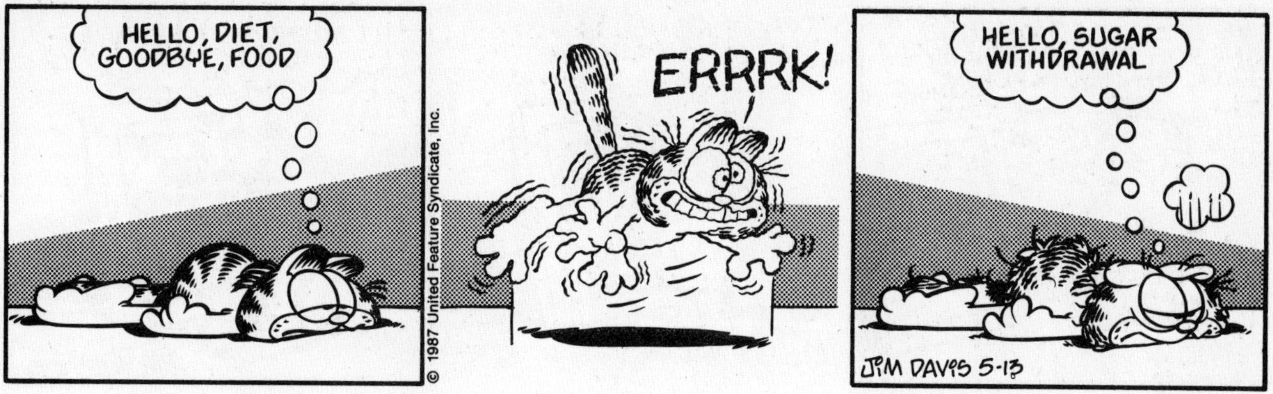
HELLO, DIET, GOODBYE, FOOD
© 1987 United Feature Syndicate, Inc.
ERRRK!
HELLO, SUGAR WITHDRAWAL
JIM DAVIS 5-13

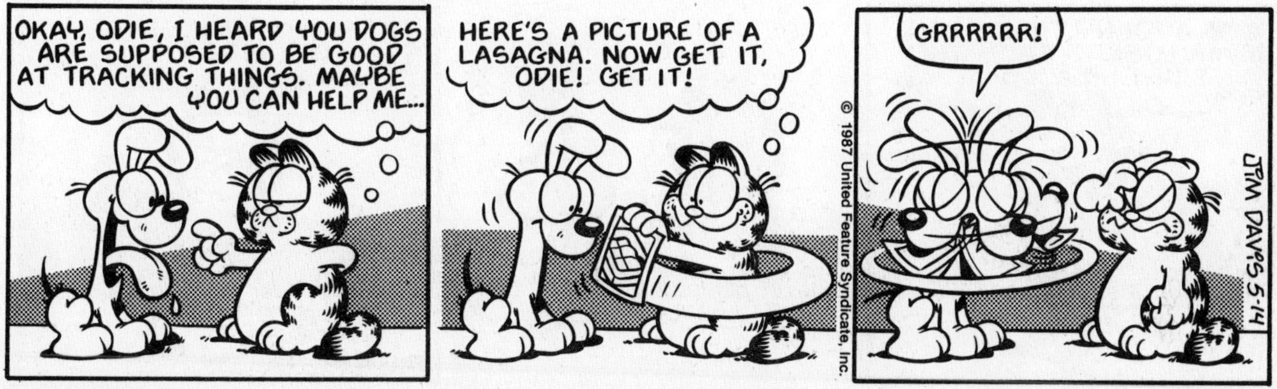
OKAY, ODIE, I HEARD YOU DOGS ARE SUPPOSED TO BE GOOD AT TRACKING THINGS. MAYBE YOU CAN HELP ME...
HERE'S A PICTURE OF A LASAGNA. NOW GET IT, ODIE! GET IT!
© 1987 United Feature Syndicate, Inc.
GRRRRRR!
JIM DAVIS 5-14

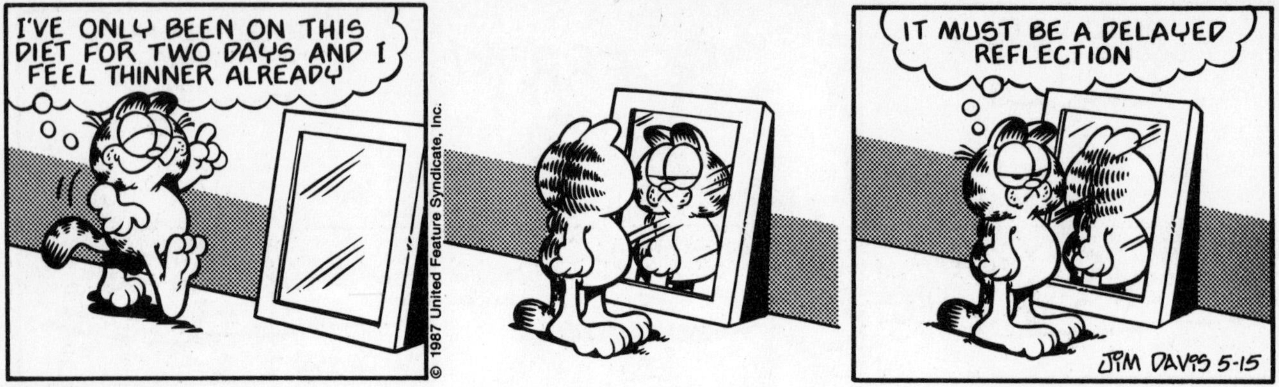
I'VE ONLY BEEN ON THIS DIET FOR TWO DAYS AND I FEEL THINNER ALREADY
© 1987 United Feature Syndicate, Inc.
IT MUST BE A DELAYED REFLECTION
JIM DAVIS 5-15

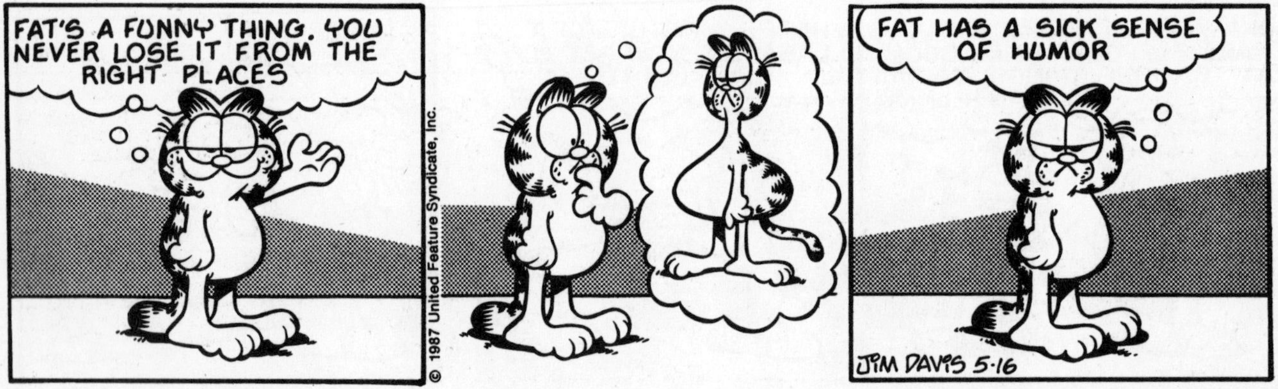
FAT'S A FUNNY THING. YOU NEVER LOSE IT FROM THE RIGHT PLACES
© 1987 United Feature Syndicate, Inc.
FAT HAS A SICK SENSE OF HUMOR
JIM DAVIS 5-16

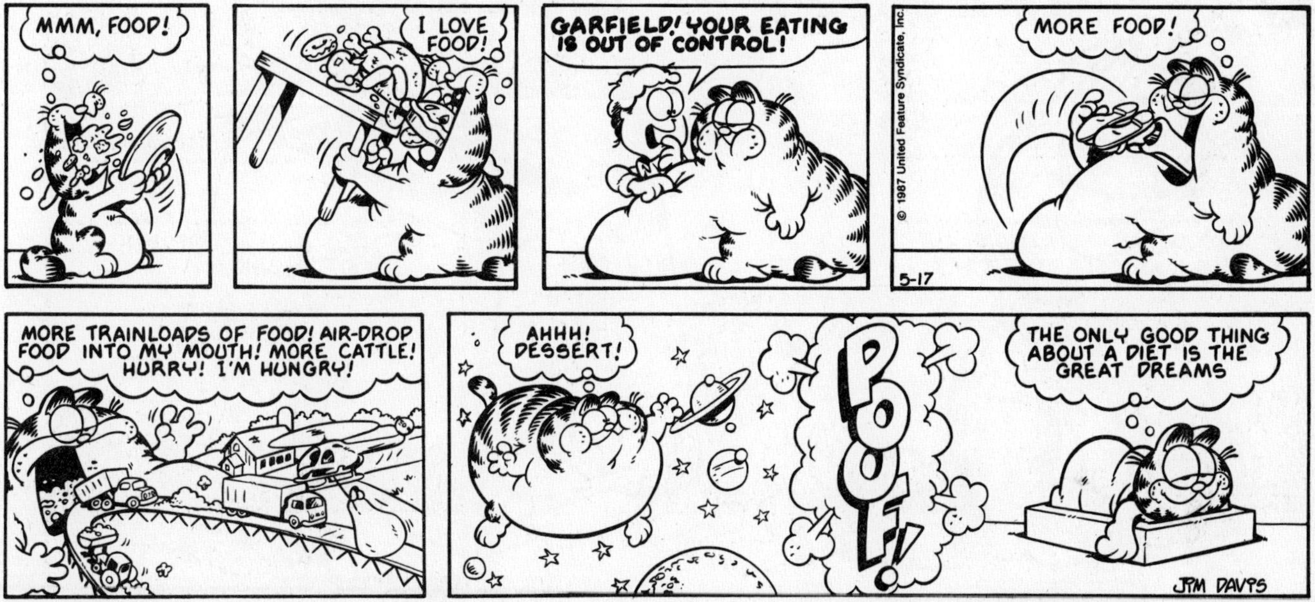
MMM, FOOD!
I LOVE FOOD!
GARFIELD! YOUR EATING IS OUT OF CONTROL!
© 1987 United Feature Syndicate, Inc.
MORE FOOD!
5-17
MORE TRAINLOADS OF FOOD! AIR-DROP FOOD INTO MY MOUTH! MORE CATTLE! HURRY! I'M HUNGRY!
AHHH! DESSERT!
POOF!
THE ONLY GOOD THING ABOUT A DIET IS THE GREAT DREAMS
JIM DAVIS

# HOW TO DRAW GARFIELD

RIGHT

WRONG

JIM DAVIS

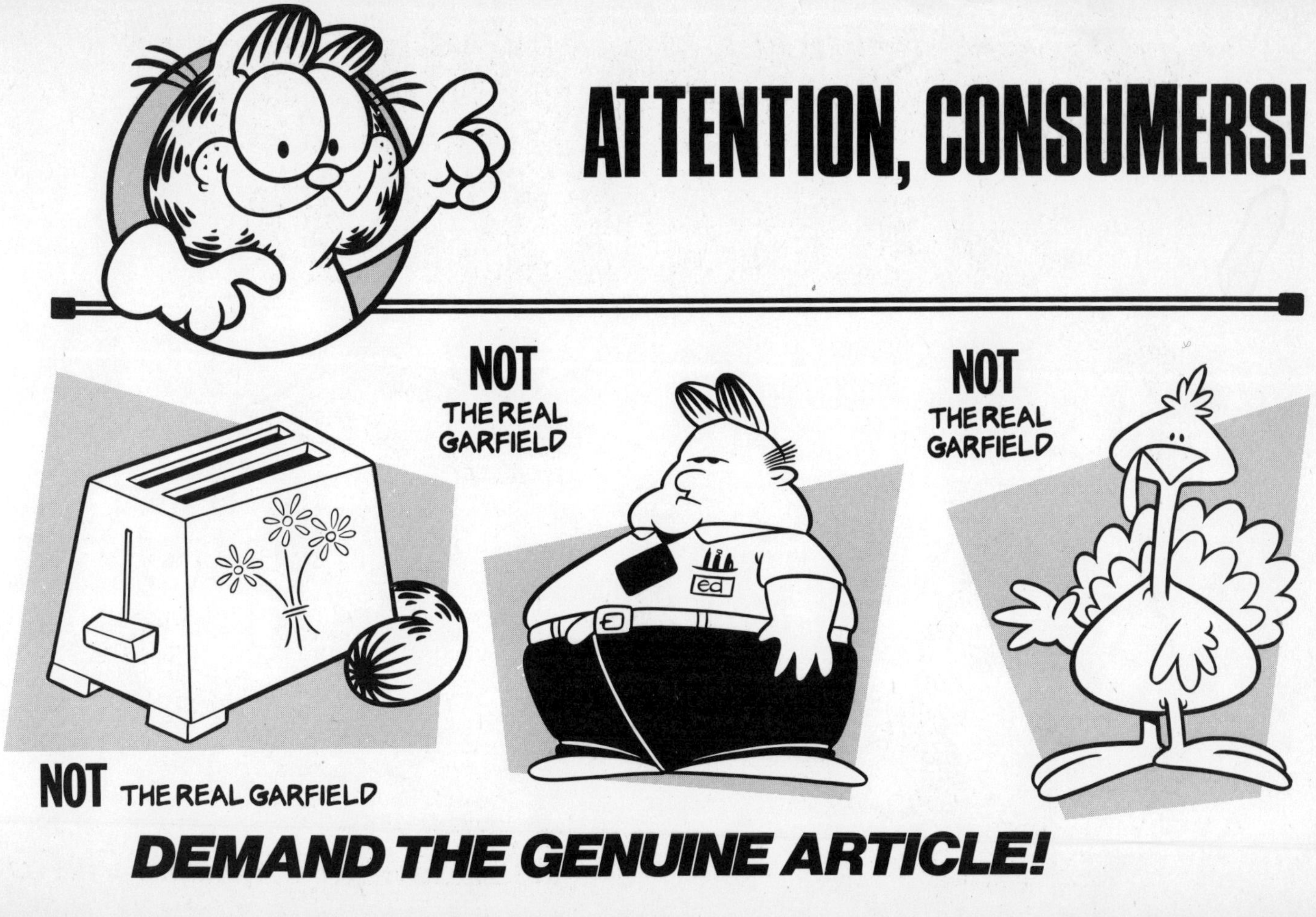
ATTENTION, CONSUMERS!
NOT THE REAL GARFIELD
NOT THE REAL GARFIELD
NOT THE REAL GARFIELD
ed
DEMAND THE GENUINE ARTICLE!